Frommer's W9-BZY-096

Nova Scotia, New Brunswick & Prince Edward Island

7th Edition

by Paul Karr

Here's what the critics say about Frommer's:

"Amazingly easy to use. Very portable, very complete."

—Booklist

"Detailed, accurate, and easy-to-read information for all price ranges."
—Glamour Magazine

"Hotel information is close to encyclopedic."

—Des Moines Sunday Register

"Frommer's Guides have a way of giving you a real feel for a place."
—Knight Ridder Newspapers

WILEY

Wiley Publishing, Inc.

Published by:

Wiley Publishing, Inc.
111 River St.
Hoboken, NJ 07030-5774

ISBN: 978-0-470-25709-8

Editor: Emil J. Ross
Production Editor: Jana M. Stefanciosa
Cartographer: Andrew Murphy
Photo Editor: Richard Fox
Production by Wiley Indianapolis Composition Services

Front cover photo: Le Pays de la Sagouine, a historic Acadian village, Bouctouche, New Brunswick
Back cover photo: Carvings from the Timmons Folk Art Studio, Cape Breton Island, Nova Scotia

For information on our other products and services or to obtain technical support, please contact our Customer Care Department within the U.S. at 800/762-2974, outside the U.S. at 317/572-3993 or fax 317/572-4002.

Wiley also publishes its books in a variety of electronic formats. Some content that appears in print may not be available in electronic formats.

Manufactured in the United States of America

5   4   3   2   1

Contents

7 Newfoundland & Labrador

248

Appendix: A Nature Guide to the Atlantic Provinces

317

Index

328

List of Maps

An Invitation to the Reader

In researching this book, we discovered many wonderful places—hotels, restaurants, shops, and more. We're sure you'll find others. Please tell us about them so we can share the information with your fellow travelers in upcoming editions. If you were disappointed with a recommendation, we'd love to know that, too. Please write to:

Frommer's Nova Scotia, New Brunswick & Prince Edward Island, 7th Edition
Wiley Publishing, Inc. • 111 River St. • Hoboken, NJ 07030-5774

An Additional Note

Please be advised that travel information is subject to change at any time—and this is especially true of prices. We therefore suggest that you write or call ahead for confirmation when making your travel plans. The authors, editors, and publisher cannot be held responsible for the experiences of readers while traveling. Your safety is important to us, however, so we encourage you to stay alert and be aware of your surroundings. Keep a close eye on cameras, purses, and wallets, all favorite targets of thieves and pickpockets.

About the Author

Paul Karr is a prize-winning writer, editor, and musician. He has written, coauthored, or edited more than 25 guidebooks, including *Frommer's Maine Coast, Vancouver & Victoria For Dummies, Vancouver: The Irreverent Guide, Frommer's New England,* and *Frommer's Canada.* He has also edited Frommer's guides to the Bahamas, Jamaica, London, Paris, San Antonio, and San Francisco and written for *The New York Times, Sierra, Sports Illustrated,* and Insight Guides to Austria, Montréal, Switzerland, and Vienna, among others. He divides his time between New York, New England, Japan, and Europe.

Other Great Guides for Your Trip:

Frommer's Canada
Frommer's Montreal and Quebec City
Frommer's Toronto
Frommer's Vancouver & Victoria
Frommer's British Columbia & the Canadian Rockies

Frommer's Star Ratings, Icons & Abbreviations

Every hotel, restaurant, and attraction listing in this guide has been ranked for quality, value, service, amenities, and special features using a **star-rating system.** In country, state, and regional guides, we also rate towns and regions to help you narrow down your choices and budget your time accordingly. Hotels and restaurants are rated on a scale of zero (recommended) to three stars (exceptional). Attractions, shopping, nightlife, towns, and regions are rated according to the following scale: zero stars (recommended), one star (highly recommended), two stars (very highly recommended), and three stars (must-see).

In addition to the star-rating system, we also use **seven feature icons** that point you to the great deals, in-the-know advice, and unique experiences that separate travelers from tourists. Throughout the book, look for:

Finds	Special finds—those places only insiders know about
Fun Fact	Fun facts—details that make travelers more informed and their trips more fun
Kids	Best bets for kids, and advice for the whole family
Moments	Special moments–those experiences that memories are made of
Overrated	Places or experiences not worth your time or money
Tips	Insider tips—great ways to save time and money
Value	Great values—where to get the best deals

The following **abbreviations** are used for credit cards:

AE	American Express	DISC	Discover	V	Visa
DC	Diners Club	MC	MasterCard		

Frommers.com

Now that you have the guidebook to a great trip, visit our website at **www.frommers.com** for travel information on more than 3,600 destinations. We update features regularly to give you instant access to the most current trip-planning information available. At Frommers.com, you'll find scoops on the best airfares, lodging rates, and car-rental bargains—and you can even book travel online through our travel booking partners. Other popular features include:

- Online updates to our most popular guidebooks
- Vacation sweepstakes and contest giveaways
- Newsletter highlighting the hottest travel trends
- Online travel message boards with featured travel discussions

What's New in the Atlantic Provinces

Things change slowly in eastern Canada, and sometimes they don't change much at all. Nevertheless, there are a few recent developments to note and a few big ones that will affect your trip planning.

PLANNING YOUR TRIP As of January 2007, **all U.S. citizens must show a passport to enter Canada and reenter the U.S.** A visa is still not required for this trip. This rule may be amended in 2008, but if you already have a passport, definitely bring it with you anyway. For more specific details on the latest entry and customs requirements, passports, and visas, consult chapter 2.

Canada has also eliminated the popular **Visitor Rebate Program.** Until 2007, the steep 14% HST (federal plus provincial) tax in the three Maritime Provinces (Nova Scotia, New Brunswick, and PEI), as well as the 10% provincial tax on PEI, were fully refundable so long as you kept receipts. From now on, you won't get anything back. Ouch.

If you prefer traveling overseas to the Atlantic Provinces rather than by air, there's been a little juggling of ferry services and schedules. There's no longer an overnight cruise service **connecting Portland, Maine, with Yarmouth, Nova Scotia;** instead, there is now a fast ferry service operating along that route three to four times per week. Note that the addition of a new route to Portland has also **cut down on ferry sailings from Bar Harbor.** The formerly twice-daily sailings from Bar Harbor have been reduced to just three to four per week.

The fast (though sometimes bumpy) Bay Ferries **CAT ferry** service (© 888/359-3760; www.catferry.com) operates both of these routes. All departures from Maine are early in the morning; returns from Yarmouth are timed for the afternoon. Check the CAT website for fares and schedules.

VIA Rail, Canada's national rail line (© 888/842-7245; www.viarail.com), continues to improve its summer-only "Easterly" class of service on the overnight run from Montréal to Halifax. The Easterly, which began operations in 2006 as a luxury version of the year-round Ocean train service, offers all-inclusive meals, sleeping accommodations, exclusive access to lounges and a panoramic car, and continuing presentations from an onboard educator about Maritime province culture and history. The Ocean runs daily each direction except Tuesdays, while the Easterly option is available from mid-June through mid-October.

Going to New Brunswick? The overnight Ocean also makes stops in Campbellton, Miramichi, Bathurst, and Moncton before noon of the following day en route to its final destination of Halifax.

EXPLORING NOVA SCOTIA The award for the best-named new festival goes to Nova Scotia's **Lobsterpalooza** (© 902/270-3330; www.lobsterpalooza. ca), a monthlong provincial bash of lobster suppers, cultural events, and tours spread across various parts of 'Scotia (though many are concentrated on Cape Breton Island). Check with the festival office about the 2008 schedule, when the events will take place from May 25 through June 30.

Halifax's farmer's market, formerly a delightful Saturday-morning-only affair, will possibly acquire a more permanent home at Pier 20 on the city's waterfront. Check with the market's website, **www. halifaxfarmersmarket.com,** for details of the project.

Tall ships will return to Halifax harbor in 2009. (They were most recently there during the summer of 2007.) The fleet, participating in a 2009 rally event, will arrive in Halifax in July after a series of races beginning in Spain.

However, there's a bit of sad news, as well: The lovely **Manse** in pretty Mahone Bay, one of Atlantic Canada's finest and friendliest inns, has closed. Up on Cape Breton Island, the **Duffus House Inn** in Baddeck has also closed.

Surfing is suddenly popping up as an outdoor option in Nova Scotia. Who knew? At least two surf schools have opened for business, capitalizing on the Atlantic surf breaks along the South Shore and off Lawrencetown Beach near Halifax. Contact the Dacane Surf Shop (© 902/ 431-7873; www.hurricanesurf.com) or the Rossignol Surf Shop (© 877/990- 3733 or 902/683-2140; www.surfnova scotia.com) for more information. Just remember to rent a wet suit: That water's *cold.*

Finally, it's getting easier to get to Nova Scotia. **American Eagle** (© 800/433- 7300; www.aa.com) recently added one daily flight in each direction between New York's LaGuardia Airport and Halifax Stanley International, in small 37-seat jets, and **Air Canada** (© 888/247-2262; www.aircanada.com) has also introduced a similar once-daily service each way, using 50-seater Bombardier jets.

EXPLORING NEW BRUNSWICK

New Brunswick continues reaping awards: **Fredericton's farmer's market** was named one of the top eight such markets in all of Canada by *Harrowsmith Magazine* (and they should know). Meanwhile, the **Lunar Rogue Pub**—also in Fredericton, curiously enough—was anointed Greatest Whisky Bar in the World by *Whisky Magazine,* who also should know.

Access to New Brunswick continues to improve. Where you once had to fly into Saint John first and then change planes, **Continental** (© 800/523-FARE; www. continental.com) now flies direct from Newark, New Jersey's Liberty International Airport to Moncton.

In the summer of 2007, **Carnival Cruise Lines** (© 888/CARNIVAL; www. carnival.com) unveiled a series of 4-day weekend summertime cruises from New York City to the Bay of Fundy and back. Optional shore excursions during the day and night at port in Saint John have previously included a bike tour of local covered bridges, visits to a dairy farm, kayak trips around the bay, and a visit to the Moosehead Brewery. A limited schedule of the cruises will continue in the summer of 2008.

EXPLORING PRINCE EDWARD ISLAND

As usual, the biggest news on PEI is *Anne*-related. The island will go gaga for the **100th anniversary** of the June 1908 publication of Lucy Maud Montgomery's novel *Anne of Green Gables* with a full program of events, including a children's literary festival, readings, plays, and the release of a new prequel novel written by a local children's author. Canada Post will also create two new stamps to commemorate the anniversary. Check the provincial tourism office's special Anne page at **www.gentleisland. com/anne** for more details and an event schedule.

And there's good news for Northeasterners who don't want to drive to the Anne proceedings: **Delta** (© **800/221-1212;** www.delta.com) has begun offering a new direct summer flight service from Boston's Logan International Airport to Charlottetown.

The **Links at Crowbush Cove** (p. 211), considered by many to be the island's best golf course, has changed its fee structure to an intriguing all-inclusive model: The greens fees now get you not only all the golf you can play but also as many pull carts, tees, buckets of range balls, and short little pencils as you can handle.

In Charlottetown, the bike-rental shop **Smooth Cycle** (p. 211) has relocated to University Avenue.

EXPLORING NEWFOUNDLAND & LABRADOR There's a new Aveda-products spa in Newfoundland, the **Found Spa,** located at the Humber Valley Resort near Corner Brook. It offers a full selection of treatments in a lovely lakeside facility broken into four treatment rooms with distinct themes: Earth, Air, Fire, and Water. There's also a deck, gardens, and an outdoor hot tub. Contact the resort (© **866/686-8100** or 709/686-8100; www.humbervalley.com) for details.

The Best of the Atlantic Provinces

Planning a trip to Atlantic Canada can present a bewildering array of choices. I've searched Nova Scotia, New Brunswick, Prince Edward Island, Newfoundland, and Labrador for the best destinations and experiences. Here are some of my personal and opinionated top choices.

1 The Best Active Vacations

- **Sea Kayaking Nova Scotia:** The twisting, convoluted coastline of this province is custom-made for snooping around by sea kayak. Outfitters are scattered all around the peninsula. For expedition kayaking, contact Coastal Adventures (© **877/404-2774** or 902/772-2774; www.coastal adventures.com), which leads trips throughout Nova Scotia and beyond. See chapter 4.

- **Biking the Cabot Trail** (Nova Scotia): This long and strenuous loop around Cape Breton Highlands National Park is tough on the legs, but you'll come away with a head full of indelible memories. See "Cape Breton Island" in chapter 4.

- **Exploring Fundy National Park and Vicinity** (New Brunswick): You'll find swimming, hiking, and kayaking at this coastal national park.

And don't overlook biking in the hills east of the park, or rappelling and rock climbing at Cape Enrage. See "Fundy National Park" in chapter 5.

- **Cycling Prince Edward Island:** This island province sometimes seems like it was created specifically for bike touring. Villages are reasonably spaced, hills virtually nonexistent, coastal roads picturesque in the extreme, and a new island-wide bike path offers detours through marshes and quiet woodlands. See "The Great Outdoors" in chapter 6.

- **Hiking Gros Morne National Park** (Newfoundland): Atlantic Canada's best hiking is found in these rugged hills. You can hike amazing coastal trails, marvel at scenic waterfalls, and stroll alongside landlocked fjords at this exceptional park. See "The Great Outdoors" in chapter 7.

2 The Best Spots for Observing Nature

- **Digby Neck** (Nova Scotia): Choose from a dozen whale-watching outfitters located along this narrow peninsula of remote fishing villages. Getting to the tip of the peninsula is half the

fun—it requires two ferries. See "Digby to Yarmouth" in chapter 4.

- **Cape Breton Highlands National Park** (Nova Scotia): The craggy geology of the west coast is impressive, but

Atlantic Canada

GREENLAND
(Denmark)

Resolution I.
(Nunavut)

Akpatok I.
(Nunavut)

C. Chidley

*Ungava
Bay*

Koksoak R.

LABRADOR

NEWFOUNDLAND

SEA

Hebron

Nutak

Baleine R.

George R.

Nain

Davis
Inlet

Caniapiscau
Res.

Postville

Rigolet

Cartwright

Smallwood Res.

Churchill
Falls

Naskaupi R.

L. Melville

Happy Valley-
Goose Bay

Labrador
City

Churchill R.

& LABRADOR

Atikonak L.

Mécatina R.

Gagnon

Red Bay

St. Anthony

Manicouagan
Res.

QUÉBEC

Port au
Choix

C. St. John

Sept-Îles

Natashquan

Grand Falls-
Windsor

Gander

Baie-
Comeau

St. Lawrence R.

Anticosti Island

Corner
Brook

Newfoundland

Bonavista

Gaspé

Rimouski Gaspé Pen.

GULF OF
ST. LAWRENCE

Stephenville

Maelpaeg
Res.

St. John's

Rivière-
du-Loup

Iles de la
Madeleine
(Que.)

C. Ray

Burgeo

Conception
Bay South

Caribou

Edmundston Bathurst

Cabot Strait

Burin Pen.

Avalon Pen.

Houlton

Newcastle

PRINCE
EDWARD
ISLAND

ST. PIERRE &
MIQUELON
(France)

Trepassey

NEW
BRUNSWICK

Charlottetown

Cape Breton I.

Fredericton Moncton

Sydney

Glace Bay

U.S.A.
MAINE

Saint
John

New-
Glasgow

C. Breton

Eastport

Truro

NOVA SCOTIA

ATLANTIC

Bangor

Windsor

Bar
Harbor

Bay of
Fundy

Bridgewater

Halifax
Lunenburg

OCEAN

Yarmouth

Sable I.

C. Sable

| 0 | 200 mi |
| 0 | 200 km |

don't let that overshadow the rest of the park, where you'll find bogs and moose in abundance. See "Cape Breton Highlands National Park" in chapter 4.

- **Grand Manan Island** (New Brunswick): This big, geologically intriguing rock off the New Brunswick coast in the western Bay of Fundy is a great base for learning about coastal ecology. Whale tour operators search out the endangered right whale and dozens of birds roost and pass through. Boat tours from the island will also take you out to see puffins. See "Grand Manan Island" in chapter 5.

- **Hopewell Rocks** (New Brunswick): The force of Fundy's tremendous tides is the most impressive at Hopewell Rocks, where great rock "sculptures" created by the winds and tides rise from the ocean floor at low tide. See "Fundy National Park" in chapter 5.

- **Avalon Peninsula** (Newfoundland): In 1 busy day you can view a herd of caribou, the largest puffin colony in North America, and an extraordinary gannet colony visible from the mainland cliffs. See "The Southern Avalon Peninsula" in chapter 7.

3 The Best Scenic Drives

- **Cape Breton's Cabot Trail** (Nova Scotia): This 300km (185-mile) loop through the uplands of Cape Breton Highlands National Park is one of the world's great excursions. You'll see Acadian fishing ports, pristine valleys, and some of the most picturesque coastline anywhere. See "Cape Breton Island" in chapter 4.

- **Cobequid Bay** (Nova Scotia): When it comes to scenery, Cobequid Bay (near Truro) is one of the region's better-kept secrets. The bay is flanked by two roads: Route 2 runs from Parrsboro to Truro; Route 215 from South Maitland to Brooklyn. Take the time to savor the rocky cliffs, muddy flats, and rust-colored bays. See "Minas Basin & Cobequid Bay" in chapter 4.

- **Fundy Trail Parkway** (New Brunswick): East of Saint John, you'll find this 11km (6¾-mile) parkway winding along the contours of the coast. Get out and stretch your legs at any of the 22 lookouts along the way for

fantastic cliffside views. Or if the tides are out, clamber down to one of the stretches of sand nestled between the rocks. See p. 177.

- **Prince Edward Island National Park:** Much of the north-central shore of PEI is part of the national park, and a quiet park road tracks along the henna-tinted cliffs and grass-covered dunes. The coastal road is interrupted by inlets, but each segment of it is worth a leisurely drive, with frequent stops to explore the beaches and walkways. See "Prince Edward Island National Park" in chapter 6.

- **Viking Trail** (Newfoundland): Travelers looking to leave the crowds behind needn't look any further. This beautiful drive to Newfoundland's northern tip is wild and solitary, with views of bizarre geology and a wind-raked coast. And you'll end up at one of the world's great historic sites—L'Anse aux Meadows. See "The Great Northern Peninsula" in chapter 7.

4 The Best Hikes & Rambles

- **Point Pleasant Park** (Nova Scotia): Overlooking the entrance to Halifax's harbor, Point Pleasant Park is a wonderful urban oasis, with wide trails for strolling along the water. Check out the stout Martello tower atop a wooded rise. See p. 102.

- **Cape Breton Highlands National Park** (Nova Scotia): You'll find bog and woodland walks aplenty at Cape Breton, but the best trails follow rugged cliffs along the open ocean. The Skyline Trail is among the most dramatic pathways in the province. See "Cape Breton Highlands National Park" in chapter 4.

- **Grand Manan Island** (New Brunswick): Grand Manan is laced with informal walking trails, through the forest and along the ocean's edge. This is a place for exploring; ask around locally for suggestions on the best hikes. See "Grand Manan Island" in chapter 5.

- **The Confederation Trail** (Prince Edward Island): This 350km (217-mile) pathway across the island is still being pieced together, but you can explore the 225km (140 miles) along the old rail line that once stitched the province together. It's best for long-distance biking but superb for a quiet stroll. See "Kings County" in chapter 6.

- **Green Gardens Trail** (Newfoundland): This demanding hike at Gros Morne National Park takes hikers on a 16km (9.9-mile) loop, much of which follows coastal meadows atop fractured cliffs. Demanding, but worth every step of the way. See "Gros Morne National Park" in chapter 7.

- **North Head Trail** (Newfoundland): Walk from downtown St. John's along the harbor, pass through the Battery neighborhood, and then climb the open bluffs overlooking the Narrows for views out to the open ocean beyond. Where else can you hike from downtown shopping to cliffside whale-watching? See "St. John's" in chapter 7.

5 The Best Family Activities

- **Upper Clements Park** (Nova Scotia): About 5 minutes south of Annapolis Royal, this wonderfully old-fashioned amusement park is full of low-key attractions that will especially delight younger kids. Highlights include a flume ride (originally built for Expo '86 in Vancouver) and a wooden roller coaster that twists and winds through trees left standing during the coaster's construction. See "Annapolis Royal" in chapter 4.

- **Waterfront Walk** (Nova Scotia): Halifax's waterfront walk is filled with wonderful distractions, from the province's finest museum to ships for exploring. Also look for buskers, delightful junk food, and sweeping views of the bustling harbor. If you're here in early August for the Busker Festival, it's all your kids will talk about for years. See "Halifax" in chapter 4.

- **Kings Landing** (New Brunswick): At this living history museum, young kids are introduced to life in early Canada between 1790 and 1910. Ask about the weeklong sessions designed to immerse kids in the past. See p. 183.

- **Prince Edward Island's Beaches:** The red-sand beaches will turn white swim trunks a bit pinkish, but it's hard to beat a day or three splashing around these lukewarm waters while admiring the pastoral island landscapes. See "The Great Outdoors" in chapter 6.
- **Terra Nova National Park** (Newfoundland): This is the less touted of Newfoundland's two national parks, but the staff has gone the extra mile to make it kid friendly. There's a marine interpretive center with activities for kids, boat tours, hikes just the right length for shorter legs, and campground activities at night. See "Terra Nova National Park" in chapter 7.

6 The Best Places for History

- **Annapolis Royal** (Nova Scotia): The cradle of Canadian civilization is found in this broad green valley, where early French settlers first put down roots. Visit Fort Anne and Port Royal, and walk some of the first streets on the continent. See "Annapolis Royal" in chapter 4.
- **Maritime Museum of the Atlantic** (Nova Scotia): Nova Scotia's history is the history of the sea, and no place better depicts that vibrant tradition than this sprawling museum on Halifax's waterfront. See p. 98.
- **Louisbourg** (Nova Scotia): This early-18th-century fort and village was part of an elaborate French effort to establish a foothold in the New World. It failed, and the village ultimately fell to ruin. In the 1960s, the Canadian government reconstructed much of it, and now it's one of the most impressive historic sites in the nation. See "Cape Breton Island" in chapter 4.
- **Village Historique Acadien** (New Brunswick): Around 45 buildings—with the number growing—depict life as it was lived in an Acadian settlement between 1770 and 1890. You'll learn all about the exodus and settlement of the Acadians from costumed guides, who are also adept at skills ranging from letterpress printing to blacksmithing. See p. 202.
- **Province House National Historic Site** (Prince Edward Island): Canadian history took shape in Charlottetown in 1864, when the idea of joining Britain's North American colonies into an independent confederation was first discussed. Learn about what transpired at this imposing Charlottetown edifice, which has been restored to appear as it did when history was made. See p. 229.
- **Bonavista Peninsula** (Newfoundland): It might seem like the edge of the earth today, but in past centuries Newfoundland was the crossroads of European culture, as nations scrapped over fishing rights and settlements. You can learn a lot about how the Old World viewed the New during a few days exploring this intriguing peninsula. Base yourself in the perfectly preserved village of Trinity, and spend at least a day exploring up to the town of Bonavista, where you can visit the Ryan's Premises National Historic Site and learn why cod was god. See "The Bonavista Peninsula" in chapter 7.
- **L'Anse aux Meadows National Historic Site** (Newfoundland): This dramatic site on Newfoundland's northern tip celebrated its 1,000th anniversary in 2000—yes, it's been a full millennium since the Vikings first landed here and established an encampment. View the intriguing ruins, enter the re-created sod huts, and hear knowledgeable interpreters' theories about why the colony failed. See p. 269.

7 The Most Picturesque Villages

- **Lunenburg** (Nova Scotia): Settled by German, Swiss, and French colonists, this tidy town is superbly situated on a hill flanked by two harbors, and it boasts some of the most unique and quietly extravagant architecture in the Maritimes. See "South Shore" in chapter 4.

- **Victoria** (Prince Edward Island): This wee village west of Charlottetown is surrounded by fields of grain and potatoes, and hasn't changed much in the last 100 years. Try to time your visit to take in an evening show at the town's wonderfully old-fashioned theater. See "Prince County" in chapter 6.

- **Trinity** (Newfoundland): Three centuries ago, Trinity was among the most important ports in the New World, when English merchants controlled the flow of goods in and out of the New World. This compact village has also been among the most aggressive in preserving its past, and the architecture and perfect scale of the village is unmatched in Atlantic Canada. See "The Bonavista Peninsula" in chapter 7.

- **Twillingate** (Newfoundland): This end-of-the-world village is located on and around the convoluted harbors and inlets of Newfoundland's north-central shore. At the mouth of the Notre Dame bay, high headlands mark the way for incoming ships; walk out here and scan the watery horizon for whales and icebergs. See "Central Newfoundland" in chapter 7.

8 The Best Inns

- **Gowrie House** (Sydney Mines, Nova Scotia; ℂ **800/372-1115** or 902/544-1050): The exquisitely decorated Gowrie House is at once resplendent and comfortable, historic and up-to-date. The smallest guest rooms are more spacious than larger rooms at many other inns. See p. 145.

- **Kingsbrae Arms** (St. Andrews, New Brunswick; ℂ **506/529-1897**): This five-star inn manages the trick of being opulent and comfortable at the same time. The shingled manse is lavishly appointed, beautifully landscaped, and well situated for exploring charming St. Andrews. See p. 165.

- **The Great George** (Charlottetown, PEI; ℂ **800/361-1118** or 902/892-0606): This connected series of restored town houses is historic, central, welcoming, and quite comfortable. Continental breakfast is served in the open-concept lobby, where you can watch the comings and goings without getting in the way. Rooms range from spacious doubles to huge family-size suites, and most of them have either a fireplace, a whirlpool bath, or both. See p. 231.

- **Inn at Bay Fortune** (Bay Fortune, PEI; ℂ **902/687-3745** or 860/296-1348 off season): This exceptionally attractive shingled compound was most recently owned by actress Colleen Dewhurst, and current innkeeper David Wilmer pulled out all the stops for his renovations. But the real draw here is the dining room, which is noted for the farm-fresh ingredients grown in the extensive gardens on the property. See p. 240.

9 The Best Bed & Breakfasts

- **Shipwright Inn** (Charlottetown, PEI; ☎ **888/306-9966** or 902/368-1905): This right-in-town, nine-room B&B is within easy walking distance of all the city's attractions yet has a settled and pastoral feel. It's informed by a Victorian sensibility without being over-the-top about it. And the rooms are surprisingly modern, with phones, VCRs, DVD players, decks, and Jacuzzis. When seeking out an inn, it doesn't get much better than this. See p. 231.

- **Tickle Inn at Cape Onion** (Cape Onion, Newfoundland; ☎ **709/452-4321** June–Sept or 709/739-5503 Oct–May): The Tickle Inn serves a family-style dinner each night, so technically it isn't a B&B at all—but this tiny and remote home has the cordial bonhomie of a B&B all the same. Set on a distant cove at the end of a road near Newfoundland's northernmost point (you can see Labrador across the straits), the Tickle Inn offers a perfect base for visiting L'Anse aux Meadows and walking on the lonesome, windy hills. See p. 271.

- **At Wit's Inn** (St. John's, Newfoundland; ☎ **877/739-7420**): This centrally located B&B is bright, cheerful, and whimsical. Opened in 1999 by a restaurateur from Toronto, the inn has managed to preserve the best of the historical elements in this century-old home while graciously updating it for modern tastes. See p. 301.

10 The Best Local Dining

- **Digby Scallops** (Nova Scotia): The productive scallop fleet based in Digby, on Nova Scotia's Bay of Fundy coast, hauls back some of the choicest, most succulent scallops in the world. Sample the fare at local restaurants, or cook up a batch on your own. Simple is better: A light sauté in butter brings out their rich flavor. See "Digby to Yarmouth" in chapter 4.

- **Rappie Pie** (Nova Scotia): When traveling between Digby and Yarmouth, watch for shops selling rappie pie—a local Acadian treat made from potatoes and meat or seafood. See "Digby to Yarmouth" in chapter 4.

- **Fresh Lobster** (Nova Scotia and New Brunswick): Wherever you see the wooden lobster traps piled on a wharf, a fresh lobster meal isn't far away. Among the most productive lobster fisheries are around Shediac, New Brunswick, and all along Nova Scotia's Atlantic coast. Sunny days are ideal for cracking open a crustacean while sitting at a wharf-side picnic table, preferably with a locally brewed beer close at hand. See chapters 4 and 5.

- **Prince Edward Island Mussels:** PEI has long been known for its wonderful potatoes, but the farmed mussels do more to thrill the taste buds. You'll see the lines of mussel buoys in inlets and harbors. Order up a mess at an island restaurant to share with your whole table. See chapter 6.

- **Newfoundland Berries:** The unforgivingly rocky and boggy soil of this blustery island resists most crops but produces some of the most delicious berries you can imagine. Look for roadside stands in midsummer, or pick your own blueberries, strawberries, partridgeberries, or bakeapples. Many restaurants serve berries (on cheesecake, in custard) when they're in season. See chapter 7.

2

Planning Your Trip to the Atlantic Provinces

The four eastern provinces of Canada are safe and scenic yet stretched out and fairly remote, with few choices of travel options. And the tourist season here is remarkably short. As such, the region requires extra care when planning if you want to be sure about getting maximum value for your travel expenditures, avoiding transit snafus, and finding available accommodations that fit both your budget and your needs.

I have tried to dispense some vital planning information in the chapter that follows. Reading it before you set out could save you money, time, and many of those headaches I've just described. In these pages, you'll get the nuts and bolts of travel in the provinces: when to come, the documentation you'll need, where to get more information, how to keep connected with the home office or family, and more. These basics just might make the difference between a smooth trip and a bumpy one.

1 The Atlantic Provinces in Brief

NOVA SCOTIA This province is the undisputed star of Canada's Atlantic coast: Its capital, Halifax, is a relative financial and cultural powerhouse compared with the rest of the hamlets scattered through eastern Canada and the surest bet for an outstanding meal, a world-class musical performance, or a great museum. But there's far more to Nova Scotia, including the South Shore (an especially photogenic stretch of fishing villages); the hardscrabble Acadian Coast, with its spruce-topped basalt cliffs and miles of sandy beaches; and astonishing Cape Breton, an enormous northerly island dominated by one of Canada's finest national parks and a tradition of Celtic music.

NEW BRUNSWICK On the other hand, New Brunswick is a strangely shaped province that's often passed over in the rush to elsewhere. Glimpsed from up close, however, it turns out to possess some of Canada's quaintest villages and highest tides. The Bay of Fundy is the place to see huge, twice-daily drops and rises of ocean against cliff and learn more about the fascinating marine ecology that has developed here. Fishing villages such as St. Andrews and Caraquet cry out to be photographed; small cities like Fredericton and Moncton offer more than initially meets the eye; and the city of Saint John contains more culture per square inch than any other place in this book except Halifax.

PRINCE EDWARD ISLAND This island leaves the razzle-dazzle to cities on the mainland, choosing instead to soothe visitors' souls by offering places for quiet relaxation. A flat island of red sands, potato farms, and purple lupine fields—plus healthy doses of fishing boats, golf, Acadian culture, and children's lit (you'll see what I mean)—PEI is the sort of place best explored by bicycle and then pondered later over a good book at night. The province's harborside capital city of Charlottetown is genuinely attractive, historic, and diverse; this was the place where the deal consolidating Canada into one nation ("the Confederation") was sealed, and it's still a little gem of a town.

NEWFOUNDLAND This is the province you need to work hardest to reach, but people here make a serious run for the title of "friendliest in all of Canada"—which is saying something. The natural wonders here are spectacular, including (to list just a few) shimmering icebergs, migrating whales, and Viking settlement sites. For good measure, there's a major city here (St. John's) with a salty, pubby pulse; fresh fish everywhere; and a hard-to-reach adjacent territory—Labrador—of native culture, fishermen, empty landscapes, and absolutely zero crowds.

2 Visitor Information & Maps

VISITOR INFORMATION It's well worth a toll-free call or postcard in advance of your trip to stock up on the free literature and maps that provincial authorities liberally bestow upon those considering a vacation in their province. Here's how to reach the official tourism folks who dispense these goodies:

- **Nova Scotia Department of Tourism, Culture & Heritage,** P.O. Box 456, Halifax, NS B3J 2R5. © **800/565-0000** or 902/425-5781; explore@gov.ns.ca.
- **New Brunswick Department of Tourism & Parks,** P.O. Box 12345, Fredericton, NB E3N 3T6. © **800/ 561-0123;** info@tourismnew brunswick.ca.
- **Tourism PEI,** P.O. Box 2000, Charlottetown, PEI C1A 7N8. © **800/463-4734** or 902/368-4444; peiplay@gov.pe.ca.
- **Newfoundland and Labrador Department of Tourism, Culture & Recreation,** P.O. Box 8700, St. John's, NL A1C 4K2. © **800/563-6353;** tourisminfo@mail.gov.nl.ca.

INFORMATION CENTERS All four provinces staff helpful visitor centers at key access points, including the main roadways running into the provinces and their major cities. Expect cordial staff and exceptionally well-stocked brochure racks overflowing with maps, menus, and booklets. Staff at these centers provide a surplus of information on local attractions, and they can also fill you in on what's happening anywhere else in the province so that you can plan a few days in advance. If the staffers don't have the information you need at their fingertips, they'll often make phone calls and track it down for you.

Centers are probably most numerous in Nova Scotia and Prince Edward Island; New Brunswick's information centers are equally helpful, though not as numerous. Newfoundland's visitor centers—with the exception of the modern information centers near the two main ferry terminals—are typically less polished than in the other provinces, yet authorities have been successful in making improvements. Look in the regional chapters of this guide for addresses and phone numbers of the main visitor centers in each area.

All four provinces publish free, magazine-size travel guides crammed with routine but often essential information on hotels, inns, campgrounds, and attractions. Nova Scotia's tome sets an international standard for high-quality information (and size), but the others are excellent and unfailingly helpful as well. If you haven't obtained a guide in advance by mail, be sure to request one at the first center you see when entering a province.

INTERNET RESOURCES Information on the Web is growing at an explosive rate, with some of the data more reliable than others. Here are a few places to start your search:

- **Nova Scotia:** The province's official website is a great whirlwind tour of accommodations and tourism sites; you can even download a bit of local music. It can be found at www.explorens.com or **www.novascotia.com.**

- **Nova Scotia Provincial Parks:** The province's website provides basic, up-to-date information about its many excellent parks at **www.parks.gov.ns.ca.**

- **New Brunswick:** The official tourism site offers a great place to start: **www.tourismnewbrunswick.ca.**

- **Prince Edward Island:** The official PEI online tourism information center can be found at both www.gentleisland.com and **www.peiplay.com.**

- **Newfoundland & Labrador:** The province's official website can be visited on the Internet at both www.gov.nl.ca/tourism and the unwieldy (but much easier to remember) alternative address **www.newfoundlandlabrador.com.**

- **National Parks:** For information about travels in the region's national parks, a good first stop is the Parks Canada official website at **www.pc.gc.ca.**

MAPS Excellent road maps are available from all the provincial tourism authorities (ask at the welcome centers). These maps are free except in Newfoundland, where the province has traditionally charged for them—though you can usually also obtain a Newfoundland map for free simply by phoning the province's tourism office in advance of your trip and requesting that a packet of visitor information about the province be mailed to you.

3 Entry Requirements

PASSPORTS

As of January 2007, U.S. citizens and permanent **residents of the United States must now show a passport to enter Canada and reenter the U.S.** This is a big change from the past, when a driver's license and a smile were often enough to get you across the border. (The two governments are considering amending this rule to require a passport *or* a driver's license plus a birth certificate in 2008, but no final decision has been reached.) For information on how to get a passport, go to "Passports" in the "Fast Facts" section at the end of this chapter—the websites listed can provide downloadable passport applications, as well as the current fees for processing passport applications. For up-to-date info and special bulletins on passport requirements to Canada, go to the "Document Requirements" section of the U.S. State Department Web page at **http://travel.state.gov**.

Even with a passport in hand, several restrictions can bar you from Canada anyway: previous involvement in criminal activity, human rights violations, or organized crime, to name three. You can also be deemed inadmissible for "security, health, or financial reasons," according to the Canadian embassy. Hopefully those won't ever come into play, but you should always have a backup plan for heading home if you're ever denied entry.

A note for teens traveling alone: If you're under 19, it's helpful to also bring a letter from a parent or guardian stating the purpose of the trip. If Customs officers are suspicious when you enter the country, they'll notify immigration officers and you might experience further delays before continuing onward. A letter can go a long way in proving that you're not running away or up to no good.

For more information about traveling into Canada, browse the "Visiting Canada" section of the Canadian website **www.goingtocanada.gc.ca**. You can also phone Canadian immigration officers at ℂ **888/242-2100** (from within Canada) or ℂ **800/992-7037** (from outside Canada).

VISAS

American travelers to Canada do not require visas and neither do residents of many other countries, including citizens of most European countries, Australia, New Zealand, Japan, Mexico, and some

present and former British territories in the Caribbean—this includes anyone holding a green card in the U.S. or anyone who is a British overseas citizen of the U.K. Needless to say, bring your identification or the relevant paperwork on your trip. If you're still not sure about whether you will need a visa or not, consult the Canadian government's up-to-date listing of countries whose residents *do* need one at **www.cic.gc.ca/english/visit/visas.asp**.

CUSTOMS

For information on what you can bring into and take out of Canada, go to "Customs" in the "Fast Facts" section at the end of this chapter.

4 When to Go

WEATHER   All the Atlantic Provinces lie within the **North Temperate Zone,** which means that they have weather much like New England in the United States. **Spring** is damp, cool, and short, though it can get warm and muggy as it eases into summer.

Summer's compact high season runs from early July to early September. That's when the great majority of travelers take to the road, enjoying the bright, clear days and warm temperatures. The average high in the southern three provinces is in the upper 70s°F (around 25°C); in Newfoundland, it's more typically in the upper 60s°F (around 20°C). Nights can become cool, even approaching freezing, by late summer.

Be aware that there is no "typical" summer weather in Atlantic Canada. The only thing typical is change, and you're likely to experience balmy, sunny days as well as howling rainstorms—quite possibly on the same day. Travelers who come here prepared for an occasional downpour, both psychologically and equipment-wise, tend to be happier than those who expect all blue skies. That's because

the weather in all four provinces is to a large degree affected by the ocean. This means frequent fogs, especially on the Fundy Coast of New Brunswick, the Atlantic Coast of Nova Scotia, and Newfoundland's Avalon Peninsula. The ocean also offers an unobstructed corridor for high winds, particularly on Prince Edward Island and Newfoundland.

Note that the ocean does provide some benefits: Prince Edward Island's summer tends to linger into fall, thanks to the warm, moderating influence of the Gulf of St. Lawrence, and you'll rarely experience a sultry hot, humid day because of the natural air-conditioning action of the sea breezes.

Fall is a time of bright leaf colors but also rapidly cooling temperatures, especially at night, and much shorter daylight hours. Bring winter sweaters and a heavy coat.

Few travelers tackle the Maritimes in the dead of **winter,** as frequent blustery storms sweep in off the Atlantic. But if you're one of those hardy souls who might, be aware that snow or ice storms are a very real possibility at any time during winter, and they can blow in suddenly; if you're driving, make sure your car is equipped with good snow tires and special antifreeze windshield wash (you can get it from any gas station). And drive cautiously: Outside the major urban areas, most of this region's high-speed arteries are two-lane roads sans medians. Watch for drivers coming your way.

Halifax Average Monthly Temperatures

	Jan	Feb	Mar	Apr	May	June	July	Aug	Sept	Oct	Nov	Dec
High (°F)	33	33	39	48	58	67	73	73	67	58	48	37
(°C)	1	1	4	9	14	19	23	23	19	14	9	3
Low (°F)	20	19	26	33	41	50	57	58	53	44	36	25
(°C)	–7	–7	–3	1	5	10	14	14	12	7	2	–4

HOLIDAYS   The national holidays in Canada are celebrated from the Atlantic to the Pacific to the Arctic oceans; for the traveler, this means all government offices and banks will be closed at these times. (Shops remain open on some but not all national holidays.) **National holidays** here include New Year's Day, Good Friday, Easter Monday, Victoria Day (the third Monday in May, always 1 week before Memorial Day in the United States), Canada Day (July 1; this is a biggie—expect fireworks), Labour Day (first Monday in September, same as in the U.S.), Thanksgiving (mid-October; the same as Columbus Day weekend in the United States), Remembrance Day (November 11), Christmas Day (December 25), and Boxing Day (December 26).

Locally observed **provincial holidays** include a civic holiday (August 2) in Nova Scotia; New Brunswick Day (the first Monday in August); and several holidays in Newfoundland and Labrador, including St. George's Day (April 26), Discovery Day (the third Monday in June), and Orangeman's Day (July 12). Check out the proceedings.

Acadian pockets of New Brunswick, Nova Scotia, or Prince Edward Island also celebrate St. Jean Baptiste Day (June 23–24), which was actually pagan in origin (for the summer solstice, known in Europe as midsummer's night) but has since become associated with Catholic, Québecois, and Franco culture. Expect tons of Franco fun on this day.

5 Getting There

BY PLANE
Airports around Atlantic Canada offer access via scheduled flights. Halifax, Nova Scotia, the region's major air hub, has frequent flights in and out of the region, as well as onward connections to local airports. Other major airports include Saint John, New Brunswick; Charlottetown, Prince Edward Island; and Gander and St. John's, Newfoundland. All offer direct flights to and from airports outside of the region.

The main air carriers serving Atlantic Canada are **Air Canada** (© 888/247-2262; www.aircanada.com) and its commuter partner **Jazz** (www.flyjazz.ca), but American carriers such as **Continental** (© 800/231-0856; www.continental.com) are jumping into the fray. See the individual "Getting There" sections at the beginning of each chapter for more information.

FLYING FOR LESS: TIPS FOR GETTING THE BEST AIRFARE

- Passengers who can book their tickets either **well in advance or at the last minute, or who fly midweek or at less-trafficked hours** may pay a fraction of the full fare. If your schedule is flexible, say so, and ask if you can secure a cheaper fare by changing your flight plans.

- **Search the Internet** for cheap fares. The most popular online travel sites are **Travelocity.com, Expedia.com,** and **Orbitz.com.** In the U.K., go to **Travelsupermarket** (© 0845/345-5708; www.travelsupermarket.com), a flight search engine that offers flight comparisons for the budget airlines whose seats often end up in bucket-shop sales (see below). Other websites for booking airline tickets online include **Cheapflights.com, Smarter Travel.com, Priceline.com,** and **Opodo** (www.opodo.co.uk). Meta search sites (which find and then direct you to airline and hotel websites for booking) include **SideStep.com** and **Kayak.com**—the latter includes fares for budget carriers like JetBlue and Spirit as well as the major airlines. **Site59.com** is a great source for last-minute flights and getaways. In addition, most **airlines** offer online-only fares that even their phone agents know nothing about. British travelers should check **Flights International** (© 800/018-7050; www.flights-international.com) for deals on flights all over the world.

- Keep an eye on local newspapers for **promotional specials** or **fare wars,** when airlines lower prices on their most popular routes.

- **Consolidators,** also known as bucket shops, are wholesale brokers in the airline-ticket game. Consolidators buy deeply discounted tickets ("distressed" inventories of unsold seats) from airlines and sell them to online ticket agencies, travel agents, tour operators, corporations, and, to a lesser degree, the general public. Consolidators advertise in Sunday newspaper travel sections (often in small ads with tiny type), both in the U.S. and the U.K. They can be great sources for cheap international tickets. On the downside, bucket-shop tickets are often rigged with restrictions, such as stiff cancellation penalties (as high as 50%–75% of the ticket price). And keep in mind that most of what you see advertised is of limited availability. Several reliable consolidators are worldwide and available online. **STA Travel** (www.statravel.com) has been the world's leading consolidator for students since purchasing Council Travel, but their fares are competitive for travelers of all ages. **Flights.com** (© 800/TRAV-800) has excellent fares worldwide. They also have "local" websites in 12 countries, including Canada. **Air Tickets Direct** (© 800/778-3447; www.airticketsdirect.com) is based in Montreal and leverages the currently weak Canadian dollar for low fares; they also book trips to places that U.S. travel agents won't touch, such as Cuba.

- Join **frequent-flier clubs.** Membership doesn't cost a cent, but it does entitle you to free tickets or upgrades when you amass the airline's required number of frequent-flier points. You don't even have to fly to earn points; frequent-flier credit cards can earn you thousands of miles for doing your everyday shopping. But keep in mind that award seats are limited, seats on popular routes are hard to snag, and more and more major airlines are cutting their expiration periods for mileage points—so check your airline's frequent-flier program

Tips   Getting Through the Airport

- Arrive at the airport at least 1 hour before a domestic flight and 2 hours before an international flight. You can check the average wait times at U.S. airports by visiting the Transportation Security Administration **Security Checkpoint Wait Times site** (http://waittime.tsa.dhs.gov).
- Know what you can and can't carry on. U.S. travelers can get the latest updates on items they are prohibited to bring as carry-on luggage at the website **www.tsa.gov/travelers/airtravel**.
- Beat ticket-counter lines by using self-service electronic ticket kiosks at the airport or even printing out your boarding pass at home from the airline's website. Using curbside check-in is another smart way to avoid lines.
- Help speed up security before you're screened: Remove jackets, shoes, belt buckles, heavy jewelry, and watches, and place them either in your carry-on luggage or in the security bins provided. Place keys, coins, cellphones, and pagers in a bin as well. If you have metallic body parts, carry a note from your doctor. Whenever possible, pack liquids in checked baggage.
- U.S. travelers would do well to use a TSA-approved lock for their checked luggage; this can speed security inspections. Look for Travel Sentry–certified locks at luggage or travel shops and Brookstone stores (or online at www.brookstone.com).

so you don't lose your miles before you use them. *Inside tip:* Award seats are offered as early as almost a year in advance, but seats also open up at the last minute, so if your travel plans are flexible, you may strike gold. To play the frequent-flier game to your best advantage, consult the community bulletin boards on **FlyerTalk** (www.flyertalk.com) or go to Randy Petersen's **Inside Flyer** (www.insideflyer.com). Petersen and friends review all the programs in detail and post regular updates on changes in policies and trends.

BY CAR & FERRY

Overland access to Atlantic Canada from the United States is through Maine. The most direct route to New Brunswick is to drive to Bangor (about 4½ hr. from Boston), then head east on Route 9 to Calais, Maine (about 2½ hr.). Here you

can cross into St. Stephen, New Brunswick, and pick up Route 1 to Saint John and beyond. If you don't plan to stop until you hit Moncton or points east of Moncton, a slightly faster alternative is to continue northeast on the Maine Turnpike—which is the northernmost end of the Eastern Seaboard's famous Interstate 95—to Houlton, then cross the border and pick up the Trans-Canada Highway. Remember that the Turnpike is a toll road for a stretch (the toll is US$4 maximum one-way for a passenger car), though it becomes toll-free north of Exit 113 at Augusta.

Between early May and late October, travelers headed to Nova Scotia can save driving time by taking a ferry. Summertime ferries to Nova Scotia depart daily from either Bar Harbor or Portland, Maine. A daily year-round ferry also connects Saint John, New Brunswick (about

---

Tips **Don't Stow It—Ship It**

Though pricey, it's sometimes worthwhile to travel luggage-free, particularly if you're toting sports equipment, meeting materials, or baby equipment. Specialists in door-to-door luggage delivery include **Virtual Bellhop** (www. virtualbellhop.com), **SkyCap International** (www.skycapinternational.com), **Luggage Express** (www.usxpluggageexpress.com), and **Sports Express** (www. sportsexpress.com).

---

a 4-hour drive from either Bangor or Bar Harbor, Maine) with Nova Scotia, as well.

Bay Ferries (© **888/249-7245;** www. catferry.com) operates the ferries. The Bar Harbor–Yarmouth and Portland–Yarmouth routes use *The Cat* (short for catamaran), which claims to be the fastest ferry in North America and, since going into service in 1998, has cut the crossing time from Bar Harbor from 6 hours to 2¾ hours, zipping along at up to 50 mph. Note that the ride can get very bumpy depending on wave and ocean conditions, so if you're sensitive to seasickness, bring and take motion-sickness medicine.

Summer rates one-way from Bar Harbor in 2007 were C$63 (US$57/£32) for adults and children age 13 to 18, C$43 (US$39/£22) for children 6 to 13, C$58 (US$52/£29) for seniors, and C$105 (US$95/£53) and up per vehicle. From Portland, it cost C$89 per adult (US$80/£45), C$59 (US$53/£30) per child age 13 to 18, C$85 (US$77/£43) per senior, and C$149 (US$134/£75) and up per vehicle. Same-day return and weekend-getaway round-trip fares are cheaper. Reservations for both routes are *vital* during the peak summer season.

The year-round ferry, known as the *Princess of Acadia*, links Saint John, New Brunswick, with Digby, Nova Scotia. The ferry sails daily year-round, with as many as three crossings per day in summer. Peak season one-way fares (charged June–Oct) in 2007 were C$40 (US$36/£20) for adults, C$25 (US$23/£13) for

children age 6 to 13, C$5 (US$4.50/£2.50) per child under age 6, C$30 (US$27/£15) for seniors, and C$80 (US$72/£40) and up per vehicle. Fares are a bit cheaper outside the peak travel months; if you walk on and return within 30 days, there are also discounts available on the round-trip. Complete up-to-the-minute schedules and fares for the *Princess of Acadia* be found at **www.nfl-bay.com** or by calling © **888/249-SAIL.**

BY BUS

Bus service into and out of the region tends to be slow and cumbersome. To get from New York to Halifax, for instance, you'd have to take the bus to Montréal (8–10 hr.), then connect to another bus line to Halifax (something like 18 hr.). A late-spring through early-fall alternative from the East Coast of the United States is to bus it from New York to either Portland or Bar Harbor, Maine (either 6 hr. or 10 hr.), stay overnight in town, and then take the early-morning ferry to Yarmouth, Nova Scotia (less than 3 hr.). Remember that you must be certain which port the boat is departing from each day; it alternates between the two ports almost daily. From Yarmouth, you can then catch a connecting bus onward to Halifax (about 4 hr.).

Greyhound (© **800/231-2222** or 214/849-8100; www.greyhound.com) offers service from diverse points around the United States to Montréal's bus station (© **514/843-4231**), from which you can connect directly to Atlantic

Canada–bound buses. Figure on spending 12 to 18 hours to get from Montréal to key cities in the eastern provinces; there is a 6am departure, for example, arriving in Halifax around midnight of the same day.

Acadian Lines (© 800/567-5151; www.smtbus.com) offers service from Bangor, Maine, to New Brunswick several times weekly and reliable daily services within Nova Scotia, New Brunswick, and Prince Edward Island. It's actually possible to circumnavigate the key points in those provinces entirely using Acadian buses.

BY TRAIN
VIA Rail (© 888/842-7245) offers train service 6 days a week between Halifax and Montréal (no service Tues), with several stops along the way (see "By Train" in the subsequent section, "Getting Around Eastern Canada"). The entire trip takes between 18 and 21 hours, depending on direction, with a basic summertime fare of about C$240 (US$216/£120) each way, not including sleeping accommodations. Discounts for those buying at least 1 week in advance are possible.

Sleeping berths and private cabins are available at extra cost—the cheapest bed, in a double-bunked cabin, is about twice the cost of the no-bed fare—and VIA has also now added a higher class of service on its overnight run known as the Easterly class, which includes better beds, presentations from an onboard guide and other activities, and a private dome car.

6 Money

It's always advisable to bring money in a variety of forms on a vacation: a mix of cash, credit cards, and traveler's checks. You should also exchange enough petty cash to cover airport incidentals, tipping, and transportation to your hotel before you leave home, or withdraw money upon arrival at an airport ATM (automated teller machine; see below).

ATMs often offer the best exchange rates; avoid exchanging money at commercial exchange bureaus and hotels, which usually have the highest transaction fees.

CURRENCY
Canadian currency, like U.S. currency, is denominated in dollars and cents, though there are some differences. Canada has no $1 bill. It does have a $1 coin (called a "loonie" because it depicts a loon) and a $2 coin (called a "twoonie"). At press time, C$1 was worth approximately US¢90 and 50p.

If you're driving into Canada, you needn't worry about stocking up on Canadian dollars before or immediately upon entry into Canada. U.S. currency is widely accepted, especially in border towns, and you'll often see signs at cash registers announcing current exchange rates. These are not always the best rates, however, so it behooves you to visit an ATM or cash some traveler's checks as soon as you're able.

You'll avoid lines at airport ATMs by exchanging at least some money before you leave home. You can exchange money at your local American Express or Thomas Cook office or at your bank. American Express offices in the U.S. also dispense traveler's checks and foreign currency via © 800/807-6233 or **www. americanexpress.com**, though they'll charge a US$15 order fee plus additional shipping costs.

For tips and telephone numbers to call if your wallet is stolen or lost, go to "Lost & Found" in the "Fast Facts" section of this chapter.

ATMS
Obtaining cash is rarely a problem for travelers in Canada. The easiest and best

way to get cash away from home is from an ATM, sometimes referred to in Canada as a "cash machine" or a "cashpoint." These are widely available in most midsize towns and cities, and the networks are often compatible with U.S. banks, allowing travelers to use their own ATM or credit cards for cash withdrawals. Your bank will convert the currency at the prevailing rate. For example, if you withdraw C$100 from a Canadian bank machine, your bank statement will show a withdrawal of around US$90 (or £50 in the U.K.). Be sure you know your personal identification number (PIN) before arriving at said ATM. If you don't know yours, call the number on the back of your credit card and ask the bank to mail it to you; this usually takes 5 to 7 business days.

The **Cirrus** (© **800/424-7787;** www.mastercard.com) and **PLUS** (© **800/ 843-7587;** www.visa.com) ATM networks span the globe. Go to your bank card's website to find ATM locations at your destination. Be sure you know your daily withdrawal limit before you depart.

Many banks impose a fee every time you use a card at another bank's ATM, and that fee can be higher for international transactions (up to US$5 or more) than for domestic ones (where they're rarely more than US$2). In addition, the bank from which you withdraw cash may charge its own fee. For international withdrawal fees, ask your bank.

Note: Banks that are members of the **Global ATM Alliance** charge no transaction fees for cash withdrawals at other Alliance member ATMs; by chance, these include Bank of America (in the U.S.) and Scotiabank (widespread in eastern Canada). The lesson? If you have a BoA account, seek out Scotiabank ATMs.

CREDIT CARDS

Credit cards are another safe way to carry money. They provide a convenient record of all your expenses and generally offer relatively good exchange rates. You can withdraw cash advances from your credit cards at banks or ATMs (provided you remember your PIN), though high fees can make credit card cash advances a pricey way to get cash. Keep in mind that you'll pay interest from the moment of your withdrawal, even if you pay your monthly bills on time. Also, note that many banks now assess a 1% to 3% "transaction fee" on *all* charges you incur abroad. Credit cards more or less universally accepted in eastern Canada include Visa, MasterCard, Interac (a Canadian card), and American Express. Diners Club and Discover are accepted by a few merchants, but not many. Remember to bring some cash, in any case: Many small establishments still accept *no* credit cards.

TRAVELER'S CHECKS

You can buy traveler's checks at most U.S. banks. They are offered in U.S. denominations of $20, $50, $100, $500, and sometimes $1,000. Generally, you'll pay a service charge ranging from 1% to 4%.

The most popular traveler's checks are offered by **American Express** (© **800/ 807-6233** or 800/221-7282 for cardholders; this number accepts collect calls, offers service in several foreign languages,

---

Tips **Small Change**

When you change money, ask for some small bills or loose change. Petty cash will come in handy for tipping and public transportation. Consider keeping the change separate from your larger bills so that it's readily accessible and you'll be less of a target for theft.

and exempts Amex gold and platinum cardholders from the 1% fee), **Visa** (© 800/732-1322), and **MasterCard** (© 800/223-9920). American Automobile Association (AAA) members can obtain Visa checks for a US$9.95 fee (for checks up to US$1,500) at most AAA offices or by calling © 866/339-3378. Auto clubs in other countries may have similar deals worked out.

Be sure to keep a record of the traveler's checks' serial numbers separate from your checks in the event that they are stolen or lost. You'll get a refund faster if you know the numbers.

American Express, Thomas Cook, Visa, and MasterCard also offer **foreign currency traveler's checks** in Canadian dollars. They're accepted at some locations where U.S.-dollar checks may not be.

7 Travel Insurance

The cost of travel insurance varies widely depending on the destination, the cost and length of your trip, your age and health, and the type of trip you're taking, but expect to pay between 5% and 8% of the vacation itself.

You can get great quick estimates of your policy cost from various providers through the website **InsureMyTrip.com.** Enter your trip cost and dates, your age, and a little more information, and the engine fires back prices from more than a dozen companies.

U.K. citizens and their families who make more than one trip abroad per year may find an annual travel insurance policy works out cheaper. They should check **www.moneysupermarket.com,** which compares prices across a wide range of providers for single and multitrip policies. Most big travel agents offer their own insurance and will probably try to sell you their package when you book a holiday; think before you sign. **Britain's Consumers' Association** recommends

that you insist on seeing a policy and reading the fine print before buying any travel insurance. **The Association of British Insurers** (© 020/7600-3333; www.abi.org.uk) gives advice by phone and publishes "Holiday Insurance," a free guide to policy provisions and prices. You might also shop around for better deals: Try **Columbus Direct** (© 0870/033-9988; www.columbusdirect.net).

TRIP-CANCELLATION INSURANCE

Trip-cancellation insurance will help you retrieve your money if you have to back out of a trip or depart early, or if your travel supplier goes bankrupt. Trip cancellation traditionally covers such events as sickness, natural disasters, and State Department advisories. The latest news in trip-cancellation insurance is the availability of **"any reason" cancellation coverage**—which costs more but covers cancellations made for any reason. You won't get back 100% of your prepaid trip cost, but you'll be

Travel in the Age of Bankruptcy

Airlines go bankrupt, so protect yourself by **buying your tickets with a credit card.** The Fair Credit Billing Act guarantees that you can get your money back from the credit card company if a travel supplier goes under (and if you request the refund within 60 days of the bankruptcy). **Travel insurance** can also help, but make sure it covers against "carrier default" for your specific travel provider. And be aware that if a U.S. airline goes bust mid-trip, a 2001 federal law requires other carriers to take you to your destination (on a space-available basis) for a fee of no more than US$25, provided you rebook within 60 days of the cancellation.

refunded a substantial portion. **TravelSafe** (© 888/885-7233; www.travelsafe.com) offers both types of coverage. Expedia also offers any-reason cancellation coverage for its air/hotel packages.

For details, contact one of the following recommended insurers: **Access America** (© 866/807-3982; www.accessamerica.com), **AIG Travel Guard** (© 800/826-4919; www.travelguard.com), **Travel Insured International** (© 800/243-3174; www.travelinsured.com), and **Travelex Insurance Services** (© 888/457-4602; www.travelex-insurance.com).

MEDICAL INSURANCE

Canadians are obviously covered when traveling within Canada. Most U.S. health plans (including Medicare and Medicaid), however, do *not* provide coverage for travel to Canada, and the ones that do often require you to pay for services upfront and reimburse you only after you return home.

As a safety net, if you're a U.S. citizen, you may want to buy travel medical insurance, particularly if you're traveling to a remote or high-risk area where emergency evacuation might be necessary. If you require additional medical insurance, try **MEDEX Travel Insurance and**

Emergency Assistance (© 410/453-6300; www.medexassist.com) or **Travel Assistance International** (© 800/821-2828; www.travelassistance.com; for general information on services, call the company's **Worldwide Assistance Services, Inc.,** at © 800/777-8710).

LOST-LUGGAGE INSURANCE

On international flights (including U.S. portions of international trips), baggage coverage is limited to approximately US$9.07 per pound, up to approximately US$635 per checked bag. If you plan to check items more valuable than what's covered by the standard liability, see if your homeowner's policy covers your valuables, get baggage insurance as part of your comprehensive travel-insurance package, or buy **AIG Travel Guard's** "BagTrak" product (© 800/826-4919; www.travelguard.com).

If your luggage is lost, immediately file a lost-luggage claim at the airport, detailing the luggage contents. Most airlines require that you report delayed, damaged, or lost baggage within 4 hours of arrival. The airlines are required to deliver luggage, once found, directly to your house or destination free of charge.

8 Health & Safety

Canada is one of the safest, cleanest countries in the world; as such, traveling in eastern Canada doesn't pose any special health threats, and food and water are generally very safe to consume. Of course, you should always prepare for every eventuality anyway.

GENERAL AVAILABILITY OF HEALTH CARE

Canada's health-care system is excellent; you shouldn't ever have trouble finding English-speaking medical help, unless you're in very remote areas of, for example, Newfoundland or Labrador. Contact the **International Association for Medical Assistance to Travellers** (© 716/754-4883 or, in Canada, 416/652-0137; www.iamat.org) for tips on travel and health concerns in Canada and lists of doctors if you need them. The United States **Centers for Disease Control and Prevention** (© 800/311-3435; www.cdc.gov) provides up-to-date information on health hazards by region or country and offers tips on food safety, though Canada is rarely affected by these. **Travel Health Online** (www.tripprep.com), sponsored by a consortium of travel medicine practitioners, may also offer helpful advice on traveling abroad. You can find listings of reliable medical clinics overseas at **The International Society of Travel Medicine** (www.istm.org).

WHAT TO DO IF YOU GET SICK AWAY FROM HOME

If you become sick in Canada, you may very well need to pay all your medical costs upfront and seek reimbursement later. Medicare and Medicaid, for example, do not provide coverage for medical costs outside the U.S. Before leaving home, find out what medical services your health insurance covers. To protect yourself, consider buying medical travel insurance (see "Medical Insurance," under "Travel Insurance," above).

Very few health insurance plans pay for medical evacuation back to the U.S. (which can cost US$10,000 and up), but a number of companies offer medical evacuation services anywhere in the world. If you're ever hospitalized more than 150 miles from home (eastern Canada is more than 150 miles from *everywhere*), **MedjetAssist** (© 800/527-7478; www.medjetassistance.com) will pick you up and fly you to the hospital of your choice virtually anywhere in the world in a medically equipped and staffed aircraft 24 hours day, 7 days a week. Annual memberships are US$225 individual, US$350 family; you can also purchase short-term memberships. See the list of **hospitals** and **emergency numbers** in the "Fast Facts" section at the end of this chapter.

If you suffer from a chronic illness, consult your doctor before your departure. Pack **prescription medications** in your carry-on luggage, and carry them in their original containers, with pharmacy labels—otherwise they won't make it through airport security. Carry the generic name of prescription medicines, in case a local pharmacist is unfamiliar with the brand name.

SAFETY

The cities of Atlantic Canada are small, well policed, and generally safe. Rowdies and drunks may occasionally be annoying or even a bit threatening, especially late on weekend nights in downtown neighborhoods, but serious crime is extremely rare in eastern Canada.

Nonetheless, whenever you're traveling in an unfamiliar place, **stay alert,** be aware of your immediate surroundings, and **take precautions** such as locking your car and hotel room and not walking alone in dark, unpopulated urban areas late at night. And carry a cellphone at all times if you have one.

The emergency number in eastern Canada is © **911.**

9 Specialized Travel Resources

TRAVELERS WITH DISABILITIES

Canada has made tremendous efforts toward eliminating barriers to mobility for its citizens and, by extension, its tourist visitors. City pavements feature curb cuts for wheelchair travel, and larger hotels and airports sport wheelchair-accessible washrooms. A growing number of restaurants and tourist attractions are now designed for wheelchair accessibility as well, although room for improvement remains.

The **Access-Able Travel Source** (www.access-able.com) is a website featuring an online database with information about hotels, tour operators, and attractions that can accommodate travelers with disabilities in the United States and Canada. The offerings for Atlantic Canada are understandably a bit slim, but the site is easy to navigate and does provide links to such resources as service animals, equipment rentals, and access guides.

The **Canadian Paraplegic Association** (www.canparaplegic.org) runs a helpful website and also maintains an office in each of the three Atlantic provinces. Consult the website for the local phone numbers.

Travelers with disabilities headed for Nova Scotia may ask about transportation or recreational facilities by contacting the **Nova Scotia League for Equal Opportunities,** 5251 Duke St., Suite 1211, Halifax, NS B3J 1P3 (© **866/696-7536** or 902/455-6942; www.novascotia leo.org).

Other organizations that offer a vast range of resources and assistance to disabled travelers include **MossRehab ResourceNet** (© **800/CALL-MOSS;** www.mossresourcenet.org), the **American Foundation for the Blind** (© **800/232-5463;** www.afb.org), and the **Society for Accessible Travel & Hospitality** (SATH; © **212/447-7284;** www.sath.org). **AirAmbulanceCard.com** is now partnered with SATH and allows you to preselect top-notch hospitals in case of an emergency.

Some travel agencies offer customized tours and itineraries for travelers with disabilities. Among them are **Accessible Journeys** (© **800/846-4537** or 610/521-0339; www.disabilitytravel.com), which can help you find a Royal Caribbean cruise touching Halifax and Saint John, for example.

Flying with Disability (www.flying-with-disability.org) is a comprehensive information source on airplane travel. **Avis Rent a Car** (© **888/879-4273**) has an "Avis Access" program that offers services for customers with special travel needs. These include specially outfitted vehicles with swivel seats, spinner knobs, and hand controls; mobility scooter rentals; and accessible bus service. Be sure to reserve well in advance.

Also check out the quarterly magazine *Emerging Horizons* (www.emerging horizons.com), available by subscription ($16.95 per year in the U.S.; $21.95 annually outside the U.S.). The "Accessible Travel" link at **Mobility-Advisor.com** offers a variety of travel resources to disabled persons as well.

Finally, **British travelers** should contact **Holiday Care** (© **0845/124-9971** in UK only; www.holidaycare.org.uk) to access a wide range of travel information and resources for disabled and elderly people.

GAY & LESBIAN TRAVELERS

Canada is considered extremely friendly to gay travelers. The Canadian website GayTraveler (**www.gaytraveler.ca**) offers ideas and advice for gay travel all over the world, while the **International Gay and Lesbian Travel Association** (© **800/448-8550** or 954/776-2626; www.iglta.org) is the trade association for the gay and lesbian travel industry and offers an online directory of gay- and lesbian-friendly travel businesses and tour operators.

Many agencies offer tours and travel itineraries specifically for gay and lesbian travelers. **Above and Beyond Tours** (© 800/397-2681; www.abovebeyond tours.com) are gay Australia tour specialists, but also run trips to New England and Canada. The San Francisco–based **Now, Voyager** (© 800/255-6951; www. nowvoyager.com) offers worldwide trips and cruises. And **Olivia** (© 800/631-6277; www.olivia.com) offers lesbian cruises and resort vacations.

Gay.com Travel (© 800/929-2268 or 415/644-8044; www.gay.com/travel or www.outandabout.com) is an excellent online successor to the popular **Out & About** print magazine. It provides regularly updated information about gay-owned, gay-oriented, and gay-friendly lodging, dining, sightseeing, nightlife, and shopping establishments in every important destination worldwide. British travelers can click on the "Travel" link at **www.uk.gay.com** for advice and gay-friendly trip ideas.

The following travel guides are available at many bookstores, or you can order them from any online bookseller: *Spartacus International Gay Guide* (www. spartacusworld.com/gayguide), *Odysseus: The International Gay Travel Planner,* and the *Damron* guides (www.damron. com), which publish separate, annual books for gay men and lesbians.

SENIOR TRAVEL

Few countries are as attentive to the needs of seniors as Canada. Discounts are extended to people over 60 for everything ranging from public transportation to museum and movie admissions. Even many hotels, tour operators, and restaurants offer discounts, so don't be bashful about inquiring, but always carry some kind of identification that shows your date of birth. (It's always best to inquire before checking in or ordering.) This discount varies widely; in practice, the gap between senior prices and full price seems to be narrowing in recent years. But ask anyway.

Members of the AARP, 601 E St. NW, Washington, DC 20049 (© 888/687-2277; www.aarp.org), get discounts when traveling to or in Canada on hotels, airfares, and car rentals. AARP offers members a wide range of benefits, including *AARP: The Magazine* and a monthly newsletter. Anyone over 50 can join.

Many reliable agencies and organizations target the 50-plus market. **Elderhostel** (© 800/454-5768; www.elder hostel.org) arranges worldwide study programs for those aged 55 and over. They manage several great tours of Atlantic Canada, including a Nova Scotia–PEI combo (10 days) and a sweeping bus tour of Newfoundland (14 days). *Bonus:* You can view the complete tour itinerary—including the actual inns and hotels you'll be staying in—online before laying down any cash.

Recommended publications offering travel resources and discounts for seniors include the quarterly magazine *Travel 50 & Beyond* (www.travel50andbeyond. com) and the best-selling paperback *Unbelievably Good Deals and Great Adventures That You Absolutely Can't Get Unless You're Over 50* (McGraw-Hill), by Joan Rattner Heilman.

FAMILY TRAVEL

Eastern Canada is a great place to take the kids: safe, clean, and sprinkled with just enough amusements and outdoor jaunts to keep them engaged. To locate accommodations, restaurants, and attractions that are particularly kid-friendly, refer to the "Kids" icon throughout this guide.

Recommended family travel websites include **Family Travel Forum** (www. familytravelforum.com), a comprehensive site that offers customized trip planning; **Family Travel Network** (www.familytravel network.com), an online magazine providing travel tips; and **TravelWithYour Kids.com** (www.travelwithyourkids.com), a comprehensive site, written by parents for parents, offering sound advice for long-distance and international travel with children.

STUDENT TRAVEL

The **International Student Travel Confederation** (www.istc.org) was formed in 1949 to make travel around the world more affordable for students. Check out its website for comprehensive travel services information and details on how to get an **International Student Identity Card,** which qualifies students for substantial savings on rail passes, plane tickets, entrance fees, and more. It also provides students with basic health and life insurance and a 24-hour help line. The card is valid for a maximum of 18 months. You can apply for the card online or in person at **STA Travel** (© **800/781-4040** in North America; www.statravel.com), the biggest student travel agency in the world; check out the website to locate STA Travel offices worldwide. If you're no longer a student but are still under 26, you can get an **International Youth Travel Card** from the same people, which entitles you to some discounts. **Travel CUTS** (© **800/ 592-2887;** www.travelcuts.com) offers similar services for both Canadians and U.S. residents. Irish students may prefer to turn to **USIT** (© **01/602-1904;** www. usit.ie), an Ireland-based specialist in student, youth, and independent travel.

SINGLE TRAVELERS

On package vacations, single travelers are often hit with a "single supplement" to the base price. To avoid it, you can agree to room with other single travelers or find a compatible roommate before you go from one of the many roommate-locator agencies. **Travel Buddies Singles Travel Club** (© **800/998-9099;** www.travel buddiesworldwide.com) is based here in Canada; runs small, intimate, single-friendly group trips; and will match you with a roommate free of charge. **TravelChums** (© **212/787-2621;** www.travel chums.com) is an Internet-only travel-companion matching service with elements of an online-personals-type site, hosted by the respected New York–based ShawGuides travel service.

Many reputable tour companies offer singles-only trips. **Singles Travel International** (© **877/765-6874;** www.singles travelintl.com) offers singles-only escorted tours to faraway places like London, Alaska, Fiji, and the Greek Islands; its fall foliage cruise touches down in Halifax. **Backroads** (© **800/462-2848;** www. backroads.com) offers "Singles + Solos" active-travel trips to destinations worldwide, including walking, cycling, and kayak tours in eastern Canada.

10 Sustainable Tourism/Ecotourism

Each time you take a flight or drive a car, CO_2 is released into the atmosphere. You can help neutralize this danger to our planet through "carbon offsetting"— paying someone to reduce your CO_2 emissions by the same amount you've added. Carbon offsets can be purchased in the U.S. from companies such as **Carbonfund.org** (www.carbonfund.org) and **TerraPass** (www.terrapass.org), and from **Climate Care** (www.climatecare. org) in the U.K.

Although one can argue persuasively that any vacation including an airplane flight can't be truly "green," you can offset carbon emissions from your flight in other ways. Choose forward-looking companies that embrace responsible

Landscape Is Not Just Scenery

The countryside of the Atlantic Provinces is not just scenery—it's home to millennia of natural history (of volcanoes, icebergs, polar bears, whales, and caribou, oh my!), as well as human history (of Vikings, native Canadians, fishermen, and hunters who predate the earliest European settlers, lobstermen). And the story this history tells continues today, creating the place we call eastern Canada. Understand the history, and these creatures and landscapes you'll be interacting with, *before* you get there and you'll have a better trip—and become a more ecologically aware traveler with a deeper respect for what you're experiencing.

Pick up the books of Canadian author Farley Mowat; a locally written book on eastern Canadian geography, geology, natural history, or native Canadian culture (library book sales and local gift shops are two great sources); or a novel by E. Annie Proulx. For information about the whales you'll be glimpsing (and how to respect them), for example, visit the **Whale and Dolphin Conservation Society** (www.wdcs.org). For info on traveling lightly in general, see **Tread Lightly** (www.treadlightly.org) online.

development practices, helping preserve destinations for the future by working alongside local people. An increasing number of sustainable tourism initiatives can help you plan a family trip and leave as small a "footprint" as possible on the places you visit.

Responsible Travel (www.responsible travel.com) contains a great source of sustainable travel ideas run by a spokesperson for responsible tourism in the travel industry. **Sustainable Travel International** (www.sustainabletravel international.org) also promotes responsible tourism practices and issues an annual Green Gear & Gift Guide.

You can find eco-friendly travel tips, statistics, and touring companies and associations—listed by destination under "Travel Choice"—at **The International Ecotourism Society (TIES)** website, **www. ecotourism.org.** Also check out **Conservation International** (www.conservation. org), which, with *National Geographic Traveler,* annually presents **World Legacy**

Awards (www.nationalgeographic.com/ traveler/worldlegacyaward.html) to those travel tour operators, businesses, organizations, and places that have made a significant contribution to sustainable tourism. **Ecotravel.com** is part online magazine and part eco-directory that lets you search for touring companies in several categories (water-based, land-based, spiritually oriented, and so on).

In the U.K., **Tourism Concern** (www. tourismconcern.org.uk) works to reduce social and environmental problems connected to tourism and find ways of improving tourism so that local benefits are increased.

The **Association of British Travel Agents** (www.abta.com) acts as a focal point for the U.K. travel industry and is one of the leading groups spearheading responsible tourism. **The Association of Independent Tour Operators** (www. aito.co.uk) is another group of interesting specialist operators leading the field in making holidays sustainable.

Tips It's Easy Being Green

Here are a few simple ways to travel lightly:

- Whenever possible, choose nonstop flights; they generally require less fuel than those that must stop and take off again.
- If renting a car is necessary (it might be, in Atlantic Canada), ask the rental agent for the smallest, most fuel-efficient car available that will serve your traveling party's needs. Not only will you use less gas, you'll save at the pump.
- At hotels, request that your sheets and towels not be changed daily. You'll save water and energy by not washing them as often, and you'll prolong the life of the towels, too. (Many hotels already have programs like this in place.)
- Turn off lights and air conditioners (or heaters) when you leave your hotel room.

---

11 Staying Connected

TELEPHONES

Pay phones are located throughout Atlantic Canada and are self-explanatory. Local calls are C25¢ to C50¢ (US25¢–US45¢/15p–25p). Calls to the United States or elsewhere abroad can be pricey, and you should check in advance whether your calling card works in Canada. Check at drugstores or convenience stores for local versions of prepaid calling cards, which usually offer a better rate for calling long distance than feeding coins into the phone. There might be a "setup" or per-call fee hidden in the cost of such cards, however.

The United States and Canada are on the same long-distance system. To make a long-distance call between the United States and Canada (in either direction), simply dial ℂ 1 first, then the area code and number. It's no different from calling long distance in the United States.

Remember that numbers beginning with 888 and 866 in Canada are toll-free—but some of these do not work when dialed from outside Canada. (And some toll-free numbers in the U.S. won't work when dialed from Canada.)

CELLPHONES

Some U.S. cellphones work in Canada, though you'll pay roaming and long-distance charges that can push call costs above the $1 per-minute level. Fortunately, national U.S. carriers offer Canadian calling plans that may reduce your roaming and long-distance charges while making calls from within Canada (but see below). Check with your carrier about switching to one such plan for the duration of your trip—without any penalties for switching back off it after you get back home.

You should be able to make and receive calls in populated areas of eastern Canada if your cellphone is from another country, works on a GSM (Global System for Mobile Communications) system, or you have a world-capable multiband phone. In the U.S., **T-Mobile** and **AT&T Wireless** (which now includes customers of the former **Cingular**) use the quasi-universal GSM system. In Canada, **Microcell** and some **Rogers** customers are GSM, and all **European** and most **Australian** phones come GSM-ready. GSM phones function with a removable plastic

SIM card, encoded with your phone number and account information.

To use your phone in Canada, simply call your wireless operator before departure and ask for "international roaming" to be activated on your account. Again, per-minute charges can be high, even if you do subscribe to some form of extended calling plan or international add-on plan that includes Canadian minutes. I have a world-calling plan with my provider, yet I still pay 20¢ per minute to call Canadian numbers with my cell—three times what it costs me to call Japan or England on the same plan. (What's up with that?) On the other hand, I passed on my provider's special Canada-only add-on plan, which would probably have reduced my per-minute cost substantially—if I were expecting to use my phone often in Canada (I wasn't).

If your cellphone doesn't work in Canada or is prohibitively expensive to use, **renting a Canadian cellphone** is a second option. While you can rent a phone from any number of overseas sites, including kiosks at Canadian airports and car-rental agencies, it's usually best to rent the phone before you leave home. Two good wireless rental companies are **InTouch USA** (© **800/872-7626;** www.intouchglobal.com) and **Roadpost** (© **888/290-1606** or 905/272-5665; www.roadpost.com). InTouch will even advise you for free on whether your existing phone will work overseas; simply call © **703/222-7161** between 9am and 4pm EST, or go to **http://intouchglobal. com/travel.htm**. Such phone rental isn't cheap, however. You'll pay a not-small weekly fee, plus airtime fees (sometimes up to a dollar a minute); the industry's price points are constantly changing, so ask carefully about what you must pay to use the phone inside Canada.

Buying a Canadian cellphone is another option, and might be economically attractive if you can locate a cheap prepaid phone system. Stop by a local cellphone shop in Halifax or wherever you're arriving and ask about the cheapest package; you'll probably pay less than

---

Frommers.com: The Complete Travel Resource

It should go without saying, but we highly recommend **Frommers.com,** voted Best Travel Site by *PC Magazine*. We think you'll find our expert advice and tips; independent reviews of hotels, restaurants, attractions, and preferred shopping and nightlife venues; vacation giveaways; and an online booking tool indispensable before, during, and after your travels. We publish the complete contents of over 128 travel guides in our **Destinations** section, covering nearly 3,600 places worldwide to help you plan your trip. Each weekday, we publish original articles reporting on **Deals & News** via our free **Frommers.com Newsletter** to help you save time and money and travel smarter. We're betting you'll find our new **Events** listings (http://events. frommers.com) an invaluable resource; it's an up-to-the-minute roster of what's happening in cities everywhere—including concerts, festivals, lectures, and more. We've also added weekly **podcasts, interactive maps,** and hundreds of new images across the site. Check out our **Travel Talk** area featuring **Message Boards** where you can join in conversations with thousands of fellow Frommer's travelers and post your trip report once you return.

$100 for a phone and a starter calling card. Local calls may be as low as 10¢ per minute, and in many countries incoming calls are free.

A final note on **service coverage in eastern Canada:** These provinces are *very* thinly populated—and as such, cell towers are few and far between. You will not be able to use your cellphone everywhere you go; even driving the Trans-Canada Highway, you'll pop in and out of service for stretches. In the major cities, you will always be reliably connected; in the smaller towns, sometimes; and, in the wilderness of the big national and provincial parks, I doubt it. Keep one on hand at all times for emergencies, but don't expect it to work anywhere and everywhere. Definitely ask park rangers about cell coverage before you venture into the backcountry.

VOICE OVER INTERNET PROTOCOL (VOIP)

If you have access to the Web while traveling, you might consider a broadband-based telephone service (in technical terms, **Voice over Internet Protocol,** or **VoIP**) such as **Skype** (www.skype.com) or **Vonage** (www.vonage.com), which allows you to make free international calls if you use their services from your laptop or in a cybercafe.

INTERNET/E-MAIL WITHOUT YOUR OWN COMPUTER

To find cybercafes in your destination, check www.cybercaptive.com and www.cybercafe.com (ideally before going); interestingly, these two search engines spit out quite different results for the same locations. Cities like Halifax and Charlottetown are rife with such cafes; anywhere else, it's catch-as-catch-can—but many towns in eastern Canada now sport at least one cybercafe. (Hey, even fishermen and sailors need to check e-mail while in port these days.) It might double as the town laundry/coffee shop, but it'll be there. Somewhere. Ask locally.

Most major airports have **Internet kiosks** that provide basic Web access for a per-minute fee that's usually higher than cybercafe prices. Check out copy shops like **FedEx Kinko's,** which offers computer stations with fully loaded software (as well as Wi-Fi).

Aside from formal cybercafes, most **youth hostels** in Canada also have at least one computer with Internet access. Many **public libraries** in Canada also offer access free or for a small charge. (Avoid hotel business centers unless you're willing to pay exorbitant rates or have no other choice.)

(Tips Hey, Google, Did You Get My Text Message?

It's bound to happen: The day you leave this guidebook back at the hotel for an unencumbered stroll through Charlottetown, you'll forget the address of the lunch spot you had set out for. If you're traveling with a mobile device, send a text message to ✆ **466453 (GOOGLE)** for a lightning-fast response. For instance, type "Rudder's Seafood Yarmouth NS" and within 10 seconds you'll receive a text message with the address and phone number. This nifty trick works in a range of search categories: Look up weather ("weather Halifax NS"), language translations ("translate goodbye in French"), currency conversions ("10 USD in Canadian dollars"), movie times ("Harry Potter B0M 1S0"), and more. If your search results are off, be more specific. For more tips and search options, see www.google.com/intl/en_us/mobile/sms/. Regular text message charges apply.

Online Traveler's Toolbox

Veteran travelers know how to navigate the Web to make their trips easier. Here are a few sites you might find useful.

- **Airplane Food** (www.airlinemeals.net)
- **Airplane Seating** (www.seatguru.com and www.airlinequality.com)
- **Maps** (maps.yahoo.ca, www.google.ca/maps, and www.mapquest.ca)
- **MasterCard ATM Locator** (www.mastercard.com)
- **Universal Currency Converter** (www.xe.com/ucc)
- **Visa ATM Locator** (www.visa.com)
- **Weather** (www.intellicast.com, www.weather.com, and www.weather.ca)

WITH YOUR OWN COMPUTER

More and more hotels, resorts, airports, cafes, retailers, and even entire cities are going **Wi-Fi** (wireless fidelity), becoming "hotspots" that offer free high-speed Wi-Fi access or charge a small fee for usage. The city of **Fredericton** in New Brunswick has won national awards in Canada for its free citywide Wi-Fi network, for instance. Most laptops sold today have built-in wireless capabilities. To find public Wi-Fi hotspots at your destination, go to **www.jiwire.com**; its hotspot finder holds the world's largest directory of public wireless hotspots.

You sign up for wireless access service much as you do for cellphone service, through a plan offered by one of several commercial companies that have made wireless service available in many airports, hotel lobbies, and coffee shops, including some locations in Canada. **TELUS** (www.telusmobility.com), a Canadian cellular phone provider, is also slowly spreading its hotspots into eastern Canada.

In some areas or hotels, you'll be forced to choose slower **dial-up access;** most business-class hotels in Canada offer dataports for laptop modems. (Don't expect a phone in your room if you're staying at a B&B in eastern Canada, however.) Business hotels will also sometimes loan or rent a **connection kit** for around C$10 (US$9/£5), but again, don't expect this service at inns or B&Bs. To be safe, bring your own connection kit: the right power and phone adapters (if needed), a spare phone line (easy to find at electronics shops), and a spare Ethernet network cable (ditto). Or find out whether your hotel supplies such items to guests by calling ahead.

Canadian hotels, inns, and private homes use the same phone jacks and electrical current as the United States: Electricity is 110–115 volts, 60 cycles. If you're traveling from the U.S., you won't need adapters for your plugs. Coming from anywhere else, you probably will.

12 Packages for the Independent Traveler

Before you start searching for the lowest airfare, you might want to consider booking your flight as part of a travel package. Package tours are not the same as escorted tours. With a package tour, you travel independently but pay a group rate. You can buy airfare, accommodations, and other elements of your trip (such as car rentals, airport transfers, and sometimes even activities) at the same time, often at

Package and Escorted Tours: The Pros & Cons

Package deals always have pros and cons. On the upside, they can **save you money** while allowing for independent travel; some even let you add on a few guided excursions or escorted day trips (often at discounted prices lower than what you would pay if you booked them yourself). But you're usually required to **make a large deposit** payment upfront; you may end up on a **charter flight;** and you have to deal with your own luggage and transfers between your hotel and the airport if transfers are not included in the package price. Packages often **don't allow for complete flexibility** or a wide range of choices of activity while on the trip, either—you may prefer a quiet inn but have to settle for a chain hotel. Choice of travel dates may be limited, too.

Before you invest in a package tour, get some answers. Ask about the **accommodations choices** and prices for each. Then look up the hotels' reviews in a Frommer's guide and check their rates online for your specific dates of travel. You'll also want to find out **what type of room** you will be getting (smoking, nonsmoking, king, twin-bedded, and so on). If you need a certain type of room, ask for it; don't take whatever is thrown your way. Request a nonsmoking room, a quiet room, a high-floor room with an ocean view, or whatever you fancy.

Watch out for **hidden expenses,** too. Ask whether airport departure fees and taxes are included in the total cost quoted—they rarely are.

Also, remember to always:

- Ask about the **cancellation policy.** Can you get your money back? Is there a deposit required?
- Request a complete **schedule** (for escorted tours only).
- Ask about the **size** and **demographics** of the group (on escorted tours only).
- Discuss what is included in the **price** (for escorted tours only): transportation, meals, tips, airport transfers?

discounted prices—sort of like one-stop shopping. These packages have been sold in bulk to tour operators, who are reselling them to you at a cost that usually undercuts the normal market price. These tours have both pros and cons (see box).

One good source of package deals is the airlines themselves, though only a few offer packages to eastern Canada. Those that do include **Air Canada** (✆ 888/AIR-CANA;** www.aircanada.com), which has the most choices to this region; **Continental Airlines Vacations** (✆ 800/301-3800;** www.coolvacations.com); **United Vacations** (✆ 800/377-1816;** www.

unitedvacations.com); and **American Airlines Vacations** (✆ 800/321-2121;** http://www.aavacations.com).

The operator with the most tours of the region is probably Newfoundland's own **Maxxim Vacations** (see the next section, "Escorted General-Interest Tours," for details). **Liberty Travel** (✆ 888/271-1584;** www.libertytravel.com), one of the biggest packagers in the northeast, also offers some good package tours to Atlantic Canada. Liberty often runs full-page ads in Sunday papers in Boston, New York, and other large cities where you can see some sample prices and itineraries spelled out. (In fact, lots of other companies' travel packages will be listed in the travel section of your local Sunday newspaper, too.)

Also check ads in national travel magazines such as *Arthur Frommer's Budget Travel Magazine, Travel + Leisure, National*

Geographic Traveler, and *Condé Nast Traveler.* Several large **online travel agencies**—Expedia, Travelocity, Orbitz, Site59, and Lastminute.com, to name a few—do a brisk business in packages as well; it can't hurt to go online and check a few of them out for specials to eastern Canada.

13 Escorted General-Interest Tours

Escorted tours are structured group tours with a group leader. Their price usually includes everything from airfare to hotels, meals, tours, admission costs, and local transportation.

Despite the fact that such tours require big deposits and predetermine all your hotels, restaurants, and itineraries, many people derive security and peace of mind from the structure they offer. Escorted tours—whether by bus, motor coach, train, or boat—let you sit back and enjoy the trip without having to drive or worry about any of the planning details. They take you to the maximum number of sights in the minimum amount of time, with the least amount of hassle. They're particularly convenient for people with limited mobility, and can be a great way to make new friends.

On the downside, you'll have little opportunity for spontaneous interactions with locals. These tours can be jam-packed with activities, leaving little room for individual sightseeing, whim, or adventure—and they often focus on

heavily touristed sites, so you may miss out on the lesser-known gems of an area.

These two firms offer escorted tours of Eastern Canada:

- **Collette Vacations,** Pawtucket, RI (© **800/340-5158;** www.collette vacations.com). Collette offers several excellent tours of eastern Canada (about 10 days long on average) that range from fly/drive packages to the escorted everything's-done-for-you variety throughout the Maritimes. Collette also maintains offices in Canada (in Delta, a suburb of Vancouver) and England (in Uxbridge, a western suburb of London).

- **Maxxim Vacations,** St. John's, NF (© **800/567-6666** or 709/754-6666; www.maxximvacations.com). Newfoundland's largest travel provider has a top-rate reputation and offers a huge range of trips, including guided and unguided excursions throughout the four Atlantic Provinces. Call and ask for their extensive and colorful brochure.

14 Special-Interest Trips

A growing number of outfitters and entrepreneurs are offering soup-to-nuts adventure tours that take care of all the planning, equipment, accommodations, and meals for a trip. Specialized vacations available in eastern Canada include learning vacations, during which you can immerse yourself in local culture, as well as more traditional sightseeing tours by bus.

LEARNING VACATIONS
The **Gaelic College of Celtic Arts and Crafts,** St. Ann's, NS (© **902/295-3411;** www.gaeliccollege.edu), offers programs for children and adults that specialize in local culture, such as Highland bagpiping, dancing, drumming, and Cape Breton fiddling, on its campus near Baddeck. More than 100 students attend classes

each session. Gaelic College also sponsors short Elderhostel-associated programs and trips, such as half-day fall walking trips on Cape Breton Island.

At **Kings Landing,** near Fredericton, NB (© **506/363-4999;** www.kings landing.nb.ca), children dress up in period costume and learn about how the early Loyalist settlers lived. The programs range from a few hours to a week, from early June through early October. Admission is charged to all visitors. Adult programs are also offered.

Sunbury Shores Arts & Nature Centre, St. Andrews, NB (© **506/529-3386;** www.sunburyshores.org), offers day- and weeklong trips and classes with topics including plant dyes, printmaking, raku pottery, and watercolor and oil painting. The center is located on the water in St. Andrews; lodging can be arranged.

At **Village Historique Acadien,** near Caraquet, NB (© **506/726-2600** or 877/721-2200; www.villagehistorique acadien.com), the lives and arts of early Acadian settlers are the focus of programs held at a re-created historic village.

ADVENTURE TRAVEL

Adventure travel is a growth industry in Atlantic Canada, just as it is worldwide. Adventure tour outfitters are especially helpful for those arriving by air—it's a bit cumbersome to fly with bikes, canoes, and so forth. You can request information on adventure outfitters currently leading trips by calling the toll-free provincial information numbers listed at the beginning of this chapter. The free provincial travel guides also list outfitters, and in each chapter, we've included a "Great Outdoors" section, which offers some pointers based on your interests.

Here's a sampling of well-regarded outfitters operating in Canada's Maritime Provinces:

- **Backroads,** Berkeley, CA (© **800/ 462-2848** or 510/527-1555; www. backroads.com). One of North America's largest adventure travel companies offers, for example, 6-day walking and biking trips through southeast Nova Scotia, among other programs in the eastern provinces. Pick according to your budget and inclination: You can stay at luxury inns or opt for more rustic camping trips.

- **Coastal Adventures,** Tangier, NS (© **877/404-2774** or 902/772-2774; www.coastaladventures.com). Sea kayak expert Scott Cunningham and his staff lead great trips ranging from 2-day paddles to weeklong adventures throughout the Maritimes and Newfoundland. He also does a range of rentals.

- **Country Walkers,** Waterbury, VT (© **800/464-9255** or 802/244-1387; www.countrywalkers.com). Country Walkers offers van-supported weeklong walking trips on Cape Breton Island.

- **Freewheeling Adventures,** Hubbards, NS (© **800/672-0775** or 902/857-3600; www.freewheeling. ca). This popular outfitter based near Halifax offers excellent guided biking, kayaking, and hiking tours throughout Nova Scotia, as well as on Prince Edward Island and two challenging, exceptionally scenic areas of Newfoundland.

15 Getting Around Eastern Canada

BY CAR & FERRY
Atlantic Canada's road network is extensive and generally well maintained. The Trans-Canada Highway enters the region north of Edmundston, New Brunswick, and continues some 1,800km (1,118

How to Buy Car-Rental Insurance (If You Need It)

When renting a car, always **ask your home insurer** first if your coverage extends to Canada (often it doesn't), and be sure to find out whether your policy covers all persons who will be driving the rental car, how much liability is covered in case an outside party is injured in an accident, and whether the type of vehicle you are renting is included under your contract.

Most **major credit cards** provide some degree of coverage as well—provided they were used to pay for the rental. Terms vary widely, however, so be sure to call your credit card company directly before you rent. If you rely on your credit card for coverage, you may want to bring a second credit card with you, as damages may be initially charged to the first card.

You can almost always **buy car-rental insurance** from an auto-rental agency, though this is expensive. The basic insurance coverage offered by most car-rental companies, known as the **loss/damage waiver (LDW)** or **collision damage waiver (CDW)**, can cost as much as US$20 or more per day. It usually covers the full value of the vehicle, with no deductible if an outside party causes an accident or other damage to the rental car. Liability coverage varies according to the company policy. If you are at fault in an accident, however, you will only be covered for the full replacement value of the car, not for any liability. Most rental companies will require a police report in order to process any claims you file, but your private insurer will not be notified of the accident.

miles) to St. John's, Newfoundland. Numerous feeder roads connect to the Trans-Canada. American travelers expecting to find six-lane highways with high-speed on- and off-ramps will be in for a surprise. With few exceptions, the highway system here is on a far smaller scale. Even main arteries, such as the inland route from Yarmouth to Halifax and Route 1 across Newfoundland, are just two lanes, albeit with frequent opportunities for passing.

If you're arriving by plane, the usual suspects offer car rentals at major airports. Despite the number of rental outfits, however, it can be difficult to reserve a car during the peak summer season when demand soars. It's best to reserve ahead. Try **Budget** (© 800/527-0700), **Dollar** (© 800/800-4000), **Hertz** (© 800/654-3131), or **National** (© 800/361-5334).

Car-rental rates vary even more than airline fares. A few key questions could save you hundreds of dollars:

- Are weekend rates lower than weekday rates?
- Is a weekly rate cheaper than the daily rate?
- Does the agency assess a drop-off charge if you don't return the car to the same location where you picked it up?
- Are special promotional rates available?
- Are discounts available for members of AARP, AAA, frequent-flier programs, or trade unions?
- How much tax will be added to the rental bill?
- What is the cost of adding an additional driver's name to the contract?

- How many free miles are included in the price?
- How much does the rental company charge to refill your gas tank if you return with the tank less than full?

Also be sure to investigate carefully about **car-rental insurance** (see box) before setting out on your trip.

DRIVING RULES   As in most of the United States, drivers may make a right turn at a red light, provided that they first stop fully and confirm that no one is coming from the left. At some intersections, signs prohibit such a turn. Radar detectors are prohibited in all the Atlantic Provinces. Drivers and all passengers are required to wear seat belts.

GASOLINE   American drivers tend to get excited about the price of gasoline when they first cross the border, thinking it to be very cheap. It is not. Gasoline is priced by the liter, not the gallon, and is actually more expensive here than in the United States. **Multiply the price you see by 3** to get a very rough idea of what it's costing you per gallon in U.S. dollars.

BY PLANE

There's a lack of competition in eastern Canada, which can mean you'll pay high fares for even a short hop to or around the region. **Air Canada** (© 888/AIR-CANA; www.aircanada.com) and its short-hop subsidiary **Jazz** (www.flyjazz.ca) are often your only choices for both domestic and international flights.

The situation is slowly improving, however. **WestJet** (© 800/538-5696; www.westjet.com) and other airlines serve small but growing segments of the Nova Scotia, New Brunswick, and Prince Edward Island air market; check for rates that are competitive with Air Canada's.

Newfoundland is the exception to this rule, with an extensive system of small airports stitching together much of the far-flung province—and a few small regional air carriers to match. Contact **Air Labrador** (© 800/563-3042; www.airlabrador.com) or **Provincial Airlines** (© 800/563-2800 or 709/576-1666; www.provincialairlines.ca).

Note that smaller airports throughout the region—such as Bathurst, Fredericton, Moncton, Yarmouth, and Sydney—offer connections to the four main provincial hubs of Halifax, Saint John, Charlottetown, and St. John's.

BY BUS

Decent bus service is offered between major cities and many smaller towns. For service between Nova Scotia, New Brunswick, and Prince Edward Island, contact **Acadian Lines** (© 800/567-5151; www.smtbus.com).

BY TRAIN

Interprovincial rail service is now but a pale shadow of its former self. Prince Edward Island and Newfoundland lack rail service completely, as does southern New Brunswick (you can no longer travel by train to either Fredericton or Saint John). There's just one train line: **VIA Rail** (© 888/842-7245; www.viarail.com) stops in a handful of towns along its single route between Montréal and Halifax, which runs six times daily (no Tues departures from either terminal). In New Brunswick, VIA trains stop at Campbellton, Charlo, Jacquet River, Petit Rocher, Bathurst, Miramichi, Rogersville, Moncton, and Sackville. In Nova Scotia, you can get on or off the train at Amherst, Springhill Junction, Truro, or Halifax. And that's it.

16 Tips on Accommodations

If you're like me, you'll want to do your best to secure safe, clean, cost-effective lodging before setting out. Here are some tips.

SURFING FOR HOTELS

In addition to the online travel booking sites **Travelocity, Expedia, Orbitz, Priceline,** and **Hotwire,** you can book hotels through **Hotels.com, Quikbook** (www.quikbook.com), and **Travelaxe** (www.travelaxe.net).

TripAdvisor.com is one of my favorite sites on the Web: chock-full of helpful independently written consumer reviews of hotels, resort properties, rental properties, and even some attractions and eateries. It really gives you the skinny on grouchy inn owners, the best rooms to book (in-room photos are sometimes posted on the site), cleanliness and hospitality issues, and so forth. If a property's average quality rating by contributors is 4.0 or higher, that's a very good sign. Less than that and you should read the individual reviews carefully.

HotelShark.com is a similar site, while **HotelChatter.com** is a daily webzine offering smart coverage and critiques of hotels worldwide.

It's a good idea to get a confirmation number and make a printout of any online booking transaction.

SAVING ON YOUR HOTEL ROOM

The **rack rate** is the maximum rate that a hotel charges for a room. Hardly anybody pays this price, however, except in high season or on holidays. To lower the cost of your room:

- **Ask about special rates or other discounts.** You may qualify for corporate, student, military, senior, frequent-flier, trade union, or other discounts.

- **Dial direct.** When booking a room in a chain hotel, you'll often get a better deal by calling the individual hotel's reservation desk rather than the chain's main number.

- **Book online.** Many hotels offer Internet-only discounts or supply rooms to Priceline, Hotwire, or Expedia at rates much lower than the ones you can get through the hotel itself.

- **Remember the law of supply and demand.** You can save big on hotel rooms by traveling in a destination's off season or shoulder seasons, when rates typically drop, even at luxury properties in eastern Canada.

- **Look into group or long-stay discounts.** If you come as part of a large group, you should be able to negotiate a bargain rate. Likewise, if you're planning a long stay (at least 5 days), you might qualify for a discount. As a general rule, expect 1 night free after a 7-night stay.

- **Sidestep excess surcharges and hidden costs.** Many hotels have adopted the unpleasant practice of nickel-and-diming their guests with opaque surcharges. When you book a room, ask what is included in the room rate and what is extra. Avoid dialing direct from hotel phones, which can have exorbitant rates. And don't be tempted by the room's minibar offerings: Most hotels charge through the nose for water, soda, and snacks. Finally, ask about local taxes and service charges, which can increase the cost of a room by 15% or more. (A few resorts may also charge an additional "resort tax.")

- **Carefully consider your hotel's meal plan,** if that's an option (at the finer resorts of eastern Canada, it invariably is). If you enjoy eating out and sampling the local cuisine, it makes sense to choose a **Continental Plan (CP),** which includes breakfast only, or a **European Plan (EP),** which doesn't include any meals and allows you maximum flexibility. If you're more interested in saving money, opt for a **Modified American Plan (MAP),** which includes breakfast and one meal, or the **American Plan (AP),** which includes three meals. If you must choose a MAP, see if you can get a free lunch at your hotel if you decide to do dinner out.

- **Book an efficiency.** A room with a kitchenette allows you to shop for groceries and cook your own meals. This is a big money saver, especially for families on long stays, and I've often enjoyed frying up fresh Digby scallops, PEI mussels, and the day's catch while traveling in eastern Canada.

- **Consider enrolling in hotel chains' "frequent-stay" programs,** which are upping the ante lately to win the loyalty of repeat customers. Frequent guests can now accumulate points or credits to earn free hotel nights, airline miles, in-room amenities, merchandise, tickets to concerts and events, and discounts on sporting facilities. Perks are awarded by most chain hotels and motels (Hilton HHonors, Marriott Rewards, Wyndham ByRequest, to name a few), but also by some individual inns and B&Bs. Many chain hotels also partner with other hotel chains, car-rental firms, airline frequent-flier programs, or credit card companies to give consumers additional incentives to do repeat business.

LANDING THE BEST ROOM

Somebody has to get the best room in the house. Why not improve your chances?

You can start by joining the hotel's frequent-guest program, which may make you eligible for upgrades. A hotel-branded credit card usually gives its owner "silver" or "gold" status in frequent-guest programs for free. Always ask about a corner room. They're often larger and quieter, with more windows and light, and often cost the same as standard rooms. When you make your reservation, ask if the hotel is renovating; If it is, request a room away from the construction. Ask about nonsmoking rooms and rooms with views. Be sure to request your choice of twin, queen- or king-size beds. If you're a light sleeper, ask for a quiet room away from vending or ice machines, elevators, restaurants, bars, and discos. Ask for a room that has been recently renovated or refurbished.

If you aren't happy with your room when you arrive and check in, ask for another one right away (that is, before you've unpacked, washed up, and put your feet up on the bed). Most lodgings will be willing to accommodate you.

Finally, remember that in eastern Canada, you're coming (and paying) for ocean views or access. Ask questions like these before finalizing your booking:

- **What's the view like?** You may be willing to pay less for a back room facing the parking lot, especially if you don't plan to spend much time in the room. On the other hand, you want to make sure your "sea view" room (with the premium charge) really does offer a full, unencumbered sea view. It's your right to ask gently.

- **Does the room have air-conditioning or ceiling fans?** Do the windows open?

- **What's included in the price?** Find out if there's some extra amenity, such as kayaks, bikes, canoes, free gelato

> **Tips** **Finding a B&B Via the WWW**
>
> One of the joys of booking travel to eastern Canada via the Internet is the surprisingly useful ratings service provided and constantly updated online (for free!) by the Canadian government. Using its website in tandem with this book, you can locate, view, and research a good B&B or hotel right from the comfort of your own home. Visit the government's Canada Select service at **www.canadaselect.com** to view its very complete listings and ratings.

(wishful thinking), or what have you. Eastern Canadian innkeepers often do provide such items free of charge—or at very fair rental rates—to their guests.

- **How far is the room from the beach/lighthouse/hiking trail?** If it's farther than walking distance, is a driving map available at the property for you so that you won't get lost?

17 Recommended Books, Films & Music

Here's a "starter kit" of films, CDs, and literature that can prepare you for a rewarding visit to the Atlantic Provinces.

BOOKS

Anne of Green Gables by L. M. Montgomery (Oxford University Press, 1997, and Children's Classics, 1998) is a children's book for all time and a lovely evocation of life on Prince Edward Island. Montgomery's fictional, ever-sunny Anne is the island's most famous export, hands down; this cycle of novels about an adopted red-haired girl remains enormously popular worldwide, thanks to both Montgomery's delineation of island characters and Anne's irrepressible optimism. It's less well known that there is an entire series of *Anne* books; *Gables,* the original in the series, only takes Anne's life through age 16. In future installments, Montgomery gave her a job as a school principal and took readers through Anne's marriage and motherhood. Montgomery was prolific beyond the *Anne* cycle as well, writing a series of spin-off novels about the lives of other townspeople in the fictional town of Avonlea; *Chronicles of Avonlea* and *Further Chronicles of Avonlea* are probably the best

known. Montgomery also authored a number of other books and short stories set on the island not involving Anne at all, although none of these has achieved anywhere near the lasting fame of the *Anne* stories; these works include *Jane of Lantern Hill, Mistress Pat,* and *Along the Shore.*

If you can locate it, the Oxford University Press edition of *Anne of Green Gables* is annotated with plenty of biographical material, excerpts from the author's girlhood journals, colloquial explanations of cookery, directions to locations featured in the book, and the like—it's a better choice for adult travelers. The Children's Classics edition is a simple hardcover version, great for kids.

No book with adult themes set in the Maritime Provinces is more famous than *The Shipping News* by E. Annie Proulx (Scribner, 1993). Proulx won both a Pulitzer Prize and a National Book Award for her second novel, the tale of a crushed down-and-out New Yorker who moves to Newfoundland and takes up a job penning articles for a shipping newspaper in the land of his forebears—a position which puts him at an intersection with some of the more fascinating characters on (or just passing through) the Rock. The protagonist must also battle the demons left him by his former wife. Yet he somehow begins to rebuild a life of dignity, hope, and purpose. Although often criticized for its overblown style, there's no denying this novel captures that peculiar blend of isolation, perkiness, and quirkiness that makes up a Newfie.

In *The Bird Artist* (Farrar, Straus and Giroux, 1994, and Picador, 1998), author Howard Norman continues the tradition of Vermont-linked authors (see E. Annie Proulx, above) heading north and finding literary gold in the Maritimes. This book, about a remote Newfoundland fishing village, was a finalist for the National Book Award, and rightly so. It spins the yarn of a local artist (with a tremendous gift for drawing birds) who has committed a murder and seeks a curious redemption for that act through his drawings and a marriage arranged by his parents. His true love, Margaret, is a hoot—a hard-drinking, sexually aware woman—and yet touching, as are many of the assembled minor characters, from the village reverend on down. It's a heartfelt novel and ought to be brought along on any trip to the Rock.

Norman is more than a one-book wonder. His novel *The Museum Guard* (Farrar, Straus and Giroux, 1994, and Picador, 1999) is set in a fictional Halifax art museum, where a downbeat guard's female companion becomes obsessed with a Dutch painting. The stories of the guard's upbringing, his lady's obsession, and their dreary lives tell much about the often claustrophobic and hard-bitten lives of Maritimers.

Norman turned to nonfiction for *My Famous Evening* (National Geographic, 2004), recounting both his own personal travels and correspondences in Nova Scotia as well as some fantastic, seemingly unreal stories of real Nova Scotians and some folk tales from the province. Definitely worth picking up if you will be in Nova Scotia.

Recently reissued, *A Whale for the Killing* by Farley Mowat (Stackpole Books, 2005) is a true story that became a touchstone for animal rights activists. The famed biologist and activist tells the tale of a huge whale stranded in a Newfoundland cove in the 1970s and the group of locals bent on killing it; the real-life Mowat becomes the whale's protector but ultimately fails—then writes about it afterward. It's interesting for the clash of ideals between local fisherfolk and an environmentalist from the "outside" (Mowat is from Ontario and Saskatchewan originally). This is not a pretty, quaint look at the Maritimes but rather a slice of real life here.

In *The Boat Who Wouldn't Float* (Little, Brown & Co., 1970, and Starfire, 1984), Mowat turned to humor, and the resulting book (now reissued) turns out to be surprisingly raucous and sidesplitting. Mowat purchases a used schooner in Newfoundland, but it doesn't hold water well, and there are serious doubts he'll ever get out of port. His subsequent misadventures and cruises among the ports of Newfoundland and beyond are wonderful fodder. Reading them, you learn about Screech (a famously powerful Newfie liquor) and much more; it's clear Mowat holds great affection for the Newfies, even as he skewers them and himself.

For historical background, try to find *Part of the Main* by Peter Neary and Patrick O'Flaherty (Breakwater Books, 1983). In it, two of the Maritime Provinces' most prolific historians lay out the history of Newfoundland and Labrador. It was published by a local St. John's publisher; the book is improved by the inclusion of several hundred photographs.

For a look at where the economy of the region is headed lately, *Lament for an*

Ocean by Michael Harris (McClelland & Stewart, 1998) is a fine nonfiction work documenting the shockingly sudden decline of the Maritime fisheries—and the consequences for both Newfoundland's way of life and its already imperiled economy.

FILMS

Many films have been made in the Maritimes but precious few have been made *about* them.

Johnny Belinda (1948) is one. The film takes place on Cape Breton Island, starring lovely Jane Wyman in a surprisingly sensitive performance as a deaf-mute woman who is sexually assaulted and then turns on her attacker. She won an Oscar for the role.

The Shipping News (2001) is an evocative picture with a stellar cast, based on the novel of the same name by E. Annie Proulx. The film was shot in Newfoundland—a condition of Proulx's sale of the screen rights, it's been said—and the visuals alone make the film an excellent watch. Kevin Spacey is the news writer Quoyle (he seems to have gained a little weight for the role), and Cate Blanchett plays his abusive wife.

MUSIC

Music in the Maritime Provinces is generally a Celtic-inflected folk, or else a pop music greatly influenced by that sound.

Nova Scotia native **Sarah McLachlan** is the exception; she has made it bigger around the globe than anyone else from eastern Canada, thanks to a continuing stream of haunting, minor-key pop classics. Among her studio albums, *Fumbling Towards Ecstasy* (Arista Records, 1994) features the single "Possession" and was her first breakout hit. *Surfacing* (BMG, 1997) features "Sweet Surrender" and "Building a Mystery." The live record *Mirrorball* (Arista Records, 1999) recaps much of McLachlan's best work in a live setting, including the often-heard gem "I Will Remember You."

Among the more folksy bands making headway, the Newfoundland band **Great Big Sea** have been the standard-bearers of modern Celtic music around the Maritimes for a while now, graduating from bar band to genuine folk influence in the best tradition of the Chieftains and the like. Of their output, I like *Turn* (Sire/Rhino, 2000) best; tunes such as "Boston and St. John's" speak closely to life in such an isolated, seafaring place.

The Rankins—a family group from little Mabou, on Cape Breton Island—were sorely underappreciated outside of eastern Canada while they were still together. The band broke up in the late 1990s, and one of its members was subsequently killed in a tragic auto accident on a twisting Cape Breton road, but their folk roots and chops came together with contemporary production (in the style of Enya or Clannad) in a way that has stood the test of time. Though a bit overproduced, there's no denying the mournful power of Jimmy Rankin's ballads, the infectious drive of the late John Morris Rankin's fiddle, and the lovely sweet harmonies of Rankin sisters Cookie, Raylene, and Heather. Among their oeuvre, *North Country* (Angel Records, 1995) is the most fitting legacy to these local kids who made good.

Cape Breton fiddler **Natalie MacMaster** is probably Canada's finest, drawing favorable comparisons to American fiddler Alison Krauss. *A Compilation* (Rounder, 1998) serves as a nice introduction to her lightning-fast yet subtle style. On *Blueprint* (Rounder, 2003), she is joined by American musicians working in the same general vein, such as Béla Fleck and Sam Bush.

Finally, any serious discussion of Maritime music cannot omit the great Hank Snow. More than a decade before there was a Bob Dylan, and around the same time Hank Williams, Sr., was shooting to prominence, there was Snow, too, born in the small Nova Scotia fishing town of Liverpool (near Lunenburg), a rambling, yodeling ranger of a crooner who made a mark on Nashville and legions of folk and country musicians to come. One of Elvis Presley's heroes, he's a member of the Country Music Hall of Fame and was a Grand Ole Opry staple for years. *The Essential Hank Snow* (RCA, 1997) includes his still-classic "I'm Movin' On," which he wrote, as well as 19 other cuts.

FAST FACTS: Atlantic Provinces

American Express American Express maintains about seven travel offices in the four Maritime Provinces, including in Halifax, Saint John, and St. John's. To report lost or stolen American Express traveler's checks, call ℂ 800/221-7282.

ATM Networks See "Money," earlier in this chapter.

Automobile Clubs The Canadian Automobile Association (CAA) extends member benefits (including maps and road service) to AAA cardholders. If you're a member, bring your membership card. For information about membership in CAA, call the eastern provinces office in Saint John at ℂ 800/561-8807. CAA's website is located at www.caa.ca. For emergency road service in a pinch, call CAA's hotline at ℂ 800/222-4357.

Business Hours Business hours in eastern Canada are generally similar to what you'd find in the United States. Most **offices** are open from 8 or 9am to 5 or 6pm Monday through Friday and are closed on weekends. Boutiques and souvenir **shops** typically open up around 10am and stay open until 6pm or so, often later during the peak tourist season. Hours vary widely for general merchandise and **grocery stores.** In general, you can expect early and late hours in the larger cities (even 24-hr. groceries are cropping up), more limited hours in the smaller towns and villages. Most general merchandise stores are closed on Sundays.

Car Rentals See "Getting Around," earlier in this chapter.

Climate See "When to Go," earlier in this chapter.

Currency See "Money," earlier in this chapter.

Customs **What You Can Bring into Canada**

Customs regulations allow adult travelers (19 or older) to bring 1.5 liters (1 bottle) of wine or 1.14 liters (40 oz.) of liquor or 24 12-oz. bottles of beer (not all three) into Canada without paying any duties or taxes. Travelers can also bring in 200 cigarettes or 50 cigars without paying duty or tax. If you're bringing gifts for Canadian friends, you're allowed to bring C$60 (US$54/£30) worth duty-free. An automated phone service can answer most of your questions about Customs regulations; call the **Canada Border Services Agency** at ℂ 800/461-9999 (within Canada only), 204/983-3500, or 506/636-5064. Also consult the Canadian Customs website located at **www.cbsa-asfc.gc.ca/travel-voyage/visitors-eng.html** (go to the "Customs Declaration Card" section) for an updated listing of Customs allowances. Regulations regarding firearms are more complicated; in short, it's best if you don't bring a gun. If you're traveling for hunting and want to bring a rifle into Canada, you should be traveling during hunting season and carry proof of your plans to hunt (a written confirmation from a guide service or hunting lodge should suffice). There are also limits on bringing some forms of ammunition.

What You Can Take Home from Canada

Returning **U.S. citizens** who have been away for at least 48 hours are allowed to bring back, once every 30 days, US$800 worth of merchandise duty-free. (*Inside tip:* This allowance can be combined by family members traveling together—US$1,600 for two family members traveling together, US$4,000 for a family of five, and so on.) You'll be charged a flat rate of 4% duty on the next US$1,000 worth of purchases above your allowance. Be sure to keep receipts handy to expedite the declaration process. On gifts mailed home, the duty-free limit is US$200. If you owe duty, you are required to pay on your arrival in the United States—either by cash, personal check, government or traveler's check, or money order (and, in some locations, a Visa or MasterCard).

To avoid paying duty on foreign-made personal items you owned before your trip, bring along a bill of sale, insurance policy, jeweler's appraisal, or receipts of purchase. Or you can register items that can be readily identified by a permanently affixed serial number or marking—think laptop computers, cameras, and CD players—with Customs before you leave. Take the items to the nearest Customs office or register them with Customs at the airport from which you're departing. You'll receive, at no cost, a Certificate of Registration, which allows duty-free entry for the life of the item.

With some exceptions, you cannot bring fresh fruits and vegetables back into the United States. For specifics on what you can bring back, download the invaluable free pamphlet "Know Before You Go" online at **www.cbp.gov**. (Click on "Travel"; then click on "Know Before You Go.") Or contact the **U.S. Customs & Border Protection (CBP),** 1300 Pennsylvania Ave. NW, Washington, DC 20229 (© **877/227-5511**), and request the same pamphlet.

U.K. citizens returning from a non-EU country have a customs allowance of 200 cigarettes, 50 cigars, or 250 grams of smoking tobacco; 2 liters of still table wine; 1 liter of spirits or strong liqueurs (over 22% volume) or 2 liters of fortified wine, sparkling wine, or other liqueurs; 60cc (ml) of perfume; 250cc (ml) of toilet water; and £145 worth of all other goods, including gifts and souvenirs. Children under 17 are not allowed the tobacco or alcohol allowances. For more information, contact HM Revenues & Customs at © **0845/010-9000** (from inside the U.K. only) or 2920/501-261 (from outside the U.K.). Also consult its website at **www.hmce.gov.uk**.

The duty-free allowance in **Australia** is A$900 or, for those under 18, A$450; these allowances can be combined for families traveling together. Travelers 18 and over can bring back 250 cigarettes or 250 grams of loose tobacco, plus up to 2.25 liters of alcohol, without paying any duties. If you're returning with valuables you already own, such as foreign-made cameras, you should file form B263. A helpful brochure available from Australian consulates or Customs offices is "Know Before You Go." For more information, call the **Australian**

Customs Service at ℂ **1300/363-263.** Also log on to the Australian Customs website at **www.customs.gov.au**.

The duty-free allowance for **New Zealand** is NZ$700. Citizens over 17 can bring in 200 cigarettes, 50 cigars, or 250 grams of tobacco (or a mixture of all three if their combined weight doesn't exceed 250g); plus 4.5 liters of wine or beer and up to three bottles containing up to 1.125 liters of liquor. Fill out a certificate of export, listing the valuables you are taking out of the country; that way, you can bring them back without paying duty. Most questions are answered in a free pamphlet available at New Zealand consulates and Customs offices: "New Zealand Customs Guide for Travellers, Notice No. 4." For more information, contact **New Zealand Customs,** The Customhouse, 17–21 Whitmore St., Box 2218, Wellington (ℂ **0800/428-786** from within New Zealand or 0064/9300-5399 from overseas). You can also phone the New Zealand embassy in Washington, D.C., at ℂ **202/328-4848** with questions. The New Zealand Customs Service website is located on the web at **www.customs.govt.nz**.

Documents See "Entry Requirements & Customs," earlier in this chapter.

Driving Rules See "Getting Around," earlier in this chapter.

Drugstores Chain drugstore and independent pharmacies are located throughout Atlantic Canada. Check the phone book under "Pharmacy." Stores in larger cities and towns are likely to be open later than those in more remote villages. One of the larger national chains is **Pharmasave** (www.pharmasave.com), with about 70 stores scattered about the four provinces (most are in Nova Scotia).

Electricity Canada uses the same electrical current as the United States: 110–115 volts, 60 cycles.

Embassies & Consulates All embassies are in Ottawa, the national capital. The **Australian High Commission** is at 50 O'Connor St., Room 710, Ottawa, ON K1P 6L2 (ℂ **613/236-0841**). The **British High Commission** is at 80 Elgin St., Ottawa, ON K1P 5K7 (ℂ **613/237-1530**). The **Irish Embassy** is at 130 Albert St., Suite 1105, Ottawa, ON K1P 5G4 (ℂ **613/233-6281**). The **New Zealand High Commission** is at 99 Bank St., Suite 727, Ottawa, ON K1P 6B9 (ℂ **613/238-5991**). The **South African High Commission** is at 15 Sussex Dr., Ottawa, ON K1M 1M8 (ℂ **613/744-0330**). The **U.S. embassy** is at 490 Sussex Dr., Ottawa, ON K1N 1G8 (ℂ **613/238-5335**). In the Maritimes, there's a **U.S. Consulate General** in Purdy's Wharf Tower 2, Suite 904, 1969 Upper Water St., Halifax, NS B3J 3R7 (ℂ **902/ 429-2480**).

Emergencies In life-threatening situations, dial ℂ **911.**

Holidays See "When to Go," earlier in this chapter.

Information See "Visitor Information," earlier in this chapter.

Internet Access See "Staying Connected," earlier in this chapter.

Liquor Laws The legal drinking age is 19 years of age in all provinces. Restaurants that serve alcoholic beverages are said to be "licensed." If you want to tipple with dinner, look for a sign or ask whether the establishment is licensed. Do not drink and drive. Canadian law takes drunken driving seriously.

Lost & Found Be sure to tell all your credit card companies the minute you discover your wallet has been lost or stolen, and file a report at the nearest police precinct. Your credit card company or insurer may require a police report number or record of the loss. Most credit card companies have an emergency toll-free number to call if your card is lost or stolen; they may be able to wire you a cash advance immediately or deliver an emergency credit card in a day or two. Visa's U.S. emergency number is ℂ **800/847-2911.** American Express cardholders and traveler's check holders should call ℂ **905/474-9280.** MasterCard holders should call ℂ **800/307-7309** or 636/722-7111. For other credit cards, try calling the toll-free number directory at ℂ **800/555-1212.**

If you need emergency cash over the weekend when all banks and American Express offices are closed, you can have money wired to you via **Western Union** (ℂ **800/325-6000;** www.westernunion.com).

Identity theft and fraud are potential complications of losing your wallet, especially if you've lost your driver's license along with your cash and credit cards. Notify the major credit-reporting bureaus immediately; placing a fraud alert on your records may protect you against liability for criminal activity. The three major U.S. credit-reporting agencies are **Equifax** (ℂ **800/766-0008;** www.equifax.com), **Experian** (ℂ **888/397-3742;** www.experian.com), and **TransUnion** (ℂ **800/680-7289;** www.transunion.com). Finally, if you've lost all forms of photo ID, call your airline and explain the situation; it might allow you to board the plane if you have a copy of your passport or birth certificate and a copy of the police report you've filed.

Mail Letters (up to 30g) mailed within Canada cost C52¢ (US47¢/26p) in postage. Letters up to 30 grams mailed to the United States cost C93¢ (US84¢/47p). For other international destinations, a letter weighing less than 30 grams costs C$1.55 (US$1.40/78p). More detailed information on heavier documents, packages, and other items can be found online at **www.canadapost.ca.**

Maps Excellent road maps are available from the provincial tourism authorities (ask at welcome centers). For more information, see "Getting Around," earlier in this chapter.

Newspapers & Magazines Publishers in the major cities of the province—including Halifax, Saint John, Fredericton, Charlottetown, and St. John's—all produce very decent daily newspapers filled with information about goings-on around the town and province. Most also maintain websites, so you can scout out happenings before your departure. Canada's two national newspapers—*The Globe and Mail* and the *National Post*—are also widely available in most cities and many larger towns. U.S. papers such as the *Wall Street Journal* and *The New York Times* can be found in larger cities, but you shouldn't count on it. When available, they often sell out early. Newsmagazines such as *Time* and *Newsweek* are not difficult to find on newsstands.

Pets Traveling into Canada with your pet dog or cat should pose no difficulties. Be sure to have with you a certificate from your veterinarian certifying that your pet is currently vaccinated against rabies. (Puppies and kittens under 3 months are exempt.)

Police For police, call ⓒ **911.**

Taxes Canada's high national and regional taxes offset some of the price advantages you gain when paying in Canadian dollars. Three of the four Maritime Provinces—New Brunswick, Nova Scotia, and Newfoundland—adopted the **Harmonized Sales Tax,** also known as the HST, in 1997. HST combines provincial and federal sales taxes into one flat rate of 14%; this tax is charged on all goods and services. On **Prince Edward Island,** you'll be charged the national sales tax (also known as the GST) of 6%, plus a hefty PEI provincial tax of 10%—the highest in Canada—on most items (including a tax on the federal sales tax!). Footwear, clothing, books, and groceries are exempt from the PEI tax.

Until very recently, non-Canadians could apply for a refund of their entire HST (or the GST only, on Prince Edward Island) upon leaving the country. That is no longer true: Canada's legislature made the Visitor Rebate Program go *poof* in June of 2007. Tear up those rebate forms. The website **www.ccra-adrc.gc.ca/visitors** has more answers on Canada's national and provincial taxes.

Time Zone Most of Atlantic Canada is on Atlantic Standard Time, 1 hour ahead of Eastern Standard Time (as observed in New England and the U.S. East Coast). The exceptions are Newfoundland and southeast Labrador, which are a half-hour ahead of Atlantic Standard Time.

Tipping As in the United States, tips provide a significant portion of the income for waiters, bellhops, and chambermaids. It's standard to leave 15% of the pre-sales tax total for basic service at a restaurant; more if the service is exceptional. Plan to tip around C$1 (US90¢/50p) per bag for assistance at your hotel and C$1 to C$2 (US90¢–US$1.80/50p–£1) per day to your chambermaid.

Toilets Generally called "washrooms" in Canada, public bathrooms are typically abundant and clean. Many towns have a visitor information center, and most of these have washrooms for visitors. In larger cities, washrooms can be found in public buildings, major hotels, some larger shops, and restaurants.

3

Suggested Itineraries in the Atlantic Provinces

The eastern provinces of Canada are big yet intimate. You drive a long way between major destinations only to find you're overwhelmed with joy by a small wooden church, a fish stand, a rock outcropping—and you end up staying longer than you intended. I've seen it happen time and again.

So I have two pieces of advice. First, leave a bit of flexibility in your itinerary, because the provinces are full of unexpected surprises. You'd hate to leave Lunenburg without jumping onto a whale-watching boat or the Friday before a weekend fisherman's festival, right? And second, allow yourself time for the long drives—better yet, bring a companion who can share the load. Except when in Prince Edward Island, you'll log more than a few hours on the road to complete these tours.

The range of possible itineraries in eastern Canada is practically endless (you could even do a kayaking itinerary, or a French-towns itinerary, for instance), but I've focused on just a few of my favorite places for this chapter. So, while even a month is not enough to see all of the Maritime Provinces, realistically most folks simply don't have that long. To help you, I've laid out four itineraries touching on the "greatest hits" of each province.

LIGHTS OUT: THE BEST OF NOVA SCOTIA IN 1 WEEK

This tour of my favorite Maritime Province takes in lighthouses, quaint villages, a surprisingly vibrant city, and dramatic headlands plunging to the ocean. Begin in Yarmouth, landing point for the ferry from Bar Harbor, Maine.

Day ❶: The Southernmost Coast

Spend an hour in **Yarmouth,** a compact port city just a few hours' ferry ride from Portland or Bar Harbor, Maine. It offers a few diversions, such as a **Firefighters' Museum** (p. 79) and a French-speaking region just a short drive to the west. It's worth a half-day. I also like to drive the coastline just west of the city, which harbors several relatively unknown (thus empty) beaches. See p. 78.

Drive 100km (62 miles) east along Route 103, exiting the main highway to reach **Shelburne** 𝒜. This compact little town has a fine **historic complex** with water views, a cooper, boatbuilders, and a few small museums. There's also a more commercial main street and one of my favorite fish-and-chips stands in eastern Canada, the aptly named **Mr. Fish.** See p. 84.

Nova Scotia in 1 Week

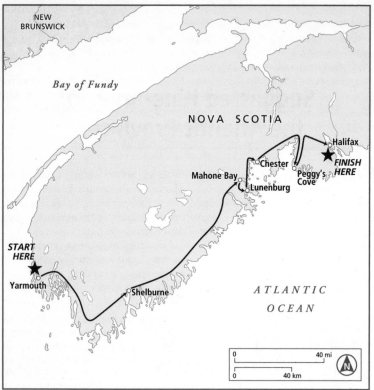

Continue another 120km (75 miles) east along Route 103 to the exit for Route 324; exit and continue about 10km (6¼ miles) east to

Days ❷–❹: Lunenburg ⚔⚔ and Mahone Bay ⚔⚔

These cute twin towns, separated by just a 15-minute drive, are easily worth 2 to 3 nights. (You'll arrive late on the first day, anyway.) You can explore remote peninsulas—preferably by bike—hit the links, visit a great ocean museum, or book a kayak tour. Some of the province's better bed-and-breakfasts are tucked into these towns, too. I like to time my visit to coincide with one of the summertime fisherman's, arts, or music festivals. See p. 84.

During your 3 days in the region, be sure to follow Route 3 about 10km (6¼ miles) northeast of Mahone Bay to

Chester ⚔⚔ (p. 90). This small port town is New England–cute, with a scenic, first-rate golf course, a little summer theater company, a handful of restaurants, and a ferry service to nearby **Tancook Island.** (If you take the ferry, just be sure to get a schedule so you don't miss the last boat back.) It's surely worth a couple hours.

From Lunenburg, Mahone Bay, or Chester, head northeast along Route 3 or Route 103 about 24km (15 miles) to the turnoff for Route 333.

Days ❺–❼: The Halifax Region

Down Route 333 about 24km (15 miles) lies **Peggy's Cove** ⚔⚔⚔. This famously picturesque village features a lighthouse, surf crashing on rocks, a somber memorial to a passenger plane crash, and more cute souvenirs than you can shake a stick at.

Sure, you can take a tour bus from Halifax, but why not just sample it on the way up? It's worth an hour or two. See p. 112.

From Peggy's Cove, backtrack 24km (15 miles) to the main highway, then continue north about 24km (15 miles) along Route 103 to **Halifax** *₭₭₭*. This is Nova Scotia's crown jewel, a place where live bands play nightly, buskers perform in the streets, and there's plenty of grog and museum-going to be had. It's not a huge place, and you'll quickly have covered all of it, but the lodging and dining are good enough that it's worth several nights. Be sure to explore the **Maritime Museum of the Atlantic,** especially for the Titanic artifacts, and **Pier 21** (p. 99), for a look at the immigrant experience in eastern

Canada. Or just wander up and down **Spring Garden Road** and back and forth along **Barrington Street,** hunting for brewpubs, record shops, and old buildings.

Bored with the bright lights? Head for a remote beach down a nearby peninsula, such as **Crystal Crescent Beach;** there are plenty, but you'll need a map to find the way. And roads are a bit rough on the suspension.

From here, rise early and you can speed back down the highway south to Yarmouth in time to catch your ferry back to Maine. Be sure not to dally, though—the 338km (210-mile) drive takes more than 3 hours.

| HIGH TIMES, HIGH TIDES: | THE BEST OF NEW BRUNSWICK IN 1 WEEK |

New Brunswick is spread out; to see it quickly and compactly, this tour takes in the highlights of the southernmost New Brunswick coast, from the province's largest city to its biggest tidal drops. Begin at St. Andrews, the first significant destination beyond the Maine state line. (I'm assuming you've driven north from Maine. If you've flown into Saint John, see it first or last and simply switch around the order below.)

Days ❶ & ❷: St. Andrews *₭₭*
This compact seaside town is the perfect stopping point after rambling through miles of the blessed emptiness that is downeast Maine. It's worth at least 1 night for shopping and walking, another day and a night if you're intent on taking a whale-watching trip or other excursion from the harbor—or playing the **Algonquin Hotel's golf course** (p. 156), one of the top courses in eastern Canada.

A day trip to the nearby islands, such as **Deer Island** or **Campobello** (p. 157), is always nice in summer.

From St. Andrews, continue about 19km (12 miles) northeast (do not backtrack) along Route 127 to Route 1, the main road. Then continue 80km (50 miles) along Route 1 to

Days ❸ & ❹: Saint John *₭*
Saint John (spelled out, please) isn't the capital of New Brunswick, but it is the province's chief economic engine. The downtown's central square is lovely and worth some time just hanging out; you can also wander the downtown streets, choosing from gourmet and midpriced restaurants or pubs with ale and live music. See p. 170.

The **farmer's market,** also within walking distance, is a must-visit if you like fresh produce.

From Saint John, continue about 90km (56 miles) northeast along Route 1 to Route 114; turn south along Route 114 and continue 15km (9⅓ miles) to its end, which puts you in

New Brunswick in 1 Week

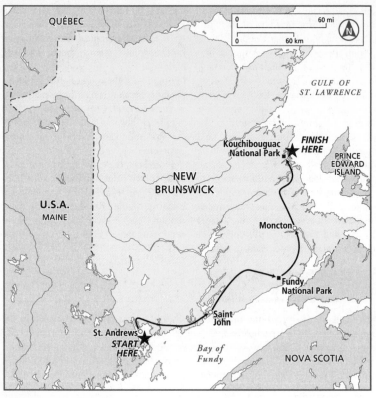

QUÉBEC

GULF OF
ST. LAWRENCE

Kouchibouguac
National Park

FINISH
HERE

PRINCE
EDWARD
ISLAND

NEW
BRUNSWICK

U.S.A.
MAINE

Moncton

Fundy
National Park

Saint
John

St. Andrews
START
HERE

Bay of
Fundy

NOVA SCOTIA

0 ___ 60 mi
0 ___ 60 km

Days ⑤ & ⑥: Fundy National Park 🎫🎫

One of the most surprising things you can do in New Brunswick is hightail it to this park, where the world's highest tides slam the narrowing "V" of the **Bay of Fundy.** Any number of tour outfits can take you down to the waterside (tide schedules in hand, of course). The weirdly shaped **Hopewell Rocks** make a good trip, and there's also an excellent road/hiking path along the bay. This is worth a day or two with the family—you'll have to stay in rustic accommodations, however—and remember to spend time on the bike or on a hike, too. See p. 188.

From the park, continue north along Route 114 80km (50 miles) to

Day ⑦: Moncton

This city at the crossroads of the Maritimes is showing new signs of life. Stay the night and use the city as a base for a day trip, or else press on to the big park an hour away. See p. 194.

Head 80km (50 miles) north, following routes 115 and 11, passing the big **Dune of Bouctouche** en route, to **Kouchibouguac National Park** 🎫🎫 (p. 198), where you can canoe, bike, or kayak, and the flat land makes for easy walking (or picnicking on the beach). Return to Moncton at night, or just stay in the park.

From Moncton, you're just 80km (50 miles) from the bridge to Prince Edward Island (see next itinerary) or a few hours from further coastal exploring. Or return south 266km (165 miles) along Highway 1 to the Maine border, about a 3½-hour trip.

REACHING THE BEACH: PRINCE EDWARD ISLAND FOR FAMILIES

This tour takes in the trifecta of the island's essential sights, giving each its due: Charlottetown, Anne's Land, and the lovely beaches of Prince Edward Island National Park. Kids will love all three places, and adults will feel a sense of tranquillity they may not have known in years.

Days ❶ & ❷: Victoria 𝒜𝒜 and Charlottetown 𝒜𝒜

Little **Victoria** makes a surprise stop en route to the "big" city. It's all too cute. An hour or two and a cup of tea ought to do it. See p. 244.

Take the Trans-Canada Highway 32km (20 miles) east to **Charlottetown.** The island's capital city has excellent restaurants, inns, a lot of history, and a plain friendly feel. Stay the night for sure. Family activities here include the **Confederation Centre of the Arts** (p. 229), which offers constantly changing program of plays and performances (including an annual run of an *Anne of Green Gables* play).

There's also excellent window-shopping and a surfeit of parks in which to push baby strollers or exercise a pet. See p. 228.

From Charlottetown, follow signs west along Route 2 to Route 13, then turn north and follow Route 13 to

Day ❸: Anne's Land 𝒜

The village of **New Glasgow** makes a good stop while heading back to the center of the island. There's a championship golf course, nice views from the country roads looping over hillsides, and the **Prince Edward Island Preserve** factory (p. 219), complete with store and cafe. Kids might enjoy sampling the jams. Give this stop an hour or two.

Continue north along Route 13 to **Cavendish** 𝒜 (p. 212), the island's most tourist-friendly and developed (some say overdeveloped) section. The fictional redheaded Anne of Green Gables is everywhere in the Cavendish area, and some of the attractions related to her and the book's author really *are* worth seeing—especially for young girls and their mothers. And in 2008, a bonus: The island will go all out celebrating the 100th anniversary of the book's publication with extra events. If you're just not into children's stories, there are still plenty of other touristy attractions for kids, from the **Ripley's Believe It or Not! Museum** and the **Wax World of the Stars** (check out Lady Di) to amusement parks like the **Sandspit.**

Where to stay? There are numerous "bungalow courts" (small cottage compounds) dotting the area, some with cooking facilities good for frying up local fish for the little ones, though my first choice might be to pitch a tent in the park (see next entry). This area is definitely worth a day or two with children.

From Cavendish, turn east on Route 6 and travel, through a series of tricky turns, to Prince Edward Island National Park.

Days ❹–❻: Prince Edward Island National Seashore 𝒜𝒜𝒜 & Souris 𝒜

Some of the best beaches in eastern Canada line the northern shores of Prince Edward Island. You'll surely want to spend a few days here with the family walking the beach, snapping photos of glorious sunsets and purple lupines against the red sand, camping among the dunes, hunting down obscure fish-and-chips shops, and just generally kicking back.

You'll find a wide range of accommodations in these parts, from Victorian

Prince Edward Island for Families

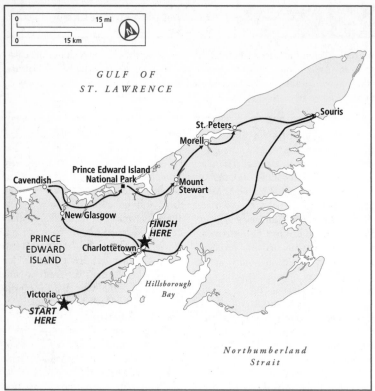

resorts to B&Bs to well-maintained campgrounds—the latter my recommended choice. Any family in the Maritimes should camp together at least 1 night; the quiet and fresh air will do you a world of good. These placid surroundings and warm waters just invite serenity, so go ahead, stay a couple nights. While staying at **Prince Edward Island National Park,** remember to take some scenic drives as well.

From the park, continue east on Route 6 to Route 2, turning east and continuing about 60 scenic kilometers (37 miles) through Mount Stewart, St. Peters, and Morell to Souris.

Some outstanding inns, scenery, and beaches lie near the postage-stamp town of **Souris** (p. 239). If you're an outdoors

sort of family, rent yourselves a bike or three and go exploring. Locals are unfailingly nice. You can even stay over in the area if you please, whether in a campground or in your pick of two of the island's most luxurious inns.

Return 80km (50 miles) along routes 2, 4, and 5 to

Day ⓻: Charlottetown ★★, Once More

I like **Charlottetown** a lot and believe it's worth a repeat visit while making a circuit of PEI. You probably didn't see everything on your first time through, anyway. Why not spend another night? Hit the **Confederation Court Mall** and wander the street snapping photos of the kids and look for souvenirs for friends.

ROLLING THROUGH THE ROCK: THE BEST OF NEWFOUNDLAND IN 2 WEEKS

This tour of "the Rock" (a local nickname for Newfoundland) brings you to the capital city as well as Viking ruins. Be prepared to burn several tanks of gas and plenty of rubber.

Days ❶–❸: St. John's 👍👍

Few places in North America are more convivial, seafaring, or musical than **St. John's.** You're absolutely required to have a pint (or fake it) in a local pub while trying to catch the next big traditional music act. I'd say it's worth 3 nights of your time if you include some sort of excursion into the countryside; the area's many outfitters can help. See p. 292.

Drive north from St. John's about 160km (99 miles) on the Trans-Canada Highway (Hwy. 1), exiting at Clarenville and continuing 65km (40 miles) east on Route 230 to Route 239. Turn south on Route 239 and continue about 2km (1¼ mile) to the turnoff for

Days ❹–❺: Trinity 👍👍

The land of icebergs, **Trinity** is a lovely town in an inaccessible place. You have to drive 72km (45 miles) down a side road off the already sparse Trans-Canada Highway just to get there; then do the same in reverse later. There's enough scenery here to eat. If it's iceberg season (that is, late spring), stay a few nights and watch for the big boys (local outfitters will help you). See p. 282.

Retrace your route back along Route 230 to the Trans-Canada Highway at Clarenville (save miles by cutting west on Rte. 233). Head north on the Trans-Canada, soon passing through

Day ❻: Terra Nova National Park 👍

This is a convenient stopping point on the way to Gros Morne (see below), with excellent family attractions—more than most anywhere else in the province. See p. 278.

Continue west along the Trans-Canada Highway about 420km (261 miles) to Deer Lake, then follow Route 430 further west to

Days ❼–❿: Gros Morne National Park 👍👍👍

Gros Morne National Park is absolutely the must-see place in Newfoundland, and if you go nowhere else, go here. You'll be tuckered out by the drive, but once here you'll know what the big deal was all about. Stay at least 2 (preferably more) nights in the park, just soaking up the grandeur of the atmosphere—not only to take in the stupendous sights (huge cliffs, waterfalls, beaches, Arctic flowers, snowshoe hares, and the like) but also to rest up for the long drive to your next wonderful destination. A true hiking enthusiast could probably spend a week here happily. See p. 260.

Drive about 338km (210 miles) north along Route 430 to the Route 436 turnoff. Continue about 9km (5½ miles) more to

Days ⓫–⓭: L'Anse aux Meadows 👍👍👍

Eleventh-century **Viking artifacts** were discovered at Newfoundland's northernmost tip in 1960. The site—and the artifacts—are well worth a visit. See p. 269.

Return about 400km (249 miles) along Route 430 to Deer Lake, then continue another 265 km (165 miles) along the Trans-Canada Highway (Hwy. 1) to

Newfoundland in 2 Weeks

Day ⑭: Port aux Basques

Traveling to **Port aux Basques** will take you the better part of a day. This town is the docking point for another ferry that carries you back to Cape Breton Island.

There's little to do here, and it's best used as a staging area—and last souvenir-grab—before the passage back to Nova Scotia. See p. 254.

Nova Scotia

Nova Scotia is difficult to characterize. It generally feels more cultured and British than wild, a better place to buy a wool sweater and shoot a round of golf than to actually get your feet wet. That is, until you stumble upon the blustery, boggy uplands and crags of Cape Breton Highlands National Park (which seems like a proper home for druids and trolls); then hear the wild strains of some local Celtic band's fiddling emanating from a tiny pub.

It's a province full of rolling hills and cultivated farms, especially near the Northumberland Straits on the northern shore—but then you find the vibrant, edgy, and lively arts and entertainment scene that is Halifax, a city possessing more intriguing street life than many cities three times its size. (It's been called a "San Francisco in miniature," and that somewhat captures its flavor, though it's probably more like a small Boston.)

This is a province that has truly earned its name—Nova Scotia is grammar-school Latin for "New Scotland"—with its Highland games and kilts and more than a touch of a brogue here and there . . . but then again, suddenly you find yourself amid enclaves of rich Acadian culture and food along the southwestern coast between Digby and Yarmouth. The province, humdrum on the surface, resists characterization at every turn—and it's friendly as all get-out.

This historic province is an ideal destination for the sort of traveler who is quicker to hit the remote control than the high mountain paths of Nepal. There's a tremendous variety of landscapes and low-key attractions, and the scene seems to change kaleidoscopically as you travel along Nova Scotia's winding roads: from dense forests to bucolic farmlands, from ragged coast to melancholy bogs, from historic villages with tall ships lazing about impressively at port to dynamic little downtowns serving up everything from fish and chips and a pint to the occasional gourmet eatery. (Pretty much the only terrain it doesn't offer is a range of towering mountain peaks. You simply don't come here for that.)

This province is twice blessed: It's compact enough that you needn't spend all your time in a car. Yet it has fewer than a million residents (and one in three live in or around Halifax), making it unpopulated enough to provide lots of empty space when you're seeking peace, quiet, or an empty beach. Even in its most populated sections, it's possible to find a sense of remoteness, of being surrounded by big space and a profound history.

More than once while traveling through the back roads of Nova Scotia, I've had the fleeting sense that I was traveling through the New England of 60 or 70 years ago—even a century ago—the one that captivated intrepid explorers and writers and painters well before anyone referred to tourism as an "industry." In 21st-century New Scotland, careful exploration is still both eminently possible and desirable.

1 Exploring Nova Scotia

Visitors to Nova Scotia should spend a little time poring over a map (and this travel guide) before leaving home. Your biggest challenge is narrowing down your options before you set off; numerous loops and circuits are possible here and the available permutations multiply once you factor in the various ferry links to the United States, New Brunswick, Prince Edward Island, and Newfoundland. Figuring out where to go—and then how to get there—is the hardest work you'll need to do in a place that is relatively easy to travel around once you're there.

The only travelers I've heard complain about Nova Scotia are those who tried to see it all at once, within a week. That sort of approach leaves you strung out and exhausted. Instead, prioritize your interests and decide accordingly. Looking for picture-perfect scenes of coastal villages? Focus mostly on the South Shore, specifically the trio of Chester, Lunenburg, and Mahone Bay. Drawn to hiking amid rocky coastal scenery? Allow plenty of time for Cape Breton. Looking for more pastoral ocean scenery? Head for the Fundy Coast. Want to spend a quiet day canoeing? Build your trip around Kejimkujik National Park. Dying for some gourmet dining and urban buzz? Factor in a few days in Halifax. Above all, schedule plenty of time for simply doing not much of anything: strolling or biking in quiet lanes; picnicking on beaches; and watching the water from docks, boat decks, and hotel porches are some of the best ways I know to let Nova Scotia's charms unfold at their own unhurried pace.

ESSENTIALS

VISITOR INFORMATION   Every traveler to Nova Scotia should have a copy of the massive (400-plus-pages) official tourism guide, which is the province's best effort to put travel-guide writers like me out of business. It's comprehensive, colorful, well-organized, and free, listing all hotels, campgrounds, and attractions within the province, with brief descriptions and current prices. (Restaurants are given only limited coverage, however; investigate those on your own using this book and your own nose for eats.)

The tome, called the *Nova Scotia Doers & Dreamers Guide,* is available starting each March by phone (✆ **800/565-0000** or 902/425-5781), fax (902/424-2668), mail (Nova Scotia Department of Tourism, Culture, and Heritage, P.O. Box 456, Halifax, NS B3J 2R5), and Internet (www.novascotia.com). If you wait until you arrive in the province before obtaining a copy, ask for one at the numerous visitor information centers, where you can also request the excellent free road map.

The provincial government administers about a dozen official **Visitor Information Centres** (known as "VICs") throughout the province, as well as in Portland and Bar Harbor, Maine. These mostly seasonal centers (see box) are amply stocked with brochures and tended by knowledgeable staffers. In addition, virtually every town of any note has a local tourist information center filled with racks of brochures covering the entire province, staffed with local people who know the area. You won't ever be short of information.

In general, the local and provincial visitor information centers are run with cordiality and brisk efficiency. I have yet to come across a single one that wasn't remarkably helpful, although the press of crowds can sometimes require a few minutes' wait to get individual attention at the more popular gateways, such as Amherst (outside Halifax) or Port Hawkesbury (entering Cape Breton Island).

Year-Round Tourist Info? Yes!

Coming to Nova Scotia off season? Fear not. Halifax's two VICs, one located at the airport and one situated downtown on the waterfront's Sackville Wharf on Lower Water Street, are both open all year round. There's also a year-round VIC located in the town of Amherst, at the westernmost entry point to the province (in other words, on the main road coming from New Brunswick). Cape Breton visitors will be cheered to know that the VIC guarding the island's entrance (it's just across the bridge from the mainland) in Port Hastings is open 8 months out of the year, closing only from early January through late April. And if you're arriving via the ferry to Yarmouth, the city's VIC is only open from mid-May through mid-October, yes—but it does have a gift shop on the premises to compensate, which is a good spot to pick up local products.

For general questions about travel in the province, call **Nova Scotia's information hot line** at $\textcircled{C}$ **800/565-0000** (North America) or 902/425-5781 (outside North America).

GETTING THERE   By Car & Ferry   Most travelers reach Nova Scotia overland by car from New Brunswick. Plan on at least a 4-hour drive from the U.S. border at Calais, Maine, to Amherst (at the New Brunswick–Nova Scotia border). Incorporating ferries into your itinerary can significantly reduce time behind the wheel. Seasonal ferries (figure June to the first week of Oct) connect both Portland and Bar Harbor, Maine, to Yarmouth, Nova Scotia, at the peninsula's southwest end, though neither runs daily; at press time, each operated three to four times per week, depending on the season.

Bay Ferries ($\textcircled{C}$ **888/249-7245;** www.catferry.com) operates the ferries. The Bar Harbor–Yarmouth and Portland–Yarmouth routes use *The Cat* (short for catamaran), which claims to be the fastest ferry in North America and since going into service in 1998 has cut the crossing time from Bar Harbor from 6 hours to 2¾ hours, zipping along at up to 50 mph. Note that the ride can get very bumpy depending on wave and ocean conditions, so if you're sensitive to seasickness, bring and take motion-sickness medicine.

Summer rates one-way from Bar Harbor in 2007 were C$63 (US$57/£32) for adults and children age 13 to 18, C$43 (US$39/£22) for children age 6 to 13, C$58 (US$52/£29) for seniors, and C$105 (US$95/£53) and up per vehicle. From Portland, it costs C$89 (US$80/£45) per adult, C$59 (US$53/£30) per child age 13 to 18, C$85 (US$77/£43) for seniors, and C$149 (US$134/£75) and up per vehicle. Same-day-return and weekend-getaway round-trip fares are cheaper. I cannot stress enough that reservations for both routes are *vital* during the peak summer season.

To shorten the slog around the Bay of Fundy, a 3-hour ferry (also operated by Bay Ferries) known as the *Princess of Acadia* links **Saint John, New Brunswick,** with **Digby, Nova Scotia.** Remarkably, this ferry sails daily year-round, with as many as three crossings per day in summer. Peak-season one-way fares (charged June–Oct) in 2007 were C$40 (US$36/£20) for adults, C$25 (US$23/£13) for children age 6 to

Nova Scotia

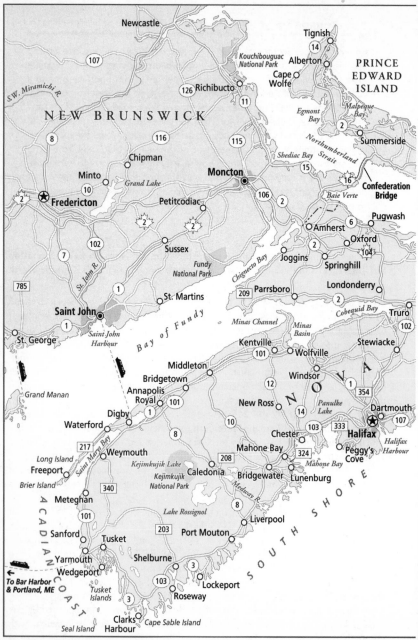

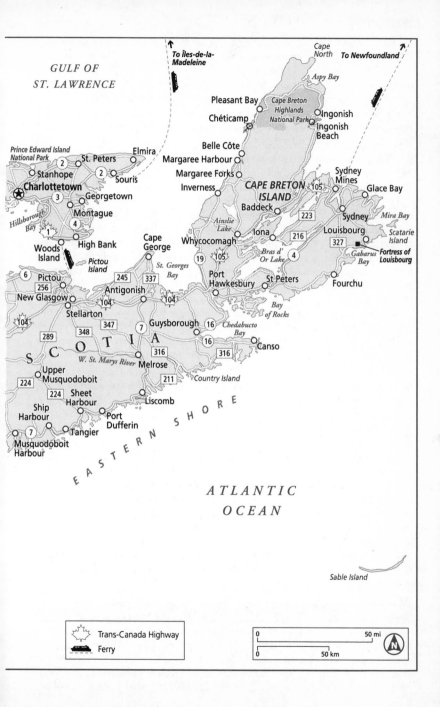

GULF OF
ST. LAWRENCE

To Îles-de-la-Madeleine

Cape North

To Newfoundland

Aspy Bay

Pleasant Bay

Cape Breton Highlands National Park

Chéticamp

Ingonish

Ingonish Beach

Prince Edward Island National Park

Elmira

St. Peters

2

Belle Côte

Margaree Harbour

Sydney Mines

2

Stanhope

Souris

Margaree Forks

105

Glace Bay

Charlottetown

Georgetown

Inverness

CAPE BRETON ISLAND

Sydney

3

Montague

Baddeck

Mira Bay

4

223

Hillsborough Bay

High Bank

1

Cape George

Ainslie Lake

Iona

216

Louisbourg

Scatarie Island

Woods Island

Pictou Island

Whycocomagh

327

Fortress of Louisbourg

6

Pictou

19

105

Bras d' Or Lake

4

Gabarus Bay

256

St. Georges Bay

245

337

Port Hawkesbury

St Peters

Fourchu

New Glasgow

Antigonish

Bay of Rocks

104

104

104

Stellarton

Guysborough

16

Chedabucto Bay

289

348

347

7

16

316

Canso

S C O T I A

W. St. Marys River

Melrose

316

Upper Musquodoboit

211

Country Island

224

Sheet Harbour

224

Ship Harbour

Liscomb

7

Port Dufferin

Tangier

EASTERN   SHORE

Musquodoboit Harbour

ATLANTIC
OCEAN

Sable Island

Trans-Canada Highway

Ferry

0   50 mi

0   50 km

N

13, C$5 (US$4.50/£2.50) per child under age 6, C$30 (US$27/£15) for seniors, and C$80 (US$72/£40) and up per vehicle. Fares are a bit cheaper outside the peak travel months; if you walk on and return within 30 days, there are also discounts available on the round-trip. Complete up-to-the-minute schedules and fares for the *Princess of Acadia* can be found at www.nfl-bay.com or by calling ✆ **888/249-SAIL.**

For those traveling farther afield, ferries also connect Prince Edward Island to Caribou, Nova Scotia, and Newfoundland to North Sydney, Nova Scotia. See chapters 6 and 7 for more detailed information.

By Plane   Halifax is the air hub of the Atlantic Provinces. **Air Canada** (✆ **888/ 247-2262;** www.aircanada.com) provides daily direct service from New York and Boston using its commuter partner **Jazz** (www.flyjazz.ca), which also flies directly to Sydney, Charlottetown, Saint John, and St. John's, as well as several more remote destinations in eastern Canada. But other contenders are jumping into the fray, as well: **Continental** (✆ **800/231-0856;** www.continental.com) flies direct from Newark to Halifax several times daily in summer, for one. American Airlines' **American Eagle** (✆ **800/433-7300;** www.aa.com) service recently added one daily flight in each direction between New York's LaGuardia Airport and Halifax, in small 37-seat jets. If you're coming from anywhere other than New York, however, you will probably need to connect in Montréal or Toronto, which can turn into a half-day excursion or more.

Also good to know: Canada's **WestJet** (✆ **800/538-5696;** www.westjet.com) flies year-round into Halifax from Toronto, Calgary, Hamilton, and St. John's, and seasonally from Montréal, Edmonton, and several Florida airports. The regional airline **CanJet** (✆ **800/809-7777;** www.canjet.com) also flies to and from Orlando, Florida—though, again, only in winter.

By Train   VIA Rail (✆ **888/842-7245;** www.viarail.com) offers train service 6 days a week between Halifax and Montréal; the entire trip takes between 18 and 21 hours depending on direction, with a basic summertime fare of about C$240 (US$216/£120) each way, not counting sleeping accommodations. Discounts for those buying at least 1 week in advance are possible.

Sleeping berths and private cabins are available at extra cost—the cheapest bed, in a double-bunked cabin, is about twice the cost of the no-bed fare—and VIA also recently added a higher class of service on its overnight run; this new summer-only Easterly class aboard the *Ocean* offers all-inclusive meals, sleeping accommodations, exclusive access to lounges and a panoramic car, and continuing presentations from an onboard educator about Maritime Province culture and history.

The *Ocean* runs daily (except Tues) each direction year-round, with standard overnight sleeper-cabin service; the Easterly option is available from mid-June through mid-October. Check the VIA Rail website for updates on routes, schedules, and online booking.

2 The Great Outdoors

Nova Scotia's official travel guide (the aforementioned *Doers & Dreamers Guide*) has a very helpful "Outdoors" section in the back that lists camping outfitters, bike shops, whale-watching tour operators, and the like. A free brochure that lists adventure outfitters is published by the **Nova Scotia Adventure Tourism Association,** 1099 Marginal Rd., Suite 201, Halifax, NS B3H 4P7 (✆ **800/948-4267** or 902/423-4480). Write or call for a copy.

Surf's Up in . . . Nova Scotia?

This is not a misprint. Surfing is suddenly popping up as an outdoor option in Nova Scotia. Who knew? At least two surf schools have opened for business, capitalizing on the Atlantic surf breaks along the South Shore and at Lawrencetown Beach outside Halifax. Contact the **Dacane Surf Shop** (© 902/431-7873; www.hurricanesurf.com) or the **Rossignol Surf Shop** (© 877/ 990-3733 or 902/683-2140; www.surfnovascotia.com) for more information about where to hang ten in the province. Just remember to buy, beg, borrow, or rent a wet suit when you go: That water's *cold*.

BIKING   The low hills of Nova Scotia and the gentle, largely empty roads make for wonderful cycling. Cape Breton is the most challenging of destinations; the south coast and Bay of Fundy regions yield wonderful ocean views while making fewer demands on cyclists. A number of bike outfitters can aid in your trip planning: **Free-wheeling Adventures** (© 800/672-0775 or 902/857-3600; www.freewheeling.ca) offers guided bike tours throughout Nova Scotia (as well as Prince Edward Island and Newfoundland). Walter Sienko's guide, *Nova Scotia & the Maritimes by Bike: 21 Tours Geared for Discovery,* is helpful in planning a bike excursion. For an Internet introduction to cycling in Nova Scotia and beyond, point your Web browser to the website of **Atlantic Canada Cycling** (www.atl-canadacycling.com).

BIRD-WATCHING   More than 400 species of birds have been spotted in Nova Scotia, ranging from odd and exotic birds blown off course in storms to majestic **bald eagles,** of which some 250 nesting pairs reside in Nova Scotia, mostly on Cape Breton Island. Many whale-watching tours also offer specialized seabird-spotting tours, including trips to **puffin colonies.**

CAMPING   With backcountry options rather limited, Nova Scotia's forte is drive-in camping. The 20 or so provincial parks offer some 1,500 campsites among them, and campgrounds are uniformly clean, friendly, well managed, and reasonably priced. For a brochure and map listing all provincial campsites, write to **Nova Scotia Department of Natural Resources, Parks and Recreation Division,** R.R. #1, Belmont, NS B0M 1C0, or call © **902/662-3030.** As usual, the province's *Doers & Dreamers Guide* contains the fullest campground listings available.

Also check with the Campground Owners Association of Nova Scotia: Its website at **www.campingnovascotia.com** lists a number of privately held campgrounds. The free and helpful *Campers Guide,* available at visitor information centers, lists this information as well.

CANOEING   Nova Scotia offers an abundance of accessible canoeing on inland lakes and ponds. The premier destination is **Kejimkujik National Park** in the southern interior, which has plenty of backcountry sites accessible by canoe. A number of other fine canoe trips allow paddlers and portagers to venture off for hours or days. General information is available from **Canoe Kayak Nova Scotia,** 5516 Spring Garden Rd., 4th floor, Halifax, NS B3J 1G6 (© **902/425-5454, ext. 316**).

FISHING   Saltwater fishing tours are easily arranged on charter boats berthed at many of the province's harbors. Inquire locally at visitor information centers or consult the "Boat Tours & Charters" section of the *Doers & Dreamers Guide*. No fishing license is required for *most* saltwater species for those on charters. For questions, current fishing regulations, or lists of licensed fishing guides, contact the Nova Scotia **Department of Fisheries and Aquaculture** in Halifax at ℂ **902/424-4560,** or go to its website at **www.gov.ns.ca/fish**.

Committed freshwater anglers come to Nova Scotia in pursuit of the tragically dwindling Atlantic salmon, which requires a license separate from that for other freshwater fish. **Salmon licenses** must be obtained from a provincial office, campground, or licensed outfitter. Other freshwater species popular with anglers are brown trout, shad, smallmouth bass, rainbow trout, and speckled trout. Again, for up-to-date information contact the Department of Fisheries and Aquaculture (see above).

GOLF   Nova Scotia lays claim to more than 50 golf courses. Among the most memorable: **Highland Links** (ℂ **800/441-1118** or 902/285-2600) in Ingonish, which features a dramatic oceanside setting; and **Bell Bay Golf Club** (ℂ **800/565-3077** or 902/295-1333) near Baddeck, which is also wonderfully scenic and has appeared in *Golf Digest*.

While the big names are fun, I really enjoy playing some of the less famous courses around the province, too. The **Bluenose Golf Club** (ℂ **902/634-4260**) has been operating on a beautiful tract of land known as Kaulbach Head overlooking Lunenburg's harbor since 1933. (It's visible in the distance from almost any point in the old town.) The short, 5,275-yard tract here plays harder than it looks because of numerous slopes and side-hill lies. Views of the ocean and town are stupendous on both the starting and finishing holes; greens fees are about C$25 (US$23/£13) for 9 holes, C$40 (US$36/£20) for 18 holes (carts cost extra), and afterward the clubhouse grill serves up some mighty fine burgers and beers on tap. Other nicely scenic tracts open to the public include the **Chester Golf Club** (ℂ **902/275-4543**), with amazing ocean views and fine course maintenance; and hilly, beautiful **Osprey Ridge** (ℂ **902/543-6666;** www.ospreyridge.ns.ca) near Shelburne, designed by the noted course architect Graham Cooke and opened in 1999.

New courses are always being constructed, too. For one-stop shoppers, **Golf Nova Scotia** (ℂ **800/565-0000,** ext. 007; www.golfnovascotia.com), run by the tourism office, represents about two dozen well-regarded properties around the province and can arrange customized golfing packages at its member courses. A handy directory of Nova Scotia's golf courses (with phone numbers) is published as a separate brochure and in the "Outdoors" section of the *Doers & Dreamers Guide* as well.

HIKING & WALKING   Serious hikers make tracks for Cape Breton Highlands National Park, which is home to the most dramatic terrain in the province. But other options abound—trails are found throughout Nova Scotia, although in many cases they're a matter of local knowledge. (Ask at the visitor information centers.) Published hiking guides are widely available at local bookstores. Especially helpful are the back-pocket-size guides published by **Nimbus Publishing;** call for a catalog (ℂ **800/646-2879** or 902/454-7404; www.nimbus.ns.ca).

SAILING   Any area with so much convoluted coastline is clearly inviting to sailors and gunkholers. Tours and charters are available almost everywhere there's a decent-size harbor. The province's premier sailing experience is an excursion aboard the *Bluenose II,* which is virtually an icon for Atlantic Canada and calls at Halifax, Lunenburg, and other ports. (See the "Lunenburg" section, later in this chapter.) Those with the inclination and skills to venture out on their own among the beautiful islands can rent 5m (16-ft.) Wayfarers or slightly larger boats by the hour at **Sail Mahone Bay** (*©* **902/624-8864**) on the South Shore near Lunenburg. A much more extensive listing of boat tour operators can be found in the "Outdoor Tours: Boat Tours & Charters" section of the *Doers & Dreamers Guide.*

SEA KAYAKING   Nova Scotia is increasingly attracting the attention of kayakers worldwide. Kayakers traveling on their own should be especially cautious on the Bay of Fundy side, since the massive tides create strong currents that overmatch even the fittest of paddlers. More than three dozen kayak outfitters do business in Nova Scotia, and they offer everything from 1-hour introductory paddles to intensive weeklong trips; once again, consult the directory in the *Doers & Dreamers Guide.*

Among the more respected outfitters is **Coastal Adventures,** P.O. Box 77, Tangier, NS B0J 3H0 (*©* **877/404-2774** or 902/772-2774; www.coastaladventures.com). The company is run by veteran kayaker and doctorate-in-biology Scott Cunningham, who leads trips throughout the Maritimes and Newfoundland. For kayaking on the eastern side of Cape Breton, check with **North River Kayak,** R.R. #4, Baddeck, NS B0E 1B0 (*©* **888/865-2925** or 902/929-2628; www.northriverkayak.com). Owner Angelo Spinazzola is a native Cape Bretoner and a professional musician with four CDs to his credit; he's been running this award-winning outfit for more than a decade.

WHALE-WATCHING   If you're on the coast, it's likely you're not far from a whale-watching operation. Around two dozen whale-watching outfits offer trips in search of finback, humpback, pilot, and minke whales, among others. The richest waters for whale-watching are found on the Fundy Coast, where the endangered right whale is often seen feeding in summer. Digby Neck (a thin strand extending southwest from the town of Digby) has the highest concentration of whale-watching excursions, but you'll find them in many other coves and harbors. Just ask the staff at visitor information centers to direct you to the whales.

3 Minas Basin & Cobequid Bay

If you're only content off the beaten track, a detour along the Minas Basin and Cobequid Bay will be one of the highlights of your trip. With the exception of Truro, this region is rural, quiet, and full of hidden surprises. You can turn down a dirt road, shut off your car's engine, and not hear much other than the wind and maybe a blackbird or two. You can trek along spectacular hiking trails or picnic alone on a long stretch of remote and misty coast, literally watching the tides roll in.

There's also a rich history here, but it tends to be hidden and subtle rather than preening and obvious. And don't look for the quaint seaside villages or the surf-washed rocky coast for which Nova Scotia is famous; that will have to wait until Yarmouth and the South Shore. The natural drama here is pegged to the region's profound remoteness and the powerful but silent tides, among the highest in the world.

WOLFVILLE ⭐

The trim and tidy Victorian village of Wolfville (pop. 3,500) has a distinct New England feel to it, in both its handsome architecture and its layout—a small commercial downtown just 6 blocks long is surrounded by shady neighborhoods of elegant homes. And it's not hard to trace that sensibility to its source: The area was largely populated in the wake of the American Revolution by transplanted New Englanders, who forced off the original Acadian settlers.

Moments   **A Scenic Drive**

If you're headed from the Truro area southwestward along the Fundy Coast toward Digby, Route 215 offers a wonderful **coastal detour** ⊛ from Maitland to Windsor. This winding, fast, and rather narrow road (not suggested for bicycling) passes through a number of quiet hamlets, some with handsome early buildings. But the chief appeal comes in the sudden vistas of lush green farmland (often accompanied by the redolent smells of cow byproduct) and broad views of expansive Minas Basin beyond. At the town of Walton, there's a handsome lighthouse on a rocky bluff with a nearby picnic area just off the main route (it's well marked). This detour runs 90km (56 miles) from South Maitland to Brooklyn. Few services for tourists are offered along the route, other than a handful of restaurants, B&Bs, and campgrounds. Look for general stores and farm stands if you need a snack.

The town's mainstay these days is handsome **Acadia University,** which has nearly as many full-time students as there are residents of Wolfville. The university's presence gives the small village an edgier, more youthful air. Don't miss the university's art gallery at the **Beveridge Arts Centre** ⊛ (© **902/585-1166**), which showcases both contemporary and historic Nova Scotian art; it's located at the corner of Main Street and Highland Avenue and is open every day (except Mon) from 1 to 4pm. Admission is free.

The town has emerged in recent years as a popular destination for weekending Halifax residents, who come to relax at the many fine inns, wander the leafy streets, and explore the countryside. Also a consistent draw is the **Atlantic Theatre Festival** (© **800/337-6661** or 902/542-4242), which has attracted plaudits in the few years it has been presenting shows. Performances are staged throughout the summer season in a comfortable 500-seat theater. Reservations are encouraged; ticket prices are C$20 to C$30 (US$18–US$27/£10–£15). Check upcoming performances on its website (www.atf.ns.ca).

EXPLORING WOLFVILLE

Strolling the village is the activity of choice. The towering elms and maples that shade the extravagant Victorian architecture provide the dappled light and rustling sounds for an ideal walk. A good place to start is the **Wolfville Tourist Bureau** at Willow Park (© **902/542-7000**) on the north edge of the downtown area.

Cape Split, the hook of land that extends far into the Bay of Fundy north of Wolfville, is home to several **walking trails** ⊛ through rugged landscapes and intriguing geological formations.

At **Blomidon Provincial Park** (© **902/582-7319**), 24km (15 miles) north of Route 101 (Exit 11), some 14km (8.7 miles) of trail take walkers through forest and along the coast. Among the most dramatic trails is the 6km (3.7-mile) **Jodrey Trail** ⊛, which follows towering cliffs that offer broad views over the Minas Basin. It's open from mid-May through early October.

For a more demanding adventure, head north of Wolfville about 25 minutes on Route 358 and park off the side of the road near the beginning of the **Cape Split Trail** ⊛. This 16km (10-mile) trail offers some of the more breathtaking vistas in Nova Scotia, specifically cresting oceanside cliffs that approach 122m (400 ft.) in height. Allow most of a day to truly enjoy this in-and-back excursion. Basic maps and additional information are available from the Wolfville Tourist Bureau (see above).

One of the more intriguing sights in town occurs each summer day at dusk, in an unprepossessing park surrounded by a parking lot a block off Main Street. At **Robie Swift Park,** a lone chimney (dating from a long-gone dairy plant) rises straight up like a stumpy finger pointed at the heavens. Around sunset, between 25 and 100 chimney swifts flit about and then descend into the chimney for the night. Alas, the swifts have been declining in number in recent years, ever since some predatory merlins started nesting nearby. But you'll learn a lot by browsing the informational plaques posted here, where you can read interesting tidbits such as this: No one knew where swifts migrated in winter until 1943, when explorers in the Peruvian jungle found natives wearing necklaces adorned with small aluminum rings. These, it turned out, were tracking bands placed on swifts by North American ornithologists.

Grand-Pré National Historic Site * Long before roving New Englanders arrived in this region, hardworking Acadians had vastly altered the local landscape. They did this in large part by constructing a series of dikes outfitted with ingenious log valves, which allowed farmers to convert the saltwater marshes to productive farmland. At Grand-Pré, a short drive east of Wolfville just off Route 1, you can learn about these dikes, along with the tragic history of the Acadians, who populated the Minas Basin from 1680 until their expulsion in 1755.

More a memorial park than a living history exhibit, Grand-Pré (which means "great meadow") has superbly tended grounds that are excellent for idling, a picnic lunch, or simple contemplation. Among the handful of buildings on the grounds is a graceful stone church, built in 1922 on the presumed site of the original church. Evangeline Bellefontaine, the revered (albeit fictional) heroine of Longfellow's epic poem, was said to have been born here; look for the statue of this tragic heroine in the garden. It was created in 1920 by Canadian sculptor Philippe Hérbert, and the image has been reproduced widely since.

2241 Grand-Pré Rd. (P.O. Box 150), Grand-Pré B0P 1M0. (*) 902/542-3631. www.grand-pre.com. Admission C$7.15 (US$6.45/£3.60) adults, C$5.90 (US$5.30/£2.95) seniors, C$3.45 (US$3.10/£1.75) children age 6–16, C$18 (US$16/£8.90) families. Daily mid-May to mid-Oct 9am–6pm. Closed mid-Oct to mid-May.

WHERE TO STAY

Gingerbread House Inn * The ornate, brightly painted Gingerbread House Inn was originally the carriage house for the building now housing Victoria's Historic Inn (see below). A former owner went woodshop-wild, adding all manner of swirly accoutrements and giving the place a convincingly authentic air. Most guest rooms here are now an updated and modern interpretation of the gingerbread style and are quite comfortable, though the two units in the back are the darkest and smallest of the lot. Each has its own private exterior entrance, adding to the privacy, and each has its own feel: The airy Gaspereau suite features luxe touches like a modernistic propane fireplace, an interior loft, a big-screen television, and a huge eight-person hot tub; the Country and Sunrise suites are more gingerbready. Even some of the simpler rooms sport hot tubs. Breakfasts tend toward the elaborate and are served by candlelight.

8 Robie Tufts Dr. (P.O. Box 819), Wolfville, NS B0P 1X0. (*) **888/542-1458** or 902/542-1458. Fax 902/542-4718. www.gingerbreadhouse.ca. 9 units. May–Oct C$115–C$129 (US$104–US$116/£58–£65) double, C$165–C$199 (US$149–US$179/£83–£100) suite; Nov–Apr C$85–C$119 (US$77–US$107/£43–£60) double, C$130–C$189 (US$117–US$170/£65–£95) suite. Rates include full breakfast. Ask about golf packages. AE, MC, V. No children permitted in suites. **Amenities:** Dining room. *In room:* A/C, TV, DVD, Jacuzzi (some), no phone.

Harwood House Bed & Breakfast 🛇 Considered by several Frommer's readers to be a jewel in the rough in Nova Scotia, Harwood House is downtown right beside Acadia University—in fact, when it was built in 1923 on a sloping lawn adjacent to the campus, it was built for then-university Provost Frank "Pa" Wheelock. Later home to a popular local family doctor, it was converted to an inn by proprietors Peter and Frances Jucker in 1999. The Juckers are incredibly warm and helpful, extending kindnesses far beyond those normally required of inn hosts; they even speak French and German, if that matters to you. Their three queen-bedded rooms are simple but cheery, with white and floral linens and prints; the Glooscap unit overlooks the university campus and has an electric fireplace.

33 Highland Ave., Wolfville, NS B4P 1Y9. ⓒ 877/897-0156 or 902/542-5707. www.harwoodhouse.com. 3 units, 1 with separate bathroom. C$100–C$160 (US$90–US$144/£50–£80) double; off-season discounts available. Rates include full breakfast. MC, V. *In room:* TV (2 units), no phone.

Tattingstone Inn 🛇🛇 "We sell romance and relaxation," says innkeeper Betsey Harwood. And that pretty well sums it up. This handsome Italianate-Georgian mansion, named after one of Harwood's forebears' ancestral town in England, dates from 1874 and overlooks the village's main drag. The inn is furnished with a mix of reproductions and antiques, traditional and modern art. The attitude isn't as over-the-top Victorian as one might guess from looking at the manse—instead the inn is decorated with a deft touch that mixes informal country antiques with regal Empire pieces. The rooms in the carriage house are a bit smaller than those in the main house, but they are still pleasant and showcase fine examples of modern Canadian art. Inquire about the blue-and-cream "Toad Hall" room in the carriage house, for instance: There's a living room downstairs with an electric fireplace and an exposed-beam ceiling, while upstairs sports a queen bed and two-person Jacuzzi. The spacious semiformal dining room is rather refined, and diners sup amid white tablecloths and stern Doric columns. The heated outdoor pool is a bonus, as is the enclosed sun porch, which captures the lambent, early evening light to good effect.

620 Main St. (P.O. Box 98), Wolfville, NS B0P 1X0. ⓒ 800/565-7696 or 902/542-7696. www.tattingstone.ns.ca. 10 units. July–Oct C$148–C$178 (US$133–US$160/£74–£89) double; Nov–June C$88–C$165 (US$79–US$149/ £44–£83) double. AE, MC, V. **Amenities:** Restaurant; outdoor pool; tennis court; steam room. *In room:* A/C, TV/VCR, hair dryer, iron/ironing board, Jacuzzi (some), fireplace (some), no phone.

Victoria's Historic Inn 🛇🛇 Victoria's Historic Inn was constructed by apple mogul William Chase in 1893 and is architecturally elaborate. This sturdy Queen Anne–style building features bold pediments and pavilions adorned with balusters and ornate Stick Style trim. Inside, it seems a bit as if you'd wandered into one of those stereoscopic views of a Victorian parlor. Whereas the nearby Tattingstone Inn resists theme decor, Victoria's Historic Inn embraces it (there's a Cranberry Room, a Sunflower Room, a Nautical Room, and so on). There's dense mahogany and cherry woodwork throughout, along with exceptionally intricate ceilings. The deluxe two-room Chase Suite features a large sitting room with a gas fireplace, double Jacuzzi, queen bed, and an oak mantle. The less expensive third-floor rooms are smaller and somewhat less historic in flavor. Several of the inn's suites have fireplaces and Jacuzzis.

600 Main St., Wolfville, NS B4P 1E8. ⓒ 800/556-5744 or 902/542-5744. Fax 902/542-7794. www.victorias historicinn.com. 15 units. Apr–Oct C$118–C$245 (US$106–US$221/£59–£123) double; Nov–Mar C$99–C$175 (US$89–US$158/£50–£88) double. Rates include full breakfast. AE, MC, V. **Amenities:** Laundry service. *In room:* A/C, TV/VCR, Jacuzzi (some).

WHERE TO DINE

If you're looking for something more elegant than the following spots, many of the inns in Wolfville open their dining rooms at night and serve fancy food to the public, though at prices to match.

Al's Homestyle Café *Value* DELI   Randy and Linda Davidson now operate this place in the nearby hamlet of Canning (about 16km/10 miles northwest of Wolfville, on Rte. 358), but Al Waddell's popular recipes for sausages live on—choose from Polish, German, hot Italian, and honey garlic. Buy some links to cook later, or order up a quick road meal. You won't find a better cheap lunch: A sausage on a bun with a cup of soup will run you less than C$5 (US$4.50/£2.50).

9819 Main St., Canning. ℂ 902/582-7270. Most selections C$2–C$4 (US$1.80–US$3.60/£1–£2). V. Mon–Sat 8am–6pm; Sun 11am–5pm.

The Coffee Merchant and Library Pub COFFEE SHOP   Get your java and coffeehouse-culture fix at possibly the hippest place in a pretty straight town. The shop also has a selection of pastries and sweets, as well as a selection of coffees and an impressive array of organic teas. Musicians sometimes show up to gig here.

472 Main St. ℂ 902/542-4315. Mon–Fri 7:30am–9pm, later on weekends.

4 Annapolis Royal ★★

Annapolis Royal is arguably Nova Scotia's most historic town—it even bills itself, with justification, as "Canada's birthplace." The nation's first permanent settlement was established at Port Royal—just across the river from present-day Annapolis Royal—in 1605 by a group of doughty settlers that included Samuel de Champlain. (Champlain called the beautiful Annapolis Basin "one of the finest harbors that I have seen on all these coasts.") The strategic importance of this well-protected harbor was proven in later tumultuous years, when a series of forts was constructed on the low hills overlooking the water.

Annapolis Royal today is truly a treat to visit. Because the region was largely overlooked by later economic growth (trade and fishing moved to the Atlantic side of the peninsula), it requires little in the way of imagination to see Annapolis Royal as it once was. (The current population is jus. 700.) The original settlement was rebuilt on the presumed site. Fort Anne overlooks the upper reaches of the basin, much as it did when abandoned in 1854. And the village itself maintains much of its original historic charm, with narrow streets and historic buildings fronting the now-placid waterfront.

Indeed, Annapolis Royal is also considered by many historians to be the birthplace of historic preservation. Starting early in this century, town residents have been unusually active in preserving the character of the place. As a testament to their dedication, some 150 buildings and homes in town are officially designated heritage sites. For anyone curious about Canada's early history, Annapolis Royal is one of Nova Scotia's don't-miss destinations.

ESSENTIALS

GETTING THERE   Annapolis is located at Exit 22 of Route 101. It is 200km (124 miles) from Halifax, and 129km (80 miles) from Yarmouth.

VISITOR INFORMATION   The **Annapolis District Tourist Bureau** (ℂ 902/ 532-5454) is 1km (⅔ mile) north of the town center (follow Prince Albert Rd. and look for the Annapolis Royal Tidal Generating Station). It's open daily in summer 8am to 8pm, and 10am to 6pm in spring and fall.

EXPLORING THE TOWN

Start at the tourist bureau, which is located at the **Annapolis Royal Tidal Power Project** (© **902/532-5454**), where the extreme fall in the tides has been harnessed since 1984 to produce electricity for the area in a generating station. It's the only such tidal generator in North America, and the world's largest straight-flow turbine. If so inclined, you can learn about the generator at the free exhibit center upstairs from the visitor center, open mid-May through mid-October.

Before leaving the center, be sure to request a copy of the free "Footprints with Footnotes" walking-tour brochure. The annotated map provides architectural and historic context for a stroll downtown and around the waterfront. Take a moment to note that as you walk down lower St. George Street, you're walking down the oldest street in Canada.

One of the more entertaining ways to learn about local history is to attend the **Old Burying Ground Walking Tour** ☆. In past years, these candlelight tours have departed Fort Anne at 9:30pm on Tuesday, Wednesday, Thursday, and Sunday evenings during summer (usually mid-June to mid-Aug); get there 15 to 30 minutes early to prep for the tour. Visitors are given candle lanterns and then are led on a 1-hour walk through the ancient cemetery next to the fort. You'll learn about fads in headstone art and hear tales of the early inhabitants of Annapolis Royal, including the flamboyant mistress of the Duke of Wellington. There's a small charge for the tours; confirm times and days at Fort Anne National Historic Site (see below).

Children and adults alike adore the **Upper Clements Parks** ☆ (© **888/248-4567** or 902/532-7557; www.upperclementsparks.com) on Route 1, about 5 minutes south of Annapolis Royal. This is a wonderfully old-fashioned amusement park (you arrive after driving through an old orchard). It's full of low-key attractions that will especially delight younger kids. Highlights include the flume ride (originally built for Expo '86 in Vancouver) and a wooden roller coaster that twists and winds through trees left standing during the coaster's construction. It's open daily in season from 11am to 7pm; admission to the grounds is C$7.50 (US$6.75/£3.75) plus tax, free for children under 2. The rate includes admission to the adjacent wild animal park. Single rides cost C$2.60 (US$2.35/£1.30), while bracelets permitting unlimited access to all rides are C$22 (US$20/£11) per day.

In the evening, there's often entertainment in downtown Annapolis Royal at **King's Theatre,** 209 St. George St. (© **902/532-5466;** www.kingstheatre.ca). Shows range from movies to musical performances to variety shows to touring plays. Stop by or call to find out what's on during your stay.

Fort Anne National Historic Site ☆   What you'll likely remember most from a visit here are the impressive grassy earthworks that cover some 14 hectares (35 acres) of high ground overlooking the confluence of the Annapolis River and Allains Creek. The French built the first fort here around 1643. Since then, dozens of buildings and fortifications have occupied this site. You can visit the 1708 gunpowder magazine (the oldest building of any Canadian National Historic Site), then peruse the museum located in the 1797 British field officers' quarters. The model of the site as it appeared in 1710 is particularly intriguing. If you find all the history a bit tedious, ask a guide for a croquet set and practice your technique on the lush rolling lawns.

A good strategy for visiting is to come during the day to tour the museum and get a feel for the lay of the land. Then return for the evening sunset, long after the bus tours have departed, to walk the **Perimeter Trail** ☆ with its river and valley vistas.

Entrance on St. George St. ☎ **902/532-2397**. Admission C$3.95 (US$3.55/£2) adults, C$3.50 (US$3.15/£1.75) seniors, C$1.95 (US$1.75/£1) children, C$9.90 (US$8.90/£4.95) families. May 15–Oct 15 9am–6pm; off season by appointment only (grounds open year-round).

Historic Gardens ☆

You don't need to be a flower nut to enjoy an hour or two at these exceptional gardens. The 4-hectare (10-acre) grounds are uncommonly beautiful, with a mix of formal and informal gardens dating from varied epochs. Set on a gentle hill, the plantings overlook a beautiful salt marsh (now diked and farmed), and they include a geometric Victorian garden, a knot garden, a rock garden, and a colorful perennial border garden. Rose fanciers should allow plenty of time—some 2,000 rose bushes track the history of rose cultivation from the earliest days through the Victorian era to the present day. A garden cafe offers an enticing spot for lunch.

441 St. George St. ☎ **902/532-7018**. www.historicgardens.com. Admission C$8.50 (US$7.65/£4.25) adults, C$7.50 (US$6.75/£3.75) seniors and students, C$23 (US$21/£12) families. July–Aug daily 8am–dusk; May–June and Sept–Oct daily 9am–5pm. Closed Nov–Apr.

North Hills Museum

On the road to Port Royal, the North Hills Museum occupies a tidy shingled home, built in 1764, that's filled with a top-rate collection of Georgian furniture, ceramics, and glassware. This compact museum will be of interest primarily to serious antiques collectors and history buffs, although anyone would be frustrated by the limited access to the opulently furnished rooms (you need to be content mostly with views from roped-off doorways).

5065 Granville Rd., Granville Ferry. ☎ **902/532-2168**. Admission C$3 (US$2.70/£1.50) adults, C$2 (US$1.80/£1) seniors and children age 6–17, C$7 (US$6.30/£3.50) families. June to mid-Oct Mon–Sat 9:30am–5:30pm, Sun 1–5:30pm. Closed mid-Oct to May.

Port-Royal National Historic Site ☆

Canada's first permanent settlement, Port Royal was located on an attractive point with sweeping views of the Annapolis Basin. After spending the dreadful winter of 1604 on an island in the St. Croix River (along the current Maine–New Brunswick border), the survivors moved to this better-protected location. Settlers lived here for 8 years in a high style that approached decadent given the harsh surroundings. Many of the handsome, compact, French-style farmhouse buildings were designed by Samuel de Champlain to re-create the comfort they might have enjoyed at home.

Although the original settlement was abandoned and eventually destroyed, this 1939 reproduction is convincing in all the details. You'll find a handful of costumed interpreters engaged in traditional handicrafts like woodworking, and they're happy to fill you in on life in the colony during those difficult early years, an "age of innocence" when the French first forged an alliance with local natives. Allow 1 or 2 hours to wander and explore.

10km (6¼ miles) south of Rte. 1, Granville Ferry (turn left shortly after passing the tidal generating station). ☎ **902/532-2898**. Admission C$3.95 (US$3.55/£2) adults, C$3.50 (US$3.15/£1.75) seniors, C$1.95 (US$1.75/£1) children, C$9.90 (US$8.90/£4.95) families. May 15–Oct 15 daily 9am–6pm. Closed Oct 16–May 14.

OUTDOOR PURSUITS

A short drive from Annapolis Royal and Port Royal are the **Delaps Cove Wilderness Trails,** which provide access to the rugged Fundy coastline. The tricky part is finding the trail head, as signs tend to vanish. Directions and a brochure are usually available from the visitor information center. Otherwise, head to Delaps Cove from Granville Ferry; veer left on the dirt road that cuts steeply downhill at a rightward bend shortly before the cove. (If you get to Tidal Cove Campground and Cabins, you've gone too far.) Follow this dirt road to the end, where you'll find parking and trail maps.

Two trails lead from an overgrown farm road to the rocky coastline. My advice is to take the **Bohaker Trail** (2km/1.25 miles) first, then decide whether you want to continue on to **Charlies Trail** (7km/4.35 miles). The Bohaker is a lovely loop through woodlands to a short coastline trail. The highlight is a cobblestone cove piled with driftwood, into which a small waterfall tumbles. This is a fine destination for a picnic. The trails are well marked—once you find them.

WHERE TO STAY

The closest campground to Annapolis Royal is on a handsome 9-hectare (22-acre) waterfront property across the embayment from the tidal generating station. The privately owned **Dunromin Campsite** ((*C*) **902/532-2808**) has full hookups for trailers and RVs and attractive tenting sites along the water's edge, as well as high-speed Internet access, an on-site cafe, and a few cabins. Sites cost C$24 to C$37 (US$22–US$33/£12–£19).

For more modern, motel-like accommodations near town, try the **Annapolis Royal Inn** ((*C*) **888/857-8889** or 902/532-2323), south of town on Highway 101, Exit 22. Doubles are C$89 to C$148 (US$80–US$133/£45–£74).

Garrison House Inn   The historic Garrison House sits across the road from Fort Anne in the town center and has bedded and fed guests since it first opened to accommodate officers at the fort in 1854. The rooms are nicely appointed with antiques, some worn, some pristine. There's no air-conditioning, but fans are provided; the top floor can still get a bit stuffy on warm days. Room no. 2 is appealing, with wide pine floors, a braided rug, and wing-back chairs, though it faces the street and at times can be a bit noisy. Room no. 7 is tucked in the back of the house, away from the hubbub of St. George Street, and it has two skylights and a big demilune window to let in the wonderfully dappled light. In addition to the restaurant (see below), there's a screened-in veranda with food (fish and lobster, mostly) and drink service. Note that there are no phones, which could be a blessing.

350 St. George St., Annapolis Royal, NS B0S 1A0. (*C*) **866/532-5750** or 902/532-5750. Fax 902/532-5501. www. garrisonhouse.ca. 7 units. C$69–C$149 (US$62–US$134/£35–£75) double. AE, MC, V. Street parking. Open May–Nov; call in advance for weekends rest of year. **Amenities:** Restaurant; bar. *In room:* AC, TV/DVD, Jacuzzi (1 unit), no phone.

Hillsdale House Inn   This pale yellow clapboard Italianate home from 1849 sits just across the road from the slightly fancier Queen Anne Inn (see below). The first floor features a Georgian-style sitting room with furniture that's both nice to look at and comfortable to sit on. The carpeted guest rooms are handsome if a little basic, furnished with antique writing desks, claw-foot tubs, poster beds, and other pieces that aren't overly elaborate—except in spots: the lovely French settee in room no. 14, for instance. Only the top-floor rooms have air-conditioning, although all units now possess flat-panel televisions (after years of holding out) as well as CD-playing clock radios. The telephones, however, are still shared.

519 St. George St. (P.O. Box 148), Annapolis Royal, NS B0S 1A0. (*C*) **877/839-2821** or 902/532-2345. Fax 902/532-0752. www.hillsdalehouse.ns.ca. 15 units. May to mid-Oct C$109–C$149 (US$98–US$134/£55–£75) double; rest of the year C$79–C$109 (US$71–US$98/£40–£55) double. Rates include full breakfast. MC, V. *In room:* A/C (top floor only), TV, no phone.

King George Inn 😊 *Kids*   The handsome King George Inn was built as a sea cap-tain's mansion in 1868 and served a stint as a rectory before becoming an inn. It's befittingly busy and cluttered for its era; guest rooms are furnished entirely with antiques, mostly country Victorian. Think commodes, bowls and pitchers, rocking chairs, Oriental rugs, and Tara-worthy lamps. (Those who prefer clean lines might find a surplus of decor and frippery here.) Most rooms have queen-size beds—ask if you want a king or twins—and the two family suites have separate bedrooms and a bathroom that's shared between them. The best in the house might be room no. 7, the Duchess of Kent suite, with its Jacuzzi and small private deck off the back of the house overlooking the garden. A second Jacuzzi room was added in 2001, in the Queen Victoria suite, which also has a king bed, bay window, and gigantic headboard (if you're into that). The inn also features a pump organ and a 19th-century grand piano, and helpfully provides bikes for guests.

548 Upper St. George St., Annapolis Royal, NS B0S 1A0. ✆ **888/799-5464** or 902/532-5286. Fax 902/532-0144. www.kinggeorgeinn.20m.com. 8 units. C$80–C$160 (US$72–US$144/£40–£80) double. MC, V. Closed Jan–Apr. **Amenities:** Bikes. *In room:* A/C, coffeemaker, hair dryer, no phone.

Queen Anne Inn 😊   You can't miss this Second Empire mansion, built in 1865, on your way into town. Like the Hillsdale House across the street, the Queen Anne (built for the sister of the Hillsdale's owner) has benefited from a preservation-minded owner, who restored the Victorian detailing to its former luster. There's a zebra-striped dining-room floor (alternating planks of oak and maple) and a grand central staircase. The guest rooms are quite elegant and furnished appropriately for the Victorian era, although they have been updated to include Jacuzzis. With their towering elms, the parklike grounds are shady and inviting. Breakfast is a three-course affair.

494 St. George St., Annapolis Royal, NS B0S 1A0. ✆ **877/536-0403** or 902/532-7850. Fax 902/532-2078. www.queenanneinn.ns.ca. 12 units. May–June C$99–C$169 (US$89–US$152/£50–£85) double; July–Oct C$119–C$209 (US$107–US$188/£60–£105) double. Rates include full breakfast. MC, V. Closed Nov–Apr. *In room:* TV, no phone.

WHERE TO DINE

The Garrison House 😊😊 ECLECTIC   The Garrison House is the most intimate and attractive of the village's restaurants. The three cozy dining rooms in this historic home each have a different feel, some with colonial colors, some contemporary, most with black Windsor chairs and modern piscine art. (My favorite room is the one with the green floors and the humpback whale.) The menu is also tricky to categorize, with yummy starters such as house-cured salmon with flatbread, Acadian seafood chowder, mussels steeped in wine, and a Thai shrimp soup; and entrees ranging from jamba-laya, shrimp and chicken in a Vietnamese curry over basmati rice, or salmon with a bourbon-maple glaze, to Digby scallops or a simple pasta with seafood or garden vege-tables. There are Jamaican influences in the cooking as well.

350 St. George St. (inside the Garrison House Inn). ✆ 902/532-5750. Reservations recommended in summer. Main courses C$14–C$27 (US$13–US$24/£7–£14). AE, MC, V. May–Oct daily 5:30–8:30pm; Nov–Apr open by arrangement.

Ye Olde Town Pub PUB FARE   For a more relaxed bite than the choice described above, swing by this local pub housed in an 1884 brick building that was once a bank (hence the bars on the windows). It's said to be the smallest pub in Nova Scotia—not only now, but in the history of the province. There's beer, a kitchen open all day, and a kids' menu.

9 Church St. ✆ 902/532-2244. Daily 11am–11pm.

5 Kejimkujik National Park ⊛

About 45km (28 miles) southeast of Annapolis Royal is a popular national park that's a world apart from coastal Nova Scotia. Kejimkujik National Park, founded in 1968, is located in the heart of south-central Nova Scotia, and it is to lakes and bogs what the South Coast is to fishing villages and fog. Bear and moose are the full-time residents here; park visitors are the transients. The park, which was largely scooped and shaped during the last glacial epoch, is about 20% water, which makes it especially popular with canoeists. A few trails also weave through the park, but hiking is limited; the longest hike in the park can be done in 2 hours. Bird-watchers are also drawn to the park in search of the 205 species that have been seen both here and at the Kejimkujik Seaside Adjunct, a 22-sq.-km (8½-sq.-mile) coastal holding west of Liverpool. Among the more commonly seen species are pileated woodpeckers and loons, and at night you can listen for the raspy call of the barred owl.

ESSENTIALS

GETTING THERE   Kejimkujik National Park is approximately midway on Kejimkujik Scenic Drive (Rte. 8), which extends 115km (71 miles) between Annapolis Royal and Liverpool. The village of Maitland Bridge (pop. 130) is near the park's entrance. Plan on about a 2-hour drive from Halifax.

VISITOR INFORMATION   The park's **visitor center** (© **902/682-2772**) is open daily and features slide programs and exhibits about the park's natural history.

FEES   The park opens daily at 8am year-round, though the visitor center cuts its hours substantially, closing at 4pm instead of 8pm, between Labor Day and mid-June. Fees are C$5.45 (US$4.90/£2.75) for adults, C$4.70 (US$4.25/£2.35) for seniors, C$2.70 (US$2.45/£1.35) for children ages 6 to 16, and C$14 (US$12/£6.80) for families. Seasonal passes can cut the cost of a longer stay; they cost C$27 (US$24/£14) adults, C$24 (US$22/£12) seniors, C$14 (US$13/£7) children ages 6 to 16, and C$68 (US$61/£34) for families.

EXPLORING THE PARK

The park's 381 sq. km (147 sq. miles) of forest, lakes, and bogs are peaceful and remote. Part of what makes the terrain so appealing is the lack of access by car. One short forked park road from Route 8 gets you partway into the park. Then you need to continue by foot or canoe. A stop at the visitor center is worthwhile, both for the exhibits on the region's natural history and for a preliminary walk on one of the three short trails. The Beech Grove loop (2km/1.2 miles) takes you around a glacial hill called a drumlin. The park has a taped walking tour available for use; ask at the information center.

   Canoeing is the optimal means of traversing the park. Bring your own, or rent a canoe at **Jake's Landing** (3km/2 miles along the park access road) for C$7.50 (US$6.75/£3.75) per hour or C$28 (US$25/£14) per day. Similar rates apply to rentals of bikes, paddleboats, kayaks, and rowboats. Canoeists can cobble together wilderness excursions from one lake to the other, some involving slight portaging. Multiday trips are easily arranged to backcountry campsites and are the best way to get to know the park. Canoe route maps are provided at the visitor center. Rangers also lead short, guided canoe trips for novices.

   The park also has 15 **walking trails,** ranging from short easy strolls to, well, longer easy strolls. (There's no elevation gain to speak of.) The 6km (3.7-mile) **Hemlocks and Hardwoods Trail** loops through stately groves of 300-year-old hemlocks; the

3km (1.9-mile) **Merrymakedge Beach Trail** skirts a lakeshore to end at a beach. A free map that describes the trails is available at the visitor center.

Mountain bikers can explore the old **Fire Tower Road,** a round-trip of about 19km (12 miles). The road becomes increasingly rugged and ends at a fire tower near an old-growth forest of birch and maple.

CAMPING

Backcountry camping is the park's chief draw. The 44 backcountry sites are so much in demand that they actually cost more than the drive-in campsites. Overnighting on a distant lakeshore is the best way to get to know the park; even if you're planning to car camp, I'd argue that it's worth the extra hassle and expense of renting a canoe and paddling off for a night just for the experience.

The canoe-in and hike-in sites are assigned individually, which means you needn't worry about noisy neighbors playing loud music on their car stereo. Backcountry rangers keep the sites in top shape, and each is stocked with firewood for the night (the wood is included in the campsite fee). Most sites can handle a maximum of six campers. Naturally, there's high demand for the best sites; you're better off here mid-week, when fewer weekenders are down from Halifax. You can also reserve backcountry sites (C$23/US$21/£12 per site) up to 60 days in advance for an additional fee; call the **visitor center** (© **902/682-2772**).

The park's drive-in campground at **Jeremy's Bay** ⚶ offers about 360 sites, a few quite close to the water's edge. Campground rates are C$18 to C$25 (US$16–US$23/ £9–£13) per night. (During the shoulder seasons in spring and fall, you get a 6th night free after 5 nights; winter camping costs less.) Note that during the off season, November to April, there are no toilets or showers—just pits. Starting early each April reservations at the drive-in campground may be made for an additional fee by calling © **877/RESERVE** or online at **www.pccamping.ca**.

6 Digby to Yarmouth

The South Shore—that stretch of coast between Yarmouth and Halifax—serves to confirm popular conceptions of Nova Scotia (small fishing villages, shingled homes), but the 113km (70-mile) shoreline from Digby to Yarmouth seems determined to confound those same conceptions. Look for Acadian enclaves, fishing villages with more corrugated steel than weathered shingle, miles of sandy beaches, and spruce-topped basalt cliffs that seem transplanted from Labrador.

The unassuming port town of **Digby** is located on the water at Digby Gap—where the Annapolis River finally forces an egress through the North Mountain coastal range. Set at the south end of the broad watery expanse of the Annapolis Basin, Digby is home to the world's largest inshore scallop fleet, which drags the ocean bottom for tasty and succulent Digby scallops. The town is an active community where life centers around fishing boats, neighborhoods of wood-frame houses, and no-frills seafood restaurants. It also serves as Nova Scotia's gateway for those arriving from Saint John, New Brunswick, via ferry. The ferry terminal is on Route 303, west of Digby.

Aside from the Digby Pines Golf Resort and Spa, which warrants its own trip (see below), the town is worth checking out if you have a few hours to kill before catching your ferry back to Saint John. If you're arriving by ferry and want to visit the town before pushing on, watch for signs directing you downtown from the bypass, otherwise you'll end up on Route 101 before you know it.

DIGBY NECK ✦

Look at a map of Nova Scotia and you'll see the thin strand of Digby Neck extending southwest from Annapolis Basin. You might guess from its appearance on the map that it's a low, scrubby sand spit. You would be wrong. In fact, it's a long, bony finger of high ridges, spongy bogs, dense forest, and expansive ocean views. The last two knuckles of this narrow peninsula are islands, both of which are connected via 10-minute ferries across straits swept with currents as strong as 9 knots.

Although neither the neck nor the islands have much in the way of services for tourists—just one real lodge, a couple of B&Bs, and a few general stores—it's worth the drive if you're a connoisseur of end-of-the-world remoteness. The town of Sandy Cove on the mainland is picture-perfect, with its three prominent church steeples rising from the forest. Both Tiverton on Long Island and Westport on Brier Island are unadorned fishing villages where pickup trucks are held together with Bondo and bailing wire. You get the distinct feeling that life hasn't changed much in the past few decades—or at least since 1960, when the roads were finally paved on Brier Island.

ESSENTIALS

GETTING THERE   Digby is Nova Scotia's gateway for those arriving from Saint John, New Brunswick, via ferry. The ferry terminal is on Route 303, west of Digby. If you've come in on the ferry and want to check the town out before continuing onward, watch for signs for downtown from the bypass or you could end up on Route 101 before you know it. From other parts of Nova Scotia, Digby is accessible via Exit 26 off Route 101.

Route 217 runs 72km (45 miles) south from Digby to Brier Island. Two ferries fill in when you run out of mainland. They leave East Ferry (about a 45 min. drive from Digby), on the mainland, for Long Island every hour on the half-hour, and then depart from Long Island for Brier Island on the hour. The ferries are timed such that you can drive directly from one ferry to the next, provided you don't dawdle. Round-trip fares are C$4 (US$3.60/£2) per car on each ferry; fares are collected on the out-bound leg only.

VISITOR INFORMATION   The province maintains a **visitor information center** (📞 **902/245-2201**) in Digby on Route 303 (on your right shortly after you disembark from the Saint John ferry). It's open April to November. There's also the municipal Visitor Information Centre located on the harbor at 110 Montague Row (📞 **902/245-5714**). It's open daily 8:30am to 8:30pm May to mid-October, and daily 9am to 5pm during spring and fall.

A seasonal **information booth** (📞 **902/839-2853**) is located at the local historical museum in Tiverton on Long Island. It's supposedly open from 9am to 7:30pm in July and August, though hours are sometimes more erratic than that. You might be better off collecting information at the aforementioned Visitor Information Centre on the Digby harbor before you set off. There's also a dependable provincial VIC at 227 Shore Rd. (📞 **902/245-2201**), open early May to early November from 8:30am to 8:30pm.

EXPLORING DIGBY NECK

BICYCLING   Brier Island offers an ideal destination for mountain bikers. At just 6.5km (4 miles) long and 2.5km (1½ miles) wide, it's the right scale for spending a slow afternoon poking around the dirt roads that lead to two of the island's red-and-white lighthouses. Brier Island maps are available free at island stores and lodges. If you park your car on the Long Island side and take your bike over on the ferry, you'll save money; there's no charge for bikes or pedestrians.

Bike rentals are available at **Backstreet Bicycles** in Digby (© **902/245-1989**).

HIKING   On Long Island, two short but rewarding woodland hikes take you to open vistas of St. Mary's Bay and the Bay of Fundy. The trailhead for the first, the half-mile hike to **Balancing Rock,** is 4km (2½ miles) south of the Tiverton ferry on Route 217; look for the well-marked parking area on the left. The trail crosses through swamp, bog, and forest and is dead straight and flat—until the last 90m (295 ft.), when you plummet nearly straight down a sheer bluff to the ocean's edge along some 169 steps. At the base, a series of boardwalks leads you over the surging ocean to get a dead-on view of the tall column of basalt balancing improbably atop another column. For the second short hike, return to the parking lot and drive 5km (3 miles) south to the picnic area on the right. From the parking lot atop the hill, a hike of 1km (.6 mile) descends gradually through a forest of moss, ferns, and roots to the remote **Fundy shore.** The coastline here is nearly lunar, with the dark rock marbled with thin streaks of quartz. You're likely to have the coast to yourself, since few venture here.

Farther along, **Brier Island** is laced with **hiking trails** ✦, offering fantastic opportunities for seaside exploration. Pick up one of the maps offered free around the island. A good place to start is the Grand Passage Lighthouse (turn right after disembarking the ferry and continue until you can't go any farther). Park near the light and walk through the stunted pines to the open meadows on the western shore, where you can pick up the coastal trail.

WHALE-WATCHING ✦   In the Bay of Fundy, ocean currents mingle and the vigorous tides cause upwelling, which brings a rich assortment of plankton to the surface. That makes it an all-you-can-eat buffet for whales, which feed on these minuscule bits of plant and animal. As the fishing industry has declined, the number of fishermen offering whale-watching tours has boomed. Most of these are down-home operations on converted lobster boats—don't expect the gleaming whale-watch ships with comfy seats and full-service cafeterias that you find in larger cities or on the New England coast.

Declining inshore herring stocks means tours need to head farther out into the bay to find whales than in years past, but you'll almost always have sightings of fin, minke, or humpback whales. Right, sperm, blue, and pilot whales, along with the seldom-seen orcas, have also been spotted over the years. Plan on spending around C$35 to C$45 (US$32–US$41/£18–£23) per adult for a 3- to 4-hour cruise, less for children.

Mariner Cruises (© **800/239-2189** or 902/839-2346) in Westport on Brier Island sails aboard the 14m (46-ft.) *Chad and Sisters Two,* which is equipped with a heated cabin. Both whale- and bird-watching tours are offered. **Pirate's Cove Whale & Seabird Cruises** (© **888/480-0004** or 902/839-2242), located in Tiverton, has been leading offshore cruises since 1990; several tours are offered daily aboard the 13m (43-ft.) *Fundy Cruiser* and *Fundy Voyager.* **Petite Passage Whale Watch** (© **902/834-2226**) sails out of East Ferry aboard the 14m (46-ft.), 45-passenger *Passage Provider 04* and has a partially covered deck. It runs two to three cruises daily from June through October.

For a saltier adventure, **Ocean Explorations** (© **877/654-2341** or 902/839-2417) offers tours on rigid-hulled inflatable Zodiacs. The largest boat holds up to a dozen passengers and moves with tremendous speed and dampness through the fast currents and frequent chop around the islands and the open bay; guests are provided with survival suits for warmth and safety. The 2- to 3-hour trips cost C$55 (US$50/£28) per adult, less for children, seniors, students, and group members.

WHERE TO STAY & DINE

Brier Island Lodge *(R)* *(Finds)*   Built to jump-start local eco-tourism, the Brier Island Lodge has a rustic-modern motif, with log-cabin construction and soaring glass windows overlooking the Grand Passage 40m (131 ft.) below. The rooms on two floors all have great views, the usual motel amenities, and some unexpected touches (double Jacuzzis in the pricier rooms). A well-regarded dining room serves up traditional favorites, and local fishermen congregate in an airy lounge in the evening to play cards and watch the satellite TV. There's a small but good selection of field guides near the upholstered chairs in the corner of the lounge; hiking trails connect directly from the lodge to the Fundy shore.

Brier Island (P.O. Box 39), Westport, NS B0V 1H0. © **800/662-8355** or 902/839-2300. Fax 902/839-2006. www.brierisland.com. 40 units. C$60–C$139 (US$54–US$125/£30–£70) double. MC, V. **Amenities:** Bike rental; game room. *In room:* A/C, TV, Jacuzzi (4 rooms).

Digby Pines Golf Resort and Spa *(R)(R)*   Digby Pines is situated on 120 hectares (297 acres) with marvelous views of the Annapolis Basin. The resort is redolent of an earlier era when old money headed to fashionable resorts for an entire summer. Built in 1929 in a Norman château style, the inn today is owned and operated by the province of Nova Scotia, and it should silence those who believe that government can't do anything right. The imposing building of stucco and stone is surrounded by the eponymous pines, which rustle softly in the wind. Throughout, the emphasis is more on comfort than historical verisimilitude, although the gracious lobby features old-world touches like Corinthian capitals, floral couches, and parquet floors. The guest rooms vary slightly in size and views (ask for a waterview room; there's no extra charge), and all now have ceiling fans, although air-conditioning is said to be on the way. The cottages have one to three bedrooms and most feature fireplaces and air-conditioning. A new Aveda spa offers a full menu of treatments and services, and an 18-hole Stanley Thompson–designed golf course threads its way through pines and over a babbling brook.

The resort's Annapolis Room is open for all three meals, and the cuisine might best be described as Nova Scotian with a French flair. Look for such entrees as roasted pork tenderloin with apples and a cider sauce, or poached char infused with green Chinese tea. Dinner reservations are advised, and dress a bit smartly at dinnertime.

Shore Rd. (P.O. Box 70), Digby, NS B0V 1A0. © **800/667-4637** or 902/245-2511. Fax 902/245-6133. www.digbypines.ca. 84 units, 30 cottages. C$160–C$325 (US$144–US$293/£80–£163) double; cottages more expensive. AE, DC, DISC, MC, V. Closed mid-Oct to mid-May. **Amenities:** Restaurant; bar; heated outdoor pool; golf course; 2 tennis courts; health club; spa; sauna; bike rentals; children's center; concierge; tour desk; courtesy car; babysitting; laundry service; dry cleaning. *In room:* A/C (cottages only), TV, dataport, coffeemaker.

ACADIAN COAST

The Acadian Coast (called the "French Shore" by English-speaking locals) runs roughly from Salmon River to St. Bernard. This hardscrabble coast, where the fields were once littered with glacial rocks and boulders, was one of the few areas where Acadians were allowed to resettle after the 1755 expulsion.

Today, you'll find abundant evidence of the robust Acadian culture, from the frequent sightings of the Stella Maris (the Acadian tricolor flag with its prominent star) to the towering churches around which each town seems to cluster. The region is more populous and developed than much of the Nova Scotia coast, and thus lacks somewhat the wild aesthetic that travelers often seek. You'll also find few tourist amenities along this stretch.

ESSENTIALS

GETTING THERE   The Acadian Coast is traversed by Route 1. Speedier Route 101 runs parallel and inland some distance; the Acadian Coast is served by exits 28 to 32.

VISITOR INFORMATION   It's best to collect information in the major towns bracketing either end of the Acadian Coast before arriving; that means heading to either the **Yarmouth Visitor Centre** (p. 79) at 228 Main St. or Digby's **information center** (p. 74) on Route 303.

EXPLORING THE ACADIAN COAST

A drive along this seaside route offers a pleasant detour, in both pace and culture. You can drive the whole length, or pick up segments by exiting from Route 101 and heading shoreward. What follows is a selected sampling of attractions along the coast, from north to south:

- **St. Mary's Church** 🎦🎦, Church Point. Many of the towns along the Acadian coast are proud of their impressive churches, but none is quite as extraordinary as St. Mary's. You can't miss it; it's adjacent to the campus of Université Sainte-Anne, the sole French-speaking university in Nova Scotia. The imposing, gray-shingled church has the stature of a European cathedral made of stone, but St. Mary's, built 1903 to 1905, is made entirely of wood.

  Outside, it's impressive—the fanciful steeple rises some 56m (184 ft.) above the grounds, with some 40 tons of rock hidden within to provide stability in the high winds. Inside, it's even more extraordinary—whole tree trunks serve as columns, although they're covered in plaster to lend a more traditional appearance. A small museum in the rear offers glimpses of church history. Admission by donation.

- **Rappie Pie.** This Acadian dish is a whole-meal pie typically made with beef or chicken. The main ingredient is grated potatoes, from which the moisture has been extracted and replaced with chicken broth. The full and formal name is "pâté a la rapure," but look for signs for "rapure" or "rappie pie" along Route 1 on the Acadian Coast.

- **Rapure Acadienne Ltd.,** Church Point (✆ **902/769-2172**). At this unassuming shop on Route 1 just south of Church Point, open daily year-round from 8am to 9pm, you can pick up a freshly baked beef or chicken rappie pie for about C$5 (US$4.50/£2.50); it costs about a dollar more for a clam pie. Commandeer an outdoor picnic table to enjoy your meal, or take it to the shady campus of Université Sainte-Anne, a few minutes' drive north.

- **La Vielle Maison** 🎦, Meteghan. This small historical museum displays artifacts of Acadian life in the 19th century. Look for the scrap of original French wallpaper uncovered during restoration of the summer bedroom. Open daily in summer. Admission is free.

- **Smuggler's Cove,** Meteghan. This small provincial picnic area a few minutes south of town has a set of steps running steeply down to a cobblestone cove. From here, you'll have a view of a tidal cave across the way. Rumrunners were said to have used this cave—about 5m (16 ft.) high and 18m (59 ft.) deep—as a hideout during the Prohibition era. Truth or local tourism boosterism? You be the judge. Admission is free.

- **Mavillette Beach** 🎦🎦, Mavillette. This beautiful crescent beach has nearly all the ingredients for a pleasant summer afternoon—lots of sand, grassy dunes, changing stalls, a nearby snack bar with ice cream, and views across the water to scenic

Cape Mary. All that's lacking is an ocean warm enough to actually swim in. It's seriously frigid here, although the courageous appear to be able to splash around for a time without lapsing into immediate cardiac arrest. The beach, managed as a provincial park, is 1km (⅔ mile) off Route 1, and the turnoff is well marked. Admission is free.

- **Port Maitland Beach** ⚓⚓, Port Maitland. Another provincial park beach—and a very long one at that—Port Maitland Beach is near the breakwater and town wharf. It isn't as scenic or pristine as Mavillette Beach; it's closer to Yarmouth and attracts larger crowds, principally families. But I really enjoy it anyway, because you can walk for miles in solitude here. This makes a good first stroll in the province if you're just off the overnight ferry. Signs direct you to the beach from the village center.

WHERE TO STAY

Accommodations are thin on the ground here; most are small, simple B&Bs offering varying degrees of comfort. They are quite affordable, however; you could pay as little as C$50 (US$45/£25) for a night in a double room here. It all depends on what you want. Push onward to the Annapolis Valley if you want a fancy inn, or backtrack to Yarmouth for a family motel or chain hotel if you'll be leaving the province by ferry or heading for the South Shore next. Traipse inland to **Kejimkujik National Park** (p. 72) if you're longing to camp in the woods.

If you're determined to stay in the land of Evangeline, no sweat. There's a good B&B, **A la Maison D'Amitie** ⚓ (© **902/645-2601**), on a cliff top down a dirt road in Mavillette, with three nice oceanfront rooms starting at C$140 (US$126/£70); the home boasts an impressive 500 ft. of ocean frontage in addition to its views. You might also try **L'Auberge au Havre du Capitaine** (© **902/769-2001**) on Route 1 in Meteghan River, a regular motel with 18 rooms at rates ranging from C$75 to C$119 (US$68–US$107/£38–£60) per night; a few even have air-jetted Jacuzzi tubs. As a bonus, there's a local-cuisine restaurant on the premises.

Still stuck? Here are two more options: the fetching **Churchill Mansion Inn** (p. 80) and the simple log **Trout Point Lodge Wilderness Resort** (p. 80), both covered below in the Yarmouth section but actually inland from the French Shore.

YARMOUTH

The constant lament of Yarmouth restaurateurs and shopkeepers is this: The summer tourists who steadily stream off the incoming ferries rarely linger long enough to appreciate the city before they mash the accelerator and speed off to higher-marquee venues along the coast.

There might be a reason for that. Yarmouth is a pleasant burg that offers some noteworthy historic architecture dating from the golden age of seafaring. But the town's not terribly unique, and thus not high on the list of places to spend a few days. It's a bit too big (pop. 7,800) to be charming, too small to generate urban buzz and vitality. It has the flavor of a handy pit stop more than a destination, though recent redevelopment efforts have spruced up the waterfront a bit and added evening entertainment during the summer months, a very welcome sign.

By all means plan to linger a few hours while awaiting the ferry (Portland-bound passengers could enjoyably spend the night here before their early morning departure) or to while away an afternoon when looping around the coast. Take the time to follow the self-guided walking tour, enjoy a meal, or wander around the waterfront, where efforts to coax it back from decrepitude have taken root.

ESSENTIALS

GETTING THERE   Yarmouth is at the convergence of two of the province's principal highways, routes 101 and 103. It's approximately 300km (186 miles) from Halifax. Yarmouth is the gateway for ferries connecting to Bar Harbor, Maine.

VISITOR INFORMATION   The **Yarmouth Visitor Centre** (© 902/742-6639 or 902/742-5033) is at 228 Main St., just up the hill from the ferry in a modern, shingled building you simply can't miss. Both provincial and municipal tourist offices are located here, open mid-May through late October daily from about 8am to 7pm.

EXPLORING THE AREA

The tourist bureau and the local historical society publish a very informative walking-tour brochure covering downtown Yarmouth. It's well worth requesting at the Yarmouth Visitor Centre (see above). The guide offers general tips on what to look for in local architectural styles (how do you tell the difference between Georgian and Classic Revival?), as well as brief histories of significant buildings. The whole tour is 4km (2½ miles) long.

The most scenic side trip—and an ideal excursion by bike or car—is to **Cape Forchu** and the **Yarmouth Light**. Head west on Main Street (Rte. 1) for 2km (1¼ miles) from the visitor center, then turn left at the horse statue. The road winds out to the cape, past seawalls and working lobster wharves, meadows, and old homes.

When the road finally ends, you'll be at the red-and-white-striped concrete lighthouse that marks the harbor's entrance. (This lighthouse dates from the early 1960s, when it replaced a much older octagonal lighthouse that succumbed to wind and time.) There's a tiny photographic exhibit on the cape's history in the visitor center in the keeper's house.

Leave enough time to ramble around the dramatic rock-and-grass bluffs—part of Leif Eriksson Picnic Park—that surround the lighthouse. Don't miss the short trail out to the point below the light. Bright red picnic tables and benches are scattered about; bring lunch or dinner if the weather is right.

Firefighters' Museum of Nova Scotia (Kids)   This two-story museum will appeal mostly to confirmed fire buffs, historians, and impressionable young children. The museum is home to a varied collection of early firefighting equipment, with hand-drawn pumpers the centerpiece of the collection. Kids love the 1933 vintage Chev Bickle Pumper because they can don helmets and take the wheel for some pretend-I'm-a-fireman time. Also showcased here are uniforms, badges, and pennants. Look for the photos of notable Nova Scotia fires ("Hot Shots").

451 Main St. © 902/742-5525. Admission C$3 (US$2.70/£1.50) adults, C$2.50 (US$2.25/£1.25) seniors, C$1.50 (US$1.35/75p) children, C$6 (US$5.40/£3) families. July–Aug Mon–Sat 9am–9pm, Sun 10am–5pm; June and Sept Mon–Sat 9am–5pm; Oct–May Mon–Fri 9am–4pm, Sat 1–4pm.

WHERE TO STAY

Fifteen kilometers (9⅓ miles) west of town on Route 1 is the **Lake Breeze Campground** (© 902/649-2332), a privately run spot with the appealingly low-key character of a small municipal campground. It has 32 sites for C$17 to C$25 (US$15–US$23/£8.50–£13), some right on the shores of tiny **Lake Darling** (you can rent a boat inexpensively), as well as five small cottages; it's all well tended to by its owners. The campground is open mid-May to mid-October.

Yarmouth is home to a number of chain motels. Among them are the **Best Western Mermaid Motel,** 545 Main St. (© 800/772-2774 or 902/742-7821), with rates of C$89 to C$180 (US$80–US$162/£45–£90) double; **Comfort Inn,** 96 Starr's Rd. (ⓒ **800/228-5150** or 902/742-1119), at C$85 to C$195 (US$77–US$176/£43–£98) double; and the **Rodd Grand Hotel,** 417 Main St. (ⓒ **800/565-7633** or 902/742-2446), C$150 to C$225 (US$135–US$203/£75–£113) double.

Churchill Mansion Country Inn   Between 1891 and 1920, the Churchill Mansion was occupied just 6 weeks a year, when Aaron Flint Churchill, a Yarmouth native who amassed a shipping fortune in landlocked Atlanta, Georgia (go figure), returned to Nova Scotia to summer. This extravagant mansion with its garish furnishings, situated on a low bluff overlooking the highway and a lake, was converted to an inn in 1981 by Bob Benson, who is likely to be found on a ladder or with a hammer in hand when you arrive. ("It never ends," he sighs.) The mansion boasts some original carpeting, lamps, and woodwork, although it can be a little threadbare, flaky, or water-stained in other spots. Note that psychics frequently visit the place. Really. If you're spooked by the thought of haunted houses, walk on by. The honeymoon suite with its Jacuzzi and little porch with lake view is the nicest room.

Rte. 1 (15km/9½ miles west of Yarmouth), Yarmouth, NS B5A 4A5. ⓒ **888/453-5565** or 902/649-2818. Fax 902/649-2801. www.churchillmansion.com. 8 units. C$69–C$140 (US$62–US$126/£35–£70) double. Meals available. DISC, MC, V. Closed mid-Nov to May. **Amenities:** Bike rental. *In room:* No phone.

Harbour's Edge B&B ⓡ *(Finds*   Now this is truth in advertising: This exceptionally attractive early Victorian home from 1864 sits on a quiet hectare (2½ acres) and has 76m (249 ft.) of harbor frontage, where the scenery changes twice per day with the tides. This was the very first parcel of land in Yarmouth to be owned by a Caucasian, but before that local native Canadians had camped and fished here. Today you can lounge on the lawn watching herons, hawks, and kingfishers below. It's hard to believe you're just a few minutes from the international ferry terminal. The inn opened in 1997 after 3 years of intensive restoration, and the rooms are lightly furnished, which nicely highlights the architectural integrity of the design. All four rooms sport high ceilings and handsome spruce floors. The attractive Audrey Kenney Room is biggest, but the Clara Caie has better views of the harbor, even if the private bathroom and its claw-foot tub are down the hall. The Georgie Allen has a private hallway and clear harbor view as well. You'll feel safe here, too: One of the innkeepers is a Royal Mountie (in other words, a Canadian cop).

12 Vancouver St., Yarmouth, NS B5A 2N8. ⓒ **902/742-2387.** www.harboursedge.ns.ca. 4 units. C$125–C$140 (US$113–US$126/£63–£70) double. Rates include full breakfast. MC, V. Head toward Cape Forchu (see above); watch for the inn shortly after turning at the horse statue. *In room:* Iron/ironing board, no phone.

Lakelawn Motel   The clean, well-kept Lakelawn Motel offers basic motel rooms in freshened bluish colors with newer carpeting very close to the ferry landing. It's been a downtown Yarmouth mainstay since the 1950s, when the centerpiece Victorian house (where the office is located) was moved back from the road to make room for the motel wings. Looking for something a bit cozier? The house also has four B&B-style guest rooms upstairs, each furnished simply with antiques. Breakfast, however, costs extra.

641 Main St., Yarmouth, NS B5A 1K2. ⓒ **877/664-0664** or 902/742-3588. www.lakelawnmotel.com. 34 units. C$59–C$99 (US$53–US$89/£30–£50) double. Meals available. AE, DC, DISC, MC, V. Closed Nov–Apr. *In room:* TV, no phone (some units).

Trout Point Lodge Wilderness Resort ⓡ   In the late 1990s, Louisiana natives Charles Leary and Vaughn Perret bought property about 25 miles north-northwest of Yarmouth and developed a small rustic property, one that emphasizes the art of cooking. Modeled loosely after an Adirondack hunting lodge, the property was built from scratch of white spruce logs and hand-cut local granite. A simple, natural feeling pervades throughout, from the windows letting in views of forest and river to roaring fireplaces in the public areas. Eight big standard rooms come with log walls, original art, handmade log-and-twig furniture, love seats, and work desks; two add stone fireplaces and decks on the river; others sport wood stoves, high ceilings, or bay windows. Two suites have canopy beds, sofas, and Jacuzzi tubs, while two cottages with differing amenities are also rented in part or whole; both possess full kitchens. The property offers free canoes, kayaks, and paddleboats for exploring the local system of rivers and lakes (there's a dock and platforms for swimming as well). If you're a serious foodie, ask about the ongoing program of cooking lessons and culinary getaways. Prix fixe dinners here cost C$95 (US$86/£48) per couple.

189 Trout Point Rd., off Rte. 203 (P.O. Box 456), E. Kemptville, NS B0W 1Y0. © 902/761-2142. www.troutpoint.com. 12 units. Peak season C$240–C$525 (US$216–US$473/£120–£263) double. Additional 15% service fee charged. Meal plans available. Ask about packages. MC, V. No meals late Oct to late May. From Yarmouth or Halifax, take Hwy. 103 to Shelburne-Ohio exit and continue 45 min. to E. Branch Rd. on right. **Amenities:** Restaurant; wood-fired hot tub; watersports equipment; massage. *In room:* Iron/ironing board, no phone.

WHERE TO DINE

Quick-N-Tasty *(Kids* SEAFOOD   The name about says it all. This country-cooking joint a mile or two from the incoming ferries from Maine has long been a hit with locals. The restaurant is adorned with the sort of paneling that was au courant in the 1970s, and meals are likewise old-fashioned and generous. The emphasis here is on seafood; you can order fish either fried or broiled, but go for the hot open-faced lobster club sandwich—it's gaining international foodie acclaim. The seafood casserole and the blueberry desserts are also notable.

Rte. 1, Dayton (from downtown Yarmouth, follow Rte. 3 west to Rte. 1). © 902/742-6606. Sandwiches C$3–C$12 (US$2.70–US$11/£1.50–£6); main courses C$7–C$18 (US$6.30–US$16/£3.50–£9). AE, DC, MC, V. Daily 11am–8pm (winter until 7:30pm). Closed mid-Dec to Feb. Original location just east of Yarmouth on the north side of Rte. 1; 2nd location across from ferry terminal.

Rudder's Seafood Restaurant & Brewpub *(R* BREWPUB   Yarmouth's first (and Nova Scotia's fourth) brewpub opened in 1997 on the waterfront. It occupies an old warehouse dating from the mid-1800s, and you can see the wear and tear of the decades on the battered floor and the stout beams and rafters. The place has been nicely spruced up, and the menu features creative pub fare, plus Acadian and Cajun specialties such as rappie pie and jambalaya, as well as lobster suppers and planked salmon. The steaks are quite good, as is the beer, especially the best bitter. In summer, there's outdoor seating on a deck with a view of the harbor across the parking lot.

96 Water St. © 902/742-7311. Sandwiches C$4–C$11 (US$3.60–US$9.90/£2–£5.50); entrees C$10–C$24 (US$9–US$22/£5–£12). AE, DC, MC, V. Mid-Apr to mid-Oct daily 11am–11pm (shorter hours in spring and fall). Closed mid-Oct to mid-Apr.

7 South Shore *(★(★*

The Atlantic coast between Yarmouth and Halifax is that quaint, maritime Nova Scotia you see on laminated place mats and calendars. Lighthouses and weathered, shingled buildings perch at the rocky edge of the sea, as if tenuously trespassing on the ocean's good graces. But as rustic and beautiful as this area is, you might find it a bit stultifying to visit every quaint village along the entire coastline—involving about 340km (211 miles) of twisting road along the water's edge. If your heart is set on exploring this fabled landscape, be sure to leave enough time to poke in all the nooks and crannies along this stretch of the coast—towns such as Lunenburg, Mahone Bay, and Peggy's Cove are well worth the time.

It's sensible to allow more time here for one other reason—fog. When the cool waters of the Arctic currents mix with the warm summer air over land, the results are predictable and soupy. The fog certainly adds atmosphere. It also can slow driving to a crawl.

SHELBURNE

Shelburne is a historic town with an unimpeachable pedigree. Settled in 1783 by United Empire Loyalists fleeing New England after the unfortunate outcome of the late war, the town swelled with newcomers, and by 1784 was believed to have a population of 10,000—larger than Montréal, Halifax, or Québec. With the decline of boat building and fishing in this century, the town edged into that dim economic twilight familiar to other seaside villages (it now has a population of about 3,000), and the waterfront began to deteriorate, despite valiant preservation efforts.

And then Hollywood came calling, hat in hand. In 1992, the film *Mary Silliman's War* was filmed here. The producers found the waterfront to be a reasonable facsimile of Fairfield, Connecticut, circa 1776. The crew spruced up the town a bit and buried power lines along the waterfront.

Two years later, director Roland Joffe arrived to film the spectacularly miscast *Scarlet Letter,* starring Demi Moore, Gary Oldman, and Robert Duvall. The film crew buried more power lines, built some 15 "historic" structures near the waterfront (most demolished after filming), dumped tons of rubble to create dirt lanes (since removed), and generally made the place look like 17th-century Boston.

When the crew departed, it left behind three buildings and an impressive shingled steeple you can see from all over town. Among the "new old" buildings is the waterfront cooperage across from the Cooper's Inn. The original structure, clad in asphalt shingles, was generally considered an eyesore and was torn down, replaced by the faux-17th-century building. Today, barrel makers painstakingly make and sell traditional handcrafted wooden barrels in what amounts to a souvenir of a notable Hollywood flop.

ESSENTIALS

GETTING THERE   Shelburne is 216km (134 miles) southwest of Halifax on Route 3. It's a short hop from Route 103 via either Exit 25 (southbound) or Exit 26 (northbound).

VISITOR INFORMATION   The **Shelburne Tourist Bureau** (© 902/875-4547) is located in a tidy waterfront building at the corner of King and Dock streets. It's open daily mid-May to October from 9am to 8pm.

EXPLORING HISTORIC SHELBURNE

The central historic district runs along the waterfront, where you can see legitimately old buildings, Hollywood fakes (see above), and spectacular views of the harbor from small, grassy parks. There's a lot more in the district, however, including a helpful little tourist office at the bend in the road (see above), gift shops, a B&B (the Cooper's Inn, reviewed below), a husband-and-wife team of coopers making barrels in an open shop (technically, it's not open to the public, but ask nicely for a look), a kayaking and outdoor adventure center, and the **Sea Dog Saloon** (© 902/875-2862, open 11am–9pm daily) at the very end of the road. A block inland from the water is

Shelburne's more commercial stretch, where you can find services that include banks, shops, and a wonderful bakery (see "Where to Dine," below).

Flower fanciers should inquire about the self-guided **garden tours** sponsored by the Shelburne County Garden Club. Some 18 gardens are open to the public. Most of the gardens are indeed quite pleasant, but almost as enjoyable is the chance to meet local gardeners and talk about a shared passion. Ask for a brochure at the tourist bureau.

Shelburne Historic Complex *Kids*   The historic complex is an association of four local museums located within steps of one another. The most engaging is the **Dory Shop Museum,** right on the waterfront. On the first floor you can admire examples of the simple, elegant boatbuilding craft (said to be invented in Shelburne) and view videos about the late Sidney Mahaney, a master builder who worked in this shop from the time he was 17 until he was 96. Then head upstairs, where all the banging is going on. While you're there, ask about the difference between a Shelburne dory and a Lunenburg dory.

The **Shelburne County Museum** features a potpourri of locally significant artifacts from the town's Loyalist past. Most intriguing is the 1740 fire pumper; it was made in London and imported here in 1783. Behind the museum is the austerely handsome **Ross-Thomson House,** built in 1784 through 1785. The first floor contains a general store as it might have looked in 1784, with bolts of cloth and cast-iron teakettles. Upstairs is a militia room with displays of antique and reproduction weaponry. The fourth museum, the **Muir-Cox Shipyard** and its Interpretive Centre, was added most recently and features, as you might guess, maritime displays of barks, sailboats, yachts, and more. If you're interested enough in these sorts of things, you could easily spend a half-day here, particularly with children. Plan to have lunch afterward in town.

Dock St. (P.O. Box 39), Shelburne, NS B0T 1W0. © 902/875-3141. Admission to all 4 museums C$8 (US$7.20/£4) adults, free for children under 16; individual museums C$3 (US$2.70/£1.50) adults, free for children under 16. June to mid-Oct daily 9:30am–5:30pm. Closed mid-Oct to May (Dory Shop closes end of Sept).

WHERE TO STAY

Just across the harbor from Shelburne is **The Islands Provincial Park** (© 902/ 875-4304), which offers 64 campsites on 193 hectares (477 acres) from mid-May to early September. Some are right on the water and have great views of the historic village across the way. No hookups for RVs. The sites cost C$19 (US$17/£9.50) apiece.

The Cooper's Inn *Finds*   Facing the harbor in the Dock Street historic area, the impeccably historic Cooper's Inn was originally built by Loyalist merchant George Gracie in 1785. Subsequent additions and updates have been historically sympathetic. The downstairs sitting and dining rooms set the mood nicely, with worn wood floors, muted wall colors (mustard and khaki green), and classical music in the background. The rooms in the main building mostly feature painted wood floors (they're carpeted in the cooper-shop annex) and are decorated in a comfortably historic-country style. The third-floor suite features wonderful detailing, two sleeping alcoves, and harbor views. It's worth stretching your budget for. The George Gracie Room has a four-poster bed and water view, the small Roderick Morrison Room has a wonderful claw-foot tub perfect for a late-evening soak, and the Harbour Suite features a harbor-view tub and massage chair. As a bonus, owners Paul and Pat DeWar leave a small bottle of wine, chocolates and biscuits, and museum passes to the historic complex in each room. The two small, elegant **dining rooms** here serve the best meals in town. Dinner is served nightly from 6 to 9pm, and reservations are strongly recommended.

36 Dock St., Shelburne, NS B0T 1W0. ℂ **800/688-2011** or 902/875-4656. Fax 902/875-4656. www.thecoopersinn.com. 7 units. C$100–C$185 (US$90–US$167/£50–£93) double. Rates include full breakfast. MC, V. **Amenities:** 2 dining rooms. *In room:* TV/VCR, kitchenette (1 unit), coffeemaker (most units), hair dryer.

WHERE TO DINE

For a full dinner out, see The Cooper's Inn, above.

Mr. Fish ⓡ *Value* SEAFOOD   You can't miss this little fried-fish stand on the side of busy Route 3, near a shopping center; what the place lacks in location, it more than makes up for in character and good simple seafood. The matronly line cooks fry up messes of haddock, scallops, and shrimp, perfectly jacketed in light crusts. As if that weren't good enough, they then dole out great fries and crunchy coleslaw on the side—plus a smile. You eat outside on the picnic tables (but watch out for bees); if it's raining, you'll have to eat in your car.

104 King St. (Rte. 3, north of town center). ℂ **902/875-3474.** Meals C$2.60–C$13 (US$2.35–US$12/£1.30–£6.50). V. Mon–Sat 10am–7pm (Fri and holidays until 9pm); Sun noon–7pm.

Shelburne Café ⓡ *Value* BAKERY/CAFE   When a family of German chefs set about opening this Shelburne pastry shop in 1995, the idea was to sell fancy pastries. But everyone who stopped by during the restoration of the Water Street building asked whether they would be selling bread. So they added bread. And today their loaves are among the best you'll taste in the province—especially the delectable Nova Scotian oatmeal brown bread. Though the place is under new ownership, it still offers great pastries (try the pinwheels) as well as satisfying sandwiches and filling meals from an expanding menu that includes seafood entrees such as almond-crusted salmon or poached haddock with a dill-wine sauce, lobster crepes and sandwiches, and seafood pastas. Everything is made from scratch, and everything (except the marked-down day-old goods) is just-baked fresh. Soft-serve ice cream and macaroons are two more new additions. You'll get good value for your loonies here.

171 Water St. ℂ **902/875-1164.** Sandwiches C$3.50–C$4.25 (US$3.15–US$3.85/£1.75–£2.15); main courses C$7.99–C$17 (US$7.20–US$15/£4–£8.50). V. Mon–Fri 8am–7pm.

LUNENBURG ⓡⓡ

Simply put, I love Lunenburg. It is one of Nova Scotia's most historic and appealing villages, a fact recognized in 1995 when UNESCO declared the old downtown a World Heritage Site. The town was first settled in 1753, primarily by German, Swiss, and French colonists. It was laid out on the "model town" plan then in vogue (Savannah, Georgia, and Philadelphia, Pennsylvania, were also set out along these lines), which meant seven north-south streets intersected by nine east-west streets. Such a plan worked quite well in the coastal plains. Lunenburg, however, is located on a harbor flanked by steep hills, and implementers of the model-town plan saw no reason to bend around these. As a result, some of the streets can be exhausting to walk.

About 70% of the downtown buildings date from the 18th and 19th centuries, and many of these are possessed of a distinctive style and are painted in bright colors. Looming over all is the architecturally unique Lunenburg Academy, with its exaggerated mansard roof, pointy towers, and extravagant use of ornamental brackets. It sets the tone for the town the way the Citadel does for Halifax. The first two floors are still used as a public school (the top floor was deemed a fire hazard some years ago), and the building is open to the public only on special occasions.

What makes Lunenburg so appealing to visitors is its vibrancy. Yes, it's historic, but this is not an ossified village. There's life, including a subtle countercultural tang that dates from the 1960s. Look and you'll see evidence of the tie-dye-and-organic crowd in the scattering of natural food shops and funky boutiques. A growing number of art galleries, crafts shops, and souvenir vendors are moving in, making for rewarding browsing.

ESSENTIALS

GETTING THERE   Lunenburg is 100km (62 miles) southwest of Halifax on Route 3.

VISITOR INFORMATION   The **Lunenburg Tourist Bureau** (© 902/634-8100 or 902/634-3656) is located at the top of Blockhouse Hill Road. It's open from May to October, daily 9am to 8pm. It's not in an obvious location, but the brown "?" signs posted around town—or helpful locals—will point you there. The staff here is especially good at helping you find a place to spend the night if you've arrived without reservations. You can also call up local information on the Web at **www.lunenburgns.com**.

EXPLORING LUNENBURG

Leave plenty of time to explore Lunenburg by foot. An excellent walking-tour brochure is available at the tourist office on Blockhouse Hill Road, though supplies are limited. If that's gone, contact the **Lunenburg Board of Trade** (© 902/634-3170) for an excellent local and regional map.

St. John's Anglican Church ✦✦ at the corner of Duke and Cumberland streets had been one of the most impressive architectural sights in all of eastern Canada. The original structure, built in 1754 of oak timbers shipped from Boston, was rendered in simple New England meetinghouse style. Between 1840 and 1880, the church went through a number of additions and was overlaid with ornamentation and shingles to create an amazing example of the "carpenter Gothic" style—one in which many local residents were baptized and attended services throughout their adult lives. All this changed on Halloween night of 2001, however: A fire nearly razed the place, gutting its precious interior and much of the ornate exterior as well. In June of 2005, however, it reopened after a painstaking 3-year restoration project.

While exploring the steep streets of the town, note the architectural influence of later European settlers—especially Germans. Some local folks undoubtedly made their fortunes from the sea, but real money was also made by carpenters who specialized in the ornamental brackets that elaborately adorn dozens of homes here. Many of these same homes similarly feature a distinctive architectural element that's known as the "Lunenburg bump"—a five-sided dormer-and-bay-window combo installed directly over an extended front door. Other homes feature the more common Scottish dormer. Also look for the double or triple roofs on some projecting dormers, which serve absolutely no function other than to give the home the vague appearance of a wedding cake.

Guided 1½-hour **walking tours** (© 902/634-3848) that include lore about local architecture and legends are hosted daily by Eric Croft, a knowledgeable Lunenburg native who's in possession of a sizable store of good stories. Tours depart at 10am, 2pm, and 9pm (by candlelight) from Bluenose Drive, across from the parking lot for the Atlantic Fisheries Museum; the cost is C$15 (US$14/£7.50) adults, C$10 (US$9/£5) children.

Several boat tours operate from the waterfront, most tied up near the Fisheries Museum. **Lunenburg Whale Watching Tours** (© 902/527-7175) sails in pursuit of several species of whales, along with seals and seabirds, on 3-hour excursions. There are four departures daily from May through October, with reservations recommended. **Star Charters** (© 902/634-3535 or 877/247-7075; www.novascotiasailing.com) takes visitors on a mellow 45-minute tour of Lunenburg's inner harbor (no swells!) in a converted fishing boat. The same folks also offer 1½-hour sailing trips on the *Eastern Star*, a 14m (46-ft.) wooden ketch, June through October.

Fisheries Museum of the Atlantic ☆ *(Kids)* The sprawling Fisheries Museum is professionally designed and curated, and it manages to take a topic that some might consider a little, well, dull and make it fun and exciting. It's also been upgraded and expanded recently. You'll find aquarium exhibits on the first floor, including a touch-tank for kids. (Look also for the massive 15-lb. lobster, estimated to be 25–30 years old.) Detailed dioramas depict the whys and hows of fishing from dories, colonial schooners, and other historic vessels. You'll also learn a whole bunch about the *Bluenose*, a replica of which ties up in Lunenburg when it's not touring elsewhere (see "The Dauntless *Bluenose*" box, below). Outside, you can tour two other ships—a trawler and a salt-bank schooner—and visit a working boat shop. Allow at least 2 hours to probe all the corners of this engaging waterfront museum.

On the waterfront. © 866/579-4909 or 902/634-4794. http://museum.gov.ns.ca/fma. Mid-May to mid-Oct admission C$9 (US$8.10/£4.50) adults, C$7 (US$6.30/£3.50) seniors, C$3 (US$2.70/£1.50) children age 6–17, C$22 (US$20/£11) families; rest of the year C$4 (US$3.60/£2) per person (children free). May–Oct daily 9:30am–5:30pm (July–Aug to 7pm); Nov–Apr Wed only, 9am–4pm.

SHORT ROAD TRIPS FROM LUNENBURG

Blue Rocks ☆☆ is a tiny, picturesque harbor a short drive from Lunenburg. It's every bit as scenic as Peggy's Cove, but without the tour buses. Head out of town on Pelham Street and keep driving east. Look for signs indicating either THE POINT or THE LANE and steer in that direction; the winding roadway gets narrower as the homes get more humble. Eventually, you'll reach the tip, where it's just fishing shacks, bright boats, and rocks, with views of spruce- and heath-covered islands offshore. The rocks are said to glow in a blue hue in certain light, hence the name. There's a small bike shop along the road to the neighborhood, the **Lunenburg Bike Barn** (© 902/634-3426; www.bikelunenburg.com) at 579 Blue Rocks Rd., whose helpful owners rent bikes for exploring the surroundings. They can also fix or otherwise service your bike in a pinch.

If you continue on instead of turning toward "the point," you'll soon come to the enclave of **Stonehurst,** another cluster of homes gathered around a rocky harbor. The road forks along the way; the narrow, winding route to South Stonehurst is somewhat more scenic. This whole area is ideal for exploring by bicycle, with twisting lanes, great vistas, and limited traffic.

Heading eastward along the other side of Lunenburg Harbor, you'll end up eventually at the **Ovens Natural Park** ☆ (© 902/766-4621; www.ovenspark.com) in Riverport, a privately owned campground and day-use park that sits on 1.6km (1 mile) of dramatic coastline. You can follow the seaside trail to view the "ovens" (sea caves, actually) for which the park was named. A closer view can be had on a **Zodiac boat tour** of the caves. The park also features a cafe that serves up basic meals and a great view. Entrance fees are C$8 (US$7.20/£4) adults, C$4 (US$3.60/£2) seniors and children age 5 to 11, and campsites cost C$25 to C$45 (US$23–US$41/£13–£23) per night, with discounts for weekly stays. The park opens from May 15 to October 15.

The Dauntless *Bluenose*

Take an old Canadian dime—one minted before 2001, that is—out of your pocket and have a close look. That graceful schooner on one side? That's the *Bluenose,* Canada's most recognized and most storied ship.

The *Bluenose* was built in Lunenburg in 1921 as a fishing schooner. But it wasn't just any schooner. It was an exceptionally fast schooner.

U.S. and Canadian fishing fleets had raced informally for years. Starting in 1920, the *Halifax Herald* sponsored the International Fisherman's Trophy, which was captured that first year by Americans sailing out of Massachusetts. Peeved, the Nova Scotians set about taking it back. And did they ever. The *Bluenose* retained the trophy for 18 years running, despite the best efforts of Americans to recapture it. The race was shelved as World War II loomed; in the years after the war, fishing schooners were displaced by long-haul, steel-hulled fishing ships, and the schooners sailed into the footnotes of history. The *Bluenose* was sold in 1942 to labor as a freighter in the West Indies. Four years later it foundered and sank off Haiti.

What made the *Bluenose* so unbeatable? A number of theories exist. Some said it was because of last-minute hull design changes. Some said it was frost "setting" the timbers as the ship was being built. Still others claim it was blessed with an unusually talented captain and crew.

The replica *Bluenose II* was built in 1963 from the same plans as the original, in the same shipyard, and even by some of the same workers. It's been owned by the province since 1971, and it sails throughout Canada and beyond as Nova Scotia's seafaring ambassador. The *Bluenose*'s location varies from year to year, and it schedules visits to ports in Canada and the United States. In midsummer, it typically alternates between Lunenburg and Halifax, during which time visitors can sign up for 2-hour harbor sailings (C$35/US$32/£18 adults, C$20/US$18/£10 children age 3 to 12). To hear about the ship's schedule, call the *Bluenose II* Preservation Trust (© 866/579-4909).

WHERE TO STAY

Lunenburg is chock-full of good inns and B&Bs, but the situation is in constant flux: Some of the properties listed below are up for sale and some have recently been sold; as a result, ownership and rates may change in the near future. Call ahead to check.

The town's most diverse set of lodgings is that run by the folks at the publike **The Grand Banker Seafood Bar & Grill** (© 902/634-3300) at 82 Montague St. Alan Creaser and company rent out a total of 17 rooms and suites around the old town. Rates depend on amenities and time of year but usually range from C$69 to C$185 (US$62–US$167/£35–£93); check directly with the inn and restaurant for current prices, availability, and to make bookings.

For budget travelers, a great little **municipal campground** is located next to (and managed by) the visitor center (© 902/634-8100) on Blockhouse Hill. It has wonderful views and hookups for RVs. Be aware that the 52 sites are packed in tightly, but the location is well situated for exploring the town. Ask about pitching your tent on the less crowded far side of the information center, up on the grassy hill next to the fort's earthworks. The cost to camp is C$18 to C$26 (US$16–US$23/£9–£13); it's generally open from May through October. If that campground's full, **Little Lake Emily Campground** (© **902/634-4308**), 3km (2 miles) outside town (in the village of Centre) has 85 sites, most with electric hookup and about half with water and sewage lines as well; they go for C$22 to C$32 (US$20–US$29/£11–£16) per night.

Alicion Bed & Breakfast 🌟🌟 *Finds*   New owners Lorne and Janet Johanson run this small B&B, formerly the Senator Bed & Breakfast, out of a large, shipshape house in a serene residential neighborhood within walking distance of Lunenburg's Old Town. It gets raves from Frommer's readers. Surprisingly for the house's size, there are only three guest rooms available here; of the three, two have Jacuzzi-like jetted "hydrotherapy" tubs, and the third—furnished with two twin beds, rather than a double—has a Victorian claw-foot tub. Cheers to the Johansons, who are going "green" with the property in future months, adding organic fabrics and foods to what is already excellent lodging.

66 McDonald St. (P.O. Box 1215), Lunenburg, NS B0J 2C0. © **877/634-9358** or 902/634-9358. www.alicionbb.com. 3 units. Peak season C$110–C$130 (US$99–US$117/£55–£65) double; off season from C$85 (US$77/£43) double. Rates include full breakfast. MC, V. **Amenities:** Bikes. *In room:* Jacuzzi (2 units), no phone.

Boscawen Inn 🌟   This imposing 1888 mansion occupies a prime hillside site just a block from the heart of town; it was built in 1888 by local Senator H.A.N. Kaulbach, an influential figure in local history, as a wedding gift for his daughter. Today it is considered one of Lunenburg's finest examples of the Queen Anne Revival style of architecture. The interior decor is Victorian, although not aggressively so, and it's almost worth staying here just to get access to the main-floor deck and its views of the harbor. Most of the simply furnished rooms are in the main building, which had a newer wing added in 1945. (Two of the spacious suites are located in the 1905 MacLachlan House, just below the main house and across Lincoln St., with its little octagonal tower.) Note that guests housed on the third floor will need to navigate some steep steps. The inn's restaurant serves reliable, sometimes imaginative dinners nightly in season from 5:30 to 9pm.

150 Cumberland St., Lunenburg, NS B0J 2C0. © **800/354-5009** or 902/634-3325. Fax 902/634-9293. www.boscawen.ca. 17 units. C$95–C$195 (US$86–US$176/£48–£98) double. Rates include continental breakfast. AE, DISC, MC, V. **Amenities:** 2 restaurants; bar; laundry service. *In room:* TV, hair dryer, iron/ironing board, Jacuzzi (1 unit), no phone (except by request).

Kaulbach House 🌟🌟   One of the few local inns to have upscaled with the times, the right-in-town Kaulbach House is decorated appropriately for its elaborate architecture: in high Victorian style, but rendered somewhat less oppressive with un-Victorian color schemes. The house also reflects the era's prevailing class structure, since the nicest room (the tower room) is on top. It features two sitting areas and a great view. (The least intriguing rooms are the former servants' quarters on street level.) The new owners have spruced up the rooms a good bit with great shower heads, fresh flowers, fluffy robes, and DVD players. The hearty three-course included breakfast alone is worth coming for. And this is a good choice in another regard: It's one of the few small Lunenburg inns in which all the guest rooms have their own private bathrooms.

75 Pelham St., Lunenburg, NS B0J 2C0. © **800/568-8818** or 902/634-8818. Fax 902/640-3036. www.kaulbach house.com. 6 units. C$109–C$169 (US$98–US$152/£55–£85) double. Rates include full breakfast. MC, V. Closed Nov–May. **Amenities:** Laundry service. *In room:* A/C, TV, hair dryer, no phone.

Lennox Inn Bed & Breakfast   In 1991, this strikingly handsome but simple house in a quiet residential area of Lunenburg was condemned and slated for demolition. Robert Cram didn't want to see it go, so he bought it and spent several years restoring it to its original 1791 appearance, filling it with antiques and period reproduction furniture. It's more rustic than opulent (translation: the wood-floored rooms are pretty spare), but this fine inn should still be high on the list for anyone fond of authentically historic houses. In fact, it claims, quite plausibly, to be the oldest unchanged inn in Canada. Three of the four spacious second-floor rooms have the original plaster, and all four have the original fireplaces (nonworking). A country breakfast is served in the former tavern; be sure to note the ingenious old bar.

69 Fox St. (P.O. Box 254), Lunenburg, NS B0J 2C0. (℃) **888/379-7605**, 902/634-4043, or 902/521-0214. www.lennox inn.com. 4 units, 2 with private bathroom. C$95–C$120 (US$86–US$108/£48–£60) double. Rates include full breakfast. MC, V. Open year-round; by reservation only mid-Oct to Apr. *In room:* No phone.

Lunenburg Arms Hotel & Spa ⋆⋆   In a town where nearly all the lodgings consist of old seamen's homes, this hotel converted from a gutted former tavern and boardinghouse stands out as a modern alternative. It's the only accommodation in town where rooms are wheelchair-accessible, there's an elevator, pets are welcomed with open paws, and each unit is wired for high-speed Internet access at no extra charge. Rooms are furnished in pleasant carpeting and queen and king beds that wouldn't look out of place in a New York boutique hotel, yet there are also thoughtfully homey touches such as wood-laminate floors and a stuffed teddy bear (or two) placed in each room. The smallish bathrooms feature pedestal sinks and all-new fixtures. No two rooms are laid out exactly alike, so examine a few if possible to get the configuration you want—some rooms have Jacuzzis, some feature the town's best harbor views, and there are two bi-level loft suites with beds up small sets of stairs. The hotel added a spa featuring Aveda products in 2006; its facilities include a soaker tub, a hot tub, and aromatherapy-delivering steam showers.

94 Pelham St., Lunenburg, NS B0J 2C0. (℃) **800/679-4950** or 902/640-4040. Fax 902/640-4041. www.lunenburgarms. com. 26 units. Peak season C$129–C$299 (US$116–US$269/£65–£150) double; off-peak C$109–C$199 (US$98–US$179/£55–£100). AE, MC, V. **Amenities:** Dining room; spa; conference room. *In room:* A/C, TV, dataport, coffeemaker, hair dryer.

WHERE TO DINE

As with Lunenburg's inns, many prominent restaurants in town also seem to be up for sale at the moment. Check ahead to ensure a given eatery is still open. Note that the Boscawen Inn (see above) also serves well-regarded meals.

Historic Grounds Coffee House ⋆ *Value* CAFE   This youthful place in decidedly unhip Lunenburg serves up more than just great coffee: Hearty breakfasts, chowders, sandwiches, salads, and fish cakes are offered throughout most of the day, and always with a smile. (They've been doing this since the mid-1990s, so this isn't one of those flash-in-the-pan designer java huts, either.) Wash it down with real Italian espresso, something called a frappé (which is not an American-style frappé but rather more like a frozen espresso), smoothies, or sodas. Ice cream and interesting dessert items are also available. Go for a table on the tiny balcony if you can snag one—they've got the best dining view in town, at a fraction of the cost of what you'd pay for a meal anywhere else. Good choices at lunch include the Caesar salad wrap, the turkey club, and even a lobster sandwich.

100 Montague St. (℃) **902/634-9995**. Lunch items C$3.95–C$8.95 (US$3.55–US$8.05/£2–£4.50). AE, DISC, MC, V. June to mid-Sept Mon–Fri 7:30am–10pm, Sat–Sun 8am–10pm; mid-Sept to May daily 7:30am–6pm.

The Knot ✦ *Value* PUB FARE   Good beers on tap and a convivial English atmosphere make this pub a great place to take a break from more upscale eateries in town. Located smack in the center of a tiny commercial district, it serves surprisingly tasty pub fare—think juicy burgers, fried fish, local sausage, and a warming mussel soup—plus a selection of bitters and ales, some of them brewed locally in Halifax. The crowd is an agreeable mixture of fishermen, local families, and tourists; and bar staff are all too happy to help you decide what's good that day.

4 Dufferin St. ⓒ **902/634-3334.** Meals C$6–C$10 (US$5.40–US$9/£3–£5). AE, MC, V. Daily 10am–midnight; kitchen closes 9pm in summer, 8:30pm in winter.

Old Fish Factory Restaurant ✦ SEAFOOD   The Old Fish Factory Restaurant is—no surprise—located in a huge old fish-processing plant, which it shares with the Fisheries Museum. This large and popular restaurant can swallow whole bus tours at once; come early and angle for a window seat or a spot on the patio. Also no surprise: The specialty is seafood, which tends to involve medleys of varied fish. At lunch you might order a fish sandwich or a salmon filet. At dinner, lobster is served four different ways, along with bouillabaisse, snow crab, local haddock and scallops, and a curried mango seafood pasta. There's steak, lamb, and chicken for more terrestrial tastes.

68 Bluenose Dr. (at the Fisheries Museum). ⓒ **800/533-9336** or 902/634-3333. www.oldfishfactory.com. Reservations recommended. Lunch C$8–C$19 (US$7.20–US$17/£4–£9.50); dinner C$14–C$35 (US$13–US$32/£7–£18). AE, DC, DISC, MC, V. Daily 11am–9pm. Closed late Oct to early May.

Rissers ✦ ECLECTIC   A relatively recent addition to Lunenburg's restaurant menu, Rissers features mostly straight-ahead seafood that's a touch classier than the fried grub that predominates elsewhere around town and definitely more interesting than it has to be. Start with steamed mussels in a saffron-tomato stew, a duck spring roll, scallops wrapped in prosciutto, or a crab-artichoke bake. Typical entrees might include a grilled steak with onion rings and béarnaise butter, a lamb shank braised in cabernet, a sage-roasted breast of chicken, or a cider-brined pork chop with a Yukon gold potato pie. Eat inside by the fireplace, at the bar, or out on the stylish terrace opening onto a quiet street. Come on Friday night to catch live music.

94 Pelham St. ⓒ **800/679-4950** or 902/640-4040. Reservations accepted. Main courses C$9–C$25 (US$8.10–US$23/£4.50–£13). AE, MC, V. Daily 7am–10pm.

MAHONE BAY ✦✦

Mahone Bay, first settled in 1754 by European Protestants, is picture-perfect Nova Scotia. It's tidy and trim with an eclectic Main Street that snakes along the bay and is lined with inviting shops. This is a town that's remarkably well cared for by its 1,100 residents, a growing number of whom live here and commute to work in Halifax. Architecture buffs will find a range of styles to keep them ogling.

A **visitor information center** (ⓒ **888/624-6151** or 902/624-6151; www.mahonebay.com) is located at 165 Edgewater St., near the three church steeples. It's open daily in summer 9am to 7:30pm, until 5:30pm in shoulder seasons.

Each year in late July, Mahone Bay celebrates the **Wooden Boat Festival** ✦, where you can see some of the most beautiful crafts on the eastern seaboard put through their paces. Entertainment and workshops are offered as well; admission is free.

EXPLORING THE TOWN

The free **Mahone Bay Settlers Museum,** 578 Main St. (ⓒ **902/624-6263**), provides historic context for your explorations from June through early September; it's open

Tuesday to Saturday 10am to 5pm, Sundays 1 to 5pm, and closed Mondays. A good selection of historic decorative arts is on display. Before leaving, be sure to request a copy of "Three Walking Tours of Mahone Bay," a handy brochure that outlines easy historic walks around the compact downtown.

Thanks to the looping waterside routes nearby, this is a popular destination for bikers. And the deep, protected harbor offers superb sea kayaking. If you'd like to give kayaking a go, contact **East Coast Outfitters** (© **877/852-2567** or 902/852-2567), based in the Peggy's Cove area near Halifax. They offer half-day introductory classes and a 5-day coastal tour of the area. Among the more popular adventures is the day-long introductory tour, in which paddlers explore the complex shoreline and learn about kayaking in the process. The price is about C$115 (US$104/£58) per person, C$35 (US$32/£18) extra for a lobster lunch. Rentals are also available, starting at about C$45 (US$41/£23) per half-day for a single kayak.

SHOPPING

Mahone Bay serves as a magnet to all manner of creative and crafty types, and Main Street has become a shopping mecca for those who treasure handmade goods. Shops are typically open late spring until Christmas, when Haligonians travel the 55 minutes here for holiday shopping. Among the more interesting options:

Amos Pewter   Watch pewter come fresh out of the molds at this spacious workshop and gallery located in an 1888 building. You can get anything from tie tacks and earrings to candle holders and vases here; the Christmas tree ornament is a popular souvenir. 589 Main St. © 800/565-3369 or 902/624-9547.

Jo-Ann's Deli, Market & Bake Shop ⊀   Gourmet and farm-fresh basic fare are sold at this wonderful food shop, where a bag of carrots serves as a counterweight on the screen door. It's the best place for miles around to stock up on local and organic produce; fresh sandwiches; and knockout cookies, sweets, and Cape Breton–influenced oat cakes—the chocolate-covered ones blend chocolate, sugar, salt, and oats to perfect effect. If you're in the mood for a picnic, this is your destination. The homemade jams, sold to benefit a local museum, are well priced, and the coffee drinks from the bar are all exceptionally good as well. 9 Edgewater St. © 902/624-6305.

Sensational Chocolates   You'll find handmade Belgian chocolates here, many cast in special shapes with local resonance. You can buy samples for C$1 (US90¢/50p). 605 Main St. © 902/624-0323.

Suttles & Seawinds   Vibrant and distinctive clothing designed and made in Nova Scotia is sold at this stylish boutique. (There are others from Halifax to Toronto, but this is the original.) The adjacent shop is crammed with quilts and resplendent bolts of fabric. 466 Main St. © 888/339-9499 or 902/624-8375.

WHERE TO STAY

You'll find a clutch of bed-and-breakfast choices in and around Mahone Bay; consult the Chamber of Commerce website (www.mahonebay.com) for a fairly complete listing. **Ocean Trail Retreat** (© **888/624-8824** or 902/624-8824; fax 902/624-8899) on Route 3 at Mader's Cove is a relatively new property with 15 airy motel-style rooms and three two-bedroom chalets. It's very popular with families, largely because of the heated outdoor swimming pool. This might be the area's best choice if you're bringing children. Rooms go for C$99 to C$119 (US$89–US$107/£50–£60) per night, and a few oceanview chalets rent for C$1,200 (US$1,080/£600) per week, or C$175 (US$158/£88) per night during the off-peak months.

Then, right in the center of town, **Mahone Bay Bed & Breakfast** at 558 Main St. (© **866/239-6252** or 902/624-6388) is a more Victorian option with four rooms at rates from C$75 to C$125 (US$68–US$113/£38–£63) per night. The restored, bright yellow 1860s-era house was built by one of the town's many former shipbuilders. There's also **Fisherman's Daughter** (97 Edgewater St.; © **902/624-0483**), with its maritime theme and four rooms costing C$100 to C$125 (US$90–US$113/£50–£63) per night.

Nature's Cottage Bed & Breakfast 🏕   This serene B&B is a bit outside town, yet still within hailing distance; it's a nice choice for those who want a quiet experience. The property features a large front porch, great bay views, a private dock on the bay, a lush garden, and an outdoor whirlpool. Guests choose from three themed rooms, each with private bathrooms (stocked with handmade soaps) in the hallway and each possessing various comfort levels; the two-room Safari suite has a television, good view, and pullout sofa bed, while the Bouquet and Rustique rooms are simpler. (An additional loft-style unit above the garage has its own entrance, kitchenette, television, and in-suite bathroom.) Full breakfast is served with your stay, and guests also share access to a sauna room.

906 S. Main St., Mahone Bay, NS B0J 2E0. © **877/607-5699** or 902/624-0196. Fax 902/624-0363. 4 units. C$90–C$150 (US$81–US$135/£45–£75) double. **Amenities:** Jacuzzi; sauna. *In room:* No phone.

WHERE TO DINE

Mahone Bay's little main street has more than its share of places at which to nosh, though most are priced for tourist dollars.

That's why the seasonally open **Gazebo Cafe** 🏕 at 567 Main St. (© **902/624-6484**), an affable and affordable waterside cafe dishing up filling, healthy sandwiches and thick bowls of seafood chowder, is my favorite. They also do juices, smoothies, and top-flight coffee. Fresh desserts are delivered several times weekly. This place is rapidly becoming the arts headquarters of the town, too; check the bulletin board for news of local art shows and musical performances, some of which take place right at the cafe.

Innlet Café 🏕🏕 SEAFOOD/GRILL   Former owners Jack and Katherine Sorensen served up great meals here for 2 decades, and new ownership is holding true to the menu they created, which brought back legions of customers. Everything is good, especially the seafood. The menu is all over the place (oven-braised lamb shank to scallop stir-fry), but the smart money is on the unadorned seafood. Notable are the "smoked and garlicked mackerel" and the mixed seafood grill. The best seats are on the stone patio, which has a view of the harbor and the famous three-steepled townscape of Mahone Bay. If you end up inside, nothing lost. The clean lines and lack of clutter make it an inviting spot, and the atmosphere is informal and relaxed.

249 Edgewater St. © **902/624-6363**. Reservations recommended for dinner. Main courses C$12–C$21 (US$11–US$19/£6–£11). MC, V. Daily 11:30am–9pm.

CHESTER 🏕🏕

Chester is a short drive off Route 103 and has the feel of an old-money summer colony, perhaps somewhere along the New England coast in the 1920s. It was first settled in 1759 by immigrants from New England and Great Britain, and today it has a population of 1,250. The village is noted for its regal homes and quiet streets, along with the numerous islands offshore. The atmosphere here is uncrowded, untram-meled, lazy, and slow—the way life used to be in summer resorts throughout the world. Change may be on the horizon: Actors and authors have discovered the place and are snapping up waterfront homes in town and on the islands as private retreats, giving a bit of an edge to the lazy feel of the spot.

The **Chester Visitor Information Centre** (© 902/275-4616; www.chesterns.com) is in the old train station on Route 3 on the south side of town. It's open daily from 9am to 7pm in July and August, from 10am to 5pm in spring and fall.

EXPLORING THE AREA

Like so many other towns in Nova Scotia, Chester is best seen out of your car. But unlike other towns, where the center of gravity seems to be in the commercial district, here the focus is on the graceful, shady residential areas that radiate out from the Lil-liputian village.

In your rambles, plan to head down Queen Street to the waterfront, and then veer around on South Street, admiring the views out toward the mouth of the harbor. Con-tinue on South Street past the yacht club, past the statue of the veteran (in a kilt), past the sundial in the small square. Then you'll come to a beautiful view of Back Harbour. At the foot of the small park is a curious municipal saltwater pool, filled at high tide. On warmer days, you'll find what appears to be half the town out splashing and shrieking in the bracing water.

Some creative shops are beginning to find a receptive audience in and around Chester, and there's good browsing for new goods and antiques both downtown and in the outlying areas. One such shop is **Fiasco,** 54 Queen St. (© **902/275-2173**), which has an appealing selection of funky and fun home accessories and clothing. Another good stop is the **Village Emporium** at 11 Pleasant St. (© **902/275-4773**), an eclectic clustering of folk-arty lavender soaps, simple pottery, knit purses, and the like; it's in the same building as the Kiwi Café (see "Where to Dine," below).

For an even slower pace, plan an excursion out to the **Tancook Islands** ✿, a pair of lost-in-time islands with 200 year-round residents. The islands, accessible via a short ferry ride, are good for walking the lanes and trails. There's a small cafe on Big Tancook, but little else to cater to travelers. Several ferry trips are scheduled daily between 6am and around 6pm. The ferry ties up each night on one of the islands, however, so don't count on making a late trip back to the mainland. Tickets are C$5 (US$4.50/£2.50) round-trip, free for children under 12.

In the evening, the intimate **Chester Playhouse,** 22 Pleasant St. (© **800/363-7529** or 902/275-3933; www.chesterplayhouse.ns.ca), hosts plays, concerts, and other high-quality performances throughout the summer season. Tickets are usually around C$20 (US$18/£10) for adults. Call for a schedule or reservations.

WHERE TO STAY

Graves Island Provincial Park ✿✿   This 50-hectare (124-acre) estatelike park is one of the province's more elegant campgrounds, as befits moneyed Chester. The park has 73 sites, many dotting a high grassy bluff with outstanding views out to the spruce-clad islands of Mahone Bay, available mid-May through early October. No hookups are available.

Route 3 (3km/1¾ miles north of the village on East River). © **902/275-4425.** 73 sites. C$19 (US$17/£9.50) per site. **Amenities:** No hookups.

Mecklenburgh Inn *Value*   This wonderfully funky and appealing inn, built around 1890, is located on a low hill in one of Chester's residential neighborhoods. The building is dominated by broad porches on the first and second floors, which invariably are populated with guests sitting and rocking and watching the town wander by. (Which it does: The post office is just next door.) Innkeeper Suzi Fraser has been running the place with casual bonhomie since the late 1980s, and she's a great breakfast cook to boot. Rooms are modern Victorian and generally quite bright. What's the catch? The four rooms share two hallway bathrooms, but guests often end up feeling like family, so it's usually not much of a bother.

78 Queen St., Chester, NS B0J 1J0. © 902/275-4638. www.mecklenburghinn.ca. 4 units, 1 with private bathroom. C$85–C$135 (US$77–US$122/£43–£68) double. Rates include full breakfast. AE, V. Closed Jan–Apr. *In room:* Hair dryer, no phone.

WHERE TO DINE

In addition to the two eateries listed below, there's also **The Rope Loft,** at 36 Water St. (© **902/275-3430**), serving dependable pastas, pizza, fried clams, Digby scallops, lobster, and other seafood by the water; ask for a deck chair, if you can get one. The restaurant also serves brunch on both weekend days, from 11am to 2pm.

Kiwi Café *Finds* CAFE   A little enclave of New Zealand culture on the nautical coast of Nova Scotia? Yes, indeed. The former Luigi's bookshop-slash-cafe right in the heart of downtown Chester was sold in 2004 and reinvented as the Kiwi, a thank-goodness-it's-still-fun place in what can be an occasionally starchy town. Proprietor Lynda Flynn—yes, she's really from New Zealand, and received training in the culinary arts in Auckland—serves up eggs and bagels (try the lobster scramble) for breakfast, plus an assortment of sandwiches, wraps, panini, fresh soups, Nova Scotian fish cakes with mango salsa, and gourmet salads for lunch. Wash it down with wine, Nova Scotia beer, or a good blended Halifax-roasted-coffee drink. On the go? No problem: Grab a "Dinner in a Box" (Flynn also runs a catering business) or some New Zealand honey from the little provisions shop on the premises.

19 Pleasant St. © **902/275-1492.** www.kiwicafechester.com. Main courses C$4.50–C$8.50 (US$4.05–US$7.65/ £2.25–£4.25). V. Daily 8:30am–4pm.

La Vista *★★* CONTINENTAL/SEAFOOD   This dining room, located inside the Oak Island Resort spa and convention center just north of Chester down a side peninsula, offers an upscale alternative to traveling diners in the Chester area. Begin with a starter like the Lunenburg seafood chowder flavored with dill, the French onion soup with Gruyère, a smoked-salmon Napoleon, Thai crab cakes, or local mussels in white wine; then move on to the sesame-crusted salmon over basmati rice, cedar-planked salmon with maple butter, pan-roasted halibut with pepper and lemongrass, roasted tenderloin with a Stilton crust, Madras seafood curry, or shrimp-and-lobster pasta.

36 Treasure Dr. (inside the Oak Island Resort), Western Shore. © **902/627-2600.** Main courses C$18–C$21 (US$16–US$19/£9–£11). MC, V. Daily 7am–2pm and 5–9pm. Take Hwy 103 to Exit 9, continue 2km (1¼ miles) to Rte 3, turn onto Rte 3, continue 5km (3 miles) to resort.

8 Halifax *★★*

Halifax's unusually pleasing harborside setting, now home to a city of some 370,000, first attracted Europeans in 1749, when Col. Edward Cornwallis established a military outpost here. (The site was named after George Montagu Dunk, second earl of Halifax. Residents tend to agree that it was a great stroke of luck that the city avoided

Halifax

ACCOMMODATIONS ■
Cambridge Suites **10**
Delta Barrington **14**
Delta Halifax **13**
Halifax Heritage
House Hostel **35**
Halifax Waverley Inn **34**
The Halliburton **33**
Lord Nelson Hotel **5**
Prince George Hotel **21**
Super 8 Dartmouth **18**

DINING ◆
Bish World Cuisine **32**
Cheapside Café **24**
Cheelin **30**
daMaurizio **30**
Henry House **36**
Il Mercato **7**
O'Carroll's Restaurant
and Lounge **20**
Ryan Duffy's Steak
and Seafood **6**
Satisfaction Feast **28**
Sweet Basil Bistro **16**
Steve-O-Reno's **9**

ⓘ **Information**
┅┅┅ **Footpath**
- - - **Ferry**

0 _____ 0.2 mi
0 _____ 0.2 km

ATTRACTIONS ●
Art Gallery of Nova Scotia **24**
Barrington Place **15**
Fairview Lawn Cemetery **1**
Halifax Citadel
National Historic Site **2**
Halifax Historic Properties **17**
Maritime Museum
of the Atlantic **26**
McNab's Island **31**
Metro Centre **11**
Neptune Theatre **27**

Nova Scotia Centre for
Craft and Design **25**
Nova Scotia Museum of
Natural History **3**
Old Burying Ground **29**
Old City Hall **19**
Pier 21 **37**
Point Pleasant Park **8**
Province House **23**
Public Gardens **4**
St. Paul's Anglican Church **22**
Scotia Square **12**

the name Dunk, Nova Scotia.) The city plodded along as a colonial backwater for the better part of a century; one historian wrote that it was generally regarded as "a rather degenerate little seaport town."

But its natural advantages—including that well-protected harbor and its location near major fishing grounds and shipping lanes—eventually allowed it to emerge as a major port and military base. In recent years, the city has grown aggressively (it annexed adjacent suburbs in 1969) and carved out a niche as the vital commercial and financial hub of the Maritimes. The city is also home to a number of colleges and universities, which gives it a youthful, edgy air—skateboards and bicycles often seem to be the vehicles of choice. In addition to the many attractions, downtown Halifax is home to a number of fine restaurants and hotels.

ESSENTIALS

GETTING THERE   Coming from New Brunswick and the west, the most direct route is via Route 102 from Truro; allow about 2 to 2½ hours from the provincial border at Amherst.

Halifax International Airport (www.hiaa.com) is 34km (21 miles) north of downtown Halifax in Elmsdale; take Route 102 to Exit 6. Nova Scotia's notorious fogs make it advisable to call before heading out to the airport to reconfirm flight times. Airlines serving Halifax include Air Canada and its commuter airline Jazz, WestJet, American Eagle, and CanJet. (See the "Getting There" section of chapter 2 for phone numbers.) The **Airporter** (✆ 902/873-2091) offers frequent shuttles from the airport to major downtown hotels daily from 6:30am to 11:15pm. The rate is C$18 (US$16/£9) one-way.

VIA Rail (✆ 888/842-7245) offers train service 6 days a week between Halifax and Montréal. The entire trip takes between 18 and 21 hours, depending on direction. Stops include Moncton and Campbellton (with bus connections to Québec). Halifax's train station, at Barrington and Cornwallis streets, is within walking distance of downtown attractions.

VISITOR INFORMATION   Halifax's two main visitor centers are conveniently located downtown, and both are open year-round. The info booth in **Scotia Square** (✆ 902/490-5963) and the VIC by the waterfront at Sackville Landing (✆ 902/424-4248) are each open daily from 8:30am to 9pm in summer (and until 5pm in winter). They're staffed with friendly folks who will point you in the right direction or help you make room reservations in a pinch. A third year-round VIC is located in the domestic arrivals area of the main terminal of the **airport** (✆ 902/873-1223), open 9am to 9pm daily. From mid-May to mid-October, still another VIC opens downtown at 1598 Argyle St. (at the corner of Sackville). Also during the summer, travel counselors cruise the waterfront and boardwalk on Segway scooters. For online information about Halifax, visit **www.halifaxinfo.com**.

GETTING AROUND   Parking in Halifax can be problematic. Long-term metered spaces are in high demand downtown, and many of the parking lots and garages fill up fast. If you're headed downtown for a brief visit, you can usually find a 2-hour meter. But if you're looking to spend a day, I'd suggest venturing out early to ensure a spot at a parking lot. The city's most extensive parking (fee charged) is available near Sackville Landing. Or try along Lower Water Street, south of the Maritime Museum of the Atlantic, where you can park all day for around C$6 (US$5.40/£3).

Metro Transit operates buses throughout the city. Route and timetable information is available at the information centers or by phone (© **902/490-4000**). Bus fare is C$2 (US$1.80/£1) adults, C$1.25 (US$1.15/65p) seniors and children.

Daily throughout the summer (early July through late Oct), a bright green bus named **FRED** (© **902/490-4000**) cruises a loop through the downtown, passing each stop about every 30 minutes from 10:30am until 5:30pm. It's free. Stops include the Maritime Museum, Water Street, the Grand Parade, the Citadel, and Barrington Place. Request a schedule and map at the visitor center. FRED, by the way, stands for Free Rides Everywhere Downtown. But it's still a cool name.

EVENTS   The annual **Royal Nova Scotia International Tattoo** (© **902/420-1114;** www.nstattoo.ca) features military and marching bands totaling some 2,000-plus military and civilian performers. This rousing event takes place over the course of a week in early July and is held indoors at the Halifax Metro Center. Tickets are C$18 to C$50 (US$16–US$45/£9–£25).

The annual **Atlantic Jazz Festival** (© **902/492-2225** or 800/567-5277; www.jazzeast.com) has performances ranging from global and avant-garde to local and traditional music each July. Venues include area nightclubs and outdoor stages, and prices vary considerably; consult the website for the latest details and specifics of performance and price.

In early August, expect to see a profusion of street performers ranging from fire-eaters to comic jugglers. They descend on Halifax each summer for the 10-day **Halifax International Busker Festival** (© **902/429-3910** or 866/773-0655; www. buskers.ca). Performances take place along the waterfront walkway all day long and are often quite remarkable. The festival is free, though donations are requested.

The **Atlantic Film Festival** (© **902/422-3456;** www.atlanticfilm.com) offers screenings of more than 150 films in mid-September. The focus is largely on Canadian filmmaking, with an emphasis on independent productions and shorts. Panel discussions with industry players are also part of the festival. Some films are free, while others cost about C$5 to C$15 (US$4.50–US$14/£2.50–£7.50) each.

EXPLORING HALIFAX

Halifax is fairly compact and easily reconnoitered on foot or by mass transportation. The major landmark is the **Citadel**—the stone fortress that looms over downtown from its grassy perch. From the ramparts, you can look into the windows of the 10th floor of downtown skyscrapers. The Citadel is only 9 blocks from the waterfront—albeit 9 sometimes steep blocks—and you can easily see both the downtown and the waterfront areas in 1 day.

A lively neighborhood worth seeking out runs along **Spring Garden Road** between the Public Gardens and the library (at Grafton St.). You'll find intriguing boutiques, bars, and restaurants along these 6 blocks, set amid a mildly Bohemian street scene. If you have strong legs and a stout constitution, you can start on the waterfront, stroll up and over the Citadel to descend to the Public Gardens, and then return via Spring Garden to downtown, perhaps enjoying a meal or two along the way.

THE WATERFRONT

Halifax's rehabilitated waterfront is at its most inviting and vibrant between Sackville Landing (at the foot of Sackville St.) and the Sheraton Casino, near Purdy Wharf. (You could keep walking, but north of here the waterfront lapses into an agglomeration of charmless modern towers with sidewalk-level vents that assail passersby with unusual odors.) On sunny summer afternoons, the waterfront is bustling with tourists enjoying the harbor, business folks playing hooky while sneaking an ice-cream cone, and baggy-panted skateboarders striving to stay out of trouble. Plan on about 2 to 3 hours to tour and gawk from end to end.

The city's most extensive parking (fee charged) is available near Sackville Landing, and that's a good place to start a walking tour. Make your first stop the waterfront's crown jewel, the **Maritime Museum of the Atlantic** (see below).

In addition to the other attractions listed below, the waterfront walkway is studded with small diversions, intriguing shops, takeout food emporia, and minor monuments. Think of it as an alfresco scavenger hunt.

Among the treasures, look for **Summit Place,** commemorating the historic gathering of world leaders in 1995, when Halifax hosted the G-7 Economic Summit. There's North America's oldest operating **naval clock,** which was built in 1767 and chimed at the Halifax Naval Dockyard from 1772 to 1993. You can visit the **ferry terminal,** which is hectic during rush hour with commuters coming and going to Dartmouth across the harbor. (It's also a cheap way to enjoy a sweeping city and harbor view.) The passenger-only ferry runs at least every half-hour, and the fare is C$2 (US$1.80/£1) per adult each way, cheaper for seniors and children age 5 to 15.

The waterfront's shopping core is located in and around the 3-block **Historic Properties,** near the Sheraton. These stout buildings of wood and stone are Canada's oldest surviving warehouses and were once the center of the city's booming shipping industry. Today, the historic architecture is stern enough to provide ballast for the somewhat precious boutiques and restaurants they now house. Especially appealing is the granite-and-ironstone **Privateers' Warehouse,** which dates from 1813.

If you're feeling that a pub crawl might be in order, the Historic Properties area is also a good place to wander around after working hours in the early evening. There's a contagious energy that spills out of the handful of public houses, and you'll find a bustling camaraderie and live music.

Maritime Museum of the Atlantic 🎐🎐 *Kids*   All visitors to Nova Scotia owe themselves a stop at this standout museum on a prime waterfront location. The exhibits are involving and well executed, and you'll be astounded at how fast 2 hours can fly by. Visitors are greeted by a 3m (10-ft.) lighthouse lens from 1906, and then proceed through a parade of shipbuilding and seagoing eras. Visit the deckhouse of a coastal steamer (ca. 1940), or learn the colorful history of Samuel Cunard, a Nova Scotia native (born 1787) who founded the Cunard Steam Ship Co. to carry the royal mail and along the way established an ocean dynasty. Another highlight is the exhibit on the tragic Halifax explosion of 1917, when two warships collided in Halifax harbor not far from the museum, detonating tons of TNT. More than 1,700 people died, and windows were shattered 100km (62 miles) away. But perhaps the most poignant exhibit is the lone deck chair from the *Titanic*—150 victims of the *Titanic* disaster are buried in Halifax, where rescue efforts were centered. Also memorable are the "Age of Steam" exhibit, Queen Victoria's barge, and the interesting new "Shipwreck Treasures of Nova Scotia" section with its stories and artifacts from more than a dozen local shipwrecks.

1675 Lower Water St. 🕐 **902/424-7490.** www.maritime.museum.gov.ns.ca. May–Oct admission C$8.50 (US$7.65/ £4.25) adults, C$7.50 (US$6.75/£3.75) seniors, C$4.50 (US$4.05/£2.25) children 6–17, C$22 (US$20/£11) family; Nov–Apr admission lower. May–Oct daily 9:30am–5:30pm (to 8pm Tues); Nov–Apr closed Mon and shorter hours Sun.

ON THE WATER

A number of boat tours depart from the Halifax waterfront. You can browse the offerings on **Cable Wharf,** near the foot of George Street, where many tour boats are based. On-the-water adventures range from 1-hour harbor tours (about C$12/US$11/£6) to 5-hour deep-sea fishing trips (about C$40/US$36/£20).

Murphy's on the Water (© 902/420-1015) runs the most extensive tour operation, with three boats and a choice of tours, ranging from a cocktail sailing cruise to whale-watching to tours of historic McNab's Island, located near the mouth of the harbor (see below).

Peggy's Cove Express (© 902/422-4200) operates 4-hour scenic boat and bus tours from Cable Wharf to the popular fishing village of Peggy's Cove; a walking tour of the town is included as part of the adventure. Cost is about C$70 (US$63/£35) per adult.

Finally, the **Harbour Hopper** (© 902/490-8687) amphibious craft crosses both land and sea during a tour, costing C$25 (US$23/£13) adults, C$24 (US$22/£12) seniors, C$15 (US$14/£7.50) children ages 6 to 15, C$9 (US$8.10/£4.50) children under 5. Families of four can travel for C$71 (US$64/£36).

CSS *Acadia*   This unusually handsome 1913 vessel is part of the Maritime Museum ("our largest artifact"), but it can be viewed independently for a small fee. The *Acadia* was used by the Canadian government to chart the ocean floor for 56 years, until its retirement in 1969. Much of the ship is open for self-guided tours, including the captain's quarters, upper decks, wheelhouse, and oak-paneled chart room. If you want to see more of the ship, ask about the guided half-hour tours (four times daily), which offer access to the engine room and more. You probably wouldn't need more than a half-hour here.

1675 Lower Water St. (on the water, in front of the Maritime Museum). © **902/424-7490.** Free admission with Maritime Museum ticket, which costs C$8.50 (US$7.65/£4.25) adults, C$7.50 (US$6.75/£3.75) seniors, C$4.50 (US$4.05/£2.25) children 6–17, C$22 (US$20/£11) family. Lower-price admission Nov–Apr. Mon–Sat 9:30am–5:30pm; Sun 1–5:30pm.

HMCS *Sackville*   This blue-and-white corvette (a speedy warship smaller than a destroyer) is tied up along a wood-planked wharf behind a small visitor center. There's a short multimedia presentation to provide some background. The ship is outfitted as it was in 1944, and it is now maintained as a memorial to the Canadians who served in World War II. Plan to spend about a half-hour here.

Sackville Landing (summer), HMC dockyard (winter). © **902/429-2132.** Admission C$3 (US$2.70/£1.50) adults, C$2 (US$1.80/£1) seniors and students. June–Oct daily 10am–5pm; off-season hours vary.

Pier 21 *Kids*   Between 1928 and 1971 more than one million immigrants arrived in Canada by disembarking at Pier 21, Canada's version of New York's Ellis Island. In 1999, the pier was restored and reopened, filled with engaging interpretive exhibits that vividly evoke the confusion and anxiety of the immigration experience. The pier is divided roughly into three sections: the boarding of the ship amid the cacophony of many languages, the crossing of the Atlantic (a 26-min. multimedia show recaptures the voyage in a shiplike theater), and the dispersal of the recent arrivals throughout Canada via passenger train. For those seeking more in-depth information (one in five Canadians today can trace a link back to Pier 21), there's a reference library and computer resources. Plan to spend at least an hour here.

1055 Marginal Rd. (on the waterfront behind the Westin Hotel). © **902/425-7770.** www.pier21.ca. C$8.50 (US$7.65/£4.25) adults, C$7.50 (US$6.75/£3.75) seniors, C$5 (US$4.50/£2.50) children 6–16, C$21 (US$19/£11) family. May–Nov daily 9:30am–5:30pm; Dec–March Tues–Sat 10am–5pm; Apr Mon–Sat 10am–5pm.

THE CITADEL & DOWNTOWN

Downtown Halifax cascades 9 blocks down a slope between the imposing stone Citadel and the waterfront. There's no fast-and-ready tour route; don't hesitate to follow your own desultory course, alternately ducking down quiet streets and striding along busy arteries. A good spot to regain your bearings periodically is the **Grand Parade,** where military recruits once practiced their drills. It's a lovely urban landscape—a broad terrace carved into the hill, presided over on either end by St. Paul's (see below) and Halifax's **City Hall.** The sandstone city hall was built between 1887 and 1890 and is exuberantly abristle with the usual Victorian architectural trifles, like a prominent clock tower, dormers, pediments, arched windows, pilasters, and Corinthian columns. Alas, there's not much to see inside. If the weather is nice, the Grand Parade is also a prime spot to bring an alfresco lunch and enjoy some people-watching.

Art Gallery of Nova Scotia   Located in a pair of sandstone buildings between the waterfront and the Grand Parade, the Art Gallery is arguably the premier gallery in the Maritimes, with a focus on local and regional art. You'll also find a selection of other works by Canadian, British, and European artists, with a well-chosen selection of folk and Inuit art. In 1998, the gallery expanded to include the Provincial Building next door, where the entire house (it's tiny) of Nova Scotian folk artist Maud Lewis has been reassembled and is on display. The museum can be comfortably perused in 60 to 90 minutes; consider a lunch break in the attractive Cheapside Café (later in this chapter).

1723 Hollis St. (at Cheapside). ℰ **902/424-5280.** Admission C\$12 (US\$11/£6) adults, C\$10 (US\$9/£5) seniors, C\$5 (US\$4.50/£2.50) students, C\$3 (US\$2.70/£1.50) children age 6–17, C\$25 (US\$23/£13) families. Daily 10am–5pm (Thurs to 9pm).

Halifax Citadel National Historic Site *★★*   Even if the stalwart stone fort weren't here, it would be worth the uphill trek for the astounding views alone. The panoramic sweep across downtown and the harbor finishes up with vistas out toward the broad Atlantic beyond. At any rate, an ascent makes it obvious why this spot was chosen for the harbor's most formidable defenses: There's simply no sneaking up on the place.

Four forts have occupied the summit since Col. Edward Cornwallis was posted to the colony in 1749. The Citadel has been restored to look much as it did in 1856, when the fourth fort was built out of concern over bellicose Americans. The fort has never been attacked.

The site is impressive, to say the least: Sturdy granite walls topped by grassy embankments form a rough star; in the sprawling gravel and cobblestone courtyard you'll find convincingly costumed interpreters in kilts and bearskin hats marching in unison, playing bagpipes, and firing the noon cannon. The former barracks and other chambers are home to exhibits about life at the fort. If you still have questions, stop a soldier, bagpiper, or washerwoman and ask.

The Citadel is the perfect place to launch an exploration of Halifax: It provides a good geographic context for the city and anchors it historically as well. This National Historic Site is the most heavily visited in Canada, and it's not hard to see why. You won't need more than 45 minutes or an hour here, though.

Citadel Hill. ℰ **902/426-5080.** Admission June to mid-Sept C\$11 (US\$9.90/£5.50) adults, C\$9.15 (US\$8.25/£4.60) seniors, C\$5.45 (US\$4.90/£2.75) children 6–16, C\$27 (US\$24/£14) families; May and mid-Sept to Dec C\$7.15 (US\$6.45/£3.60) adults, C\$5.90 (US\$5.30/£2.95) seniors, C\$3.45 (US\$3.10/£1.75) children 6–16, C\$18 (US\$16/£9) families; free admission Jan–Apr. July–Aug daily 9am–6pm; May–June and Sept–Oct daily 9am–5pm. Visitor center closed, grounds open Nov–Apr; no guides in fall or winter.

Nova Scotia Centre for Craft and Design   The provincial government runs this center with the idea of encouraging and developing crafts- and design-based industries across the province. Of interest to travelers is the first-floor gallery, where visitors can view oft-changing exhibits of the best of what Nova Scotia craftspeople have produced. Depending on your interest, plan to spend between a half-hour to an hour here.

1683 Barrington St. *(C)* 902/492-2522. www.craft-design.ns.ca. Free admission. Mon–Wed 11am–5pm; Thurs 11am–8pm; Fri 11am–4pm; Sat 10am–5pm; Sun noon–4pm.

Nova Scotia Museum of Natural History   Situated on the far side of the Citadel from downtown, this modern, midsize museum offers a good introduction to the flora and fauna of Nova Scotia. Galleries include geology, botany, mammals, and birds, plus exhibits of archaeology and Mi'kmaq culture. Especially noteworthy is the extensive collection of lifelike ceramic fungus and the colony of honeybees that freely come and go from their indoor acrylic hive through a tube connected to the outdoors. Allow about 1 hour.

1747 Summer St. *(C)* 902/424-7353. Admission June to mid-Oct C$5.50 (US$4.95/£2.75) adults, C$5 (US$4.50/£2.50) seniors, C$3.50 (US$3.15/£1.75) children 6–17, C$11–C$16 (US$9.90–US$14/£5.50–£8) families; free admission Wed nights. Admission mid-Oct to May C$3.50 (US$3.15/£1.75) adults, C$3 (US$2.70/£1.50) seniors, C$2.50 (US$2.25/£1.25) children 6–17, C$7.50–C$10 (US$6.75–US$9/£3.75–£5) families. June to mid-Oct Mon–Sat 9:30am–5:30pm (Wed until 8pm), Sun 1–5:30pm; mid-Oct to May Tues–Sat 9:30am–5pm (Wed until 8pm), Sun 1–5pm.

Province House   Canada's oldest seat of government, Province House has been home to the Nova Scotian legislature since 1819. This exceptional Georgian building is a superb example of the rigorously symmetrical Palladian style. And like a jewel box, its dour stone exterior hides gems of ornamental detailing and artwork inside, especially the fine plasterwork, rare for a Canadian building of this era.

A well-written free booklet is available when you enter that provides helpful background about the building's history and architecture. (My favorite legend: It's said the headless falcons in several rooms were decapitated by an agitated, free-swinging legislator with a cane who mistook them for eagles during a period of feverish anti-American sentiment in the 1840s.) If the legislature is in session, you can obtain a visitor's pass and sit up in the gallery and watch the business of the province take place. History buffs should allow an hour for this visit.

1776 Hollis St. (near Prince St.). *(C)* 902/424-4661. Free admission. July–Aug Mon–Fri 9am–5pm, Sat–Sun and holidays 10am–4pm; Sept–June Mon–Fri 9am–4pm.

St. Paul's Anglican Church 👁   Forming one end of the Grand Parade, this classic white Georgian building was the first Anglican cathedral established outside of England and is Canada's oldest Protestant place of worship. Part of the 1750 church was fabricated in Boston and erected in Halifax with the help of a royal endowment from King George II. A piece of flying debris from the explosion of 1917 ("Maritime Museum of the Atlantic," p. 98) is lodged in the wall over the doors to the nave. Just a quick drop in is enough to get a sense of the place, especially the fine stained-glass windows; take one of the summer-only guided tours if you want to see more.

1749 Argyle St. (on the Grand Parade near Barrington St.). *(C)* 902/429-2240. Mon–Fri 9am–4:30pm; Sun services 8, 9:15, and 11am. Free guided tours June–Aug Mon–Sat.

GARDENS & OPEN SPACE

Fairview Lawn Cemetery 👁   When the *Titanic* went down April 15, 1912, nearly 2,000 people died. Ship captains from Halifax were recruited to help retrieve the corpses (you can learn about this grim mission at the Maritime Museum, described on p. 98). Some 121 victims, mostly ship crewmembers, were buried at this quiet cemetery located a short drive north of downtown Halifax. Some of the simple graves have names, others just numbers. Signs highlight some of the stories that survived the tragedy. A brochure with driving directions to this and two other *Titanic* cemeteries may be found at the Maritime Museum and visitor information centers. It's definitely worth an hour or more for *Titanic* fans; others might just spend a few minutes here. Without a car, skip it.

Chisholm Ave., off Connaught Ave. (about 4km/2½ miles northwest of the Citadel). © 902/490-4883. Daylight hours year-round.

McNab's Island   This island wilderness is located within city limits near the mouth of the harbor, and it's a world apart from downtown Halifax. Once part of the city's military defenses and later the site of a popular amusement park, McNab's hasn't had any permanent residents since 1985. You'll find miles of wooded roads and trails to explore, some 200 species of birds, and great views of the city skyline and Point Pleasant. Fort McNab at the island's south tip dates from 1888, and it was manned during both world wars—all ships visiting the harbor were required to signal the fort, and those that failed to comply were warned with a shot across the bow. Bring a picnic (and a ferry schedule) and plan to spend 2 hours or so.

In Halifax Harbor. © 902/465-4563 (ferry service). Admission to island free; ferry from Eastern Passage C$10 (US$9/£5) round-trip adult, C$8 (US$7.20/£4) round-trip senior and children 5–17.

Old Burying Ground   Fully restored in 1991, this was the first burial ground in Halifax, and between 1749 and 1844 some 12,000 people were interred here. (Only one in 10 graves is marked with a headstone, however.) You'll find wonderful examples of 18th- and 19th-century gravestone art—especially winged heads and winged skulls. (No rubbings allowed.) Also exceptional is the Welsford-Parker Monument from 1855, which honors Nova Scotians who fought in the Crimean War. This ornate statue near the grounds' entrance features a lion with an unruly Medusa-like mane. Go at dusk; the grounds are imbued with a quiet grace a couple of hours before sunset, when the light slants through the trees and the traffic seems far away. Cemetery buffs could spend an hour or more; others can easily drop by for 10 minutes en route to downtown attractions or eateries.

Corner of Spring Garden and Barrington. © 902/429-2240. Free admission. June–Sept 9am–5pm; guides until late Aug. Closed rest of year.

Point Pleasant Park ✦   Point Pleasant is one of Canada's finer urban parks, and there's no better place for a walk along the water on a balmy day. This 74-hectare (183-acre) park occupies a wooded peninsular point, and it served for years as one of the linchpins in the city's military defense. You'll find the ruins of early forts and a nicely preserved Martello tower. Halifax has a 999-year lease from Great Britain for the park, for which it pays 1 shilling—about US10¢—per year. You'll also find a lovely gravel carriage road around the point, a small swimming beach, miles of walking trails, and groves of graceful fir trees. The park is located about 2km (1¼ miles) south of the Public Gardens. No bikes are allowed on weekends or holidays.

Point Pleasant Dr. (south end of Halifax). Free admission. Daylight hours. Head south on S. Park St. near Public Gardens and continue on Young.

Public Gardens *Kids* The Public Gardens took seed in 1753, when it was founded as a private garden. It was acquired by the Nova Scotia Horticultural Society in 1836, and it assumed its present look in 1875, during the peak of the Victorian era. As such, the garden is one of the nation's Victorian masterpieces, more rare and evocative than any mansard-roofed mansion. You'll find wonderful examples of many 19th-century trends in outdoor landscaping, from the "natural" winding walks and ornate fountains to the duck ponds and fussy Victorian bandstand. (Stop by at 2pm on Sun in summer for a free concert.) There are lots of leafy trees, lush lawns, cranky ducks who have long since lost their fear of humans, and tiny ponds, and you'll usually find dowagers and kids feeding pigeons and smartly uniformed guards slowly walking the grounds. The overseers have also been commendably stingy with memorial statues and plaques.

Spring Garden Rd. and S. Park St. Free admission. Spring to late fall 8am–dusk.

BOAT TOURS

Murphy's on the Water (*©* 902/420-1015) runs daily boats from Cable Wharf in downtown Halifax daily in summer for C$15 (US$14/£7.50) and up round-trip; a range of harbor, whale-watching, nature, and sightseeing tours are offered by Captain Gerard Murphy and his family. Or, to see McNab's Island, drive instead to Eastern Passage (south of Dartmouth), park free at Government Wharf, and take the McNab's Island Ferry (*©* 902/465-4563). For the brief trip, captain Mike Tilley (known locally as "Red Beard") charges C$10 (US$9/£5) adults, C$8 (US$7.20/£4) children ages 4 to 15, free for children under 4, and there's no extra charge for bikes or dogs. Captain Tilley will also charter you around the harbor for C$49 (US$44/£25) per hour.

SHOPPING

Halifax has a pleasing mix of shops, from mainstream retailers to offbeat boutiques. There's no central retail district to speak of; shops are scattered throughout downtown. Two indoor malls are located near the Grand Parade—**Scotia Square Mall** and **Barrington Place Shops,** flanking Barrington Street near the intersection of Duke Street. Another downtown mall, the 85-shop **Park Lane Shopping Centre,** is on Spring Garden Road about 1 block from the Public Gardens.

For souvenir shopping, head to the Historic Properties buildings on the waterfront; for idle browsing, try the shops on and around Spring Garden Road between Brunswick and South Park streets.

Almanac Used Furniture and Antiques A classic, old-fashioned antiques shop crammed to the eaves with everything from bureaus to barber chairs, the Almanac is a short drive from downtown. 2810 Windsor St. *©* 902/455-1141.

Art Gallery of Nova Scotia Shop The museum's gift shops feature limited but choice selections of local crafts, ranging from creative postcards to birdhouses and table-top sculptures. There's also work by Mi'kmaq artisans. 1723 Hollis St. *©* 902/424-4203.

Drala Books & Gifts This serene shop specializes in Asian imports, including raku-style pottery, incense, calligraphy materials, paper screens, chopsticks, teas, teapots, and books on design and philosophy. Classes in the store teach meditation, Japanese tea ceremony, and the like. 1567 Grafton St. *©* 902/422-2504 or 877/422-2504.

Geddes Furniture and Antiques Elegant and formal mahogany reproduction Chippendale and Queen Anne pieces, including dining room chairs and highboys, are the specialty at this shop, which is filled with lovely pieces priced for less than you might expect. Delivery trucks travel to the northeastern United States regularly. 2739 Agricola St. ℂ **902/454-7171** or 866/443-3337.

Janet Doble Pottery Studio   Doble's bright and festive pottery is inspired by European majolica; anything purchased here is certain to brighten a drab kitchen. Note that hours are quirky, as befits a working artist. 2641 Fuller Terrace. ℂ **902/455-6960.**

Thornbloom, The Inspired Home   This tidy shop in a small indoor mall on Spring Garden features housewares, knives by Henckels, good bed linens, and intriguing tile "memory blocks" by Vancouver-based Sid Dickens. 5640 Spring Garden Rd. ℂ **902/425-8005.**

Urban Cottage   This consignment store in the middle of downtown has an eclectic and sizable selection of furniture, housewares, and collectibles, nicely displayed and generally reasonably priced. 1819 Granville St. ℂ **902/423-3010.**

WHERE TO STAY
EXPENSIVE
Cambridge Suites Hotel Halifax ⋇ *Kids*   The attractive, modern Cambridge Suites is nicely located near the foot of the Citadel and is well positioned for exploring Halifax. It's perfect for families—40 of the units are two-room suites featuring kitchenettes with microwaves, two phones, coffeemakers, and hair dryers. Expect above-average service and comfortable, inoffensive decor; everything in the place was freshened up in 2001. Dofsky's Grill on the first floor is open for all three meals, which are palatable if not exciting. Look for pasta, blackened haddock, burgers, and jerk chicken.

1583 Brunswick St., Halifax, NS B3J 3P5. ℂ **888/417-8483** or 902/420-0555. Fax 902/420-9379. www.cambridge suiteshalifax.com. 200 units. C$119–C$299 (US$107–US$269/£60–£150) suite. Children under 18 stay free in parent's room. AE, DC, MC, V. Valet or self-parking C$14 (US$13/£7). **Amenities:** Restaurant; health club; Jacuzzi; sauna; concierge; room service; babysitting; coin-op laundry; dry cleaning. *In room:* A/C, TV, dataport, kitchenette (some units), minibar, fridge (some units), coffeemaker, hair dryer, iron.

Delta Barrington ⋇   Convenience and location form the cornerstones of the Delta Barrington, located just 1 block from the waterfront and 1 block from the Grand Parade and connected to the Metro Centre and much of the rest of downtown by a covered walkway. It's a large modern hotel but has been designed and furnished with an eye more to comfort than to flash. The guest rooms are decorated with a contemporary country decor, with pine headboards and country-style reproduction furniture. The king rooms are spacious, furnished with sofas and easy chairs. Some rooms face the pedestrian plaza and have been soundproofed to block the noise from the evening rabble, but these windows don't open (most other rooms have opening windows). The quietest rooms face the courtyard but lack a view. The hotel restaurant, the Stone Street Café, serves an attractive upscale menu of tea-smoked chicken breast, yogurt-crusted rack of lamb, seafood pappardelle, pistachio-crusted Arctic char, sesame salmon, and the like. Also ask about the hotel's affordable four-course "Seafood Festival" lobster dinner specials.

1875 Barrington St., Halifax, NS B3J 3L6. ℂ **877/814-7706** or 902/429-7410. Fax 902/420-6524. www.deltabarrington. com. 200 units. C$134–C$294 (US$121–US$265/£67–£147) double. AE, DC, DISC, MC, V. Valet parking C$22 (US$20/£11), self-parking C$19 (US$17/£10). Small pets allowed. **Amenities:** Restaurant; indoor pool; Jacuzzi; sauna; children's programs; concierge; room service; babysitting; laundry service; dry cleaning. *In room:* A/C, TV, dataport, minibar, coffeemaker, hair dryer, iron.

Delta Halifax The Delta Halifax (formerly the Hotel Halifax, which was formerly the Chateau Halifax) is a slick and modern downtown hotel that offers premium service. It's located just a block off the waterfront, which it's connected to via skyway, but navigating the skyway involves an annoying labyrinth of parking garages and charmless concrete structures. The lobby is street-side and guests—largely business travelers during the week—take elevators up above a six-floor parking garage to reach their rooms. Ask for a room in the "resort wing" near the pool, which feels a bit farther away from the chatter of downtown and the press of business. A number of rooms have balconies and many have harbor views; ask when you book. Rooms are in two classes—either 300 or 500 square feet—and all are furnished simply and unexceptionally with standard-issue hotel furniture. The Crown Bistrot restaurant (run by the same chef as the Delta Barrington's cafe) offers good Continental, Asian, and Maritime-inflected cuisine, while Sam Slick's Lounge next door features Friday-night piano and a surprisingly varied bar menu.

1990 Barrington St., Halifax, NS B3J 1P2. © **877/814-7706** or 902/425-6700. Fax 902/425-6214. www.deltahalifax. com. 296 units. C$134–C$284 (US$121–US$265/£67–£142) double. AE, MC, V. Valet parking C$22 (US$20/£11), self-parking C$19 (US$17/£10). **Amenities:** Restaurant; bar; indoor pool; health club; Jacuzzi; sauna; concierge; car-rental desk; shopping arcade; limited room service; babysitting; laundry service; dry cleaning. *In room:* A/C, TV, dataport, minibar, coffeemaker, hair dryer, iron.

The Halliburton The Halliburton is a well-appointed, well-run, and elegant country inn located in the heart of downtown. Named after former resident Sir Brenton Halliburton (Nova Scotia's first chief justice), the inn is spread among three town house-style buildings, which are connected via gardens and sun decks in the rear but not internally. The main building was constructed in 1809 and was converted to an inn in 1995, when it was modernized without any loss of its native charm. All guest rooms are subtly furnished with fine antiques, but few are so rare that you'd fret about damaging them. The rooms are rich and masculine in tone and light on frilly stuff. Among the best: room no. 113, relatively small but with a lovely working fireplace and unique skylighted bathroom. Room nos. 102 and 109 are both suites with wet bars and fireplaces; there's also a studio apartment. Halliburton is popular with business travelers, yet it's also a romantic spot for couples to hide out in. The intimate first-floor dining room **Stories** serves nightly; it's dusky and wonderful, with a menu that's small yet inventive. The seafood has always been reliable, but there's also a new emphasis on other tastes such as game and duck.

5184 Morris St., Halifax, NS B3J 1B3. © **888/512-3344** or 902/420-0658. Fax 902/423-2324. www.halliburton. ns.ca. 29 units. C$145–C$350 (US$131–US$315/£73–£175) double; off-season rates cheaper. All rates include continental breakfast and parking (limited). AE, MC, V. **Amenities:** Restaurant; room service; babysitting; dry cleaning. *In room:* A/C, TV, coffeemaker, hair dryer.

The Lord Nelson Hotel & Suites The Lord Nelson was built in 1928 and was for years the city's preeminent hostelry. It gradually sank in esteem and eventually ended up as a flophouse. In 1998, it was purchased and received a long-overdue top-to-bottom renovation. It certainly has location going for it: It's right across from the lovely Public Gardens and abuts lively Spring Garden Road. Rooms are furnished with Georgian reproductions. The business-class Flagship Rooms feature desks, ergonomic office chairs, robes, free local calls, and morning newspapers. The hotel charges a premium for rooms that face the street or the gardens, but it's worth it; others face into a rather bleak courtyard filled with service equipment. Off the handsome coffered lobby you'll find the Victory Arms, a cozy and convincing English-style pub. There's

British pub fare like bangers and mash and fish and chips, but also more inventive cuisine such as Singapore noodles, nan pizzas, and Cajun-spiced cod sandwiches.

1515 South Park St., Halifax, NS B3J 2L2. (© **800/565-2020** or 902/423-6331. Fax 902/491-6148. www.lordnelson hotel.com. 260 units. C$139–C$259 (US$125–US$233/£70–£130) double. Valet parking C$20 (US$18/£10), self-parking C$15 (US$14/£7.50). AE, DC, DISC, MC, V. Pets allowed with C$100 (US$90/£50) deposit. **Amenities:** Restaurant; bar; health club; sauna; concierge; limited room service; babysitting; laundry; dry cleaning. *In room:* A/C, TV, coffeemaker, hair dryer, iron.

The Prince George Hotel ⟨⟩

This contemporary and large downtown hotel features understated styling, polished wainscoting, carpeting, and the discreet use of marble; everything was renovated in 2000, though it stills feels a bit sterile and stuffy. In any case, expect modern and comfortably appointed rooms, most with balconies and all with a selection of complimentary tea and coffee, coffeemakers, and hair dryers. This hotel is nicely situated near the Citadel and restaurants and is linked to much of the rest of downtown via underground passageways; parking is beneath the hotel. The hotel's Gio restaurant on the first floor features contemporary bistro styling, with a zippy menu to match: Recent dinner options have included Kobe burgers, crab club sandwiches, Thai noodles, grilled tuna, steak frites, and haddock in almond-butter sauce. An attractive Sunday brunch at the hotel's Terrace restaurant is C$30 (US$27/£15) per person.

1725 Market St., Halifax, NS B3J 3N9. (© **800/565-1567** or 902/425-1986. Fax 902/429-6048. www.princegeorge hotel.com. 203 units. C$169–C$299 (US$152–US$269/£85–£150) double. AE, DC, DISC, MC, V. Valet parking C$20 (US$18/£10), self-parking C$15 (US$14/£7.50). **Amenities:** Restaurant; indoor pool; Jacuzzi; sauna; concierge; business center; limited room service; massage; babysitting; laundry; dry cleaning. *In room:* A/C, TV, dataport, minibar, coffeemaker, hair dryer, iron.

MODERATE

Another good choice for families, if you have a car and don't need to stay downtown, is the former Maranova Suites property across the bridge in Dartmouth, recently made over as the **Super 8 Dartmouth** (© **902/463-9520** or 888/561-7666). Yes, I know, but this suite hotel is right across the harbor from Halifax and a 2-minute walk to frequent ferry service to downtown—definitely one of the better options in town for travelers with kids on a ginger-ale budget instead of a champagne one. Housed in a modern concrete building, it features rooms that are large and tidy. Many of the 84 units have separate sitting areas, kitchenettes, balconies, and flat-screen televisions. Don't expect anything fancy; these rooms are basic, simple, and clean, but some have wonderful views of the harbor—ask when you book. Rates range from as low as C$89 (US$80/£45) per night up to C$350 (US$315/£175). It's located at 65 King St., reached by crossing the Angus MacDonald bridge from Halifax's waterfront and quickly exiting onto Windmill Road (east), which becomes Alderney; go left at Queen Street, then left again on King.

Waverley Inn ⟨⟩

The Waverley is adorned in high Victorian style, as befits its 1866 provenance. Flamboyant playwright Oscar Wilde was a guest in 1882, and one suspects he had a hand in the decorating scheme. There's walnut trim, red upholstered furniture, and portraits of sourpuss Victorians at every turn. The headboards in the guest rooms are especially elaborate—some look like props from Gothic horror movies. Room no. 130 has a unique Chinese wedding bed and a Jacuzzi (about 10 rooms have private Jacuzzis).

1266 Barrington St., Halifax, NS B3J 1Y5. (© **800/565-9346** or 902/423-9346. Fax 902/425-0167. www.waverley inn.com. 34 units. mid-May to Dec C$125–C$279 (US$113–US$251/£63–£140) double; Nov to mid-May C$99–C$279 (US$89–US$251/£50–£140). Rates include continental breakfast, snacks, afternoon tea, and parking. DC, MC, V. *In room:* A/C, TV, hair dryer (some units), Jacuzzi (some units), no phone (some units).

INEXPENSIVE

The 75-bed **Halifax Heritage House Hostel** (© 902/422-3863) is located at 1253 Barrington St., within walking distance of downtown attractions. You'll usually share rooms with other travelers (several private and family rooms are available); there are lockers in each room, shared bathrooms, and a shared, fully equipped kitchen. Rates are C$20 (US$18/£10) and up per person in dormitories, C$50 (C$45/£25) for a double bed in a private room.

A short way from downtown but convenient to bus lines are university dorm rooms open to travelers during the summer, when school isn't in session (that is, mid-May through mid-Aug). **Dalhousie University** (© 902/494-8840 or 888/271-9222) rents out a range of one-, two-, and three-bedroom units—furnished with plain single beds each—to the public. Many rooms have private bathrooms and kitchenettes (you rent the dishes for a small fee). During past summers, single rooms have begun at about C$40 (US$36/£20), double rooms around C$60 (US$54/£30), and apartments cost more than that, but check with the university about current pricing and options. Note that a 2-night minimum stay is required for some of these units.

WHERE TO DINE

Coffee emporia have cropped up throughout Halifax in the last couple of years, as they have in urban areas everywhere. Many also stock sandwiches, pastries, and light snacks in addition to the java. A few of the best downtown options are **Caffé Ristretto** (© 902/425-3087) at 1475 Lower Water St. (Bishop Landing) with its nice harbor views; **Timothy's World Coffee,** which has locations at Barrington and Upper Water streets; **Cabin Coffee** (© 902/422-8130) at 1554 Hollis St. with its Bohemian feel and good espresso and cappuccino; and the dependable Canadian chain **Second Cup,** with outlets in Scotia Square and on Spring Garden Road.

For chain fast-food meals (if you must), again stick to Spring Garden Road. For a quick snack on the same street, the plastic patio furniture outside belies the good snacks, pastries, coffees, teas, and light meals inside **Annie's Place** (© 902/420-0098) at 1513 Birmingham St. (corner of Spring Garden); outstanding bargain lunch specials include changing offerings such as a slab of grilled meatloaf on focaccia. For more upscale fare, explore downtown or some of the tiny side streets that cross Spring Garden.

The **Brewery** ✺✺ complex, on the uphill side of Lower Water Street just above the docks, is perhaps the city's most interesting one-stop shopping and dining experience. Originally the site of the Alexander Keith brewery, North America's oldest, the space was eventually redesigned and renovated to enclose some courtyards from the weather, link up the various structures of the brewery, and create a kind of interior market of shops and restaurants. Today the complex houses the city's finest Italian restaurant (see daMaurizio, below), as well as a range of other drinking, dining, and shopping options. While navigating its labyrinthine courtyards to find a particular establishment can be a bit confusing, it's also great fun to see what pops up around the next corner.

The **Saturday morning farmer's market** ✺✺ held within the Brewery's walls is a weekly highlight for local Haligonians, rain or shine. It's Canada's oldest—and possibly its most interesting—such market. The market runs between 7am and 1pm each Saturday, but come early in the day for the widest selection of donuts, fruits, vegetables, coffee, baked goods, smoked meats, crafts, Greek pastries, wine and chocolate samples, and dynamite crepes—among many other items.

There's also a more **permanent farmer's market** that will apparently become established year-round at Pier 20 on the waterfront once funds are secured. Check with the market's website, www.halifaxfarmersmarket.com, for the latest details and opening hours.

EXPENSIVE

Bish World Cuisine ★★★ *(Finds)* FUSION   Maurizio strikes again! The culinary wizard behind the deservedly popular daMaurizio (see below) in The Brewery market has daringly opened a second high-tone eatery—practically across the street from his first—and, against the odds in a tough economic moment, it's already supplanting his original fine-dining establishment as the "in" place. Tucked into a harborside location at the back of the upscale Bishop's Landing development (hence the name—I think), this place combines Asian and Continental influences to fine effect, much like a hot young chef in Manhattan might do. Exhibit A: appetizers and first courses of mussels in garlic and wine, pulled-pork quesadillas, a tomato-chêvre tart, foie gras with blueberries and cassis, tempura scallops with ponzu sauce, a lobster-corn chowder, and the like. Exhibit B: main courses such as seared Angus medallions and cremini mushrooms, lamb served with mint or curry, Kobe beef burgers, roasted duck with wild cherries and port sauce, sesame-crusted tuna, or a peanutty chicken and shrimp pad thai. There's also local lobster, of course, here split and garlic-broiled. Finish your meal off with house-made ice creams or sorbets, crème caramel, a rhubarb-ginger crisp, an outstanding peanut brittle sundae, or perhaps a lemon tart. The water views, professional service, and fine bar and wine list only enhance the experience of having temporarily traded in New Scotland for New York. Dress smartly, expect Halifax's finest to be out in force on the weekends, and reserve early in anticipation of that fact.

1475 Lower Water St. (in Bishop's Landing, entrance at end of Bishop St.). © **902/425-7993.** Reservations highly recommended. Main courses C$20–C$27 (US$18–US$24/£10–£14). AE, DC, MC, V. Mon–Sat 5:30–10pm.

daMaurizio ★★★ ITALIAN   daMaurizio does everything right. Located in a cleverly adapted former brewery, the vast space has been divided into a complex of hives with columns and exposed brick that add to the atmosphere and heighten the anticipation of the meal. The decor shuns decorative doodads for clean lines and simple class. Much the same might be said of the menu. You could start with an appetizer such as squid quick-fried with olive oil, tomato, and chiles, pick through a romaine salad with grapefruit and candied walnuts, go for risotto or minestrone, or just order simple ravioli with sausage. The main courses tax even the most decisive of diners: On a given night, they might include pastas featuring lobster, leeks, white wine, cream, and fresh ginger; gnocchi with Bolognese sauce; pumpkin ravioli with citrus and roasted duck sauce; pasta with king crab and mascarpone, drizzled with curry sauce; a few variations on veal scaloppine; pan-seared scallops with chili and port sauce; or a whole lobster gratinéed with sweet peppers, onions, brandy, and cream. Desserts run beyond tiramisu and gelati to cake; panna cotta; a fruit, nut, and cheese plate; and tartufo, a molded almond gelato filled with chocolate and topped with crumbled amaretti, with crème anglaise and a chocolate ganache on the side. These simple dishes aren't meant to dazzle with outlandish creativity but rely instead on the best ingredients and the kitchen's close eye for perfect preparation.

1496 Lower Water St. (in The Brewery). © **902/423-0859.** Reservations highly recommended. Main courses C$28–C$33 (US$25–US$30/£14–£17); pasta dishes C$11–C$16 (US$10–US$14/£5.50–£8). AE, DC, MC, V. Mon–Sat 5–10pm.

MODERATE

O'Carroll's ⍟ SEAFOOD/CONTINENTAL   O'Carroll's is one of the best options for a fulfilling seafood meal in Halifax, though it's changed direction recently, becoming a lot fancier than the average fish house about town. The kitchen has taken a rather creative slant to the food, with global dinner offerings from Chef Colin Stone such as planked salmon, mixed seafood in a lemon-chive crème, raspberry-brie chicken, and duckling with star anise and cassis. Lunch is equally classy, with lamb burgers, lobster salad, crab cakes, finnan haddie, linguine with pesto and chicken, and peppered halibut. Options available in the pub section include more comfortable grub such as nachos and wings, but even here the menu still leans more heavily toward the Continental (cheese plates) than to fish and chips or steak-and-kidney pie; in fact, those two dishes don't even appear on the menu anymore. Sign o' the times. The restaurant remains a dusky, Gaelic-influenced spot laid out in white tablecloths, potted plants, and stained-glass lamps, though, and there's still live Celtic music in the pub, making that section a worthwhile stop.

1860 Upper Water St. ⓒ 902/423-4405. Reservations recommended. Main courses C$9–C$17 (US$8.10–US$15/£4.50–£8.50) at lunch, C$24–C$30 (US$22–US$27/£12–£15) at dinner, C$6–C$10 (US$5.40–US$9/£3–£5) in the pub. AE, MC, V. Restaurant daily 11am–2:30pm and 5–11pm; pub daily 11am–11pm; weekend hours may vary.

Ryan Duffy's ⍟ STEAKHOUSE   Located on the upper level of a small shopping mall on Spring Garden, Ryan Duffy's may at first strike diners as a knockoff of a middlebrow chain like T.G.I. Friday's. It's not. It's a couple of notches above. The house specialty is steak, for which the place is justly famous. The beef comes from corn-fed Hereford, Black Angus, and Shorthorn, and it is nicely tender. (When the waiter delivered me an oversize steak knife, he said, "You don't really need this, but it's all part of the show.") Steaks are grilled over a natural wood charcoal and can be prepared with garlic, cilantro butter, or other extras upon request. The more expensive cuts, such as the strip loin, are trimmed right at the table. If you move away from steak on the menu, expect less consistency—the shrimp cocktail is disappointing; the Caesar salad is wonderful. Americans who are disappointed that they can't order rare steak much anymore owing to liability concerns will like it here—you can even order it "blue-rare."

5640 Spring Garden Rd. ⓒ 902/421-1116. Reservations recommended. Main courses C$9–C$15 (US$8.10–US$14/£4.50–7.50) at lunch, C$19–C$38 (US$17–US$34/£9.50–£19) at dinner. AE, DC, MC, V. Mon–Fri 11:30am–2pm and 5–10pm; Sat–Sun 5–10pm.

Sweet Basil Bistro ⍟⍟ *Finds* FUSION   Of the waterfront's many highbrow and lowbrow spots, Sweet Basil might be my very favorite. It has the casual feel of a local trattoria, but the elegant menu transcends the limited regional offerings you might expect. The chef somehow manages to meld Thai influences, pasta, cream sauces, and local seafood cooked in fusion style without going overboard, resulting in truly interesting creations: a bouillabaisse of lobster, scallops, mussels, shrimp, and haddock, for example; pork tenderloin with a crab-apple butter; pistachio-crusted chicken breast with chèvre, pears, and basil cream; a Guinness-brined rack of lamb; vanilla-poached salmon; a cocoa-and-chili-dusted steak with brandy cream; and a partridgeberry-stuffed duck breast with a white truffle demi-glace. Desserts such as a warmed apple cake, Nova Scotia blueberry cheesecake, a caramelized banana split over a coconut macaroon, a raspberry mousse torte with white-chocolate shavings, or a Grand Marnier–flavored chocolate pâté make very fitting finishes. A recent addition to this winner is the weekend brunch, from 10am to 3pm Saturdays and Sundays: Look for crepes, breakfast burritos, egg dishes, fish cakes, and a hearty brioche French toast filled with pears, walnuts, and brie—all for just C$10 (US$9/£5) per person.

1866 Upper Water St. ✆ **902/425-2133.** Reservations recommended. Main courses C$8–C$16 (US$7.20–US$14/ £4–£8) at lunch, C$14–C$24 (US$13–US$22/£7–£12) at dinner. AE, DC, MC, V. Daily 11:30am–10pm.

INEXPENSIVE

Cheapside Café *Value* *Kids* CAFE   Yes, it's cheap, but the name actually comes from an open market that once occupied this street, named after a similar market in London. The cheerful and lively Cheapside Café is tucked inside the Provincial Building, one of two structures housing the Art Gallery of Nova Scotia. The interior is almost like a little museum, with its fun artwork on the walls and table settings. The daily card of soups and sandwiches might feature choices like chicken breast with avocado and mango chutney, roast beef with fried onions, or smoked salmon served with an egg pancake and asparagus. Other daily fare might include jerk pork, pasta primavera, fish cakes, Thai chicken salads with peanut sauce, quiche, poached salmon, and cold open-faced shrimp sandwiches. Desserts are delicious—especially notable is the Cheapside Café torte, with its hazelnut crunch.

1723 Hollis St. (inside the Art Gallery of Nova Scotia). ✆ **902/425-4494.** Sandwiches and entrees C$10–C$13 (US$9–US$12/£5–£6.50). MC, V. Tues–Sat 10am–5pm; Sun noon–5pm.

Cheelin ✿ CHINESE   The city's best Chinese restaurant, Cheelin manages to achieve a seemingly improbable balance between authentic Asian cuisine—in such normally hard-to-find dishes as *mapo* tofu (spicy tofu, cubed and stir-fried, often mixed with ground pork or beef) and *yu xiang* pork (pork with Szechuan sauce, usually made from some combination of ginger, garlic, sesame, vinegar, or fish flavoring)—and a funkier, Haligonian vibe (from the brightly painted interior and the hip young staff and crowd to dishes such as scallops paired with mango sauce). Despite the low prices, this is definitely not a hole-in-the-wall Chinese eatery. Go for the haddock, the excellent vegetable spring rolls, orange beef, shredded pork with bitter melon, or a daily special such as peppery mala shrimp with sautéed bok choy and squash. They also deliver to the downtown area—good to know when you're hungry late at night.

1496 Lower Water St. (inside The Brewery). ✆ **902/422-2252.** Main courses C$10–C$19 (US$9–US$17/£5–£9.50). AE, MC, V. Mon 11am–2:30pm; Tues–Sat 11am–2:30pm and 5:30–10pm; Sun 5:30–10pm.

Henry House ✿ BREWPUB   Eastern Canada's pioneer brewpub—this was the first—is housed in an austere building far down Barrington Street. The starkly handsome 1834 stone building has a medium-fancy dining room upstairs with red tablecloths and captains' chairs. (The pub downstairs is more boisterous and informal.) You can order off the same menu at either spot, and it's what you'd expect at a brewpub, only better-tasting: Entrees include beer-battered fish, steak sandwiches, an excellent smoked-salmon club sandwich, burgers, beef-and-beer stew, salads, and meatloaf. The beer here is fresh and good; they also do Sunday brunches.

1222 Barrington St. ✆ **902/423-5660.** Main courses C$7–C$14 (US$6.30–US$13/£3.50–£7). AE, DC, MC, V. Mon–Sat 11:30am–12:30am; Sun noon–11pm.

Il Mercato ✿✿ ITALIAN   Light-colored Tuscan sponged walls and big rustic terracotta tiles on the floor set an appropriate mood at this popular spot amid the clamor of Spring Garden. Come early or late or expect to wait a bit (no reservations accepted), but make the effort either way—it's worth it. You'll find a great selection of meals at prices that approach bargain level. Start by selecting antipasti from the deli counter in the front (you point; the waitstaff will bring them to your table). The focaccias are superb and come with a pleasing salad, while the ravioli with roast chicken and wild mushrooms is sublime. There are plenty of pastas and thin-crust pizzas on the menu to satisfy your fix, while non-Italian entrees include grilled rack of lamb with Dijon, a seafood medley cooked up with peppers, and a strip steak topped with gorgonzola.

5650 Spring Garden Rd. (C) **902/422-2866.** Reservations not accepted. Main courses C$12–C$20 (US$11–US$18/£6–£10). AE, DC, MC, V. Mon–Sat 11am–11pm.

Satisfaction Feast VEGETARIAN   Located along the newly cool stretch of Grafton Street, Halifax's original vegetarian restaurant (it turns 25 in 2006) has been voted one of the top 10 veggie restaurants in Canada by the *Globe and Mail.* It's funky and fun, with a certain spare grace inside and a canopy and sidewalk tables for summer lounging. Entrees include lasagna, bean burritos, pesto pasta, veggie burgers, and a macrobiotic rice casserole. There's also "neatloaf" and tofu-and-rice-based "peace burgers" for those who like their food with cute names. The vegan fruit crisp is the dessert to hold out for. They also do takeout; consider a hummus-and-pita picnic atop nearby Citadel Hill.

1581 Grafton St. (C) **902/422-3540.** Main courses C$5–C$12 (US$4.50–US$11/£2.50–£6). AE, DC, MC, V. Daily 11:30am–9:30pm (winter to 8:30pm).

Steve-O-Reno's (★) (*Value*) CAFE   Tucked off Spring Garden, this coffee shop is also a popular lunch stop for locals. You'll have your choice of potent coffee and coffeelike beverages (such as chai tea latte), along with inventive fruit smoothies, a small selection of sandwiches and salads, and a pleasantly relaxed atmosphere. They do everything well and inexpensively, and the hip young staff is as friendly and cheerful as can be. There's now a second location on Robie Street as well.

1536 Brunswick St. (C) **902/429-3034.** Meals C$4–C$6 (US$3.60–US$5.40/£2–£3). No credit cards. Mon–Sat 7:30am–6pm; Sun 8am–6pm.

HALIFAX BY NIGHT

For starters, stop by the visitor center or the front desk of your hotel and ask for a copy of *Where Halifax,* a comprehensive monthly guide to the city's entertainment. Among the city's premier venues for shows are the downtown **Halifax Metro Centre,** 1800 Argyle St. ((C) **902/421-8000**), which hosts sporting events and concerts by a wide variety of artists.

PERFORMING ARTS

Shakespeare by the Sea ((C) **902/422-0295**) stages a whole line of bardic and non-bardic productions July through August at several alfresco venues around the city. Most are held at Point Pleasant Park, where the ruins of old forts and buildings are used as the stage settings for delightful performances, with the audience sprawled on the grass, many enjoying picnic dinners with their *Taming of the Shrew.* Shows are technically free, though the players suggest a donation of C$10 (US$9/£5) per person. The occasional more elaborate productions at other locations (past shows have included *King Lear* at the Citadel and *Titus Andronicus* at the park's Martello tower) have limited seating, with ticket prices that might range up to C$30 (US$27/£15).

The **Neptune Theatre,** 1593 Argyle St. ((C) **902/429-7070**), benefited from a C$13.5-million renovation and now also includes an intimate 200-seat studio theater. Top-notch dramatic productions are offered throughout the year. (The main season runs Sept–May, with a summer season filling in the gap with eclectic performances.) Main-stage tickets range generally from around C$15 to C$45 (US$14–US$41/£7.50–£23).

A Road Trip to Peggy's Cove

About 42km (26 miles) southwest of Halifax is the fishing village of **Peggy's Cove** 𝕲𝕲 (pop. 120), which offers postcard-perfect tableaus: an octagonal lighthouse (surely one of the most photographed in the world), tiny fishing shacks, and graceful fishing boats bobbing in the postage stamp-size harbor. The bonsai-like perfection hasn't gone unnoticed by the big tour operators, however, so it's a rare summer day when you're not sharing the experience with a few hundred of your close, personal bus-tour friends. The village is home to a handful of B&Bs and a gallery, but scenic values draw the day-trippers with cameras and lots of film. While there, make sure to check out the touching **Swissair Flight 111 Memorial** 𝕲 among the rocks just before the turnoff to the cove; this site memorializes the passengers of that flight, which crashed into the Atlantic just off this coast. Want to stay awhile? One good lodging choice in the area is **Peggy's Cove B&B** (𝒞 888/634-8973 or 902/634-4543), a three-bedroom restored fisherman's home close to the lighthouse with rooms at C$95 to C$165 (US$86–US$149/£48–£83) per night. If it's full, **Code's Oceanside Inn** (𝒞 888/823-2765), about 3km (2 miles) away in West Dover, has two rooms and a suite for C$105 to C$195 (US$95–US$176/£53–£98) per night.

For a more informal dramatic night out, there's the **Grafton Street Dinner Theater,** 1741 Grafton St. (𝒞 902/425-1961), which typically offers light musicals and mysteries with a three-course dinner (choice of prime rib, salmon, or chicken). Adult tickets cost about C$35 (US$32/£18), half-price for children 12 and under.

CLUB & BAR SCENE

The young and restless tend to congregate in pubs, in nightclubs, and at street corners along two axes that converge at the public library: Grafton Street and Spring Garden Road. If you're thirsty, wander the neighborhoods around here and you're likely to find a spot that could serve as a temporary home for the evening. One of the coolest places to hang out is **Economy Shoe Shop** (𝒞 902/423-7463) at 1663 Argyle St., not a shop but rather a cafe-slash-bar where many of Halifax's prettiest people wind up sooner or later. Helpfully, they serve some sort of food all the way until 2am, and the wine list is impressive. In the evening (and late afternoons on Sat), you'll also find lively Maritime music and good beer at the **Lower Deck Pub** (𝒞 902/425-1501), one of the popular restaurants in the Historic Properties complex on the waterfront. There's music nightly, and often on Saturday afternoons. Among the clubs offering local rock, ska, and the like are the **Marquee Club,** 2041 Gottingen St. (𝒞 902/423-2072), and **The Attic,** 1741 Grafton St. (𝒞 902/423-0909). **Maxwell's Plum** at 1600 Grafton St. (𝒞 902/423-5090) is a free-for-all English pub where peanut shells litter the floor and there are dozens upon dozens of selections of import and Canadian draft and bottled beers. Happy-hour specials run about C$2.50 (US$2.25/£1.25) a bottle for a selected import each night.

Check *The Coast,* Halifax's free weekly newspaper (widely available), for listings of upcoming performances.

9 The Eastern Shore

Heading from Halifax toward Cape Breton Island (or vice versa), you need to choose between two basic routes. If you're burning to get to your destination, take Route 102 to Route 104 (the Trans-Canada Highway, the one with the maple leaf). If you're in no particular hurry and are most content venturing down narrow lanes, destination unknown, by all means allow a couple of days to wind along the Eastern Shore, mostly along Route 7. (Note that official tourism materials refer to this stretch as the Marine Drive instead of the Eastern Shore, for whatever reason.) Along the way you'll be rewarded with glimpses of a rugged coastline that's wilder and more remote than the coast south of Halifax. Communities here tend to be farther apart, less genteel, and stocked with far fewer services—or tourists. With its rugged terrain and remote locales, this region is a good bet for those drawn to the outdoors and seeking coastal solitude.

Be forewarned that the Eastern Shore isn't breathtakingly scenic if you limit yourself to the main road. You'll drive mostly through cutover woodlands and scrappy towns. To get the most out of this section of the coast, become committed to making periodic wanders and detours, the more impetuous the better. Drive down dead-end roads ending in coastal peninsulas, where you might come upon wild roses blooming madly in the fog, or point your car inland to the enormous interior forest instead, where you can still find moose and an enveloping quiet.

ESSENTIALS

GETTING THERE   Routes 107 and 7 run along or near the coast from Dartmouth to Stillwater (near Sherbrooke). A patchwork of other routes—including 211, 316, 16, and 344—continues onward along the coast to the causeway to Cape Breton. An excursion along the entire coastal route—from Dartmouth to Cape Breton Island with a detour to Canso—is 407km (253 miles).

VISITOR INFORMATION   Several tourist information centers are staffed along the route. You'll find the best stocked and most helpful centers in **Sheet Harbour,** next to the waterfall (© 902/885-2595; open daily in summer 10am–7pm); in **Sherbrooke Village,** at the museum (© 902/522-2400; open daily in summer 9:30am–5:30pm), and in **Canso** at 1297 Union St. (© 902/366-2170; open daily in summer 9am–6pm).

A DRIVING TOUR OF THE EASTERN SHORE

This section assumes travel northeastward from Halifax toward Cape Breton. If you're traveling the opposite direction, hold this book upside down (just kidding).

Between Halifax and Sheet Harbour, the route plays hide-and-seek with the coast, touching the water periodically before veering inland. The most scenic areas are around wild and open **Ship Harbour,** as well as **Spry Harbour,** noted for its attractive older homes and islands looming offshore.

At the **Fisherman's Life Museum** (© 902/889-2053) in Jeddore Oyster Pond, you'll get a glimpse of life on the Eastern Shore a century ago. The humble white-shingle-and-green-trim cottage was built by James Myers in the 1850s; early in this century it became the property of his youngest son, Ervin. Ervin and his wife raised a dozen daughters here ("This was quite a popular spot among the young men in the area," reported the laconic guide), and the home and grounds have been restored to look as they might have around 1900 or 1920. A walk through the house and barn and down to the fishing dock won't take much more than 20 minutes or so. The museum is open June to mid-October, Monday through Saturday 9:30am to 5:30pm and Sunday 1 to 5:30pm. Admission is C$3.25 (US$2.95/£1.65) adults, C$2.25 (US$2.05/£1.15) seniors and children age 6 to 17, C$7.50 (US$6.75/£3.75) families. It's located on Route 7 and is well marked.

At the town of Lake Charlotte you can opt for a side road that weaves along the coast (look for signs for Clam Harbour). The road alternately follows wooded coves and passes through inland forests; about midway you'll see signs for a turn to **Clam Harbour Beach Provincial Park.** A broad crescent beach attracts sunbathers and swimmers from Halifax and beyond, with lifeguard-supervised swimming on weekends. A picnic area is set amid a spruce grove on a bluff overlooking the beach. There's no admission charge, and gates close at 8pm. Continue on up the coast from the park and you'll reemerge on Route 7 in Ship Harbour.

Between Ship and Spry harbours is the town of Tangier, home to **Coastal Adventures** (© 877/404-2774 or 902/772-2774), which specializes in kayak tours. It's run by Scott Cunningham, who literally wrote the book on Nova Scotia kayaking (he's the author of the definitive guide to paddling this coast). This well-run operation is situated on a beautiful island-dotted part of the coast, but it specializes in multiday trips throughout Atlantic Canada. You're best off writing (P.O. Box 77, Tangier, NS B0J 3H0) or calling for a brochure well in advance of your trip.

There's also a terrific little fish-smoking business just outside Tangier, **Willie Krauch & Sons Smokehouse** ☆ (© 800/758-4412 or 902/772-2188). Krauch (pronounced "craw") and family sell wood-smoked Atlantic salmon, mackerel, and eel in an unpretentious little store; they'll also give you a tour of the premises, if you like, where you can check out the old-style smoking process in action. Take some to go for a picnic. It's open until 6pm daily.

Sheet Harbour (pop. 900) is a pleasant small town with a campground open May through September, a couple of small grocery stores, two motels, and a **visitor information center** (© 902/885-2595), behind which is a short nature trail and boardwalk that descends along low, rocky cascades. Inland from Sheet Harbour on Route 374 is the **Liscomb Game Sanctuary,** a popular destination for hearty, self-contained explorers equipped with maps, compasses, canoes, and fishing rods. There are no services to speak of for casual travelers. Continuing eastward from Sheet Harbour, you'll pass through the wee village of **Ecum Secum,** which has little to attract the tourist but is unusually gratifying to say out loud to others in the car.

Adjacent to the well-marked Liscombe Lodge (see below) and just over the main bridge is the **Liscomb River Trail** system. Trails follow the river both north and south of Route 7. The main hiking trail follows the river upstream for 5km (3 miles), crosses it on a suspension bridge, and then returns on the other side. The Mayflower Point Trail follows the river southward toward the coast, then loops back inland.

Continuing on Route 211 beyond historic Sherbrooke Village (see description below), you'll drive through a wonderful landscape of lakes, ocean inlets, and upland bogs and soon come to the scenic **Country Harbour Ferry** (© 902/389-2200). The 12-car cable ferry crosses the broad river encased by rounded and wooded bluffs each direction every half-hour when open. The fare is C$5 (US$4.50/£2.50) per car, which includes driver and passengers. If the ferry isn't running, you'll have to turn right around and head back, so it's wise to check at the Canso or Sherbrooke visitor centers before detouring this way.

Farther along (you'll be on Rte. 316 after the ferry), you'll come to **Tor Bay Provincial Park.** It's 4km (2½ miles) off the main road but well worth the detour on a sunny day. The park features three sandy crescent beaches backed by grassy dunes and small ponds that are slowly being taken over by bog and spruce forest. The short boardwalk loop is especially worth a walk.

Way out on the eastern tip of Nova Scotia's mainland is the end-of-the-world town of Canso (pop. 1,200). It's a rough-edged fishing and oil-shipping town, often windswept and foggy. The chief attraction here is **Grassy Island Fort National Historic Site (© 902/295-2069),** part of the newly created Canso Islands National Historic Site. A park-run boat takes you out to the island, which once housed a bustling community of fishermen and traders from New England. The small interpretive center on the waterfront (open daily 10am–6pm June to mid-Sept) features artifacts recovered from the island and boat schedules. A trail also links several historic sites within the island, which feels a bit melancholy whether it's foggy or not. Boat fares are by donation; I always give them a few dollars per person. If you're coming to Canso in summer, also watch out for the annual folk music festival created to honor Nova Scotia's own Stan Rogers.

Route 16 between the intersection of Route 316 and Guysborough is an uncommonly **scenic drive.** The road runs high and low along brawny hills, affording soaring views of Chedabucto Bay and grassy hills across the way. Also pleasant, although not quite as distinguished, is Route 344 from Guysborough to the Canso causeway. The road twists, turns, and drops through woodlands with some nice views of the strait. It will make you wish you were riding a large and powerful motorcycle.

Sherbrooke Village *(Kids)*   About half of the town of Sherbrooke comprises Sherbrooke Village, a historic section surrounded by low fences, water, and fields. (It's managed as part of the Nova Scotia Museum.) You'll have to pay admission to wander around, but the price is well worth it. This is the largest restored village in Nova Scotia, and it's unique in several respects. For one, almost all of the buildings are on their original sites (only two have been moved). Also, many homes are still occupied by local residents, and private homes are interspersed with the buildings open to visitors. About two dozen buildings have been restored and opened to the public, from a convincing general store to an operating blacksmith shop and post office. Look also for the former temperance hall, courthouse, printery, boatbuilding shop, drugstore, and schoolhouse. These are all staffed by genial costumed interpreters, who can tell you about what life was like in the 1860s around here. Be sure to ask about the source of the town's early prosperity; you might be surprised. Plan to spend up to a half-day here, depending on your (and your kids') interest level.

Rte. 7, Sherbrooke. © **902/522-2400.** Admission C$9 (US$8.10/£4.50) adults, C$7.25 (US$6.55/£3.65) seniors, C$3.75 (US$3.40/£1.90) children, C$25 (US$23/£13) families. June to mid-Oct daily 9:30am–5pm.

WHERE TO STAY & DINE

Other than a handful of motels and B&Bs, few accommodations are available on the Eastern Shore. If the following two are full, you might also inquire at the **Salmon River House Country Inn (© 800/565-3353** or 902/889-3353) in Salmon River Bridge, with seven rooms plus a cottage ranging from around C$100 to C$145 (US$90–US$131/£50–£73) per night; there's a lobster restaurant on the premises, though this is only 45 minutes from Halifax and you may want to push farther north in your explorations.

Liscombe Lodge 🏕🏕 _Kids_   This modern complex, owned and operated by the province, consists of a central lodge and a series of smaller cottages and outbuildings. It's situated in a remote part of the coast, adjacent to hiking trails and a popular boating area at the mouth of the Liscomb River. The lodge bills itself as "the nature lover's resort," and indeed it offers access to both forest and water. But it's not exactly rustic, with well-tended lawns, bland modern architecture, a shuffleboard, a marina, and even an oversize outdoor chessboard. Plenty of kid-friendly offerings (table tennis, horseshoe pitches, and so forth) make this a good choice for vacationing families, though. The rooms are modern and motel-like; the cottages and chalets have multiple bedrooms and are good for families. The dining room is open to the public and serves resort fare.

Rte. 7, Liscomb Mills, NS B0J 2A0. © **800/665-6343** or 902/779-2307. Fax 902/779-2700. www.signatureresorts.com. 68 units. C$140–C$350 (US$126–US$315/£70–£175) double. Inquire about packages. AE, DISC, MC, V. Closed mid-Oct to mid-May. Pets allowed in chalets. **Amenities:** Restaurant; indoor pool; tennis court; fitness center; free bikes; shuffleboard; coin-op washers and dryers. _In room:_ TV w/VCR (some units), fridge (some units), hair dryer, iron, no phone.

SeaWind Landing Country Inn 🏕🏕   What to do when your boatbuilding business collapses because the fisheries business is on the downturn? How about opening an inn instead? That's what Lorraine and Jim Colvin decided to do, and their 8-hectare (20-acre) oceanfront compound is the delightful result. Some of the guest rooms here are located in the 130-year-old main house, which has been tastefully modernized and updated. The rest are in a more recent outbuilding, where any historic charm that's been lost is made up for by the brightness, great ocean views, and double Jacuzzis these units possess. The Colvins are especially knowledgeable about local art (much of the work on display here was produced in the area), and they have compiled a literate and helpful guide to the region for guests to use while exploring. The property also has three private sand beaches, and coastal boat tours and picnic lunches can easily be arranged for an extra charge. The inn also serves **dinner** 🏕 nightly, to inn guests only, featuring local products prepared in country-French style washed down with wines from the inn's own wine cellar.

1 Wharf Rd., Charlos Cove, NS B0H 1T0. © **800/563-4667** or 902/525-2108. Fax 902/525-2108. www.seawindlanding. com. 10 units. C$95–C$169 (US$86–US$152/£48–£85) double. AE, MC, V. Closed mid-Oct to mid-May. **Amenities:** Dining room; laundry service. _In room:_ Hair dryer, Jacuzzi (most units), no phone.

10 Amherst to Antigonish

The north shore of Nova Scotia—dubbed the Sunrise Trail at visitor information centers and in provincial tourism publications—is chock-full of rolling hills and pastoral landscapes that rarely fail to enchant. Driving along Route 6, you pass through farmlands along the western reaches from Amherst to Pugwash and beyond; around Tatamagouche the landscape at times mirrors that found on the other side of the straits, on Prince Edward Island—softly rolling fields of grain punctuated by a well-tended farmhouse and barn, rust-red soil appearing where the ground cover has been scraped off. Cows dominate one field, and in the next are those massive bull's-eyes of rolled hay. The Amherst-to-Pictou drive is especially scenic early or late on a clear day, when the low sun highlights the fields and forests. After Pictou, back on the Trans-Canada Highway, you'll see more forest and hills as you make your way toward Cape Breton Island.

AMHERST

Amherst is best known for the busy and bustling information center staffed by the province just off the Trans-Canada (see below). But it's a lovely small town perched on a low hill at the edge of the sweeping Amherst Marsh, which demarcates the border between Nova Scotia and New Brunswick. It's worth slowing and taking a detour through town just to appreciate the historic streetscapes.

ESSENTIALS

GETTING THERE   Amherst is the first Nova Scotia town you'll encounter heading east on the Trans-Canada Highway and is the terminus for both routes 6 (to the north) and 2 (to the south). It's about 40 minutes east of Moncton and a stop on the **VIA Rail** (✆ **888/842-7245**) train between Montréal and Halifax.

VISITOR INFORMATION   The huge **Nova Scotia Visitor Information Centre** (✆ **902/667-8429**) is on Amherst's western edge, just off Exit 1 of the Trans-Canada Highway. In addition to the usual vast library of brochures and pamphlets, there's an ice-cream stand, videos, helpful staff, extraordinary views across the usually windy marsh, and often a bagpiper providing the appropriate mood out in front. It's open year-round: daily from 8am to 9pm during the summer; weekdays only from 8am to 9pm during the rest of the year. A portion of the center that includes washrooms, vending machines, and payphones is open 24 hours a day in summer.

Just east of the provincial visitor center is the **Amherst Visitor Information Centre** (✆ **902/667-0696**), housed in a handsome 1905 rail car. It's a good bet for more detailed information on activities in the immediate area. It's open daily from 10am to 6pm from late May to early September.

EXPLORING AMHERST

Downtown Amherst is compact (just a few blocks, really), though attractive in a brick-and-sandstone way perhaps best appreciated by those who are Scots, or were in a previous life. A half-dozen or so buildings are rough gems of classical architecture, nicely offset by the trees—including a few elms that continue to soldier on despite Dutch elm disease. Note the elaborately pedimented 1888 courthouse at the corner of Victoria and Church; a short stroll north is the sandstone Amherst First Baptist Church with its pair of prominent turrets. Farther north are the stoutly proportioned Doric columns on the 1935 Dominion Public Building.

Driving east on Route 6 you'll pass through a residential area of large, attractive historic homes dating from the last century and a half or so. They display an eclectic range of architectural styles and materials.

Those seeking more information on Amherst's history can visit the **Cumberland County Museum,** 150 Church St. (✆ **902/667-2561**), located in the 1836 home of R. B. Dickey, one of the Fathers of Canadian Confederation. (Historical note: Four of the Fathers of Confederation were from Amherst.) The museum is especially strong in documenting details of local industry and labor; it's open Monday through Saturday from 9am to 5pm from May through September, closed Mondays in the off season. Admission costs C$3 (US$2.70/£1.50) adult, C$5 (US$4.50/£2.50) family.

While this is not really a town to linger in before jumping off into such a lovely province, a Frommer's reader has written me to recommend the **Old Germany Restaurant** (✆ **902/667-2868**) in Amherst, located at 80 Church St. Said traveler described it thus: "We stumbled upon this fabulous and quaint place where the owners cook traditional German cuisine. We also had fantastic desserts." That's good enough for me; go forth and dine. Owners Heidi Renner-Dembour and Holger Renner are, as you may have just guessed from their names, German in origin.

PUGWASH & TATAMAGOUCHE

If you're in the planning phase of your trip, note that it takes roughly 2 hours to drive from Amherst to New Glasgow via the Trans-Canada Highway (which dips southward through Truro) or via Route 6 along the northern shore. On the Trans-Canada the driving is typically steady and fast, but you'll likely glaze over and find yourself punching the radio's scan button for entertainment.

Route 6 has far more visual interest, and you'll speed along sprawling farms, fields of wheat and corn, azure ocean inlets, and verdant coastal marshes. You'll spot the wide straits dotted with sails, with Prince Edward Island in the distance. The landscape changes frequently enough to prevent it from ever growing repetitious. As I mentioned, both routes require the same amount of time—assuming you don't stop. But traveling on Route 6 you most likely *will* stop to walk on beaches, to order up a mess of french fries and vinegar, or to shop at one of the handful of specialized crafts stores. It's worth the sacrifice in time.

ESSENTIALS

GETTING THERE Both towns are located on Route 6; you can't miss them from either direction.

VISITOR INFORMATION The **Tatamagouche Visitor Information Center** (*© 902/657-3285*) is in the Fraser Cultural Center at 362 Main St.

EXPLORING THE REGION

This region is home to a number of picnic parks, as well as local and provincial beaches. Signs along Route 6 point the way; most require a detour of a few miles. Pack a picnic and make an afternoon of it.

Pugwash, which comes from the Mi'kmaq word *pagweak,* meaning deep waters, has a slightly industrial feel, with its factory and a midsize cargo port on the Pugwash River. **Seagull Pewter** (*© 902/243-3850*) is well known throughout the province and is made in a factory on the east side of town; look for the retail store (which also stocks antiques) on the other side of town, just west of the Pugwash River bridge on Route 6. It's open 7 days a week in the summer.

Between Pugwash and Tatamagouche you'll drive through the scenic village of Wallace (motto: "A Friendly Place"), where the road winds along the water and you'll take in fine views of the forested shores on the far side of Wallace Bay. East of Wallace, watch for the remains of ancient Acadian dikes in the marshes, built to reclaim the land for farming (signs point these out).

Tatamagouche is a pleasant fishing village with a surprisingly large annual Oktoberfest, and it's also home to the **Fraser Cultural Centre** (362 Main St.; *© 902/657-3285*), which strives to preserve the region's cultural heritage through ongoing exhibits, as well as to promote activities that encourage greater involvement in the arts and crafts. It's open daily June through August from 10am to 5pm (1–4pm in Sept), and admission is free.

Also in Tatamagouche is the shop of **Sara Bonnyman Pottery** (*© 902/657-3215*), where you'll find rustic country-style plates, mugs, and more in a speckled pattern embellished with blueberries and other country motifs. The shop is on Route 246, 1 mile from the post office.

Days of Wine and Rosé

Near Malagash, itself quite close to Tatamagouche, look for the highway signs crafted of casks along the road; these will direct you to the **Jost Vineyards** 𝒜𝒜 ((℃ **800/565-4567** or 902/257-2636), which produces wines you may have sipped in many of Nova Scotia's better restaurants. The vineyard's success is an instructive story of persistence. The winemaking Jost family emigrated here from Germany in 1970 and began growing grapes in the local soil 8 years later; finally, in 1985, Jost's first wines were bottled and sold. Today they are highly regarded throughout Eastern Canada.

You can take a free tour of the winery, enjoy a picnic (a deli opens on the premises during the summer), or sample the wines produced here and stock up on those that impress you. Don't miss the "ice wine," a Canada specialty made from naturally frozen grapes and usually associated with the province of Ontario; Jost's Vidal ice wine, however, trumped all comers in a competition a few years back. The vineyard is open Monday through Saturday 9am to 6pm, noon to 6pm on Sunday; the tours are offered twice daily, at noon and 3pm, from mid-June through mid-September. To get there from Tatamagouche, simply follow Route 6 to Malagash and turn right at the wine barrel, following grape signs to the vineyard.

WHERE TO STAY

Train Station Inn *(Finds* This is one of the most unique lodgings in the province . . . or in Canada, for that matter. You won't find Jacuzzis here, but you will get a souvenir-worthy digital photo of your digs at least. Located down a side street in and around a weedy rail yard, the Train Station offers three rooms in, yes, a lovely century-old brick train station—but also seven rooms in a set of Canadian National cabooses and train cars that have been refurbished as rather simple guest rooms. I am not kidding. The station rooms are like your grandmother's spare bedroom, and they lack TVs and air-conditioning; the cabooses vary in comfort and character but are generally more plush, relatively speaking. All have been nicely done over, though, in various styles and decor—some decorated in regal Edwardian parlor motifs with bead-board paneling and striped wallpaper, other (later-model) cars outfitted with hardwood floors, gas woodstoves, kitchenettes, king beds, and small private elevated sitting areas with plastic patio chairs for lounging. Rates include a continental breakfast served in the men's waiting room, which is lined with lanterns and other railway memorabilia and doubles as a cafe. The reception and gift shop is located in the ladies' waiting room; pick up an engineer's cap if you like. Amazingly, there is even a dining car, with lunches and dinners of salmon, steak, lobster, and the like served daily. The fleet is still growing, too: In December 2006, a new addition—a 1905 Vice Regal car—arrived on the scene.

21 Station Rd., Tatamagouche, NS B0K 1V0. (℃ **888/724-5233** or 902/657-3222. Fax 902/657-9091. www.trainstation. ca. 10 units. Apr–Oct C$90–C$170 (US$81–US$153/£45–£85) double. Rates include light breakfast. Closed Nov–Mar. AE, DC, MC, V. Pets allowed with advance notice. **Amenities:** Restaurant; kitchenette; laundry. *In room (caboose only):* A/C, TV, kitchenette (2 units), fridge, coffeemaker.

PICTOU

Pictou was established as part of a development scheme hatched by speculators from Philadelphia in 1760. Under the terms of their land grant, they needed to place some 250 settlers at the harbor. That was a problem: Few Philadelphians wanted to live there. So the company sent a ship called the *Hector* to Scotland in 1773 to drum up some impoverished souls who might be more amenable to starting life over in North America.

This worked out rather better, and the ship returned with some 200 passengers, mostly Gaelic-speaking Highlanders. The stormy voyage was brutal, and the passengers were threatened with starvation. But they eventually arrived at Pictou, and they disembarked wearing tartans and playing bagpipes.

The anniversary of the settlers' arrival is celebrated mid-August each year with the **Hector Festival** (© **800/353-5338** or 902/485-8848), when you might spot members of the clans wearing kilts and dining out in high style in memory of their ancestors; tickets cost around C$15 to C$20 (US$14–US$18/£7.50–£10). Pictou is Scottish enough that you might find haggis slipped into your meal when you're not paying attention.

ESSENTIALS

GETTING THERE   Pictou is located on Route 106, which is just north of Exit 22 off Route 104 (the south branch of the Trans-Canada Hwy.). The **Prince Edward Island ferry** is several kilometers north of town at the coast near Caribou. (See chapter 6 for details on the ferry.)

VISITOR INFORMATION   The provincial **Visitor Information Centre** (© **902/ 485-6213**) is located just off the rotary at the junction of routes 106 and 6. It's open daily 8am to 10pm in summer, 9am to 6pm in fall, and 9am to 5pm the rest of the year.

EXPLORING PICTOU

Pictou is a pleasant and historic harborside town with an abundance of interesting architecture. There's a surfeit of dour sandstone buildings adorned with five-sided dormers, and at times you might think you've wandered down an Edinburgh side street. Water Street is especially attractive, and it offers an above-average selection of boutiques, casual restaurants, and pubs. Look for the headquarters and factory outlet of **Grohmann Knives,** 116 Water St. (© **888/756-4837** or 902/485-4224). At Grohmann's, located in a 1950s-mod building with a large knife piercing one corner, you'll find a good selection of quality knives (each with a lifetime guarantee) at marked-down prices. It's open daily; free half-hour factory tours for groups of at least four are offered Monday through Friday from 9am to 3:30pm.

The harbor is well protected and suitable for novices who want to explore by sea kayak or canoe. Also look in on the **Hector Heritage Quay Visitor's Marina** (© **902/ 485-6960**) on the waterfront at 37 Caladh Ave., with its twice-weekly live music in summer and a variety of other events.

Hector Heritage Quay   Learn about the hardships endured on the 1773 voyage of the singularly unseaworthy *Hector*—which brought Scottish settlers to the region—at this modern small museum on the waterfront in downtown Pictou. You'll pass by intriguing exhibits en route to the museum's centerpiece: a full-size replica of the 33m (108-ft.) *Hector* at the water's edge. Stop by the blacksmith and carpentry shops to get a picture of life in the colonies in the early days.

33 Caladh Ave. © **902/485-4371**. Admission C$7 (US$6.30/£3.50) adults, C$5 (US$4.50/£2.50) seniors, C$15 (US$14/£7.50) families. Mid-May to mid-Oct Mon–Sat 9am–5pm, Sun noon–5pm; longer hours July–Aug.

CLOSED
due to accidental demolition

WEGEN BISSIGEN
EICHHÖRNCHEN GESCHLOSSEN

CERRADO
CABRAS

Κλειστό
Μετεωρίτες

POOL CLOSED
プールも
ELECTRIC EELS
閉鎖中

Hotel closed for facelifting

FERMÉ POUR
RAISON
DE GRÈVE
DES BONNES

FECHADO!
POR CAUSA DE
ATAQUES DOS CROCODILOS

I don't speak sign language.

A hotel can close for all kinds of reasons.

Our Guarantee ensures that if your hotel's undergoing construction, we'll
let you know in advance. In fact, we cover your entire travel experience.
See www.travelocity.com/guarantee for details.

travelocity
You'll never roam alone.

WHERE TO STAY

Auberge Walker Inn ✦   This handsome downtown inn is located in a brick town house-style building dating to 1865 that overlooks one of Pictou's more active intersections. The innkeepers have done a commendable job of giving the place a comfortable feel while retaining its historic sensibility. Some rooms (such as the queen-bedded room no. 10 on the third floor) have nice harbor views. A first-floor suite has a small kitchen, Jacuzzi, and dark bedroom in the back. All rooms have private bathrooms, but the conversions have come at some sacrifice—upstairs rooms have showers only, and one Frommer's reader wrote that his was so small he couldn't bend over to wash his legs. On the upside: The inn is perfectly situated to enjoy Pictou's restaurants and attractions.

34 Coleraine St. (P.O. Box 629), Pictou, NS B0K 1H0. ✆ 800/370-5553 or 902/485-1433. Fax 902/485-1222. www.walkerinn.com. 11 units. C$79–C$89 (US$71–US$80/£40–£45) double; C$149 (US$134/£75) suite. Rates include breakfast. AE, MC, V. Parking on street, at rear of building, and in lot 1 block away. *In room:* Kitchenette (1 unit), no phone.

Braeside Inn   This three-story hotel on a hill at the edge of downtown was built in 1938 as an inn, and it has been one of the town's more enduring hostelries. The public rooms are done up in pinks and greens; one has a herd of wingback chairs and is a good spot to settle in with a book before dinner. Guest rooms are all carpeted and comfortable, if a bit small. Some units now have Jacuzzis, and all now sport ceiling fans, TVs, and VCRs (previously, guests gathered around the tube in a common television room for the nightly news). The dining room has hardwood floors and views down a lawn to the harbor. Meal choices here aren't terribly daring but you can certainly get all the standards, with hearty selections on offer including prime rib with Yorkshire pudding, scallops, duck, salmon, and a rack of lamb. Reservations for dining are suggested.

126 Front St., Pictou, NS B0K 1H0. ✆ 800/613-7701 or 902/485-5046. Fax 902/485-1701. www.braesideinn.com. 18 units. C$65–C$175 (US$59–US$158/£33–£88) double. AE, MC, V. At the end of Water St., make a right on Coleraine St., then left on Front St. **Amenities:** Dining room. *In room:* A/C, TV, fridge (some units), hair dryer, Jacuzzi (some units).

Consulate Inn ✦   No surprise: This doughty 1810 historic home of sandstone and ivy was originally a consulate. Three guest rooms are upstairs in the main building and share a handsome sitting area; seven larger and more modern rooms are located next door; and there's another room off-property. The decor tends more toward the cute (think simple white walls, understated furniture, and floral-print bedspreads) than the elegant, with innkeepers Debbie and Garry Jardine striving to impart a romantic mood to appeal to couples. Two newer rooms are located in a walk-in basement and are a tad small, but feature nice touches such as Jacuzzis and mood lighting; three other suites also have Jacuzzis, VCRs, and luxury touches. The Prince Edward Island ferry is located just a short 10-minute drive away, making this a handy stop for excursions onward, and the inn is well situated for exploring Pictou as well. The included breakfast is hot and filling, served farmhouse-style in the breakfast room.

157 Water St., Pictou, NS B0K 1H0. ✆ 800/424-8283 or 902/485-4554. Fax 902/485-1532. www.consulateinn.com. 11 units. C$79–C$159 (US$71–US$143/£40–£80) double. Rates include full breakfast. Ask about off-season rates Nov–May. AE, DC, MC, V. **Amenities:** Laundry service. *In room:* A/C, TV/VCR, fridge (some units), Jacuzzi (some units).

The Customs House Inn ✦   This hulking brick-and-sandstone building with heroic arches and dentils was built in 1872 and thoroughly renovated in 1997. Once an office building, today it contains some amazingly spacious and dramatic guest rooms with high ceilings, maple floors, fireplaces, and a certain Spartan grace; the innkeepers have held back on the decorating, letting the architectural space speak for itself. Three rooms have kitchenettes with refrigerators; all have whirlpool tubs, phones, and air-conditioning. Many are also adorned with the nautical paintings of contemporary local painter Dave Macintosh. Among the best rooms is 2F, a bright corner room with a kitchenette and water views; in the basement is a pub with beers on tap and live Celtic music some evenings—when it's open (call ahead about this if it's important). Note that this is *not* a warm and fuzzy place where the innkeepers sit around a fire with you and chat helpfully, and the inn's breakfast is best skipped. Still, the rooms are eye-popping.

38 Depot St., Pictou, NS B0K 1H0. ℂ **902/485-4546.** Fax 902/485-1657. www.customshouseinn.ca. 8 units. C$79–C$169 (US$71–US$152/£40–£85) double. Rates include breakfast. AE, DC, MC, V. **Amenities:** Bar. *In room:* A/C, TV, dataport, kitchenette (some units), Jacuzzi.

Pictou Lodge Resort ⟨ The original rustic log lodge and a handful of log out-buildings have gone through a number of owners—including the Canadian National Railway—since entrepreneurs built the compound on a far-off grassy bluff overlooking a pristine beach early in the 20th century. It's now owned by Maritime Inns and Resorts and has been modestly upgraded and improved with two new family suites. The lodge is located about a 10-minute drive from downtown yet has a wonderfully remote feel. Those older log rooms, most of which have kitchenettes, have considerably more char-acter (though some travelers still regard them as a bit dowdy); the newer rooms have the blandness of modern motel rooms anywhere. Lunch and dinner are served in an oceanside Adirondack-style lodge, its soaring spaces hammered together with time-bur-nished timbers. Dinner entrees might be termed "creative traditional," though they mostly feature the expected fare: rack of lamb, rib-eye steaks, halibut, game hen, pork tenderloin. The flourishes occur with the sauces and sides. Note that some of the lodge's cottages, part of the original log accommodations, were newly renovated in 2006.

Shore Rd. (P.O. Box 1539), Pictou, NS B0K 1H0. ℂ **888/662-7484** or 902/485-4322. Fax 902/485-4945. www. maritimeinns.com. 51 units. C$145–C$289 (US$131–US$260/£73–£145) double. AE, DC, DISC, MC, V. Closed mid-Oct to mid-May. Follow Shore Rd. from downtown toward PEI ferry; watch for signs. **Amenities:** Restaurant; outdoor pool; boats; bikes; playground; game room; room service. *In room:* A/C, TV (some units), kitchenette (some units), fridge (some units), Jacuzzi (some units).

WHERE TO DINE

Piper's Landing TRADITIONAL   This contemporary, attractive dining room on a stretch of residential road outside of Pictou remains a local favorite and your best bet in the area for a sophisticated meal, despite sometimes frustrating service. The interior is sparely decorated and understated. Likewise, the menu looks simple—entrees include grilled beef tenderloin, pork schnitzel, and a filling seafood platter—but you'll be impressed by the flair in preparation. The wine list, alas, is small and tired.

Rte. 376, Lyons Brook. ℂ **902/485-1200.** Reservations recommended. Main courses C$16–C$25 (US$15–US$23/ £8–£13). AE, MC, V. Mon–Sat 5:30–9pm; Sun 11am–9pm. From the Pictou Rotary take Rte. 376 toward Lyons Brook; it's 3km (1¾ miles) on your left.

Stone House Cafe & Pizzeria CAFE   For an unhurried, relaxed meal in unstuffy environs, try the decent selection of pizza (including a lobster, scallop, and haddock pizza) here. Other basic meals include smoked pork chops, lasagna, croquettes, and roast chicken.

13 Water St. ℂ **902/485-6885.** Main courses C$10–C$15 (US$9–US$14/£5–£7.50). Mon–Fri 11am–midnight; Sat–Sun 11am–1am.

ANTIGONISH

Antigonish traces its European roots back to the 1650s, when the French arrived, only to be driven off by the Mi'kmaq. The French returned a century later, only to be driven off this time by Irish Loyalists. These Irish settlers established the first permanent community, and today there thrives a handsome town of 5,500 residents with a bustling main street and the respected St. Francis Xavier University, which was founded in 1853.

The town has a bustling commercial center (be prepared for some traffic midsummer) and is a good spot to stock up on groceries or get a bite for lunch. There are several cafes on and around Main Street and a shop or two that merit browsing. For mild outdoor adventure, drive 9km (5½ miles) northeast of town on Route 337 and look for the **Fairmont Ridge Trail** ✦. Here you'll find 12km (7.5 miles) of hiking that will take you through ravines and into forests with old-growth trees. Nearby is the home base of **Shoreline Adventures** (✆ **902/863-5958**), which offers sea kayaking tours in the Antigonish Harbor area. For self-motivated travelers, sea kayak rentals with instructions on where to go are also available. Advance reservations are requested.

ESSENTIALS

GETTING THERE   Antigonish is on Route 104 (Trans-Canada Hwy.) 53km (33 miles) west of the Canso Causeway (the connection to Cape Breton Island).

VISITOR INFORMATION   The **Tourist Office** (✆ **902/863-4921**) is located at 56 West Rd. (Exit 32 on the Trans-Canada Hwy.). It's open daily from 9:30am to 8pm in summer, 9am to 6pm in June, September, and October.

SPECIAL EVENTS   The **Highland Games** ✦ have been staged in mid-July annually since 1861. What started as a community diversion has become an international event—and these are now the oldest continuously played Highland games in North America. This is the place for everything Scottish, from piping to dancing to tossing the caber. Contact the **Antigonish Highland Society** (✆ **902/863-4275**) for dates and details. Rooms are scarce during the 3-day games (Fri–Sun), so if you plan to attend, be sure to book well ahead. You can buy daily tickets or a 3-day pass.

Festival Antigonish ✦ (✆ **800/563-7529** or 902/867-3333) features a variety of plays and live performances held on the campus of St. Francis Xavier University from late June to late August. Shows range from locally written productions to Agatha Christie tales and *Rumpelstiltskin*. Tickets for children's productions are usually under C$10 (US$9/£5); tickets for adult performances range from C$10 to C$27 (US$9–US$24/ £5–£14).

WHERE TO STAY

Antigonish is conveniently located just off the Trans-Canada Highway and is the last town of any consequence before you reach Cape Breton Island. As such, it's home to

---

⸢ Fun Fact **The Name Game**

The name Antigonish (correctly pronounced "an-*tee*-gun-ish" . . . I think) creates some contention among linguists. In the original native dialect it means either "five-forked rivers of fish" or "place where the branches are torn off by bears gathering beechnuts." There's no consensus.

a number of chain motels, both in town and on the strip outside of town. If nightfall is overtaking you and you're pushing for Cape Breton, I'd suggest overnighting here and pushing onward early the next morning. Port Hastings and Port Hawkesbury—the first two towns you will pass through on Cape Breton—also have a slew of chain motels, but both towns tend toward the sprawling and charmless. Antigonish is a better choice for staging an assault on the island, and has better restaurants to boot.

Budget travelers can book a no-frills dorm room at **St. Francis Xavier University** (✆ **902/867-2855** or 877/STAY-AT-X) from May through August. Rooms are mostly simple and share hallway washrooms, but they include all the basics: linens, pillows, towels, and soap. Rates are about C$50 (US$45/£25) for two, including tax, with apartments going for around C$115 to C$145 (US$104–US$131/£58–£73). Four-bedroom apartments are also for rent. All-you-can-eat meals are available in the Morrison Dining Hall; figure on about C$5 (US$4.50/£2.50) for breakfast or C$10 (US$9/£5) for dinner. If you're looking for a room and it's after business hours, head to the Security Office in the basement of MacKinnon Hall and plead. I mean, ask.

At the west edge of town on the Trans-Canada, you'll find the **Chateau Motel,** 112 Post Rd. (✆ **877/339-8544** or 902/863-4842), which is unexciting, but in a good way. It has 16 rooms and cottages and a laundromat on the premises. Rates are C$69 to C$99 (US$62–US$89/£35–£50) for two.

Maritime Inn Antigonish   The basic, modern Maritime Inn Antigonish has benefited from new management and renovation. The rooms here are comfortable and clean, if unexceptional. The best thing about the place? Its location right on Antigonish's Main Street, where you can easily walk to the city's best restaurant (Sunshine on Main; see below) and take care of your basic shopping needs without getting back in that car you've been caged up in for the past 2 days. A restaurant on the premises—Main Street Café and Lounge—serves three meals daily.

158 Main St., Antigonish, NS B2G 2B7. ✆ **877/768-3969** or 902/863-4001. Fax 902/863-2672. www.maritime inns.com/antigonish. 32 units. C$105–C$175 (US$95–US$158/£53–£88) double. AE, DC, DISC, MC, V. Take Exit 33 off the Trans-Canada; follow Church St. to Main St. and turn right. **Amenities:** Restaurant. *In room:* A/C, TV, dataport (some units), coffeemaker.

WHERE TO DINE
Lobster Treat *Kids* SEAFOOD   Housed in a red-shingle former schoolhouse (note the original hanging lamps) just west of town on the Trans-Canada Highway, Lobster Treat has been doing seafood justice for the past quarter-century. It's not fancy, and it features the usual family-restaurant decor like potted plants and mauve carpeting. But the seafood here is fresh, the service friendly. The menu ranges from the traditional Nova Scotia boiled lobster dinner (which most people seem to order) to surf-and-turf combos to a few spicy seafood concoctions. You can get haddock just about anywhere in the Maritimes, but here it's soaked in lemon, lime juice, and olive oil and seasoned with oregano before being pan-fried or broiled. Complete meals for kids are available for under C$5 (US$4.50/£2.50), and the place also serves pasta, chicken, and steaks for landlubbers. But come on, now—it's not called Chicken Treat, right? You know what to do.

241 Post Rd. (Rte. 104). ✆ **902/863-5465.** Reservations not necessary. Main courses C$7.95–C$30 (US$7.15–US$27/£4–£15) at dinner; most dishes under C$20 (US$18/£10). AE, DC, MC, V. Daily 11am–10pm. Closed late Dec to mid-Apr.

Sunshine on Main Café & Bistro ✿ ECLECTIC   You'll need to detour a bit off the Trans-Canada Highway and venture downtown, but it's worth it if you're in the mood for simple but creative bistro fare offered at attractive prices. The interior is dominated by a large and lovely wall mural, the other walls painted a cool lemon-sherbet yellow. The creative lunch menu includes a healthy selection of sandwiches and salads. Come evening, the selections expand and get fancier, with an emphasis on pastas (such as fettuccine mixed with various kinds of fish, or linguine with roasted veggies and baby clams). There's also a good selection of grilled steaks, thin-crust pizzas, and chicken and fish dishes such as parchment paper-steamed filet of tilapia and a chicken piccata.

332 Main St. © 902/863-5851. Reservations recommended. Main courses C$8–C$14 (US$7.20–US$13/£4–£7) at lunch, C$14–C$23 (US$13–US$21/£7–£12) at dinner. AE, DC, MC, V. Sun–Thurs 7am–9:30pm; Fri–Sat 7:30am–10pm.

11 Cape Breton Island ★★★

Isolated and craggy Cape Breton Island—Nova Scotia's northernmost landmass—should be high on the list of don't-miss destinations for travelers, especially those with an adventurous bent. The island's chief draw is **Cape Breton Highlands National Park,** far north on the island's western lobe. But there's also the historic fort at **Louisbourg** and scenic **Bras d'Or Lake,** the inland saltwater lake that nearly cleaves the island in two. Above all, there are the drives: It's hard to find a road that's not a scenic route in Cape Breton. By turns the vistas are wild and dramatic, then settled and pastoral.

When traveling on the island, be alert to the cultural richness. Just as southern Nova Scotia was largely settled by English Loyalists fleeing the United States after they lost the War of Independence, Cape Breton was principally settled by Highland Scots whose families came out on the wrong side of rebellions against the crown. You can still see that heritage in the accents of elders in some of the more remote villages, and in the great popularity of Scottish-style folk music.

You'll often hear references to the **Cabot Trail** ★★★ when on the island. This is the official designation for the 300km (186-mile) roadway around the northwest part of the island, which encompasses the national park. It's named after John Cabot, who many believe first set foot on North American soil near Cape North. (However, many disagree, especially in Newfoundland.)

If you're in a hurry, you might do well to base yourself in Baddeck, which is centrally located (if a bit twee) and offers the most accommodations and restaurants. It's well positioned for day excursions to the island's two best attractions: the national park and the reconstructed historic settlement of Louisbourg. The southeastern portion of the island—near Isle Madame and Port Hawkesbury—can be beautiful in parts, but isn't nearly as inviting as the rest of the island. I would encourage you to focus more on the west and central sections given a short amount of time. One more thing: If you've got golf clubs and you enjoy a challenge, definitely bring 'em here.

For your reading pleasure (or at least ease), I've divided Cape Breton into two sections: Cape Breton Island and Cape Breton Highlands National Park. For information on adventures in the park itself, jump ahead to the next section.

ESSENTIALS

GETTING THERE   Cape Breton is connected to the mainland via the Canso Causeway, a 24m-wide (79-ft.), 65m-deep (213-ft.), 1,290m-long (4,232-ft.) stone causeway built in 1955 with 10 million tons of rock. (You can see a half-mountain, the other half of which was sacrificed for the cause, as you approach the island on the Trans-Canada Hwy.) The causeway is 262km (163 miles) from the New Brunswick border at Amherst, 272km (169 miles) from Halifax.

VISITOR INFORMATION   Nine tourist information centers dot the island. The best stocked (and a much-recommended first stop) is the bustling **Port Hastings Info Centre** (© **902/625-4201**), located on your right just after crossing the Canso Causeway. It's open daily from 8am to 8:30pm most of the year and closed from January through late April.

SPECIAL EVENTS   **Celtic Colours** ✿✿✿ (© **877/285-2321** or 902/562-6700; www.celtic-colours.com) is a big annual music shindig timed to approximate the peak of the lovely highland foliage. Few tourists know about it—until now, that is—and the concentration of local Celtic musicians getting together for good times and music beneath lovely foliage is simply astounding if you're into this sort of thing. It usually begins around the second week of October and lasts a full foot-stompin', penny-whistlin', fiddle-playin' week. The musical performances, by such international stars as the Chieftains—or, even better, the up-and-coming *next* Chieftains—are the obvious highlight, though they can cost as much as C$60 (US$54/£30) per person for a real headline act. More typical ceilidh nights (see below) cost about C$20 (US$18/£10), and popular local performers sell out months in advance; call well ahead if you've got your heart set on some particular act or another. Otherwise, just buy a ticket to anything. You almost can't go wrong.

MABOU & VICINITY ✿✿

The little village of Mabou (pop. 600) sits on a deep, protected inlet along the island's western shore. This former coal-mining town has made itself over as a lobster-fishing town, though you don't come here for crustaceans; instead, scenery and culture beckon. Attractive drives and bike rides are easy to find in the area; almost any road you choose will yield opportunities to break out the camera or just lean against your vehicle and enjoy the panorama. The town itself consists of a short main street, a clump of homes, a gas station, a few eateries and services, and (if you can find it) a scenic little beach.

But there's a hidden bonus to the area, giving it an importance disproportionate to its size: Local residents are strongly oriented toward **music,** even more so than is usual on already-musical Cape Breton Isle. The local kids, nearly all of Scots descent, grow up playing instruments, singing, and dancing; amazingly, this tiny town has produced not only several international hit Celtic music acts, but also the current premier of Nova Scotia (Rodney MacDonald), a former step dancer and fiddler elected to the post in February 2006 at the age of just 34.

Evening entertainment here revolves around fiddle playing, square dancing, or the traditional gathering of musicians and storytellers known as a **ceilidh** ✿✿✿ (pronounced *kay*-lee). These events take place in pubs, civic buildings, outdoors, people's homes . . . anywhere.

To find out where things are going on, your best bet is to stop by the village grocery store and **The Mull** pub across the road (see below) and scope out the bulletin boards there. You might also check out the calendar for the **Strathspey Place Theatre** (© **902/945-5300;** www.strathspeyplace.com) on Route 19. This is a more formal place, but it does serve up Celtic music. Tickets for performances generally run C$15 to C$20 (US$14–US$18/£7.50–£10) per person.

In a handsome valley between Mabou and Inverness is the distinctive post-and-beam **Glenora Distillery** ✿ (© **800/839-0491** or 902/258-2662). This modern distillery—said to be North America's only single-malt whiskey producer—began producing spirits from a pure local stream in 1990 and began selling it in 2000; they'll

tell you that the Cape Breton water is what makes all the difference and is the reason the owner chose to put the factory here—seemingly in the middle of nowhere. Glenora has since modified the process slightly to employ Kentucky bourbon casks, which its distillers believe impart a mellower taste to the spirit than the traditionally used sherry casks.

Production runs take place in the fall, but tours of the facility are offered throughout the year. Tours cost C$7 (US$6.30/£3.50) and last about a half-hour (offered daily 9am–5pm), culminating in free samples; they also conveniently end near the gift shop, where you can buy local music CDs, gift glasses, and even bottles of the whisky itself for about C$80 (US$72/£40) a pop. The owner can't call the product Scotch, by the way, since it isn't made in Scotland (hence "Canadian single malt whiskey")—but that's what it is. Swing by and savor this newer contribution to the island's lore.

The distillery complex also includes an adjoining **restaurant** (open late June to late Oct) and a nine-room **hotel** with rooms and some pretty spiffy chalets with knockout views on a hillside overlooking the valley (see below); traditional music is often scheduled for weekends or evenings in the contemporary pub.

WHERE TO STAY

Duncreigan Country Inn   The Duncreigan occupies a wooded bluff just across the bridge from the village. Modern and airy, it was built in 1991 by two wayward Connecticut Yankees and mixes contemporary with traditional stylings. Guest rooms are located in the main lodge and an outbuilding known as the Spring House (connected via boardwalk). Many rooms are furnished with Nova Scotian antiques, with headboards creatively designed by a local artisan to match the furnishings, and are decorated in dark, burgundy tones. There's no charge to use the inn's bikes or canoe, and dinners are served nightly from July through mid-October.

Rte. 19 (P.O. Box 59), Mabou, NS B0E 1X0. ✆ 800/840-2207. Fax 902/945-2206. www.duncreigan.ca. 8 units. C$120–C$195 (US$108–US$176/£60–£98) double. Rates include continental breakfast. MC, V. **Amenities:** Restaurant (seasonal); free bikes and canoes. *In room:* A/C, TV, fridge (2 units).

Glenora Inn & Distillery 🍴🍴   So, when was the last time you spent the night at a distillery? This distiller of single-malt whiskey added nine modern rooms in a building next to the pub (which in turn is located next to the actual distillery). It all has the feel of being in a remote vale in the Scottish highlands. The architecture is contemporary yet rustic, but the real attraction is easy access to said pub and restaurant on the premises, which often features live performers from the area. Honeymooners will appreciate the half-dozen modern chalets, located on the hills overlooking the distillery: Each has a Jacuzzi, satellite TV, and a wonderful view of the mist-covered valley below. (Do be prepared for a bone-rattling ride up the hill on a gravel road.) These chalets are available in one-, two-, or three-bedroom configurations.

Rte. 19, Glenville, NS B0E 1X0. ✆ 800/839-0491 or 902/258-2662. Fax 902/258-3572. www.glenoradistillery.com. 15 units. C$120–C$150 (US$108–US$135/£60–£75) double; C$175–C$240 (US$158–US$216/£88–£120) chalet. AE, MC, V. Closed mid-Oct to mid-May. **Amenities:** Restaurant; bar. *In room:* TV, Jacuzzi (some units).

Haus Treuburg Country Inn and Cottages 🍴   Located a few miles from Mabou in the undistinguished oceanside fishing village of Port Hood, Haus Treuburg is a handsome Queen Anne–style home dating from 1914. The three guest rooms in the main building (one is a suite) are nicely furnished in a spare style, with down duvets and a lot of wood. As nice as they are, though, the better deals are the small two-bedroom cottages behind the house, each with a private deck, an ocean view, and a gas barbecue. German and Italian specialties are featured in the two downstairs dining rooms. Dinner is served at one seating, and it might include beef stroganoff with spaetzle, or lobster bordelaise on homemade fettuccine. Four-course meals are about C$30 to C$34 (US$27–US$31/£15–£17) prix fixe. The German "Sunday morning breakfast" is available every morning.

175 Main St. (P.O. Box 92), Port Hood, NS B0E 2W0. ✆ 902/787-2116. Fax 902/787-3216. www.haustreuburg.com. 6 units. C$95–C$115 (US$86–US$104/£48–£58) double; C$135 (US$122/£68) cottage. Breakfast C$10 (US$9/£5) extra. AE, DC, MC, V. **Amenities:** 2 dining rooms; babysitting. *In room:* TV/VCR.

Mabou River Inn 🍴🍴 *Finds*   Located not far from the river and adjacent to the Mother of Sorrows Pioneer Shrine (dedicated to the settlers of the Mabou area), this former boarding school was converted twice, first into a winning youth hostel and then into this homey little inn just off the main road. Hosts Donna and David Cameron keep things running smoothly and dispense great advice; nature lovers will appreciate the opportunity to hike, kayak, fish, and mountain-bike on the scenic Ceilidh Trail using the inn's rental equipment, while night owls can stroll a few minutes across the bridge and into town to check out the local traditional music offerings that fill Mabou in summer. Note that while all nine of the main inn rooms come with their own private bathrooms, you have to put on your slippers and walk to get to seven of them. There are also three two-bedroom apartment suites good for families, since they come with TVs, VCRs, kitchens, and phones. The kitchen and dining room for guests are useful: At night the staff cooks up some good pizzas and serves beer and wine with them.

19 Southwest Ridge Rd. (P.O. Box 255), Mabou, NS B0E 1X0. © 888/627-9744 or 902/945-2356. Fax 902/945-2605. www.mabouriverinn.com. 12 units. C$75–C$99 (US$68–US$89/£38–£50) double; C$125–C$155 (US$113–US$140/£63–£78) suite. AE, MC, V. **Amenities:** Restaurant; bike and sea kayak rentals; game room. *In room:* TV/VCR (some units), kitchenette (some units), no phone (some units).

WHERE TO DINE

The Mull CAFE   Owned by the same folks who own the Duncreigan (see above), The Mull is a simple country deli that serves simple food. Lunches include such basics as seafood chowder, fish and chips, pasta, burgers, and deli-style sandwiches. After 5pm, the dinner menu kicks in, with such entrees as grilled halibut, a T-bone steak, and scallops in a light wine sauce. Don't expect to be wowed by fancy food; do expect a filling meal and good company. One bonus for nonsmokers: The dining is completely nonsmoking, a marked contrast with some of the other eating places in Mabou.

Rte. 19 (just north of the village), Mabou. © 902/945-2244. Reservations accepted for parties of 6 or more. Sandwiches C$5.50–C$8.50 (US$4.95–US$7.65/£2.75–£4.25); main courses C$13–C$22 (US$12–US$20/£6.50–£11). AE, MC, V. Daily 11am–8pm (from 7am summer and fall, closes 7pm in winter).

The Red Shoe Pub ★ *Finds* PUB FARE   You won't find a more local pub than "the Shoe," which was formerly operated by the famous Rankin family of musicians. The menu here features basic pub fare such as soups, salads, ribs, and wings; there are a few beers on tap, plus all the obvious bottles. The real highlight, though, is the frequent musical performances in the pub—the next Celtic music star might be playing for peanuts on the night you swing by. Be aware that the place is small and, when crowded, can get a bit claustrophobic; it helps to know a local, though the influx of summer tourists coming for music and beer keeps the mix interesting. With modern times has come another change: This is now a completely nonsmoking venue (even the patio), which was definitely not the case for many years here. A small kids' menu and a line of surprisingly upscale desserts like sticky toffee pudding, gingerbread, lemon pavlova with lemon curd, and berry cobbler have also been added.

Main St. (Hwy. 19), Mabou. © 902/945-2996. Meals C$5–C$12 (US$4.50–US$11/£2.50–£6). MC, V. Mon–Wed daily 11:30am–midnight; Thurs–Sat 11:30am–2am; Sun noon–midnight.

Shining Waters Bakery CAFE   This bakery, smack in the center of what passes for downtown, is a locals-only kind of place, with a simple menu of breakfast items and sandwiches and a cooler full of canned and bottled drinks. Don't come expecting atmosphere or service here; instead, you'll get a slightly hectic (and smoky) meal, elbow-to-elbow with the real Mabou.

11497 Main St., Mabou. © 902/945-2728. Meals C$2.25–C$8 (US$2.05–US$7.20/£1.15–£4). MC, V. June to mid-Oct Mon–Sat 6:30am–8pm, Sun 9am–8pm; shorter hours off season.

MARGAREE VALLEY ⸙

West of Baddeck and south of Chéticamp, the Margaree Valley region consists of the area from the village of Margaree Valley near the headwaters of the Margaree River to Margaree Harbor, down the river on Cape Breton's west coast. Some seven small communities are clustered along the valley floor, and it's a world apart from the rugged drama of the surf-battered coast—it's vaguely reminiscent of, say, the rolling farm country of upstate New York. The Cabot Trail gently rises and falls on the shoulders of rounded hills flanking the valley, offering views of the farmed floodplains and glimpses of the shining river. In autumn, the foliage here is often among eastern Canada's best.

The **Margaree River** has been accorded celebrity status in fishing circles—it's widely regarded as one of the most productive Atlantic salmon rivers in North America, and salmon have continued to return to spawn here in recent years, which is unfortunately not the case in many other waterways of Atlantic Canada. The river has been closed to all types of fishing except fly-fishing since the 1880s, and in 1991 it was designated a Canadian Heritage River.

Learn about the river's heritage at the **Margaree Salmon Museum** ⸙ (© 902/248-2848) in North East Margaree. The handsome building features a brief video about the life cycle of the salmon, and exhibits include fisherman photos by the score as well as antique rods (including one impressive 5m/16-footer), examples of poaching equipment, and hundreds of hand-tied salmon flies. Museum docents can help you find a guide to try your hand on the water; late spring and early fall are the best times to get a catch. The museum is open June to mid-October daily from 9am to 5pm. Admission is C$1 (US90¢/50p) adult, C25¢ (US25¢/15p) child. The whole area is best explored by slow and aimless driving, or by bike or canoe if you've brought one along with you.

Make a point of dropping by **Cape Breton Clay** ⸙⸙ (© 902/248-2467; www.capebretonclay.com), northeast of the salmon museum. Margaree Valley native Bell Fraser's work is truly unique. Fish, crab, lobster, starfish, ear-of-corn, and other motifs are worked into her platters and bowls in ways that will surprise and delight even pottery haters. Her colorful hand-painted lobster and starfish platters, for instance, bring a whole new interpretation to the serving plate, while Bell's fish-handled serving bowl is reminiscent of the Margaree's leaping, silvery trout. Open daily year-round from around 9am to 6pm, it's definitely worth a stop; pieces run from C$60 to C$300 (US$54–US$270/£30–£150). Don't miss the "Koop" next door, a place where real—and Bell's ceramic—chickens mingle. See it, believe it.

WHERE TO STAY

Normaway Inn and Cabins ⸙. Down a drive lined with Scotch pines, the Normaway is a throwback. It was built in 1928 and has been run by the same family since the 1940s; while it might have once been the sort of place you would run into gentlemen anglers dressed in tweed, it's neither a fishing resort nor a truly luxury getaway today. Instead, it appeals to families and honeymooners interested in fresh air, the sounds of crickets, the strain of pipes, and nothing more. Nine of the rooms on the 200-hectare (494-acre) property are situated in the main lodge; the first-floor rooms, which are larger and have corner windows for better ventilation, are probably best here. The cottages, with hardwood floors and spare interiors, are spread around the property but an easy walk to the main lodge. The oldest of these cottages were built in the 1940s and are a bit smaller and rougher around the edges; eight newer cottages have Jacuzzis, all but two have wood stoves, and some have two bedrooms. The dining room, decorated in a simple country farmhouse style, is known for its salmon and lamb, which is raised specially for the inn about 16km (10 miles) away. (No, those sheep wandering the property are not destined for your dinner plate.) The Normaway's strong suit is its laid-back evening entertainment, with events ranging from films to live performances—Acadian music, storytelling, local fiddling, and the like. A weekly square dance, held in the inn's barn, attracts hundreds of locals and tourists alike; there's a small fee to attend.

P.O. Box 121, Margaree Valley, NS B0E 2C0. (℃ **800/565-9463** or 902/248-2987. Fax 902/248-2600. www. normaway.com. 26 units. C$79–C$249 (US$71–US$224/£40–£125) double and cottage. Late-afternoon same-day booking discounts. Breakfast about C$11 (US$9.90/£5.50) extra. DC, MC, V. Closed late Oct to May. Pets allowed in cottages only. **Amenities:** Dining room; tennis court; free bikes. *In room:* No phone.

CHÉTICAMP ✫

The Acadian town of Chéticamp is the western gateway to Cape Breton Highlands National Park and the center for French-speaking culture on Cape Breton. The change is rather obvious as you drive northward from Margaree Harbour—the family names suddenly go from MacDonald to Doucet, and the cuisine turns on its head all at once.

The town itself is an assortment of restaurants, boutiques, and tourist establishments spread along Main Street, which closely hugs the harbor. A winding boardwalk follows the harbor's edge through much of town and offers a good spot to stretch your legs and get your bearings. (Chéticamp Island sits just across the water; the tall coastal hills of the national park are visible just up the coast.) This is an adequate stop for provisioning, topping off the gas tank, and finding shelter.

Chéticamp is noted worldwide for its hooked rugs, a craft perfected by early Acadian settlers. Those curious about the craft should allow time for a stop at Les Trois Pignons, which houses the **Elizabeth LeFort Gallery and Museum** (℃ **902/ 224-2642;** www.lestroispignons.com). It is located on Main Street in the north end of town and displays some 300 fine tapestries, many created by Elizabeth LeFort, who was Canada's premier rug-hooking artist for many decades until she passed away in 2005. It's open daily from 8am to 7pm in July and August, 9am to 5pm spring and fall, and 8:30am to 4:30pm in winter. Admission is C$4.50 (US$4.05/£2.25) adult, C$4 (US$3.60/£2) seniors, C$3.50 (US$3.15/£1.75) students, C$15 (US$14/£7.50) families, free for ages 12 and under.

In the 1930s, artisans formed the **Co-operative Artisanale de Chéticamp,** located at 5067 Main St. (℃ **902/224-2170**). A selection of hooked rugs—from the size of a drink coaster on up—are sold here, along with other trinkets and souvenirs. There's often a weaver or other craftsperson at work in the shop. A small museum downstairs (admission is free) chronicles the life and times of the early Acadian settlers and their descendants. It's closed from mid-October to May.

Several boat tour operators are based in Chéticamp Harbor. **Love Boat Seaside Whale and Nature Cruises** (℃ **800/959-4253** or 902/224-2400) sets out in search of whales, seals, and scenery, and has hydrophones on board for listening to any whales you may encounter. (No, Captain Stubing will not be your captain.)

The most pleasing drive or bike ride in the area is out to Chéticamp Island, connected to the mainland by road. Look for the turn south of town; the side road is just north of Flora's gift shop on the Cabot Trail.

WHERE TO STAY

A handful of motels service the thousands of travelers who pass through each summer. **Laurie's Motor Inn,** on Main Street (© **800/959-4253** or 902/224-2400), has more than 50 motel rooms in three buildings well situated right in town, with rates of C$99 to C$149 (US$89–US$134/£50–£75) double. The inn also manages some nicer suites and apartments around town; inquire if you're interested in something larger, coming with a family, staying a while, or need cooking facilities.

Parkview Motel   The basic yet comfortable Parkview's best claim is its location—within walking distance of the national park's visitor center and away from the hubbub of Chéticamp's downtown. Don't expect anything fancy and you won't be disappointed; at least it has cable television and recently upgraded bathrooms. There's a dining room and lounge in a separate building across the street, where the six newest rooms are located. These units offer additional amenities to the traveler, such as coffeemakers, refrigerators, and microwave ovens, unavailable in the main building.

Cabot Trail, Chéticamp, NS B0E 1H0. © **902/224-3232.** Fax 902/224-2596. www.parkviewresort.com. 17 units. C$75–C$109 (US$68–US$98/£38–£55) double. AE, MC, V. Closed mid-Oct to early May. **Amenities:** Dining room; bar; bike rentals. *In room:* A/C (some units), TV, fridge (some units), coffeemaker (some units).

Pilot Whale Chalets 🐾   These spare, modern cottages (constructed in 1997) each have two bedrooms and full housekeeping facilities, including microwaves. They may have a bit of an antiseptic condo air, but they are nevertheless well equipped with TVs and VCRs, gas barbecues for firing up steaks, coffeemakers, decks, and wood stoves; some even have Jacuzzis and fireplaces as well. The best feature, though, is the grand view northward toward the coastal mountains. (Cottage nos. 1, 2, 4, and 5 have the best vistas.) The lodge added apartments to the walkout basements beneath two of the cottages in 1999, which impinges slightly on the privacy of those both upstairs and down, and also added a three-bedroom cottage very recently.

Rte. 19, Chéticamp, NS B0E 1H0. © **902/224-1040.** Fax 902/224-1540. www.pilotwhales.com. 13 units. C$95–C$199 (US$86–US$179/£48–£100) double. AE, MC, V. *In room:* TV/VCR, kitchenette (some units), coffeemaker, Jacuzzi (some units), no phone.

WHERE TO DINE

La Boulangerie Aucoin (© **902/224-3220**) has been a staple of Chéticamp life since 1959. Located just off the Cabot Trail between the town and the national park (look for signs), the bakery is constantly restocking its shelves with fresh-baked goods; ask what's warm when you order at the counter. Among the options: croissants, scones, loaves of fresh bread, and berry pies. This is a recommended stop to fuel up on snack foods before setting off into the park.

For an informal and quick lunch in town, there's **L&M Chéticamp Seafoods, Ltd.** (© **902/224-1688**) on Main Street. It's a takeout spot with a few picnic tables inside and outside. It's best known for its fish and chips, but also offers hamburgers and chicken fingers. If you're camping in the park, this is also the spot for fresh fish for the grill. It's open from 8am to 8pm daily May to mid-September.

Restaurant Acadien ACADIAN   This restaurant is attached to a crafts shop on the south side of town (the Co-operative Artisanale; see above) and has the uncluttered feel of a cafeteria. Servers here wear costumes inspired by traditional Acadian dress, and the menu draws on local Acadian traditions. Look for *fricot* (a kind of chicken-and-potato soup), stewed potatoes, and the meat pies for which this region is renowned. Also on the menu: blood pudding, for the brave, and butterscotch pie.

15067 Main St. 🕾 **902/224-3207.** Reservations recommended. Breakfast C$3.50–C$5 (US$3.15–US$4.50/ £1.75–£2.50); lunch and dinner C$3.50–C$17 (US$3.15–US$15/£1.75–£8.50). AE, MC, V. Daily 7am–9pm. Closed Nov to mid-May.

PLEASANT BAY ⭑

At the north end of the Cabot Trail's exhilarating run along the western cliffs, the road turns inland at the village of Pleasant Bay. The attractive, active fishing harbor, protected by a man-made jetty, is a short walk off the Cabot Trail and sits at the base of rounded, forested mountains that plunge down to the sea.

The newly opened **Whale Interpretive Center** (🕾 **902/224-1411**), built on a rise overlooking the harbor, features exhibits to help explain why the waters offshore are so rich with marine life—not to mention life-size models (yes, really) of some of the local whales. It's open June through mid-October from 9am to 5pm; admission is C$4.50 (US$4.05/£2.25) adults, C$3.50 (US$3.15/£1.75) children and seniors, C$14 (US$13/£7) families.

Whale-watching tours are offered daily June through mid-October from the harbor by Capt. Mark Timmons of **Capt. Mark's Whale and Seal Cruise** (🕾 **888/754-5112** or 902/224-1316; www.whaleandsealcruise.com). The 2½-hour cruise on the 42-ft. *Bay Hookup* provides unrivaled glimpses at the rugged coast both north and south, and often a close-up look at whales (almost always pilot whales, frequently finbacks and minkes, occasionally humpbacks). The boat has a hydrophone on board, so you can hear the plaintive whale calls underwater. Trips are C$25 (US$23/£13) per adult, C$12 (US$11/£6) children, and reservations are encouraged. The outfit runs three to five tours daily during the season. Zodiac sea tours are also offered in those 21-foot inflatable boats, though you'll spend more—and get considerably wetter—if you take one.

As you entered town you may have noticed the **Timmons Folk Art Studio** (🕾 **902/224-3575**) near the fork in the road. Inside and out you'll find colorful, whimsical folk art by Reed Timmons (Capt. Mark Timmons's cousin). Reed carves fish, cows, seagulls, and sailors that are rustic and visually arresting.

If you bear right at the "Y" and continue northward, the road wraps around the coastal hills and turns to gravel after 5km (3 miles). Keep going another 4km (2½ miles). Here you'll come to a spectacular **coastal hiking trail** ⭑⭑, which runs to **Pollett's Cove,** about 10km (6 miles) up the coast. A dozen families once lived here; all that remain are two cemeteries. The cove and the trail are on private land, but hiking and other quiet recreation are allowed.

CAPE NORTH ⭑

Cape North is a much-recommended detour for adventurous travelers hoping to get off the trafficked Cabot Trail. Folks say that Cape North is much like the Cabot Trail used to be 20 or 30 years ago, before the travel magazines started trumpeting its glories and large numbers of tourists started showing up. It's worth the extra driving and backtracking.

Cape North is reached via a turnoff at the northern tip of the Cabot Trail, after you descend into the Aspy Valley. You'll soon come to Cabot Landing Provincial Park, where local lore claims that John Cabot first made landfall in North America in 1497. You can debate the issue near the Cabot statue or take a long walk on the lovely 3km (2-mile) ochre-sand beach fronting Aspy Bay. The views of the remote coast are noteworthy.

The road winds onward to the north; at a prominent fork, you can veer right to Bay St. Lawrence, where you can sign up for a summertime whale-watching trip. Try

---

(Moments **Baywatch**

The 8km (5-mile) trip from Bay St. Lawrence to Meat Cove is ideal for a mountain bike ride if you thought to bring one along. This is one of very few places in Canada where you can pedal and whale-watch at the same time—a terrific daily double, to be sure.

Captain Cox's Whale Watch (© 888/346-5556 or 902/383-2981) or **Oshan Whale Cruise** (© 877/383-2883). Both offer 2½-hour whale-watching cruises for about C$25 (US$23/£13) adults and C$12 (US$11/£6) children; the *Oshan* folks can also take you deep-sea fishing (and clean your fish for cooking afterward), and their cruise schedule operates longest, usually until the end of October.

Turn left at the fork and continue along a remarkable cliffside road to Meat Cove. The last 5km (3 miles) track along a dirt road that runs high along the shoulders of coastal mountains, then drops into shady ravines to cross brooks and rivers. The road ends at this rough-hewn settlement that's been home to fishermen (seemingly all named McClellan) for generations.

There's a private campground here, the **Meat Cove Campground** ⚡ (© 902/383-2379), which is open June through October. The 25 campsites here may have the most dramatic ocean views of any campground in Nova Scotia; they start at about C$20 (US$18/£10) apiece. Whether you're staying or not, ask owner Kenneth McClellan about the hiking trails in the hills above the campground (there's a day-use fee for noncampers).

WHERE TO STAY

Four Mile Beach Inn ⚡ (Value   This handsome inn, which opened in 1998, has quickly become one of the more interesting hotels on Cape Breton. Located in an old inn and general store dating from 1898, it's run by John Cuthbert and Janet Conner, who have done a superb job fixing the place up, making it feel comfortable and historic yet not cloying. The old general store has been spruced up and stocked with (not-for-sale) items that turned up in the basement and attic; two parlors are perfect for evening reading or card playing, and there's sometimes traditional Maritime music played live or piped throughout the downstairs. The breakfast is all you can eat, and tasty. Two of the regular rooms share a bathroom, while another has a private bathroom across the hall; the best of the lot might be no. 2, a snug spot with low eaves, a ceiling fan, and a great bathroom with wainscoting and a tub fit for serious relaxing. The innkeepers recently opened a small cafe that serves meals summer and fall. They also rent kayaks, canoes, and bikes; you can paddle North Bay after a short stroll down a dirt road through their backyard. This place offers good value for the money.

R.R. No. 1 (Box 3), Cape North, NS B0C 1G0. © 888/503-5551 or 902/383-2282. www.fourmilebeachinn.com. 8 units. C$79–C$169 (US$80–US$152/£40–£85) double. Rates include full breakfast. AE, MC, V. Closed mid-Oct to mid-June. Pets in efficiency only. **Amenities:** Canoe, kayak, and bike rentals. *In room:* Kitchenette (some units), coffeemaker (some units), safe (some units), no phone.

Markland Coastal Resort   The Markland is sited on 28 hectares (69 acres) where a meandering river meets a long sand beach fronting spectacular Aspy Bay. It's hard to imagine a more idyllic spot, especially when the morning sun illuminates the coastal range to the north. The resort features two kinds of accommodations, both furnished in uncluttered style: One- and two-bedroom cottages have kitchens, sitting areas, and porches—most with views of the bay—though some visitors have complained that some are dated. Motel units are narrow and a bit dark, though air-conditioning was recently added. Canoes are available to explore the river, or you can linger on shore. The resort's dining room offers a contrast of modern furniture in a rustic setting with ocean views; it serves three meals daily, including the best dinners in northern Cape Breton. The Markland also hosts cultural performances at the gemlike **Octagon** ⚜, a performance space on the grounds shaped like a . . . you guessed it. Friday nights typically feature Cape Breton music and traditional tunes or ceilidhs; on Sunday, there's a chamber music series.

Cabot Trail, Dingwall, NS B0C 1G0. ⓒ 800/872-6084 or 902/383-2246. Fax 902/484-5762. www.marklandresort. com. 12 units, 13 cottages. C$99–C$139 (US$89–US$125/£50–£70) double; C$169–C$289 (US$152–US$260/ £85–£145) log cabins. Ask about packages. Children 16 and under stay free in parent's room. AE, DC, DISC, MC, V. Closed mid-Oct to mid-June. "Well-behaved pets" allowed. **Amenities:** Outdoor pool; bike rentals; canoes; game room; babysitting. *In room:* A/C (some units).

WHERE TO DINE

For upscale dining, see the **Markland Coastal Resort,** above.

Morrison's Restaurant ⚜ *(Value)* SEAFOOD   Morrison's is a favorite with locals and travelers, and with good reason. It serves good food at a good price. It's a comfortable, rustic spot with old wood floors, baskets hanging from the ceiling, moose antlers on the wall . . . you get the picture. The menu tends toward comfort food, with selections such as fettuccine and tasty beer-battered fish. Other options might include braised halibut in a dill cream sauce or a sinful "Cape Islander"—consisting of scallops and lobster in velouté sauce sandwiched between halibut and salmon, served with hollandaise. Desserts are traditional: cheesecake, gingerbread, bumbleberry pie, and the like. Bus tours often stop here, however—and when they do, the service can sometimes be aggravatingly slow for smaller groups of travelers.

Cabot Trail, Dingwall. ⓒ 902/383-2051. Main courses C$5.95–C$11 (US$5.35–US$9.90/£3–£5.50) lunch, C$11–C$17 (US$9.90–US$15/£5.50–£8.50) dinner. AE, MC, V. Daily 8am–9pm. Closed late Nov to mid-May.

WHITE POINT & NEIL'S HARBOUR

From South Harbor (near Dingwall) you can drive on the speedy Cabot Trail inland to Ingonish, or stick to the coast on an alternate route that arcs past White Point, continues onward to Neil's Harbour, then links back up with the Cabot Trail. If the weather's agreeable, the **coast road** ⚜⚜ is the recommended route. Initially, the road climbs upward along abrupt and jagged cliffs with sweeping views of Aspy Bay; at White Point, you can veer out to the tip for even more expansive views of the coast.

The road then tracks inland before emerging at **Neil's Harbour** ⚜, a postcard-perfect fishing village. On a rocky knob located on the far side of the bay is a square red-and-white lighthouse (now an ice-cream parlor). Just beyond that is the **Chowder House** ⚜ (ⓒ 902/336-2463), a low-key, pine-paneled takeout restaurant that specializes in excellent, stuffed-with-seafood chowder and platters of good deep-fried fish and crab cakes. Meals cost about C$4.50 to C$16 (US$4.05–US$14/£2.25–£8). It's open as late as 8pm some nights. There's a grassy area outside the restaurant for picnicking as you admire the panorama of the rocky shoreline shaded with pinkish-orange rock. Consider yourself warned, though: It's a popular spot with bus tours. From Neil's Harbour, it's just a 2-minute drive back to the Cabot Trail.

INGONISH 𝒢

The Ingonish area includes a gaggle of similarly named towns (Ingonish Centre, Ingonish Ferry, South Ingonish Harbor), which together have a population of 1,300 or so. Like Chéticamp on the peninsula's east side, Ingonish serves as a gateway to the national park and is home to a park visitor information center and a handful of motels and restaurants. Oddly, there's really no critical mass of services here—instead, they're spread along a lengthy stretch of the Cabot Trail, so there's never any real sense of having arrived in town. You pass a liquor store, some shops, a bank, a post office, and a handful of cottages. And that's it—suddenly you're there, in the park. Highlights in the area include a sandy beach (near Keltic Lodge) good for some chilly splashing around, and a number of shorter hiking trails. (See "Cape Breton Highlands National Park," later in this chapter.)

For golfers, the windswept **Highlands Links course** 𝒢𝒢𝒢 (© **800/441-1118** or 902/285-2600; www.highlandslinksgolf.com)—adjacent to the Keltic Lodge (see "Where to Stay," below) but under completely separate management—is considered one of the best in Nova Scotia, if not all of Atlantic Canada. Rounds cost about C$88 (US$79/£44) per golfer, less if you tee off in the late afternoon, in spring and fall, or if you're a teenager or child. Ask about packages whenever booking a hotel room in the area, and be sure to reserve your tee times well in advance—it's popular.

South of Ingonish, the **Cabot Trail** 𝒢𝒢𝒢 climbs and descends the hairy 300m-high (984-ft.) promontory of Cape Smokey, which explodes into panoramic views from the top. At the highest point, there's a provincial park where you can cool your engine and admire the views. An 11km (6.8-mile) hiking trail studded with unforgettable viewpoints leads to the tip of the cape along the high bluffs.

Sea kayak tours are offered in protected Ingonish Harbor by burly and gregarious raconteur Mike Crimp of **Cape Breton SeaCoast Adventures** (© **877/929-2800** or 902/929-2800). Both full-day and half-day tours are offered from June through October, and both are designed for novices who've never set bottom in a kayak. You'll look for whales but are more likely to spot bald eagles or blue herons. The landscape hereabouts is dramatic, with Cape Smokey rising powerfully to the south, Middle Head to the north, and marsh grasses serving as home to a mix of shorebirds.

WHERE TO STAY

A number of serviceable cottage courts and motels are located in this area. (If booking by phone, be sure to find out which Ingonish you're staying in; the town names around here all sound the same, leading to possible confusion.)

In addition to the choices below, **Glenghorm Beach Resort** in Ingonish (© **800/565-5660** or 902/285-2049) has about 75 units on a spacious 8-hectare (20-acre) property that fronts a sandy beach. Some rooms feature painted cinderblock walls, and the decorating is a bit dated, with avocado or gold hues that recall a bygone era. Options include motel rooms and efficiencies, along with cottages and some elaborate suites. Prices are C$80 to C$129 (US$72–US$116/£40–£65) for the motel rooms, C$120 to C$189 (US$108–US$170/£60–£95) for the cottages, and C$195 to C$399 (US$176–US$359/£98–£200) for the suites.

Castle Rock Country Inn   The Castle Rock Country Inn sits boldly on a high hill overlooking Ingonish Harbor—a little too boldly, say some locals, who feel the inn's bulldozers greatly altered the pristine view of the hillside flanking Cape Smokey. The inn opened in 1997 and is a square two-story lodge clad in wood shingles. The dozen rooms and one suite are surprisingly basic—furnished the way you might expect in a midrange chain hotel. Rooms facing north have outstanding ocean views and cost extra. The inn's **dining room** ⭐ has, no surprise, stunning water views and features a menu of what might be called "new traditional cuisine." Entrees on a given night could include maple-glazed salmon, mussels with pasta, and cheese crepes with salad.

39339 Cabot Trail, Ingonish Ferry, NS B0C 1L0. ⓒ **888/884-7625** or 902/285-2700. Fax 902/285-2525. www. ingonish.com/castlerock. 15 units. C$114–C$173 (US$103–US$156/£57–£87) double. Packages available. AE, MC, V. **Amenities:** Restaurant; bar; laundry service. *In room:* TV, hair dryer, iron, no phone.

Keltic Lodge Resort and Spa ⭐ The Keltic Lodge is reached after a series of dramatic flourishes: You pass through a grove of white birches, cross an isthmus atop cliffs, then arrive at a vaguely Tudor-looking resort. The views are extraordinary. Owned and operated by the province, this resort is comfortable without being slick, worn without being threadbare. Some rooms are painted in a soothing mint green that was popular in the 1940s; most are furnished rather plainly with run-of-the-mill motel furniture. (You might expect more for the price.) The cottages are set amid birches and have three bedrooms each, but you share some space with other travelers; if you rent just one bedroom, you will share a common living room with two other sets of guests. Some units are located in the more modern Inn at Keltic building a few hundred meters away, which has better views though a more sterile character. (One reader wrote to lament the inadequate soundproofing in this annex, recommending an upstairs room here to avoid hearing heavy footfalls.) There is also a recently opened Aveda-products spa on the grounds. The food in the **Purple Thistle main dining room** ⭐⭐ (open 6–9pm nightly) is among the best on the island; the excellent fixed-price dinner menu—which is included in your room rates—offers selections such as prime rib, lemon-pepper salmon filet, and the like. A less formal option is the newer Atlantic Restaurant, with its high post-and-beam ceiling, views, and lighter fare.

Middle Head Peninsula, Ingonish Beach, NS B0C 1L0. ⓒ **800/565-0444** or 902/285-2880. Fax 902/285-2859. www.kelticlodge.ca. 72 standard units, 10 cottage units. C$175–C$442 (US$158–US$398/£88–£221) double and cottage. Rates include breakfast and dinner. Packages available. AE, DC, DISC, MC, V. Closed late Oct to late May. **Amenities:** 2 restaurants; outdoor pool; golf course; spa; game room; laundry service. *In room:* A/C (2 units), TV (most units), fridge (some units), hair dryer, iron, no phone.

ST. ANN'S

Traveling clockwise around the Cabot Trail, you'll face a choice when you come to the juncture of Route 312. One option is to take the side road to the Englishtown ferry and cross over St. Ann's Harbor in slow but dramatic fashion. The crossing of the fjordlike bay is very scenic, and takes just about 2 minutes (when there's no line). The ferry runs around the clock, and the fare is nominal.

In Englishtown, one of Nova Scotia's more unique museums is the **Giant MacAskill Museum,** on Route 312 (ⓒ **902/929-2925**). This spot honors the memory of local Angus MacAskill, who lived from 1825 to 1863. At 7 feet 9 inches tall and weighing 425 pounds, MacAskill was the tallest natural giant who ever lived, and, according to the 1981 *Guinness Book of World Records,* the strongest man in history. Children will enjoy sitting on his massive chair (if they can reach it) and trying on his sweater. The replica coffin that MacAskill was buried in is astounding, as are many of the stories about him. The museum is open daily mid-June to mid-September from 9am to 6pm. Admission is C$1 (US90¢/50p) adults, C75¢ (US70¢/40p) seniors and youth, C50¢ (US45¢/25p) under 12.

Your second option for making the Cabot Trail circuit is not to cross via ferry but rather to stay on the Trail, heading down along the western shore of St. Ann's Harbor. A good launching point for exploring the waters is North River, where kayak guide Angelo Spinazzola offers tours through his **North River Kayak Tours** (✆ **888/ 865-2925** or 902/929-2628) from mid-May through mid-October. The full-day tour (C$99/US$89/£50 per person) includes a steamed-mussel lunch on the shore; there's also a romance tour offered, where couples camp overnight on a remote beach—the owner cooks dinner, then departs for the night. Most every trip, says Spinazzola, includes sightings of a bald eagle or two. Kayaks can also be rented.

In the village of St. Ann's you'll pass the **Gaelic College of Celtic Arts and Crafts** ⚘ (✆ **902/295-3411**), located 1km (⅔ mile) off the Trans-Canada Highway at Exit 11. The school was informally founded in 1938, when a group of area citizens began offering instruction in Gaelic language in a one-room log cabin. Today, both the campus and the curriculum have expanded significantly, with classes now offered in bagpiping, fiddle, Highland dance, weaving, spinning, and Scottish history.

The 140-hectare (346-acre) campus is home to the Great Hall of Clans, where visitors can get a quick lesson in Scottish culture. A number of exhibits provide answers to many questions, such as, what is the deal with tartan plaid, how did Scotsmen get reputations as fierce warriors, and what do Scotsmen really wear under a kilt? (Alas, the question "Is bagpiping really music?" is not addressed.) Poet Robert Burns's walking stick is on display, and you can buy intriguing clan histories as well. The Hall of Clans is open daily June through September from 9am to 5pm; admission is about C$5 (US$4.50/£2.50) per adult, C$4 (US$3.60/£2) students, C$15 (US$14/£7.50) families. A campus crafts shop has shelves full of Gaelic items, including bolts of tartan plaid and tapes of traditional music. Live performances are also offered throughout the summer; call ahead or ask at the crafts shop for a schedule.

WHERE TO STAY

Luckenbooth Bed & Breakfast   Built in 1999, this modern, log-accented B&B has three bedrooms and is nicely located on 300m (984 ft.) of wooded shore frontage (with a trail down to the water). Guests have the run of several common areas, including the main living room with its cozy fireplace and soaring cathedral ceiling and a yellow-tartan-themed basement room with satellite television, a VCR, and games. (It's decorated in the clan tartans of proprietors Frances and Wayne McClure; Frances is also a bagpiper.) The guest rooms each have modern furnishings. The best of the lot is no. 3 upstairs, with hardwood floors, views of the bay, and a sitting area just outside the door. The other two rooms are in the walkout basement and feature cork floors. The inn has a no-shoes-inside policy, and slippers are furnished to guests. Breakfast is served by candlelight, a nice touch.

R.R. 4, Baddeck, St. Ann's, Cabot Trail, NS B0E 1B0. ✆ **877/654-2357** or 902/929-2722. Fax 902/929-2503. 3 units. C$120–C$140 (US$108–US$126/£60–£70) double. Rates include breakfast. MC, V. *In room:* No phone.

BADDECK

Although Baddeck (pronounced *Bah*-deck) is at a distance from the national park, it's often considered the de facto "capital" of the Cabot Trail. The town offers the widest selection of hotels and accommodations along the whole loop, an assortment of restaurants, and a handful of useful services like grocery stores and laundromats. Baddeck is also famed as the summer home of inventor Alexander Graham Bell, memorialized at a national historic site here. It's a compact and easy town to explore by foot, scenically located on the shores of Bras d'Or Lake and within striking distance of the fortress at Louisbourg. That makes it the most practical base for those with limited vacation time who are planning to drive the Cabot Trail in 1 day (figure on 6–8 hr.).

If, however, your intention is to spend a few days exploring the hiking trails, bold headlands, and remote coves of the national park (which I recommend), you're better off finding a base farther north; the town's single street, frankly, can get claustrophobically packed with tourists and tour buses, and beyond Bell's home there's little of lingering interest here.

The useful **Baddeck Welcome Center** (© **902/295-1911**) is located just south of the village at the intersection of routes 105 and 205. It's open daily in season (June to mid-Oct) from 9am to 7pm.

EXPLORING THE TOWN

Baddeck is much like a modern New England village, skinny and centered around a single commercial boulevard (Chebucto St.) just off the lake. Ask for a free walking-tour brochure at the welcome center. A complete tour of the village's architectural highlights won't take much more than 15 or 20 minutes.

Government Wharf (head down Jones St. from the Yellow Cello restaurant) is home to boat tours, which is the best way to experience **Bras d'Or Lake.** For fishing buffs, Captain Donald Tutty's outfit, **Fan-A-Sea** (© **902/295-1900**), runs charter fishing trips from Baddeck mid-May through mid-October, and with some luck you may land cod, haddock, or trout. Bait and rods are supplied; the rate is about C$40 (US$36/£20) per person, and a minimum of two people is required per tour. Cheaper harbor tours are also offered.

Also in Baddeck, **Loch Bhreagh Boat Tours** (© **902/295-2016**) offers thrice-daily sightseeing tours on a 42-foot cruiser motorboat. They pass Alexander Graham Bell's palatial former estate and other attractions at this end of the lake from May through October. Moonlight tours are available by arrangement, if you've got a group together.

About 180m (591 ft.) offshore from the downtown wharf is Kidston Island, owned by the town. It has a wonderful sand beach with lifeguards and an old lighthouse to explore. The Lion's Club offers frequent pontoon boat shuttles across St. Patrick's Channel; the crossing is free, but donations are encouraged.

Alexander Graham Bell National Historic Site ★★ (Kids)   Each summer for much of his life, the inventor Alexander Graham Bell—of Scottish descent, his family emigrated to Canada when he was young—fled the oppressive heat and humidity of Washington, D.C., for this hillside retreat perched above Bras d'Or Lake at the northern end of Baddeck. The mansion, still owned and occupied by the Bell family, is visible across the harbor from various spots around town. But to learn more about the inventor's career and restless mind, you should visit the modern exhibit center. You'll find extensive exhibits about Bell's invention of the telephone at age 29, as well as considerable information about his less lauded contraptions: ingenious kites, hydrofoils, and airplanes, among others. (Bell also invented the metal detector.) Science buffs will love it, and it's surprising to learn Bell actually died in this home and is buried on the mountaintop. There's an extensive "discovery" section as well, where kids are encouraged to apply their intuition and creativity to solving problems. All in all, it's a very well-thought-out diversion—and attractive, besides.

Chebucto St., Baddeck. © **902/295-2069**. Admission C$7.15 (US$6.45/£3.60) adults, C$5.90 (US$5.30/£2.95) seniors, C$3.45 (US$3.10/£1.75) youth age 6–16, C$18 (US$16/£9) families. June daily 9am–6pm; July to mid-Oct daily 8:30am–6pm; May and mid- to late Oct daily 9am–5pm. Nov–Apr by appointment only.

WHERE TO STAY

If the places below are booked, try **Auberge Gisele's,** 387 Shore Rd. (✆ **800/304-0466** or 902/295-2849), a modern 75-room hotel that's open May to late October and popular with bus tours; regular rooms cost C$135 to C$175 (US$122–US$158/£68–£88) and suites are C$40 to C$100 (US$36–US$90/£20–£50) more. Or try the **Cabot Trail Motel,** Route 105, 1.6km (1 mile) west of Baddeck (✆ **902/295-2580**), with 38 motel units and four chalets overlooking the lake, as well as a heated outdoor pool and private saltwater beach. Doubles run around C$95 to C$115 (US$86–US$104/£48–£58), the cabins a bit more.

Green Highlander Lodge   The Green Highlander is located atop the Yellow Cello, a popular in-town eatery. The three rooms are nicely decorated in a sort of gentleman's fishing camp motif. Rooms are named after Atlantic salmon flies: Blue Charm, for instance, has a private sitting room and blue-quilted twin beds. All three have private decks with views looking out toward Kidston Island, with Lady Amherst perhaps having the best. Ask about the moonlight paddle trips, kayak rentals, and the private beach located a mile away.

525 Chebucto St., Baddeck, NS B0E 1B0. ✆ **902/295-2303** or 902/295-2240. Fax 902/295-1592. www.green highlanderlodge.com. 3 units. C$90–C$120 (US$81–US$108/£45–£60) double. Rates include full breakfast. AE, MC, V. Closed Nov to mid-May. **Amenities:** Kayak rentals, laundry. *In room:* TV, hair dryer, no phone.

Inverary Resort ✦ (Kids)   This sprawling resort, located on 5 lakeside hectares (12 acres) within walking distance of town, is a good choice for families with active kids. The slew of activities runs the gamut from fishing and paddleboats to nightly bonfires on the beach. Sports fans will love the volleyball, tennis, and shuffleboard courts. Guest rooms and facilities are spread all over the well-maintained grounds, mostly in buildings painted dark-chocolate brown with white trim and green roofs. The rooms vary in size and style, but most are comfortable, even the snug motel-style units in the cottages; several two-bedroom units are offered, and a few units have kitchens. The resort has two dining rooms: A cafe overlooking the resort's small marina serves informal fare such as various pastas; the more formal dining room in the main lodge serves classier food on a sun porch.

Shore Rd. (P.O. Box 190), Baddeck, NS B0E 1B0. ✆ **800/565-5660** or 902/295-3500. Fax 902/295-3527. www.cape bretonresorts.com. 138 units. C$119–C$189 (US$107–US$170/£60–£95) double; C$159–C$390 (US$143–US$351/£80–£195) suite. AE, DC, MC, V. Closed Dec–May. **Amenities:** 2 restaurants; pub; indoor pool; 3 tennis courts; spa; Jacuzzi; sauna; watersports equipment; bike; playground; room service. *In room:* A/C, TV (VCR in some units), kitchenette (some units).

Telegraph House   The rooms in this 1861 hotel right on Baddeck's bustling main street are divided between the original inn and motel units on a rise behind the main building. This is where Alexander Graham Bell stayed when he first visited Baddeck, and the units are still rooming-house small. Four rooms on the top floor share two bathrooms between them, an arrangement that works fine for families but might give others a bit of pause. The larger, if unexciting, motel rooms in back (especially room nos. 22–32) are actually better—some with small sitting decks and glimpses of the lake outside their front doors—unless you want to watch the town's coming and goings. For that, guests can linger on a front or side porch (there are several sitting nooks) and watch the commerce on the main drag. The dining room serves traditional meals at lunch and dinner. Expect shepherd's pie, meatloaf, turkey, fish cakes, and big desserts.

Chebucto St. (P.O. Box 8), Baddeck, NS B0E 1B0. ℂ 902/295-1100. Fax 902/295-1136. www.baddeck.com/
telegraph. 41 units. C$70–C$119 (US$63–US$107/£35–£60) double; C$150–C$195 (US$135–US$176/£75–£98)
cabin. AE, MC, V. **Amenities:** Restaurant. *In room:* A/C (1 unit), TV, no phone.

WHERE TO DINE

Many of Baddeck's larger hotels have dining rooms, where you'll find some of the
town's more refined fare. **Auberge Gisele's** dining room (see above) features Continental cuisine, although try to come later in the evening after the bus tours have fin-
ished feeding. At the Inverary Resort (see above), the aptly named **Lakeside Cafe** is a
popular spot, with a view of the marina and a moderately priced menu with pastas and
stir-fries. The resort's main dining room, Flora's, features more creative (and more
expensive) fare. At the **Silver Dart Lodge,** on Shore Road (ℂ **902/295-2340**), there's
the informal **McCurdy's Dining Room,** which has a good reputation for seafood.

Baddeck Lobster Suppers *(Overrated* SEAFOOD   This no-frills restaurant has the
charm of a Legion Hall and charges an arm and a leg, but tourist crowds contentedly
and noisily chow down here every summer nonetheless. The lobster dinner—which
virtually everyone gets—is only available from 4 to 9pm, and includes one smallish
steamed crustacean, plus all-you-can-eat mussels, chowder, biscuits, dessert, and soda.
Beer and wine cost extra and can push the bill for a family into the "unexpectedly
expensive" category. Not in the mood for lobster? There's also cedar-planked salmon
cooked out back by a chef happy to talk about the process—if you've never eaten it,
it might taste a little dry—for a bit less, and a cold ham plate that nobody seems to
order. A kids' menu is available.

Ross St. ℂ **902/295-3307.** Reservations accepted for groups of 10 or more. Lobster dinner around C$30 (US$24);
lunch items C$4–C$9 (US$3.60–US$8.10/£2–£4.50). MC, V. Daily 11:30am–1:30pm and 4–9pm. Closed Nov–May.

Yellow Cello Café PUB FARE   Despite its arty name, this eatery located inside the
Green Highlander Lodge (see "Where to Stay," above) is a pubby, family-restaurant
sort of place, not a gourmet lunchery. If you don't set your culinary expectations too
high, it's a convivial spot to while away an afternoon or evening. Angle for a seat outdoors under the awning facing Chebucto Street. There are two decks, and the decor
features the work of local artist David Stephens. The menu will be familiar to those
who watch a lot of sports on TV: pizza, pasta, nachos, chili, sandwiches, and the like.

525 Chebucto St. ℂ **902/295-2303.** Reservations suggested during peak season. Main courses C$7–C$12
(US$6.30–US$11/£3.50–£6). AE, MC, V. May–Oct daily 8am–11pm.

BRAS D'OR LAKE

With so much beauty around the perimeter of Cape Breton Island, Bras d'Or Lake
hardly gets noticed. This in itself is remarkable. Almost anywhere else in the world,
Bras d'Or (pronounced brah-*door*), a vast inland sea that nearly cleaves Cape Breton
Island right in two, would be a major tourist attraction ringed by motels, lodges, boat
tour operators, water parks, and chain restaurants. But today, along the twisting shoreline of this 114km-long (71-mile) saltwater lake, you'll find . . . almost nothing.
Granted, roads circumnavigate the whole lake, but you'll generally run into few services for tourists, or tourists themselves, for that matter. Is this good or bad? It really
depends on your outlook.

Bras d'Or is a difficult lake to characterize, since it changes dramatically from one
area to the next—wilderness here, rolling farmland there, a summer home colony at
another bend of the road. But wherever you go around this lake, keep an eye peeled

for the regal silhouettes of **bald eagles** 🦅🦅🦅 soaring high above, or for the telltale spot of vivid white in the trees, indicating a perched eagle. Dozens of pairs of these eagles nest along the lake's shores or nearby, making this one of the best areas in the Maritimes—heck, North America—for eagle sightings.

EXPLORING BRAS D'OR LAKE

What's a good strategy for touring the lake? For starters, I would caution against trying to drive around it in 1 day—or even 2 days. There's no equivalent to the Cabot Trail around the lake's perimeter. The road serves up breathtaking views from time to time, but much of the route is dull and uninteresting, running some distance from the lakeshore and offering mostly views of the scratchy woods. It's better to select one or two portions of the lake and focus your travels there.

For **scenic drives,** three segments lend themselves best to touring by car. One is the quiet shore near Iona and along the St. Andrew's Channel on **Route 223.** Another is the hump between **St. Peters and Dundee,** which winds high and low and in recent years has become an area of choice for the summer homes of vacationing Germans. A third segment is **Route 4** running from East Bay to St. Peters, where you'll get the most uninterrupted views of the lake and the best sense of its surprisingly vast size.

Off-the-beaten-track explorers would do well to roam the road that snakes along western shore backwaters between the towns of Marble Mountain through Orangedale to Estmere, though obtaining a decent map for this trip is essential beforehand. This is a good area to explore by canoe or mountain bike; bring your own or rent in one of the larger towns, because you won't find outfitters (or any other service providers) around this part of the lake. Several boat tours are offered from **Baddeck** (see above), however.

On the southeastern shore is the town of **St. Peters,** where the lake comes within 800m (2,625 ft.) of breaking through to the Atlantic Ocean and splitting Cape Breton into two islands. Nature couldn't quite manage to split the mass, but humans did when they built **St. Peter's Canal** in 1854. This canal still operates, and you may see some rather impressive pleasure craft making their way up-canal to the lake. The pathway along the canal makes for good strolling as well.

The village of **Marble Mountain,** on the southwestern shore, offers an intriguing glimpse into history. The town was once a bustling metropolis of sorts. In 1868 a lustrous seam of marble was located here, and by the early part of this century a full-scale mining operation was in effect, supplying builders worldwide. At its peak, the quarry employed 750, and the town was home to more than 1,000. Today, it's reverted to a sleepy backwater. The free **Marble Mountain Museum and Library** (✆ **902/ 756-3289**), in a former schoolhouse, is open daily in July and August from 10am to 5pm; it provides a glimpse at the former prosperity of the area.

Afterward, drive north of town to the overlook high above the island-dotted lake. On the uphill side, look for the gravel lane across the road that angles upward to the right. It's just a 5- or 10-minute walk up to the quarry, a hulking and melancholy hole encroached upon by thistles and Queen Anne's lace. There's an even better view of the lake from here.

Hot and bothered? You can cool off down at the lake, and in style. The **town beach,** which looks from above to be of white sand, really isn't. It's marble chips from the old quarrying operation. You can scramble down from the overlook, or drive into the village and make your way to the lakeshore.

Also worth a quick detour is **Isle Madame** (actually a group of small islands), just south of the lake off Route 4 between St. Peter's and Port Hawkesbury; it's almost entirely French-speaking. Drop by a local bakery or restaurant for a croissant or other French treat. Near the village of Arichat, the **Duke of York Cranberry Meadow** (© **902/226-0001;** www.cranberrytreats.com) has been cultivating the sour berry since 1892. The proprietors operate tours and sell berries, drinks, and other products.

Nova Scotia Highland Village Museum ★ *Kids*   The Highland Village is located near Iona, on a grassy hillside with sweeping views over the lake. When you finally turn your back on the panorama, you'll be at a living history museum—a 17-hectare (42-acre) village featuring 10 buildings that reflect the region's Gaelic heritage, including historic structures moved here from locations around the island and exacting replicas. These range from the Black House (ca. 1790), a stone-and-sod hut of the sort an immigrant would have lived in prior to departing Scotland, to a schoolhouse and general store from the 1920s. Staffers dressed in historical costume will answer any questions you may have about early island life and happily answer kid-size questions, too. Take a Living History Tour (a daylong event allowing visitors to immerse themselves in daily life) or a candlelight tour after-hours (summer only, if available), pick up a Breton oat cake, and drop by the genealogy center if you suspect your family has local roots. It's worth spending at least an hour here.

Rte. 223, Iona. © **902/725-2272.** http://museum.gov.ns.ca/hv. Admission C$9 (US$8.10/£4.50) adults, C$7 (US$6.30/£3.50) seniors, C$4 (US$3.60/£2) children 5–18, C$22 (US$20/£11) families. June to mid-Oct daily 9:30am–5:30pm. Closed mid-Oct to May.

WHERE TO STAY

Highland Heights Inn ★ *Value*   New owners have taken over the Highland Heights, which was already a well-managed motel with clean, well-maintained rooms. But it's different from all the other well-run motels in one critical way: the views. Every room has a view of the lake bordering on the spectacular. The second-floor rooms cost a little more, but they're worth the splurge if only for the included balconies from which you can watch the water's shifting moods. (These rooms are also a bit larger and brighter.) All the motel's units have fans and windows that open. The motel's dining room is cheerful and sunny in a 1970s sort of way (the inn *was* built in 1972), with lake views from the tables along the windows. It's open for three meals daily and features home-style cooking.

Rte. 223 (P.O. Box 19), Iona, NS B0A 1L0. © **800/660-5660** or 902/725-2360. Fax 902/725-2800. www.highland heightsinn.ca. 32 units. C$72–C$119 (US$65–US$107/£36–£60) double. Ask about multinight packages. DISC, MC, V. Closed mid-Oct to mid-May. **Amenities:** Dining room. *In room:* TV.

WHERE TO DINE

Rita's Tea Room ★ *Finds* CAFE   Singer/songwriter Rita MacNeil grew up in Big Pond, and she never forgot her roots during her rise to fame. She always told audiences to stop by for a cup of tea if they were in the neighborhood. Problem was, they did. So Rita opened a tearoom for her fans, housing it in a converted 1939 schoolhouse. Today it contains a thriving gift shop (offering the music of Rita and others), with a comfortable and homey dining room where you can get baked goods, sandwiches, and soup. Rita herself periodically shows up for meet-and-greets with her fans here, and a tea-leaf reader also sometimes comes and reads diners' tea for a fee (if they want).

Rte. 4, Big Pond (about 40km/25 miles southwest of Sydney). © **902/828-2667.** Snacks, soups, and sandwiches C$7–C$14 (US$6.30–US$13/£3.50–£7); afternoon tea sets C$10–C$12 (US$9–US$11/£5–£6). V. Mid-June to mid-Oct daily 10am–6pm. Closed mid-Oct to mid-June.

SYDNEY

The province's third-largest city (pop. 30,000) was northern Nova Scotia's industrial hub for decades, and to this day three out of four Cape Breton Islanders live in or around Sydney. Recent economic trends have not been kind to the area, however, and the once-thriving steel mills and coal mines are no longer so prosperous. This gritty port city has thus been striving to reinvent itself as a tourist destination, though success has been elusive—in part because Cape Breton's other natural charms offer such tough competition.

Although the commercial downtown is a bit workaday, some of the historic residential areas might appeal to architecture and history aficionados. Three early buildings are open to the public in summer, and all are within easy walking distance of one another. The **Cossit House Museum,** 75 Charlotte St. (© **902/539-7973**), is Sydney's oldest house, built in 1785. It's been lovingly restored and furnished with a fine collection of 18th-century antiques. It's open June through mid-October, Monday through Saturday from 9:30am to 5:30pm and Sunday from 1pm. Admission costs C$2 (US$1.80/£1) adults, C$1 (US90¢/50p) seniors and children age 6 to 17. The **Jost Heritage House,** 54 Charlotte St. (© **902/539-0366**), was built in 1787 and had a number of incarnations in the intervening years, including service as a store. It's open June through August Monday through Saturday from 9:30am to 5:30pm, Sunday from 1:30pm; hours are shorter during the fall. Highlights of the home include an early apothecary, and again there's a small entry fee to view it.

St. Patrick's Church Museum, 87 Esplanade (© **902/539-1572**), locally known as "St. Pat's," is in Cape Breton's oldest Roman Catholic church (which dates to 1828) and opens to the public Monday through Saturday in summer from 9:30am to 5:30pm (1:30–5:30pm Sun). There's an old burying ground and a collection of local artifacts. It's free. Plan to spend a few hours visiting this trifecta if you're a fan of old buildings.

PUFFIN TOURS

Thirty minutes west of Sydney (just off the Trans-Canada Hwy. en route to St. Ann's or Baddeck) is the home port of **Bird Island Boat Tours** (© **800/661-6680** or 902/674-2384; www.birdisland.net). On a 2½-hour narrated cruise you'll head out to the Bird Islands, home to a colony of around 300 nesting puffins. You'll get within about 18m (59 ft.) of the colorful birds (they nest in grassy burrows above rocky cliffs), and you may also see razorbills, guillemots, and the occasional bald eagle. Three tours are offered daily from mid-May through mid-September; the fare is about C$32 (US$29/£16) adults, C$15 (US$14/£7.50) children 6 to 12; free for children under 5. Reservations are suggested. The outfit also maintains rental cottages in the area.

AN UNDERGROUND TOUR

Northeast of Sydney is the town of Glace Bay, a former coal-mining center. The mines have slipped into a long economic twilight of late, but the province has made lemonade from lemons by inaugurating the surprisingly intriguing **Cape Breton Miners' Museum** ★★, 42 Birkley St. (© **902/849-4522**; www.minersmuseum.com). The museum provides some background on the geology of the area and offers insight into the region's sometimes-rough labor history.

The highlight of the trip is the 20-minute descent into the mine itself, with damp walls and cool temperatures (it's always around 50°F/10°C down there). Retired miners, who can tell you what it was like to work these mines better than anyone else could hope to do, lead the tours. One Frommer's reader reported her two teenage sons were all groans and eye rolls when she announced their destination—but then the two came away in awe of the place afterward. Plan to spend at least an hour here.

Admission is C$5 (US$4.50/£2.50) adults, C$4 (US$3.60/£2) children for the museum, and then an additional C$5 (US$4.50/£2.50) adults or C$4 (US$3.60/£2) children if you want to take the mine tour; there is no combined ticket for both. The museum is open daily in summer from 10am to 6pm (Tues until 7pm), and open weekdays only in winter from 9am to 4pm.

WHERE TO STAY & DINE

Gowrie House Country Inn ★★   Located across the harbor from Sydney and a few minutes' drive north of the Newfoundland ferry, Gowrie House is at once resplendent and comfortable, historic and up-to-date. Portions of the home were built in 1820, and the building has since been expanded and decorated with Oriental carpets, Asian ceramics, stout Regency furniture, and splashes of modern art. Some guest rooms are a bit frilly, but even the smallest are more spacious than the largest units at many other inns. Especially nice is the Caretaker's Cottage, lavishly furnished and accompanied by its own small deck, garden, and French doors; it costs considerably more than the inn. But the four big rooms in the modern Garden House are almost as nice; they are carpeted and airy, with microwaves and refrigerators. The only problem? Getting a room. The whole summer is often booked up by mid-June, so call as far in advance as you can. The **dining room** ★★ serves a tasty four-course prix fixe dinner of regional cuisine and ingredients such as halibut, lamb, seared scallops, or a dessert of phyllo shells filled with raspberry ice cream. There's one seating nightly at 7:30pm; the price is about C$40 (US$36/£20) per person. Houseguests receive a carafe of wine; outside guests, who should reserve 3 or 4 days in advance at least, must BYOB.

840 Shore Rd., Sydney Mines, NS B1V 1A6. ☎ 800/372-1115 or 902/544-1050. Fax 902/736-0077. www.gowriehouse.com. 11 units. C$145–C$175 (US$131–US$158/£73–£88) double; C$265 (US$239/£133) cottage. Rates include continental breakfast. AE, MC, V. Closed Jan–Mar. Pets allowed with advance notice. **Amenities:** Dining room. *In room:* A/C, kitchenette (some units), fridge (some units), coffeemaker (some units), hair dryer, Jacuzzi (some units), no phone.

LOUISBOURG ★★

In the early 18th century, **Louisbourg on Cape,** Breton's remote and windswept easternmost coast, was home to an ambitious French fortress and settlement. Despite its brief prosperity and durable construction of rock, the colony virtually disappeared after the British finally forced the French out (for the second time) in 1760. Through the miracle of archaeology and historic reconstruction, much of the imposing settlement has been re-created, and today Louisbourg is among Canada's most ambitious national historic parks. It's an attraction everyone coming to Cape Breton Island should make an effort to visit.

And a visit does require some effort. The site, 36km (22 miles) east of Sydney, isn't on the way to anyplace else, and it's an inconvenient detour from Cape Breton Highlands National Park. As such, it's easy to justify skipping it. But if you're interested in Louisbourg, commit yourself to going. A few hours spent wandering the wondrous rebuilt town, then walking amid ruins and out along the coastal trail, might be one of the highlights of your trip to Atlantic Canada.

EXPLORING THE VILLAGE

The hamlet of Louisbourg—which you'll pass through en route to the historic park—is low-key, still looking for ways to rebound from the cessation of the local railway, the decline in local boatbuilding, and the decline of local fisheries. Louisbourg is now striving to gear its economy more toward tourism, and it's making progress on this front.

A short **boardwalk** with interpretive signs runs along the town's tiny waterfront. (You'll get a glimpse of the national historic site across the water.) Nearby is a faux-Elizabethan theater, the **Louisbourg Playhouse** (© 902/733-2996; www.louisbourg playhouse.com), at 11 Aberdeen St. This was originally built near the old town by Disney for the movie *Squanto.* After the production wrapped up, Disney donated it to the village, which dismantled it and moved it to a side street near the harbor. Various performances and concerts are staged here throughout the summer.

As you come into town on Route 22, you'll pass the **Sydney and Louisbourg Railway Museum** (© 902/733-2720), which shares the gabled railway depot with the local **visitor information center** (© 902/733-2720). The museum commemorates the former railway, which shipped coal from the mines to Louisbourg harbor between 1895 and 1968. You can visit some of the old rolling stock (including an 1881 passenger car), and view the roundhouse. It's open daily mid-May to mid-October; hours in July and August are 8am to 8pm, in spring and fall 9am to 5pm. Admission is free.

You might detour a couple of miles out of your way to **Lighthouse Point,** the site of Canada's first lighthouse. (The lighthouse you see today is a replacement, however.) The rocky coastline here is dramatic and undeveloped, a perfect spot for a picnic or to idle away an afternoon. The road, which is partly gravel, diverges from the main paved road near the visitor information center.

Fortress of Louisbourg National Historic Site 🇫🇷🇫🇷 🄺ids   The historic village of

Louisbourg has had three lives. The first was early in the 18th century, when the French colonized this area aggressively in a bid to stake their claim in the New World. They built an imposing fortress of stone. It was imposing but not impregnable, as the British would prove when they captured the fort in 1745. The fortress had a second short-lived heyday when it was returned to the French following negotiations in Europe. War soon broke out again, however, and the British recaptured it in 1758; this time they blew it up for good measure. The final resurrection came during the 1960s, when the Canadian government decided to rebuild a quarter of the stone-walled town—creating a whole settlement from some grass hummocks and a few scattered documents on what once had been. The park was built to re-create life as it might have looked in 1744, when this was still an important French military capital and seaport; visitors today arrive at the site after walking through an interpretive center and boarding a bus for the short ride to the site. (Keeping cars at a distance does much to enhance the historic flavor.) You come through an impressive gatehouse—perhaps after being challenged by a costumed guard on the lookout for English spies—then begin wandering narrow lanes and poking around faux-historic buildings, some of which contain informative exhibits, others that have been restored and furnished with convincingly worn reproductions. Chicken, geese, and barnyard animals peck and cluck, and vendors hawk freshly baked bread out of wood-fired ovens. It really does feel like old Europe. Ask for a free tour, and don't hesitate to question the costumed guides, who are knowledgeable and friendly. Allow at least 4 hours here.

Louisbourg, NS. © 902/733-2280 or 902/733-3546. www.pc.gc.ca/lhn-nhs/ns/louisbourg. June–Sept admission C$16 (US$14/£8) adults, C$14 (US$13/£7) seniors, C$8 (US$7.20/£4) children, C$41 (US$37/£21) families; May and

Oct admission discounted 60%. July–Aug daily 9am–5:30pm; mid-May to June and Sept to mid-Oct daily 9:30am–5pm. Costumed interpreters limited in off season. Closed Nov to mid-May.

WHERE TO STAY

Cranberry Cove Inn ✿ You can't miss this attractive in-town inn en route to the fortress—it's the three-story Victorian farmhouse painted cranberry red. Inside, it's decorated in a light Victorian motif. Upstairs rooms are carpeted and furnished on themes—Anne's Hideaway is the smallest but has a nice old tub and butterfly collection; Isle Royale is done up in Cape Breton tartan. The quirky Field and Stream room has a twig headboard, a mounted deer head, and a stuffed pheasant. The meals in the dining room match the inn's exterior—breakfast includes cran-apple sauce and "cran-bran" muffins; dinner is served nightly from 5 to 8:30pm in a handsome first-floor dining room of polished wood floors and cherrywood tables and chairs. Entrees could range from charbroiled Atlantic salmon to (you guessed it) cranberry-marinated breast of chicken. Note that, due to the three-story open staircase, this inn isn't suitable for toddlers.

12 Wolfe St., Louisbourg, NS B1C 2J2. ✆ 800/929-0222 or 902/733-2171. www.louisbourg.com/cranberrycove. 7 units. C$105–C$160 (US$95–US$144/£53–£80) double. Rates include breakfast. MC, V. Closed Nov–Apr. **Amenities:** Dining room. *In room:* TV (some units), hair dryer, no phone (some units).

Louisbourg Harbour Inn Bed & Breakfast ✿✿ This golden-yellow, century-old clapboard home is conveniently located a block off Louisbourg's main street and overlooks the fishing wharves, the blue waters of the harbor, and, across the way, the fortress of Louisbourg. The inn's lovely pine floors have been nicely restored, and all guest rooms are tidy and attractive. Some are fussier than others, but all are comfortable. The best rooms are on the third floor, requiring a bit of a trek: Room no. 6 is bright and cheerful, with a Jacuzzi tub; room no. 7, one of my favorites, is spacious and also boasts an in-room Jacuzzi, plus a handsome wooden bed and a pair of rockers from which to monitor the happenings at the fish pier. Room nos. 1 and 3 also have private balconies and Jacuzzis. A three-course dinner is sometimes available by advance reservations to guests in the first-floor dining room. All in all, an excellent choice.

9 Lower Warren St., Louisbourg, NS B1C 1G6. ✆ 888/888-8466 or 902/733-3222. www.louisbourg.com/louisbourg harbourinn. 8 units. C$100–C$180 (US$90–US$162/£50–£90) double. Rates include breakfast. MC, V. Closed mid-Oct to mid-June. *In room:* Fridge (some units), coffeemaker, Jacuzzi (some units), no phone.

WHERE TO DINE

Louisbourg has a handful of informal, family-style restaurants, plus upscale dining at Cranberry Cove (see above). My choice for more casual eating out would be **The Grubstake** ✿, 7499 Main St. (✆ **902/733-2308**), open mid-June to early October from noon to about 9pm. The place was founded by a few friends in 1972, and ever since it has embraced the philosophy that food should be fresh and honest. Expect good food at good prices and served with a winning attitude—steaks, pastas, pork, burgers, and the like. The seafood (wine-poached scallops, lobsters, fish and chips) is especially tasty.

12 Cape Breton Highlands National Park ✿✿✿

Cape Breton Highlands National Park is one of the two crown-jewel national parks in Atlantic Canada (Gros Morne in Newfoundland is the other). Covering some 950 sq. km (367 sq. miles) and stretching across a rugged peninsula from the Atlantic to the Gulf of St. Lawrence, the park is famous for its starkly beautiful terrain. It also features one of the most dramatic coastal drives east of Big Sur, California. One of the great pleasures of the park is that it holds something for everyone, from tourists who prefer to sightsee from the comfort of their car to those who prefer backcountry hiking in the company of bear and moose.

The mountains of Cape Breton are probably unlike those you're familiar with elsewhere. The heart of the park is fundamentally a huge plateau. In the vast interior, you'll find a flat and melancholy landscape of wind-stunted evergreens, bogs, and barrens. This is called the taiga, a name that refers to the zone between tundra and the northernmost forest. In this largely untracked area (which is also Nova Scotia's largest remaining wilderness), you might find 150-year-old trees that are only knee-high.

It's the park's edges that really capture the attention, though. On the western side of the peninsula, the tableland has eroded into the sea, creating a dramatic landscape of ravines and ragged, rust-colored cliffs pounded by the ocean. The Cabot Trail, a paved road built in 1939, winds dramatically along the flanks of the mountains, offering extraordinary vistas at every turn. On the park's other coastal flank—the eastern, Atlantic side—the terrain is less spectacular, with a coastal plain interposed between mountains and sea. But the lush green hills still offer a backdrop that's exceptionally beautiful.

Note that this section focuses only on the park proper, which offers no lodging or services other than camping. You will find limited lodging and restaurants in the handful of villages that ring the park. See "Cape Breton Island," earlier in this chapter, for those.

ESSENTIALS

GETTING THERE   Access to the park is via the Cabot Trail, one of several tourist routes well marked by provincial authorities. The entire loop is 300km (186 miles). The distance from the park entrance at Chéticamp to the park entrance at Ingonish is 105km (65 miles). Although the loop can be done in either direction, I would encourage visitors to drive it in a clockwise direction solely because the visitor center in Chéticamp offers a far more detailed introduction to the park.

VISITOR INFORMATION   **Visitor information centers** are located at both Chéticamp and Ingonish and are open daily in the summer from 8am to 8pm. The Chéticamp center has more extensive information about the park, including a 10-minute slide presentation, natural history exhibits, a large-scale relief map, and a very good bookstore specializing in natural and cultural history. The park's main phone number is ✆ **902/224-2306.**

FEES   Entrance permits are required from mid-May through mid-October and can be purchased either at information centers or at tollhouses at the two main park entrances. Permits are required for any activity along the route, even stopping to admire the view. Daily fees are C$6.90 (US$6.20/£3.45) adults, C$5.90 (US$5.30/£2.95) seniors, C$3.45 (US$3.10/£1.75) children age 6 to 16, and C$17 (US$15/£8.50) families.

EXPLORING THE PARK
SCENIC DRIVES

Cape Breton Highlands National Park offers basically one drive, and with few lapses it's scenic along the entire route. The most breathtaking stretch is the 43km (27-mile) **route from Chéticamp to Pleasant Bay** along the western coast. Double the time you figure you'll need to drive this itinerary, because you'll want to spend lots of time at the pullouts gawking at the views, perusing the signs, and snapping digital

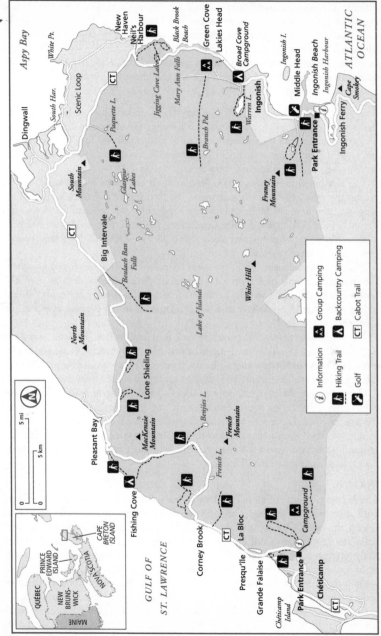

Aspy Bay

White Pt.

New Haven
Neil's Harbour

Black Brook Beach

Green Cove

Lakies Head

South Har.

Scenic Loop

CT

Broad Cove Campground

Ingonish I.

Ingonish Beach

Middle Head

Ingonish Harbour

ATLANTIC OCEAN

Dingwall

Paquette L.

Jigging Cove Lake

Mary Ann Falls

Warren L.

Ingonish

Branch Pd.

Park Entrance

Ingonish Ferry

Cape Smokey

South Mountain

Glasgow Lakes

Big Intervale

Franey Mountain

CT

Beulach Ban Falls

White Hill

Lake of Islands

Information

Hiking Trail

Golf

Group Camping

Backcountry Camping

CT Cabot Trail

North Mountain

Lone Shieling

Benjies L.

MacKenzie Mountain

French L. French Mountain

Pleasant Bay

5 mi

5 km

Fishing Cove

Corney Brook

La Bloc

Campground

CT

Presqu'ile

Grande Falaise

Park Entrance

Chéticamp

Chéticamp Island

GULF OF ST. LAWRENCE

CAPE BRETON ISLAND

QUÉBEC

PRINCE EDWARD ISLAND

NEW BRUNSWICK

NOVA SCOTIA

MAINE

CT

photos. (If it's foggy, though, save yourself the entrance fee and gas money. Without the views, there's little reason to travel and you'd be well advised to wait until the fog lifts.) You can also hike in the foggy forest or across the upland bogs, or explore some of the nearby villages in an atmospheric mist.

For an excellent detour at the northern apex of the loop, consider a side trip to Meat Cove (see the "Cape North" section, earlier in this chapter).

HIKING

The park offers no fewer than 27 distinct hiking tracks departing from the Cabot Trail. Many excursions are quite short and have the feel of a casual stroll rather than a vigorous tromp, but those determined to be challenged will find suitable destinations. All trails are listed, with brief descriptions, on the reverse side of the map you'll receive when you pay your park entry fee at the gates.

The **Skyline Trail** 🐾🐾🐾 offers oodles of altitude and views, but no climbing. You ascend the tableland from Chéticamp by car, then follow a 7km (4.3-mile) hiking loop out along dramatic bluffs and through wind-stunted spruces and firs. A spur trail descends to a high, exposed point overlooking the surf; it's capped with blueberry bushes. Moose are often spotted along this trail. The downside: It's a very popular trek, and thus often crowded.

Farther along the Cabot Trail, the .8km (.5-mile) **Bog Trail** 🐾 offers a glimpse of the tableland's unique bogs from a dry boardwalk. **Lone Shieling** 🐾 is an easy .8km (.5-mile) loop through a verdant hardwood forest in a lush valley home to 350-year-old sugar maples. A re-creation of a hut of a Scottish crofter (shepherd) is a feature along this trail.

If you're looking to leave the crowds behind, the **Glasgow Lake Lookoff** 🐾 is a relatively gentle 8km (5-mile) round-trip hike that takes you through barrens and scrub forest to a rocky bald overlooking with distant views of the ocean and the pristine highland lakes. The trail is alternately swampy and rocky, so rugged footwear is advised.

On the eastern shore, try the superb 4km (2.5-mile) **hike to Middle Head** 🐾🐾, beyond the Keltic Lodge resort. This dramatic, rocky peninsula thrusts well out into the Atlantic. The trail is wide and relatively flat, and you'll cross open meadows with wonderful views north and south. The tip is grassy and open, and it offers a fine spot to scan for whales or watch the waves crash in following a storm. Allow about 2 hours for a relaxed excursion out and back.

BIKING

The 282km (175-mile) **Cabot Trail loop** 🐾🐾🐾 is the ironman tour for bike trekkers, both arduous and rewarding. The route twists up ravines and plummets back down toward the coast. One breathtaking vista after another unfolds, and the plunging, brake-smoking descent from Mt. MacKenzie to Pleasant Bay will be one you're not likely to forget soon. Campgrounds and motels are well spaced here for a 3- or 4-day excursion. As for disadvantages, the road is uniformly narrow and almost universally without shoulders, and cyclists may often get the sense that motor-home drivers don't really know where the far side of their rig is located. That can be a bit harrowing.

If you're not inclined to pedal the whole loop, pick and choose. Especially scenic stretches for fit bikers include **Chéticamp to Pleasant Bay** 🐾🐾 and back, and the climb and descent from **Lone Shieling eastward into the Aspy Valley** 🐾🐾. See also the "Cape North" section, earlier in this chapter.

Tips   Check Your Brakes

You'll want to be *very* confident about your car's brakes before setting out on the Cabot Trail: The road rises and falls with considerable drama, and while cresting some ridges you may feel a mild sense of vertigo. Especially stressful on the brakes (when traveling the Trail clockwise) are the descents to Pleasant Bay, into the Aspy Valley, and off Cape Smokey. The moral of the story? Test your brakes *before* you get here . . . not when you're flying down your first hill.

Note that mountain bikes are allowed on just a few trails within the park—check with the visitor center when you arrive for details about restrictions. The longest backcountry trail is the 13km (8-mile) route into the **Lake of Islands** ⚔, which doesn't appear on all maps. Ask about it at one of the park's two visitor centers.

CAMPING

The park has five drive-in campgrounds. The largest are at **Chéticamp** (on the west side) and **Broad Cove** (on the east), both of which have the commendable policy of never turning campers away. Even if all regular sites are full, they'll find a place for you to pitch a tent or park an RV. All the national park campgrounds are well run and well maintained. Chéticamp and Broad Cove offer three-way hookups for RVs. Rates run from around C$18 to C$35 (US$16–US$32/£9–£18) per night, depending on the level of services you require and the campground you've selected. Remember that you're also required to buy a day-use permit when camping at Cape Breton, and that you can only make advance reservations at Chéticamp, where half the sites are set aside for advance bookings using the website **www.pccamping.ca**. At all the other campgrounds, it's first-come, first-served.

Cape Breton also has some backcountry campsites at **Fishing Cove** ⚔, set on a pristine cove that is especially attractive; just remember to plan for an 8km (5-mile) hike in from the Cabot Trail and your car. Once there, however, you can watch for pilot whales at sunset from the cliffs. The current fee is C$9.90 (US$8.90/£4.95) per person per night; make arrangements at one of the visitor information centers.

5

New Brunswick

Sometimes New Brunswick seems like it could be the Rodney Dangerfield of Atlantic Canada—it just gets no respect. It's probably better known within Canada for its pulp mills, industrial forests, cargo ports, and oil refineries (the huge Irving Oil conglomerate is based here) than for its many quaint villages and charming byways. And that's a shame. Travelers also tend to view New Brunswick as a place to be driven through as quickly as possible en route from Québec or Maine to the rest of Atlantic Canada—and the building of a fast toll road through the western section of the province hasn't helped mitigate that impression at all.

Rest assured, though: New Brunswick *does* in fact have pockets of wilderness and scenic beauty equal to those anywhere in eastern Canada. The province's appeal is just a bit more hidden. With a little homework, you can easily cobble together memorable excursions through exquisite landscapes. You might discover surprisingly warm ocean waters lapping up on sand beaches that hold their own to anything Prince Edward Island's got to offer; rocky, surf-pounded headlands that could be in the farthest reaches of Newfoundland; huge tides that will stun you with their drop; and a salty, pubby maritime city (Saint John) that makes a nice run at Halifax as a developing hub.

Culturally, New Brunswick is Canada in microcosm. It's seemingly split between Anglophone and Francophone populations (one-third of the province's residents speak French), and its heritage is both proudly Acadian and proudly British—in fact, New Brunswick is sometimes called the Loyalist Province, since so many Loyalists fleeing the United States after the American Revolution settled here.

Despite this, the cultural divide is much less contentious here than in Québec. Maybe that's because the French-speaking residents of New Brunswick share few cultural roots with the French-speaking Québecois: New Brunswick's French settlers came mostly from central and western France, while the Québecois trace their ancestry to the extreme northwestern *départements* of Brittany and Normandy. As a result, Acadians here celebrate the Feast of the Assumption (in mid-Aug) as their big national holiday instead of St. Jean Baptiste Day (in late June), which is biggest in Québec. With its unusually harmonious détente between two cultures, New Brunswick likes to think of itself as a model for Québec, even if Québec more or less ignores its neighbor. Too bad; they're missing an unsung national treasure next door.

1 Exploring New Brunswick

Come to New Brunswick with a strategy in mind; the key points are not close to one another, and there are no superspeedways to get you from here to there quickly. If you're drawn to rugged beauty, you should plan to focus on the Fundy Coast with its

QUÉBEC

Matapedia — Tide Head — Dalhousie — Campbellton — New Richmond
132
Chaleur Bay — Miscou I.
L. Témiscouata — Kedgwick — 11 — Caraquet — Lamèque I. — Shippagan
17 — MOUNT CARLETON PROV. PARK — Bathurst
Edmundston — 2 — Ste.-Anne-de-Madawaska — Nepisiguit — 11 — GULF OF ST. LAWRENCE
St. John R. — St.-Léonard — 8 — Neguac
Square L. — Grand Falls
Caribou — Chatham — Newcastle — KOUCHIBOUGUAC N.P.
Presque Isle — Perth-Andover — Alberton — P.E.I.
161 — SW Miramichi — St. Louis de Kent — Northumberland Strait — Summerton
MAINE — 1 — 2 — Doaktown — Salmon R. — Bouctouche — 11 — Shediac
Hartland — 126
Houlton — Woodstock — 8 — Chipman — Moncton — Pt. Elgin
Grand L.
Fredericton — Petitcodiac — Sackville
95 — Oromocto — Washademoak L. — Amherst — Oxford
Grand L. — 4 — Sussex — 1 — 114 — NOVA SCOTIA
Spednic L. — McAdam — 7 — Norton — Alma — FUNDY N.P.
West Grand L. — Long Reach
6 — Grand Bay — Quispamsis — Chignecto Bay
St. Stephen — St. George — Saint John — Kentville
1 — 101 — Windsor
St. Andrews — Passamaquoddy Bay — BAY — OF — FUNDY — Middleton
Bangor — 9 — Eastport — Campobello I. — Digby
Grand Manan I.

Trans-Canada Highway
Ferry

0 — 50 mi
0 — 50 km

stupendous dropping tides, rocky cliffs, and boreal landscape. This part of the coast actually feels a lot more remote and northerly than the more densely settled (and tamer-looking) northeastern coast.

Those interested in Acadian history or sandy beaches, on the other hand, should veer toward the Gulf of St. Lawrence and its fishing heritage and laid-back feel. And those who want to sip a pint to the strains of traditional music and shop at a great farmer's market should swing through Saint John and its lovely associated fishing towns.

Those simply interested in hurrying through the province to get to Prince Edward Island or Nova Scotia . . . well, you've turned to the wrong chapter of this book. But take at least a day anyway to detour down through Fundy National Park, visiting Cape Enrage and Hopewell Rocks, which number among eastern Canada's more dramatic attractions. If nothing else, you'll agree that New Brunswick should never be completely written off on any tour of eastern Canada.

ESSENTIALS

VISITOR INFORMATION   New Brunswick publishes several free annual directories and guides that are helpful in planning a trip to the province, including *Experience New Brunswick,* with listings of attractions, accommodations, campgrounds, and multiday and daylong adventure packages, as well as an official New Brunswick travel map. Contact the **New Brunswick Department of Tourism and Parks,** P.O. Box 12345, Campbellton, NB E3N 3T6 (© **800/561-0123;** www.tourismnewbrunswick.ca).

The province staffs seven official visitor information centers; most cities and larger towns also have their own municipal information centers. A complete listing of phone numbers for these centers can be found in the *Experience New Brunswick* guide, or look for "?" direction signs on the highway. Phone numbers and addresses for the appropriate visitor information centers are provided in each section of this chapter.

GETTING THERE   By Car and Ferry   The Trans-Canada Highway bisects the province, entering from Québec at St. Jacques. It follows the Saint John River Valley before veering through Moncton and exiting into Nova Scotia at Aulac. The entire distance is about 530km (329 miles).

The fastest route from New England to southwestern New Brunswick is to take the Maine Turnpike to Bangor, then head east on Route 9 to connect to Route 1 into Calais, which is just across the river from St. Stephen, New Brunswick. A more scenic variation is to drive to Campobello Island across the bridge from Lubec, Maine (see the "Passamaquoddy Bay" section, below), then take a ferry to Deer Island, drive the length of the island, and board a second ferry to the mainland. Those headed to Fredericton or Moncton will speed their trip somewhat by following U.S. I-95 to Houlton, then connecting with the Trans-Canada after crossing the border.

Bay Ferries (© **888/249-7245;** www.nfl-bay.com) operates the 3-hour ferry known as the *Princess of Acadia* that links Saint John with Digby, Nova Scotia. The ferry sails year-round, with as many as three crossings daily each way in summer. One-way summer fares in 2007 were C$40 (US$36/£20) for adults, C$30 (US$27/£15) for seniors, C$25 (US$23/£13) for children ages 6 to 13, C$5 (US$4.50/£2.50) per child under 6, and C$80 (US$72/£40) and up per vehicle; all fares are cheaper in the off season, and you also get a discount if you buy a ticket to complete a round-trip within 30 days. Reservations are advised.

By Air   The province's main airports are at Fredericton (the provincial capital), Saint John, and Moncton, all of which are chiefly served by **Air Canada** (© **888/AIR-CANA;** www.aircanada.com) and the major car-rental companies. **Continental** (© **800/523-FARE;** www.continental.com) now also flies nonstop from Newark, New Jersey's, Liberty International Airport to Moncton.

By Train   Canada's government-operated national rail line, **VIA Rail** (© **888/842-7245;** www.viarail.com), offers train service through the province from Montréal (on the way to Halifax) 6 days a week (no Tues) year-round. The train follows a northerly route with stops in Campbellton, Miramichi, and Moncton. Check out the website for more details on routes, schedules, and stopping times in New Brunswick, and online booking.

By Cruise Ship   Yes, indeed, you read that correctly. In the summer of 2007, the popular **Carnival Cruise Lines** outfit (© **888/CARNIVAL;** www.carnival.com) unveiled a series of 4-day weekend summertime cruises from New York City to the Bay of Fundy and back. Optional shore excursions during the day and night at port in Saint John have previously included a bike tour of local covered bridges, visits to a dairy farm, kayak trips around the bay, and a visit to the Moosehead Brewery. Another limited schedule of the cruises will continue in the summer of 2008; contact the cruise line to book a cabin or for more information.

2 The Great Outdoors

The province has put together a well-conceived campaign to encourage visitors of all budgets to explore its outdoor attractions and activities. The provincial travel guide outlines dozens of multiday and day adventures ranging from a C$10 (US$9/£5) guided hike at Fundy National Park to C$276 (US$248/£138) biking packages that include inn accommodations and gourmet dinners. For more information on the program, call the tourism department at ℂ **800/561-0123.**

I recommend that readers with an adventurous bent think seriously about visiting the outdoor center at **Cape Enrage** (see the "Fundy National Park" section, later in this chapter), where you can canoe, rappel, rock-climb, and kayak—all in one dramatic coastal setting.

BACKPACKING   Among the best destinations for a backcountry tromp are **Mount Carleton Provincial Park** and **Fundy National Park,** both of which maintain backcountry campsites for visitors. These two landscapes are quite different to hike through, however; see the appropriate sections later in this chapter for more information on each park, then make your choice.

BICYCLING   The islands and peninsulas of **Passamaquoddy Bay** lend themselves nicely to cruising in the slow lane—especially Campobello, which also has good dirt roads for mountain biking. **Grand Manan** holds appeal for cyclists, although the main road (Rte. 776) has rather narrow shoulders and some fast local cars. Some of the best coastal biking is around **Fundy National Park**—especially the back roads to Cape Enrage and the **Fundy Trail Parkway,** an 11km (6.8-mile) multiuse trail that hugs the coast west of the national park. Along the Acadian Coast, **Kouchibouguac National Park** has limited but unusually nice biking trails through mixed terrain (rentals available).

A handy guide is *Biking to Blissville,* by Kent Thompson. It covers 35 rides in the Maritimes, and costs about C$15 (US$14/£7.50). Look in local bookshops, check online bookstores, or contact the publisher directly: Goose Lane Editions, 500 Beaverbrook Ct., Suite 500, Fredericton, NB E3B 5X4 (ℂ **888/926-8377;** www.gooselane.com).

BIRD-WATCHING   **Grand Manan** is probably the province's most noted destination for birders, located right on the Atlantic flyway. (John James Audubon lodged here when studying bird life more than 150 years ago.) Over the course of a typical year, as many as 275 species can be observed on the island, with September usually the best month for sightings. Boat tours from Grand Manan can take you to Machias Seal Island, with its colonies of puffins, Arctic terns, and razorbills. It's fun to swap information with other birders: On the ferry, look for excitable folks with binoculars and floppy hats dashing from port to starboard and back.

On **Campobello Island,** the mixed terrain also attracts a good mix of birds, including the sharp-shinned hawk, common eider, and black guillemot. Ask for a checklist and map at the visitor center. Shorebird enthusiasts flock to **Shepody Bay National Wildlife Area,** which maintains preserves in the mud flats between Alma (near Fundy National Park) and Hopewell Cape. Also offering excellent birding is the marsh that surrounds **Sackville,** near the Nova Scotia border.

CANOEING   New Brunswick has 3,500km (2,175 miles) of inland waterways, plus lakes and protected bays. Canoeists can find everything from glass-smooth waters to daunting rapids. In Kouchibouguac National Park, for example, there is a rental and tour concession based at **Ryans Recreational Equipment Rental Centre** (© 506/ 876-8918) from mid-May to mid-September (open weekends only Sept–June). More experienced canoeists looking for a longer expedition should head to the **St. Croix River** on the U.S. border, where you can embark on a multiday paddle trip and get lost in the woods, spiritually if not in fact.

FISHING The **Miramichi River** has long attracted anglers famous and obscure, lured by the wily Atlantic salmon. In some considered opinions, this ranks among the best salmon rivers in the world, even though diminished runs have plagued recent years (as they have all rivers in the Maritimes). There are strict laws regarding river fishing of the salmon: The fish must be caught using flies, and nonresidents must hire a licensed guide when fishing for them. (There are occasional exemption periods from these rules, called Fish New Brunswick Days in early June, when you don't need to use a guide but still need a license; check ahead with your lodging if you are interested.) For other freshwater species, including bass, as well as open-ocean saltwater angling, the provincial restrictions are less onerous. Get up to date on the rules and regulations by requesting two brochures: "Sport Fishing Summary" and "Atlantic Salmon Angling." These are available from the **Fisheries Section** of the Department of Natural Resources, reached by phone at © 506/453-2440 or by snail mail at P.O. Box 6000, Fredericton, NB E3B 5H1. The website can be found at the always-memorable address www.gnb.ca/0254.

GOLF In St. Andrews, the **Algonquin hotel**'s newly expanded and redesigned golf course is a beauty—easily among eastern Canada's top 10, right behind the bigger-name stars on Cape Breton Island and Prince Edward Island. It features 9 newer inland holes (the front 9) and 9 older seaside holes that become increasingly spectacular as you approach the point of land separating New Brunswick from Maine. (All 18 of them are challenging, so bring your "A" game.) Service and upkeep are impeccable here, and there's both a snack bar on premises and a roving club car with sandwiches and drinks. Greens fees are C$79 to C$99 (US$71–US$89/£40–£50) for 18 holes (carts extra; discount at twilight time). Lessons are offered, and there's a short-game practice area in addition to a driving range; call © 888/460-8999 or 506/529-8165 for tee times. In Fredericton, **Kingswood** (© 800/423-5969 or 506/443-3333; www.golfnb.com/kingswood1.html) was recognized by *Golf Digest* as the best new Canadian golf course in 2003. It features 27 holes, a par-3 course, and a double-ended driving range. A round of 18 holes cost C$50 to C$65 (US$45–US$59/£25–£33) in 2007.

HIKING The province's highest point is in the center of the woodlands region, at **Mount Carleton Provincial Park.** Several demanding hikes in the park yield glorious views. There's also superb hiking at **Fundy National Park,** with a mix of coastal and woodland hikes on well-marked trails. The multiuse, 11km (6.8-mile) **Fundy Trail Parkway** has terrific views of the coast and is wheelchair accessible. **Grand Manan** is a good destination for independent-minded hikers who enjoy the challenge of finding the trail as much as the hike itself.

An excellent resource is *A Hiking Guide to New Brunswick,* published by Goose Lane Editions. It's C$15 (US$14/£7.50) and available in bookstores around the province, or directly from the publisher, Goose Lane Editions, at 500 Beaverbrook Ct., Suite 500, Fredericton, NB E3B 5X4 (© 888/926-8377; www.gooselane.com).

SEA KAYAKING The huge tides that make kayaking so fascinating along the **Bay of Fundy** also make it exceptionally dangerous—even the strongest kayakers are no match for a fierce ebb tide if they're in the wrong place. Fortunately, the number of skilled sea-kayaking guides has really boomed in recent years.

Among the most extraordinary places to explore is **Hopewell Rocks.** The rocks stand like amazing Brancusi statues on the ocean floor at low tide, then offer sea caves and narrow channels to explore at high tide. **Baymount Outdoor Adventures** (© 877/601-2660 or 506/734-2660), run by the Faulkners in Hillsborough, offers 90-minute sea kayak tours of Hopewell Rocks for C$55 (US$50/£28) adults, C$45 (US$41/£23) children. Other good kayak outfitters along the Fundy Coast include **FreshAir Adventure** (© 800/545-0020 or 506/887-2249) in Alma and **Seascape Kayak Tours** (© 866/747-1884 or 506/747-1884) on Deer Island, both charging basically the same rates as Baymount.

SWIMMING   Parts of New Brunswick offer surprisingly good ocean swimming. The best beaches are along the **Acadian Coast,** especially near Shediac and within Kouchibouguac National Park. If you're coming to this province mostly to dip your toes and set out a blanket, bear in mind that the water is much warmer (and the terrain more forgiving) along the Gulf of St. Lawrence than in the Bay of Fundy.

WHALE-WATCHING   The **Bay of Fundy** is rich with plankton, and therefore rich with whales. Some 15 types of whales can be spotted in the bay, including finback, minke, humpback, the infrequent orca, and the endangered right whale. Whale-watching expeditions sail throughout the summer from Campobello Island, Deer Island, Grand Manan, St. Andrews, and St. George. Any visitor information center can point you in the right direction; the province's travel guide also lists many of the tours, which typically cost around C$40 to C$50 (US$36–US$45/£20–£25) for 2 to 4 hours of whale-watching.

3 Passamaquoddy Bay

The Passamaquoddy Bay region is often the first point of entry for those arriving overland from the United States. The deeply indented bay is wracked with massive tides that produce currents powerful enough to stymie even doughty fishing boats. It's a place of lasting fogs, spruce-clad islands, bald eagles, and widely scattered development. It's also home to a grand old summer colony and a peninsula that boasts two five-star inns and a rambling turn-of-the-20th-century resort.

CAMPOBELLO ISLAND ⊛

Campobello is a compact island (about 16km/10 miles long and 5km/3 miles wide) at the mouth of Passamaquoddy Bay. It's connected by a graceful modern bridge to Lubec, Maine, and is thus easier to get to from the United States than from Canada. (To get here from the Canadian mainland without driving through the United States requires two ferries, one of which operates only during the summer.) This is a great quick trip into Canada for a quick taste of New Brunswick when you're already in downeast Maine.

Campobello has been home to both humble fishermen and wealthy families over the years, and both have coexisted nicely. (Locals approved when summer folks built golf courses earlier this century, for example, since it gave them a place to graze their sheep.) Today, the island is a mix of elegant summer homes and humble local dwellings.

Campobello offers excellent shoreline **walks** ⊛ at both **Roosevelt Campobello International Park** (see below) and **Herring Cove Provincial Park** (© 506/752-7010), which opens from mid-May to mid-October. The landscapes are extraordinarily diverse. On some trails you'll enjoy a Currier & Ives tableau of white houses and church spires across the channel in Lubec and Eastport; 10 minutes later you'll be walking along a wild, rocky coast pummeled by surging waves. Herring Cove's 425 hectares (1,050 acres) include a 1.6km-long (1-mile) beach that's perfect for a slow stroll in the fog; camping (88 sites) and golf are also offered at the park. Watch for bald eagles and osprey.

ESSENTIALS

GETTING THERE   Campobello Island is accessible year-round from the United States. From Route 1 in Whiting, Maine, take Route 189 to Lubec, where a bridge links Lubec with Campobello. In the summer, there's another option: From the Canadian mainland, take the free ferry to Deer Island, drive the length of the island, and then board the small seasonal ferry to Campobello. The ferry is operated by **East Coast Ferries** (© **506/747-2159**) and runs from late June to September. The fare is C$14 (US$13/£7) for car and driver, C$3 (US$2.70/£1.50) for each additional passenger.

VISITOR INFORMATION   The **Campobello Welcome Center,** 44 Rte. 774, Welshpool, NB E5E 1A3 (© **506/752-7043**), is on the right side just after you cross the bridge from Lubec. It's open mid-May to early September from 9am to 7pm, and from 10am to 6pm until mid-October.

Roosevelt Campobello International Park ★★   Like a number of other affluent Americans, the family of Franklin Delano Roosevelt made an annual trek to the prosperous summer colony at Campobello Island. The island lured folks from the sultry cities with the promise of cool air and a salubrious effect on the circulatory system. ("The extensive forests of balsamic firs seem to affect the atmosphere of this region, causing a quiet of the nervous system and inviting sleep," read an 1890 real-estate brochure.) The future U.S. president came to this island every summer between 1883, the year after he was born, and 1921, when he was stricken with polio. Franklin and his siblings spent those summers exploring the coves and sailing around the bay, and he always recalled his time here fondly. (It was his "beloved island," he said, coining a phrase that gets no rest in local advertising.)

You'll learn much about Roosevelt and his early life at the visitor center, where you can watch a brief film, and during a self-guided tour of the elaborate mansion, covered in cranberry-colored shingles. For a "cottage" this huge, it's surprisingly comfortable and intimate.

The park is truly international; run by a commission with representatives from both the United States and Canada, it's like none other in the world. It offers scenic coastlines and 14km (8.7 miles) of walking trails among its 1,120 hectares (2,768 acres). While the park's visitor center closes on Canada's Thanksgiving Day in late October, these extensive grounds and parklands remain open to the public year-round. Maps and walk suggestions are available at the visitor center. Campobello Park, should you find your way here, is easily worth a half-day.

459 Rte. 774, Welshpool. © **506/752-2922**. www.fdr.net. Free admission. Daily 10am–6pm; last tour at 5:45pm. Visitor center closed mid-Oct to mid-May; grounds open year-round.

WHERE TO STAY & DINE

There is camping at **Herring Cove Provincial Park** (© **506/752-7010**) for C$22 to C$24 (US$20–US$22/£11–£12), with discounts for seniors. For indoor options, see below.

Lupine Lodge ⚓ *Value* *Kids*   In 1915, cousins of the Roosevelts built this handsome compound of log buildings not far from the Roosevelt cottage. A busy road runs between the lodge and the water, but the buildings are located on a slight rise and have the feel of being removed from the traffic. Guest rooms are in two long lodges adjacent to the main building and restaurant. The rooms with bay views cost a bit more but are worth it—they're slightly larger, and better furnished in a rustic style. All guest rooms have queen beds (some rooms add another double bed or fireplace) and access to a deck that overlooks the bay. You won't find phones, TVs, luxury bathrooms, or wireless Internet, but you will find a pleasing vibe—they welcome even small children and will pack a lunch for your explorations, though they cannot accept pets. The lodge's attractive **dining room** ⚓ is a great place for a meal, exuding rustic summer ease with log walls, a double stone fireplace, bay views of the fishing fleets, and mounted moose and swordfish. Three meals are served daily (go for blueberry pancakes at breakfast), and dinners have been recently upscaled: Entrees now include such choices as maple-glazed salmon and a turkey dinner, in addition to longtime favorites like rib-eye steak, seafood, and lobster chowder.

610 Rte. 774, Welshpool, Campobello Island, NB E5E 1A5. © 888/912-8880 or 506/752-2555. www.lupinelodge.com. 11 units. C$99–C$150 (US$89–US$135/£50–£75) double. MC, V. Closed Nov–Apr. **Amenities:** Restaurant. *In room:* No phone.

Owen House, A Country Inn & Gallery   This three-story clapboard captain's house dates from 1835 and sits on 4 tree-filled hectares (10 acres) at the edge of the bay. The first-floor common rooms are nicely decorated in a busy Victorian manner with Persian and braided carpets and mahogany furniture; view the water from the nautical-feeling airy sun room and its big windows. The guest rooms are a mixed lot, furnished with an eclectic mix of antique and modern furniture; some are bright and filled with salty air (room no. 1 is the largest, with waterfront views on two sides); others, like room no. 5, are tucked under stairs and a bit dark, though the Owens are renovating the house. Third-floor rooms share a single bathroom but also have excellent views. A filling hot breakfast served family-style is included in the room rates, and ask to see the owner's in-house watercolor gallery if you're an art buff.

11 Welshpool St., Welshpool, Campobello Island, NB E5E 1G3. © 506/752-2977. www.owenhouse.ca. 9 units, 2 with shared bathroom. C$107–C$210 (US$96–US$189/£54–£105) double. Rates include full breakfast. MC, V. Closed Nov–Apr. No children under 6 in Aug. *In room:* No phone.

ST. STEPHEN

St. Stephen is the gateway to Canada for many travelers arriving from the United States. It's directly across the tidal St. Croix River from Calais, Maine, and the two towns share a symbiotic relationship—it's a local call across the international border from one town to the other, fire engines from one country will respond to fires in the other, and during an annual summer parade, bands and floats have sometimes marched right through customs. Though downtown St. Stephen is hardly a destination in and of itself, it is a handy pit stop—and the smell of chocolate (as you'll read below) does sneakily attempt to entice you into a longer stay.

ESSENTIALS

VISITOR INFORMATION   The **Provincial Visitor Information Centre** (© **506/466-7390**) is open daily from 9am to 8pm mid-June to August and 9am to 6pm in the shoulder seasons (May, June, Sept, and early Oct). It's in the old train station at

Milltown Boulevard and King Street, about a mile from Canadian customs; turn right after crossing the border (following signs for St. Andrews and Saint John), and watch for the information center at the light where the road turns left.

EXPLORING ST. STEPHEN

St. Stephen is a town in transition. The lumber industry and wood trade that were responsible for those handsome brick and stone buildings that line the main street have mostly dried up. The town now depends on its paper mill, the large Ganong chocolate factory, and pass-through tourists like yourself for its economic mainstays. (For the truly cocoa bean–obsessed, there's also a small chocolate festival in summer.) As a regional commercial center, St. Stephen has a gritty, lived-in feel to it, though not much in the way of stylish shopping or restaurants to keep you more than a moment.

Still, you can learn about the region's history with a brief stop at the **Charlotte County Museum,** 443 Milltown Blvd. (© **506/466-3295**), open June through September only; it's quite close to the tourist office described above.

The Chocolate Museum *Kids*   St. Stephen's claim to fame is that it's the home of the chocolate bar—the first place where somebody thought to wrap chocolate pieces in foil and sell them individually (in 1910). At least that's according to local lore. Chocolate is still big around here—not as big as in Hershey, Pennsylvania, but still a big part of the local psyche and economy. The Ganong brothers began selling chocolate from their general store here in 1873, and from that an empire was built, employing some 700 people by the 1930s. Ganong was also the first place to package chocolates in heart-shaped boxes for Valentine's Day and still holds 30% of the Canadian market for heart-box chocolates. The new modern plant on the outskirts of town isn't open to the public, but in 1999 this museum was opened in one of the company's earlier factories, a large brick structure on the main street. Here you can view an 11-minute video about the history of local chocolates. Displays and exhibits explain 19th-century chocolate boxes, and there are interactive multimedia displays about the making of candy and games for young children (such as "Guess the Centers"). One highlight is watching the expert hand-dippers make chocolates the old-fashioned way; samples, of course, are available afterward. Want more? Ganong's Chocolatier, an old-fashioned candy shop, is located in the storefront adjacent to the museum. (Don't miss the budget bags of factory seconds.) There's also a "Heritage Chocolate Walk" offered, which combines a factory tour with a walk through the downtown's historic areas. Plan to spend about an hour here altogether.

73 Milltown Blvd. © **506/466-7848.** www.chocolatemuseum.ca. Admission C$5 (US$4.50/£2.50) adults, C$4 (US$3.60/£2) students and seniors, C$3 (US$2.70/£1.50) children under 6, C$15 (US$14/£7.50) families. Downtown tour plus museum C$10 (US$9/£5) adult, C$8 (US$7.20/£4) seniors and students, C$6 (US$5.40/£3) children under age 6, C$25 (US$23/£13) families. Mid-June to Aug Mon–Sat 9:30am–6:30pm, Sun 11am-3pm; mid-Mar to June and Sept–Nov Mon–Fri 10am–4pm (Sept also open Sat). Closed Dec to mid-Mar.

ST. ANDREWS *★★*

The village of St. Andrews—or St. Andrews by-the-Sea, as the chamber of commerce persists in calling it—traces its roots back to the days of the Loyalists. After the American Revolution, New Englanders who supported the British in the struggle were made to feel unwelcome. They decamped first to lovely little Castine, Maine, which they presumed was safely on British soil. But it wasn't; the St. Croix River was later determined to be the border between Canada and the United States. Forced to uproot

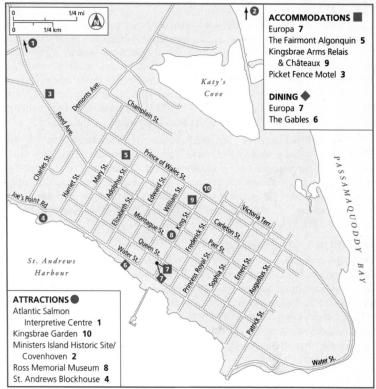

ACCOMMODATIONS ■
Europa **7**
The Fairmont Algonquin **5**
Kingsbrae Arms Relais
  & Châteaux **9**
Picket Fence Motel **3**

DINING ◆
Europa **7**
The Gables **6**

ATTRACTIONS ●
Atlantic Salmon
  Interpretive Centre **1**
Kingsbrae Garden **10**
Ministers Island Historic Site/
  Covenhoven **2**
Ross Memorial Museum **8**
St. Andrews Blockhouse **4**

once again, the Loyalists dismantled their new homes, loaded the pieces aboard ships, and rebuilt them on the welcoming peninsula of St. Andrews, which is not so far away by water. Some of these remarkably resilient saltbox houses still stand in town today.

This community later emerged as a fashionable summer resort in the late 19th century, when many of Canada's affluent and well-connected built homes and gathered annually here for social activities. The Tudor-style Algonquin hotel (now known as the Fairmont Algonquin) was then built in 1889 on a low-rise overlooking the town and quickly became the town's social hub and defining landmark.

St. Andrews is beautifully situated at the tip of a long, wedge-shaped peninsula. Thanks to its location off the beaten track, the village hasn't been spoiled much by modern development, and walking the wide, shady streets—especially those around the Algonquin—invokes a more genteel era. Some 250 homes around the village are more than a century old. A number of appealing boutiques and shops are spread along Water Street, which stretches for some distance along the town's shoreline, and it's easy to grab a boat tour from the waterfront as well. I definitely recommend this town if you're seeking a tame, easy tourism dip into New Brunswick. Also don't miss the weekly farmer's market, held Thursday mornings in summer on the waterfront.

ESSENTIALS

GETTING THERE   St. Andrews is located at the apex of Route 127, which dips southward from Route 1 between St. Stephen and St. George. It's an easy drive north from St. Stephen or south from Saint John (but more scenic coming from Saint John), and the turnoff is well marked from either direction. In case you don't have wheels, **Acadian Bus Lines** (② **800/567-5151** or 506/529-3101; www.smtbus.com) runs one daily bus trip between St. Andrews and Saint John; the one-way fare in 2007 was C$22 (US$20/£11) adult one-way, C$37 (US$33/£19) round-trip. Even better, the bus line offers discounts of 15% to 40% for children, students, and seniors.

VISITOR INFORMATION   St. Andrews' seasonal **Welcome Centre** (② **506/ 529-3556**) is located at 46 Reed Ave., on your left as you enter the village. It's in a hand-some 1914 home overarched by broad-crowned trees. It's open daily from 8am to 8pm in July and August, and from 9am to 5pm in May, June, and from September until it closes in early October. The rest of the year, contact the **Chamber of Commerce** in the same building (② **800/563-7397** or 506/529-3555) by writing P.O. Box 89, St. Andrews, NB E0G 2X0.

EXPLORING ST. ANDREWS

The chamber of commerce produces two brochures, the town map and directory and the St. Andrews by-the-Sea historic guide, both of which are free and can be found at the two visitor information centers. Also look for *A Guide to Historic St. Andrews,* produced by the St. Andrews Civic Trust. With these in hand you'll be able to launch an informed exploration. To make it even easier, many of the private dwellings in St. Andrews feature plaques with information on their origins. Look in particular for the saltbox-style homes, some of which are thought to be the original Loyalist structures that traveled here by barge.

The village's compact and handsome downtown flanks Water Street, a lengthy commercial street that parallels the bay. You'll find low, understated commercial architecture, much of it from the turn of the 20th century, that encompasses a gamut of styles. Allow an hour or so for browsing at boutiques and art galleries. There's also a mix of restaurants and inns.

Two blocks inland on King Street, you'll get a dose of local history at the **Ross Memorial Museum,** 188 Montague St. (② **506/529-5124**). The historic home was built in 1824; in 1945 it was left to the town by Rev. Henry Phipps Ross and Sarah Juliette Ross, complete with their eclectic and intriguing collection of period furniture, carpets, and paintings. The museum is open June to early October, Monday through Saturday from 10am to 4:30pm. Admission is by donation. Up the hill from the museum, at the head of King Street, is the steadily growing **Kingsbrae Garden,** worth a look (see below).

On the west end of Water Street, you'll come to Joe's Point Road at the foot of Harriet Street. The stout wooden **blockhouse** that sits just off the water behind low grass-covered earthworks was built by townspeople during the War of 1812, when the British colonials anticipated a U.S. attack that never came. This structure is all that remains of the scattered fortifications created around town during that war.

Across the street from the blockhouse is the peaceful Centennial Gardens, established in 1967 to mark the centenary of Canadian Confederation. The compact, tidy park has views of the bay and makes a pleasant spot for a picnic.

At the other end of Water Street, headed east from downtown, is the open space of Indian Point and the Passamaquoddy Ocean Park Campground. The views of the bay are panoramic; somehow it's even dramatic on foggy days, and swimming in these icy waters will earn you definite bragging rights.

Look for history right at your feet when exploring the park's rocky beaches: You'll sometimes turn up worn and rounded flint and coral that has washed ashore. It's not native but rather imported—early traders sailing here from afar loaded up their holds with flint from Dover, England, and coral from the Caribbean to serve as ballast on their crossings. When they arrived, the ballast was just dumped offshore, and today it still churns up from the depths.

For a more protected swimming spot, wander down **Acadia Drive,** which runs downhill behind the Algonquin. You'll come to popular Katy's Cove, where floating docks form a sort of natural saltwater swimming pool along a lovely inlet. You'll find a snack bar, a playground, and an affable sense of gracious ease here, and it's a fine place for families to while away an afternoon. There's a small fee.

BOAT TOURS

St. Andrews is an excellent spot to launch an exploration of the bay, which is very much alive, biologically speaking. On the water you'll look for whales, porpoises, seals, and bald eagles, no matter which trip you select. Two- to 3-hour tours generally run C$45 to C$50 (US$41–US$45/£23–£25) per adult, less for children.

Quoddy Link Marine (© 877/688-2600 or 506/529-2600) offers seasonal (late June to early Oct) whale-watch tours on a 17m (56-ft.) power catamaran, and the tour includes seafood snacks and use of binoculars; the tours take 2½ to 3 hours. Two-hour tours in search of wildlife aboard 7.2m (24-ft.) rigid-hull Zodiacs are offered by **Fundy Tide Runners** (© 506/529-4481); passengers wear flotation suits as they zip around the bay. This outfitter is open for a longer season than many others, from mid-May to mid-October.

For a more traditional experience, sign up for a trip aboard the 72-foot square-rigged cutter the *Jolly Breeze of St. Andrews* ⊛ with **Tall Ship Whale Watching** (© 506/529-8116). The outfit offers 3-hour tours under sail three times daily from mid-June through mid-October; tickets cost C$45 (US$41/£23) per adult, C$34 (US$31/£17) children 12 and under. A discount for families of four or more is available. Watch for seals, dolphins, and eagles—all have been sighted from the ship's deck.

Seascape Kayak Tours (© 866/747-1884 or 506/747-1884), in nearby Deer Island (see "Getting There," in the Campobello Island section, earlier), offers an up-close and personal view of the bay on half-day tours, with snacks provided during the 2½-hour run. No kayaking experience is needed. The trip costs C$59 (US$53/£30) adults, C$45 (US$41/£23) children. The outfit also offers a number of 3-day, 2-night trips for the serious kayaker throughout the summer.

Atlantic Salmon Interpretive Centre   The splashy visitor center of the Atlantic Salmon Federation, sometimes called Salar's World after the main exhibit, is dedicated to educating the public about the increasingly rare and surprisingly intriguing Atlantic salmon. Located in a bright and airy post-and-beam facility, the center allows visitors to get oriented through exhibits and presentations and by viewing salmon through underwater windows or strolling the outdoor walkways along Chamcook Stream. Plan to spend about a half-hour here.

24 Chamcook Rd. (6.5km/4 miles from St. Andrews via Rte. 127). ℂ **506/529-1384**. Admission C$5 (US$4.50/£2.50) adults, C$3.50 (US$3.15/£1.75) seniors and college students, C$3 (US$2.70/£1.50) children, C$13 (US$12/£6.50) families. Daily 9am–5pm. Closed Oct to mid-May.

Kingsbrae Garden *(Kids)*   This 11-hectare (27-acre) public garden opened in 1998, using the former grounds of a long-gone estate. The designers incorporated the existing high hedges and trees and have ambitiously planted open space around the mature plants. The entire project is very promising, and as the plantings take root and mature it's certain to become a noted stop for garden lovers. The grounds include almost 2,000 varieties of trees (including old-growth forest), shrubs, and plants. Among the notable features: a day lily collection, an extensive rose garden, a small maze, a fully functional Dutch windmill that circulates water through the two duck ponds, and a children's garden with an elaborate Victorian-mansion playhouse.

With views over the lush lawns to the bay below, the on-site Garden Cafe is a pleasant place to stop for lunch. (Try the thick, creamy seafood chowder and one of the focaccia-bread sandwiches.) There's also a gift shop and art gallery. Those with a horticultural bend should plan to spend at least a few hours here.

220 King St. ℂ **866/566-8687** or 506/529-3335. Admission C$9 (US$8.10/£4.50) adults, C$7.60 (US$6.85/£3.80) students and seniors, C$24 (US$22/£12) families, free for children under 6. Daily 9am–6pm. Closed early Oct to mid-May.

Ministers Island Historic Site/Covenhoven *(★★)*   This rugged, 200-plus-hectare (494-acre) island is linked to the mainland by a sandbar at low tide, and the 2-hour tours are scheduled around the tides. (Call for upcoming times.) You'll meet your tour guide on the mainland side, then drive your car out convoy-style across the ocean floor to the magical island estate created in 1890 by Sir William Van Horne.

Van Horne was president of the Canadian Pacific Railway and the person behind the extension of the rail line to St. Andrews. He then built a sandstone mansion (Covenhoven) with some 50 rooms (including 17 bedrooms), a circular bathhouse (where he indulged his passion for landscape painting), and one of Canada's largest and most impressive barns. The estate also features heated greenhouses, which produced grapes and mushrooms along with peaches that weighed up to 2 pounds each. When Van Horne was home in Montréal, he had fresh dairy products and vegetables shipped daily (by rail, of course) so that he could enjoy fresh produce year-round. You'll learn all this, and more, on the tours.

Rte. 127 (northeast of St. Andrews), Chamcook. ℂ **506/529-5081**. Admission C$8 (US$7.20/£4) adults, C$7 (US$6.30/£3.50) seniors and students, C$25 (US$23/£13) families, free for children 6 and under. Closed mid-Oct to mid-May.

WHERE TO STAY

Those traveling on a budget instead of seeking the luxury digs below might head for the **Picket Fence Motel,** 102 Reed Ave. (ℂ **506/529-8985**). This trim and tidy property is near the handsome, newly expanded Algonquin golf course (see "Golf," earlier in this chapter) and within walking distance of St. Andrews' village center. Rooms cost C$69 to C$85 (US$62–US$77/£35–£43) double.

Or, for something slightly more upscale yet unlikely to break your bank, contact the **Europa** *(★★)* restaurant (see "Where to Dine," below); the owners rent out a series of rooms, suites, and an apartment collectively rated at 3½ stars by Canada's government hotel-rating agency for C$69 to C$149 (US$62–US$134/£35–£75) double. The suites and apartment have kitchenettes.

The Fairmont Algonquin ⭐⭐   The Algonquin's distinguished pedigree dates from 1889, when it opened its doors to wealthy vacationers seeking respite from city heat. The original structure was destroyed by fire in 1914, but the surviving annexes were rebuilt in Tudor style; in 1993 an architecturally sympathetic addition was built across the road, linked by a gatehouse-inspired bridge. The red tile–roofed resort commands one's attention through its sheer size and aristocratic bearing (not to mention through its kilt-wearing, bagpipe-playing staff). The inn is several long blocks from the water's edge; it's perched on the brow of a hill and affords panoramic bay views from the second-floor roof garden and many guest rooms. The rooms have been refreshed and are comfortable and tasteful. In addition to the outstanding seaside golf course (see "Golf," earlier), there's a spa at the hotel featuring a full card of treatments ranging from facials and nail services to body wraps and massage. Note that the hotel markets itself to bus tours and conferences, and if your timing is bad you might feel a bit overwhelmed by one or more of them. On the upside, the resort's main **dining room** ⭐⭐, open May to October, is one of the more enjoyable spots in town—it's often bustling with summer folks (which means good people-watching), and the kitchen produces some surprisingly creative meals. Informal dining options include The Library Lounge & Bistro (just off the main lobby) and the downstairs lounge. Farther afield, the food at the Clubhouse Grill on the resort's golf course is worth the drive; it's open May through October.

184 Adolphus St., St. Andrews, NB E5B 1T7. ☏ 800/441-1414 or 506/529-8823. Fax 506/529-7162. www.fairmont.com. 234 units. C$99–C$459 (US$89–US$413/£50–£230) double; C$299–C$1,169 (US$269–US$1,052/£150–£585) suite. Rates include continental breakfast. AE, DC, MC, V. Valet parking. Small cats and dogs C$25 (US$24/£13) per night. **Amenities:** 2 restaurants; 2 bars; outdoor heated pool; golf course; 2 tennis courts; health club; spa; Jacuzzi; sauna; bike rentals; children's programs; game room; concierge; salon; babysitting; laundry service; dry cleaning. *In room:* TV, dataport, minibar, coffeemaker, hair dryer, iron.

Kingsbrae Arms Relais & Châteaux ⭐⭐⭐   Kingsbrae Arms, part of the Relais & Châteaux network, is a five-star inn with an upscale European feel. Located at the top of King Street, it occupies an 1897 manor house, where the furnishings all seem to have a story to tell. The home, built by prosperous jade merchants in 1897, occupies .4 hectares (1 acre), all of which have been well employed. A heated pool sits amid rose gardens at the foot of a lawn, and immediately next door is the 11-hectare (27-acre) Kingsbrae Horticultural Gardens; some guest rooms have wonderful views of the gardens, while others offer a panoramic sweep of the bay. Guests will feel pampered, with amenities including 325-thread-count sheets, plush robes, and a complete guest-services suite stocked with complimentary snacks and refreshments. Some rooms have Jacuzzis; all have gas fireplaces. Guests can also enjoy a five-course meal around a stately table in the dining room during peak season. (This dining room is not open to the public.) One meal is offered nightly, and the *nouveau* Canadian-style cuisine is ever-changing and good. Entrees on a given visit might include Fundy salmon, PEI mussels, roasted guinea hen, goat cheese in a hazelnut crust New Zealand rack of lamb, or Alberta steaks; quality wines are carefully paired with these meals. Note that rates are in American dollars, rather than Canadian.

219 King St., St. Andrews, NB E5B 1Y1. ☏ 506/529-1897. Fax 506/529-1197. www.kingsbrae.com. 8 units. US$585–US$985 (C$650–C$1,094/£325–£547) double. 2-night minimum; 3-night minimum July–Aug weekends. 5% room service charge additional. AE, MC, V. Closed Nov–Apr. Pets allowed with advance permission. **Amenities:** Babysitting; laundry service; dry cleaning. *In room:* A/C, TV, coffeemaker, hair dryer, iron/ironing board, Jacuzzi (some units).

WHERE TO DINE

Europa ★★ (Finds) CONTINENTAL   In an intriguing yellow building that once housed a movie theater and dance hall, Bavarian husband-and-wife transplants Markus and Simone Ritter whip up great French-, Swiss-, and German-accented Continental cuisine for a 35-seat room. Starters include smoked salmon with *rösti* and capers; a house specialty of seared scallops in Mornay sauce, baked with cheese; French onion soup; and escargots. Main courses run to several versions of schnitzel (grilled pork or veal steak), each with distinct fillings, toppings, and sauces; beef stroganoff; duck a l'Orange; rack of lamb; haddock in lemon butter or champagne sauce; steak in béarnaise sauce; and tiger shrimp in mango-curry sauce. All are prepared with skill and restraint. Finish with chocolate mousse, homemade almond parfait, or one of about a dozen homemade ice creams or sorbets. The wine list is also surprisingly strong given that this is such a small, out-of-the-way town. All in all, consider this restaurant a gem—a should-get-there spot if you're at all in the area.

48 King St. © 506/529-3818. Reservations recommended. Main courses C$18–C$27 (US$16–US$24/£9–£14). MC, V. Mid-May to Sept daily 5–9pm; Oct Tues–Sat 5–9pm; Nov to mid-Feb Thurs–Sat 5–9pm. Closed mid-Feb to mid-May.

The Gables SEAFOOD/PUB FARE   This informal eatery is located in a trim home with prominent gables fronting Water Street, though you enter down a narrow alley where sky and water views suddenly break through a soaring window from a spacious outside deck. Inside, expect a bright and lively local spot with a casual maritime decor and fare; outside there's a plastic porch-furniture informality. Breakfast is served during peak season only, with homemade baked goods and rosemary potatoes. Lunch and dinner options include burgers, steaks, and seafood items such as breaded haddock, daily catches, and a lobster clubhouse—a chopped lobster salad with cheese, cucumber, lettuce, and tomato. There's a kid's menu as well, while margaritas and sangria are available by the pitcher for the adults in the party. The view tends to pull rank on the menu, but if you like simple fare, both will satisfy.

143 Water St. © 506/529-3440. Main courses C$3.95–C$6.95 (US$3.55–US$6.25/£2–£3.50) at breakfast, C$7.50–C$25 (US$6.75–US$23/£3.75–£13) at lunch and dinner. MC, V. July–Aug daily 8am–11pm; Sept–June daily 11am–9pm.

4 Grand Manan Island (★)

Geologically rugged, profoundly peaceful, and indisputably remote, this handsome island of 2,800 year-round residents is a 90-minute ferry ride from the port of Blacks Harbour, which is just southeast of St. George. Despite being located incredibly close to Maine (and the U.S.), Grand Manan is a much-prized destination for adventurous travelers—sometimes a highlight of their vacation. Yet the island also remains a mystifying puzzle for others who fail to be smitten by its rough-edged charm. Either this is your kind of place or it isn't; perhaps there's no in-between. The only way to find out is to visit.

Grand Manan is a special favorite both among serious **birders** and serious enthusiasts of Pulitzer Prize–winning novelist Willa Cather, who found her way from Nebraska and New York to a summer cottage here. Hiking the island's famous trails, don't be surprised to come across knots of very quiet people peering intently through binoculars. These are the birders, not the Cather fans. Nearly 300 different species of birds either nest here or stop by the island during their long migrations, and it's a good place to add to your "life list," if you're into such a pursuit—with birds ranging from bald eagles to puffins (though you'll need to sign up for a boat tour to catch a glimpse of the latter), you're sure to see something with wings you've never seen before.

Cather wrote some of her books while staying on the island. Her die-hard fans are as easy to spot as the birders, say locals, and something of a wild breed; during one Cather conference some years ago, several dozen got up, wrapped themselves in sheets, and danced around a bonfire during the summer solstice—I'm not sure what that was all about, but there you have it.

ESSENTIALS

GETTING THERE   Grand Manan is connected to Blacks Harbour on the mainland via frequent ferry service in summer. **Coastal Transport ferries** (© **506/ 642-0520;** www.coastaltransport.ca), each capable of hauling 60 cars, depart from the mainland and the island every 2 hours between 7:30am and 5:30pm during July and August; a ferry makes three to four daily trips the rest of the year. The round-trip fare was C$11 (US$9.90/£5.50) per passenger, C$5.20 (US$4.70/£2.60) for ages 5 to 12, and C$31 (US$28/£16) per car in 2007. Boarding the ferry on the mainland is free; you purchase tickets when you leave the island.

Reserve your return trip at least a day ahead to avoid getting stranded on the island, and get in line early to secure a spot. A good strategy for departing from Blacks Harbour is to bring a picnic lunch, arrive an hour or two early, put your car in line, and head to the grassy waterfront park adjacent to the wharf. It's an attractive spot; there's even an island to explore at low tide.

VISITOR INFORMATION   The island's **Visitor Information Centre,** Route 776, Grand Manan, NB E5G 4E9 (© **888/525-1655** or 506/662-3442), is open Monday to Friday in summer (8am–5pm; Sun 9am–1pm) in the town of Grand Harbour. It's closed mid-September to early June; if so, ask at island stores or inns for a free island map published by the **Grand Manan Tourism Association** (www.grandmanannb.com), which has a listing of key island phone numbers.

EXPLORING THE ISLAND

Start your explorations before you arrive. As you come abreast of the island aboard the ferry, head to the starboard side. You'll soon see **Seven Days' Work** in the rocky cliffs of Whale's Cove, where seven layers of hardened lava and sill (intrusive igneous rock) have come together in a sort of geological Dagwood sandwich.

You can begin to open the puzzle box that is local geology at the **Grand Manan Museum** (© **506/662-3424**) in Grand Harbour, one of three villages on the island's eastern shore. The museum's geology exhibit, located in the basement, offers pointers about what to look for as you roam the island. Birders will enjoy the Allan Moses collection upstairs, which features 230 stuffed and mounted birds in glass cases. The museum also has an impressive lighthouse lens from the Gannet Rock Lighthouse, and a collection of stuff that's washed ashore from the frequent shipwrecks. The museum is open from June to September, Monday through Friday, 10am to 4pm; it's also open Sundays 1 to 5pm in July and August. Admission is C$4 (US$3.60/£2) adults, C$2 (US$1.80/£1) seniors and students, and free for children under 12.

This relatively flat and compact island is perfect for exploring by bike; the only stretches to avoid are some of the faster, less scenic segments of Route 776. All the side roads offer **superb biking.** Especially nice is the paved **cross-island road** ❀❀ to **Dark Harbour,** where you'll find a few cabins, dories, and salmon pens. The route is wild and hilly at times, but offers a memorable descent to the ocean on the island's west side.

Bike rentals are available at **Adventure High** ✿ (𝒞 **800/732-5492** or 506/662-3563) in North Head, not far from the ferry. (Day-trippers who are fit enough should consider leaving their cars at **Blacks Harbour** and exploring the island by bike alone, then returning on the last ferry.) Adventure High also offers sea kayak tours of the island's shores for those who prefer a **cormorant's-eye view** ✿ of the impressive cliffs. Bikes rent for C$22 (US$20/£11) per day, C$16 (US$14/£8) for a half-day. Kayak tours run from C$39 (US$35/£20) for a 2-hour sunset tour to C$99 (US$89/£50) for a full day's excursion. The company even rents out cabins.

While Grand Manan is very quiet, you can find more solitude and cross one more island off your "life list" on **White Head Island.** To get there, drive to Ingalls Head (follow Ingalls Head Rd. from Grand Harbour) and catch the half-hour ferry to this rocky island, home to about 200 locals. On the island, you can walk along the shore to the lighthouse guarding the way between Battle Beach and Sandy Cove. The ferry holds 10 cars, is free of charge, and sails up to 10 times daily in summer.

HIKING

Numerous hiking trails lace the island, and they offer a popular diversion throughout the summer. Trails can be found just about everywhere, but most are a matter of local knowledge. Don't hesitate to ask at your inn or the tourist information center, or to ask anyone you might meet on the street. *A Hiking Guide to New Brunswick* (Goose Lane Editions; 𝒞 **506/450-4251**) lists 12 hikes with maps; this handy book is often sold on the ferry.

The most accessible clusters of trails are at the island's northern and southern tips. Head north up Whistle Road to Whistle Beach, and you'll find both the **Northwestern Coastal Trail** ✿ and the **Seven Days' Work Trail** ✿, both of which track along the rocky shoreline. Near the low lighthouse and towering radio antennae at Southwest Head (follow Rte. 776 to the end), trails radiate out along cliffs topped with scrappy forest; the views are remarkable when the fog's not in.

WHALE-WATCHING & BOAT TOURS

A fine way to experience island ecology is to mosey offshore. Several outfitters offer complete nature tours, providing a nice sampling of the world above and beneath the sea. On an excursion you might see minke, finback, or humpback whales, along with exotic birds including puffins and phalaropes. **Sea Watch Tours** (𝒞 **506/662-8552**), run by Peter and Kenda Wilcox, operates a series of 5-hour excursions from mid-June to early August, with whale sightings guaranteed or your money back, aboard a 13m (43-ft.) vessel with canopy. The rate is C$59 (US$53/£30) for adults and C$39 (US$35/£20) per child.

WHERE TO STAY

Anchorage Provincial Park ✿ (𝒞 **506/662-7022**) has about 100 campsites scattered about forest and field, available late May to mid-September. There's a small beach and a hiking trail on the property, and it's well situated for exploring the southern part of the island. It's very popular midsummer; call before you board the ferry to ask about campsite availability. Sites are C$22 to C$35 (US$20–US$32/£11–£18), some with hookups for RVs and some better suited for a simple tent.

Inn at Whale Cove Cottages ✿✿   The Inn at Whale Cove is a delightful, family-run compound set in a grassy meadow overlooking a quiet cove. The original building is a cozy farmhouse that dates to 1816. It's been restored with a nice selection of simple country antiques. The three guest rooms in the main house are comfortable (Sally's Attic has a small deck and a large view); the living room has a couple years' worth of good reading and a welcoming fireplace. Five cottages are scattered about the property, and they vary in size from one to four bedrooms; some only rent by the week, others daily. One of the older units was author Willa Cather's famous cottage, while the newer John's Flat and Cove View cottages are the most modern, with such amenities as extra bedrooms and dining rooms, decks, televisions, laundry service, and in one case a Jacuzzi. Views are lovely. The 4-hectare (10-acre) grounds, especially the path down to the quiet cove-side beach, are wonderful to explore. Innkeeper Laura Buckley received her culinary training in Toronto, and her **dining room** ⚜ demonstrates a deft touch with local ingredients. The changing daily menu might include a rack of lamb cooked Provence-style, a scallop ravioli, a pork tenderloin with a rhubarb sauce, steaks, or local seafood. From June through mid-October, dinner is served nightly. It's served weekends only from May to early June.

Whistle Rd. (P.O. Box 233), North Head, Grand Manan, NB E0G 2M0. © 506/662-3181. 3 rooms, 5 cottages (some only rented by week). C$105–C$150 (US$95–US$135/£53–£75) double; C$800–C$900 (US$720–US$810/£400–£450) weekly cottage. Rates include full breakfast. MC, V. All but 1 unit closed Nov–Apr. Pets accepted for C$5 (US$4.50/£2) per day. **Amenities:** Dining room. *In room:* TV (2 units), kitchenette (3 units), Jacuzzi (1 unit).

Shorecrest Lodge ⚜ (Value) (Kids)   This century-old inn is a place to put your feet up and unwind. Located just a few hundred yards from the ferry, the inn is nicely decorated with a mix of modern furniture and eclectic country antiques. Most of the guest rooms have private bathrooms, a rarity for Grand Manan. The best might be Room no. 8 with its burgundy leather chairs and harbor view. Kids like the TV room in back, which also stocks games and a library that's long on local natural history. The country-style dining room has a fireplace and hardwood floors, and a menu of local fresh seafood, pizza, chicken, and beef tenderloin. Most entrees are around C$24 (US$22/£12), and the Shorecrest's owners also offer a fondue meal, for groups reserving at least 1 day in advance. The dining room is open daily from 5 to 9pm during peak season; hours are limited, however, during the shoulder seasons. Don't feel like sitting indoors? The lodge also maintains an outdoor grill area for firing up your mini–Iron Chef competition.

100 Rte. 776, North Head, Grand Manan, NB E5G 1A1. © 506/662-3216. www.shorecrestlodge.com. 10 units, 8 with private bathroom. C$65–C$119 (US$59–US$107/£33–£60) double. Rates include continental breakfast. MC, V. Closed Nov–May. **Amenities:** Restaurant; fitness room. *In room:* No phone.

WHERE TO DINE

Options for dining out aren't exactly extravagant on Grand Manan. The inns listed above offer good meals, and you'll encounter a few more family restaurants and grocers along the road as well. If you're here on Saturday morning, check out the weekly **farmer's market** in North Head.

In the mood for a dare? Try walking into **North Head Bakery** ⚜⚜ (© 506/ 662-8862) at 199 Rte. 776 and walking out without buying anything. It cannot be done. This superb bakery (open Tues–Sat 6am–6pm) has used traditional baking methods and whole grains since it opened in 1990. Breads made daily include a crusty, seven-grain Saint John Valley bread and a delightful egg-and-butter bread—nor should the chocolate-chip cookies be overlooked. The bakery is on Route 776 on the left when you're heading south from the ferry.

5 Saint John ⭑

Centered on a good-size commercial harbor, Saint John is New Brunswick's largest city and the center of much of the province's industry. Spread out over a low hill with good rocky views, the downtown boasts wonderfully elaborate Victorian flourishes on its rows of commercial buildings. (Be sure to look high along the cornices to appreciate the intricate brickwork.) A handful of impressive mansions lord over the side streets, their interiors a forest of intricate wood carving—appropriately so, as timber barons built most of them.

There's an industrial grittiness to Saint John, which some find unappealing and others find charming. It all depends on your outlook. Just don't expect a tidy garden city with lots of neat homes; this isn't that sort of place. Instead, Saint John offers a surfeit of brick architecture in various states of repair. Throughout the downtown you'll get glimpses of its past and present industry: large shipping terminals, oil storage facilities, and paper mills of the sort that were so popular with Ashcan artists. (A 1978 book on New Brunswick put it diplomatically: "Saint John's heavy industries ensure that the city is not famed for beauty, but the setting is magnificent.")

More or less, that's the truth. Don't let this put you off, though—instead take a detour from the main coastal highway downtown. It does take some effort—the traffic engineers have been very mischievous, leading you around rather than into the city. When you finally arrive, though, you'll discover an intriguing place to take an afternoon stroll while awaiting the ferry to Digby, grab a delicious bite to eat and a pint of ale, and possibly stay the night while breaking up your driving and cute-village-hopping routine. The streets here often bustle with everyone from skateboarders to out-for-the-weekenders to dowagers shopping at the public market.

Note that Saint John is *always* spelled out, just as I have done in this sentence. It's never abbreviated as "St. John." That's to keep mail destined for St. John's in Newfoundland from ending up here by mistake, and vice versa. Good thinking. But don't worry if you get it mixed up: The locals will be quick to correct you if you err.

ESSENTIALS

GETTING THERE   Saint John is located on Route 1. It's 106km (66 miles) from the U.S. border at St. Stephens and 427km (265 miles) from Halifax, Nova Scotia.

Year-round ferry service connects Saint John to Digby, Nova Scotia. See "Exploring New Brunswick" at the beginning of this chapter for more information. Saint John's **airport,** coded YSJ (© **506/696-0200;** www.saintjohnairport.com), has regular flights to and from Montréal, Toronto, and Halifax on **Air Canada Jazz** (© **888/AIR-CANA;** www.flyjazz.ca). **WestJet** (© **800/538-5696;** www.westjet.com) also runs occasional service from Toronto. There are auto-rental kiosks in the terminal, and a taxi ride into the city costs about C$30 (US$27/£15).

VISITOR INFORMATION   Saint John (www.tourismsaintjohn.com) is fully stocked with *three* (count'em) **visitor information centers.** Arriving from the west, look for a contemporary triangular building near the Route 1 off-ramp, open mid-May to early October, where you'll find a trove of information and brochures (© **506/658-2940**). A smaller seasonal **information center,** off exits 119A and 119B of Route 1, is located inside the observation building overlooking Reversing Falls on Route 100 (© **506/658-2937**). It's also open mid-May to early October.

Saint John

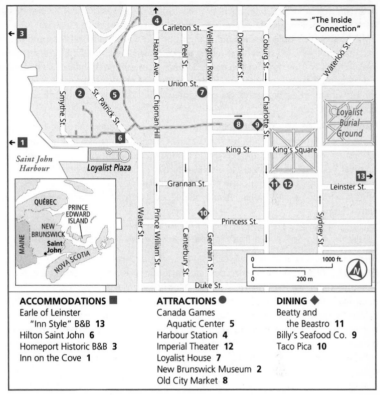

```
                                                    ↑
                                    ④  Carleton St.            ╌╌╌ "The Inside
                                                                   Connection"
```

ACCOMMODATIONS ■
Earle of Leinster
  "Inn Style" B&B **13**
Hilton Saint John **6**
Homeport Historic B&B **3**
Inn on the Cove **1**

ATTRACTIONS ●
Canada Games
  Aquatic Center **5**
Harbour Station **4**
Imperial Theater **12**
Loyalist House **7**
New Brunswick Museum **2**
Old City Market **8**

DINING ◆
Beatty and
  the Beastro **11**
Billy's Seafood Co. **9**
Taco Pica **10**

If you've already made your way downtown, or need info outside of the peak seasons, look for the city's **City Centre Tourist Information Centre** (☎ 886/GO-FUNDY or 506/658-2855) inside Market Square, a downtown shopping mall just off the waterfront reached via Exit 122 off Route 1. Find the info center by entering the square at street level at the corner of St. Patrick and Water streets. During peak season (mid-June to mid-Sept) the center is open daily from 9am to 7pm. The rest of the year it's open daily 9am to 5:30pm.

EXPLORING SAINT JOHN

If the weather's cooperative, start by wandering around near the **waterfront.** Tourism Saint John has published three walking-tour brochures that offer plenty of history and architectural trivia, including a rundown of the odd and interesting gargoyles and sculpted heads that adorn the brick and stone 19th-century buildings downtown. If you have time for only one tour, I'd opt for **"Prince William's Walk,"** an hour-long, self-guided tour of the impressive commercial buildings. Obtain the tour brochures at the **Market Square information center.**

Try to end your walk at the **Old Burial Ground** across from King's Square, which is an especially attractive spot to wander while reading the old headstones or simply to sit and rest your feet. The cemetery dates from 1784 but was recently renovated—note the new beaver fountain, symbolic of the town's hardworking citizens.

If the weather's disagreeable (and it might be), just head indoors. Over the past 2 decades, Saint John has been busy linking its downtown malls and shops with an elaborate network of underground and overhead pedestrian walkways, dubbed **"The Inside Connection."** It's not only for shopping—two major hotels, the provincial museum, the city library, the city market, the sports arena, and the aquatic center are all part of this network.

Canada Games Aquatic Centre   The gleaming and modern Aquatic Centre was built right downtown in 1985 for the Canada Games. It remains a remarkably popular destination for exercise and recreation among locals, and it's also open to the public most hours all week long. You do have to pay admission, however. The facilities include an eight-lane Olympic-size pool, warm-up and leisure pools, water slides, rope swings, whirlpools, and saunas. Also available are weight and exercise rooms (for an extra charge).

50 Union St. ℂ **506/658-4715.** Admission C$7.50 (US$6.75/£3.75) adults, C$5 (US$4.50/£2.50) children, C$20 (US$18/£10) families. Summer Mon–Thurs 6am–9pm, Fri 6am–8pm; rest of year Mon–Thurs 6am–10pm, Fri 6am–9pm.

Loyalist House   A mandatory destination for serious antiques buffs, this stately Georgian home was built in 1817 for the Merritt family, who were wealthy Loyalists from Rye, New York. Inside is an extraordinary collection of furniture dating from before 1833; most pieces were original to the house and have never left. Especially notable are the extensive holdings of Duncan Phyfe Sheraton furniture and a rare piano-organ combination. The house also features doors steamed and bent to fit into the curved sweep of the stairway, and intricate carvings on the wooden chair rails. Tours last 30 to 45 minutes, depending on the number of questions you ask. Note that this house is open only 2 months out of the year, though it does sometimes open in the fall when cruise ships are at port in the harbor. Failing to catch one of those in town, you might get together a small interested group or big family, give these folks a call, and ask them nicely to open the house.

120 Union St. ℂ **506/652-3590.** C$3 (US$2.70/£1.50) adults, C$1 (US90¢/50p) children, C$7 (US$6.30/£3.50) families. July–Aug daily 10am–5pm; June Mon–Fri 10am–5pm; Sept–Apr by appointment only.

New Brunswick Museum ⚓ *Kids*   The New Brunswick Museum is an excellent stop for anyone the least bit curious about the province's natural or cultural history. The collections are displayed on three open floors, and they offer a nice mix of traditional artifacts and quirky objects. (Among the more memorable items is a frightful-looking "permanent wave" machine from a 1930s beauty parlor.) The exhaustive exhibits include the complete interior of Sullivan's Bar (where longshoremen used to slake their thirst a few blocks away), a massive section of a ship frame, a wonderful geological exhibit, and even a sporty white Bricklin from a failed New Brunswick automobile-manufacturing venture in the mid-1970s. The Wind, Wood, and Sail exhibit describes 19th-century shipbuilding in the province. Allow at least 2 hours to enjoy these eclectic and uncommonly well-displayed exhibits.

1 Market Sq. ℂ **506/643-2300.** Admission C$6 (US$5.40/£3) adults, C$4.75 (US$4.30/£2.40) seniors, C$3.25 (US$2.95/£1.65) students and children 4–18, C$13 (US$12/£6.50) families. June–Oct Mon–Fri 9am–5pm (Thurs until 9pm), Sat 10am–5pm, Sun noon–5pm. Closed Mon Nov–May.

Old City Market 🎖🎖 Hungry travelers venture here at their peril! This spacious, bustling, and bright marketplace is crammed with vendors hawking meat, fresh seafood, cheeses, flowers, baked goods, and bountiful fresh produce. You can even sample *dulse,* a snack of dried seaweed from the Bay of Fundy. (One traveler has compared the experience to licking a wharf.) The market was built in 1876, and it has been a center of commerce for the city ever since. Note the construction of the roof—local lore says it resembles an inverted ship because it was made by boat builders who didn't know how to build anything else. And watch for the small, enduring traces of tradition: The handsome iron gates at either end have been in place since 1880, and the loud bell is rung daily by the Deputy Market Clerk, who signals the opening and closing of the market. A number of vendors offer meals to go, and there's a bright seating area in an enclosed terrace on the market's south side. It's worth an hour or two (including a stop to eat, of course).

47 Charlotte St. ⓒ **506/658-2820**. Mon–Thurs 7:30am–6pm; Fri 7:30am–7pm; Sat 7:30am–5pm. Closed Sun and holidays.

OUTDOOR PURSUITS

Irving Nature Park Located along the coast across the Saint John River (take Exit 119A off Rte. 1 and follow Bleury St. to Sand Cove Rd.), the Irving Nature Park consists of 240 dramatic coastal hectares (593 acres) where as many as 240 species of birds have been spotted. Soft wood-chipped trails and marsh boardwalks provide access to a lovely forest and wild, salty seascapes. The observation tower on the "Squirrel Trail" gives a fine vantage of the park and its mud flats, where migrating sandpipers devour shrimp for a week to double their weight before flying 4 days nonstop to Surinam. Seals throng the park in mid-June and mid-October and are so thick on the rocks that they've been described as "a great gray noisy carpet." This park can get very busy—there are some 125,000 visitors a year—and Sundays are most popular. Call beforehand to ask about the excellent tours; otherwise, you can see everything in an hour.

Sand Cove Rd. ⓒ **506/653-7367**. Free admission and tours. Daily dawn–dusk; early May to mid-Nov information booth staffed daily.

Reversing Falls *Overrated* Just west of downtown is Reversing Falls, located within an impressive rocky gorge. Because of the huge local tides, sets of rapids, small waterfalls, and big, slurping whirlpools flow one way up through the gorge during the incoming tide, then reverse during the opposite tide. It's a sometimes-dramatic sight, but few publicity photos or descriptions include the important fact that there's a huge paper mill right next door and an active train trestle and a busy highway spanning the gorge over the falls. Don't come expecting a wild natural place. There are several ways to observe the spectacle: Scramble down the wooden steps to a park along the river's edge, or climb up atop a rooftop viewing platform, both for free. Across the river is **Fallsview Park** (turn left on Douglas Ave., then left again on Fallsview Ave.), where you can get a duck's-eye view of the river from another small park directly across from the mill. At **The Falls Restaurant** (ⓒ **506/635-1999**), open year-round, you're paying for the view, not the food. If you can't get a table overlooking the falls, skip it.

If you've got the courage and cash, check this out: Departing from a narrow cove at Fallsview Park are **Reversing Falls Jet Boat Rides** (ⓒ **888/634-8987** or 506/634-8987), which offer fun, fast boat trips through the falls at all tides and also out through the harbor. The always-breezy, sometimes-damp trips take 20 minutes and cost about C$32 (US$29/£16) adults, C$26 (US$23/£13) children, C$106

(US$95/£53) families; all include use of raincoats. Reservations are recommended during peak season.

Rte. 100. ℂ **506/658-2937.** Free admission to viewing platform. Early June to mid-Oct daylight hours, but best at low or high tide. Call for tidal schedule.

Rockwood Park   The footpaths attract walkers and joggers to this 880-hectare (2,175-acre) urban preserve of lakes, forest, and rocky hills. But there is also swimming at sandy lake beaches, golf at an 18-hole municipal course (ℂ **506/634-0090;** greens fees C$18–C$35/US$16–US$32/£9–£18), picnic areas, a campground, and a small zoo with 38 species of exotic animals (including six species of monkeys, all on the endangered species list). Boat rentals include canoes and kayaks. There's also an aquatic driving range, where duffers practice their swings by hitting floating golf balls into a lake, which are later harvested by boat. The park, located just 5 minutes' drive north of downtown, is especially popular on weekends.

Lake Dr. S. ℂ **506/658-2883.** Free admission; fees charged for various activities. Interpretation Centre late May to early Sept daily 8am–dusk.

WHERE TO STAY

Budget travelers should head to Manawagonish Road for lower-priced motels. Unlike many other motel strips, which tend to be notably unlovely, Manawagonish Road is reasonably attractive. It winds along a high ridge of residential homes west of town, with views out to the Bay of Fundy. It's about a 10-minute drive into downtown. Rates at most motels here are approximately C$50 to C$60 (US$45–US$54/£25–£30) during peak season. The **Econo Lodge,** 1441 Manawagonish Rd. (ℂ **800/55-ECONO** or 506/635-8700), is somewhat more expensive but a bit more comfortable, and the rooms have sweeping views.

In-town camping is available summers at **Rockwood Park** (ℂ **506/652-4050**). Some 80 sites are spread across a rocky hill; many overlook downtown, the highway, and a rail yard (expect nighttime noise). RVs requesting full hookups are directed to an area resembling a parking lot, but it's quite serviceable. Other sites vary widely in privacy and scenic attributes. Rates range from about C$18 (US$16/£9) for a tent site to around C$24 (US$22/£12) for hookups. Follow signs to the park from either Exit 122 or Exit 125 off Route 1.

EXPENSIVE

Hilton Saint John 🏵   This 12-story waterfront hotel was built in 1984 and has the amenities one would expect from an upscale chain hotel. Rooms on the top two Plaza Floors were repainted, redecorated, and upgraded to include perks such as electronic safes, cordless phones, bigger desks, and terry-cloth robes. This property boasts the best location in Saint John, overlooking the harbor yet just steps from the rest of downtown by street or indoor walkway. Windows in all guest rooms open, a nice touch when the breeze is coming from the sea. The Hilton is connected to the convention center and attracts major events; ask whether anything's scheduled before you book if you don't want to be overwhelmed by conventioneers.

The hotel's lounge offers light meals from 11:30am to midnight daily. For more refined fare, head for the main dining room, which serves three meals daily in an understated and classical harborside setting. Entrees include creatively prepared steaks, pheasant, and salmon.

1 Market Sq., Saint John, NB E2L 4Z6. ℂ **800/561-8282** in Canada, 800/445-8667 in the U.S., or 506/693-8484. Fax 509/657-6610. www.hiltonsaintjohn.com. 197 units. C$119–C$219 (US$107–US$197/£60–£110) double. AE, DC,

DISC, MC, V. Self-parking C$15 (US$14/£7.50) per day. Pets allowed. **Amenities:** 2 restaurants; bar; indoor pool; fitness room; Jacuzzi; sauna; game room; concierge; car-rental desk; business center; salon; 24-hr. room service; babysitting; laundry service. *In room:* A/C, TV, dataport, minibar, coffeemaker, hair dryer, iron, safe.

Homeport Historic Bed & Breakfast 🍂🍂 *Kids*   This architecturally impressive Italianate home built by a prominent shipbuilding family sits high atop a rocky ridge on the north side of Route 1, overlooking downtown and the harbor. Built around 1858 (that's before Canada was even Canada), this is one of southern New Brunswick's best options for an overnight if you're a fan of old houses and furnishings. Rooms are fitted with materials gleaned from local auctions and shops; look for such touches as sleigh beds and (nonworking) marble fireplaces. The Veranda Room in particular is spacious, has fine harbor views, and gets superb afternoon sun. The walls are decorated with steel engravings commemorating the laying of the first trans-Atlantic cable, floors are wide-board hand-cut pine, and there's locally made antique furniture. The Harbour Master Suite has a four-posted bed and a small, separate sitting room that's ideal for those traveling with a child or two. All units also have individually controlled heat, a rarity in such an inn. "Come-hungry" breakfasts are served family-style around a long antique table in the formal dining room.

80 Douglas Ave. (take exit 121 or 123 to Main St.), Saint John, NB E2K 1E4. © **888/678-7678** or 506/672-7255. Fax 506/672-7250. www.homeport.nb.ca. 10 units. C$110–C$175 (US$99–US$158/£55–£88) double. Rates include full breakfast. Free parking. AE, MC, V. *In room:* A/C, TV, dataport, kitchenette (1 unit), fridge (1 unit).

Inn on the Cove & Spa 🍂🍂   Inns like to tout celebrity connections, but the Inn on the Cove has one of the thinnest links to fame you'll encounter: It was built by Alexander Graham Bell's gardener. Nevertheless, it's a lovely place in a lovely setting, on a quiet road overlooking the water, about a 15-minute drive from the city center. The Irving Nature Park is next door; guests can hike right from the inn to dramatic Sheldon's Point. The house, built in 1910, was once a classic late Victorian; subsequent changes to the architecture created bright, spacious rooms that take full advantage of the amazing views. A few of the Superior rooms offer some of the best bathtub views in the Maritimes; on the other hand, the least expensive room has a detached private bathroom down the hall with the same view. All rooms have complimentary high-speed Internet. Meals here are excellent, and there's a day spa offering mud wraps, facials, and more for an extra charge, as well as a hair salon. This is a much-celebrated and written-about inn, and with good reason.

1371 Sand Cove Rd. (mailing address: P.O. Box 3113, Station B, Saint John, NB E2M 4X7). © **877/257-8080** or 506/672-7799. Fax 506/635-5455. www.innonthecove.com. 8 units. Late June to mid-Oct C$175–C$225 (US$158–US$203/£88–£113) double; rest of the year C$125–C$195 (US$113–US$176/£63–£98) double. Rates include full breakfast. MC, V. Small dogs allowed in kennels. Children 12 and up welcome. **Amenities:** Restaurant; day spa; salon. *In room:* A/C, TV/DVD, kitchenette (1 unit), coffeemaker, hair dryer.

MODERATE

Earle of Leinster "Inn Style" Bed & Breakfast *Value*   For more than a decade, Lauree and Stephen Savoie have operated the Earle of Leinster, a handsome Victorian row house in a working-class neighborhood a 5-minute walk from King's Square. It's a welcoming and casual place, nothing fancy, with a kitchen for guests to make themselves at home and a pool table and TV in the basement. The Fitzgerald and Lord Edward rooms in the main house are the most historic, with high ceilings and regal furniture. Most of the remaining rooms are in the carriage house and are a bit more motel-like, although the second-floor loft is quite spacious. (Some rooms can be musty after a rainy spell.) The bathrooms are private, but they're also small. Added bonus: There's a free self-serve washer and dryer, plus VCRs in all rooms and a small library of films to select from. Recently the owner has expanded some of the smaller rooms, making them into minisuites with small kitchenette facilities.

96 Leinster St., Saint John, NB E2L 1J3. (C) **506/652-3275**. http://earleofleinster.tripod.com. 7 units. C$65–C$96 (US$59–US$86/£33–£48) double. Rates include full breakfast. AE, DC, MC, V. Pets allowed. **Amenities:** Laundry service. *In room:* TV/VCR, fridge, hair dryer, no phone.

WHERE TO DINE

For lunch, don't overlook the Old City Market, mentioned above. With a little snooping you can turn up tasty light meals and fresh juices in the market, then enjoy your finds in the alley atrium.

Beatty and the Beastro (★) *Finds* CONTINENTAL   Ignore the jokey name: This large-windowed establishment is the most handsome eatery in Saint John with its attractive interior fronting King's Square and a mild European-*moderne* look. Service is cordial and efficient, and the meals are among the best in the city. Lunch includes soups, salads, omelets, curry wraps, and elaborate gourmet sandwiches (but the simple grilled fish sandwich isn't bad, either). Critics have praised the lamb dinner entree, the preparation of which varies nightly according to the chef's desire; the house curry dish is also recommended, as are the chicken parmigiana, the schnitzel served with spaetzle, the steaks, the fish, and a pepper-chicken dish of the restaurant's creation. When dessert time rolls around, be aware that both the butterscotch pie and the lemon chess pie have large local followings.

60 Charlotte St. (on King's Sq.). (C) **506/652-3888**. Reservations recommended weekends and when shows are slated at the Imperial Theatre. Main courses C$7–C$10 (US$6.30–US$9/£3.50–£5) at lunch, C$20–C$22 (US$18–US$20/£10–£11) at dinner. AE, DC, MC, V. Mon–Fri 11:30am–3pm and 5–9pm; Sat 5–10pm.

Billy's Seafood Co. (★) SEAFOOD   Billy Grant's restaurant off King's Square boasts a congenial staff, exceptionally fresh seafood (they sell to City Market customers by day), and slightly better prices than the more tourist-oriented waterfront seafood restaurants. And the chef at this classy yet casual eatery knows how to prepare fish without overcooking. Specialties include cedar-planked salmon, and Billy's bouillabaisse is also quite good. Lunch entrees are surprisingly versatile, too, including Thai curried mussels and seafood crepes, among other choices. Offerings of beef, veal, and pasta fill out the menu for those not in the mood for fish.

49–51 Charlotte St. (at City Market). (C) **506/672-3474**. Reservations suggested. Light meals C$5.95–C$11 (US$5.35–US$9.90/£3–£5.50); dinner entrees C$16–C$29 (US$14–US$26/£8–£15). AE, DC, MC, V. Mon–Thurs 11am–10pm; Fri–Sat 11am–11pm; Sun 4–10pm.

Taco Pica LATIN AMERICAN   This cooperative is owned and run by a group of Guatemalans and their friends. It's bright, festive, and just a short stroll off King Street. The restaurant has developed a devoted local following since it opened in 1994, featuring a menu that's a notch above the usual staid Canadian adaptations of Mexican and Latin American fare. Among the most reliable dishes are *pepian* (a spicy beef stew with chayote); garlic shrimp; and the shrimp taco with potatoes, peppers, and cheese. Vegetarian offerings are available as well. There's a good selection of fresh juices here, and the restaurant possesses a liquor license—which means you can quaff any of a variety of fruit margaritas to put out the fire.

96 Germain St. (C) **506/633-8492**. Reservations recommended on weekends. Main courses C$7.95–C$17 (US$7.15–US$15/£4–£8.50). AE, MC, V. Mon–Sat 10am–10pm. Closed Sun and holidays.

SAINT JOHN AFTER DARK

The best entertainment destination in town is the **Imperial Theatre** ⚜ (*℃* **800/ 323-7469** or 506/674-4100) on King's Square—not always because of the acts that appear here, but because the performances are in what the Toronto *Globe and Mail* called the "most beautifully restored theatre in Canada." The theater originally opened in 1913 and hosted performances by such luminaries as Edgar Bergen, Al Jolson, and Walter Pidgeon (the latter a Saint John native). After being driven out of business by movie houses, then serving a long interim as home to a Pentecostal church, the theater was threatened with demolition in the early 1980s. That's when concerned citizens stepped in, raising funds to ensure that it would survive.

The Imperial reopened to much fanfare in 1994, and it has since hosted a wide range of performances, from Broadway road shows to local theatrical productions and concerts. Even if nothing is slated during your stay, in the summer a guide is stationed on the premises to give you a tour, during which you can admire the intricate plaster-work and the 2.7m (8¾-ft.) chandelier. Thirty-minute tours are offered Monday through Saturday between 9am and 5pm by appointment only; there's a small charge of C$2 (US$1.80/£1) per person.

Nightlife revolves around the seemingly innumerable pubs, most featuring live music, concentrated in the city's central downtown district. If you're looking to catch a big-time recording act, though, **Harbour Station** (*℃* **800/267-2800** or 506/ 657-1234) at 99 Station St. is the place to go; acts might range anywhere from Mötley Crüe (we'll pass) to Willie Nelson (we're in).

ROAD TRIP TO FUNDY TRAIL PARKWAY

Fundy Trail Parkway ⚜ *(Kids)*   The parkway is an ambitious project that will eventually extend some 50km (31 miles) up the coast (it's currently 11km/6.8 miles) and link up with the Trans-Canada Trail. This multiuse trail is nicely integrated with the natural environment and makes the Fundy Coast accessible without despoiling its beauty. The trail is wide and easy to hike or bike, and it has wheelchair-accessible pullouts with spectacular coastal views. Additional hiking trails lead to various beaches, some of which can only be reached at low tide. If you don't have the time or energy to walk, you can drive the paved road that parallels the trail, or catch the shuttle (free with paid admission; runs noon–6pm weekends and holidays) that stops at each of the parkway's eight parking lots. To make life even simpler, there are judiciously placed water stations and covered picnic tables at various locations along the way. The interpretive center has some interesting displays and a short film on the logging history of the area; guided tours of the parkway are also offered. A 2-hour tour costs C$2 (US$1.80/£1), a half-day excursion C$25 (US$23/£13) for adults and C$12 (US$11/£6) per child.

Rte. 111 (at St. Martins). *℃* 866/386-3987 or 506/833-2019. www.fundytrailparkway.com. Day pass C$3 (US$2.70/£1.50) adult, C$2 (US$1.80/£1) child, C$10 (US$9/£5) family. Mid-May to mid-Oct trail gates daily 6am–8pm, interpretive center from 8am. Take Rte. 111 east; entrance is 10km (6¼ miles) east of St. Martins (watch for signs). Leashed dogs allowed.

6 Fredericton

New Brunswick's provincial capital is a compact, historic city of brick and concrete that unfolds lazily along the banks of the wide Saint John River. The handsome buildings, broad streets, and wide sidewalks make the place feel more like a big, tidy village than a small city. Keep an eye out for two icons that mark Fredericton: the stately elm

Fredericton: The Land of Wi and Fi?

Surprisingly, Fredericton has been named one of the most "wired" cities in all of North America; it's easy to find a "hot spot" with your laptop anywhere in the city, thanks to the 2003 installation of citywide Wi-Fi. Known as Fred-e-Zone, the project now offers hundreds of access points—not only downtown, but at the Greater Fredericton Airport, in shopping malls, and even in parks and sports arenas (think hockey) throughout the city. Fredericton was the first city in Canada to offer such a service—far ahead of Montréal, Calgary, and Vancouver, for example, which still do not offer such a service. Remarkably, so far it remains free of charge; there's a C$30 (US$27/£15) or so monthly fee for public Wi-Fi access in most every other large Canadian city that has it. You can even rent a portable PC from the **Lighthouse Adventure Centre** (© 506/460-2939) for just C$3 (US$2.70/£1.50) per half-hour. Thumbs up, guys. Now get me my laptop.

trees that have stubbornly resisted Dutch elm disease and still shade the occasional park and byway, and the Union Jack, which you'll occasionally see fluttering from various buildings, attesting to long-standing historic ties with the Loyalists who shaped the city.

The city can be seen as divided into three zones: the malls and motels atop the hills and near the Trans-Canada Highway; the impressive, Georgian-style University of New Brunswick on the hillside just south of town; and the downtown itself, with its casual blend of modern and historic buildings.

Most visitors focus on downtown. The main artery—where you'll find the bulk of the attractions and restaurants—is Queen Street, which parallels the river between 1 and 2 blocks inland. An ill-considered four-lane road separates much of downtown from the river, but you can still reach water's edge via the Green, a pathway that follows the river, or by crossing a pedestrian bridge at the foot of Carleton Street.

Once you've seen the water, it's time to get to know the place. With a population of roughly 80,000, Fredericton is low-key and appealing in an understated way. There's really no single must-see attraction here, but the collective impact of strolling the streets gives the traveler a full sense of history and place. My advice: If eastern Canada's allure for you is the shimmering sea, deep woods, and wide open spaces, you won't miss much by bypassing Fredericton. If your passions include history—especially the history of British settlement in North America—then it's well worth the detour.

ESSENTIALS

GETTING THERE   A major relocation and widening of the Trans-Canada Highway near Fredericton has relieved traffic congestion somewhat. Look for signs directing you downtown; from the west, follow Woodstock Road, which tracks along the river. From Saint John, look for Route 7 to Regent Street, and then turn right down the hill.

The **Fredericton Airport** (© 506/444-6100; www.frederictonairport.ca), coded YFC, is located 10 minutes southeast of downtown on Route 102 and is served by cab and rental-car companies. For flight information, contact **Air Canada Jazz** (© 888/AIR-CANA; www.flyjazz.ca). There's also a new direct **Delta Connection** (© 800/221-1212; www.delta.com) shuttle service from Boston.

Fredericton

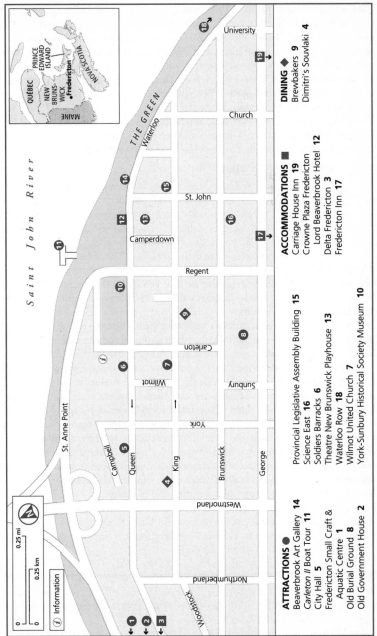

ATTRACTIONS ●
Beaverbrook Art Gallery **14**
Carleton II Boat Tour **11**
City Hall **5**
Fredericton Small Craft &
Aquatic Centre **1**
Old Burial Ground **8**
Old Government House **2**

Provincial Legislative Assembly Building **15**
Science East **16**
Soldiers Barracks **6**
Theatre New Brunswick Playhouse **13**
Waterloo Row **18**
Wilmot United Church **7**
York-Sunbury Historical Society Museum **10**

ACCOMMODATIONS ■
Carriage House Inn **19**
Crowne Plaza Fredericton
Lord Beaverbrook Hotel **12**
Delta Fredericton **3**
Fredericton Inn **17**

DINING ◆
Brewbakers **9**
Dimitri's Souvlaki **4**

VISITOR INFORMATION   Always careful to cater to visitors, Fredericton maintains no fewer than three center-city visitor information centers: the original in **City Hall** at 397 Queen St. (✆ **506/460-2041**), open daily 8am to 5pm (to 8pm in the summer); and a second newer one at **11 Carleton St.,** which also has racks of information year-round (open normal business hours weekdays 8:15am–4:30pm). Call ✆ **888/888-4768** or 506/460-2041 to reach either. There's a third information center at **King's Landing** (✆ **506/460-2191**), just west of town in River Valley, open from mid-May through early October. No matter which one you find first, ask for a Visitor Parking Pass, which allows visitors from outside the province to park free at city lots and meters in town for up to 3 days without penalty. You can also request travel information in advance by visiting the city's website at **www.tourismfredericton.ca**.

EXPLORING FREDERICTON

The free *Fredericton Visitor Guide,* available at the information centers and many hotels around town, contains a well-written and informative **walking tour** of the downtown. It's worth tracking down before launching an exploration of the city.

City Hall, at 397 Queen St., is an elaborate Victorian building with a prominent brick tower and a 2.4m (8-ft.) clock dial. The second-floor City Council Chamber occupies what was Fredericton's opera house until the 1940s. Small, folksy tapestries adorn the **visitor's gallery** and tell the town's history. Learn about these and the rest of the building during the free building tours, which are offered twice daily from mid-May to mid-October (both in English and French). In the off season, call ✆ **506/460-2120** to schedule a tour.

Officers' Square, on Queen Street between Carleton and Regent, is now a handsome city park. In 1785, the park was the center of military activity and used for drills, first as part of the British garrison and later (until 1914) by the Canadian Army. Today, the only soldiers are local actors who put on a show for the tourists. Look also for music and dramatic events staged at the square in the warmer months. The handsome colonnaded stone building facing the parade grounds is the former officer's quarters, now the **York-Sunbury Historical Society Museum** (p. 183).

In the center of the square, the prominent statue of the robed figure is Lord Beaverbrook. That's a name you'll hear a lot of in Fredericton—a street, a museum, and a hotel bear his name—though it wasn't *actually* his name. . . . In fact, Lord Beaverbrook was born Max Aitken, a native of Newcastle, New Brunswick, who amassed a fortune, primarily in publishing. Although he spent much of his life in Britain (he was made a lord in 1917, taking the name after a stream near Newcastle where he had fished as a young man), he maintained close ties to Canada. He donated an art collection and a modern building to house it (the Beaverbrook Art Gallery), along with a modern playhouse, which now is home to **Theatre New Brunswick.** The playhouse was built in 1964, the same year Lord Beaverbrook died.

Two blocks upriver from Officers' Square are the Soldiers' Barracks, housed in a similarly grand stone building. Check your watch against the sundial high on the end of the barracks, a replica of the original timepiece. A small exhibit shows the life of the enlisted man of the 18th century. Along the ground floor, local craftspeople sell their wares from small shops carved out of former barracks.

Fredericton is well noted for its distinctive architecture, especially the fine Victorian and Queen Anne residential architecture. Particularly attractive is **Waterloo Row** ✪, a group of privately owned historic homes—some grand, some less so—just downriver from the downtown area.

One entertaining and enlightening way to learn about the city's history is to sign up for a walking tour with the **Calithumpians Theatre Company** ⚔. Costumed guides offer free tours daily in July and August, pointing out highlights with anecdotes and dramatic tales. Recommended is the nighttime "Haunted Hike" tour, done by lantern light, which runs 5 nights each week. This evening tour is about 2 hours and costs C$13 (US$12/£6.50) for adults, C$8 (US$7.20/£4) for children; call ℭ **506/457-1975** for more information.

If you happen to be in town on a Saturday, a worthy detour is to the **Boyce Farmers' Market** ⚔ (ℭ **506/451-1815**), located on George Street, behind the old jail at 668 Brunswick St. This award-winning market, which runs from about 6am until about 1pm, has existed here in one form or another since the late 18th century. The current building was constructed in 1951 and expanded in 1990. More than 200 vendors offer everything fresh, from seasonal vegetables to meats, baked goods, and crafts. *Harrowsmith* magazine named the market one of the top eight farmer's markets in Canada. The market is adjacent to **Science East** (see below).

OUTDOOR PURSUITS

Fredericton recently expanded its trail system for walkers and bikers. The centerpiece of the system is **The Green** ⚔, a 5km (3-mile) pathway that follows the river from the Sheraton hotel to near the Princess Margaret Bridge. It's a lovely walk, and you'll pass the **Old Government House** (see below), downtown, and the open parklands near Waterloo Row.

Connecting with The Green is a well-used pedestrian bridge that crosses an abandoned railroad trestle just east of downtown. From this vantage point you'll get wonderful views of the downtown and river valley. If you continue onward, the **Nashwaak/Marysville Trail** ⚔ follows an abandoned rail bed along the attractive Nashwaak River; after about 4km (2.5 miles) you can cross the Nashwaak at Bridge Street and loop back to the pedestrian rail bridge via the **Gibson Trail.**

A number of other trails link up to this expanding network, which stretches more than 60km (37 miles). A free trail guide is available at the information centers, or contact the **New Brunswick Trails Council,** which builds and maintains bridges and trails throughout the system, at ℭ **800/526-7070.**

Bikes may be rented by the hour or the day at the **Lighthouse Adventure Centre** (ℭ **506/460-2939**) near **Regent St. Wharf** in the Fredericton Lighthouse, or at **Radical Edge,** 386 Queen St. (ℭ **506/459-3478**). Rentals are around C$20 to C$25 (US$18–US$23/£10–£13) per day or C$5 to C$7.50 (US$4.50–US$6.75/£2.50–£3.75) per hour.

The *Carleton II* (ℭ **506/454-2628;** www.carleton2.com) offers 1-hour excursions on the river aboard a 100-passenger ship. You'll learn about local history, take in an alternate view of the city, and perhaps spot a bald eagle flying along the shoreline. The tours depart several times daily in summer from the wharf near the **Fredericton Lighthouse** (at the foot of Regent St.). Rates are C$10 (US$9/£5) adults, C$5 (US$4.50/£2.50) children.

Another option for getting on the water is the **Small Craft Aquatic Centre,** on Woodstock Road (behind the Victoria Health Centre and near the Old Government House; ℭ **506/460-2260**). It's open daily from the middle of May to early October and rents rowing shells, canoes, and kayaks. Also ask about naturalist-guided tours of the river.

Finally, the **Kingswood** golf course (ℭ **800/423-5969** or 506/443-3333; www.golfnb.com/kingswood1.html) was recognized by *Golf Digest* as the best new

Canadian golf course in 2003. It features 27 holes, a par-3 course, and a double-ended driving range. A round of 18 holes costs C$50 to C$65 (US$45–US$59/£25–£33).

ATTRACTIONS DOWNTOWN

Beaverbrook Art Gallery ✦ *Value*   This surprisingly impressive museum overlooks the waterfront and is home to an extensive collection of British paintings, including works by Reynolds, Gainsborough, Constable, and Turner. Antiques buffs gravitate to the rooms with period furnishings and early decorative arts. Most visitors find themselves drawn to Salvador Dalí's massive *Santiago El Grande,* and studies for an ill-fated portrait of Winston Churchill. A new curator has brought in more controversial modern art exhibits of late; one focused on nudity, featuring various artistic perceptions of the unclothed human form, for example. Other shows have touched on more conventional ground, such as 19th-century French realism and a show on the cities of Canada drawn from The Seagram Collection. Stop by to find out what's currently on display.

703 Queen St. ⓒ **506/458-2028.** www.beaverbrookartgallery.org. Admission C$5 (US$4.50/£2.50) adults, C$4 (US$3.60/£2) seniors, C$2 (US$1.80/£1) students, C$10 (US$9/£5) families; Thurs evenings pay what you wish. Daily 9am–5:30pm (Thurs until 9pm).

Old Government House   The wonderfully severe Government House, constructed in 1828, was the official residence of the lieutenant governor, who was the official representative of the British Crown. It was built of locally quarried sandstone in a rigorously classical style, featuring Palladian symmetry, intricate plasterwork, and other haute touches. It remained the official residence until 1890, after which it housed a school and later a detachment of Mounties. Recently spared from the wrecking ball, the home underwent an exhaustive restoration and reopened in 1999. It once again is the official residence of the lieutenant governor, who has an apartment on the third floor and an office on the second floor.

The bilingual tours begin in a basement interpretive center and last about 45 minutes. You'll hike up sweeping staircases and view the extraordinarily high-ceilinged ground-floor reception rooms and have a chance to peruse art displayed in the second-floor art gallery. Guides are loaded with stories and anecdotes. The tour will be of special interest to those who are passionate about historic architecture, and those attracted to the grandeur of bygone days.

51 Woodstock Rd. (next to the Sheraton hotel). ⓒ **506/453-2505.** Free admission. June–Sept tours Mon–Sat 10am–5pm and Sun noon–5pm; off season by appointment. Tours leave on the hour; last tour at 5pm.

Provincial Legislative Assembly Building ✦   The Legislative Assembly Building, built in 1880, boasts an exterior designed in that bulbous, extravagant Second Empire style. But that's just the prelude: Inside, it's even more dressed up. Entering takes a bit of courage if the doors are closed; they're heavy and intimidating, with slits of beveled glass for peering out. (They're reminiscent of the gates of Oz.) Inside, it's creaky and wooden and comfortable, in contrast to the cold, unyielding stone of many seats of power. In the small rotunda, look for the razor-sharp prints from John James Audubon's elephant folio, on display in a special case.

The assembly chamber nearly takes the breath away, especially when viewed from the heights of the visitor gallery on the upper floors. (You ascend via a graceful wood spiral stairway housed in its own rotunda.) The chamber is ornate and draped in that fussy Victorian way, which is quite a feat given the vast scale of the room. Note all the regal trappings, including the portrait of the young Queen Elizabeth. This place just feels like a setting for high drama, whether or not it actually delivers when the chamber is in session. Half-hour-long tours are available; plan to spend at least an hour here.

706 Queen St. (across from the Beaverbrook Art Gallery). (C) 506/453-2527. Free admission. June to mid-Aug daily 9am–7pm (last tour at 6:30pm); off season Mon–Fri 9am–4pm.

Science East (*Value* *Kids*)   Children will enjoy a visit to this science center for two reasons: First, it's located in the old county jail, a sturdy stone structure built in the 1840s. (It was still being used as a jail as late as 1996.) And then there are the great exhibits—more than 100 interactive displays indoor and out, including a huge kaleidoscope, a periscope for people-watching, a solar-powered water fountain, and a mini-tornado. It's an ideal destination for a family on a chilly or rainy day, and there's plenty to do in the outdoors portion on nice days, too—a garden of native New Brunswick plants is in the works, for example. If you have kids, this place is easily worth up to 2 hours of your time.

668 Brunswick St. (C) 506/457-2340. www.scienceeast.nb.ca. Admission C$5 (US$4.50/£2.50) adults, C$3 (US$2.70/£1.50) students and seniors, C$14 (US$13/£7) families. June–Aug Mon–Sat 10am–5pm, Sun 1–4pm; rest of year Mon–Fri noon–5pm, Sat 10am–5pm, Sun 1-4pm.

York-Sunbury Historical Society Museum (*Kids*)   This small museum lures visitors with the promise of a stuffed 42-pound frog, which supposedly belonged to one Fred Coleman, who in the late 19th century fed it a nasty mixture of June bugs, cornmeal, buttermilk, and whiskey to inflate it to Rubenesque proportions. After it perished at the hands of some miscreants, the famous frog was displayed at the Burke House Hotel until 1959, when it traveled with little ceremony to this museum. It's displayed on the top floor to ensure that you wander through all the exhibits looking for it—a clever trick on the part of the curator. When you get there, the frog is something of a disappointment. (Not to mention suspect; it looks like bad papier-mâché.)

Still, the rest of the museum is nicely done. Displays feature the usual artifacts of life gone by, but several exhibits rise well above the clutter, including a fine display on Loyalist settlers. Kids will love the claustrophobic re-creation of a German World War II trench on the second floor—and likely will end up talking more about that on the way home than Fred's portly frog. Plan to spend about a half-hour here.

571 Queen St. near Regent St. (C) 506/455-6041. Admission C$3 (US$2.70/£1.50) adults, C$2 (US$1.80/£1) seniors, C$1 (US90¢/50p) students, C$6 (US$5.40/£3) families. July–Aug daily 10am–5pm; spring and fall Tues–Sat 1–4pm. Closed Nov–May.

ATTRACTIONS OUTSIDE OF TOWN

Kings Landing Historical Settlement (*Value*)   Kings Landing, on the bank of the Saint John River, is 34km (21 miles) and about 150 years from Fredericton. The authentic re-creation brings to life New Brunswick from 1790 to 1910, with 10 historic houses and nine other buildings relocated here and saved from destruction by the flooding during the Mactaquac hydro project. The aroma of freshly baked bread mixes with the smell of horses and livestock, and the sound of the blacksmith's hammer alternates with that of the church bell. More than 160 costumed "early settlers" chat about their lives.

You could easily spend a day exploring the 120 hectares (297 acres), but if you haven't that much time, focus on the Hagerman House (with furniture by Victorian cabinetmaker John Warren Moore), the Ingraham House (with its fine New Brunswick furniture and formal English garden), the Morehouse House (where you'll see a clock Benedict Arnold left behind), and the Victorian Perley House. The Ross Sash and Door Factory is an imitation turn-of-the-20th-century manufacturing plant.

Afterward, hitch a ride on the sloven wagon or relax at the Kings Head Inn, which served up grub and grog to hardy travelers along the Saint John River a century or more ago. Today it serves lemonade, chicken pie, and corn chowder, along with other traditional dishes. Lunch prices are around C$8 to C$13 (US$7.20–US$12/£4–£6.50), and dinner is about C$13 to C$19 (US$12–US$17/£6.50–£9.50).

Exit 253 off the Trans-Canada Hwy. (Rte. 2 west). © 506/363-4999. www.kingslanding.nb.ca. Admission C$15 (US$14/£7.50) adults, C$13 (US$12/£6.50) seniors, C$12 (US$11/£6) students over 16, C$10 (US$9/£5) children 6–16, C$36 (US$32/£18) families. June to early Oct daily 10am–5pm. Closed early Oct to May.

SHOPPING

Fredericton is home to a growing number of artists and artisans, as well as entrepreneurs who have launched a handful of offbeat shops. It's worth setting aside an hour or two for browsing.

Aitkens Pewter   This well-known shop sells classically designed pewter dishes and mugs based on historic patterns, as well as modern adaptations and jewelry. 408 Queen St. © 800/567-4416 or 506/453-9474.

Cultures Boutique   This is one of a chain of YMCA-run shops that promote alternative trade to benefit craftspeople in the Third World. Look for goods from foreign lands as well as North American native cultures, mostly from community-based cooperatives. 383 Mazzucca Lane (off York St. between King and Queen). © 506/462-3088.

Gallery Connexion   Expect vibrant modern artwork, much of it experimental and in all sorts of media, at this lively nonprofit gallery run by area artists. Studios are within the same building, and you may have a chance to see the artists at work. 453 Queen St. (behind the Justice Building). © 506/454-1433.

Gallery 78   An exceptionally solid and handsome Queen Anne–style mansion is home to the province's oldest private art gallery. Sunny spaces upstairs and down showcase a range of local art, much of it sold at affordable prices. 796 Queen St. (near the Beaverbrook Art Gallery). © 506/454-5192.

WHERE TO STAY

A handful of motels and chain hotels are located in the bustling mall zone on the hill above town, mostly along Regent and Prospect streets. Allow about 10 minutes to drive downtown from here.

Among the classiest of the bunch is the **Fredericton Inn,** 1315 Regent St. (© 800/561-8777 or 506/455-1430), situated between two malls. It's a soothing-music-and-floral-carpeting kind of place that does a brisk business in the convention trade. But with its indoor pool and classically appointed rooms, it's a comfortable spot for vacation travelers as well, and there's a fitness facility on-site for working out. Peak season rates are C$119 to C$135 (US$107–US$122/£60–£68), and up to C$199 (US$179/£100) for suites.

Also near the malls are the **Comfort Inn,** 797 Prospect St. (© 506/453-0800), at C$99 to C$199 (US$89–US$179/£50–£100) double; **City Motel,** 1216 Regent St. (© 800/268-2858 or 506/459-9900), with rooms for C$85 (US$77/£43) and up; and the **Lakeview Inn and Suites,** 655 Prospect St. (© 877/355-3500 or 506/459-0035), with rooms for C$87 to C$117 (US$78–US$105/£44–£59) and laundry facilities for guest use.

The Carriage House Inn   Fredericton's premier bed-and-breakfast is located a short stroll from the riverfront pathway in a quiet residential neighborhood. A former mayor built the imposing three-story Victorian in 1875. Inside, it's a bit somber in that Victorian way, with dark wood trim and deep colors, and feels solid enough to resist glaciers. The hotel and its rooms are furnished with art and antiques, but it's comfortable without being overly opulent. High-speed wireless Internet is available throughout the inn, and delicious, elaborate breakfasts included with your rate are served in a sunny ballroom in the rear of the house.

230 University Ave., Fredericton, NB E3B 4H7. © **800/267-6068** or 506/452-9924. Fax 506/452-2770. www.carriagehouse-inn.net. 10 units. C$95–C$125 (US$86–US$113/£48–£63) double. Rates include full breakfast. AE, MC, V. "Small, well-trained pets" allowed. **Amenities:** Restaurant. *In room:* A/C, TV, hair dryer.

Crowne Plaza Fredericton Lord Beaverbrook Hotel 🐾 *Kids*   This hulking 1947 waterfront hotel is severe and boxy in an early-deco kind of way, a look that may at first suggest that it houses the Ministry of Dourness. But inside, the mood lightens considerably, with composite stone floors, Georgian pilasters, and chandeliers. The downstairs indoor pool and recreation area are positively whimsical, a sort of tiki-room grotto that kids adore. The guest rooms are nicely appointed with traditional reproduction furniture in dark wood—and they've been seriously freshened up since the Crowne Plaza folks acquired the property. Standard rooms can be somewhat dim, and most of the windows don't open (ask for a room with opening windows when you book). However, the suites are spacious, and many have excellent river views. This is the best accommodation for those who want the convenience of a downtown location and who enjoy the solid architectural touches of an old-fashioned hotel. Those looking for a modern polish may be more content at the Delta.

You've got three choices for dining. The Terrace Room is the main dining area, with an indoor gazebo, mahogany, tapestries, and a lovely seasonal outdoor deck overlooking the river. The menu here corrals resort standards, starting with relish trays and puffy white dinner rolls. Main courses might range from Asian shrimp stir-fry to chicken fettuccine Alfredo. The more intimate Governor's Room has higher aspirations, with French-inflected dinner entrees, such as duck breast with a raspberry–and–Grand Marnier coulis. Finally, the Maverick room (formerly known as the James Joyce Irish Pub) is the spot for a pint and a snack.

659 Queen St., Fredericton, NB E3B 5A6. © **866/444-1946** or 506/455-3371. Fax 506/455-1441. www.cpfredericton.com. 168 units. C$139–C$199 (US$125–US$179/£70–£100) double. AE, DC, MC, V. **Amenities:** 3 restaurants; pub; indoor pool; Jacuzzi; sauna; business center; babysitting; laundry service; dry cleaning. *In room:* A/C, TV, dataport, coffeemaker; hair dryer; iron.

Delta Fredericton 🐾🐾   This modern resort hotel built in 1992 occupies a prime location along the river about a 10-minute walk from downtown via the riverfront pathway. In the summer, life revolves around the outdoor pool (with its own poolside bar) on the deck overlooking the river, and on Sundays the lobby is surrendered to an over-the-top brunch buffet. Although decidedly up-to-date, the interior is done with classical styling and is comfortable and well appointed. The hotel lounge is an active and popular spot on many nights, especially weekends. Across the lobby is Bruno's Seafood & Chophouse, which offers a good alternative to the restaurants downtown. The chef wisely focuses on whatever's fresh at the city's farmer's market; thus, look for seasonal and regional specialties, including fiddleheads in early summer and local vegetables and fruits in season. Bruno's also cooks good steaks.

225 Woodstock Rd., Fredericton, NB E3B 2H8. © **888/462-8800** or 506/457-7000. Fax 506/457-7000. www.deltafredericton.com. 222 units. C$99–C$229 (US$89–US$206/£50–£115) double; royal suites up to C$800 (US$720/£400). AE, DC, MC, V. Free parking. Pets accepted. **Amenities:** Restaurant; 2 bars; heated indoor pool and heated outdoor pool; fitness room; Jacuzzi; sauna; salon; room service; babysitting. *In room:* A/C, TV, minibar, coffeemaker, hair dryer, iron/ironing board.

On the Pond Country Retreat & Spa 🏊 *Finds*   In 1999, Donna Evans opened On the Pond, about 15 minutes west of Fredericton, with the idea of creating a comfortable retreat where guests could be pampered with spa treatments after indulging in soft adventures at the adjacent provincial park and surrounding countryside. The lodge is lovely, constructed in a sort of William Morris–inspired style with dark wood trim, slate floors in the entryways, and fieldstone fireplaces. The two downstairs common rooms—one with a wood fireplace and one lined with bookshelves—invite lingering and chatting with other guests. Upstairs guest rooms each feature a queen and a double bed, and are slightly larger than the average hotel room, with nice extras such as bathrobes and duvets. The basement spa includes two massage rooms, a hot tub, a sauna, an aesthetics room (offering manicures, pedicures, and facials), and a fitness center. Keeping with the theme, heart-healthy meals are served in the Parkview Dining Room daily from 6:30am to 11pm.

The lodge sits on "The Arm"—an impoundment of the Saint John River behind the nearby hydroelectric dam—in a marshy setting that's better for bird-watching than swimming. There's a small wharf here, with canoes, kayaks, and bikes that guests may use for free. Also nearby are a golf course and the Kings Landing Historical Settlement (see above). Beach swimming is available across the road at the provincial park.

20 Scotch Settlement Rd. (Rte. 615), Mactaquac, NB E6L 1M2. © **800/984-2555** or 506/363-3420. Fax 506/363-3479. www.onthepond.com. 8 units. C$125–C$145 (US$113–US$131/£63–£73) double. MC, V. Drive west of Fredericton on Woodstock Rd.; cross the Mactaquac Dam and continue to the Esso station; turn right and look for sign on right. No children. **Amenities:** Dining room; spa; Jacuzzi; sauna; watersports equipment. *In room:* A/C, TV/VCR, dataport, hair dryer.

WHERE TO DINE

Brewbakers 🏊 ITALIAN   Brewbakers is a convivial pub, cafe, and restaurant, located on three levels in a cleverly adapted downtown building. It's a bustling and informal spot, creatively cluttered with artifacts and artworks, and it does boomtown business during lunch hours and early evenings. The cafe section is quieter, as is the mezzanine dining room above the cafe, while the third floor bustles with its open kitchen. Pastas are the main attraction here, served up with the usual array of sauces, and recent years have brought a few more upscaled versions (a maple-curry-chicken-cream pasta is just one). Also good here are the personal pizzas, the roasted chicken, the grilled strip loin, and the herb-crusted tenderloin. Lunch features sandwiches that are getting fancier all the time, with choices like smoked salmon, a Moroccan salsa-topped sirloin burger, and a sandwich of oven-roasted peppers and garlicky mayo.

546 King St. © **506/459-0067**. Reservations recommended. Main courses C$9–C$14 (US$8.10–US$13/£4.50–£7) at lunch, C$12–C$24 (US$11–US$22/£6–£12) at dinner. AE, DC, MC, V. Mon–Wed 11:30am–10pm; Thurs–Fri 11:30am–midnight; Sat 4pm–midnight; Sun 4–10pm.

Dimitri's Souvlaki *Value* GREEK   Dimitri's is hard to find, and easy to walk past even after you've found it. But the generic, chain-restaurant interior belies better-than-average cooking that will appeal to budget-conscious diners. You'll get a big plate of food here without dropping a lot of money. Greek specialties include moussaka (with and without meat), souvlakia, and *dolmades,* and all are quite good. (Avoid the mystery-meat *donairs,* though.) Deluxe dinner plates are served with delicious potatoes—hearty wedges that are cooked crispy on the outside and remain hot and soft on the inside. The meats are sometimes on the tough side, but most budget-happy diners will find this place to be a good value.

349 King St. (in Piper's Lane area). © 506/452-8882. Main courses C$8.25–C$18 (US$7.45–US$16/£4.15–£9). AE, DC, MC, V. Mon–Wed 11am–11pm; Thurs–Sat 11am–11:30pm.

FREDERICTON AFTER DARK

Fredericton's downtown is often lively with university students and young professionals after hours. Your best bet is the **Lunar Rogue** ⚘⚘, 625 King St. (© **506/450-2065**), which features more than 100 single-malt whiskeys and a dozen draft beers in a comfortable, pubby atmosphere. It was anointed "Greatest Whisky Bar in the World" by *Whisky* magazine, who should know what they're talking about. Tuesday remains nacho night, which lures out the local folks in droves; other light-food specials are available Mondays and Thursdays. The pub is open 9am to 1am weekdays, from 10am Saturdays and from 11am to 10pm Sundays.

Dolan's Pub, 349 King St. (© **506/454-7474**), is the place to go for live Maritime music, which is on tap most Thursdays through Saturdays. Also on tap is the city's largest selection of microbrews. Don't miss the barrel of free peanuts, either.

ROAD TRIP TO GAGETOWN ⚘

About 55km (34 miles) southeast of Fredericton is the untroubled, unassuming village of **Gagetown.** (The village can be visited via a scenic driving detour en route to or from Saint John.) It's been named one of the 10 prettiest villages in Canada, and has remained largely unchanged over the years—still backed by farm fields on one side, and cozied up to Gagetown Creek, a placid inlet off the Saint John River. The peaceful surroundings and simple country architecture have attracted the attention of craftspeople and artists, who have settled here and slowly made it a quiet arts colony—quaint and creative, but never annoyingly so. Look for a handful of low-key enterprises including art galleries, a cafe, a decoy carver, a bookstore, a cider press, a crafts cooperative, and several potters.

You can also **bird-watch** and explore here; the region is noted for its avian life, with a wide range of birds enjoying the mixed terrain that includes marsh grass, forest, and field. Nearly 150 species of bird have been reliably identified in and around Gagetown. Gagetown Island is just offshore (easily accessible by kayak or canoe, which inn guests may borrow; see below). The island is 400 hectares (988 acres) in size and features a glacial deposit that rises 23m (75 ft.) high, the ruins of a stone house that dates from the early 19th century, and an osprey-viewing platform.

While in Gagetown, you might also visit the **Queens County Museum** (© **506/488-2483**), birthplace of Sir Samuel Leonard Tilley, one of the fathers of Canadian Confederation. His 1786 home, located at 69 Front St., is open to the public in summer.

If you want to stay the night, check with two simple bed-and-breakfast inns in town about availability: the **Doctor's Hill B&B** (© **506/488-8989**) at 16 Doctor's Hill Rd. and the **Step Aside B&B** (© **506/488-1808**) at 58 Front St.

7 Fundy National Park 🅐🅐

The Fundy Coast between Saint John and Alma is for the most part wild, remote, and unpopulated. It's plumbed by few roads other than the Fundy Drive, making it difficult to explore unless you have a boat. The best access to the wild coast is through Fundy National Park, a gem of a destination that's hugely popular with travelers with an outdoor bent. Families often settle in here for a week or so, filling their days with activities in and around the park that include hiking, sea kayaking, biking, and splashing around a seaside pool. Nearby are lovely drives and an innovative adventure center at **Cape Enrage.** If a muffling fog moves in to smother the coast, head inland for a hike to a waterfall or through lush forest. If it's a day of brilliant sunshine, venture along the rocky shores by foot or boat.

ESSENTIALS

GETTING THERE Route 114 runs through the center of Fundy National Park. If you're coming from the west, follow the prominent national park signs just east of Sussex. If you're coming from Prince Edward Island or Nova Scotia, head southward on Route 114 from Moncton.

One word of warning for travel from Moncton: Beware the signs at the Route 15 rotary directing you to Fundy National Park. Moncton's traffic czars send tourists on a silly detour far around the city's outskirts, apparently to avoid downtown traffic; after 16km (10 miles) of driving you'll end up within sight of the rotary again, just across the river. It's far more sensible to just head straight downtown via Main Street, cross the river on the first steel bridge (you can see it from everywhere); then turn left onto Route 114.

VISITOR INFORMATION The park's main **Visitor Centre** (⊙ 506/887-6000) is located just inside the Alma (eastern) entrance to the park. The stone building is open daily during peak season from 8am to 10pm (only to 4:30pm in the spring and fall). You can watch a video presentation, peruse a handful of exhibits on wildlife and tides, and shop at the nicely stocked nature bookstore.

The smaller **Wolfe Lake Information Centre** (⊙ 506/432-6026) is at the park's western entrance and is open daily, mid-June to mid-August only, from 10am to 6pm. The small town of **Alma** also maintains an information center at 8584 Main St. (⊙ 506/887-6127).

FEES Park entry fees are charged from mid-May to mid-October. The fee is C$6.90 (US$6.20/£3.45) adults, C$5.90 (US$5.30/£2.95) seniors, C$3.45 (US$3.10/ £1.75) children ages 6 to 16, and C$17 (US$15/£8.50) families. Seasonal passes and spring-season discount rates are also available.

EXPLORING FUNDY NATIONAL PARK

Most national park activities are centered around the Alma (eastern) side of the park, where the park entrance has a cultivated and manicured air, as if part of a landed estate. Here you'll find stone walls, well-tended lawns, and attractive landscaping, along with a golf course, amphitheater, lawn bowling, and tennis.

Also in this area is a **heated saltwater pool,** set near the bay with a sweeping ocean view. There's a lifeguard on duty, and it's a popular destination for families. The pool is open late June to August. The cost is about C$3 (US$2.70/£1.50) adults, C$2.50 (US$2.25/£1.25) seniors, C$1.50 (US$1.35/75p) children, and C$7.50 (US$6.75/ £3.75) families.

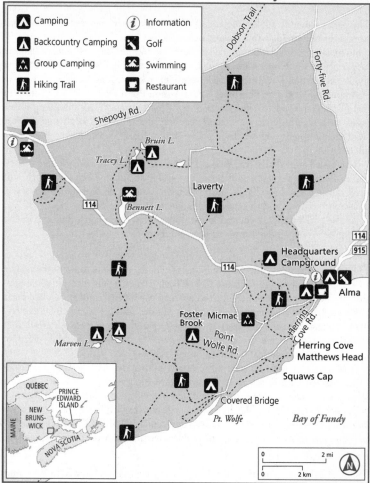

Fundy National Park

Legend:
- Camping
- Information
- Backcountry Camping
- Golf
- Group Camping
- Swimming
- Hiking Trail
- Restaurant

Dobson Trail
Forty-five Rd.
Shepody Rd.
Bruin L.
Tracey L.
Laverty
114
Bennett L.
Headquarters
Campground
114
915
114
Alma
Foster
Brook
Micmac
Point
Wolfe Rd.
Marven L.
Herring Cove Rd.
Herring Cove
Matthews Head
Squaws Cap
Covered Bridge
Pt. Wolfe
Bay of Fundy

QUÉBEC
PRINCE EDWARD ISLAND
NEW BRUNS-WICK
MAINE
NOVA SCOTIA

0   2 mi
0   2 km

Also unique to the park are two **auto trails**—basically overgrown dirt roads that you can explore with the family car. **Hastings Auto Trail** is one-way so you needn't worry about oncoming vehicles. It's a good way to see some of the great outdoors without suffering the indignities that often result from actual encounters with nature (rain, bugs, blisters, and so on).

Sea kayaking tours are a way to get a good, close look at the ocean landscape and the tides. **FreshAir Adventure** (℃ **800/545-0020** or 506/887-2249) in Alma offers tours that range from 2 hours to several days. The half-day tours explore marsh and coastline (C\$45–C\$57/US\$41–US\$51/£23–£29 including lunch); the full-day adventure includes a hot meal and 6 hours of exploring the wild shores (C\$85–C\$105/US\$77–US\$95/£43–£53).

HIKING

The park maintains 105km (65 miles) of trails for hikers and walkers. These range from a 20-minute loop to a 4-hour trek, and they pass through varied terrain. The trails are arranged such that several can be linked into a 48km (30-mile) backpacker's loop, dubbed the **Fundy Circuit,** which typically requires 3 nights in the backcountry. Preregistration is required for the overnight trek, so ask at the visitor center.

Among the most accessible hikes is the **Caribou Plain Trail** ✿, a 3km (2-mile) loop that provides a wonderful introduction to the local terrain. You'll hike along a beaver pond, on a boardwalk across a raised peat bog, and through lovely temperate forest. Read the interpretive signs to learn about deadly "flarks," which lurk in bogs and can kill a moose.

The **Third Vault Falls Trail** ✿✿ is a 7.5km (4.7-mile) in-and-back hike that takes you to the park's highest waterfall (about 14m/46 ft. high). The trail is largely a flat stroll through leafy woodlands, until you begin a steady descent into a mossy gorge. You round a corner and there you are, suddenly facing the cataract.

All the park's trails are covered in the pullout trail guide you'll find in *Salt & Fir,* the booklet you'll receive when you pay your entry fee.

BIKING

The roads east of Alma offer superb bicycling terrain, at least if you get off busy Route 114. Especially appealing is **Route 915** ✿ from Riverside-Albert to Alma, along with a detour to Cape Enrage. Along this scenic road you'll pedal through rolling farmland and scattered settlements, past vistas of salt marshes and the wonderfully named Ha Ha Cemetery. The hills are low but can be steep and require a serious grind, so you should be in reasonable shape. Route 915 runs 27km (17 miles), with the spur to Cape Enrage an additional 6.5km (4 miles) each way.

Also note that the park allows **mountain biking** on the following trails: Goose River, Marven Lake, Black Hole, Bennett Brook (only to the top of Point Wolfe valley), East Branch (must take right-hand side trail only and return from river on same path), and Maple Grove. Bike rentals have not been available in Alma in recent years, but check with the Alma visitor information center (✆ **506/887-6127**) to see if the situation has changed. Otherwise, bikes may be rented in Saint John or Moncton.

CAMPING

The national park maintains four drive-in campgrounds and about 15 backcountry sites. The two main campgrounds are near the Alma entrance. **Headquarters Campground** ✿ is within walking distance of Alma, the saltwater pool, and numerous other attractions. Since it overlooks the bay, this campground tends to be cool and subject to fogs. **Chignecto North Campground** ✿ is higher on the hillside, sunnier, and warmer. You can hike down to Alma on an attractive hiking trail in 1 to 2 hours. Both campgrounds have hookups for RVs, flush toilets, and showers, and sites can be reserved in advance (✆ **877/737-3783;** www.pccamping.ca); sites cost C$15 to C$33 (US$14–US$30/£7.50–£17) per night, depending on services offered.

The **Point Wolfe** and **Wolfe Lake** campgrounds lack RV hookups and are slightly more primitive, but they are the preferred destinations for campers seeking a quieter camping experience. Rates at Point Wolfe, where showers and flush toilets are available, are about C$25 (US$23/£13); Wolfe Lake lacks showers and has only pit toilets—thus a night there costs only about C$15 (US$14/£7.50).

Backcountry sites are scattered throughout the park, with only one located directly on the coast (at the confluence of the coast and Goose River). Ask at the visitor centers for more information or to reserve a site (mandatory). Backcountry camping fees are about C$10 (US$9/£5) per person per night.

ROAD TRIP TO CAPE ENRAGE 🗲🗲

Cape Enrage is a blustery and bold cape that juts impertinently out into Chignecto Bay. It's also home to a wonderful adventure center that could be a model for similar centers worldwide.

Cape Enrage Adventures 🗲 traces its roots to 1993, when a group of Harrison Trimble High School students in Moncton decided to do something about the decay of the cape's historic lighthouse, which had been abandoned in 1988. They put together a plan to restore the light and keeper's quarters and establish an adventure center. It worked. Today, with the help of experts in kayaking, rock climbing, rappelling, and other rugged sports, a couple dozen high-school students staff and run this program throughout the summer months. The program closes in late August, when the student-managers head back to school.

Part of what makes the program so notable is its flexibility. You can pick and choose from day adventures, which are scheduled throughout the summer, as if from a menu. These include **rappelling workshops, rock-climbing lessons, kayak trips,** and **canoeing excursions.** Prices are about C$50 (US$45/£25) per person for a 2-hour rock-climbing or rappelling workshop, about C$60 (US$54/£30) for a half-day kayak trip. Parents should note that this is an ideal spot to drop off restless teens while you indulge in scenic drives or a trip to Hopewell Rocks.

Families looking to endure outdoor hardships together should inquire about **custom adventures.** For about C$200 to C$300 (US$180–US$270/£100–£150) per person, the center can organize a 2- to 5-night adventure vacation that includes equipment, instruction, food, and lodging. You pick your own activities—for example, a sea-kayak trip early one morning followed by an afternoon of rappelling.

As if running the center didn't keep the students busy enough, they also operate a restaurant (open to the public), called the **Keepers' Lunchroom.** Light but tasty meals include a notable fish chowder made with fresh haddock from a recipe provided by a local fisherman's wife, served with hot biscuits. A few other selections are offered—like grilled cheese and cheesecake—but the smart money gets the chowder. Finish with blueberry-and-whipped-cream-topped biscuits.

For more information about the program, which runs May through September, contact **Cape Enrage Adventures** (📞 **888/280-7273** or 506/887-2273; www.capenrage.com).

ROAD TRIP TO THE HOPEWELL ROCKS

There's no better place to witness the extraordinary power of the Fundy tides than at **Hopewell Rocks** 🗲 (📞 **877/734-3429;** www.thehopewellrocks.ca), located about 40km (24 miles) northeast of Fundy National Park on Route 114. Think of it as a natural sculpture garden. At low tide (the best time to visit), eroded columns as high as 15m (49 ft.) tower above the ocean floor. They're sometimes called the "flowerpots," on account of the trees and plants that still flourish on their narrowing summits.

When you arrive, park at the visitor center and restaurant and wander down to the shore. (There's also a shuttle service that runs from the interpretive center to the rocks for a small fee.) Signboards here will fill you in on the natural history of the rocks. If you've come at low tide, you can descend the steel staircase to the sea floor and admire these wondrous free-standing rock sculptures, chiseled by waves and tides.

The visitor center is a pleasant place to spend some time. It not only has intriguing exhibits (in particular look for the satellite photos of the area, and the time-lapse video of the tides) but the cafeteria-style restaurant has terrific views from its floor-to-ceiling windows and serves good, simple food. Salads and various sandwiches (salmon burgers, steak hoagies, lobster rolls, and so on) are satisfying, and a harvest vegetable bisque is the perfect antidote to the often chilly, damp weather. There's also a children's menu.

The site can be crowded, but that's understandable. If your schedule allows it, come early in the day when the sun is fresh over Nova Scotia across the bay, the dew is still on the ground, and most travelers are still sacked out in bed. The park charges an entry fee of C$8 (US$7.20/£4) adults, C$6.75 (US$6.10/£3.40) seniors, C$5.75 (US$5.20/£2.90) children ages 5 to 18, and C$20 (US$18/£10) families. It's open mid-May to mid-June, 9am to 5pm, then 8am to 8pm from mid-June until mid-August (mid-Aug to late Aug only to 6pm), and from 9am to 5pm through the end of September.

If you arrive at the top half of the tide, consider a sea kayak tour around the islands and caves. **Baymount Outdoor Adventures** (© **877/601-2660** or 506/734-2660) runs 90-minute tours daily for C$55 (US$50/£28) adults, C$45 (US$41/£23) youths. Caving tours at nearby caverns are also offered; inquire for details.

WHERE TO STAY

Broadleaf Guest Ranch 𝒜 (Kids)   The two-bedroom cottages at this homey, family-operated ranch are a great choice for families or couples traveling together, particularly those with an interest in horses: The ranch offers trail rides of varying duration, cattle checks, and some basic spa packages. Think of it as a dude ranch without the rattlesnakes. The cottages feature full kitchens; a small sitting area with gas stove, TV and VCR; and lovely, sweeping views of the ranch's 600 hectares (1,483 acres) and the bay. Bedrooms are furnished with bunk beds (a single over a double) plus a single bed. You won't mistake these lodgings for a luxury experience, but staying here is like sinking into a favorite armchair at the end of the day: comforting and satisfying. The same could be said of the home-cooking Broadleaf dishes up in its large, cafeteria-style dining area. There are also three simple bed-and-breakfast rooms in the main house (known as Broadleaf "Too") and a campground as well.

5526 Rte. 114, Hopewell Hill, Albert County, NB E4H 3N5. © 800/226-5405 or 506/882-2349. Fax 506/882-2075. www.broadleafranch.com. 7 units. Main inn rooms C$60–C$75 (US$54–US$68/£30–£38) double; chalets and apartments C$150–C$200 (US$135–US$180/£75–£100). Ask about packages. MC, V. **Amenities:** Restaurant; spa; watersports equipment; bike rentals; business center; room service; laundry service. *In room:* TV/VCR (some units), kitchenette (some units), no phone.

Fundy Highlands Inn and Chalets 𝒜 (Kids)   This recently renovated property was brought to my attention by several Frommer's readers, who wrote me to give it high recommendations. Indeed, its 24 cottages and 20 motel rooms—managed by New Brunswick natives Doug and Donna Stewart—are each furnished with color televisions, beach towels, and kitchenette units. Some of the cottages even have built-in bunk beds, making those a good choice for travelers with young children. It's also notable for its expansive grounds, 7 hectares (17 acres) in all of grassy knolls, rose beds, and the like, and the good views of the bay and coastline from many of the rooms and cottages.

8714 Rte. 114, Fundy National Park, NB E4H 4V3. ℂ **888/883-8639** or 506/887-2930. Fax 506/887-2453. www.
fundyhighlandchalets.com. 44 units (24 cabins, 20 rooms). Cottages C$74–$C105 (US$67–US$95/£37–£53); motel
rooms C$65–C$85 (US$59–US$77/£33–£43). MC, V. *In room:* TV, kitchenette.

Fundy Park Chalets   These rather simplistic cabins are set amid birch and pines
just inside the park's eastern entrance and might appeal to fans of classic motor courts.
The gabled white clapboard units have interiors that bring to mind a national park
vacation—from the 1950s. Imagine painted wood floors, pine paneling, metal shower
stalls, and small kitchenettes. Two beds in the main rooms of the cottages are separated by hospital-style track curtains that pull around one bed to provide "privacy."
Should you stay? Frankly, only if everywhere else in the area is booked. At least the
park's golf course, playground, tennis courts, lawn bowling, and saltwater pool are all
within walking distance.

23 Fundy Chalet Rd. (P.O. Box 72), Alma, NB E4H 4Y8. ℂ **877/887-2808** or 506/887-2808. www.fundyparkchalets.
com. 29 cabins. Summer C$99 (US$89/£50) double; off season C$69 (US$62/£35) double. Discounts in spring and fall.
MC, V. Closed Dec–Apr. Pets accepted. *In room:* Kitchenette, no phone.

Parkland Village Inn *Value* *Kids*   The Parkland opened the same day as the park in
1948. It's an old-fashioned seaside hotel in the village of Alma, with five two-room
suites that have been modernized and thinly furnished in a sort of budget-motel modern style. Some rooms have been set up as two-bedroom units, others with a sitting
room and bedroom. All have fine views of the bay. It's not deluxe by any means, but
it's handy to the park and offers good value for families. The inn also manages a small
cottage about 10km (6 miles) away, renting for C$125 (US$113/£63) per night with
a 3-night minimum stay required. The downstairs dining room of the inn, the Tides,
has 110 seats and specializes in (of course) seafood, prepared with little fuss or flair.
It's open for breakfast as well, in July and August only.

8601 Main St. (Rte. 114), Alma, NB E4H 1N6. ℂ **866/668-4337** or 506/887-2313. Fax 506/887-2315. www.parkland
villageinn.com. 5 units. C$75–C$135 (US$68–US$122/£38–£68) double. Discounts in off season. MC, V. Closed
Dec–Apr. **Amenities:** Restaurant. *In room:* TV, Jacuzzi (some units), no phone.

WHERE TO DINE

Amid the scattering of seafood takeout and lobster shops in and around the park, one
good self-catering pick is **Butland's** (ℂ **506/887-2190;** www.fundylobster.com) at
8607 Main St. in Alma beside the town wharf. As you would expect, the shop pur-
veys locally caught crustaceans, scallops, and salmon (you can do the cooking yourself
back in your cabin, or have these guys do it). It's open daily from mid-May through
Labor Day and then weekends until New Year's. There's also a **bakery** in Alma at 8587
Main St. (ℂ **506/887-2460**), open year-round, with locally famous sticky buns.

Seawinds Dining Room PUB FARE   Seawinds overlooks the park's golf course,
and it serves as a de facto clubhouse for hungry duffers—and tourists in the area. The
handsome and open dining room has hardwood floors, a flagstone fireplace, and
wrought-iron chandeliers. The menu offers enough variations to please most anyone;
lunch selections include a variety of hamburgers, fish and chips, and bacon-and-cheese
dogs. Dinner is somewhat more refined, with main courses like grilled trout, roast
beef, and fried clams.

47 Fundy Park Chalet Rd. (near park headquarters), Fundy National Park, NB E4H 4Y8. ℂ **506/887-2808.** Reservations recommended. Sandwiches C$3–C$7 (US$2.70–US$6.30/£1.50–£3.50); main courses C$9–C$16
(US$8.10–US$14/£4.50–£8). AE, MC, V. Summer daily 8am–9:30pm. Closed Oct–May.

8 Moncton

Moncton makes the plausible claim that it's at the crossroads of the Maritimes, and it hasn't been bashful about using its geographic advantage to promote itself as a business hub. As such, much of the hotel and restaurant trade caters to people in suits, at least on weekdays. But walk along Main Street in the evening or on weekends, and you're likely to spot spiked hair, grunge flannel, skateboards, and other youthful fashion statements from current and lapsed eras. There is some life here.

For families, Moncton offers a decent stopover if you're traveling with kids. Magnetic Hill and Crystal Palace both offer entertaining (albeit somewhat pricey) ways to fill an afternoon.

ESSENTIALS

GETTING THERE   Moncton is at the crossroads of several major routes through New Brunswick, including Route 2 (the Trans-Canada Hwy.) and Route 15. The airport is about 10 minutes from downtown on Route 132 (head northeast on Main St. from Moncton and keep driving). **Air Canada** (℃ **888/AIR-CANA;** www.aircanada. com) has traditionally served the city, but the upstart carrier **WestJet** (℃ **888/937-8538;** www.westjet.com) now also connects Moncton with Halifax, Toronto, St. John's, and Calgary, and from those hubs you can fly onward to Florida, Los Angeles, and Las Vegas without switching airlines.

VIA Rail's (℃ **888/842-7245;** www.viarail.com) train from Montréal to Halifax stops in Moncton 6 days a week. The rail station is downtown on Main Street, next to Highfield Square.

VISITOR INFORMATION   Moncton has three staffed visitor information centers, all open seasonally. One is located at the **Moncton airport** (℃ **506/877-7782**), open from late May through Labor Day. The second is near **Magnetic Hill,** in a McDonald's restaurant off Exit 450 of the Trans-Canada Highway (℃ **506/855-8622**); it's also open from late May until Labor Day. Then there's a downtown visitor information center located centrally in **Bore Park,** just off Main Street at 10 Bendview Court (℃ **506/853-3540**), open daily from late May until early October.

The rest of the year, you can find an unstaffed kiosk of tourist information in the lobby of the modern **City Hall** at 655 Main St. The city's tourism website is located at **www.gomoncton.com.**

EXPLORING MONCTON

Moncton's downtown can be easily reconnoitered on foot—once you find parking, which can be vexing. (Look for the paid lots a block or so north and south of Main St.) **Downtown Moncton Inc.** publishes a nicely designed "Historic Walking Tour" brochure that touches on some of the most significant buildings; ask for it at one of the visitor centers.

The most active stretch of Main Street is the few blocks between City Hall and the train underpass. Here you'll find cafes, newsstands, hotels, and restaurants, along with a handful of intriguing shops. Note the sometimes-jarring mix of architectural styles, the earlier examples of which testify to Moncton's historic prosperity as a commercial center.

Exploring by bike offers some wonderful dividends, especially when pedaling along Riverfront Park or through the popular 120-hectare (297-acre) Centennial Park. A local nonprofit called Hub City Wheelers schedules group bike rides nearly every day throughout the summer, and nonmembers are welcome; it's a good way to meet some of the local bikers and find the best routes. Ask at the visitor information center for a brochure with a schedule.

Crystal Palace *(Kids*   The indoor amusement park at Crystal Palace will make an otherwise endless rainy day go by quickly. The spacious enclosed park includes a four-screen cinema, shooting arcades, numerous games (ranging from old-fashioned Skee-Ball to cutting-edge video games), a medium-size roller coaster, a carousel, a swing ride, laser tag, bumper cars, miniature airplane and semitruck rides, minigolf, batting cages, and a virtual-reality ride. From late June to early September, outdoor activities include go-karts and bumper boats. The park will particularly appeal to kids under the age of 12, although teens will likely find a video game to occupy them. To really wear the kids down, you can stay virtually inside the park by booking a room at the adjoining Ramada Plaza Crystal Palace Hotel (see below).

At Champlain Place Shopping Centre (Trans-Canada Hwy., Exit 504-A W.), 499 Paul St., Dieppe. © 877/856-4386 or 506/859-4386. www.crystalpalace.ca. Free admission. Rides are 1–4 tickets each (book of 25 C$20/US$18/£10); unlimited ride bracelets C$20 (US$18/£10) adults, C$17 (US$15/£8.50) children, C$62 (US$56/£31) families. July and Aug daily 10am–10pm; rest of year Mon–Thurs noon–8pm, Fri noon–9pm, Sat 10am–9pm, Sun 10am–8pm.

Magic Mountain Water Park *(Kids*   This water park, adjacent to the famous/infamous Magnetic Hill (see below), features wave pools and numerous slides, including the towering Kamikaze Slide, where daredevils can reach speeds of 40 miles per hour. Your kids can also race their friends side-by-side down a slide on a tube or mat (count me in) and play minigolf at the site. Little kids might be more interested in the Splash-pad, a more passive attraction that sprays water in four directions (from a plastic whale, boat, and lighthouse) onto shrieking kiddies.

2875 Mountain Rd. (Trans-Canada Hwy., Exit 488), Moncton. Admission C$23 (US$21/£12) adults full day, C$12–C$17 (US$11–US$15/£6–£8.50) children 4–11, C$74 (US$67/£37) families. Afternoon rates (enter after 3pm) 33% lower. July–Aug 10am–7pm; mid-June to end of June till 6pm.

Magnetic Hill *(Overrated (Kids*   Magnetic Hill, located on Moncton's northwest outskirts a few miles from downtown, began as a simple quirk of geography. Cars that stopped at the bottom of a short stretch of downhill started to roll back uphill! Or at least what *appeared* to be uphill. . . . It's a nifty illusion. Not to pull back the curtain, but it works because the slope is on the side of a far larger hill, which tilts the whole countryside and effectively skews one's perspective. Starting in the 1930s, locals capitalized on the phenomenon by opening canteens and gift shops nearby. By the 1950s, the hill boasted the largest souvenir shop in the Maritimes. The atmosphere is a bit more glossy than a half-century ago, however. You enter a well-marked drive with magnet-themed road signs and streetlights, pay a small toll at a gatehouse, and wind around a comically twisting road to wait your turn before being directed to the hill.

You might find the "uphill roll" entertaining—for a few meters. But only come if you have kids; they will be riveted by two amusement complexes that have sprouted in the fields on either side of the road. Attractions within a few hundred yards of the hill include Wharf Village (a collection of souvenir shops and snack bars designed to look like a seaside village), a popular **zoo** *&*, video arcades, go-kart racing, batting cages, a driving range, a kiddie train, and bumper boats. The chief attraction is the Magic Mountain Water Park (see previous entry).

Despite—or perhaps because of—the unrepentant cheesiness, Magnetic Hill is actually a decent destination for families weary of beaches, hikes, and the dreary natural world. Just be aware that nothing's cheap after you fork over the C$5 (US$4.50/£2.50) to roll up the hill; an afternoon here can put a serious hurt on your wallet.

Mountain Rd. (Trans-Canada Hwy., Exit 488), Moncton. No phone. Admission Magnetic Hill C$5 (US$4.50/£2.50) per car, free if the gate is open and unstaffed; Magnetic Hill Zoo C$9.50 (US$8.55/£4.75) adults, C$8.50 (US$7.65/£4.25) seniors and children 12–18, C$6.50 (US$5.85/£3.25) children 4–11, C$22 (US$20/£11) families in summer, cheaper off-season. June–Oct Mon–Fri 10am–6pm, weekends 9am–6pm; off season some attractions closed, call for info. Closed Nov to mid-May.

WHERE TO STAY

Chain hotels have set up shop near the complex of services that have sprouted around Magnetic Hill (from the Trans-Canada Hwy., take Exit 450 to reach these hotels). These include the **Comfort Inn,** 2495 Mountain Rd. (© **800/228-5150** or 506/384-3175); **Country Inn & Suites,** 2475 Mountain Rd. (© **800/456-4000** or 506/852-7000); and **Holiday Inn Express,** also just off the exit at 2515 Mountain Rd. (© **866/402-7666**). At these clean, convenient hotels, rooms generally range from around C$85 to C$199 (US$77–US$179/£43–£100).

Delta Beauséjour ✦ The downtown Delta Beauséjour, constructed in 1972, is boxy, bland, and concrete, and the entrance courtyard is sterile and off-putting in a Cold War Berlin sort of way. But inside, the decor is inviting in a spare, international-modern manner. The property is well maintained, with rooms and public areas recently renovated. The third-floor indoor pool offers year-round swimming. (There's also a pleasant outdoor deck overlooking the distant marshes of the Petitcodiac River.) The hotel is a favorite among business travelers, but in summer and on weekends, leisure travelers largely have it to themselves. In addition to the elegant Windjammer (see below), the hotel has a basic cafe/snack bar; a piano bar and lounge; and a rustic, informal restaurant called L'Auberge that serves three meals a day.

750 Main St., Moncton, NB E1C 1E6. © **888/351-7666** or 506/854-4344. Fax 506/858-0957. www.deltahotels.com. 310 units. C$129–C$199 (US$116–US$179/£65–£100) double. Rates include continental breakfast. AE, DC, MC, V. **Amenities:** 3 restaurants; bar; indoor heated pool; fitness center; business center; shopping arcade; salon; 24-hr. room service; babysitting; laundry service; dry cleaning. *In room:* A/C, TV, fax (some units), dataport, minibar, cof-feemaker, iron/ironing board.

Ramada Plaza Crystal Palace Hotel *(Overrated* This modern, three-story chain hotel (built in 1990) adjoins the Crystal Palace amusement park and is a short walk from the region's largest mall. As such, it's surrounded by acres of asphalt and has lit-tle in the way of native charm. Most rooms are modern but unexceptional—not counting the 12 fantasy suites that go over the top with themes like "Deserted Island" (sleep in a thatched hut) or "Rock'n' Roll" (sleep in a 1959 replica pink Cadillac bed). Some rooms face the indoor pool; others the vast parking lot. For entertainment nearby, there's the amusement park, obviously. Also within the amusement complex is the hotel's restaurant, McGinnis Landing, which offers basic pub fare. Prices are high for what you get for main dinner courses, but specials are always available, and the restaurant caters well to younger appetites.

499 Paul St., Dieppe, NB E1A 6S5. © **800/528-1234** or 506/858-8584. Fax 506/858-5486. www.crystalpalace hotel.com. 115 units. C$90–C$275 (US$81–US$248/£45–£138) double. Ask about packages, some of which include amusement-park passes. AE, DC, DISC, MC, V. **Amenities:** Restaurant; bar; indoor pool; Jacuzzi; sauna; limited room service; babysitting; dry cleaning. *In room:* A/C, TV, minibar, coffeemaker.

WHERE TO DINE

Boomerang's Classic Grill ✦ *(Kids* STEAK Though it has changed its name to reduce confusion, Boomerang's is still likely to remind diners of the Aussie-themed

Outback Steakhouse chain, right down to the oversize knives here. Though there is now a second location in the town of Dartmouth, this is *not* a chain; service is rather more personal, and the Aussie-whimsical decor is done with a lighter hand. It's a handsome spot with three dining rooms, all quite dim with slatted dividers, drawn shades, and ceiling fans, which create the impression that it's blazingly hot outside (a real trick in Feb in New Brunswick). The menu features lobster and all the usual stuff from the barbie, including grilled chicken breasts and ribs. But the steak selection is the reason you come, ranging from an 8-ounce bacon-wrapped tenderloin to a 14-ounce porterhouse; you can even get them "blue-rare" if you want. Side it with an Aussie baked potato if you like. Boomerang's burgers are also excellent, and the plethora of lunch offerings and "cut lunch" specials is nothing short of amazing—every kid and parent can find something good to eat here.

130 Westmoreland St. © **506/857-8325.** Call-ahead seating in lieu of reservations. Lunches C$9–C$15 (US$8.10–US$14/£4.50–£7.50); dinners C$17–C$28 (US$15–US$25/£8.50–£14). AE, DC, DISC, MC, V. Sun–Wed 4–10pm; Thurs–Sat 4–11:30pm.

The Windjammer 🏮🏮 SEAFOOD/CONTINENTAL   Tucked off the lobby of Moncton's best hotel is The Windjammer, probably its best restaurant; this dining room is considered in some circles to be one of Canada's top hotel eateries. With its heavy wood and nautical theme, it resembles the private officer's mess of an exclusive ship. Yet this isn't a fish-and-chips joint: The menu is ambitious, and the dining room has garnered an excellent reputation for its dishes, including appetizers of oysters or a cold seafood "martini," or entrees such as squid-ink linguine with fiddleheads, a ginger-garlic filet salmon, the pan-roasted black cod, an herbed Arctic char, and simple lobster. Despite the seafaring decor, the chef serves up plenty of treats for carnivores, including a bison ragout appetizer, a roasted New Brunswick rack of lamb, a chateaubriand of bison, and a tenderloin flambé prepared tableside and then garnished with a peppercorn sauce.

750 Main St. (in the Delta Beauséjour). © **506/877-7137.** Reservations recommended. Main courses C$22–C$42 (US$20–US$38/£11–£21). AE, DC, MC, V. Mon–Sat 5:30–10pm.

EN ROUTE TO KOUCHIBOUGUAC NATIONAL PARK

If you decide to head directly to Kouchibouguac from Moncton, **La Dune de Bouctouche** makes for a good stop along the way. To reach the dune, take Route 15 east out of Moncton, then go north on Route 11 at its intersection with Shediac. The drive takes about an hour.

This striking white sand dune stretches an impressive 12km (7½ miles) across Bouctouche Bay and is home to the endangered piping plover, a unique butterfly species, and some rare plants. The sensitive dune area itself can be viewed from a wheelchair-accessible, 2km (1¼-mile) boardwalk that snakes along its length. On a sunny day, the sand beach is a lovely spot to while away a couple of hours, or even to take a dip in the warm seawater. The visitor center is fairly straightforward in its explanations of the flora and fauna indigenous to the dune; kids will probably be most amused by the larger-than-life baby plover puppet that can be removed from its just-hatched "egg." Admission is free; the boardwalk is open year-round (in good weather) and the visitor center is open daily from10am to 8pm (until 5pm in the off season).

If you're interested in spending the night in the area or grabbing a bite to eat, stop by the **Dune View Inn** 🏮, 589 Rte. 875 (© **877/743-9893** or 506/743-9993; www. aubergevuedeladune.com), open year-round, where the new owners (one's a trained chef who previously cooked in Montréal) serve up French-inflected local seafood. The rooms feature TVs, telephones, and private bathrooms; they're pretty and light but rather cramped. A double with breakfast costs from C$90 to C$135 (US$81–US$122/ £45–£68). The inn can also arrange local golf and kayaking packages or a romance package featuring handmade soaps.

9 Kouchibouguac National Park (★

Much is made of the fact that this sprawling park has all sorts of ecosystems worth studying, from sandy barrier islands to ancient peat bogs. But that's a little bit like saying Disney World has nice lakes: It entirely misses the point. In fact, this artfully designed national park is a wonderful destination for biking, hiking, and beach-going. If you can, plan to spend a couple of days here doing a whole lot of nothing. The varied ecosystems (which, incidentally, are spectacular) are just an added attraction.

Kouchibouguac is, above all, a place for bikers and families. The park is laced with well-groomed bike trails made of finely crushed cinders that traverse forest and field and meander along rivers and lagoons. Where bikes aren't permitted (such as on boardwalks and beaches), there are usually clusters of bike racks for locking them up while you continue on foot. If you camp here and bring a bike, there's no need to ever use your car.

The only contingent the park might disappoint is gung-ho hikers. This isn't for serious hiking, just walking and strolling. The pathways are wide and flat and invite a leisurely pace. Most trails are very short—on the order of 1 or 2km (.6–1.2 miles)— and seem more like detours than destinations. In fact, approaching the park as a sort of desultory tour with intriguing detours might be the best way to go about a visit here.

Although the park is ideal for campers, day-trippers also find it a worthwhile destination. Plan to remain here until sunset. The trails tend to empty out, and the dunes, bogs, and boreal forest take on a rich, almost iridescent hue as the sun sinks over the spruce.

Be aware that this is a fair-weather destination—if it's blustery and rainy, there's little to do except take damp and melancholy strolls on the beach. So it's best to save a visit here for more cooperative days. Check the weather before coming, if you can. (The ungainly name, by the way, is a Mi'kmaq Indian word meaning "river of the long tides." It's pronounced "Koosh-uh-*boog*-oo-whack." If you don't get it right, don't worry; few do.)

ESSENTIALS

GETTING THERE   Kouchibouguac National Park is between Moncton and Miramichi. The exit for the park off Route 11 is well marked.

VISITOR INFORMATION   The park is open from mid-May to mid-October. The **Visitor's Centre** (© **506/876-2443**) is just off Route 134, a short drive past the park entrance. It's open from 8am to 8pm during peak season, with shorter hours in the off season. There's a slide show to introduce you to the park's attractions, and a small collection of field guides to peruse.

FEES   A daily pass is C$6.90 (US$6.20/£3.45) adults, C$5.90 (US$5.30/£2.95) seniors, C$3.45 (US$3.10/£1.75) children 6 to 16, and C$17 (US$15/£9) families. (April–June and Oct–Nov, rates are discounted about 40%.) Seasonal passes are also available but are only worth the dough if you're planning to visit for more than 3 days.

You should have permits for everyone in your car when you enter the park; though there are no formal checkpoints, occasional roadblocks during the summer ensure compliance. Note that, for a small extra charge, you can also get a helpful map of the park at the information center.

CAMPING

Kouchibouguac is at heart a camper's park, best enjoyed by those who plan to spend at least a night. **South Kouchibouguac** ☆, the main campground, is centrally located and very nicely laid out with 311 sites, most rather large and private. The 46 or so sites with electricity are nearer the river and somewhat more open. The newest sites (nos. 1–35) lack grassy areas for pitching a tent, and campers have to pitch tents on gravel pads. It's best to bring a good sleeping pad or ask for another site. Sites are about C$21 to C$30 (US$19–US$27/£11–£15) per night, depending on time of year and the level of comfort you require. Reservations are accepted for about half of the campsites; call © **506/876-2443** starting in late April. The remaining sites are doled out first-come, first-served.

Other camping options within the park include the more remote, semiprimitive **Côte-à-Fabien,** across the river on Kouchibouguac Lagoon. It lacks showers and some sites require a short walk, but it's more appealing for tenters. The cost is about C$15 (US$14/£7.50) per night. The park also maintains three backcountry sites. **Sipu** is on the Kouchibouguac River and is accessible by canoe or foot, **Petit Large** by foot or bike, and **Pointe-à-Maxime** by canoe only. Backcountry sites cost C$9.90 (US$8.90/£4.95) per night.

BEACHES

The park features some 15km (9⅓ miles) of sandy beaches, mostly along barrier islands of sandy dunes, delicate grasses and flowers, and nesting plovers and sandpipers. **Kellys** ☆ is the principal beach, and it's one of the best-designed and best-executed recreation areas in eastern Canada. At the forest's edge, a short walk from the main parking area, you'll find showers, changing rooms, a snack bar, and some interpretive exhibits. From here, you walk some 540m (1,772 ft.) across a winding boardwalk that's plenty fascinating on its own. It crosses a salt marsh, lagoons, and some of the best-preserved dunes in the province.

The long, sandy beach features water that's comfortably warm, with waves that are usually quite mellow—they lap rather than roar, unless a storm's offshore. Lifeguards oversee a roped-off section of about 90m (295 ft.); elsewhere, you're on your own. For very young children who still equate waves with certain death, there's supervised swimming on a sandy stretch of the quiet lagoon.

BOATING & BIKING

Ryans (© **506/876-8918**)—a cluster of buildings between the campgrounds and Kellys Beach—is the place for renting bikes, kayaks, paddleboats, and canoes seasonally. Bikes rent for around C$5 (US$4.50/£2.50) per hour. Most of the watersports equipment (including canoes and pedal boats) rent for around C$7 (US$6.30/£3.50) per hour, with double kayaks at C$12 (US$11/£6) per hour. Canoes may be rented for longer excursions; they're around C$30 (US$27/£15) daily, or C$45 (US$41/£23) for 2 days. Ryans is located on the lagoon, so you can explore around the dunes or upstream on the winding river.

The park offers a **Voyageur Canoe Marine Adventure** in summer, with a crew paddling a sizable canoe from the mainland to offshore sandbars, where the naturalist-guide will help identify the wildlife encountered. Expect to see osprey and bald eagles. The 3-hour excursion usually costs about C$30 (US$27/£15) adults, C$14 (US$13/£7) children 6 to 16. Inquire about the trip at the park's information center.

HIKING

The hiking and biking trails are as short and undemanding as they are appealing. The one hiking trail that requires slightly more fortitude is the **Kouchibouguac River Trail,** which runs for some 13km (8 miles) along the banks of the river.

The **Bog Trail** ⊛ is just 2km (1.2 miles) each way, but it opens the door to a wonderfully alien world. The 4,500-year-old bog is a classic domed bog, made of peat from decaying shrubs and other plants. At the bog's edge you'll find a wooden tower ascended by a spiral staircase that affords a panoramic view of this eerie habitat.

The boardwalk crosses to the thickest, middle part of the bog. Where the boardwalk stops, you can feel the bouncy surface of the bog—you're actually standing on a mat of thick vegetation that's floating atop water. Look for the pitcher plant, a carnivorous species that lures flies into its bell-shaped leaves, where downward-pointed hairs prevent them from fleeing. Eventually, the plant's enzymes digest the insect, providing nutrients for growth in this hostile environment.

Callanders Beach and **Cedar Trail** ⊛ are both located at the end of a short dirt road. There's an open field with picnic tables here, a small protected beach on the lagoon (there are fine views of dunes across the way), and a 1km (.6-mile) hiking trail on a boardwalk that passes through a cedar forest, past a salt marsh, and through a mixed forest. This is a good alternative for those who'd prefer to avoid the larger crowds at Kellys Beach.

WHERE TO STAY & DINE

Habitant Hotel and Restaurant ⊛ *(Value)* About 15km (9⅓ miles) from the park entrance, the Habitant is the best choice for overnighting if you're exploring Kouchibouguac by day. It's a modern, mansard-roofed, Tudor-style complex—well, let's just say "architecturally mystifying"—with a restaurant and small campground on the premises. The rooms are decorated in a contemporary motel style and are very clean. The motel features a distinctive indoor pool, along with a fitness center and sauna. The restaurant next door serves three meals a day and is informal, comfortable, and reasonably priced. Seafood dinners are the specialty, including a heaping "fisherman's feast" for about C$25 (US$23/£13). One nice touch: There's a self-serve wine cellar, where wines are sold at liquor-store prices, many under C$20 (US$18/£10).

9600 Main St. (Rte. 134), Richibucto, NB E4W 4E6. © **888/442-7222** or 506/523-4421. Fax 506/523-9155. www.habitant.nb.ca. 29 units. C$65–C$140 (US$59–US$126/£33–£70) double. AE, DC, MC, V. "Small, well-trained pets" allowed. **Amenities:** Restaurant; indoor pool; sauna. *In room:* A/C, TV.

10 Acadian Peninsula

The Acadian Peninsula is that bulge on the northeast corner of New Brunswick, forming one of the arms of the Baie des Chaleurs (Québec's Gaspé Peninsula forms the other). It's a land of tidy if generally nondescript houses, miles of shoreline (much of it beaches), modern concrete harbors filled with commercial fishing boats, and residents proud of their Acadian heritage. You'll see the Stella Maris flag—the French tricolor with a single gold star in the field of blue—everywhere.

On a map it looks like much of the coastline would be wild and remote here. But it's not. Although a number of farmhouses dot the route, and you'll occasionally come upon brilliant meadows of hawkweed and lupine, this part of the coast is more defined by manufactured housing that's been erected on square lots between the sea and the fast two-lane highways. Other than the superb Acadian Village historical museum near Caraquet, there are few organized attractions in this region. It's more a place to unwind while walking on a beach or sitting along harbors while watching fishing boats come and go.

ESSENTIALS

VISITOR INFORMATION   Each of the areas mentioned below maintains a visitor information center. The **Caraquet Tourism Information,** 35 du Carrefour Ave. (© 506/726-2676), is a seasonal (late May to mid-Sept) office that offers convenient access to other activities in the harbor (see below) and has plenty of parking. Shippagan dispenses information from a wooden lighthouse near the Marine Centre at 200 Hotel de Ville Ave. (© 506/336-3993).

GETTING THERE   Route 11 is the main highway serving the Acadian Peninsula.

SHIPPAGAN & MISCOU ISLAND

Both of these destinations require a detour off Route 11 but are worthwhile if you're interested in glimpsing Acadian New Brunswick in the slow lane. As an added bonus, Miscou Island boasts some fine beaches.

Shippagan is a quiet, leafy village that's home to a sizable crabbing fleet. It's also home to the modern **Aquarium and Marine Centre** ✹, 100 Aquarium St. (© 506/336-3013). The center is on the water near the harbor (prominently posted signs around town will direct you there) and is a good destination if you're the least bit curious about local marine life. You'll learn about the 125 species of native fish hereabouts, many of which are on display. Kids are especially drawn to the **harbor seal tank** outside, where trainers prompt the sleek beasts to show off their acrobatic skills. Little ones will also love watching the twice-daily feedings, when the seals down pounds of herring. Admission is C$7 (US$6.30/£3.50) adults, C$5.25 (US$4.75/£2.65) seniors, C$4.35 (US$3.90/£2.20) children, and C$12 (US$11/£6) families. The center is open mid-May to September from 10am to 6pm daily; seal feedings are at 11am and 4pm.

Keep driving north on Route 113 and you'll soon cross a low drawbridge to Lamèque Island. If you're traveling through in mid-July, don't be surprised to hear fine baroque music wafting from the Ste-Cecile Church. Since 1975, the island has hosted the **Lamèque International Baroque Music Festival** (© 506/344-5846 or 800/320-2276 from Canada only). For about 10 days each summer, talented musicians perform an ambitious series of concerts, held in an architecturally striking, acoustically wonderful church in a small village on the island's north coast. Tickets often sell out well in advance, and most are priced at C$20 to C$35 (US$18–US$32/£10–£18) per adult.

North of Lamèque is **Miscou Island** ✹, which for decades was served by a modest ferry. That era ended in the mid-1990s, when a shiny, arched bridge was erected across the strait. The bridge made some islanders a bit grumpy, but happily the island still retains a sense of remoteness, especially north of the village of Miscou Centre, where you get into bog territory. The extraordinary view of the islands and ocean from the crest of the bridge serves as some consolation for the breach of isolation.

Drive northward on Route 113 until you run out of road and you'll come to New Brunswick's oldest lighthouse. **Point Miscou Lighthouse** marks the confluence of the Gulf of St. Lawrence and the Baie des Chaleurs.

The dominant natural feature of Miscou is the bog. The **bog landscape** is as distinctive as that of the Canadian Rockies. It's flat and green and can stretch for miles. You'll see much of this on northern **Miscou Island** (some of the bogs have been harvested for peat).

A finely constructed **interpretive nature trail** is on Route 113 north of Miscou Centre. A boardwalk loops through the bog around an open pond. Learn about the orchids and lilies that thrive in the vast and spongy mat of shrubs and roots. Look for the fascinating carnivorous plants (the pitcher plants are relatively easy to spot). The loop takes about 20 minutes, and it's free.

WHERE TO STAY

Miscou Beach Cottage & Camping   Far up Miscou Island are these simple, unpretentious cottages right on the beach. Six of them sit side by side facing the dunes and the ocean; small decks front each cottage and invite idleness. All considered, the place has an English caravan-park feel, with camp trailers crowded in a field behind the cottages. There's also a no-frills family restaurant on the premises. Not much else goes on here (unless you consider the bare-bones minigolf course), so plan to spend most of your day exploring the long sandy strand out front. Note that cottage rentals here are now only by the week (but ask about cancellations and open dates anyway). Campsites are also available, for C$16 to C$28 (US$14–US$25/£8–£14) each. Beware of the voracious local mosquito population, however, descending at dusk early in the season.

Rte. 113 (mailing address 118 Paradis du Campeur Lane), Miscou, NB E8T 2A2. ✆ **506/344-1015** or 506/344-8463. 6 units. Cottages C$670 (US$603/£335) weekly. MC, V. Closed Sept 15–June 15. **Amenities:** Restaurant. *In room:* Kitchenette, no phone.

CARAQUET ✿

The historic beach town of Caraquet—widely regarded as the spiritual capital of Acadian New Brunswick—just keeps on going and going . . . geographically speaking, anyway. It's spread thinly along a commercial boulevard parallel to the beach. Caraquet once claimed the honorific "longest village in the world" when it ran to some 21km (13 miles) long. As a result of its length, Caraquet lacks a well-defined downtown or any sort of urban center of gravity; there's one stoplight, and that's where Boulevard St-Pierre Est changes to Boulevard St-Pierre Ouest. (Most establishments mentioned below are somewhere along this boulevard.)

A good place to start a tour is the **Carrefour de la Mer** (51 Blvd. St-Pierre Est), a modern complex overlooking the man-made harbor. It has a spare, Scandinavian feel to it, and you'll find the tourist information office (see above), a seafood restaurant, a snack bar, a children's playground, and two short strolls that lead to picnic tables on jetties with fine harbor views.

Village Historique Acadien ✿   New Brunswick sometimes seems awash in Acadian museums and historic villages. If you're interested in visiting just one such site, this is the place to hold out for. Some 45 buildings—most of which were dismantled and transported here from other villages on the peninsula—depict life as it was lived in an Acadian settlement between the years 1770 and 1890. The historic buildings are set throughout 183 hectares (452 acres) of woodland, marsh, and field. You'll learn all about the exodus and settlement of the Acadians from costumed guides, who are also adept at skills ranging from letterpress printing to blacksmithing. Plan on spending at least 2 to 3 hours exploring the village.

In June 2002, the village opened a major addition, which focuses on a more recent era. Some 26 buildings (all but one are replicas) are devoted to continuing the saga, showing Acadian life from 1890 to 1939, with a special focus on industry. The attractive yellow Chateau Albert Hotel, which mostly houses students enrolled in multiday workshops in traditional Acadian arts and crafts, was part of this new construction project; the simple rooms lack phones and televisions, but there is a dining room, convivial bar area, and a thrown-back-in-time vibe (which is intentional). Rooms run from about C$70 to C$125 (US$63–US$113/£35–£63) double.

Rte. 11 (10km/6 miles west of Caraquet). ⓒ 506/726-2600. www.villagehistoriqueacadien.com. Admission C$15 (US$14/£7.50) adults, C$13 (US$12/£6.50) seniors, C$10 (US$9/£5) children, C$30 (US$27/£15) families. June to mid-Sept daily 10am–6pm; mid-Sept to mid-Oct 10am–5pm. Closed mid-Oct to May.

WHERE TO STAY

Auberge de la Baie   The Auberge de la Baie is your basic year-round motel that has dressed itself up with a modern lobby and dining room. The rooms are cheerless but adequate (some have cinder-block walls, some have bay views). Particularly inviting is the broad lawn that descends from the property toward the water; stake your claim to a lawn chair and dive into a book. There's a small beach for swimming as well. The oaky and spare restaurant is open daily for all three meals, specializing in seafood dinners. Look for such items as salmon, fish and chips, and the ever-present fried clams with tartar sauce.

139 Blvd. St-Pierre Ouest, Caraquet, NB E1W 1B7. ⓒ 506/727-3485. 54 units. C$79–C$139 (US$71–US$125/£40–£70) double. AE, MC, V. **Amenities:** Dining room; bar. *In room:* A/C, no phone.

Hôtel Paulin 𝕬𝕬   This attractive Victorian hotel, built in 1891 as the first hotel in Caraquet, has been operated by the Paulin family for the past three generations and has recently gone a bit more upscale with added units . . . and rising prices to match. It's a three-story red clapboard building with a green-shingled mansard roof, located just off the main boulevard and overlooking the bay. (Some of the charm has been compromised by buildings nearby, however.) The lobby immediately puts one in mind of summer relaxation, with royal blue wainscoting, canary yellow walls, and stuffed furniture upholstered in white with blue piping. Expect rooms, including four suites, to be comfortably but sparely furnished with antiques; only one suite has an ocean view. The hotel's first floor houses a handsome, well-regarded **restaurant** 𝕬. Specialties might include a delectable crab mousse or a piece of brown-sugar pie.

143 Blvd. St-Pierre Ouest, Caraquet, NB E1W 1B6. ⓒ 506/727-9981 or 866/727-9981. Fax 506/727-4808. www.hotelpaulin.com. 12 units. Mid-June to mid-Sept C$199–C$315 (US$179–US$284/£100–£158) double; mid-Sept to mid-June C$179–C$235 (US$161–US$212/£90–£118) double. MC, V. **Amenities:** Restaurant; massage. *In room:* A/C, TV, hair dryer, iron, no phone.

WHERE TO DINE

Caraquet is a good place for seafood, naturally. My preference is still with the Hôtel Paulin's restaurant for its charm, but the several inexpensive-to-moderate spots along the main drag all serve fresh seafood nicely, if simply, prepared.

For a delicious and sophisticated snack, head to **Les Blancs d'Arcadie** 𝕬, 340-A Blvd. St-Pierre Est (ⓒ 506/727-5952), a handsome compound of yellow farm buildings set against the forest just east of town. The specialties here are cheese and yogurt from the milk of a Swiss breed of goats called Saanen. The goats are raised indoors year-round; you can learn about the goats and the cheese- and yogurt-making process on a tour of the operation, which includes tastings. The 90-minute tour costs about

C$6 (US$5.40/£3). There's also a small shop to buy fresh cheeses and milk. (The peppercorn and the garlic soft cheeses are very good.) Les Blancs d'Arcadia is en route to Bas Caraquet on Route 145; watch for the goat sign on the right shortly after you pass the road to St-Simon. Reservations for tours are appreciated.

GRANDE-ANSE

Grande-Anse is a wide-spot-in-the-road village of low, modern homes near bluffs overlooking the bay. The town is lorded over by the stone Saint Jude church. The best view of the village, and a good spot for a picnic, is along the bluffs just below the church. (Look for the sign indicating QUAI 45m/148 ft. west of the church.) Here you'll find a small man-made harbor with a fleet of fishing boats, a tiny sand beach, and some grassy bluffs where you can park overlooking the bay.

If you'd prefer picnic tables, head a few miles westward to **Pokeshaw Park** (© **506/732-5423**), open mid-June through August. Just offshore is a large kettle-shaped island ringed with ragged cliffs that rise from the waves, long ago separated from the cliffs on which you're now standing. An active cormorant rookery thrives among the skeletons of trees, lending the place a bit of a haunted and melancholy air. There's a small picnic shelter for use in inclement weather. The park is open daily from 9am to 9pm; a small admission fee is charged.

For the full-blown ocean swimming experience, head to **Plage Grande-Anse,** located 2km (1¼ miles) east of town. This handsome beach has a snack bar near the parking area and is open from 10am to 9pm daily. There's a small entrance fee for adults.

11 Mt. Carleton Provincial Park ⟨★

In 1969, New Brunswick carved out some of the choicest land and set it aside as wilderness park. Mt. Carleton Provincial Park contains 2,821 hectares (6,971 acres) of azure lakes, pure streams, thick boreal forest, and gently rounded mountains, the largest of which afford excellent views. When visiting, look for moose, black bear, coyotes, bobcat, and more than 100 species of birds. And, of course, black flies.

ESSENTIALS

GETTING THERE   Mt. Carleton Provincial Park is 42km (26 miles) east of Saint-Quentin on Route 180. Be aware that Saint-Quentin is the nearest community for supplies; there are no convenient general stores just outside the park gates. The park is also accessible from Bathurst to the east, but it's a 111km (69-mile) drive on a road that's mostly paved but gravel in spots. There are no services along the road and frequent logging trucks.

VISITOR INFORMATION   There is no admission fee. The park's gates are open daily in summer from 7am to 10pm (8am–8pm in spring and fall). A small **interpretive center** (© **506/235-0793**), located at the entrance gate, offers background on the park's natural and cultural history from mid-May through early September. The park remains open, though unstaffed, the rest of the year.

CAMPING

Armstrong Brook ⟨★⟨★ is the principal destination for visiting campers coming to Mount Carleton. It has 88 sites split between the forest near Lake Nictau's shore (no lakeside sites) and an open, grassy field. Campers can avail themselves of hot showers and a bathhouse for washing up. A path leads to the lake's edge; there's a spit of small, flat pebbles that's wonderful for swimming and sunbathing. Camping fees are C$11 (US$9.90/£5.50) weekdays, C$14 (US$13/£7) weekends.

Four backcountry sites are located high on the slopes of Mt. Carleton (preregistration required). The sites, which require a 4km (2.5-mile) hike, offer views into a rugged valley and a great sense of remoteness. Water is available but should be treated (beavers are nearby). No fires are permitted, so bring a stove. The fee is C$5 (US$4.50/£2.50) per night. Two other remote campsites on the shores of Lake Nictau are accessible by either canoe or a moderate walk. Register in advance; the fee is C$8 to C$9 (US$7.20–US$8.10/£4–£4.50) per night.

HIKING & BIKING

The park has 10 hiking trails that total 68km (42 miles). The helpful park staff at the gatehouse will be happy to direct you to a hike that suits your experience and mood.

The park's premier hike is to the summit of **Mount Carleton,** the province's highest point at 820m (2,690 ft.). Although that elevation is not going to impress those who've hiked in the Canadian Rockies, size is relative here, and the views seem endless. A craggy comb of rocks with a 360-degree view of the lower mountains and the sprawling lakes marks the summit. The trail head is about a 25-minute drive from the gatehouse; allow about 4 hours for a round-trip hike of about 10km (6 miles). Overlooking Nictau Lake is **Mount Sagamook,** at an altitude of 777m (2,549 ft.). It's a steep and demanding hike of about 3km (1.9 miles) to the summit, where you're rewarded with spectacular views of the northern park.

For the truly gung-ho, there's the ridge walk that connects Sagamook and Carleton via **Mount Head.** The views from high above are unforgettable; you'll need to set up a shuttle with two cars to do the whole ridge in 1 day.

If you have a **mountain bike,** bring it. The gravel roads are perfect for exploring. Motor vehicles have been banned from two of these roads, which take you deep into the woods past clear lakes and rushing streams.

WHERE TO STAY & DINE

Auberge Evasion de Rêves ⚅ (Kids)   In inclement weather, or if you're just not into camping in the park with the kiddies, check out this property in nearby Saint-Quentin; its name roughly translates from the French as "Dream-Escape Inn," though that might be a bit generous. Inside, it's made up of simply furnished business-hotel-type rooms of the Courtyard This or Homewood That ilk, but with small flourishes of design on various themes (nature, golf, and so forth). The unpretentiousness and unfrilliness is refreshing, and kids will enjoy the indoor swimming pool. All rooms have TVs, DVD players, and high-speed Internet access; some have extras like settees, minifridges, armoires, and the like. There's also a dining area, a lounge, and a nice high-ceilinged, lodgelike common area of plush stuffed chairs and good wood floors. It's certainly a decent choice when in the area.

11 Canada St., Saint-Quentin, NB E8A 1J2. ② **866/443-7383** or 506/235-3551. Fax 506/235-3518. www. aubergeevasion.com. 14 units. C$120–C$150 (US$108–US$135/£60–£75) double. Rates include continental breakfast. MC, V. **Amenities:** Restaurant; bar; indoor pool; Jacuzzi. *In room:* A/C, TV, fridge (some units), coffeemaker, hair dryer, iron/ironing board.

6

Prince Edward Island

Prince Edward Island (PEI) may not be the the world's leading manufacturer of relaxation, but it's certainly a major distribution center.

Visitors soon realize there's something about the richly colored landscape of azure seas, henna-tinged cliffs capped with purple, and green farm fields that trigger some obscure relaxation hormone, resulting in a pleasant ennui. It's sometimes difficult to believe that PEI and boggy, blustery Newfoundland share the same planet, never mind the same gulf.

The northerly coast is lined with red-sand beaches, washed by the warm waters of the Gulf of St. Lawrence. Swimming here isn't quite like taking a tepid dip in North Carolina, but it's warmer than one in Maine or New Hampshire, farther south down the eastern seaboard. Away from these beaches you'll find low, rolling hills blanketed in trees and crops, especially potatoes, for which the island is justly famous. Small farms make up the island's backbone—one-quarter of the island is dedicated to agriculture, with that land cultivated by more than 2,300 individual farms.

The island was first explored in 1534 by Jacques Cartier, who discovered Mi'kmaq native Canadians living here. Over the next 2 centuries, dominion over the island bounced between Great Britain and France (who called the island Isle-St-Jean). Great Britain was awarded the island in 1763 as part of the Treaty of Paris; a little more than a century later, the first Canadian Confederation was held at Charlottetown and resulted in the creation of Canada in 1867 (though PEI didn't actually *join* the new confederation until 1873).

The island is compact and its roads are usually well marked. It's difficult to become disoriented—but you should try. Whether you're on bicycle or traveling by car, it can be quite pleasurable indeed getting lost on PEI's back roads.

This island is still steeped in the slower pace of an earlier era; milkmen still make their quiet rounds, and you return soda bottles for refilling, not only recycling. Gas attendants cheerfully pump full-serve style and wash your windows without your needing to ask. Indeed, the island's population has only grown from 109,000 in 1891 to about 140,000 today. Take your cue from this comfortable cadence and do yourself a favor: Schedule 1 or 2 extra days into your vacation, and make absolutely no plans. You won't regret it.

This chapter is divided into the counties that trisect the province. They're easy to remember: They rise in order of royal hierarchy—Prince to Queens to Kings—in the direction of England.

One final note: The island has, somewhat remarkably, managed to retain the bucolic flavor of a century ago, and pockets of sprawl are still happily few. But the handwriting is on the wall, especially in the central part of the island. That handwriting reads COTTAGE LOTS FOR SALE. These sorts of signs have been springing up in ever-greater numbers in the alfalfa and potato fields, and in coming years more and more of the island is certain to be claimed by subdivisions, luxe resorts, and malls.

The sooner you can visit, the better.

1 Exploring Prince Edward Island

PEI is Canada's smallest province—just about 193km (120 miles) at its greatest length—which keeps the scuttling about down to a minimum and makes it very manageable for day explorations from one or two bases. However, traffic on the island roads tends to be slower than you would expect elsewhere, for various reasons—speed limits, leisurely drivers, terrain—so don't count on the sort of speedy travel you'd expect in a place like the neighboring U.S. Just enjoy the scenery.

In recent years, a number of PEI hotels and attractions have banded together to market some 80 different vacation packages that offer discounts ranging from moderate to generous. There are some good values hidden within. Call the provincial tourism office at ✆ **800-463-4734** or 902/368-4444 to request information on discount packages.

ESSENTIALS

VISITOR INFORMATION   Tourism PEI publishes a comprehensive **free visitor's guide** to island attractions and lodgings that's well worth picking up. It is available at all information centers on the island, or in advance by calling ✆ **800/463-4734** or 902/368-4444. You can also request it by fax (to ✆ 902/368-4438), e-mail (gentle island@gov.pe.ca), or good old-fashioned mail (P.O. Box 2000, Charlottetown, PEI C1A 7N8). The official PEI website is located at **www.gentleisland.com**.

PEI's splashy main information center is in something called **Gateway Village** (✆ **902/437-8570**), just as you arrive on the island via the Confederation Bridge (see below). It's a good spot for gathering brochures and asking last-minute questions. There's also a well-laid-out interpretive center featuring nicely designed exhibits about island history and culture. The exhibits on venturing to the mainland by iceboat in winters past are especially intriguing. The whole 12-hectare (30-acre) Gateway development, which features a number of retail shops selling island products, is a little odd, however. As the promoters put it, "Gateway Village portrays a turn-of-the-century PEI streetscape encompassing an exposition pavilion, food and retail services, liquor store, visitor information center, and the Festivals at Gateway." Huh? My suggestion: Stop for brochures, maps, maybe a quick walk through the interpretive center, and then push on. This island's got a lot to offer. Why not experience the real thing rather than this faux version?

WHEN TO GO   PEI's peak tourism season is rather brief, running for 6 or 7 weeks from early July to late August. Most attractions don't open fully until July and a few even close before August is done.

Officials and more serious entrepreneurs are striving to convince shops and attractions to maintain more regular hours during the shoulder seasons, but they still have a way to go. If you do plan to visit in June or September, expect to be disappointed when a few (or more) restaurants and attractions are closed; check the listings in this book carefully for opening seasons. It will behoove you to base yourself in Charlottetown for part of the time if you're making a shoulder-season visit, since the capital city's restaurants all keep year-round hours.

GETTING THERE   If you're coming from the west by car, you'll arrive via the **Confederation Bridge,** which opened with great fanfare in June 1997. On the island, you'll sometimes hear it referred to instead as the "fixed link," a reference to the

Who *Is* This Prince Edward Guy, Anyway?

Prince Edward Island is named for Prince Edward Augustus (1767–1820), who was the son of King George III of England. A strict disciplinarian, Augustus rose swiftly through the British military ranks and was posted to Halifax in 1791 with the elite Fusiliers unit; his rise continued, until he was promoted to the position of official commander in chief of all British forces in North America in 1799—a post he seems to have held for only 1 year. After returning to England, his career languished, and his retirement as a duke to a Devonshire cottage seems to have been his ultimate undoing: After a walk in the cool mists, he caught a cold or pneumonia and expired at the age of just 52.

However, Edward's true lasting claim to fame occurred only after he married very late in life and his wife bore him a daughter, who was less than 1 year old when he died. Because Edward's father and uncle did not have any other surviving grandchildren—by legitimate wives, anyway—she became, by default, the Queen of England. (Get an encyclopedia if you want to understand the rules of British succession.)

In 1837, Prince Edward's daughter acceded to the throne, and she would preside over one of the most impressive expansions of empire in world history. We remember her today as Queen Victoria—the face that launched an era.

guarantee Canada made in 1873 to provide a permanent link from the mainland. Whatever you call it, the dramatic 13km (8-mile) bridge is open 24 hours a day and takes about 10 to 12 minutes to cross. Unless you're high up in a van, a truck, or an RV, however, the views are mostly obstructed by the concrete Jersey barriers that form the guardrails along the sides.

The bridge toll in 2007 was C$41 (US$37/£21) round-trip for cars, more for vehicles with more than two axles. No fare is paid when you travel to the island; the entire toll is collected when you leave. Credit cards are accepted. Call © 888/437-6565 for more information.

If you didn't bring wheels to Canada, **PEI Express Shuttle** (© 877/877-1771; www.peishuttle.com) offers transportation by van from Halifax to Charlottetown for C$55 (US$50/£28) one-way for adults, C$50 (US$45/£25) for students and seniors, C$45 (US$41/£23) for children under age 5.

By Ferry   For those arriving from Cape Breton Island or other points east, **Northumberland Ferries Limited** (© 888/249-7245; www.nfl-bay.com) provides seasonal service between Caribou, Nova Scotia (just north of Pictou) and Woods Island, PEI. Ferries with a 250-car capacity run from May to mid-December. During peak season (June to mid-Oct), ferries depart each port approximately every 90 minutes throughout the day, with the last ferry departing at 7:30pm or 9pm, depending on which direction you are traveling. The crossing takes about 75 minutes.

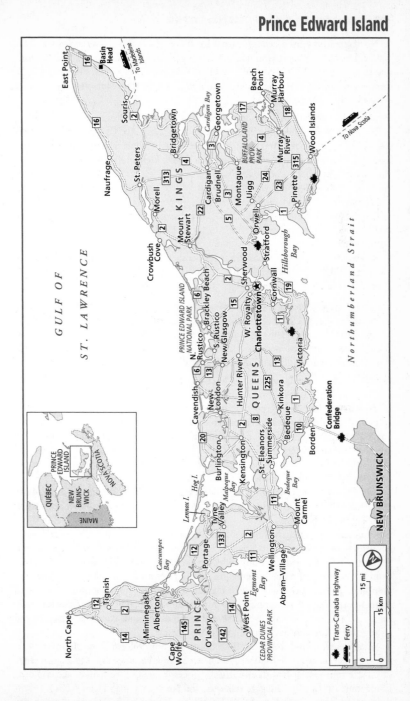

Prince Edward Island

No reservations are accepted, except for buses; it's best to arrive at least an hour before departure to boost your odds of securing a berth on the next boat. Early-morning ferries tend to be less crowded. Fares are C$12 to C$14 (US$11–US$13/£6–£7) per person and C$59 (US$53/£30) for a regular-size car (more for campers and RVs). Major credit cards are honored.

By Air   The island's main airport, Charlottetown Airport (call sign YYG; www.fly pei.com), is a few miles north of the city. The daily **Air Canada Jazz** (© **888/ 247-2262;** www.flyjazz.com) commuter flights from Halifax take just a half-hour, and Jazz also flies to Toronto and Montréal. In 2007, **Delta** (© **800/221-1212;** www. delta.com) announced a new direct summertime service from Boston, joining **Northwest** (© **800/447-4747;** www.nwa.com), which has flown onto the island from Detroit daily in summer for several years.

Calgary-based **WestJet** (© **888/937-8538;** www.westjet.com) also connects Charlottetown with Toronto, where you can fly to Florida, Los Angeles, and Las Vegas without switching airlines.

A taxi ride into the city from the airport costs C$11 (US$9.90/£5.50) for the first passenger, C$3 (US$2.70/£1.50) for additional passengers. There are also limousine firms and four auto-rental outfits represented in the terminal.

2 The Great Outdoors

Prince Edward Island doesn't have any wilderness, or even much wildness, to speak of. It's all about cultivated landscapes that have long ago been tamed by farmers. That doesn't mean you can't find outdoor adventure. Here are some places to start.

BICYCLING   There's perhaps no finer destination in Atlantic Canada for relaxed road biking than Prince Edward Island. The modest size of the island, the gentleness of the hills (the island's high point is just 142m/466 ft.), and the loveliness of the landscapes all conspire to provide a memorable biking trip. Although you won't find much rugged mountain biking here, you will find a surfeit of idyllic excursions, especially in the northern and eastern portions of the island. Avoid the Trans-Canada Highway on the south coast and main arterials like Route 2, and you'll find superb biking throughout the secondary road network.

The main off-road bike trail is the **Confederation Trail** 🐾. Eventually, the trail will cover some 350km (217 miles) along the old path of the ill-fated provincial railway from Tignish to Souris.

At present, more than half the trail has been completed, mostly in Prince and Kings counties; Queens County is still largely under development, however. The pathway is covered mostly in rolled stone dust, which makes for good travel with a mountain bike or hybrid. Services are slowly developing along the route, with bike rentals and inns cropping up. Ask at the local tourist bureaus for updated information on completed segments. An excellent place to base for exploring the trail is the **Trailside Café** (p. 242) in Mount Stewart, where several spurs of the trail converge. The cafe can arrange for return shuttles if you'd prefer one-way cycling.

MacQueen's Island Tours & Bike Shop (© **800/969-2822** or 902/368-2453; www.macqueens.com), located at 430 Queen St. in Charlottetown, organizes a range of bicycle tour packages with all-inclusive prices covering bike rentals, accommodations, route cards, maps, luggage transfers, and emergency road repair service. Seven-night tours, for example, start at C$1,350 (US$1,215/£675) double occupancy; 5-day tours are also offered. Bike rentals alone are available for C$25 (US$23/£13) and up per day, C$125 (US$113/£63) and up per week; kids' bikes are cheaper.

For rentals and repairs, you might also try **Smooth Cycle** (© 800/310-6550 or 902/566-5530), in a new location at 330 University Ave. in Charlottetown. Rentals include helmet, water bottle, and a lock and cost C$25 (US$23/£13) per day. Note that the shop is closed Sundays.

FISHING   For a taste of deep-sea fishing, head to the north coast, where you'll find plenty of outfitters happy to take you out on the big swells. The greatest concentrations of services are at North Rustico and Covehead Bay; see the "Queens County" section, below. Rates are quite reasonable, generally about C$20 (US$18/£10) for 3 hours or so.

Trout fishing holes attract inland anglers, although, as always, the best spots are a matter of local knowledge. A good place to start your inquiries is at **Going Fishing** in the Sherwood Shopping Centre at 161 St. Peter's Rd. in Charlottetown (© 902/367-3444), which specializes in fly-fishing equipment. Information on required fishing licenses can be had from any visitor information center, or by contacting the **Division of Fisheries and Aquaculture,** P.O. Box 2000, Charlottetown, PEI C1A 7N8 (© 902/368-6330).

GOLF   PEI's reputation for golf has soared in the last few years. That's due in part to a slew of new and expanded courses and in part because the greens fees haven't followed the same sharply upward trajectory of those in the United States. As a result, you can golf along the ocean at fees just a fraction of what you'd expect in similarly dramatic settings elsewhere. One of the best-regarded courses is the **Links at Crowbush Cove** ✦ (© 800/235-8909 or 902/368-5761). Sand dunes and persistent winds off the gulf add to the challenge at this relatively young course, which is on the northeastern coast. Another perennial favorite is the **Brudenell River Golf Course** (© 800/235-8909 or 902/652-8965) near Montague along the eastern shore; in the late 1990s the course added a second 18-holer, designed by Michael Hurdzan, who has also created well-regarded courses in Toronto and Vancouver. As part of its expansion, the course also launched the **Canadian Golf Academy** (© 888/698-4653 or 902/894-6880). Programs take place on the two golf courses as well as at the 475-yard double-ended driving range, and on the 1.6 hectares (4 acres) of tee decks.

Golf PEI publishes a booklet outlining the essentials of about 20 island courses. Request a copy from island information centers or from the provincial tourist information office (© 902/368-4653), or write 565 N. River Rd., Charlottetown, PEI C1E 1J7. The information is also available online at **www.golfpei.com.**

SEA KAYAKING   PEI has 1,260km (783 miles) of attractive coastline and relatively warm water, making for excellent sea kayaking.

Paddlers can vary the scene from broad tidal inlets ringed with marsh to rusty-red coastline topped with swaying waves of marram grass. **Outside Expeditions** (© 800/207-3899 or 902/963-3366; www.getoutside.com) in North Rustico hosts half- and full-day excursions and clinics daily at the national park and nearby for C$50 to C$100 (US$45–US$90/£25–£50). More ambitious paddlers can sign up for 1- to 7-day kayak trips departing throughout the summer. Excursions are also available from Peake's Wharf in Charlottetown and at Brudenell River Provincial Park in eastern PEI. Outside Expeditions also rents kayaks.

SWIMMING   Among PEI's chief attractions are its red sand beaches. You'll find them all around the island, tucked in among dunes and crumbling cliffs. Thanks to the moderating influence of the Gulf of St. Lawrence, the water temperature is more humane here than elsewhere in Atlantic Canada, and it usually doesn't result in unbridled shrieking among bathers. The most popular beaches are at Prince Edward Island National Park along the north coast, but you can easily find other beaches with great swimming.

Among my favorites: Cedar Dunes Provincial Park on the southwest coast, Red Point Provincial Park on the northeast coast, and Panmure Island Provincial Park on the southeast coast.

3 Queens County

Queens County occupies the center of the province, is home to the island's largest city, and hosts the greatest concentration of traveler services.

The county is neatly cleaved by the Hillsborough River, which is spanned by a bridge at Charlottetown. Cavendish on the north shore is the most tourist-oriented part of the entire province; if the phrase "Ripley's Believe It or Not Museum" lacks positive associations for you, you might consider avoiding this area, which has built a vigorous tourist industry around a fictional character, Anne of Green Gables. On the other hand, much of the rest of the county—not including Charlottetown—is quite pastoral and untrammeled.

Two parts of Queens County merit their own sections within this chapter: the capital city of Charlottetown on the south shore and Prince Edward Island National Park on the north shore. Flip ahead for more detailed information on these destinations.

ESSENTIALS

GETTING THERE   Route 2 is the fastest way to travel east or west through the county, although it lacks charm. Route 6 is the main route along the county's north coast; following the highway involves a number of turns at intersections, so keep a sharp eye on the directional signs.

VISITOR INFORMATION   The snazzy, well-stocked little **Cavendish Visitor Information Centre** (✆ **902/963-7830**) is open daily from 8am to 9pm mid-May to mid-October (only until 4:30pm in shoulder seasons) and is located just north of the intersection of routes 13 and 6.

CAVENDISH

Cavendish is the home of the fictional character Anne of Green Gables. If you mentally screen out the tourist traps constructed over the past couple of decades, you'll find the area a bucolic mix of woodlands and fields, rolling hills, and sandy dunes—a fine setting for a series of pastoral novels.

However, the tremendous and enduring popularity of the novels has attracted droves of curious tourists, who in turn have attracted droves of entrepreneurs who've constructed new buildings and attractions. The bucolic character of the area has thus become somewhat compromised. There are wax museums and loud amusements, all of which would probably alarm Anne, along with a surfeit of motels and cottage courts. The new developments don't approach the garishness of, say, Niagara Falls, but they're quite unavoidable, especially along Route 6 west of Route 13. Happily, most

Cavendish 2008: Anne Hits the Century Mark

As usual, the biggest news in 2008 on the island is Anne-related. The island will go gaga for the 100th anniversary of the June 1908 publication of Montgomery's novel—and that means (hold your breath) *even more Anne!* You would think the Olympic Games are coming to town . . . but no, it's just a precocious, redheaded girl in pigtails. The very full program of events from spring through fall will include a children's literary festival, readings, plays, and the release of a new prequel novel written by a local children's author. Check the provincial tourism office's "Anne" page at **www.gentle island.com/anne** for details and schedules. Not so much into Anne? Grin and bear it. You have been warned.

attractions are set off the road and spread well apart from one another. I wouldn't go so far as to say that the new developments harmonize with the landscape, but the collateral damage has been slight compared to what might have occurred. And the development is rather limited—you need only head east or west of Cavendish on Route 6 for a few miles to be back into the lovely landscapes of rolling farm fields that made the region famous in the first place.

Of the village of Cavendish, you should be aware that there's no *there* there, to steal from Gertrude Stein. There's no discernible village center; everything is sprawled out along the approach roads. A commercial development called Avonlea (see below) is seeking to manufacture a new village center, but it's just not quite the same. Those who like their villages quaint and are not terribly interested in the cult of Anne are better off steering for North or South Rustico, among other villages in the area.

EVERYTHING ANNE

Visitors to Prince Edward Island owe it to themselves to think about picking up a copy of *Anne of Green Gables* at some point. Not that you won't enjoy your stay here without doing so, but if you don't read it, you might feel a bit out of touch and unable to understand the inside references that seem to seep into many aspects of PEI culture. (Gas stations in Cavendish even sell little Anne dolls—something that might appear disturbing, at first glace, if you didn't know where you were.) In fact, Anne has become so omnipresent and popular on the island that a licensing authority was created in 1994 to control the crushing glacier of Anne-related products.

Some background: In 1908, island native Lucy Maud Montgomery published *Anne of Green Gables,* her first book—and it was an instant smash. The book is a fictional account of one Anne Shirley, a precocious and bright 11-year-old who's mistakenly sent from Nova Scotia to the farm of the taciturn and dour Matthew and Marilla Cuthbert. (The plot device driving the conflict? The Cuthberts had requested an orphan *boy* to help them with their farm chores.)

Anne's vivid imagination and outsize vocabulary get her into a series of ever-more-hilarious pickles, from which she generally emerges beloved by everyone who encounters her. It's a bright, bittersweet story, and it went on to huge popular success, spawning a number of sequels and becoming an international hit. The book is even taught in most elementary schools in Japan—I'm not exactly sure why, but it must have something to do with Anne's ever-plucky attitude and drive in the face of crushing reality to the contrary. Whatever the reason, throngs of Japanese tourists (the overwhelming majority of whom are women) come to Cavendish each year to celebrate Anne's fictional life. You're all but sure to run through the fields of their clicking cameras at some point.

As corny as the attractions and hoopla are, there is a certain sweetness to both Anne's story and the landscape in which she lived—which still looks more or less the same today as it did in the time Montgomery created her. Except, ironically, for Cavendish itself, which has been eaten alive by the tourist services and attractions that have inexorably sprung up around the Anne phenomenon. If you can overlook that and have a fondness for things English (or characters in children's literature), you might enjoy yourself here. But if you're a traveler who has never heard of Anne and are more interested in fine foods and weeklong bike tours, you might want to skip this town.

Anne of Green Gables Museum at Silver Bush

About 20km (12 miles) west of Cavendish near the intersection of routes 6 and 20 is the Anne of Green Gables Museum at Silver Bush. It's located in the home of Montgomery's aunt and uncle; the author was married here in 1911. The building still holds some of Montgomery's furniture, linens, photos, and other personal effects. For the best view of the "Lake of Shining Waters," take the wagon ride. It's hardly essential, but a half-hour visit might be in order if you're ticking off Anne destinations.

Rte. 20, Park Corner. ℂ **800/665-2663** or 902/886-2884 (weekends only). Admission C$3 (US$2.70/£1.50) adults, C$1 (US90¢/50p) children age 6–16. May and Oct daily 11am–4pm; June and Sept 10am–4pm; July–Aug daily 9am–5pm.

Anne of Green Gables—The Musical

This sprightly, professional musical has been playing for years at the downtown arts center—43 years, in fact; a Cal Ripkenesque streak making it Canada's longest-running musical and kicking the tail of anything running on Broadway. It brings to the stage many of Montgomery's stories and characters from late June through September. The 2-hour show takes place once or twice daily, at 2 and/or 7:30pm, though on some days there are no shows at all. Definitely call ahead, as tickets go fast in the limited summer season.

Confederation Centre of the Arts, 145 Richmond St., Charlottetown. ℂ **800/565-0278** or 902/566-1267. Tickets C$38–C$68 (US$34–US$61/£19–£34).

Avonlea (Kids)

This development of faux historic buildings was opened in the summer of 1999 with the idea of creating the sort of a village center you might find in reading the Anne novels. It's located on a large lot amid amusement parks and motels, and the new buildings have been constructed with an eye to historical accuracy. Several Anne-related buildings and artifacts are located on the site, including the schoolhouse in which Montgomery taught (moved here from Belmont) and a Presbyterian church (moved from Long River) that Montgomery occasionally attended. There's also a variety show, hayrides, staff in period dress, a restaurant, several stores (including an art gallery and music shop), and a spot for ice cream and candy. It's a bit overpriced, however.

Rte. 6, Cavendish. (©) **902/963-3050**. www.avonlea.ca. Day-pass admission C$19 (US$17/£9.50) adults, C$17 (US$15/£8.50) seniors, C$15 (US$14/£7.50) children 6–16, C$64 (US$58/£32) families. Musical variety show, small extra charge. June daily 10am–5pm; July–Aug 10am–6pm; Sept 10am–4pm. Closed Oct–May.

Cavendish Cemetery

Cavendish Cemetery   This historic cemetery was founded in 1835 and is best known as the final resting spot for author Lucy Maud Montgomery. It's not hard to find her gravesite: Follow the pavement blocks from the arched entryway, which is across from the Anne Shirley Motel.

Intersection of rtes. 13 and 6, Cavendish. Free admission. Open daily dawn–dusk.

Green Gables Heritage Site *Overrated*

Green Gables Heritage Site *Overrated*   The best place to start an Anne tour is at Green Gables itself. The house is operated by Parks Canada, which also operates a helpful visitor center on the site. You can watch a short video presentation about Montgomery, view a handful of exhibits, and then head out to explore the farm and trails. The farmhouse dates from the mid–19th century and belonged to cousins of Montgomery's grandfather. It was the inspiration for the Cuthbert farm, and it has been furnished according to descriptions in the books.

If you're a die-hard Anne fan, you'll delight in the settings where characters ventured, such as the Haunted Woods and Lover's Lane. But you might need as active an imagination as Anne's to edit out the golf carts puttering through the landscape at the adjacent Green Gables Golf Course, or the busloads of tourists crowding through the house and moving herdlike down the pathways. Come very early or very late in the day to avoid the largest crowds, and plan to spend 45 minutes or so. (Rumors persist that Green Gables burned down a few years ago. It didn't. These tenacious fictions evidently stem from news reports of a minor fire in 1997.)

2 Palmers Lane (just off Rte. 6), Cavendish (just west of intersection with Rte. 13). (©) **902/963-7874**. Admission C$7.15 (US$6.45/£3.60) adults, C$5.90 (US$5.30/£2.95) seniors, C$3.45 (US$3.10/£1.75) children, C$18 (US$16/£9) families. Discounted rates spring and fall. May–Oct daily 9am–8pm; off season Wed 10am–4pm only.

Lucy Maud Montgomery Birthplace

Lucy Maud Montgomery Birthplace   Very near the Anne of Green Gables Museum is the Lucy Maud Montgomery Birthplace, where the author was born in 1874. The house is decorated in the Victorian style of the era, and it includes Montgomery mementos like her wedding dress and scrapbook. It's worth 45 minutes, but only for die-hard Anne fans.

Intersection of rtes. 6 and 20, New London. (©) **902/886-2099** or 902/836-5502. Admission C$3 (US$2.70/£1.50) adults, C50¢ (US45¢/25p) children 6–12. Mid-May to mid-Oct daily 9am–5pm. Closed mid-Oct to mid-May.

Site of Lucy Maud Montgomery's Cavendish Home

Site of Lucy Maud Montgomery's Cavendish Home   Montgomery lived with her grandparents, Alexander and Lucy Macneill, from 1876 (when she was just 21 months old) to 1911. Montgomery wrote *Anne of Green Gables,* among other books, while living in their farmhouse. Alas, the building is no longer standing, but visitors can roam the grounds and read interpretive signs about the property's literary history: This is now a National Historic Site, believe it or not. There's also a small bookshop featuring books by and about the author. Once again, the site will be mainly of interest to true Anne buffs, but does give a nice flavor of the surrounds in which she worked.

Rte. 6, Cavendish (just east of Rte. 13 intersection). (©) **902/963-2231**. Admission C$3 (US$2.70/£1.50) adults, C$1 (US90¢/£0.50) children, C$8 (US$7/£4) families. Mid-May to mid-Oct daily 9am–5pm (July–Aug to 6pm). Closed mid-Oct to mid-May.

Kids Family Fun

Cavendish has capitalized on its tourist allure with a handful of "museums" and theme parks to appeal to younger kids. All are located along Route 6 westward from the intersection with Route 13. The small, manageable **Sandspit** (© **902/963-2626**) has go-kart racing, an 18m (59-ft.) Ferris wheel, a roller coaster, bumper cars, and the like. There's no admission charge to visit the grounds—you can pay as you go. Rides cost three to five tickets, totaling about C$3 to C$5 (US$2.70–US$4.50/£1.50–£2.50) each—or buy a bracelet that covers all rides for C$18 to C$21 (US$16–US$19/£9–£11). It's open daily from mid-June to Labor Day.

Rainy-day diversions include **Ripley's Believe It or Not! Museum** (© **902/963-2242**), which is about what you'd expect it to be, and **Wax World of the Stars** (© **902/963-4444**), which renders Hollywood stars like Julia Roberts, Jim Carrey (who's Canadian, of course), and Tom Cruise forever in wax. One, er, interesting scene features John Travolta dancing with Lady Di. Both of these attractions are located near the intersection of routes 6 and 13 in Cavendish.

WHERE TO STAY

Cottage courts are to Cavendish what 19th-century inns are to Vermont—they're everywhere, and vary tremendously in quality. Be aware that many of the cottage courts and motels are more interested in high volume and rapid turnover than personal attention to guests. A number also believe that hanging a straw hat or two on a door allows them to boast of "country charm," when they have anything but.

If you arrive in town without reservations, check the board at the visitor information center (see above), which lists up-to-the-minute vacancies.

Also, you might ask around among local residents about under-the-table rentals. A talented writer I know once rented a handsome three-bedroom Cavendish farmhouse built in 1910 and set in a barley field. The way he tells it, it was a lovely 10-minute stroll to the beach down a dirt lane, and the cost of paradise was just C$100 (US$90/£50) per night. How did he learn about it? Why, from a scrap of paper tacked to the wall of the local laundromat, of course. So keep your eyes open.

Cavendish Beach Cottages ⍟ Location, location, location. This compound of 13 cottages is located on a grassy rise within the national park, just past the gatehouse into the park. The pine-paneled cottages are available in one-, two-, or three-bedroom configurations, and all feature ocean views, kitchenettes with microwaves, and outdoor propane barbecue grills. Some of the better-equipped cottages have dishwashers, making them great for families, and all are a 2-minute walk from the beach. There's also easy access to Gulf Shore Drive, where you'll find some of the island's premier biking trails.

Gulf Shore Dr., Cavendish (mailing address 166 York Lane, Charlottetown, PEI C1A 7W5). © **902/963-2025.** Fax 902/963-2025. www.cavendishbeachcottages.com. 13 units. C$115–C$209 (US$104–US$188/£58–£105) double. MC, V. Closed Oct to mid-May. **Amenities:** Laundry. *In room:* A/C, TV, kitchenette, no phone.

Green Gables Bungalow Court ⍟ Located next to the Green Gables house, this pleasant cluster of one- and two-bedroom cottages began as a government make-work project promoting tourism in the 1940s. As a result, they're quite sturdily built, and nicely arrayed among the grass and pines. All have kitchens with refrigerators and coffeemakers, and many have outdoor gas grills for an evening barbecue. The linoleum floors and Spartan furnishings take on a certain retro charm after a few hours of settling in. Some cabins were trimmed with cheap sheet paneling, while others have the original pine paneling; ask for one with the latter. The beach is about 1km (⅔ mile) away, and there's a small heated outdoor pool on the premises.

Rte. 6 (Hunter River R.R. 2), Cavendish, PEI C0A 1N0. © **800/965-3334** or 902/963-2722. www.greengablesbungalow court.com. 40 cottages. C$65–C$135 (US$59–US$122/£33–£68 [up to 4 people]) nightly, C$655–C$899 (US$590–US$809/£328–£450) weekly. AE, MC, V. Closed Oct–June. **Amenities:** Outdoor heated pool. *In room:* TV, kitchenette, fridge, no phone.

WHERE TO DINE

Cavendish itself offers limited opportunities for creative dining, although it's well stocked with restaurants offering hamburgers, fried clams, and the like. Both places mentioned below require a 10- to 15-minute drive from Cavendish proper, but they're worth it. See also the "Lobster Suppers" box, below.

Café on the Clyde ★★ *Value* *Kids* ECLECTIC   This cafe is part of the noted Prince Edward Island Preserve Co. (p. 219), itself a worthwhile stop for the delicious homemade preserves. Light meals are served in the bright and modern dining room just off the preserve showroom; in this popular and often crowded spot, you can order from a menu that has expanded to include breakfast, lunch, and dinner. A smoked-fish platter or the lobster chowder are just the ticket on a drizzly afternoon, and they've also got pastas, crepes, sandwiches and wraps, island fish cakes, lobster rolls, and even a cheesy potato pie with maple cream. There's beer and wine, a kids' menu, and pies, cakes, and cheesecakes, making this a legitimate dining destination in a rural area with few restaurants besides the Olde Mill (see next entry). Just be prepared for the tour bus crowd: Buses get their own parking lot here, close to the door.

Intersection of rtes. 224 and 258 (6.5km/4 miles south of Rte. 6 on Rte. 13), New Glasgow. © **902/964-4301.** Main courses C$6–C$13 (US$5.40–US$12/£3–£6.50) at breakfast and lunch, C$11–C$18 (US$10–US$16/£5.50–£9) at dinner. AE, DC, MC, V. July–Aug daily 9am–9pm; June and Sept limited hours. Closed Oct–May.

Olde Glasgow Mill Restaurant ★ REGIONAL   This casual restaurant, formerly a 19th-century feed mill in twee little New Glasgow, is nicely shielded from the tourist throngs at Cavendish. The place overlooks a small pond and features an eclectic assortment of regional food. Appetizers include seafood chowder, along with salads and PEI mussels. Lunch entrees are uncomplicated, but dinner is more serious. Besides Atlantic salmon and scallops, you'll find rack of lamb swabbed in Dijon mustard and rosemary herb crust served with a rosemary peppercorn sauce, cheese-and-spinach-stuffed chicken breast in puff pastry, peppery strip loin, and the like. There's a leisurely brunch on the weekends.

Rte. 13, New Glasgow. © **902/964-3313.** Reservations recommended. Lunch C$9–C$12 (US$8.10–US$11/£4.50–£6); dinner C$14–C$29 (US$13–US$26/£7–£15). AE, MC, V. June–Oct Mon–Sat noon–10pm, Sun 10am–10pm; shorter hours in winter.

NORTH & SOUTH RUSTICO TO BRACKLEY BEACH

A few miles east of Cavendish are the Rusticos, of which there are five: North Rustico, South Rustico, Rusticoville, Rustico Harbour, and Anglo Rustico. The region was settled by Acadians in 1790, and many residents are descendants of those original settlers. This was one of the first Canadian regions to be populated by Acadians following the Treaty of Paris, and is the oldest Acadian presence on PEI. North and South Rustico are both attractive villages that have fewer tourist traps and are more amenable to exploring by foot or bike than Cavendish. Although out of the hubbub, they still provide easy access to the national park and Anne-land, with beaches virtually at your doorstep.

North Rustico clusters around a scenic harbor with views out toward Rustico Bay. Plan to park and walk around, perusing the deep-sea fishing opportunities (see below) and peeking in the shops. The village curves around Rustico Bay to end at North Rustico Harbour, a sand spit with fishing wharves, summer cottages, and a couple of informal restaurants. A wood-decked promenade follows the water's edge from the town to the harbor and is a worthy destination for a quiet afternoon ramble or a picnic. Also here in the bright yellow wharf building is **Outside Expeditions** (© 800/207-3899 or 902/963-3366; www.getoutside.com), which offers sea kayak excursions of the harbor and surrounding area (see "Sea Kayaking," earlier in this chapter).

In **South Rustico** 🌟🌟, turn off Route 6 onto Route 243 and ascend the low hill overlooking the bay. Here you'll find a handsome cluster of buildings that were home to some of the more prosperous Acadian settlers. Among the structures is the sandstone **Farmers' Bank of Rustico Museum** 🌟 (© 902/963-3168), beside the church. The bank was established with the help of a visionary local cleric, Reverend Georges-Antoine Belcourt, in 1864 to help local farmers get ahead of the hand-to-mouth cycle; the father and his parishioners actually built it themselves, timber by timber, stone by stone. It then operated for some 30 years and helped inspire the credit union movement in Canada and North America before it was forced to close by sweeping bank reforms. Renovations to the building have been ongoing for several years, and it's looking much better these days; the bank is open for tours June through September, Monday through Saturday, 9:30am to 5pm, and Sundays 1 to 5pm. It's free.

Next door to the bank are two more structures worth investigating. **Doucet House** 🌟, a sturdy log building of Acadian construction dating from 1772, was the home of one Jean Doucet, who arrived in these parts by boat. (The house was moved from its waterside location in 1999 and completely restored—which it badly needed.) Period furnishings have been added to bring back that 2-plus-centuries-ago flavor.

Then there's the handsome **St. Augustine's Parish Church** (dating from 1838, with a cemetery beyond). If the church's door is open, head in for a look at this graceful structure.

Brackley Beach is the gateway to the eastern section of the national park, and has the fewest services of all. It's a quiet area with no village center to speak of; it will be best appreciated by those who prefer their beach vacations unadulterated.

DEEP-SEA FISHING

PEI's north shore is home to the island's greatest concentration of deep-sea fishing boats. For C\$20 to C\$35 (US\$18–C\$32/£10–£18) per person, you'll get 3 hours out on the seas in search of mackerel, cod, and flounder. Don't worry about lack of prior experience: Equipment is supplied, crewmembers are very helpful, and most will even clean and fillet your catch for you.

In North Rustico, about a half-dozen captains offer fishing trips. Among them are Aiden's Deep Sea Fishing (© **866/510-3474** or 902/963-3522) and Bearded Skipper's Deep-Sea Fishing (© **902/963-2334**). Or try Richard's Deep-Sea Fishing (© **902/ 672-2376**) or Salty Seas Deep-Sea Fishing (© **902/672-3246**), both a 20-minute drive east of North Rustico, at Covehead Harbour (within the national park).

SHOPPING

Between Cavendish and Brackley Beach you'll find a number of shops offering unique island crafts and products. Browsing is a good option when you can't get to the beach.

Cheeselady's Gouda (Finds) This is a short detour off Route 6, but well worth it. Watch a brief video about the making of Gouda cheese, and then get down to business: buying some of the excellent cheeses produced here. If you don't want to stick with the traditional aged Gouda, try the flavored varieties, including peppercorn, garlic, and herb. Sizes ranging from a wedge to a wheel are available. Rte. 223, Winsloe North, southeast of Oyster Bed Bridge. ✆ 902/368-1506.

The Dunes Café and Studio Gallery This architecturally striking modern gallery on the way to the eastern section of PEI National Park is among the best spots on the island to browse the fine works produced by island artisans and craftspeople. Situated on two open levels, the gallery features pottery, furniture, lamps, woodworking, sculpture, and paintings, along with more accessible crafts including handmade soaps and jewelry. The gallery is also home to an appealing cafe, a good spot for a coffee; a lunch break; or even a fancy full-blown dinner of lamb, steak, or seafood. It's open May through October. Rte. 15, Brackley Beach. ✆ **902/672-2586.**

Gaudreau Fine Woodworking ✦ All woodworking sold here is made on the premises. Items range from elegant timeless sushi trays to modern wrist rests for computer keyboards crafted from birds-eye maple. Also sold are crafts and paintings from selected island artisans. The recent expansion here allows better viewing of the woodworkers, and a new gallery space displays the work of Maritime craftspeople. It's open June through October, off-season by appointment. Rte. 6, South Rustico. ✆ **902/963-2273.**

Prince Edward Island Preserve Co. PEI Preserve sells accessible luxury—a little piece of PEI to take home, if you will. The company makes a variety of tasty preserves at a small factory in a lovely valley; you can sample those that are currently on sale and watch the preserve-making process through a glass window. It's pricey for a jar of jam (about C$7/US$6.30/£3.50 at last visit), but that never deters me from stocking up on raspberry and champagne jam, sour cherry marmalade, or whatever looks good. There's also an excellent cafe on-site, Café on the Clyde, open from mid-May through mid-October. See "Where to Dine" in the Cavendish section above. Intersection of rtes. 224 and 258 (just off Rte. 13), New Glasgow. ✆ **902/964-4300.**

Seasway Hammock Shop The sturdy, attractive hammocks at this shop are crafted on the premises during the winter months by retired fisherman Keith Smith; then sold in the summer tourist season. They not only look good; they're made to last. Churchill Ave., North Rustico. ✆ **902/963-2846.**

WHERE TO STAY

Barachois Inn ✦✦ (Finds) The proudly Victorian Barachois (say bar-a-*schwa*) Inn was built in 1870, and it is a soothing retreat for road-weary travelers located amid a cluster of historic buildings on a gentle rise overlooking Rustico Bay (see "North & South Rustico to Brackley Beach," above). Factor in some time to just stroll around the neighborhood and enjoy both the village and the inn's tidy garden. It's topped with a lovely mansard roof adorned with pedimented dormers, and it boasts a fine garden and historic furnishings throughout. Innkeepers Judy and Gary MacDonald bought the place as derelict property in 1982 and have done an outstanding job bringing it back from the brink, adding modern art along the way to soften the staid Victorian architecture.

The main house is furnished with quality period antiques; the two rooms on the third floor are a bit cozier than the spacious second-floor suites, but those guests will feel far from the world when tucked beneath the slanted eaves. Room no. 1 has a canopy bed dating from the 1840s and an unusually large bathroom; room no. 3 has a claw-foot tub and a stall shower. There's a second, newer building known as Mac-Donald House next door with four additional executive-style rooms and perks like a sauna, exercise bike, and meeting room. Its architecture nicely echoes that of the original structure. Be sure to inquire about the 3-night "special occasions" package if you're celebrating an anniversary, which includes an Anne of Green Gables–themed carriage ride, a gourmet dinner at a local restaurant, and a packed picnic lunch with your accommodations.

2193 Church Rd. (Hunter River R.R. 3), Rustico, PEI C0A 1N0. © **902/963-2194.** Fax 902/963-2906. www.barachois inn.com. 8 units, 1 with private bathroom in hallway. June–Sept C$160–C$275 (US$144–US$248/£80–£138) double; Oct–May rates lower. Rates include full breakfast. Ask about packages. AE, MC, V. Closed Nov–Mar. **Amenities:** Sauna; laundry service. In room: A/C, VCR, kitchenette, hair dryer, iron, no phone.

Shaw's Hotel ⊛   Shaw's is a delightfully old-fashioned compound located down a tree-lined dirt road along a marsh-edged inlet. It's been in the same family since 1860, and even with its regimen of modernization—new in 1999 were a sun deck, a bar, and a dining-room addition that accommodates 40 more people—the place still has the feel of a farm-stay vacation in the 19th century. It remains mostly the kind of place where the aging carpets in the hallways add to the charm rather than detract from it.

The hotel's centerpiece is a Victorian farmhouse with a lipstick-red mansard roof. Fifteen guest rooms are located upstairs; they are "boardinghouse style," which is to say, small. The cottages vary in size and vintage. None are lavish, but most have the essentials (some with kitchenettes, some just with cube refrigerators) and some are downright comfy (double Jacuzzis have been installed in a few of them). While the new cottages are fine, older ones—like no. 6 with its dark beadboard paneling and brick fireplace—have a creaky, summer-home charm all their own, too. This is still the kind of place where you walk down a sandy lane to get to the beach, and where signs admonish you not to let the dog follow you to the beach. (Since the beach is just a quarter-mile away, he might anyway.) The spare, handsome dining room serves breakfast and dinner daily; the menu changes frequently, but typical dinner entrees might be filet mignon au poivre, poached halibut with béarnaise, penne with smoked salmon in a vodka cream sauce, prime rib, rack of lamb, or—a few times a week—lobster. There's also a Sunday-night buffet that's well attended.

Rte. 15, Brackley Beach, C1E 1Z3. © **902/672-2022.** Fax 902/672-3000. www.shawshotel.ca. 41 units. Inn rooms July–Aug C$145–C$240 (US$131–US$216/£73–£120) double, rest of the year C$75–C$135 (US$68–US$122/£38–£68); cottages C$190–C$710 (US$171–US$639/£95–£355). Meal plans available. AE, MC, V. Closed Nov to late May. Pets allowed in cottages only. **Amenities:** 2 restaurants; canoes, kayaks, and bike rental; secretarial services; babysitting; laundry. In room: TV (some units), kitchenette, no phone.

WHERE TO DINE

For fine dining in the area in addition to the selections below, also consider the dining room at **Shaw's Hotel** (above) and **Dalvay-by-the-Sea** ⊛⊛ (under "Prince Edward Island National Park," below), as well as the great little **Dunes Café** ⊛ in Brackley Beach (listed in "Shopping," above).

Dayboat ⊛⊛ SEAFOOD   Native island chef Sean Furlong and his sous chef Andrew Smith (another local) run one of the island's best recently opened (2005) kitchens, in the attractive little hamlet of Oyster Bed Bridge. Dayboat replaces Café

Lobster Suppers

The north shore of Prince Edward Island is home to famous lobster suppers, which are a good bet if you have a craving for one of the succulent local crustaceans. These suppers first took root years ago as informal gatherings held in local church basements, in which parishioners would bring covered hot dishes to share and the church would provide a lobster. Everyone would contribute some money, and the church netted a few dollars from the fun get-together. Outsiders (and travel writers like me) began discovering these good deals and showing up, the fame of the dinners spread, and today several establishments offer the bountiful lobster dinners, which have become almost a cottage industry.

Expect a large and impersonal dining experience—Fisherman's Wharf (see below) can accommodate 500 diners at a time—especially if you have the misfortune to pull up just after a couple of bus tours have unloaded. Lobster is naturally the main feature, although you'll usually find roast beef, ham, or other alternatives. These are typically accompanied by an all-you-can-eat buffet with a button-bursting selection of rolls, salads, chowder, mussels, desserts, and more. The cost? Figure on C$25 to C$50 (US$23–US$45/£13–£25) per person, depending on the size lobster you want and the options available.

St. Ann's Church Lobster Suppers (© **902/621-0635**) remains a charitable organization, as it was in 1963 when it claims it created the first lobster supper on PEI. Located in a modern church hall in the small town of St. Ann, just off Route 224 between routes 6 and 13, St. Ann's has a full liquor license and the home-cooked food is served at your table (no buffet lines). Lobster dinners are served mid-June to late September Monday through Saturday from 4 to 8:30pm. (As befits a church, it's closed Sun.) Credit cards are accepted.

Fisherman's Wharf Lobster Suppers (© **902/963-2669** or 877/289-1010) in North Rustico boasts an 18m (59-ft.) salad bar to go with its lobster; it's open daily from noon to 9pm, mid-May to mid-October (shorter hours in May and June). It offers a children's menu. And near the PEI Preserve Company in New Glasgow is the barnlike **New Glasgow Lobster Suppers** (© **902/964-2870**). Meals here include unlimited mussels and chowder, so it's a bit pricier. It's on Route 258 (just off Rte. 13) and is open June to mid-October daily from 4 to 8:30pm. This eatery also offers roast beef suppers and a kids' menu.

St. Jean, which was truly a fun place to eat and listen to good music, but this eatery's more upscale take succeeds wonderfully as a replacement. The menu here leans heavily on natural themes and textures, right down to the way it's organized according to ingredients' roots in either earth or water. Start with a small plate of corn-breaded oysters with avocado mousse and local-tomato salsa, an island scallop-mussel chowder, or some lobster bruschetta made with crumbled feta cheese. Then move on to main "Water" courses of grilled or cedar-planked salmon, scallops seared in a garlic-citrus butter, or local halibut with an orange-vanilla vinaigrette. "Earth" entrees might include chicken breast with a pesto-risotto cake or a PEI pork chop with Nova Scotia apples. The lunch menu has some additional lobster specials.

5033 Rustico Rd., Hunter River. © **902/963-3833**. www.dayboat.ca. Dinner main courses C$25–C$30 (US$23–US$27/ £13–£15). MC, V. Early June to late Sept daily noon–3pm and 5–9pm; late Sept to late Oct daily 5–9pm. Closed late Oct to May.

Jo-Joe's Take Out *Value* *Kids* SEAFOOD   This little shack overlooking Rustico Bay at a bend in the road is the place to go when you don't have the time for a sit-down dinner on the far shores of the island. The menu is simple—fried fish, clams, and scallops, basically—and not particularly healthful. But portions are big; they serve ice cream and burgers, too; and they'll even make a "snackasaurus" (to be exact, a hot dog—see what I mean) for the kids. Take a seat on the back deck to get a nice view of the water. This property is also home to a deep-sea fishing outfit called Joey's—bad for the fish, good for you.

Rte. 6, Rusticoville, at the bridge over Hunter River. © **902/963-2295**. Meals C$3–C$15 (US$2.70–US$14/£1.50–£7.50). No credit cards. Daily 11am–8pm. Closed Sept to mid-June.

ORWELL

In southeastern Queens County, the village of Orwell offers a historic detour off speedy Route 1 between Charlottetown and the Wood Islands ferry. Both sites mentioned below are near each other on a side road; there are few landmarks other than simple signs directing you here, so keep a sharp eye out.

The **Orwell Corner Historic Village** ✦ (© **902/651-8510**) is one of the most aesthetically pleasing historic villages in the province. It's one of several sites island-wide managed by the Prince Edward Island Museum and Heritage Foundation. Set on a gentle slope amid a profusion of leafy trees, the village re-creates life in a small agricultural town in the 1890s. You can visit the general store, stop by the blacksmith shop, or wander the lush gardens. If it works out, plan to visit around lunchtime and pick up a picnic from the community hall to enjoy under a shady tree on the grounds. Ask about the lively ceilidhs (Scottish concerts) with traditional music, held Wednesday evenings in the community hall (extra charge). It's open 9:30am to 4:30pm daily in July and August, the same hours but weekdays only in June, and Sunday to Thursday from September to mid-October. Admission is C$7.50 (US$6.75/£3.75) for adults, C$3 (US$2.70/£1.50) for children 6 to 18, free for children under 6, and C$20 (US$18/£10) families.

A few minutes' drive from the village is the modest, white-shingled home of **Sir Andrew Macphail,** a gifted polymath born here in 1864. Macphail found renown as a medical doctor, pathologist, professor, writer, editor, and agricultural tinkerer. You'll learn about his exceptional career while walking through the house, which includes a handful of exhibits and period furniture. (There's also a restaurant; see below.) But the real allure of the site is a stroll through the 56-hectare (138-acre) farm grounds, which are accessible via several **trails.** They're lush and pastoral, filled with the summer sounds of crickets and songbirds. Admission to this national historic site (© **902/651-2789**) is free, with donations happily accepted. It's open daily in summer, shorter hours in the shoulder seasons; see the restaurant ("Where to Dine," below) for hours.

WHERE TO DINE
Sir Andrew Macphail Homestead ✦ *Value* TRADITIONAL   The simple, sparely decorated restaurant is located in the Macphail homestead (see above) and features a limited menu of classic dishes. Arrive early enough for a leisurely walk through the

Impressions

The man who farms only for the money . . . is a fool, because one who can make money out of farming can make a good deal more out of something else. But for the man who would live a quiet, interesting, reasonable, and useful life there is no other occupation which affords so favorable an opportunity. It demands the exercise of every facility. Every movement of the day is full of surprise, and every effort has its immediate reward either in success or failure. For the finest minds it affords an outlet for activity; for the poorest it affords a living without the sordid accompaniment of poverty. And Prince Edward Island presents a field the freest for all who would live this life.

—Sir Andrew Macphail, 1912

grounds; then request a table on the sun porch, which is always bright and summery. The menu includes the Macphail haggis, a modern adaptation of the traditional Scottish meal ("There are no sheep stomachs involved," the hostess assured me). Other dishes range from roast lamb to sole amandine, and the menu always includes a vegetarian selection. Lunches feature soups, sandwiches, and salads.

Off Rte. 1, Orwell. ℂ 902/651-2789. Reservations requested for dinner. Main courses C$3–C$10 (US$2.70–US$9/£1.50–£5) at lunch, C$12–C$16 (US$11–US$14/£6–£8) at dinner. V. Thurs–Sat 11:30am–4:30pm; Wed and Sun 11am–7:30pm. Closed early Oct to late June.

4 Prince Edward Island National Park (★(★

Prince Edward Island National Park encompasses 40km (25 miles) of red-sand beaches, wind-sculpted dunes topped with marram grass, vast salt marshes, and placid inlets. The park is located along the island's sandy north-central coast, which is broached in several spots by broad inlets that connect to harbors. As a result, you can't drive along the entire park's length in one shot. The coastal road is disrupted by inlets, requiring backtracking to drive the entire length. And, actually, there's little point in trying to tour the whole length. It's a better use of your time to pick one spot, then settle in and enjoy your surroundings.

The reddish sand and abstract dunes define the park for many. But also look for woods and meadows nearby, as well as wildlife. You might spot the tracks of red fox, mink, or muskrat. In the marshes and tidal flats, dozens of great blue heron stalk their aquatic prey near sunset. Where beach and dune meet, watch for the piping plover, a small and endangered beach bird.

The national park also oversees the Green Gables house and grounds; see "Cavendish," earlier in this chapter.

ESSENTIALS

GETTING THERE From Charlottetown, Route 15 offers the most direct route to the eastern segments of the park. To head to the Cavendish area, take Route 2 to Hunter River, then head north on Route 13.

VISITOR INFORMATION The **Cavendish Visitor Information Centre** (ℂ 902/963-7830), near the intersection of routes 6 and 13, furnishes information on the park's destinations and activities; it's open daily from 9am to 10pm in the peak summer season (it closes earlier during the shoulder seasons).

Inside the park, the modern **Greenwich Interpretation Centre** (© **902/961-2514**) is open from 9am to 5pm, mid-May through early October. For other questions or during the off-season, the park administration (located in Charlottetown) can be reached at © **902/672-6350.**

FEES The park is open year-round. Between mid-June and mid-October, however, visitors to the national park must stop at one of the tollhouses and pay entry fees. Daily rates are C$6.90 (US$6.20/£3.45) adults, C$5.90 (US$5.30/£2.95) seniors, C$3.45 (US$3.10/£1.75) children ages 6 to 16, and C$17 (US$15/£8.50) per family; all rates are lower in June. Ask about multiday passes if you plan to visit for more than 3 days.

BEACHES

PEI National Park is home to two kinds of sandy strands: popular and sometimes crowded beaches with changing rooms, lifeguards, snack bars, and other amenities; and all the other beaches. Where you go depends on your temperament. If it's not a day at the beach without the aroma of other people's coconut tanning oil, head to Brackley Beach or Cavendish Beach. The latter is within walking distance of the Green Gables house and many other amusements (see "Cavendish," earlier in this chapter) and makes a good destination for families.

If you'd just as soon be left alone with the waves, sun, and sand, you'll need to head a bit farther afield, or just keep walking far down the beaches away from parking-area access points until you have left the crowds behind. I won't reveal the best spots here for fear of crowding. But suffice it to say they're out there.

HIKING & BIKING

Hiking is limited here compared to Atlantic Canada's other national parks, but you can still find a handful of pleasant strolls. Of course, there's also the beach, which is perfect for long leisurely walks.

The park maintains eight trails, adding up to a total of 20km (12 miles). Among the most appealing is the **Homestead Trail** ⓡ, which departs from the Cavendish campground. The trail offers a 5.2km (3.2-mile) loop and an 8km (5-mile) loop. The trail skirts wheat fields, woodlands, and estuaries, with frequent views of the distinctively lumpy dunes at the west end of the park. Mountain bikes are allowed on this trail, and it's a busy destination on sunny days. The two **short trails** at the Green Gables house—Balsam Hollow and Haunted Wood—are lovely but invariably crowded. Avoid them if you're looking for a relaxing walk in the woods.

Biking along the seaside roads in the park is sublime. The traffic is light, and it's easy to make frequent stops to explore beaches, woodlands, or the marshy edges of inlets. The two **shoreline roads** ⓡⓡ within the national park—between Dalvay and Rustico Island, and from Cavendish to North Rustico Harbour—are especially beautiful on a clear evening as sunset edges into twilight. Snack bars are located at Brackley Beach and Covehead Bay.

You can rent bikes easily in **Charlottetown.** Try **Smooth Cycle** (© **800/310-6550** or 902/566-5530) in its new location at 330 University Ave. Rentals including a helmet, water bottle, and lock cost C$25 (US$23/£13) per day. The shop is closed Sundays.

You can often find rentals closer to the beach as well. In Brackley Beach, a good option is **Northshore Rentals** (© **902/672-2022**), located at Shaw's Hotel; their rentals cost C$7 (US$6.30/£3.50) per hour and C$20 (US$18/£10) per day.

CAMPING

Prince Edward Island National Park maintains three excellent campgrounds, which open for the short season in early June. Reservations are not accepted, so plan to arrive early in the day for the best selection of sites. Campground fees start at about C$25 (US$23/£13) per night, with serviced sites costing up to C$33 (US$30/£17). For more information, contact the **Cavendish Visitors Centre** (© **902/963-7830**).

The most popular (and first to fill) is **Cavendish,** located just off Route 6 west of Green Gables. It has more than 300 sites spread among piney forest and open, sandy bluffs; the sites at the edge of the dunes overlooking the beach are the most popular. The sites aren't especially private or scenic. A limited number of two-way hookups are available for RVs, and the campground has free showers, kitchen shelters, and evening programs. Note that this campground closes for the season in late August.

The **Stanhope** ⊛ campground lies just across the park road from lovely Stanhope Beach, which is on the eastern segment of the park (enter through Brackley Beach). The road isn't heavily traveled, so you don't feel much removed from the water's edge. Most sites are forested, and you're afforded more privacy here than at Cavendish. Two-way hookups, free showers, and kitchen shelters are offered. It's also open later, until early October.

WHERE TO STAY & DINE

Also see listings for "Cavendish" and "North & South Rustico to Brackley Beach," earlier in this chapter.

Dalvay by the Sea ⊛⊛   This imposing Tudor mansion was built in 1895 by Alexander MacDonald, a partner of John D. Rockefeller. It is unusually large for a private home, yet rather intimate for a luxury inn. There are glimpses of the ocean across the road from the upper floors, even as the landscaping largely focuses on a beautiful freshwater pond out front. Inside, you'll be taken aback by the extraordinary cedar woodwork in the main entryway, and by the grand stone fireplace. The guest rooms are elegantly appointed and wonderfully solid and quiet, though they have intentionally been kept free of any phones or televisions; this is true rusticating. As a result, in the evening you'll hear mostly the roar of the sea, since the inn overlooks one of the park's best beaches. Rates are steep, though that partly disguises the fact that breakfast and dinner are included in all rates, whether you want it or not. (So eat up.) The eight newer, lovely three-bedroom pine cottages are in big demand thanks to their size, open design, and amenities like wet bars and propane stoves.

Dalvay added a new pavilion-style dining room to the main inn in 1999. Not to worry—it's been constructed in a classic style that blends nicely with the original architecture. The net result has been to add some much-needed seats, along with improved views of the gardens and pond. The highly regarded kitchen might feature such dishes as a steamed island lobster, a piece of honey-roasted venison, or tea-smoked Atlantic salmon with artichoke salad and crème fraîche. (Ordering some of these entrees requires a small supplement above your room rate, but they're worth it.) For dessert, try the sticky date pudding with toffee sauce, which was once featured in *Gourmet* magazine. The hotel also serves afternoon tea each day from 2 to 4pm. Next morning? Hike off all those extra calories at one of the many walking trails nearby.

Off Rte. 6, Grand Tracadie (P.O. Box 8, Little York), PEI C0A 1P0. © **902/672-2048.** Fax 902/672-2741 (summer only). www.dalvaybythesea.com. 34 units. June to late Sept C$270–C$390 (US$243–US$351/£135–£195) double, C$450–C$490 (US$405–US$441/£225–£245) cottages; extra charges for children and infants. All rates include breakfast and dinner. Ask about packages. National park entrance fees also charged. 2-night minimum in summer. AE, DC, MC, V. Closed late Sept to May. **Amenities:** Tennis court; bike rentals; croquet; lawn bowling; horseshoes; canoeing. *In room:* Minibar (cottages only), fridge (cottages only), coffeemaker (cottages only), no phone.

5 Charlottetown ✶

It's not hard to figure out why early settlers put the province's political and cultural capital where they did: It's on a point of land between two rivers and within a large protected harbor. For ship captains plying the seas, this quiet harbor with ample anchorage and wharf space must have been a welcome sight. Of course, travelers rarely arrive by water these days (unless a cruise ship is in port), but the city's harborside location translates into a lovely setting for one of Atlantic Canada's most graceful and relaxed cities.

Named after Queen Charlotte, consort of King George III, Charlottetown is home to some 40,000 people—nearly one of every three islanders. Within Canada, the city is famous for hosting the 1864 conference that 3 years later led to the creation of the independent Dominion of Canada. For this reason, you're never far from the word *confederation,* which graces buildings, malls, and bridges. (In a historic twist, PEI itself actually declined to join the new confederation until 1873.)

Today, the downtown has a brisk and busy feel to it, with a pleasing mix of modern and Victorian commercial buildings, as well as government and cultural centers. Outside the business core, you'll find leafy streets and large, elegant homes dating from various eras, with the most dramatic from the late 19th century. Charlottetown is also blessed with a number of pocket parks, which provide a quiet respite amid the gentle clamor. Its only charmless moment? The outlying suburbs off Route 2, where you'll find traffic and strip malls of the sort that have proliferated throughout the rest of North America. But if you're hankering for gasoline, fast food, or discount clothes, this is your last pit stop before entering the gracious historic center of town.

Charlottetown is centrally located and serves admirably as a base for exploring the rest of the island (only the far western coast is a bit distant for relaxed day-tripping). You can be touring Green Gables, relaxing on a north-shore beach, or teeing off at Brudenell Provincial Park—all within 45 minutes of leaving Charlottetown. The capital has by far the island's best selection of inns and hotels, and a fine assortment of restaurants that ensure you can dine out every night for a week and still be pleasantly surprised.

As for scheduling time for exploring the city itself, save that for a rainy day or those early-morning or late-afternoon moments. You don't really need much more than a day to take in the highlights, but it's an exceedingly nice place to simply stroll the cobbles when you have an odd hour and chat with locals you encounter along the way. In that sense, it is much like the downtown quarters of a Boston, Portland, Halifax, or Savannah: more enjoyable than you realized it would be, once the commercial hubbub of the working day has faded out.

ESSENTIALS

GETTING THERE　Coming by car from the mainland, both Route 1 (the Trans-Canada Hwy.) and Route 2 pass through or near Charlottetown. For information on arriving by air, see "Exploring Prince Edward Island," at the beginning of this chapter. If you're coming from Montréal by train, debark at Moncton and take an **Acadian bus** (🕿 **800/567-5151;** two or three trips daily) to Charlottetown; the cost is C$30 (US$27/£15) adults for the 3-hour trip. Or, if you have flown into Halifax, **PEI**

Charlottetown

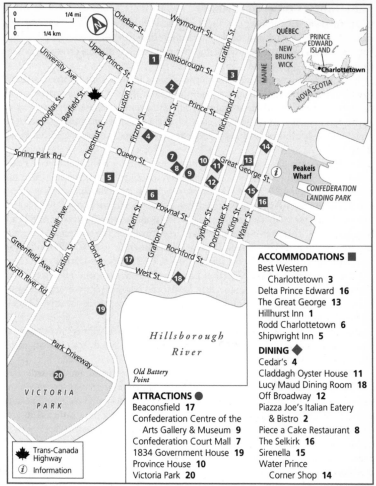

ACCOMMODATIONS ■
Best Western
    Charlottetown **3**
Delta Prince Edward **16**
The Great George **13**
Hillhurst Inn **1**
Rodd Charlottetown **6**
Shipwright Inn **5**

DINING ◆
Cedar's **4**
Claddagh Oyster House **11**
Lucy Maud Dining Room **18**
Off Broadway **12**
Piazza Joe's Italian Eatery
    & Bistro **2**
Piece a Cake Restaurant **8**
The Selkirk **16**
Sirenella **15**
Water Prince
    Corner Shop **14**

ATTRACTIONS ●
Beaconsfield **17**
Confederation Centre of the
    Arts Gallery & Museum **9**
Confederation Court Mall **7**
1834 Government House **19**
Province House **10**
Victoria Park **20**

Express Shuttle (© 877/877-1771; www.peishuttle.com) offers transportation by van between Charlottetown and Halifax for C$55 (US$50/£28) one-way for adults, C$50 (US$45/£25) students and seniors, C$45 (US$41/£23) children under age 5.

VISITOR INFORMATION The city's main **Visitor Information Centre** (© 902/ 368-7795) is a modern structure known as **Founders Hall** at 6 Prince St. (the end of the street, at the entrance to Confederation Landing Park). Look for brown "?" signs to direct you to this brick building with helpful staffers, an interactive computer kiosk, a cafe, free Internet, and an ample supply of brochures. There's also a vacancy board to let you know where rooms are currently available. The center is open daily in July and August from 8am to 10pm, weekdays only in the off-season from 8am to 5pm. Charlottetown's **City Hall** also maintains an info kiosk, though it is less comprehensive.

EXPLORING CHARLOTTETOWN

Charlottetown is a compact city that's easy to walk once you park your car. Three main areas merit exploration: the waterfront, the downtown area near Province House and the Confederation Court Mall, and the parks and residential areas near Victoria Park.

You're best off first heading to the main **Visitor Information Centre** (see above), by the waterfront, and then starting your tour from there. Parking is generally scarce downtown, but it's relatively abundant near the visitor center, both on the street and in free and paid lots. At the visitor center, be sure to ask for a map and one of the free walking-tour brochures, such as "The First Five Hundred: Heritage and History Walks."

The **waterfront** has been spruced up in recent years with the addition of **Peake's Wharf,** a collection of touristy boutiques and restaurants that attracts hordes in summer (it's open mid-May to mid-Oct). The complex is attractive and offers good people-watching and a kid-friendly "touch tank" (watch out for those lobster spines), though it also has a somewhat formulaic "festival marketplace" feel to it and is a bit lacking in local character—except for the exceptional **free concert series.** To see the city from the water, sign up with **Peake's Wharf Boat Cruises** (© 902/566-4458), which offers three tours daily for about C$16 to C$22 (US$14–US$20/£8–£11).

Next to the wharf is **Confederation Landing Park** ⊕, an open, modern park with a boardwalk along the water's edge, lush lawns, and benches nicely situated for indolence. There's also a 220-boat marina, where you can scope out newly arrived pleasure craft.

From Peake's Wharf, stroll up **Great George Street** ⊕⊕⊕. This is surely one of the most handsome streets in all of Canada, with leafy trees, perfectly scaled Georgian row houses, and stately churches.

At the top of Great George Street, stop by the **Province House** and **Confederation Centre of the Arts** (see below); then explore the shops and restaurants of downtown Charlottetown. Watch for historical characters: Students dressed in period costume lead free 1-hour walking tours; others portray the Fathers of the Confederation, the politicians who were the key players in the confederation conference. Check with the visitor center for times.

For a pleasant walk affording fine water views, head southwest on Kent Street (just north of the Confederation Mall). At 2 Kent St., you'll see **Beaconsfield** (© 902/368-6603), a mansard-roofed mansion designed in 1877 by locally prominent architect William Harris for a prosperous shipbuilder. The architecture boasts an elegant mix of Georgian symmetry and Victorian exuberance, and the rooms are furnished in high Victorian style. The home, which is part of the Prince Edward Island Museum and Heritage Foundation, hosts lectures and events throughout the year, or you can just stop in and look around. It's open daily in summer from 10am to 5pm, but call ahead for opening hours if you'll be visiting outside of the July-to-August season; it is open sporadically at those times. Admission is C$4.25 (US$3.85/£2.15) adults, C$3.25 (US$2.95/£1.65) students, C$12 (US$11/£6) families, free for children under 12.

From Beaconsfield, look for the boardwalk that follows the edge of the harbor for 1.6km (1 mile) into **Victoria Park** ⊕⊕, which is home to ball fields and grassy picnic areas. The walk along the water has unobstructed views of the harbor and Northumberland Strait beyond.

Along the walk look for the **Government House** ⊕ (© 902/368-5480), also known as Fanningbank. Built in 1834, this sturdy white-shingled residence with Ionic columns is set back on a broad lawn and is the official home to the island's lieutenant governor. Only the gatehouse is open to the public, and you're also welcome to explore the grounds daily from 10am to 4pm (both are only open to the public in July and Aug, however). There are tours of the house weekdays on the half-hour. The famous picture of the Fathers of the Confederation (you'll see it most everywhere around town) was taken on the front portico.

Confederation Centre of the Arts Gallery and Museum   Part of the Confederation Centre of the Arts (which includes three theaters; see "Charlottetown After Dark," later in this chapter), this is the largest art gallery in Atlantic Canada. The center is housed in a bland and boxy modern complex of glass and rough sandstone; about the best that can be said of it is that it doesn't detract too much from the stylishly classical Province House next door. (Canadian writer Will Ferguson has referred to the building as "one of the greatest unprosecuted crimes of urban planning in Canadian history.") Inside, however, the gallery is spacious and nicely arranged on two levels, and it features displays from the permanent collection as well as imaginatively curated changing exhibits. Admission is free. Shows might range from an exhibit on Canadian legal history to Uruguayan paintings to knit works or photographs of islands, but mostly the museum focuses on hanging the work of up-and-coming Canadians such as prize-winning Inuit artist Annie Pootoogook (who hails from the Northwest Territories). Spend an hour here if you enjoy art.

145 Richmond St. ⓒ **902/628-6142.** www.confederationcentre.com. Late May to early Oct daily 9am–5pm; off season Wed–Sat 11am–5pm, Sun 1–5pm.

Province House National Historic Site ⭐   This neoclassical downtown landmark was built in 1847 in an area set aside by town fathers for colonial administration and church buildings. When it served as a colonial legislature, the massive building rose up from vacant lots of dust and mud; today, as the provincial legislature, it's ringed by handsome trees, an inviting lawn, and a bustling downtown just beyond. This stern and imposing sandstone edifice occupies a special spot in Canadian history as the place where the details of the Confederation were hammered out in 1864. In the early 1980s, the building was restored to appear as it would have looked in that year.

Start your tour by viewing a well-made film that documents the process of confederation. Afterward, wander the halls and view the Legislative Assembly, where legislators have been meeting since 1847. It's surprisingly tiny, but perhaps appropriate given that PEI's legislature has just 27 members, making it the smallest in Canada. Especially impressive is the second-floor Confederation Chamber, where a staffer is usually on hand to explain what took place and to answer that burning question: Why did PEI wait 9 years to join Canada? Plan to spend about an hour here.

2 Palmer's Lane. ⓒ **902/566-7626.** Free admission (donations requested). July–Sept daily 8:30am–5pm; rest of the year Mon–Fri 8:30am–5pm.

SHOPPING

Charlottetown has a number of shops and boutiques, but not many are all that impressive—with a few notable exceptions. Better quality and more creative crafts can be found in outposts elsewhere on the island, especially along the north shore.

Peake's Wharf on the waterfront has an abundance of shops, most of which are tourist-oriented. This is a good destination if you're in search of a souvenir emblazoned with PRINCE EDWARD ISLAND. You'll also find casual dining, ice cream, and harbor cruises here.

The **Confederation Court Mall** (✆ **902/894-9505**) is located downtown across from the Province House, at 134 Kent St. Architecturally, this 90-store mall blends in nicely with its neighbors. Inside, however, the place is less distinctive; it's all very nice, though the food courts, escalators, and chain stores might give you a shudder of déjà vu. Come chiefly if you (or your kids) need a rainy-day mall fix.

Anne of Green Gables Store   Everything Anne, from dolls to commemorative plates. 110 Queen St. ✆ 902/368-2663.

The Bookman   Located across from the mall, this small shop has the city's best selection of used books, with a strong inventory of PEI and Canadian titles. 177 Queen St. ✆ 902/892-8872.

Cows   PEI's answer to Ben & Jerry's. It's as much a clothing store as an ice-cream shop; fans of the premium ice cream scoop up T-shirts and other bovine whimsy. Ice-cream flavors include Wowie Cowie Coffee Toffee Crunch and Cotton Candy Bunny Tails. Look for other locations popping up around town and the island. 150 Queen St. ✆ 902/892-6969.

Great Northern Knitters   This knit shop has recently expanded its retail operations. It sells a diverse line of unusually well-made sweaters handcrafted on PEI. Every sweater is guaranteed for life; also look for factory seconds. 133 Queen St. ✆ 800/565-9665 or 902/566-5850.

The Kitchen Store   Serious amateur cooks trek here to buy the elegant stainless-steel Paderno brand cookware made with heat-conducting pads; these high-quality pots and pans, which come with a 25-year warranty, are made right on PEI. The store also sells other high-quality kitchen items. There's a smaller shop in the Charlottetown Mall. (If you want even more Paderno, there are a half-dozen outlet stores scattered across the island.) Confederation Court Mall (Grafton St.). ✆ 800/263-9768 or 902/629-2217.

The PEI Company Store   This is a great place to pick up locally made island products in one fell swoop. If you didn't get out to the factory in New Glasgow to pick up Prince Edward Island Preserve Co.'s great preserves, for example, stop here to stock up: Products are priced the same here as at the factory. Confederation Court Mall (Grafton St.). ✆ 902/566-5267.

WHERE TO STAY

For those traveling on a tight budget, there are a number of moderately priced motels situated along the main access roads running into town (coming from the Confederation Bridge) and beside the airport. These offer few pleasures beyond the savings to your pocketbook, but if cost is a prime consideration in your planning, two properties with rooms under C$100 (US$90/£50) are **Royalty Maples Cottages and Motel** on Route 2 (✆ **800/831-7829** or 902/368-1030) and the **Winfield Motel** on Route 1 (✆ **800/267-5525** or 902/566-2675).

For a motel situated a lot closer to town—in fact, within easy walking distance of the main attractions—try the **Best Western Charlottetown** (✆ **800/528-1234** or 902/892-2461), in two buildings (one a brick '70s mélange, one surprisingly attractive in a Cape Cod–shingled cottage sort of way) across the street from each other at 238 Grafton St., a couple blocks east of the Confederation Court Mall. Of course, you're paying more for the central location: Rooms and suites range from about C$90 to C$235 (US$81–US$212/£45–£118). The hotel has 146 units in all.

EXPENSIVE

Delta Prince Edward ★★ *Kids*   A modern, boxy, 10-story hotel overlooking the harbor, the Prince Edward Hotel is part of the Canadian Pacific chain and has all the amenities expected by business travelers and upscale tourists, including coffeemakers, hair dryers, free exercise bikes delivered to your room, and even cordless phones (in about half the rooms). You enter the hotel to a two-story atrium, home to a very well-regarded restaurant, then head up to the guest rooms. The better rooms are furnished with reproduction Georgian-style furniture; others have those oak and beige laminate furnishings that are virtually invisible. Higher rooms have better views; there's a premium for water views, but the city views are actually nicer and you can usually still glimpse the water. Kids will love the "kiddie" wading pool indoors, while adults hang out in the adjacent heated lane pool and hot tub, or work the Nordic Tracks in the fitness center. The in-hotel Selkirk restaurant (see below) might be the city's best, with upscale service and presentation to complement a fine menu. There's also a pubby lounge. A more informal restaurant serves tasty lunches on a patio near the harbor, but only during the summer. Raining? No problem: Try out the hotel's golf simulator.

18 Queen St., Charlottetown, PEI C1A 8B9. ⓒ **888/890-3222** or 902/566-2222. Fax 902/566-2282. www.delta princeedward.com. 211 units. Peak season C$169–C$390 (US$152–US$351/£85–£195) double, C$225–C$905 (US$203–US$815/£113–£453) suite; call for off-season rates. AE, DC, DISC, MC, V. Valet parking C$18 (US$16/£9), self parking C$14 (US$13/£7) per day. Pets allowed. **Amenities:** 2 restaurants; indoor pool; fitness room; Jacuzzi; sauna; concierge; business center; shopping arcade; salon; room service; babysitting; laundry service; dry cleaning; golf simulator. *In room:* A/C, TV, minibar, coffeemaker, hair dryer, iron/ironing board.

The Great George ★★★   The Great George opened in 1997 and has already established itself as one of Charlottetown's classiest addresses. Actually a complex rather than a single inn, the property encompasses a collection of striking buildings on and near historic Great George Street, most of which were jacked up and renovated from states of former disrepair. (You can learn the story from a series of black-and-white photographs in the attractive lobby.)

Two dozen rooms are located in the 1846 Pavilion Hotel; others are in smaller, brightly painted town houses and homes nearby. All have been thoroughly updated and refurbished with antiques, down duvets, and early black-and-white prints; all but two rooms are carpeted. The more expensive rooms have fireplaces and Jacuzzis, but many of the others have claw-foot tubs, perfect for soaking in after a day of roaming the city. Room no. 403 has buttery pine floors, a wonderful tub, and lots of light. Room no. 308 has a Shaker-style canopy bed, an in-room two-person Jacuzzi, and a gas fireplace. Families or couples traveling together should ask about room no. 662, an attractive three-bedroom suite, or one of a number of other renovated suites. The addition of a garden space in back only makes this place more desirable—and since your address is C-town's most famous street, you couldn't be any closer to the pubs, shops, and historic buildings.

58 Great George St., Charlottetown, PEI C1A 4K3. ⓒ **800/361-1118** or 902/892-0606. Fax 902/628-2079. www. thegreatgeorge.com. 54 units. C$165–C$499 (US$149–US$449/£83–£250) double; C$299–C$899 (US$269–US$809/ £150–£450) suite. Rates include continental breakfast. AE, DC, MC, V. Free parking. **Amenities:** Fitness room; limited room service; babysitting; laundry service; dry cleaning. *In room:* A/C, TV (some units), hair dryer, iron.

Shipwright Inn ★★★   This understated Victorian home was built by a shipbuilder and has been expertly renovated and refurbished. It's decorated with period furniture and a deft touch—no over-the-top Victoriana here—and equipped with surprisingly modern amenities such as telephones and VCR or DVD players in all rooms. All rooms have lovely wood floors (some with original ship-planking floors), and three are in a recent addition, which was built with a number of nice touches. Among the best rooms are those with extra somethings: the Officer's Wardroom, a suite with an Asian feel, living-room fireplace, and skylight-view bathtub; the airy Crow's Nest luxury apartment, with its plush king bed, claw-foot Jacuzzi (yes, really), and lovely unvarnished wood furniture; and even the simpler Purser's Stateroom, which shares a lovely deck with another room. The business center, with its computer and fax machine, is a nice bonus; afternoon tea service is a good introduction to the island; and innkeepers Judy and Trevor Pye and their staff are unfailingly helpful. This inn is located right in the city, yet it has a settled, pastoral farmhouse feel to it—a perfect combination.

51 Fitzroy St., Charlottetown, PEI C1A 1R4. ℂ 888/306-9966 or 902/368-1905. Fax 902/628-1905. www.shipwright inn.com. 9 units. May–Oct C$149–C$289 (US$134–US$260/£75–£145) double; Nov–Apr C$99–C$199 (US$89–US$179/£50–£100) double. Rates include full breakfast. AE, DC, MC, V. Free parking. **Amenities:** Dining room; business center. *In room:* A/C, TV, kitchenette (some units), fridge (most units), minibar, hair dryer, iron, Jacuzzi (some units).

MODERATE

Hillhurst Inn 🎯   Another fine mansion built in 1897 in another fine neighborhood (3 blocks northeast of Province House), Hillhurst features an abundance of nice touches, not the least of which is the extraordinarily detailed woodworking carved by some of the city's shipbuilders. When built, locals called it "the crystal palace" because of its profusion of windows. The rooms are varied in size and style and have been upgraded over time; all now have phones, air-conditioning, televisions, and so forth. Two even have Jacuzzis. As is often the case, third-floor rooms require a bit of a hike, and are smaller and cozier than rooms on the second floor. Only drawback? Many of the bathrooms are small (often shoehorned into closets). Also, the furnishings are a bit less historic and creative than those at the comparatively priced Shipwright.

181 Fitzroy St., Charlottetown, PEI C1A 1S3. ℂ 877/994-8004 or 902/894-8004. Fax 902/892-7679. www. hillhurst.com. 9 units. Mid-June to mid-Sept C$135–C$235 (US$122–US$212/£68–£118) double; spring and fall C$99–C$165 (US$89–US$149/£50–£83) double. Closed Dec–Apr. Rates include full breakfast. AE, DISC, MC, V. Free parking. **Amenities:** Business center. *In room:* A/C, TV, dataport, hair dryer, Jacuzzi (2 units).

Rodd Charlottetown 🎯   This 1940s-era business hotel—part of the Rodd Hotel chain—is located in a five-story brick building next to a shady park, just a few minutes' walk from most downtown attractions. The hotel features Georgian flourishes inside and out, and has been updated and remodeled with a nod to its heritage. The dusky lobby has the feel of a prewar New York City apartment building, with a vaulted ceiling and echoey composite floors. The rooms, which have opening windows, were tastefully remodeled in the mid-1990s with reproduction-period furniture. Five suites were added in 1999; the rooftop patio is also worth a look. The hotel will certainly appeal to travelers drawn to the solid construction and understated styling of yore, though some of the public areas are perhaps overdue for remodeling. A low-ceilinged indoor pool is open to guests on the ground floor.

The in-hotel Chambers Restaurant is open daily for dinner and features hotel favorites including prime rib, jumbo shrimp, Atlantic salmon, and a popular shellfish buffet. Across the lobby, a dinner theater performs nightly in July and August, and there's also a new lobby bar.

Kent and Pownal sts. (P.O. Box 159), Charlottetown, PEI C1A 7K4. ℂ 800/565-7633 or 902/894-7371. Fax 902/ 368-2178. www.rodd-hotels.ca. 115 units. C$109–C$250 (US$98–US$225/£55–£125) double; C$185–C$350 (US$167–US$315/£93–£175) suite. AE, DC, DISC, MC, V. Free parking. Pets accepted with C$10 (US$9/£5) charge.

Amenities: Restaurant; bar; indoor pool; Jacuzzi; sauna; limited room service; babysitting, laundry service; dry cleaning. *In room:* A/C, TV, dataport, coffeemaker, hair dryer, iron/ironing board.

WHERE TO DINE

For a late-afternoon pick-me-up, try **Beanz,** 38 University Ave. (© **902/892-8797**), for its industrial-strength cappuccino. They also sell pastries and offer light lunches.

A locally popular spot for inexpensive meals is **Cedar's Eatery** at 81 University Ave. between Fitzroy and Kent (© **902/892-7377**). Lebanese dishes are the specialty here, such as *yabrak* (stuffed vine leaves) and kibbe (ground beef with crushed wheat and spices). There are also sandwiches and burgers. Specials start around C$5 (US$4.50/£2.50).

Claddagh Oyster House ⚓ SEAFOOD Despite the Irish name and the Olde Dublin Pub located downstairs, the Claddagh Room isn't the place for corned beef. Instead, as the rest of its name indicates, it's a place for seafood—starting with oysters, which have become a focus of the recently retooled menu. The seafood chowder is very tasty, or go for seared scallops over sweet potato pancakes, mussels of the day, or oysters Rockefeller. For the main meal, you might choose from the raw oyster bar or go for a boiled lobster, lemony shrimp, sesame seed-encrusted salmon, citrus-shallot haddock, and the like; there are also strip-loin steaks, maple pork chops, and other landlubber entrees. There are no harbor views, as there are at other seafood places in town, but the preparation and service here are a notch above. Live Irish entertainment is often featured downstairs in the pub during the summer months.

131 Sydney St. © **902/892-9661.** Reservations recommended. Main courses C$18–C$29 (US$16–US$26/£9–£15); oysters C$1.60–C$1.90 (US$1.45–US$1.70/80p–95p) each. AE, DISC, MC, V. Mon–Fri 11:30am–2pm; Sun–Thurs 5–10pm; Fri–Sat 5–10:30pm.

Lucy Maud Dining Room ⚓⚓ REGIONAL The Lucy Maud Dining Room is located on the respected Culinary Institute of Canada's Charlottetown campus. The building itself is a bit institutional and charmless, and the 80-seat dining room has much the feel of a hotel restaurant. But plenty of nice touches offset the lack of personality. Among them: custom china and a beautiful view of the bay and Victoria Park from oversize windows. Best of all, diners get to sample some of the best of island cuisine, prepared and served by Institute students eager to please. The lunch and dinner menus change each semester, but typical dinner entrees might include duck breast with a sour cherry sauce or venison loin with a blueberry-peppercorn sauce (the kitchen is noted for its venison). There's always salmon on the menu here, and often a curry-flavored seafood chowder with fresh tarragon. A short wine list is also available.

4 Sydney St. © **902/894-6868.** Reservations recommended June–Sept for lunch and dinner. Main courses C$8–C$13 (US$7.20–US$12/£4–£6.50) at lunch, C$15–C$28 (US$14–US$25/£7.50–£14) at dinner. AE, MC, V. Tues–Fri 11:30am–1:30pm; Tues–Sat 6–8pm. Closed holiday weekends.

Off Broadway ⚓ CANADIAN Affiliated with The Great George (see above), this friendly upscale restaurant has the feel of an intimate, wood-paneled English eating house. At dinner, its dimness can be downright romantic, though the proximity of other diners might be a slight deterrent to popping the question then and there. It's known for an unusually wide selection of crepes (some filled with seafood), as well as hearty steaks, salmon, island shellfish, and the like; the 42nd Street Lounge upstairs is also quite nice.

125 Sydney St. © **902/566-4620.** Reservations recommended. Lunch C$6–C$12 (US$5.40–US$11/£3–£6); dinner C$14–C$22 (US$13–US$20/£7–£11). AE, DISC, MC, V. Mon–Thurs 11:30am–10pm; Fri–Sat 11:30am–11pm; Sun 11am–10pm.

Piazza Joe's Italian Eatery and Bistro ITALIAN   Piazza Joe's, located in a hand-some, historic building 1 long block from the Confederation Mall, has gone a bit overboard with the Tuscan-style washed tones and fake ivy climbing fake trellises. But it works in a comic-book kind of way. The place is pleasantly casual and can be loud on weekends, but it offers friendly service, a long menu, and lots of comic-book-type mixed drinks to match the decor. (It's the best spot for a late-night meal if you get into town behind schedule.) The wood-fired pizza is consistently quite good, and there's a build-your-own-pasta entree option; take your chances on the rest of the selections, such as five-vegetable lasagna or veal *a la limone.* There's also a bistro menu, with items that include burgers, chicken wings, and fish and chips.

189 Kent St. ⓒ **902/894-4291.** Reservations accepted. Main courses C$10–C$39 (US$9–US$35/£5–£20); individ-ual pizzas C$7 (US$6.30/£3.50) and up. AE, DC, MC, V. Mon–Thurs 11am–midnight; Fri–Sat 11am–1am; Sun 10am–midnight.

Piece a Cake Restaurant 🏵🏵 ECLECTIC   This modern, handsome restaurant occupies the second floor of a building that's part of the Confederation Court Mall. With hardwood floors, high ceilings, rich custard-colored walls, and window frames suspended whimsically from the ceiling, there's a welcoming, airy grace to it. It's the kind of place where friends who don't see each other often get together and relax over a lively meal. The menu is wonderfully far-ranging, and it's hard to imagine someone not finding something appealing—lunches might range from a teriyaki salmon wrap to Thai scallop salad to Tuscan grilled chicken sandwiches. Dinners are similarly diverse and include a range of adventurous pastas, such as "penne on fire" (with charred onions, grilled zucchini, toasted pecans, and a tangerine relish). Other dinner options have included a medley of Thai seafood, blackened salmon, and a pecan-encrusted pork loin. Also ask about the gourmet brown-bag lunches, about C$10 to C$14 (US$9–US$13/£5–£7), each including dessert and beverage, with choices that could run from a lobster-salad croissant to a jerk-chicken pasta salad.

119 Grafton St. (upstairs in the Confederation Court Mall). ⓒ **902/894-4585.** Reservations recommended. Main courses C$6–C$12 (US$5.40–US$11/£3–£6) at lunch, C$9–C$18 (US$8.10–US$16/£4.50–£9) at dinner. AE, DC, MC, V. Mon–Sat 11am–10pm.

The Selkirk 🏵🏵🏵 NEW CANADIAN   Charlottetown's most stylish restaurant is smack in the middle of the lobby of the high-end Delta Prince Edward Hotel. Yet it has a more informal character than many upscale hotel restaurants, with an eclectic mix of chairs and a piano player providing the live soundtrack. The menu is also more ambi-tious and creative than you'll find elsewhere in the city. Start with a local seafood chow-der or some island-smoked salmon. Main courses from chef Mark Gregory could include a bouillabaisse; spicy smoked beef ribs; a pan-roasted pork loin chop; a potato-crusted filet of salmon with a spinach-onion confit stuffing and a ruby grapefruit *gas-trique;* or a salt-boiled PEI lobster accompanied by chowder, mussels, potatoes, and veggies. Ask about the seasonal three-course dinner prix-fixe meals (C$35/US$32/£18). The lobby location gets noisy at times, especially when conferees are in town, so ask for a table under the mezzanine, nearer the piano.

18 Queen St. (in the Delta Prince Edward). ⓒ **902/566-2222.** Reservations recommended. Main courses C$11–C$25 (US$10–US$23/£5.50–£13) at dinner. AE, DC, DISC, MC, V. Mon–Fri 7am–1:30pm and 5:30–9pm; Sat 7–11am and 5:30–9pm; Sun 7am–2pm and 5:30–9pm.

Sirenella *Kids* ITALIAN   Sirenella is a locally popular spot that offers good value when the service staff and kitchen are operating smoothly, which is not always the case. But if all systems are go, it's a decent family drop-in. You'll soon understand why locals swear by reliable dishes such as grilled calamari; ravioli with ricotta, spinach, and prosciutto; veal dishes; and seafood pastas. This restaurant is tucked on a quiet side street and is tiny enough that it can be considered either romantic and intimate or claustrophobic, depending on your mood. There's a patio for outdoor dining and a kids' menu for the little ones.

83 Water St. ℰ 902/628-2271. Reservations recommended. Main courses C$13–C$26 (US$12–US$23/£6.50–£13) at dinner. AE, MC, V. Mon–Fri 11:30am–2pm and 5–10pm; Sat 5–10pm.

Water Prince Corner Shop ★★ *Finds* SEAFOOD   This place is a real hidden gem, tucked into an attractive corner building at Water and Prince streets (thus the name) that looks at first glance like a simple newsstand or convenience store. Inside, though, you'll find one of the city's most convivial seafood joints, serving lobster dinners, superb seafood chowder, cooked mussels, and even lobster rolls to an appreciative mixture of tourists and locals. There's a liquor license if you want to tip a few (and you might). If the weather's good, try to get a seat on the street near sundown: You can see the waterfront from some tables. Even if it's not, don't miss the exceptionally rare blue lobster kept here on display (alive)—it was caught off the west coast of PEI in 2002.

141 Water St. ℰ 902/368-3212. Reservations recommended. Lunch C$4.95–C$11 (US$4.45–US$10/£2.50–£5); dinner C$6.95–C$25 (US$6.25–US$23/£3.50–£13). AE, DISC, DC, MC, V. May–June and Sept–Oct daily 9am–8pm; July–Aug daily 9am–10pm.

CHARLOTTETOWN AFTER DARK

A good resource for evening adventure is *Buzz,* a free monthly newspaper that details ongoing and special events around the island with an emphasis on Charlottetown. It's widely available; look for it in visitor centers or area bars and restaurants.

For high culture, check out the **Confederation Centre of the Arts Gallery and Museum** (ℰ **800/565-0278** or 902/628-1864; p. 229), where three stages bustle with activity in the warm-weather months. The musical *Anne of Green Gables,* a perennial favorite, is performed here throughout the summer, as are revivals and new shows.

For low culture, head to the **Charlottetown Driving Park** (ℰ **902/892-6823**), located at Kensington Road on the Hillsborough River at the northeast edge of downtown. Harness racing is slated most afternoons and evenings of the week from June to September; call for the current schedule. Parimutuel betting is offered, and there's a club on the upper level for enjoying snacks and drinks while handicapping the ponies, as well as a new casino section featuring slot machines and poker tables.

The art house **City Cinema,** 64 King St. (ℰ **902/368-3669**), has an excellent lineup of domestic and foreign films throughout the year; typically, there's a choice of two films each evening.

Outdoor libations are on tap at **Victoria Row,** on pedestrian-only Richmond Street behind the Confederation Centre. Several restaurants and pubs cluster here and serve meals and drinks on street-side patios; some offer live music. The row is a popular destination for university students and younger locals.

For live Celtic-flavored music and occasional roast-beef buffet dinners, head no farther than the fun and popular **Olde Dublin Pub,** above the Claddagh Oyster House (see above) at 131 Sydney St. (ℰ **902/892-6992**). **Myron's,** at 151 Kent St. (ℰ **902/ 892-4375**), features a dance club and cabaret located on two floors with a robust 2,044 square meters (22,001 sq. ft.) of entertainment space; performers range from country to rock.

6 Kings County

After a visit to Charlottetown and the island's central towns, Kings County comes as a bit of a surprise. It's far more tranquil and uncluttered than Queens County (Anne's reach is much diminished here), and the landscapes feature woodlots alternating with corn, grain, and potato fields. Although much is made of the county's two great commercial centers on the coast—Souris and Montague—it's good to keep in mind that each of these has a population of around 1,500. In some parts of North America, that wouldn't even rate a dot on the map.

Don't arrive here expecting attractions that go out of their way to amuse and entertain you. You'll have to do that yourself. It's prime biking territory, though, and walks on the empty beaches are a good tonic if you're suffering from a hectic schedule in your real (nonvacation) life. Long drives in the country with occasional stops are similarly relaxing.

If you're headed to southeastern Kings County from Charlottetown, you'll pass through Orwell and its historic sites en route. See the listings earlier in this chapter, in Queens County.

ESSENTIALS

GETTING THERE   Several main roads—including Highways 1, 2, 3, and 4—connect eastern PEI with Charlottetown and western points. The ferry to Nova Scotia sails from Woods Island on the south coast. See "Exploring Prince Edward Island," earlier in this chapter, for more information about the ferry.

VISITOR INFORMATION   There's a provincial **Visitor Information Centre** (© 902/687-7030) at 95 Main St. in Souris, open daily from mid-June to mid-October. There's another VIC in St. Peter's Bay (© **902/961-3540**), on Route 2 at the intersection of routes 313 and 16; this center, bordering the lovely Confederation Trail, opens daily June through October.

MURRAY RIVER & MURRAY HARBOUR ✯

It's not especially hard to guess the name of the family that originally settled this area—it seems that "Murray" is appended to every natural landmark of note. These two small and tidy villages offer little drama, but lots of repose. It's hard to imagine a better place to listen to the crickets and the wind in the trees. As you drive, watch for the tight lines of buoys in the coastal waterways: The island's widely acclaimed blue mussels (you see them on Manhattan menus all the time) are cultivated here in mesh bags suspended from ropes attached to those buoys, and then shipped worldwide when they've grown to proper eating size.

EXPLORING THE MURRAYS

Seals are practically as common as crows in this part of PEI. You just have to know where to look. The best way to view these sleek creatures is close up, from the water. Visit the island's largest **seal colony** ✯✯ with **Marine Adventures Seal Watching** (© **800/496-2494** or 902/962-2494; www.sealwatching.com), based in Murray River. You'll travel in enclosed boats (tours offered rain or shine) and see seals, mussel farms, herons, and, with luck, bald eagles. Tours are offered daily in summer; the cost is C$19 (US$17/£9.50) adults, C$17 (US$15/£8.50) students and seniors, C$12 (US$11/£6) children and students. Allow at least 2 hours for the entire trip.

Young children rarely fail to enjoy the wonderful (if slightly corny) **Kings Castle Provincial Park** ★ (© **902/962-7422**), an old-fashioned kiddy wonderland of the sort that was popular in the 1950s and 1960s. This pleasant picnic park on the shores of the Murray River (there's swimming at a small beach) features life-size kids' story-book characters scattered about the fields and woodlands. Kids can visit with the likes of Goldilocks and the Three Little Pigs, and then scamper about on an array of play-ground equipment or lick an ice cream at the park's canteen. It's open daily from 9am to 9pm from mid-June to mid-October; best of all, admission is free. The park is on Route 348 just east of the town of Murray River, on the south bank of the river.

A couple of beaches are worthy of note: A short drive from Murray River along the north bank of the river is remote and peaceful **Poverty Beach** ★★. Dunes back this long strand of eastward-facing beach. You can park at the end of the road and walk along the beach watching for bird life. Swimming is problematic; the beach is pebbly at low tide, and the currents can sometimes be troublesome. But it's a great getaway: You might not see another soul, even in summer. It's free.

North of Poverty Beach (and also free of charge) is **Panmure Island Provincial Park,** open early June through the middle of September. The island is connected to the mainland via a sand-dune isthmus; the contrast between the white sands (on the ocean side) and the red beach of the inner cove is striking. It's a lovely spot, with swim-ming on the ocean side and views northward to a striking lighthouse.

There's also a 9-hole golf course, shopping, and tour outfits in the Murrays.

WHERE TO STAY

Forest and Stream Cottages ★   These cottages are located on 8 hectares (20 acres) of peaceful woodlands near a narrow lake and the site of an old gristmill. The grounds are shady, lovely, and laced with nature trails; you can also swim in the lake or use the rowboats and life jackets for free. The cottages themselves are fairly bland and dated, with 1950s-style kitchenettes and linoleum floors, TVs, and screened-in porches with picnic tables and gas grills outside. However, the owners have recently upgraded the remainder of the property, adding bed-and-breakfast rooms and a loft suite in the main house and a hot tub in a gazebo outdoors. There's a playground for kids, and the staff rents bikes at good rates if you need one.

Fox River Rd. (off Rte. 18), Murray Harbour, PEI C0A 1V0. © **800/227-9943** or 902/962-3537. Fax 902/962-2130. www.forestandstreamcottages.com. 5 cottages (3 1-bedroom, 2 2-bedroom). Mid-June to mid-Sept cottages C$85– C$125 (US$77–US$113/£43–£63), slightly lower May to mid-June and mid-Sept to Oct; inn rooms C$99–C$149 (US$89–US$134/£50–£75). Inn-room rates include full breakfast. Weekly rates available for all units. MC, V. Closed Nov–Apr. Small pets allowed. **Amenities:** Hot tub; bike rentals; laundry facility. *In room:* TV/DVD (cottages), kitch-enette (cottages), no phone.

Fox River Cottages ★   These four modern two-bedroom cottages with kitch-enettes are beautifully situated on 5.2 hectares (13 acres) down a winding dirt road at the edge of a field overlooking the islands of Murray Bay. The cottages are all tidy units of exposed wood, furnished with televisions and VCRs; they're near one another, yet also staggered to create a sense of personal privacy. You can relax on the screened porches or wander to the river beach and dabble around in the canoe. One unit has a wood stove, and all have electric heat and gas barbecues for evening grilling. If you have a croquet set, by all means bring it.

Machon Point Rd., Murray Harbour, PEI C0A 1V0. © **902/962-2881.** www.foxriver.ca. 4 units. Cottages C$75– C$140 (US$68–US$126/£38–£70) double, weekly C$500–C$925 (US$450–US$833/£250–£463) double. 3- to 7-night minimum stay sometimes required. Off-season rates available. V. Closed Nov–May. **Amenities:** Laundry facility. *In room:* TV/VCR, kitchenette, coffeemaker, no phone.

MONTAGUE

Montague may be the Kings County region's main commercial hub, but it's a hub in low gear: compact and attractive, with a handsome business district on a pair of flanking hills sloping down to a bridge across the Montague River. (In fact, a century and a half ago, the town was called Montague Bridge.) Shipbuilding was the economic mainstay in the 19th century; today, it's dairy and tobacco.

EXPLORING THE OUTDOORS

Cruise Manada (© **800/986-3444** or 902/838-3444; www.cruisemanada.com) offers seal- and bird-watching tours daily during peak season aboard restored fishing boats; the cost is C$22 (US$20/£11) adults, C$20 (US$18/£10) seniors and students, C$12 (US$10/£5.75) children ages 5 to 13. Trips depart from the marina on the Montague River (just below the visitor center in the old railway depot) three times daily in July and August, once daily from mid-May to June and in September. Reservations are advised; allow at least 2 hours. Cruise Manada also does "floating ceilidhs" for about C$36 (US$32/£18) per adult.

Southeast of Montague (en route to Murray River) is the **Buffaloland Provincial Park** (© **902/652-8950**), where you'll spot a small herd of buffalo. These magnificent animals were a gift to PEI from the province of Alberta, and they now number about two dozen. Walk down the 90m (295-ft.) fenced-in corridor into the paddock and ascend the wooden platform for the best view of the shaggy beasts. Often they're hunkered down at the far end of the meadow, but they sometimes wander nearer. The park is right off Route 4; watch for signs. It's open daily year-round, and—like so many of PEI's parks—free to enter.

A few minutes north of Buffaloland on Route 4, between routes 216 and 317, is **Harvey Moore Park,** a delightful place for a stroll. A privately owned park named after a famous local naturalist who created the sanctuary in 1949, this park's centerpiece is its 45-minute trail that loops around a pond and through varied ecosystems. A well-written nature guide is available free at the signboard. Watch especially for waterfowl, with which Moore had an unusually close rapport; avian visitors include black ducks, blue-winged teal, ring-necked ducks, pintails, and an abundance of Canada geese. It's open daylight hours June to mid-September. Once again, admission is free.

Brudenell River Provincial Park is one of the province's better-bred parks and is a great spot to work up an athletic glow on a sunny afternoon. On its 600 riverfront hectares (1,483 acres) you'll find two well-regarded golf courses, a golf academy, a full-blown resort (see below), tennis, lawn bowling, a wildflower garden, a playground, a campground, and nature trails. Kids' programs—including Frisbee golf, shoreline scavenger hunts, and crafts workshops—are scheduled daily in summer. You can also rent canoes, kayaks, and jet skis from private operators located within the park. The park is open daily mid-May to early October from 9am to 9pm; free admission. Head north of Montague on Route 4, then east on Route 3 to the park signs.

WHERE TO STAY

Rodd Brudenell River Resort ★★ *Kids*   The attractive Brudenell River Resort was built in 1991, and its open, vaguely Frank Lloyd Wright–esque design reflects its recent vintage. This is an especially popular destination for golfers—it's set among two

golf courses that have hosted international tournaments and exhibitions and have garnered rave reviews. Guests choose from three types of rooms. The hotel proper has
nearly 100 well-appointed guest rooms, most with a balcony or terrace. The expensive
cottages each have two bedrooms, cathedral ceilings, fireplaces, and large-screen TVs;
then, there are a set of more basic cabins—the best choice for those traveling on a
budget, though these aren't as fresh and the units are clustered together oddly like
pavilions in a long-gone world exposition. In addition to the two excellent golf courses
(one with a Golf Academy offering lessons), the resort maintains indoor and outdoor
pools, as well as a newer **spa** ⊛, which opens from mid-May through mid-October
only. The dining room on the first level of this property overlooks one of the golf
courses—it's huge, but the high-backed chairs carve out a sense of intimacy. The
kitchen serves dinners of what might be described as creative country-club cuisine,
with entrees including charbroiled steak, sole in puff pastry, and pasta primavera.

Rte. 3 (P.O. Box 67), Cardigan, PEI C0A 1G0. ⓒ **800/565-7633** or 902/652-2332. Fax 902/652-2886. www.rodd-
hotels.ca. 165 units. C$131–C$353 (US$118–US$318/£66–£177) double, C$87–C$178 (US$78–US$160/£44–£89)
cabin, C$167–C$536 (US$150–US$482/£84–£268) cottage. AE, DC, MC, V. Closed mid-Oct to mid-May. Pets allowed
with C$10 (US$9/£5) fee per pet per night. **Amenities:** 2 restaurants; 2 bars; indoor and outdoor pools; golf course
(with academy); 2 tennis courts; fitness center; spa; Jacuzzi; sauna; canoe/kayak/bike rentals; children's center;
babysitting; dry cleaning. *In room:* A/C, TV, dataport, kitchenette (some units), minibar (some units), fridge (some
units), coffeemaker, hair dryer, iron.

WHERE TO DINE
Windows on the Water Café ⊛ SEAFOOD   If you haven't yet dined on PEI
mussels, this is the place to let loose. The blue mussels are steamed in a root *mirepoix*
(soup base) with sesame, ginger, and garlic—a great idea. Main courses might include
sole stuffed with crab and scallop and topped with hollandaise; or a filet mignon
served with sweet peppers, red onion, and mushrooms in a peppercorn sauce. Lunches
are lighter, with choices that could include a grilled chicken and mandarin salad or
house-made fish cakes. The appealing, open dining room features press-back chairs
and a lively buzz, but if the weather's agreeable, angle for a seat under the canopy on
the deck and enjoy the great view of the Montague River.

106 Sackville St. (corner of Main St.), Montague. ⓒ **902/838-2080.** Reservations recommended. Main courses
C$7.50–C$9.95 (US$6.75–US$9/£3.75–£4.50) at lunch, C$15–C$21 (US$14–US$19/£7.50–£11) at dinner. AE, DC,
MC, V. June–Oct daily 11:30am–9:30pm. Closed Nov–May.

SOURIS & NORTHEAST PEI
Some 42km (26 miles) northeast of Montague is the town of Souris, an active fishing
town attractively set on a gentle hill overlooking the harbor. Souris (pronounced Soo-
ree) is French for "mouse"—so named because early settlers here were beset by voracious field mice that destroyed their crops. The town is the launching base for an
excursion to the Magdalen Islands, and it also makes a good base for exploring northeastern PEI, which is considered by some Charlottetown types to be the island's version of either Mayberry, RFD, or the Outback—in other words, a place that's remote
and sparsely populated. You'll find it to be somewhat less agricultural and more
forested (especially away from the coast) than the rest of the island, too.

EXPLORING THE AREA
Several good beaches can be found ringing this wedge-shaped peninsula that points
like an accusing finger toward Nova Scotia's Cape Breton Island. **Red Point Provincial Park** (ⓒ **902/357-3105**) is 13km (8 miles) northeast of Souris. Open from June

until mid-September, it offers a handsome beach and supervised swimming, along with a campground that's popular with families; sites cost about C$19 to C$25 (US$17–US$23/£9.50–£13). Another inviting and often empty beach is a short distance northeast at Basin Head, which features a **"singing sands" beach** ⚘ that allegedly sings (actually, it's more like squeaks) when you walk on it. The dunes here are especially appealing.

Look also for the nearby **Basin Head Fisheries Museum** ⚘ (📞 **902/357-7233**), a provincially operated museum that offers insight into the life of the inshore fisherman. Admission is C$4 (US$3.60/£2) adults, C$3.50 (US$3.15/£1.75) students, and C$12 (US$11/£6) families (free for children under 12). It's open daily 9am to 5pm, then closed from October through May.

At the island's far eastern tip is the aptly named **East Point Lighthouse** ⚘ (📞 **902/357-2718**). You can simply enjoy the dramatic setting or take a tour of the building (mid-June to Aug only). Ask for your East Point ribbon while you're here. If you make it to the North Cape Lighthouse on the western shore, you'll receive a Traveler's Award documenting that you've traveled PEI tip-to-tip. Admission to the octagonal lighthouse tower is C$3 (US$2.70/£1.50) adults, C$2 (US$1.80/£1) seniors and students, C$1 (US90¢/50p) children, and C$8 (US$7.20/£4) families. There are daily tours in season; from September to mid-June, you'll need to call to try to schedule one. There's also a craft shop on-site purveying jewelry, soap, sand paintings, local books and music, and other island goods.

A spur of the Confederation Trail ends in Souris, making this a good spot from which to launch a bike excursion of the area. One suggested day trip would be to link to the main trunk trail, then venture northeast to East Point Lighthouse.

WHERE TO STAY

Inn at Bay Fortune ⚘⚘   This exceptionally attractive shingled compound on 18 hectares (44 acres) was built by playwright Elmer Harris in 1910 as a summer home, and it quickly became the nucleus for a colony of artists, actors, and writers. (Most recently the home was owned by Canadian actress Colleen Dewhurst, who sold it to current innkeeper David Wilmer in 1988.) Wilmer pulled out the stops in renovating, bringing it back from the brink of decay. In 1998 he added a wing with six new rooms (several with Jacuzzis), including the wonderful North Tower Room no. 4, with a high ceiling and balcony overlooking the lodge and bay beyond. The best room, though, remains South Tower Room no. 4, which requires a hike up a narrow staircase—but feels like another world once you reach the perchlike destination. Newer rooms are bigger than older ones, yet all are cozy with mixes of antiques and custom-made furniture. About half of the units have wood-burning fireplaces. This is also home to one of PEI's best restaurants (see below).

Rte. 310 (off Rte. 2), Bay Fortune, PEI C0A 2B0. 📞 **902/687-3745** or off season 860/296-1348. Fax 902/687-3540. www.innatbayfortune.com. 18 units. C$150–C$335 (US$135–US$302/£75–£168) double. Rates include full breakfast. DC, MC, V. Closed mid-Oct to mid-May. **Amenities:** Restaurant.

Inn at Spry Point ⚘⚘ (Finds)   This inn was founded in the 1970s on a remote point of land as a United Nations–funded, self-sufficient community affiliated with the New Alchemy Institute—think windmills, solar power, greenhouses, trout ponds, and some serious hippy-dippy talk. But oil prices dropped, interest in conservation waned, and the experiment faded. Enter David Wilmer, owner of the Inn at Bay Fortune (see above). He bought the 32-hectare (79-acre) property and has undertaken the monumental task of bringing it up to date. All 15 rooms have canopied king-size beds and are tastefully appointed with comfortable sitting areas. Most have their own private balconies, and four have a garden terrace. Beyond the grounds, there are 2,440m (8,005 ft.) of undeveloped shorefront that invite exploration, and you can walk along trails that traverse red-clay cliffs with views of the Northumberland Strait. Later, dine in the outstanding contemporary **dining room** ⟡⟡ featuring locally grown organic vegetables and island seafood; prix-fixe meals cost about C$45 (US$41/£23) per person, and you can also order a la carte.

Spry Pt. Rd. (off Rte. 310), Little Pond, PEI COA 2BO. ℂ **902/583-2400.** Fax 902/583-2176. www.innatsprypoint.com. 15 units. C$185–C$335 (US$167–US$302/£93–£168) double. Rates include full breakfast. DC, MC, V. Closed Oct to mid-June. **Amenities:** Restaurant. *In room:* A/C.

Matthew House Inn ⟡   Kimberly and Franco Olivieri came to PEI on vacation from Italy in 1995. They fell in love with the island's grand old homes, and before their holiday had ended they found themselves owners of this fine B&B. ("My husband is very impulsive by nature," says Kimberly.) Located atop a pleasant lawn overlooking the harbor and ferry to the Magdalen Islands, this stately Victorian dates from 1885 and maintains many of the original flourishes inside and out. Eastlake-style furnishings and William Morris touches give the place an architectural richness without

An Excursion to the Magdalen Islands

The **Magdalen Islands (Les Isles de la Madeleine),** located a 5-hour ferry ride north of PEI, consist of a dozen low sandy islands linked to one another by sand spits. About 14,000 people live here, and the islands are dotted with peaceful fishing villages and farming communities. The islands, part of the province of Québec, also boast some 299km (186 miles) of beaches, a fact that has not gone unnoticed by urban Québecois in search of leisure. (The island is linked by air and a 2-day ferry from Québec.) It's also famous for its persistent winds, which rake across the Gulf and find little resistance here.

Advance planning is needed for a trip to the islands, since the demand for accommodations often outstrips supply. A free island tourist guide is available by calling ℂ **877/624-4437** or 418/986-2245. On the Web, head to **www.tourismeilesdelamadeleine.com.**

Ferry service from Souris to Cap-aux-Meules is provided by the **Coopérative de Transport Maritime** (ℂ **888/986-3278** or 418/986-3278; www.ctma. ca), also known as the CTMA. The long river crossing takes 5 hours one-way on a seven-deck ferry that can carry 95 cars and 400 passengers. The boats sail as many as 11 times weekly in summer; the schedule is reduced to as few as three weekly boats in the off season, so check on the schedule before arriving.

One-way summer rates in 2007 were C$43 (US$39/£22) adults, C$35 (US$32/ £18) seniors, C$22 (US$20/£11) children 5 to 12, and C$80 (US$72/£40) for a normal-size automobile (more for vans and campers). These rates plunge 30% to 50% in the off season.

seeming too grandmotherly about it; for big families, a two-bedroom cottage adjacent to the inn rents by the week and is equipped with a kitchen and laundry. This place will be appreciated by those passionate about historic architecture.

15 Breakwater St. (P.O. Box 151), Souris, PEI C0A 2B0. © **902/687-3461.** Fax 902/687-3461. www.matthewhouse inn.com. 8 units. C$105–C$175 (US$95–US$158/£53–£8) 8double. Rates include full breakfast. AE, MC, V. Closed early Sept to mid-June. Children over 10 welcome. **Amenities:** Dining room; fax service; laundry service. *In room:* TV/VCR, hair dryer.

WHERE TO DINE

Inn at Bay Fortune ✿✿✿ CONTEMPORARY   To fully appreciate a meal at the Inn at Bay Fortune, arrive early enough to wander the gardens behind the inn. The herbs and edible flowers are a short walk from the kitchen; a little farther beyond is the 1.2 hectare (3-acre) vegetable garden. This is good introduction to the local products emphasized on the menu. Chef Warren Barr worked with founding chef Michael Smith to develop the inn's cuisine and its vaunted openness—how many restaurants feature a KITCHEN—WELCOME sign inviting diners to stop in for a visit? The place is wildly successful, with an always-shifting menu that rarely fails to produce a great meal. For those with a serious interest in cooking, ask about the coveted chef's table (a glass-enclosed booth within the kitchen in which dinner is served just once nightly; parties dine on seven courses) and another five-course tasting menu.

Rte. 310 (off Rte. 2), Bay Fortune, PEI C0A 2B0. © **902/687-3745.** Reservations strongly recommended. Main courses C$24–C$32 (US$22–US$29/£12–£16); tasting menu about C$70 (US$63/£35); chef's table about C$95 (US$86/£48). AE, MC, V. Daily 5–9pm. Closed mid-Oct to late May.

ST. PETERS BAY & ENVIRONS

The easternmost sector of Kings County attracts few tourists—other than those speeding through en route to East Point and the goal of a tip-to-tip car crossing of the entire island. Yet it's worth slowing down for—the pastoral landscapes are sublime, and the best vistas are found off the paved roads. It's also an area blessed with a number of appealing bike routes and what may be the island's top golf course. And although this region has few prominent natural landmarks, **St. Peters Bay** ✿, a narrow and attractive inlet that twists eastward from the coast, is a worthy exception. Impatient travelers may grow irritated, wishing for more clearly defined attractions along the way, but a bit of rambling around here is not a bad way to spend an afternoon.

EXPLORING THE AREA

Follow Route 313 along the north shore of St. Peter's Bay to its tip and you'll come to the **Greenwich Dunes** ✿, a stunning area of uniquely wind-carved migrating sand dunes capped with grasses. This region was slated for vacation-home development until 1997, when it was acquired (and thus saved) by Parks Canada and added as an extension to the existing Prince Edward Island National Park. Thank goodness for that.

The little town of **Mount Stewart** (on Rte. 2, just over the county line in Queens County) is located near the confluence of several spurs of the **Confederation Trail,** the excellent island-wide recreation trail that's slowly replacing an abandoned rail line. The Mount Stewart area is home to some of the better-developed and better-maintained segments of this trail.

The trail's popularity and potential didn't pass unnoticed by a father-and-son team, who opened **Trailside Inn, Café & Adventures** ✿ (© **888/704-6595** or 902/676-3130; www.trailside.ca) and set up a bike-rental operation (see below for a review of the restaurant and hotel). Today, they rent a fleet of 80 mountain bikes at inflation-proof

(*Finds* **Golf Along the Gulf**

Hidden away in this quiet part of the island are the **Links at Crowbush Cove** 👀👀👀 (📞 **800/235-8909** or 902/368-5761), considered by many to be the island's best golf course for both its lovely aesthetics and its sturdy challenge. (The course captured five stars from no less than *Golf Digest*.) The 6,900-yard, par-72 course, built in 1994, is located along the Gulf of St. Lawrence; it has 9 water holes and 8 that run along the dunes, making it a true links-style course in the best Scottish tradition. The 11th tee tends to be a bottleneck, as golfers are momentarily distracted from their game by sweeping views up and down the island's coast. Reserved tee times are available for C$75 to C$90 (US$68–US$81/£38–£45) per round, less if you begin in the afternoon; rates include not only unlimited golf (play more than 18 if you have the stamina) but also pull carts, tees, and buckets of practice-range balls. Kids play free after 3pm every day. Crowbush Cove is located west of the village of Morell; take Route 2 to Route 350 and continue driving northwest until you reach the course.

rates of C$15 (US$14/£7.50) per half-day, C$20 (US$18/£10) per full day, and C$80 (US$72/£40) per week. The staff is very helpful with suggestions and directions, and they can arrange for a van shuttle to pick you up at your destination if you'd prefer a one-way trip; among the most popular trips is the northeast ride toward **East Point** (64km/40 miles; see above), along lovely St. Peters Bay, which takes you over several low train trestles retrofitted for bikes.

Greenwich Interpretation Centre 👀   An annex of the island's national park, this interpretive center offers a look at the unique dune formations adjacent to St. Peters Bay. In addition to programs and displays, there are guided tours for individuals and groups. You can also take a cool break by making use of the beach, where supervised swimming is allowed from late June to the end of August. There are also bathrooms, changing facilities, showers, and an observation tower here. A visit here is worth at least 20 minutes of your time to get oriented before plunging into the area.

Rte. 313, Greenwich, Prince Edward Island National Park. 📞 **902/961-2514**. Call for rates. Late May to Oct daily, summer 9am–7pm, spring and fall 10am–4pm.

WHERE TO STAY & DINE
Trailside Inn Café & Adventures   The Trailside Inn is housed in a 1937 grocery store that's been converted to an inn, cafe, and outdoor adventure center (see "Exploring the Area," above, regarding bike rentals). There's nothing fancy here, but the four rooms (each with private bathroom) are comfortable and simply furnished, and have nice touches like radiant heat under the hardwood floors. Few guests spend much time lingering in their rooms. The clientele consist primarily of bicyclists, who migrate here for its location smack on the Confederation Trail, but everyone benefits from the live local music (there are thrice-weekly shows of Celtic or gospel music).

The funky, informal cafe on the first floor is a fine spot for hanging out, especially when there's live music. Dinner and entertainment packages invariably sell out; reservations are strongly suggested. The cafe serves lunch and dinner daily in summer. The menu is basic, but everything is homemade and tasty. Soups and chowders are perfect for drizzly or blustery days; there's also a smoked-salmon plate, lobster rolls, crepes, poached Digby scallops, pizza, and a dish of chicken with vegetables.

109 Main St., Mount Stewart, PEI C0A 1T0. (✆ 888/704-6595 or 902/676-3130. www.trailside.ca. 4 units. C$80 (US$72/£40) double, C$450 (US$405/£225) weekly. MC, V. Closed late Sept to mid-June. **Amenities:** Restaurant, bike rentals. *In room:* TV, no phone.

7 Prince County

Prince County encompasses the western end of PEI and offers a varied mix of lush agricultural land, rugged coastline, and unpopulated sandy beaches. With a few exceptions, this region is a bit more ragged around the edges in a working-farm, working-waterfront kind of way. It lacks the pristine-village charm or polish of Kings County or much of Queens County.

Within this unrefined landscape, however, you'll find pockets of considerable charm, such as the village of Victoria on the south coast at the county line and in Tyne Valley near the north coast, which is reminiscent of a Cotswold hamlet.

In addition, the **Confederation Trail** offers quiet access to the rolling countryside throughout much of northwest Prince County. Several provincial parks here rank among the most inviting on the island.

ESSENTIALS
GETTING THERE   Route 2 is the main highway connecting Prince County with the rest of the island. Smaller feeder roads typically lead you to or from Route 2. The Confederation Bridge from the mainland connects to Prince County at Borden Point, southeast of Summerside.

VISITOR INFORMATION   The best source of travel information for the county is **Gateway Village** (✆ **902/437-8570**) at the end of the Confederation Bridge. It's open daily year-round.

VICTORIA 🏵🏵
The town of Victoria—located a short detour off Route 1 between the Confederation Bridge and Charlottetown—is a tiny and unusually scenic village that has attracted a number of artists, boutique owners, and craftspeople. The village is perfect for strolling—parking is near the wharf and off the streets, keeping the narrow lanes free for foot traffic. Wander the short, shady lanes while admiring the architecture, much of which is in elemental farmhouse style, clad in clapboard or shingle and constructed with sharply creased gables. (Some elaborate Victorians break the mold.) What makes the place so singular is that the village, which was first settled in 1767, has utterly escaped the creeping sprawl that has plagued so many otherwise attractive places. The entire village consists of 4 square blocks, which are surrounded by potato fields and the Northumberland Strait. It's not hard to imagine that the village looked much the same a century ago.

EXPLORING VICTORIA
The **Victoria Seaport Museum** (no phone) is located inside the shingled, square **lighthouse** near the town parking lot. (You can't miss it.) You'll find a rustic local history museum with the usual assortment of artifacts from the past century or so. In summer, it's open most afternoons; admission is by donation.

In the middle of town is the well-regarded **Victoria Playhouse** (✆ **902/658-2025**). Built in 1913 as a community hall, the building has a unique raked stage (it drops 18cm/

7 in. over 6.5m/21 ft.) to create the illusion of space, four beautiful stained-glass lamps, and a proscenium arch (also unusual for a community hall). Plays staged here from late June through September attract folks out from Charlottetown for the night. It's hard to say what is more enjoyable: the high quality of the acting or the wonderful big-night-out air of a professional play in a small town where nothing else is going on. There's also a Monday-night concert series, with performers offering up everything from traditional folk to Latin jazz. Most tickets are C$24 (US$22/£12) adults, C$22 (US$20/£11) seniors, and C$18 (US$16/£9) students, though a few performances are priced higher; matinees cost about C$18 (US$16/£9).

Among the two dozen or so businesses in the village, the most intriguing is **Island Chocolates** (© **902/658-2320**), where delicious Belgian-style chocolates are made; the shop is open daily or nearly so from June through September. You'll also find a quilt maker, a candle maker, a used-book store, art galleries, and an antiques shop.

WHERE TO STAY

Orient Hotel ⚐ The Orient has been a Victoria mainstay for years—a 1926 guide notes that the inn had 20 rooms at C$2.50 (US$2.25/£1.25) per night (of course, back then a trip to the bathroom required a walk to the carriage house). It has been modernized in recent years (all rooms now have private bathrooms), but it retains much of its antique charm. The century-old building with its yellow shingles and maroon trim is at the edge of the village overlooking fields lurid with purple blooms in late summer. Rooms are painted in warm pastel tones and furnished with flea-market antiques; most have good water views. Some of the updating diminished the charm a bit, but the place has a friendly low-key demeanor, much like the village itself; the enthusiastic owners have also added a combination television/games room set up for cribbage and crokinole (an old-fashioned Maritime game), and ceilidhs (Celtic folk dances) have been known to pop up, too.

Mrs. Proffit's Tea Shop, on the first floor, serves lunch and afternoon tea and is gaining a reputation for its scones. The light lunches here are appropriate for a tearoom—think tea sandwiches, lobster rolls, soups, and salads.

34 Main St. (P.O. Box 55), Victoria, PEI C0A 2G0. © **800/565-6743** or 902/658-2503. 8 units. C$80–C$150 (US$72–US$135/£40–£75) double. Rates include full breakfast. Dinner and theater packages available. MC, V. Closed mid-Oct to mid-May. Not suitable for children under 12. **Amenities:** Tearoom. *In room:* TV.

WHERE TO DINE

Landmark Café CAFE Located across from the Victoria Playhouse, the Landmark Café occupies a small, cozy storefront teeming with shelves filled with crockery, pots, jars, and more, some of which is for sale. But the effect is more funky than Ye Olde Quainte, and the limited menu is inviting. Daily offerings might include steamed mussels, vine leaves with feta cheese, salads, lasagna, a meat pie, or a salmon steamed in tarragon.

12 Main St. © **902/658-2286.** Reservations recommended. Sandwiches around C$5.50 (US$4.95/£2.75); main courses C$11–C$16 (US$10–US$14/£5.50–£8). MC, V. Daily 11am–9:30pm. Closed mid-Sept to late June.

TYNE VALLEY ⚐

The village of Tyne Valley is just off Malpeque Bay and is one of the most attractive and pastoral areas in all of western PEI. There's little to do here but much to admire. Verdant barley and potato fields surround a village of gingerbreadlike homes, and azure inlets encroach on the view from afar; these are the arms of the bay, world-famous for its succulent Malpeque oysters. A former 19th-century shipbuilding center, the village now attracts artisans and others in search of a quiet lifestyle within sight of gorgeous scenery. A handful of good restaurants, inns, and shops here cater to visitors.

EXPLORING TYNE VALLEY

Just north of the village on Route 12 is lovely **Green Park Provincial Park** ✿ (✆ **902/831-7912**), open from mid-June through early September. Once the site of an active shipyard, the 88-hectare (217-acre) park is now a lush riverside destination with emerald lawns and leafy trees, and it has the feel of a turn-of-the-20th-century estate, which, in fact, it was. In the heart of the park is the extravagant 1865 ginger-bread mansion once owned by James Yeo, a merchant, shipbuilder, and landowner who in his time was the island's wealthiest and most powerful man.

The historic Yeo House and the **Green Park Shipbuilding Museum** (✆ **902/ 831-7947**), open June through September, are now the park's centerpieces. Managed by the Prince Edward Island Museum and Heritage Foundation, exhibits in two buildings provide a good view of the prosperous life of a shipbuilder and the golden age of PEI shipbuilding. The museum and house are open daily from mid-June through summer, 9am to 5:30pm, closing for the season around Labor Day. Admission is C$5 (US$4.50/£2.50) plus tax for adults, C$3.50 (US$3.15/£1.75) students, C$12 (US$11/£6) families, and free for children under 12.

Frequent musical and stage performances are held summers at the 125-seat **Britannia Hall Theatre** (✆ **902/831-2191**), on Route 178. Prices are reasonable, usually under C$10 (US$9/£5) for both plays and concerts. Call for information on upcoming shows.

When leaving the area, consider taking the highly scenic drive along the bay on Route 12 from Tyne Valley to MacDougall.

WHERE TO STAY

Green Park Provincial Park ✿✿ (✆ **902/831-7912**) may be the most gracious and lovely park on the island, and it offers camping on 58 grassy sites overlooking an arm of Malpeque Bay for about C$19 to C$25 (US$17–US$23/£8.50–£23) per night.

Caernarvon Cottages, B&B, and Gardens _Kids_   The sense of quiet and the views over Malpeque Bay across the road are the lure at this attractive, well-maintained cottage complex on 2 hectares (5 acres) a few minutes' drive from Tyne Valley. The four modern (ca. 1990) pine cottages are furnished simply but comfortably. Each has two bedrooms and a sleeping loft, an outdoor gas barbecue, a cathedral ceiling, and a porch with a bay view. This is a good choice if you're looking to get away, but it's also popular with families—there's a playground out back—so it may not be the best option for a romantic escape, even with the pretty 10m (33-ft.) high gazebo on the lawn just steps from the bay. (The gazebo is encircled by three large flower beds filled with peonies, lilies, and hardy roses.) Three simply furnished rooms are available in the main house; a full breakfast is included in those rates.

4697 Hwy. 12 (Richmond R.R. 1), Bayside, PEI, C0B 1Y0. ✆ **800/514-9170** or 902/854-3418. www.cottagelink.com/caernarvon. 7 units. Main inn C$120 (US$108/£60) double; cottages C$110 (US$99/£55) double, C$770 (US$693/£385) weekly for two. Inn rates include full breakfast. V. Cottages closed mid-Sept to mid-June. Pets in cottages only. _In room:_ TV/VCR (some units), kitchenette (some units), hair dryer, iron, no phone.

The Doctor's Inn ✿ _Value_   A stay at the Doctor's Inn is a bit like visiting relatives you didn't know you had. Upstairs in this handsome in-town farmhouse are just two guest rooms, which share a bathroom. (Note that you could rent both for less than the cost of a room at many other PEI inns.) There's an upstairs sitting area, and extensive organic gardens out back to peruse. It's a pleasant retreat, and innkeepers Jean and Paul Offer do a fine job of making guests feel relaxed and at home. (There's also a cottage available for rent.) The Offers serve up one of Atlantic Canada's most memorable dining experiences in their **dining room** ★★ (reservations by prior arrangement for up to six diners): You gather for appetizers and wine in a sitting room, then move to the large oval dining-room table for extraordinary salads featuring produce from the gardens. Entrees are cooked on the wood stove in an old-fashioned kitchen; look for scallops, arctic char, salmon, veal, and fresh-baked desserts. Reservations are requested at least 24 hours in advance; dinner is served as a four-course meal with wine for C$45 to C$55 (US$41–US$50/£23–£28) per person.

Rte. 167, Tyne Valley, PEI C0B 2C0. © **902/831-3057.** www.peisland.com/doctorsinn. 2 units, both with private bathroom. C$60 (US$54/£30) double; cottage C$360–C$450 (US$324–US$405/£180–£203) weekly. All rates include breakfast. MC, V. "Well-mannered" pets allowed. **Amenities:** Dining room. *In room:* No phone.

WHERE TO DINE

Also see the "The Doctor's Inn," above, for fine dining.

The Shipwright's Café REGIONAL   This locally popular restaurant moved to the village of Margate in the summer of 2001. It's elegant yet informal, and you'd be comfortable here in either neat jeans or predinner sport clothes. Expect good service, a modest but useful wine list, and salads with organic greens from the Offers just down the street (see The Doctor's Inn, in "Where to Stay," above). Justly popular dishes include local oysters broiled with spinach and cheese, island-raised lamb, Atlantic salmon, and a seafood chowder rich with plenty of those famous plump PEI mussels.

11869 Rte. 6 (at junction of Rte. 33), Margate, PEI C0B 1M0. © **902/836-3403.** Reservations recommended in summer. Lunch C$9.95–C$17 (US$8.95–US$15/£5–£8.50); dinner C$15–C$20 (US$14–US$18/£7.50–£10), more for lobster. MC, V. June–Sept daily 11:30am–8:30pm. Closed Oct–May.

Newfoundland & Labrador

Newfoundland and Labrador are the sorts of places that instantly cue strong sensations in the intrepid (or even the *imagines*-oneself-to-be-intrepid) traveler unfurling his or her first maps of the region: images of remote, fly-in-only harbors, isolated lakes, and towering cliffs; ideas about icebergs floating by with imagined polar bears decamping atop them; salty shanty tales of shipwreck, heartache, and whales that got away. Lumbering moose. Verified Viking ruins. And, oh, the extraordinary places and names covering those maps: Jerry's Nose, Snook's Arm, Leading Tickles, Heart's Delight, Happy Adventure, Chapel Island, Mistaken Point, Misery Hill, Breakheart Point, and Shuffle Board.

This might be the Eastern Seaboard's last best place. (These two distinct geographic areas are administered as one province; thus, the phrase "Newfoundland and Labrador" sometimes refers to a single province of Canada, sometimes to the two physically separate places.) Wild, windswept, and secluded, the province often reveals a powerful paradox. Although the landscape is as rocky and raw as expected—at times it looks as though the glaciers had only receded a year or two ago, instead of a hundred thousand—residents here display a warmth that puts visitors to shame even as it makes them feel right at home.

Tourists only recently started arriving here in numbers, and longtime residents more often than not love to chat up the place, offering advice and curious to hear outsiders' impressions. Even the sort of traveler who's usually reluctant to engage a stranger is likely to drop that hesitation after an encounter or two here.

An excursion to The Rock, as the island of Newfoundland is often called in Canada, can be experienced on many levels—not only for, say, the extraordinary northern landscape and curious northern lights but also for the rich history that catches many first-time visitors off guard. This is where European civilization made landfall in the New World—twice. First by Vikings, then later by fishermen and settlers in the wake of John Cabot's arrival in 1497.

You'll therefore find traces of North America's original history at almost every turn here. Although other parts of eastern North America—Savannah, Boston, New Orleans, and Montréal leap to mind—can claim equally historic lineages, there are few other places in the New World where one feels so strongly that not a whole lot has transpired *since* those first settlers sailed into harbor centuries ago. History isn't buried here; it's right on the surface.

And Mother Nature is never far away; witness the changing weather, huge cliffs, and fishing boats braving brawny winds and waves. (Locals hardly seem to notice the climate.)

At the very least, learn how to pronounce "Newfoundland" like a local: Say "new-fun-*land*" quickly. (There's emphasis on the final syllable, but it's subtle.) Here's a trick: Memorize the rhyme, "You just won't understand, till you've been to Newfound*land*." There. Easy, wasn't it?

1 Exploring Newfoundland & Labrador

Don't let maps of the Atlantic Provinces fool you. Newfoundland (and sometimes Labrador) is commonly published as an inset map alongside Nova Scotia, Prince Edward Island, and New Brunswick, which makes it look smaller than the aforementioned. But carefully check out the scale. Whereas an inch might equal 30km (19 miles) in Nova Scotia, it might be 60 or 70km (37 or 43 miles) in Newfoundland. This is a big place, and the amount of time to travel anywhere on the island goes up accordingly. In fact, the island has about the same landmass as Pennsylvania (which is pretty decent-sized), and even *that's* misleading because it's all twisted and pulled as though made of taffy, and thus seems bigger, higher, longer, and more time-consuming when you're actually traveling it from one end to another. An example: The peninsula that extends northward along the west coast takes 8 to 9 hours to drive from Port aux Basques (where the ferry from Nova Scotia docks) to the tip at St. Anthony's—no Sunday drive, and one that requires planning and decision-making beforehand.

So you need to extend your time here. A weekend in this province isn't even in the realm of the possible. A couple of weeks is enough for a bare-bones tour of the island, though you'll still be frustrated by all that gets left out. You're better off selecting a few regions and focusing on those.

For those arriving by ferry, try this itinerary: If you've got less than a week, you should come and go via Port aux Basques and focus on Gros Morne National Park, which is usually the highlight of a stay here, especially for outdoor-oriented travelers. If you're planning on at least 2 weeks, arrive on and leave The Rock from opposite ports (see below), completing a traverse of the island.

For those arriving by air, St. John's is well situated for exploring the wonderful Avalon Peninsula, and the intriguing Bonavista Peninsula isn't too distant. If you have your heart set on venturing to Gros Morne or beyond, though, plan to spend a couple of weeks more—or be prepared to spend some serious hours behind the wheel. It's about 7 to 8 hours driving from St. John's to the national park. The best option in that case would be to fly in to St. John's and depart via Deer Lake if you can arrange it.

ESSENTIALS

WEATHER & TIME   The weather in Newfoundland can charitably be called "mercurial." You might well experience all four seasons during a weeklong trip to the place—from decently warm and sunny days (the average high temperature in summer is about 70°F/21°C) to downright frigid ones (it can dip into the range of 40°F/4°C or lower on summer evenings). If you have a rain suit, bring it. When the rain pairs up with the high winds, the results can be, well, less than comforting. If you have sweaters, bring a few. Shorts? Only for hiking, mate.

Note that Newfoundland keeps its own clock. The "Newfoundland time zone" is a half-hour ahead of Atlantic time (which the rest of the Atlantic provinces keep) and 1½ hours ahead of Eastern Standard (that is, New York) time.

It's All in a Name

The official name of this province is "Newfoundland and Labrador." But if I kept writing that out, this book would be twice as long (and heavy). So I'm going to abbreviate it to just "Newfoundland" for most purposes in this chapter. Labradoreans, bear with us. We know you're there.

> ### *Tips* Sailing by Night
>
> You may find it more convenient to take an **overnight ferry** from North Sydney to Port aux Basques; the ferry sails most nights of the week, departing around midnight and arriving early in the morning. Of course, you'll need to pay extra for your bunk bed or private cabin—but you'll also wake up refreshed for the long drive ahead. In 2007, dormitory-style bunks cost C$16 (US$14/£8) per person and private cabins (which sleep four passengers) cost C$99 (US$89/£50). Check with Marine Atlantic ferries for the latest details and fares of the sleeper service.

VISITOR INFORMATION   Visitor information centers aren't as numerous or well organized in Newfoundland as they are in Nova Scotia or Prince Edward Island, where every small community has a place to stock up on truckloads of pretty color brochures. In Newfoundland, you're better off stocking up on maps and information either in St. John's or just after you disembark from the ferries, where excellent centers are maintained.

The Newfoundland and Labrador Travel Guide, published by the province's department of tourism, is hefty and helpful, with listings of all attractions and accommodations. Request a free copy before arriving by calling © **800/563-6353.** You can also request it by e-mail (tourisminfo@mail.gov.nf.ca) or regular mail (P.O. Box 8700, St. John's, NL A1B 4J6). The guide is available on the ferries and at the province's information centers.

Newfoundland is also better wired than you might expect when it comes to the Internet, and many residents and businesses maintain websites—a big help when trying to cobble together your travel plans.

GETTING THERE   Air transportation to Newfoundland is typically through Gander or St. John's, although scheduled flights are also available to Deer Lake and St. Anthony. Flights originate in Montréal, Toronto, Halifax, and London, England. Airlines serving the island include **Air Canada** (© **888/AIR-CANA;** www.aircanada.com), **Air Labrador** (© **800/563-3042;** www.airlabrador.com), and **Provincial Airlines** (© **800/563-2800** or 709/576-1666; www.provincialairlines.ca). Flight time from Toronto to St. John's is about 3 hours. Calgary-based **WestJet** (© **888/937-8538;** www.westjet.com) also connects St. John's with Halifax and Toronto.

Marine Atlantic (© **800/341-7981;** www.marine-atlantic.ca) operates a year-round ferry service from North Sydney, Nova Scotia, to Port aux Basques, with as many as four sailings each way daily during the peak summer season. The crossing is about 5 hours; one-way fares are C$28 (US$25/£14) adults, plus C$78 (US$70/£39) for an automobile. A seasonal ferry (mid-June through late Sept) also connects North Sydney with Argentia on the southwest tip of the Avalon Peninsula. Remember that this crossing is offered only three times per week, in summer only, and takes 14 to 15 hours. The one-way fare is C$77 (US$69/£39) adults, C$160 (US$144/£80) for regular-size vehicles. On both ferries, children 5 to 12 years old ride for half-price, and the ride's free for children under 5.

Map legend:
- Trans-Canada Highway
- Ferry

QUÉBEC

Red Bay
Str. of Belle I.
L'Anse aux Meadows
Blanc-Sablon
430
St. Anthony
St. Barbe
432
Roddickton
Port au Choix
Northern Peninsula
Englee

ATLANTIC OCEAN

GULF OF ST. LAWRENCE
430
Horse Is.
Baie Verte
La Scie
GROS MORNE N.P.
Baie Verte Pen.
Notre Dame Bay
Fogo I.
Rocky Harbour
410
Twillingate
Woody Point
Springdale
Musgrave Harbour
Bottle Cove
Deer Lake
Botwood
Lewisporte
330
Wesleyville
331
Corner Brook
1
Grand L.
Badger
Gander
Hare Bay
Port au Port Pen.
Grand Falls-Windsor
Red Indian L.
Gambo
Bonavista
Stephenville
TERRA NOVA N.P.
Bonavista Pen.
235
Catalina
St. George's Bay
St. George's
Victoria L.
360
Trinity
230
Shoal Harbour
Baccalieu I.
Maelpaeg Res.
70
Heart's Content
Jeddore L.
1
Goobies
480
Milltown
210
Carbonear
Torbay
St. John's
Port aux Basques
Burgeo
Harbour Grace
Brigus
Conception Bay South
Rose Blanche
Harbour Breton
Fortune Bay
Argentia
Witless Bay
Marystown
Placentia
Avalon Pen.
AVALON W.R.
Ferryland
Fortune
Placentia Bay
100
Miquelon
Burin Pen.
Burin
90
10
ST. PIERRE AND MIQUELON (France)
220
St. Lawrence
St-Pierre
Trepassey
To Nova Scotia

0 — 50 mi
0 — 50 km

N

If you're traveling between the two landmasses, a much shorter ride on the MV *Apollo* connects Blanc-Sablon, Labrador, with St. Barbe, Newfoundland. The one-way trip takes 20 minutes and costs C$7.50 (US$6.75/£3.75) for adults, C$6 (US$5.40/£3) for students, and C$23 (US$21/£12) for autos. Call ☎ **866/535-2567** for more information.

For all ferries, advance reservations are strongly advised during the peak travel season. The terminals all have snack bars, restrooms with free showers, television lounges, and up-to-date facilities.

GETTING AROUND   To explore the countryside, you'll almost certainly need a car (bus service is sporadic). Major rental companies with fleets in St. John's include **Avis** (☎ **800/879-2847** or 709/722-6620), **Dollar** (☎ **800/800-4000** or 709/726-1791), **Hertz** (☎ **800/263-0600** or 709/722-4333), **Thrifty** (☎ **800/367-2277** or 709/722-6000), and **Rent-A-Wreck** (☎ **800/239-7990** or 709/753-2277). Many of these car-rental chains, as well as some small independent outfits, rent cars in other gateway communities in the province such as Corner Brook, Deer Lake, Happy Valley–Goose Bay, and Port aux Basques; consult the visitor guide or call the rental chains directly for details about some of these other locations.

Sock away some extra cash for gasoline when traveling the island, however: The price of fuel on Newfoundland tends to be a bit higher than in other Atlantic Provinces.

2 The Great Outdoors

BIKING   Bike touring in Newfoundland is not for the out-of-shape. It's not that the hills here are necessarily brutal (though many are). It's the *weather* that can be downright demoralizing. Expect more than a handful of blustery days, complete with horizontal rains that seem to swirl from every direction and can bring forward-pedaling progress to a standstill. The happiest bike tourists seem to be those who allow themselves frequent stays in motels or inns, where they can find hot showers and places to dry their gear.

Freewheeling Adventures, P.O. Box 100, Norris Point, NL A0K 3V0 (✆ **800/ 672-0775** or 902/857-3612; www.freewheeling.ca), runs van-supported trips based in hotels and B&Bs. Its Viking Tour of the northern coast of Newfoundland is a week of pure pleasure; it costs C$2,000 to C$2,400 (US$1,800–US$2,160/£1,000–£1,200), depending on whether you use their guides or make up your own itinerary. Lodging is included in both plans, but the full monty includes all your meals, equipment rental, van transfers, a bonus fjord boat trip, and a whale/iceberg-watching boat trip in the package. Needless to say, go for that one. Freewheeling offers a similar 8-day tour of the Avalon Peninsula (very near St. John's) as well.

Aspenwood Tours, P.O. Box 622, Springdale, NL A0J 1T0 (✆ **709/673-4255**), arranges mountain-biking trips in and around the central sections of Newfoundland.

BIRD-WATCHING   If you're from a temperate climate, bird-watching doesn't get much better than in Newfoundland and Labrador—the province is home to some of the most concentrated bird populations on the continent (and in the world). Seabirds typically attract the most attention, and eastern Newfoundland and the Avalon Peninsula are especially rich in bird life. Just south of St. John's, offshore from Route 10, near Deer Lake, is **Witless Bay Ecological Reserve** (✆ **709/635-4520**), a cluster of several islands hosting the largest colony of breeding puffins and kittiwakes in the western Atlantic. On the southern Avalon Peninsula, **Cape St. Mary's** features a remarkable sea stack that's home to a cacophonous colony of northern gannets. (See the section on the Avalon Peninsula later in this chapter.)

CAMPING   In addition to the two national parks, Newfoundland maintains a number of provincial parks open for car camping. (About a dozen of these were "privatized" in 1997 and are now run as commercial enterprises, although many still appear on maps as provincial parks.) These are all listed in the provincial travel guide, where you'll also find information about most of the province's private campgrounds.

CANOEING   A glance at a map shows that rivers and lakes abound in Newfoundland and Labrador. Canoe trips can range from placid puttering around a pond near St. John's to world-class descents of Labrador rivers hundreds of miles long. The Department of Tourism produces a free brochure outlining several canoe trips; call ✆ **800/563-6353.** A popular guide to provincial canoeing is sold in bookstores around the province.

FISHING   Newfoundland and Labrador are legendary among serious anglers, especially those stalking the cagey Atlantic salmon, which can weigh up to 18kg (40 lbs.). Other prized species include landlocked salmon, lake trout, brook trout, and northern pike. More than 100 fishing-guide services on the island and mainland can provide everything from simple advice to complete packages that include bush-plane transportation, lodging, and personal guides. One fishing license is needed for Atlantic salmon and one for other fish, so be sure to read the current *Newfoundland &*

Pit Stop: "Gravel-Pit" Camping on The Rock

Campgrounds can be in short supply in remote areas of Newfoundland, and if you're properly equipped, you might want to try out a traditional activity known as "gravel-pit camping" (which the official tourism office officially discourages). Basically, this means pulling over to the side of the road—typically in a gravel pit or parking lot—and spending the night away from organized campgrounds. (Always ask permission first.) You'll see gravel-pit campers from time to time around the island, often in beautiful and dramatic spots overlooking coves or ponds. So long as you don't pitch your tent or park your RV right in someone's driveway, you usually won't be hassled—and you might be entertained by the curious local folks who show up to say hello and suss out the passers-through.

Labrador Hunting and Fishing Guide closely for current regulations. It's available at most visitor centers, or by calling © **800/563-6353.** To request it by mail, write the provincial tourism office at P.O. Box 8700, St. John's, NL A1B 4J6.

HIKING & WALKING   Newfoundland has an abundance of trails, but you'll have to work a bit harder to find them here than in the provinces to the south. The most obvious hiking trails tend to be centered around national parks and historic sites, where they are often fairly short—good for a half-day's hike, rarely more. But Newfoundland has hundreds of trails, many along the coast leading to abandoned communities. Some places are finally realizing the recreational potential for these trails, and are now publishing maps and brochures directing you to them. The Bonavista Peninsula and the Eastport Peninsula, both on Newfoundland's east coast, are two areas that are attracting attention for world-class trails that were all but overlooked until recently.

The best-maintained trails are at **Gros Morne National Park** ⋒⋒⋒, which has around 100km (62 miles) of trails. In addition to these, there's also off-track hiking on the dramatic Long Range for backpackers equipped to set out for a couple of days. Ask at the park visitor center for more information.

SEA KAYAKING   With all its protected bays and inlets, Newfoundland is ideal for exploring by sea kayak. But there's a catch: the super-frigid water. There's a reason you'll see icebergs offshore: It's called the Labrador Current. You'll need to be well prepared in the event you end up in the drink, because you won't have a lot of time for a rescue before the cold gets you in its grip. Experts traveling with their own gear can pick and choose their destinations; the area northeast of **Terra Nova National Park,** with its archipelago centering around St. Brendan's Island, is one great choice.

Novices should stick to guided tours. The aforementioned **Aspenwood** (© **709/ 673-4255**) in Springdale does half- and full-day guided paddles and rentals, in addition to its mountain-biking options; **Eastern Edge Kayak Adventures** (© **866/782-5925** or 709/773-2201) offers tours and clinics of 1 day and up, mostly on the Avalon Peninsula.

Coastal Safari (© **877/888-3020** or 709/579-3977; www.coastalsafari.com), based in St. John's, is a similar outfitter offering extended paddling tours from May through the end of August. Its eponymous 8-day "coastal safari" begins with a pickup from the St. John's airport on a Saturday, then includes 5 days' paddling in and out of an Avalon Peninsula base camp, plus several overnights in the St. John's area and Harbour Mille. All kayaks, transport, food (and wine, if you wish), camping gear, and even snorkels are included in this package. You sleep in tents with comfortable support pads or bed-and-breakfast inns. Contact Coastal for latest prices and schedules.

At **Terra Nova National Park,** 2-hour sea kayak tours leave from the Marine Inter-pretation Centre to explore protected Newman's Cove. (See the "Terra Nova National Park" section, later in this chapter.)

3 Southwestern Newfoundland

For most travelers arriving by ferry, this region is their first introduction to The Rock. It's like starting a symphony without a prelude, jumping right to the crescendo: There's instant drama in the brawny, verdant Long Range Mountains that run paral-lel to the Trans-Canada Highway en route to Corner Brook. Then come the towering seaside cliffs of the Port au Port Peninsula and intriguing coastal villages just waiting for your exploration. This is a polar-opposite travel experience to, say, flying into Charlottetown and lazing along the backroads of Prince Edward Island.

PORT AUX BASQUES

Port aux Basques is a major gateway for travelers arriving in Newfoundland, with fer-ries connecting the town to Nova Scotia year-round. It's a good way station for those arriving late on a ferry or departing early in the morning; otherwise, it can comfort-ably be viewed in a couple of hours while either coming or going, or even skipped over altogether en route to much greater scenic treasures.

This appealing harborside village is situated on treeless emerald hills that define the terrain around the harbor. Downtown consists of bright boxy homes set on the hills around a compact commercial zone. A narrow boardwalk snakes along the water's edge and links the ferry terminal with the town; it's worth a walk if you've got an hour to kill, especially at sunset, which brings out the contours of the surrounding hills. At the edge of town are a tiny mall and newer residential neighborhoods. The town also has a one-screen movie theater and a few family-style restaurants.

ESSENTIALS

GETTING THERE Port aux Basques is commonly reached via ferry from Nova Scotia. See "Exploring Newfoundland & Labrador," earlier, for ferry information. The Trans-Canada Highway (Rte. 1) links the major communities of southwestern Canada. Port aux Basques is 874km (543 miles) from St. John's via the Trans-Canada Highway.

VISITOR INFORMATION In Port aux Basques, the **Provincial Interpretation and Information Centre** (© 709/695-2262) is located on the Trans-Canada High-way about 3km (2 miles) from the ferry terminal. You can't miss it: It's the modern, ecclesiastical-looking building on the right. Inside are displays to orient you to the island's regions and racks aflutter with great forests of brochures. It's open from mid-May to the middle of October daily from 6am to 11pm.

EXPLORING PORT AUX BASQUES

The Gulf Museum, 118 Main St. (© **709/695-7604**), across from the Town Hall, has a quirky assortment of artifacts related to local history. The museum's centerpiece is a Portuguese astrolabe dating from 1628, which was recovered from local waters in

1981. Also intriguing is a display about the *Caribou,* a ferry torpedoed by a German U-boat in 1942; 137 people died in the tragedy. The museum is open daily in summer from 9am to 7pm; admission is C$3.50 (US$3.15/£1.75) adults, C$1 (US90¢/ 50p) children, C$5 (US$4.50/£2.50) families.

On the way out of town you'll pass the **Port aux Basques Railway Heritage Centre,** Route 1 (© **709/695-2646**), dedicated to the memory of the Newfie Bullet, a much-maligned but now much-reminisced-about passenger train that ran between Port aux Basques and St. John's from 1898 to 1969. (The highway across the island opened in 1966, dooming the train.) The train required 27 hours to make the trip (going a respectable average speed of 48kmph/30 mph), and during a tour of several restored rail cars you'll learn how the train made the run through deep snows of winter, how the passengers slept at night (very cozily, it turns out), and what life aboard the mail car and caboose was like. Tours given by railway-costumed staff last 15 minutes and cost C$2 (US$1.80/£1) for adults, free for students, C$5 (US$4.50/£2.50) families. It's a good quick pit stop for rail enthusiasts or those with kids. The museum is open daily from mid-June through mid-September, 9am to 9pm.

Departing from the edge of Railway Heritage Centre is the **T'Railway** ✻, a coast-to-coast, nearly 900km (559-mile) pathway being converted from the old train line. It's used by pedestrians, bikers, and ATVers, and in this stretch it runs through marsh and along the ocean to Cheeseman Park (see below) and beyond. It's a good spot to get your mountain bike limbered up for further adventures.

J. T. Cheeseman Provincial Park ✻ (© **709/695-2222**) is 15km (9⅓ miles) west of town on Route 1 (confusingly, you have to follow the highway marked "Rte. 1 East" to get there). Much of the park lies along sandy dunes, which are home to the **piping plover,** an endangered species; these plucky birds scratch shallow nests out of the sand but are very vulnerable to beach walkers. Tread lightly. An observation platform offers a view of the plover's habitat; bring binoculars and patience (they're present from early May to mid-Aug). Swim at the park's pretty Cape Ray Beach if you dare (it's chilly and unsupervised by any lifeguards), or just stroll its length, beachcombing the mussels, sea urchins, and other goodies fetching up in the wake of the tide.

The park also maintains about 100 campsites costing C$13 (US$12/£6.50) per night if you want to stay. One bonus: You're right alongside a section of the T'Railway, which is good for walking or mountain biking. Admission to the park is C$5 (US$4.50/£2.50) per car.

WHERE TO STAY

About a half-dozen hotels and B&Bs offer no-frills shelter to travelers at Port aux Basques. The two largest are **Hotel Port aux Basques,** Route 1 (© **877/695-2171** or 709/695-2171), and **St. Christopher's Hotel,** Caribou Road (© **800/563-4779** or 709/695-3500). Both might be described as "budget modern," with clean, basic rooms in architecturally undistinguished buildings. I'd give St. Christopher's the edge since it's located on a high bluff with views of the town and the harbor. Both have around 50 rooms and charge C$75 to C$150 (US$68–US$135/£38–£75) for a double.

WHERE TO DINE

Dining opportunities are limited. Both hotels mentioned above have dining rooms serving basic, filling meals. A short walk from the ferry terminal on the boardwalk is the **Harbour Restaurant,** at easy-to-remember 1 Main St. (© **709/695-3238**). It's a family-style restaurant that serves budget-friendly meals with entrees around C$5 to C$14

(US$4.50–US$13/£2.50–£7), most C$10 (US$9/£5) or less. Expect fried fish, fried chicken, fish cakes, sandwiches, and the like. Most tables have good views of the harbor.

CORNER BROOK

Corner Brook is Newfoundland's second-largest city. Like St. John's, it's also dramatically sited—in this case, on the banks of the glimmering Humber River, which winds down through verdant mountains from beyond Deer Lake, then turns the corner to flow into Humber Arm. The hills on the south shore of the Humber are nearly as tall as those in **Gros Morne National Park,** making a great backdrop for the town, which has gradually expanded up the shoulders of the hills.

This is a young city with a long history. The area was first explored and charted in 1767 by Capt. James Cook, who spent 23 days mapping the islands at the mouth of the bay. But it wasn't until early in the 20th century that the city started to take its present shape. Copper mines and the railroad brought in workers; the paper mill, which still dominates downtown, was constructed in the early 1920s. By 1945 it was the largest paper mill in the world.

The city has grown beyond its stature as a mill town and has a more vibrant feel than other spots anchored by heavy industry. This is no doubt aided in large part by the energy from two institutions of higher learning: **Sir Wilfred Grenfell College of Memorial University of Newfoundland** and the **College of the North Atlantic.** You'll also find well-developed services and suppliers, including grocery stores, banks, hotels, and restaurants. This is your last chance to stock up and indulge if you're headed to Gros Morne—from here on out, you'll be dependent on small grocery stores and mom-and-pop restaurants.

ESSENTIALS

GETTING THERE   Corner Brook is on the Trans-Canada Highway 217km (135 miles) north of Port aux Basque. Air access is via **Deer Lake Regional Airport** (© 709/635-3601; www.deerlakeairport.com), call sign "YDF," with incoming flights from Provincial, Air Labrador, WestJet, and Air Canada.

VISITOR INFORMATION   Corner Brook maintains a tourism information kiosk just off the Trans-Canada Highway, uphill at the intersection of West Valley Road and Confederation Drive (near the Mamateek Inn). It's usually open daily from mid-June to September, and on weekdays during spring and fall. Check the city's very good tourism website, **www.cornerbrook.com**, before coming.

EXPLORING CORNER BROOK

Downtown Corner Brook looks promising on your approach—it's located on the hill-flanked Humber Arm, a well-protected ocean inlet and famed salmon-fishing area. With the residential areas stacked neatly on the hills around the commercial center in the valley, it's got great topographical interest. Alas, the actual city center is likely to disappoint sightseers—it consists mostly of a large paper mill and two small malls. The enclosed malls offer basic goods but little charm; the mill offers an, er, interesting olfactory experience when the wind is blowing right.

It's still worth a quick detour into town, though: Tree-lined **West Street** is fun to explore (you'll find coffee shops, restaurants, and pharmacies), while **Broadway** has a frontier-town look to it.

The **Corner Brook Museum and Archive,** 2 West St. (© 709/634-2518), is housed in a solid 1920s-era building that once was home to customs offices, the court, and the post and telegraph offices. A visit here offers a quick way to learn just how young the city really is (grainy black-and-white photos show empty hills surrounding the paper mill as late as the 1920s), and how civilized it has become since its establishment. An assortment of locally significant artifacts (a prominent doctor's desk, ship models) rounds out the collection. The museum is open daily from 9am to 7pm, mid-June through August, the rest of the year by appointment only. Admission is C$5 (US$4.50/£2.50) adults, C$3 (US$2.70/£1.50) students, and children under age 12 enter for free.

Nearby, at Glynmill Inn, you can follow a connector trail to the **Corner Brook Stream Trail** ⍟, which runs right through the heart of the city along gravel paths and over footbridges. The trail is being developed along the 19km (12-mile) length of the stream (formerly the city's water supply), but for now it offers access to a narrow and pleasantly green sanctuary within the city. From Glynmill Inn you'll round a man-made pond; from here you can head upstream to **Margaret Bowater Park** (a locally popular spot with a swimming pool and playground), or downstream toward Main Street and City Hall. Note also the family of swans at Glynmill Inn Pond.

The **Newfoundland Emporium,** 7 Broadway (② **709/634-9376**), is a traditional downtown stop for travelers. It stocks a mix of antiques, crafts, books, and—in the owner's words—"flotsam and jetsam." It's the city's best destination for souvenirs.

OUTDOOR PURSUITS

For outdoor enthusiasts, Corner Brook makes an excellent base for exploring outlying mountains and waters.

Mountain bikers should plan a stop by **TNT Professional Bicycles,** 8 Maple Valley Rd. (② **709/634-6799**). These guys know their business; ask for suggestions on where to go and for the free map of backcountry bike routes. Didn't bring your bike? You can also rent one here, and the shop leads group rides twice a week in summer, starting around 7pm (it stays light late here). Note that the shop is closed Sundays.

Some of the region's best **hiking** is found along Route 450 toward Bottle Cove (see "A Road Trip from Corner Brook," below). But other hikes will get you quickly up into the hills around Corner Brook. At Marble Mountain ski area (see below), east of town on the Trans-Canada Highway, you can park at the ski lodge parking lot and follow a 1km (.6-mile) trail up to **Steady Brook Falls,** which is especially impressive after a summer rain. More extensive hikes are outlined in the "Corner Brook Hiking Guide and Map," available free at the visitor information center.

Anglers in search of the noted Atlantic salmon that spawn in the Humber have a wide selection of outfitters who provide an all-inclusive **fishing** experience; one price covers transportation from the airport, accommodations, meals, and a guide. For a reputable guide, try the **Strawberry Hill Resort** in Little Rapids (② **877/434-0066** or 709/634-0066) or the **Humber Valley Resort** in the Humber Valley near Corner Brook (② **866/686-8100** or 709/686-8100). Other outfitters are listed in the province's "Hunting and Fishing Guide," available at provincial information centers or by calling ② **800/563-6353.**

Atlantic Canada has just one downhill ski area that I'd classify as a destination resort, and that's **Marble Mountain** ⍟, a 10-minute drive from Corner Brook. You can see its steep hills just north of the city. With a location near the Gulf of St. Lawrence, in the path of persistent northwest winds, it gets plenty of powder dumps, and the 1,700-ft. vertical drop is respectable. There are 35 runs on the 14-hectare (35-acre) property, including many open to snowboarding. Many skiers take advantage of packages that include airfare, lodging, lift tickets, and a rental car; ask for a brochure by calling ℂ **888/462-7253** or 709/637-7600, or pointing your browser at **www.ski marble.com**. The park is reached by taking Exit 8 off the Trans-Canada Highway.

WHERE TO STAY

Corner Brook is home to several convenient chain motels. Among others, you'll find the **Mamateek Inn,** 64 Maple Valley Rd. (ℂ **800/563-8600** or 709/639-8901), near the tourist information booth, and the **Greenwood Inn & Suites,** 47 West St. (ℂ **800/ 399-5381** or 709/634-5381), which is within walking distance of the city's best restaurant (see below); it recently changed hands and was upgraded by the new owners. Double rooms go for C$90 up to C$120 (US$81–US$108/£45–£60) at the Mamateek, and up to C$195 (US$176/£98) at the Greenwood.

Camping is offered on the north banks of the Humber at **Kinsmen Prince Edward Park** 🌟🌟 (ℂ **709/637-1580**), with 80 sites spread along a bluff from which you can often spot osprey and bald eagles. Both fully serviced (C$20/US$18/£10) and unserviced sites (C$15/US$14/£7.50) are available. Exit the Trans-Canada Highway at Marble Mountain and follow Route 440 until you see the signs. It's about 10 minutes' drive from downtown. The campground is open June to mid-September.

Glynmill Inn 🌟 *Value*   This Tudor inn is set in a quiet, parklike setting—an easy stroll to the services and shops of West Street. Built in 1924 and extensively renovated in 1994, the four-story hotel's appealing detailing will charm you. (The place was designated a Registered Heritage Structure in 2001.) Rooms are tastefully decorated with colonial reproductions; the popular Tudor Suite has a private Jacuzzi. You'll get far more character here than at the chain motels in town, for about the same price. The inn's two eating rooms, the Carriage Room and the Wine Cellar, are quite popular among local diners; the setting can feel a bit institutional (they do a rousing business with conventions and banquets), but the food is nevertheless pretty good. There's also a commodious pub and a little art gallery on the inn's premises.

1 Cobb Lane (near West St.), Corner Brook, NL A2H 6E6. ℂ **800/563-4400** or 709/634-5181. Fax 709/634-5106. www.glynmillinn.ca. 81 units. C$79–C$155 (US$71–US$140/£40–£78) double. AE, DC, MC, V. **Amenities:** 2 dining rooms; bar; fitness center; business center; laundry service. *In room:* A/C, TV, fridge (some units), coffeemaker, hair dryer, iron/ironing board.

WHERE TO DINE

Thirteen West 🌟🌟 GLOBAL   Western Newfoundland's best restaurant can easily hold its own with the top restaurants in St. John's, both in terms of quality of food and with its casual but professional service. Tucked along shady West Street in an unobtrusive building (there's a patio fronting the street for that rare balmy night), the kitchen does an outstanding job preparing top-notch meals, and the staff makes good service look easy. At lunchtime, look for offerings like grilled strip loin spiced Montréal-style; salmon salad; or a warm seafood salad of mussels, shrimp, scallops, and bacon. In the evening, you might find a menu of such items as grilled salmon with a dill pesto, roasted rack of lamb, barbecued chicken with Cajun shrimp and black-pepper sauce, or a seafood platter. Don't leave without sampling at least one of the delightful desserts, which have usually included such standards as crème caramel and profiteroles along with more inventive selections such as sautéed bananas with a rum-pecan caramel sauce and vanilla ice cream.

13 West St. ℂ **709/634-1300**. Reservations recommended. Main courses C$6–C$13 (US$5.40–US$12/£3–£6.50) at lunch, C$16–C$28 (US$14–US$25/£8–£14) at dinner. AE, DC, MC, V. Mon–Fri 11:30am–2:30pm and 5:30–9:30pm (Fri until 10:30pm); Sat 5:30–10:30pm; Sun 5:30–9:30pm (summer until 10:30pm).

A Road Trip from Corner Brook

One of western Newfoundland's most scenic drives is between Corner Brook and Bottle Cove, driving west on Route 450, also known as Captain Cook's Trail. It takes about 45 minutes to an hour to drive to the end of the road at Bottle Cove if you don't make any stops. But you should. The region stands up well to a leisurely excursion.

The road is winding and dramatic, running between the looming Blow Me Down Mountains and the dark dappled waters of Humber Arm. Near Lark Harbour is **Blow Me Down Provincial Park** 🎿 ((℃ 709/681-2430), a fine destination for a hike and a picnic. Start off with the 1km (.6-mile) hike to the lookout tower. Along the way you can view the Governor's Staircase, a rock formation 450 million years old. Continue along the up-and-down trail for 3km (1.9 miles) one-way to Tortoise Point, with its exceptional views of the Bay of Islands. The park is open daylight hours; admission is C$5 (US$4.50/£2.50) per car. They also have a campground; see "Where to Stay & Dine" under Deer Lake.

On the way back to Corner Brook is the **Blow Me Down Nature Trail** 🎿🎿, west of the village of Frenchman's Cove and about 500m (1,640 ft.) west of the bridge over the brook. This is an especially appealing walk on a warm day, since this easy 1km (.6-mile) trail leads to great swimming holes in Blow Me Down Brook. Bring towels.

DEER LAKE

Deer Lake is an unassuming crossroads town near the head of the Humber River where travelers coming from the south either continue on the Trans-Canada Highway toward St. John's or veer northwest to Gros Morne National Park, some 69km (43 miles) distant. Deer Lake is the gateway for those coming by air directly to western Newfoundland. There's little to detain a visitor here; it's a good spot to buy gas, peruse the brochures at the provincial information center, and then push on.

Deer Lake is located 48km (30 miles) north of Corner Brook on the Trans-Canada Highway. **Deer Lake Regional Airport** (℃ 709/635-3601; www.deerlakeairport.com) is the air hub for western Newfoundland, with scheduled flights both within the island and to Halifax on several different airlines. Car rentals are available from the terminal.

EXPLORING DEER LAKE

Lucky is the traveler who arrives here during the short wild strawberry season (mid- to late July some years; early Aug in others). If you're here at the right time, do your-self a favor and stop at one of the several seasonal roadside stands for a pint or two. These berries are plump, cheap, and sinfully sweet and flavorful—nothing at all like those tasteless commercial berries filling the aisles in big grocery stores.

The **Newfoundland Insectarium** (℃ 866/635-5454 or 709/635-4545; www.nf insectarium.com) opened in 1999 on Route 440, half a kilometer from the Trans-Canada Highway. Funded privately and operated as a for-profit venture, the insectar-ium will appeal to impressionable children and anyone fascinated with bugs. It's housed in a retrofitted dairy farm framed in red cedar, with most of the exhibits on a spacious second floor. These include more than 4,000 mounted, actual insects (no faux bugs are displayed here) and 28 terrariums with live insects, including tiger beetles, American cockroaches, and honeybees. A walking trail and bug-themed gift shop (including, um, chocolate-coated crickets) round out the experience.

It's open daily in July and August 9am to 8pm, May through June and September on weekdays from 9am to 5pm, and weekends from 10am to 5pm; the place is closed the rest of the year, from October through April. Admission is C$10 (US$9/£5) adults, C$8.50 (US$7.65/£4.25) seniors, C$6.50 (US$5.85/£3.25) children ages 5 to 14, C$30 (US$27/£15) families. You could spend the better part of an hour here—but only if you *really* dig bugs.

WHERE TO STAY & DINE

Blow Me Down Provincial Park ✦ (© 709/681-2430) has camping for C$13 (US$12/£6.50) per site. See "A Road Trip from Corner Brook," above, for more information.

Deer Lake Motel   This serviceable motel is located right on the Trans-Canada Highway and has 54 clean, basic rooms. On the premises are a coffee shop, a pubby lounge, and a dining room. This is a place to lay your head if you're arriving late en route to Gros Morne or points north or east; otherwise, there's little call to remain overnight in Deer Lake.

Trans-Canada Hwy., Deer Lake, NL A0K 2E0. © **800/563-2144** (from Newfoundland only) or 709/635-2108. Fax 709/635-3842. www.deerlakemotel.com. 54 units. C$85–C$129 (US$77–US$116/£43–£65) double. AE, DC, MC, V. **Amenities:** 2 restaurants; bar. *In room:* A/C, TV, coffeemaker, hair dryer, iron/ironing board.

4 Gros Morne National Park ✦✦✦

"Gros Morne" translates roughly from the French as "big gloomy," and if you arrive on a day when ghostly bits of fog blow across the road and scud clouds hover in the glacial valleys, you'll get a pretty good idea how this area got its name. Even on brilliantly sunny days, there's something imposing about the stark mountains, lonely fjords cut off from the ocean, and miles of tangled spruce forest.

That's not to say you shouldn't come, though. **Gros Morne National Park** is one of Canada's greatest natural treasures, and few who visit here fail to come away with a sense of awe. In fact, it's been officially designated as one of the *world's* greatest natural treasures: In 1987, the park was declared a UNESCO World Heritage Site, largely due to the importance of a section of the park known as **the Tablelands.** This geological quirk formed eons ago, when a portion of the earth's mantle broke loose during continental drifting and was forced to the surface, creating an eerie, rust-colored tableau. (See "Journey to the Center of the Earth," p. 262, for more information.)

The park is divided into two sections, north and south, riven by the multiarmed Bonne Bay (locally pronounced like "Bombay"). Alas, a ferry connecting the two areas has not operated for years, so exploring both sections by car requires some backtracking. The park's visitor center and most tourist services are found in the village of **Rocky Harbour** in the north section—but you'd be shortchanging yourself to miss a detour through the dramatic **southern section,** a place that looks to have had a rough birth, geologically speaking.

To do Gros Morne justice, plan on spending at least 3 days here. (A week would not be too much if you're an ardent hiker.) The dramatic terrain throughout the park is on a scale large enough to be appreciated even if you never get out of your car. But to *really* get a sense of the place, think about getting out to see the place on foot, by bike, or in a boat. Excellent hikes and awe-inspiring boat rides can take you right into the heart of the park's wildest places.

If you'd prefer to let someone else do the planning for you, contact **Gros Morne Adventures** (© 800/685-4624 or 709/458-2722; www.grosmorneadventures.com), which organizes guided sea kayaking and hiking excursions throughout the park.

ESSENTIALS

GETTING THERE   From the Trans-Canada Highway in Deer Lake, turn west on Route 430 (the Viking Trail). This runs through the northern section of the park; it's 71km (44 miles) in all from Deer Lake to Rocky Harbour. To reach the southern section, turn left (south) on Route 431 in Wiltondale; from the turn, it's 27km (17 miles) to Woody Point.

VISITOR INFORMATION   The park's main **visitor information center** (© 709/458-2417) is just south of Rocky Harbour on Route 430. It's open daily from 9am to 9pm in summer, from 9am to 5pm most days in spring and fall (but weekdays only in early May and Oct), and closed from November through April. The center features exhibits on park geology and wildlife; there's also a short film about the park that's picturesque but not terribly informative. Interactive media kiosks are exceptionally well done; you can view video clips depicting highlights of all hiking trails and other attractions simply by touching a video screen. The center is also the place to stock up on field guides, as well as to request backcountry camping permits.

Across the bay just outside of Woody Point on Route 431 en route to Trout River is the new **Discovery Centre.** This building is an enlightening stop, with interactive exhibits, a fossil room, and a multimedia theater to help make sense of the Gros Morne landscape. It's open mid-May through early October; more information is available at the visitor center.

FEES   All visitors must obtain a permit for any activity within the park. From mid-May through early October, the daily entrance fees are C$8.90 (US$8/£4.45) adults, C$7.65 (US$6.90/£3.85) seniors, C$4.45 (US$4/£2.25) children 6 to 18, and C$18 (US$16/£9) families; in the off season, fees are somewhat lower. Annual passes are available for about C$45 (US$41/£23) per adult or C$89 (US$80/£45) per family, a great deal if you'll be entering the park on at least 3 different days.

GROS MORNE'S SOUTHERN SECTION ๙๙๙

The road through the southern section of Gros Morne dead-ends at Trout River, and accordingly it seems to discourage convenience-minded visitors who prefer loops and through-routes. That's too bad, because the south contains some of the park's most dramatic terrain. Granted, you can glimpse the rust-colored Tablelands from north of Bonne Bay near Rocky Harbour and call it a day, thereby saving the 48km (30-mile) detour. But without actually walking through that desolate landscape, you miss much of its impact. The southern section also contains several lost-in-time fishing villages that predate the park's creation in 1973, and a new Discovery Centre (see above) with exhibits documenting the park's natural history.

The region's scenic centerpiece is **Trout River Pond,** a landlocked fjord some 15km (9⅓ miles) long. You can hike along the north shore to get a great view of the Narrows, where cliffs nearly pinch the pond in two. For a more relaxed view, sign up for a boat tour, which surrounds you with breathtaking panoramic views. The **Trout River Pond Boat Tour** ๙ (© 866/751-7500 or 709/451-7500) is an excursion on

Journey to the Center of the Earth

If you see folks wandering around the **Tablelands** 🐟🐟 looking all twitchy and excited, they're probably amateur geologists. The Tablelands are one of the world's great geological celebrities, and a popular destination among pilgrims who come to worship at the altar of classic rock. Not rock 'n' roll—*rocks*.

To the uninitiated, the Tablelands area—south of Woody Point and the south arm of Bonne Bay—seems rather bleak and barren. These muscular hills rise up, rounded and rust-colored, devoid of trees or even the slightest green haze of vegetation. Up close, you discover just how barren they are— little plant life seems to have established a toehold here yet.

There's a reason for that. Some 570 million years ago, this rock was part of the earth's mantle—the part of the earth lying just underneath its crust. Riding on continental plates, two landmasses collided forcefully, and this piece of mantle was driven up and over the crust, rather than being forced under (as is usually the case). Years of erosion followed, and what's left is a rare x-ray of the earth's oldest bones. But this rare, ancient rock is so rich in magnesium that few plants can stand to live here, giving the landscape a barrenness that seems more appropriate for a desert landscape than for the rainy mountains of Newfoundland.

the pond aboard a 40-passenger boat that runs from late May through mid-October. The 2½-hour trips are offered three times daily in summer, once daily in the shoulder seasons; cost is C$35 (US$32/£18) per adult, C$18 (US$16/£9) children ages 7 to 17, and C$75 (US$68/£38) families. Tickets are sold at a gift shop between the village of Trout River and the pond; watch for signs.

HIKES & WALKS

For a superb panorama encompassing ocean and mountains, watch for the **Lookout Trail** 🐟, just outside of Woody Point en route to Trout River. This steep trail is about 5km (3 miles) round-trip.

The **Tablelands Trail** departs from barren Trout River gulch and follows an old gravel road up to Winterhouse Brook Canyon. You can bushwhack along the rocky river a bit farther upstream, or turn back. It's about 2km (1.2 miles) each way, depending on how adventurous you feel. This is a good trail to get a feel for the unique ecology of the Tablelands. Look for the signboards that explain the geology located at the trail head and at the roadside pull-off on your left before reaching the trail head.

Experienced hikers looking for a challenge should seek out the **Green Gardens Trail** 🐟🐟🐟. There are two trailheads to this loop; I recommend the second one (closer to Trout River). You begin by trekking through a rolling, infertile landscape, and then plunge down, down, and down wooden steps and a steep trail toward the sea. The landscape grows more lush by the moment, until you're walking through extraordinary coastal meadows on crumbling bluffs high above the churning surf.

The trail then follows the shore northward for about 4 or 5km (2.5 or 3.1 miles) more, and this next stretch might be one of the most breathtaking coastal trails in the world. In July, the irises and a whole symphony of wildflowers bloom wildly. The entire loop is about 16km (9.9 miles) and is rugged and very hilly; allow about 5 or 6 hours for the hike. An abbreviated version involves walking clockwise on the loop to the shore's edge, then retracing one's steps back uphill. That's about 9km (5.6 miles) in total.

CAMPING

The two **drive-in campsites** in the southern section—**Trout River Pond** and **Lomond**—both offer showers and nearby hiking trails. Of the two, Trout River Pond is more dramatic, located on a plateau overlooking the pond; a short stroll brings you to the pond's edge with wonderful views up the fjord. Lomond is near the site of an old lumber town and is popular with anglers. Camping is about C$18 to C$25 (US$16–US$23/£9–£13) per site.

Three exceptional **backcountry campsites** are located along the Green Garden Trail; registration at the park visitor center is required, and the fee is about C$10 (US$9/£5) per night. The northernmost site is near the coast in a ravine where Wallace Brook meets the ocean. The two southern sites are on grassy bluffs above pebble beaches, and both have outstanding coastal views.

WHERE TO STAY

Victorian Manor B&B   This 1920s home is one of the most impressive in the village, though that doesn't mean it's extravagant. It's more solid than flamboyant, set in a residential neighborhood near the town center and a few minutes' walk to the harbor. The attractive guesthouse has its own whirlpool. If that's booked, ask for one of the efficiencies, which cost about the same as the inn rooms but afford much greater convenience, especially considering the slim dining choices around town.

Main Rd. (P.O. Box 165), Woody Point, NL A0K 1P0. (C) **866/453-2485** or 709/453-2485. www.grosmorne.com/victorianmanor. 7 units. C$60–C$95 (US$54–US$86/£30–£48) double. Rates include continental breakfast. AE, MC, V. **Amenities:** Jacuzzi; coin-op washers and dryers. In room: TV, kitchenette, fridge, coffeemaker, no phone.

WHERE TO DINE

Seaside Restaurant ⸙ SEAFOOD   The Seaside has been a Trout River institution for years; it's a notch above the tired fare you often find in tiny coastal villages, though service can be slow if the place fills up. The restaurant is nicely polished without being swank, and it features magnificent harbor views. The pan-fried cod is superb, as are a number of other seafood dishes. (Sandwiches and burgers are at hand for those who don't care for seafood.) Desserts are quite good; inquire about whether the partridge-berry parfait is on the menu.

Main St., Trout River. (C) **709/451-3461.** Main courses C$10–C$19 (US$9–US$17/£5–£9.50). MC, V. Daily noon–8pm. Closed mid-Oct to June.

GROS MORNE'S NORTHERN SECTION ⸙⸙

Gros Morne's northern section flanks Route 430 for some 72km (45 miles) between Wiltondale and St. Paul's. The road winds through the abrupt, forested hills south of Rocky Harbour; beyond these, the road levels out, following a broad coastal plain covered mostly with bog and tuckamore. East of the plain rises the extraordinarily dramatic monoliths of the Long Range. This section contains the park's visitor center as well as its one must-see attraction: **Western Brook Pond.**

The hardscrabble fishing village of Rocky Harbour is your best bet for tourist services, including motels, B&Bs, laundromats, and such. One caveat: This area lacks a good, big grocery store or supply depot of the sort you would expect to be located near a big national park of such international significance. What you'll find instead are a few modest grocers.

EXPLORING THE NORTHERN SECTION

If you have time for only one activity in Gros Morne—and heaven forbid that's the case—make it the **BonTours boat trip** (© 888/458-2016 or 709/458-2016; www. bontours.ca) up **Western Brook Pond** ☆☆. The trip begins with a 20-minute drive north of Rocky Harbour. Park at the Western Brook Pond trail head, then set off on an easy 2-mile, 45-minute hike across the northern coastal plain, with interpretive signs explaining the wildlife and bog ecology you'll see along the way. (Keep an eye out for moose.) Always ahead, the mighty monoliths of the Long Range rise high above, inviting and mystical, more like a 19th-century scene from the Rockies than the Atlantic seaboard.

You'll soon arrive at pond's edge, where there's a small collection of outbuildings near a wharf. This is where the tour boats dock up. Once aboard one of the vessels (there are two), you'll set off into the maw of the mountains, winding between the sheer rock faces that define this landlocked fjord. The spiel on the boat is recorded, but even that unfortunate bit of cheese fails to detract from the grandeur of the scene. You'll learn about the glacial geology and the remarkable quality of the water, which is considered among the purest in the world. Bring lots of film and a wide-angle lens. The trip lasts about 2½ hours and costs C$39 (US$35/£20) adults, C$18 (US$16/£9) students 12 to 16 (must be accompanied by an adult), C$12 (US$11/£6) children under 11, and C$79 (US$71/£40) per family; they only take cash; no credit cards. Buy tickets for the tour at the dock, or at the Ocean View Motel in Rocky Harbour. Also note that you must acquire a **park admissions pass** before arrival to take this tour.

If rain or heavy fog puts a damper on outdoor activities, there's a modern indoor pool at the **Gros Morne Recreation Complex** on Route 430 high above Rocky Harbour; it's open in summer only. The view of Bonne Bay from the outdoor terrace is great, and the pool is inviting. This is also a good spot for a shower if you're staying at a campground lacking one. Tickets good for a 1-hour swim cost about C$3 (US$2.70/£1.50) for adults, C$2 (US$1.80/£1) for children.

If you're looking for diversion that requires minimal physical effort, both the **SS *Ethie* shipwreck** ☆☆ and **Broom Point** ☆ (both near Western Brook Pond) are worth stopping for. The coastal steamer *Ethie* met its fate during a storm in 1919; all passengers were saved, including an infant shuttled to shore in a mailbag. The wreck has long been prominent in song and story, but the years have taken their toll on the rusting scrap. The hull is all but gone, leaving only the massive boiler and some other stray parts. But the cobbles nearby are beautiful.

Broom Point is an easy stroll out to a rocky peninsula where active fishing operations take place. The views from the point are outstanding; don't miss the superb sand beach down a side trail to your left as you walk toward the point.

HIKES & WALKS   Gros Morne Mountain ☆☆ is the Mount Everest of this national park—at 793m (2,602 ft.) it's the highest peak in the park, and the most demanding. What makes it especially challenging isn't so much the height or the length (about 16km/10 miles round-trip); it's the terrain. You expend considerable energy scrambling over loose scree on the upper reaches. But the views of the bay and beyond to the Gulf of St. Lawrence are well worth it if the weather cooperates. Allow about 7 or 8 hours for the whole excursion, and bring plenty of water and food. Pick up a trail brochure at the information center. (If you're traveling with a pet, note that this is the one park trail on which dogs aren't allowed.)

Even if you're not planning on signing up for the Western Brook Pond boat tour, you owe yourself a walk up to the pond's wharf and possibly beyond. The 45-minute one-way trek from the parking lot north of Sally's Cove follows a well-trod trail and boardwalk through bogs and boreal forest. When you arrive at the wharf, the **view** 𝕂𝕂 to the mouth of the fjord will take your breath away. A well-executed outdoor exhibit explains how glaciers shaped the dramatic landscape in front of you.

Two spur trails continue on either side of the pond for a short distance. The **Snug Harbour Trail** 𝕂𝕂, which follows the northern shore to a primitive campsite (registration required), is especially appealing. After crossing a bridge at the pond outlet, you'll pass through scrubby woods before emerging on a long and wonderful sand and pebble beach; this is a great destination for a relaxed afternoon picnic and requisite nap. The hike all the way to Snug Harbour is about 8km (5 miles) one-way.

Three easy but enjoyable strolls depart from the **Berry Hill Campground** just north of Rocky Harbour. The 2km-long (1.2-mile) Berry Hill Pond loop is a perfect place for walking off your meal in the evening. The equally short 1.5km (.9-mile) round-trip hike up **Berry Hill** 𝕂 is an easy stroll, except for a demanding set of steps at the end; a short trail around the summit affords excellent views. Departing from the same parking area is the somewhat more demanding **Baker Brook Falls Trail** 𝕂. This level trail runs 10km (6.2 miles) round-trip, ending at a wooden platform overlooking tumultuous, wild cascades. The trail crosses big stretches of bog via boardwalks.

CAMPING   The northern section has three campgrounds open to car campers. The main campground is **Berry Hill,** which is just north of Rocky Harbour. There are nearly 150 drive-in sites, plus a handful of walk-in sites on the shores of the pond itself. It's just 10 minutes' drive from the visitor center, where evening activities and presentations are held. **Shallow Bay** 𝕂 has 50 campsites and is near the park's northern border and an appealing 4km (2.5-mile) sand beach. Both of these campgrounds have showers and flush toilets; sites at each cost C$18 to C$25 (US$16–US$23/ £9–£13) per night depending on the time of year.

Green Point 𝕂𝕂 is an intimate, popular campground with just 18 sites; bear in mind that it's a "primitive" campsite, meaning there are only pit toilets (no flush toilets) and showers. Green Point is divided into two areas: The upper area is more open and has views of the gulf; the lower area is set amid evergreens and offers more privacy and shelter from the wind.

In midsummer, these northern-section campgrounds tend to fill up fast; it's best to arrive as soon after the 2pm checkout time as possible to secure a site. Reservations are very helpful for all three sites during the peak summer season; call 🕻 **800/563-6353** for more details.

BACKPACKING   Backcountry camping is available at **Snug Harbour** on Western Brook Pond, an 8km (5-mile) hike from the road. Register for a site at the visitor center; the cost is C$15 (US$14/£7.50).

For an unforgettable—though very demanding—adventure, inquire at the visitor center about backpacking trips along the **Long Range** 𝕂𝕂 and the **North Rim** 𝕂𝕂. On both of these, you strike out cross-country, bushwhacking through the high subarctic terrain. These traverses require 2 or 3 nights to complete. You must be in good physical condition and well-versed in a range of backcountry skills, including proficiency with

Visiting More Than One Park? I'll Take a (Viking) Pass

If you're going to be visiting Gros Morne National Park, and then also folding one or another of the province's natural and historic treasures into your trip before or after going there—L'Anse aux Meadows, Red Bay, Port au Choix, or the Grenfell Historic Properties—pick up a **Viking Trail Pass** (valid for 7 days from the date of issue) at any of the park offices listed. This pass gives you unlimited admission to all of them for one flat fee. It costs C$40 (US$36/£20) per adult, C$34 (US$31/£17) seniors, C$21 (US$19/£11) children, and C$81(US$73/£41) for a family of four.

maps and compasses. A brief pretrip orientation at the visitor center is mandatory, as is the rental of a small (pager-size) locator beacon to help pinpoint your location should you become disoriented. There's a one-time fee of C$20 (US$18/£10) charged to reserve these trips, plus an activity fee of C$54 to C$79 (US$49–US$71/£27–£40) per hike or C$109 (US$98/£55) for both trails, which includes the locator rental and camp fees.

WHERE TO STAY

Rocky Harbour has more tourist services than any other village in or around the park yet still has trouble handling the sudden torrent of travelers in July and August. Two or three bus tours can pretty well fill up a town, as can droves of overnight arrivals in good weather. It's unwise to arrive in the park area without a reservation.

The largest motel in town is the **Ocean View Motel** (© **800/563-9887** or 709/458-2730), located on the harbor. It has 52 rather basic rooms (some with small balconies and bay views). The motel is popular with bus tours and often fills up early in the day. Rooms are C$115 to C$155 (US$104–US$140/£58–£78) for a double in season.

Gros Morne Cabins The best thing about the Gros Morne Cabins? Pulling up and seeing long lines of freshly laundered sheets billowing in the sea breeze, like a Christo installation. Two dozen trim, tidy log cabins are clustered along a grassy rise overlooking Rocky Harbour, and all have outstanding views toward the Lobster Cove Head Lighthouse. Inside they're new and clean (even sporting good televisions and wireless Internet access), more antiseptic and modern than time-worn. Each is equipped with a kitchenette, while gas barbecues are scattered about the property. The complex also includes a store and a laundromat, and there's a pizza place across the street for relaxed sunset dining at your own picnic table.

Main St. (P.O. Box 151), Rocky Harbour, NL A0K 4N0. © 888/603-2020 or 709/458-2020. Fax 709/458-2882. 25 units. C$99–C$179 (US$89–US$161/£50–£90) double. AE, DC, MC, V. Pets allowed. **Amenities:** Laundry service. *In room:* TV, kitchenette, Jacuzzi (1 unit).

Sugar Hill Inn 🔊 This appealing green-shingled inn opened in 1991 on the road between Rocky Harbour and Norris Point. The six rooms are quite comfortable, though some guests might find them a bit condolike or sterile. Nice touches abound, like hardwood floors in all units, plenty of natural wood trim, well-selected furnishings, phones and televisions throughout, and a shared sauna and hot tub in a cedar-lined common room. The upstairs sitting room is spacious and bright, with a fireplace and modern furnishings; it's a good spot to swap local adventure ideas with other guests. There's also a cottage with queen bed and Jacuzzi for rent. The inn's dining room serves breakfast and dinner daily, and surprisingly, this inn is open all year round—a bonus if you're visiting off-season.

115–129 Sexton Rd. (P.O. Box 100), Norris Point, NL A0K 3V0. ℂ 888/299-2147 or 709/458-2147. Fax 709/458-2166. www.sugarhillinn.nf.ca. 7 units. C$89–C$175 (US$80–US$158/£44.50–£87.50). Rates include continental breakfast. AE, MC, V. **Amenities:** Restaurant; bar; Jacuzzi; sauna; laundry service. *In room:* A/C, TV, fridge, Jacuzzi (some units).

Wild Flowers Bed and Breakfast This 1930s home near the village center was modernized and updated with a casual country look before it opened as a B&B in 1997. Rooms here are tastefully appointed, if a bit small, though two newer rooms have private bathrooms and are a bit larger. The neighborhood isn't especially scenic (there's an auto repair shop across the way, for instance), but the house is peaceful, the innkeepers exceptionally friendly, and this is a great choice for those seeking reasonably priced lodging with a comfortable, homey feel.

Main St. N. (P.O. Box 291), Rocky Harbour, NL A0K 4N0. ℂ 888/811-7378 or 709/458-3000. Fax **709/458-3080**. www. wildflowerscountryinn.com. 6 units. C$89–C$129 (US$80–US$116/£45–£65) double. Rates include full breakfast. Mid-Oct to May, call about availability. MC, V. **Amenities:** Restaurant; bar; laundry service. *In room:* TV, no phone.

WHERE TO DINE
Fisherman's Landing SEAFOOD With its industrial carpeting and generic chain-restaurant tables and chairs, Fisherman's Landing is lacking in homespun character. But it does offer efficient service and dependable meals, with specialties including fish and chips, cod tongues, and squid rings. For breakfast, there's the traditional Newfie fisherman's breakfast of a mug of tea served with homemade bread and molasses. Meals are quite reasonably priced, and you can get in and out faster than at most other joints. There's also a glimpse of the harbor from a few tables, provided not too many RVs have parked themselves out front.

Main St., Rocky Harbour. ℂ 709/458-2060. Sandwiches C$3–C$7 (US$2.70–US$6.30/£1.50–£3.50); main courses C$7–C$17 (US$6.30–US$15/£3.50–£8.50). MC, V. Late June to early Sept 6am–11pm; limited hours off season.

5 The Great Northern Peninsula ✸

On a map, the Great Northern Peninsula looks like a stout cudgel threatening the shores of Labrador. If Newfoundland can even be said to have a beaten track, rest assured that this peninsula is well, well off it. It's not nearly as mountainous or starkly dramatic as Gros Morne, but the road here unspools for miles through tuckamore and evergreen forest, along coastline at the feet of geologically striking hills. There are few services and even fewer organized diversions. But it has early history in spades, a handful of fishing villages clustering along its rocky coast, and some of the most unspoiled terrain you'll find in North America. The road here is in good condition, the chief hazard being the occasional stray moose or caribou—or, in spring, the infrequent polar bear wandering through, hungry after a long trip south on an ice floe.

How nice is it? A talented writer I know drove down the rocky road one evening to make dinner and watch the sun sink over the Labrador hills across the straits. He came upon a waterfall that tumbled into a cobblestone cove where driftwood was piled chest-high for firewood. A beautiful grassy plateau—perfect for a tent—overlooked the sea. He had recently stocked up on food and had brought a milk crate full of books I wanted to read.

Long story short: It was 3 days before this guy was finally able to extricate himself from that idyllic spot.

ESSENTIALS

GETTING THERE   Route 430, which is also called the Viking Trail, runs from Deer Lake (at the Trans-Canada Hwy.) to St. Anthony, a 419km (260-mile) jaunt. Shorten it by taking a flight to tiny **St. Anthony Airport** (airport code YAY; ℂ 709/ 454-3192), where rental cars are available. The airport is on Route 430 approximately 30km (19 miles) west of St. Anthony. Two Newfoundland airlines service the airstrip: **Air Labrador** (ℂ 800/563-3042 or 709/758-0002; www.airlabrador.com) and **Provincial Airlines** (ℂ 800/563-2800 or 709/576-1666; www.provincialairlines.ca).

VISITOR INFORMATION   For information about the Great Northern Peninsula and the Viking Trail, contact the **Viking Trail Tourism Association,** P.O. Box 251, St. Anthony, NL A0K 4T0 (ℂ 877/778-4546 or 709/454-8888; www.vikingtrail.org).

PORT AU CHOIX

A visit to Port au Choix (pronounced port-a-*shwaw*) means a short, 13km (8-mile) detour off the Viking Trail, out to a knobby peninsula that's home to a sizable fishing fleet. The windswept landscape overlooking the sea here is low, predominantly flat, and lush with windblown grasses. Simple homes speckle the landscape; most are of recent vintage.

The town's chief attraction is the Port au Choix historic site (see below), but if you're coming be sure to also visit the site of former archaeological excavations at **Philip's Garden** 𝕱𝕱. Reaching the garden requires a 20-minute hike over low coastal cliffs of fissured slabs splashed with rust-orange lichens. It doesn't take much to imagine the ancient community, although there's only a placard or two marking the site of the millennia-old native settlement. Should you hunker down behind a rock to find solace from the persistent, howling winds, look carefully in the grass for the local tasty wild strawberries, which are a bit hard to see—they're no bigger than wild blueberries.

Ask for directions to the garden at the historic site's visitor center.

Port au Choix National Historic Site 𝕱𝕱 *Kids*   Back in 1967, a local businessman began digging the foundation for a new movie theater in Port au Choix. Seems innocent enough. Suddenly, he came upon some bones. A lot of bones. In fact, what he stumbled upon turned out to be a remarkable burying ground for what are now called the Maritime Archaic Indians. This group of hunters populated parts of Atlantic Canada beginning about 7,500 years ago, predating the Inuit (who "only" arrived perhaps 4,000 years ago). These early natives relied chiefly on the sea, and among the artifacts recovered here are slate spears and antler harpoon tips, which featured an ingenious toggle that extended into the fish as a sort of delayed-action mechanism after being thrust into flesh. One of the enduring historical mysteries is the disappearance of these people from the province about 3,500 years ago; to this day, no one can explain their sudden departure.

You'll learn about this historic episode at the modern visitor center. Staff here can also direct you to nearby sites including the original burial ground, now surrounded by village homes. (Don't miss Philip's Garden; see above.) You can also visit a nearby **lighthouse,** scenically located on a blustery point thrusting into the Gulf of St. Lawrence. Plan to spend about 90 minutes exploring the area.

Point Riche Rd., Port au Choix. ℂ 709/861-3522. Admission C$7.15 (US$6.45/£3.60) adults, C$5.90 (US$5.30/ £2.95) seniors, C$3.45 (US$3.10/£1.75) children 6–16, C$18 (US$16/£8) families. Visitor center June to early Oct daily 9am–6pm.

Knaar She Blows! Seeing the Park by Boat

One way to fire up your Viking fantasies is by taking a tour on the *Viking Saga*, a replica of one of the horned ones' early ships. These tours, run by **Viking Boat Tours**, depart in August only. Based in Noddy Bay (about 1.5km/1 mile south of L'Anse aux Meadows), the outfitter's handsome *knaar* (a type of Viking work boat) was built after extensive study of a ship recovered from the bottom of a fjord near Roskilde, Denmark. The boat has been upgraded to meet current safety standards, which require an engine, so you must travel by motor instead of sail. But you'll still get a taste of life aboard the compact boats as you motor along the remote coast, and you'll probably see whales and possibly icebergs. The tours are offered three times daily in August; they take about 2½ hours, and the fare is about C$40 (US$36/£20) adults, C$25 (US$23/£13) children 5 to 12, and C$10 (US$9/£5) for children under 5. Make reservations on the boat by calling © **709/623-2100.**

L'ANSE AUX MEADOWS ✫✫✫

Newfoundland's northernmost tip is not only exceptionally remote and dramatic, it is also one of the most historically significant archaeological sites in the world. A Viking encampment dating from A.D. 1000 was discovered here in 1960 and has been thoroughly documented by archaeologists in the decades since. An especially well-conceived and managed national historic site (see below) probes this earliest chapter in European expansion, and an afternoon spent here will pique your imagination.

L'Anse aux Meadows National Historic Site ✫✫✫ *Kids* *Value*   In the late 1950s, a pair of determined archaeologists named Helge Ingstad and Anne Stine Ingstad pored over 13th-century Norse sagas searching for clues about where the Vikings might have landed on the shores of North America. With just a few bits of description to go on, the Ingstads began cruising the coastlines of Newfoundland and Labrador, asking locals about unusual hummocks and mounds.

In 1960, at L'Anse aux Meadows, they finally struck gold. In a remote cove noted for its low, grassy hills, they found the remains of an ancient Norse encampment that included three large halls, along with a forge where nails were made from locally mined pig iron. As many as 100 Vikings lived here for a time, including some women; the Vikings abandoned the settlement after a few years to return to Greenland and Denmark, thus ending the first experiment in the colonization of North America by Europeans. It's telling that no graves have ever been discovered here.

Start your visit by viewing the recovered artifacts in the visitor center and watching the half-hour video about the site's discovery. Then sign up for one of the free guided tours of the site. The guides here offer considerably more information than the simple markers around the grounds do.

Near the original encampment are several re-created sod-and-timber buildings depicting how life was lived 1,000 years ago. These are tended by costumed interpreters who stay in character and answer questions without making you feel silly. If you time it right, you might be rewarded with a bit of flatbread cooked old-style over

Tips **Readers Recommend**

In Newfoundland you directed us to the Viking boats near L'Anse aux Meadows, which may have been fun. But I feel we found an excellent alternative in St. Anthony that I'd like to share with the world. It goes by the name Northland Discovery Tour.

Paul Alcock is an enthusiastic host, taking life's lemons and making lemonade. His father and uncle, forced into early retirement by the cod-fishing ban, had an unused boat. Paul seized the opportunity. Seating 10, the open boat is perfect for a personalized tour of icebergs and wildlife. This 2½-hour ride is an educational experience. We saw everything from whales to jellyfish, bald eagles to Arctic terns. We went inside a cave, and we tasted an iceberg. I can't recommend this highly enough. Paul was delightfully informative about the land he obviously loves.

Northland Discovery Boat Tours, P.O. Box 728, St. Anthony, NL A0K 4S0 (© 877/632-3747 or 709/454-3092). Tours mid-May to late Sept C$48 (US$43/£24) adults, C$25 (US$23/£13) children age 13 to 17, C$20 (US$18/£10) children age 5 to 12, C$8 (US$7.20/£4) children age 2 to 4.

—Marianne J. Heintz, Aurora, Illinois

an open fire. This is one of eastern Canada's major attractions; stick around for at least a couple hours or a half-day and soak it all up with the family.

Rte. 436, L'Anse aux Meadows. © 709/623-2608. Admission C$10 (US$9/£5) adults, C$8.90 (US$8/£4.45) seniors, C$5.20 (US$4.70/£2.60) children 6–16, C$26 (US$23/£13) families. June to early Oct daily 9am–8pm; rest of the year, call ahead for status.

ST. ANTHONY ☆

The seaport town of St. Anthony—named by explorer Jacques Cartier in 1534—was first visited by 16th-century French and Basque fishermen. Today, with its 3,200 residents, St. Anthony is the northern peninsula's largest town and its undisputed commercial center. It's a good place to restock on basic supplies or secure a motel room for day trips to L'Anse aux Meadows, about 50km (31 miles) north of town.

Be sure to visit **Fishing Point Park** ☆☆, at the end of a dirt road at the mouth of the harbor. With propitious timing and some luck, you'll be able to view icebergs and whales from the rugged, rocky bluffs. A series of short trails and wooden platforms makes life easy for the casual explorer.

In the evening, there's live entertainment at the **Great Viking Feast at Leifsburdur** (© 877/454-4900 or 709/454-4900). In a replica sod hut—the "only sod-covered restaurant in North America," a dubious distinction to be sure—as many as 85 diners at a time feast on local fare such as Jigg's dinner (boiled meat and potatoes), moose stew (yes, really), cod tongues, and baked cod, while being amused by a crew of boisterous faux Vikings. The show is staged daily at 7:30pm from July to early September (reservations required), and costs about C$35 (US$32/£18) per person. Corny? Sure. Fun and filling? Yes.

Grenfell House Museum and Interpretation Centre ☆☆   Dr. Wilfred Grenfell is more or less the patron saint of St. Anthony. A devout Christian, Grenfell was born

in England and as a young man became active in providing medical care to North Sea fishermen. In 1892, he visited Newfoundland and Labrador. Appalled by the conditions, he founded the first hospital; he was to spend much of the rest of his life ministering to residents of remote outports and agitating for better services from the government. In 1912, he established the International Grenfell Association, which built hospitals and nursing homes throughout the region. Grenfell was relentless in trying to improve the lot of the northland's residents and the delivery of medicines and services. One example: In 1909, he experimented using reindeer rather than sled dogs for winter travel, having observed that the dogs had the unfortunate habit of savaging the driver if he fell down in the deep snow.

An interpretive center features two floors of exhibits that nicely fill visitors in on the Grenfell's history. There's also a short video worth watching. Afterward, you can tour the handsome house that the grateful town built for Grenfell and his wife, Anne, in 1910. It's furnished with numerous artifacts and interesting exhibits about Grenfell's life and works. You'll also learn about Grenfell cloth, a versatile fabric invented in 1922, which was made of Egyptian cotton specifically to withstand the rigors of severe winter travel. Garments made of Grenfell cloth are available at **Grenfell Handicrafts,** in the interpretation center. Plan to spend about an hour here.

West St., St. Anthony (across from the hospital). ✆ **709/454-4010.** Admission C$6 (US$5.40/£3) adults, C$5 (US$4.50/£2.50) seniors, C$2.75 (US$2.50/£1.40) children 6–16, C$12 (US$11/£6) families. May–Sept daily 9am–8pm (Sept until 5pm).

WHERE TO STAY & DINE
Lightkeeper's Seafood Restaurant ✦ SEAFOOD   Located at scenic Fishing Point Park, this cafe with an amazing view is housed in a simple but handsome white building with fire-engine-red trim overlooking the ocean. Inside, it's sparely decorated and flooded with natural light. You can't beat the panoramic scenery, and the proprietors have helpfully placed binoculars on the windowsills for you to scope out the whales and icebergs while waiting for your meal. The daily specials are fresh and tasty. Perennial favorites include butter-fried cod, cod tongues, steaks, burgers, ribs, and seafood chowder; the truly famished can order the Commissioner's Feast, which includes samples of "all the seafood in the house" plus lobster or crab.

Fishing Point Park. ✆ **877/454-4900** or 709/454-4900. Reservations not accepted. Main courses C$8–C$22 (US$7.20–US$20/£4–£11); Feast costs more. AE, MC, V. Daily 11:30am–9pm. Closed Nov–May.

Tickle Inn at Cape Onion ✦ *Finds*   If you're seeking that end-of-the-world flavor, you'll be more than content here. Set on a remote cove at the end of a road near Newfoundland's northernmost point (you can see Labrador across the straits), the Tickle Inn occupies a solid fisherman's home built by the great-grandfather of the current innkeeper, David Adams, in 1890. (Adams is a retired school counselor from St. John's.) After lapsing into decrepitude, the home was expertly restored in 1990 and has recaptured the charm of a Victorian outport home. Its rooms are small but comfortable; all of them share three communal bathrooms. Before dinner, guests often gather in the parlor and enjoy snacks and complimentary cocktails; afterward, there's often music or other entertainment. **Dining room** ✦ meals are served family-style each evening. (Your only other option is to drive a considerable distance to the nearest restaurant.) The food is excellent, featuring local cuisine—Cape Onion soup with a touch of port, or paella with local seafood, for instance. Time your visit for berry season and you can expect them to pop up in the flan or other desserts. One of the highlights of a stay here is the small but superb network of hiking trails maintained by the Adams family; they ascend open bluffs to amazingly beautiful views of the Labrador Straits. The inn is about a 40-minute drive from L'Anse aux Meadows.

R.R. 1 (Box 62), Cape Onion, NL A0K 4J0. (℗ 866/814-8567 or 709/452-4321. Fax 709/452-2030. www.tickleinn.net. 4 units, none with private bathroom. C$55–C$70 (US$50–US$63/£28–£35) double. Rates include deluxe continental breakfast. MC, V. Closed Oct–May. **Amenities:** Dining room. *In room:* No phone.

6 Central Newfoundland

Spruce. Larch. Spruce. Bog. Spruce. Lake. Spruce. Bog.

You get the idea. This 350km (217-mile) stretch of the Trans-Canada Highway is long and, if you're in a grumpy mood, awfully tedious. Travelers crossing the interior typically spend more of their time cursing slow-moving RVs and wishing for passing lanes than admiring the scenery. The vast forest is certainly monumental, and along the way you'll crest some hills and take in panoramic views of lakes or ocean inlets that finger their way down from the north. You can also detour to some appealing fishing villages on the north coast. These notwithstanding, Newfoundland's interior is widely regarded as an area you should pass through en route to more inviting areas, rather than one in which to linger. If you've been saving a book on tape in the trunk, this is the time to rummage around and get it out.

Grand Falls–Windsor and Gander are both regional service centers and are reasonable stopping points for stretching your legs, taking in an attraction, gassing up, getting a bite to eat, and perhaps spending a night if evening is encroaching. But neither offers much as a destination for travelers, with the exception of hunters, fishermen, canoeists, and backpackers who might choose to employ the towns as bases from which to explore the woody, boggy, lake-filled interior. The area around Twillingate is a distinct exception—it's well worth the northward detour off the Trans-Canada Highway and could easily occupy a traveler who enjoys low-key, off-the-beaten-path destinations.

GRAND FALLS–WINDSOR

The settlement of Grand Falls dates from 1903, when British tycoons Lord Northcliffe and Lord Rothermere grew concerned that a restless Germany might disrupt the supply of newsprint from the Continent. They liked what they found at Grand Falls, where the Exploits River rushed over cascades amid a seemingly endless supply of timber. An ambitious paper mill was constructed on the banks of the river; it cost C$7.5 million at the time—which would be roughly C$160 million (US$144/£80 million) today—to build, employing some 15,000 mill- and woodworkers when it was finally completed in 1909. The mill took root and expanded over the decades; today, it's a major regional employer owned and operated by the Montréal-based Abitibi-Consolidated conglomerate.

The once-independent towns of Grand Falls and Windsor were joined as a single municipality in 1991, resulting in the ungainly name. It's also a bit cumbersome to get from one town to the other, because the Trans-Canada Highway neatly bisects the two. There's really little need to venture to Windsor, however; focus your attention on Grand Falls, which is south of the highway.

There's a **visitor information center** ((℗ 709/489-6332) is just off the Trans-Canada Highway on the west side of town. It's well marked from the highway.

EXPLORING GRAND FALLS–WINDSOR

You'll find a worthwhile detour to the **Salmonid Interpretation Centre** ((℗ 709/489-7350), across the river from the mill. Finding the place is a bit of a trick; you should stop at the visitor information center on the Trans-Canada Highway west of town and ask for a map, which the staff will happily supply.

The interpretation center is more intriguing than you might think. Not only will you get a good view of the rocky gorge through which the river tumbles lustily, but you also will be able to watch the Atlantic salmon laboring their way up the fish ladder, which opened in 1992. The ladder is a series of concrete pools linked by short waterfalls that leads to a main holding tank, where the fish are counted before a final gate is opened and they continue their upstream journeys.

Inside the exhibit center you can descend to an observation area below ground and see the impatient salmon through aquariumlike walls. The fish are surprisingly majestic, though the exhibits themselves are a bit dull. If you're passing through town around lunch or dinner, the cozy restaurant, located at the interpretation center, offers basic and reasonably priced meals. The center is open mid-June to mid-September daily from 8am to dusk. Admission is about C$3 (US$2.70/£1.50) adults, C$2 (US$1.80/ £1) seniors and children.

Back across the river in Grand Falls is the **Mary March Regional Museum** at 24 St. Catherine St. (© **709/292-4522**). It honors a Beothuk Indian who was captured in 1819 at Red Indian Lake; she died of tuberculosis after a year in captivity. The museum covers Newfoundland's 5,000-year history of inhabitation, from the early Maritime Archaic Indians on through the Paleo-Eskimo, Beothuk, Mi'kmaq, and, eventually, Europeans. Intriguing artifacts such as ancient stone gouges and the geometrically incised game pieces and pendants of the Beothuk are displayed. The museum also offers a perspective on the local pulp and paper industry, and the coming of the railway. It's open late April to late October daily from 9am to 4:45pm. Admission is C$2.50 (US$2.25/£1.25) adults, free for visitors under 18.

The area around Grand Falls–Windsor is good for backcountry exploring, although you need guidance owing to the extensive logging operations that feed the mill. **Red Indian Adventures** (© **709/486-0892**) is located 18km (11 miles) west of Grand Falls–Windsor in Aspen Brook, right off the Trans-Canada Highway. Proprietors Paul and Joy Rose offer a full range of canoe, kayak, and raft excursions and classes, ranging from white-water courses (the rapids on the Exploits River are vigorous and challenging) to daylong sea kayaking trips in Notre Dame Bay. Rates for day tours are C$69 to C$105 (US$62–US$95/£35–£53) per person. Overnight trips cost C$199 to C$249 (US$179–US$224/£100–£125) per person.

WHERE TO STAY & DINE

The simple brick **Mount Peyton Hotel** (© **800/563-4894** or 709/489-2251; www. mountpeyton.com) is the town's largest hotel and motel. (Take your pick: The seasonal motel is on the north side of the Trans-Canada Hwy., the year-round hotel on the south.) It has 102 hotel rooms and 48 motel and housekeeping units; all the hotel rooms are air-conditioned, and it's a good enough option. You might prefer the slower pace of the Hotel Robin Hood (below), however; the Mount Peyton can be noisy with highway sounds and is often bustling with meetings or conference attendees. Doubles range from C$87 all the way up to C$250 (US$78–US$225/£44–£125).

Hotel Robin Hood   This modern, basic, comfortable hotel is in a quiet area between the residential and commercial neighborhoods of Grand Falls. The building was constructed in 1997 and has been well maintained; all the rooms are larger than standard-issue motel rooms. (Note that rooms on the second floor are slightly bigger than those on the first.) It's the hotel closest to the salmon interpretation center. With its beadboard wainscoting, the in-house restaurant is more intimate than one might expect. The restaurant is open for dinner and lunch; its menu includes traditional favorites along the lines of fish and chips, chops, salmon, and steak.

78 Lincoln Rd., Grand Falls–Windsor, NL A2A 1N2. ℂ **709/489-5324.** Fax 709/489-6191. www.hotelrobinhood.com. 22 units. C$80–C$110 (US$72–US$99/£40–£55) double. Rates include continental breakfast. AE, DC, MC, V. Pets allowed. **Amenities:** Restaurant; room service. *In room:* A/C, TV.

TWILLINGATE 🐟🐟

The islands of North and South Twillingate are a photographer's dream. You'll find a bit of everything here—historic fishing harbors, gently rolling forested ridges, jagged cliffs washed by the surf, and open rocky barrens that roll down to the sea. There's also a good chance of spotting whales and icebergs—a good many of the Greenland icebergs seem to drift into Notre Dame Bay to the west of Twillingate, where they can be spotted in late spring and early summer.

Twillingate was named by early French fishermen, who noted a striking resemblance between the rocky cliffs of this region and the stone shores of their hometown of Toulinguet, near Brest, France. (The spelling was subsequently Anglicized.) The region around Twillingate is actually an archipelago linked by a series of causeways, and the drive northward on Route 340 from Boyd's Cove follows inlets and harbors cropping up between the low, green, forested hills. Twillingate (pop. 5,000) itself is a surprisingly active commercial center, with a number of bustling stores lining the road down to the old harbor. It's been connected to the mainland by causeway since 1972.

The communities around Twillingate have shown more entrepreneurial drive in offering services to travelers than you might typically find among Newfoundland's villages. A number of homes have been converted to B&Bs, and the route on to the two Twillingates is lined with homemade billboards touting boat tours, inns, restaurants, and the like.

ESSENTIALS

GETTING THERE   Twillingate is 142km (88 miles) northeast of Grand Falls–Windsor. Coming from the west, turn north on Route 340 approximately 50km (31 miles) east of Grand Falls–Windsor. From the east, head north on Route 330 at Gander, then take Route 331 to connect with Route 340 at Boyd's Cove. From Gander to Twillingate, it's about 101km (63 miles).

VISITOR INFORMATION   The **regional visitor information center** (ℂ **709/ 628-7454**) is located on Route 340 in Newville. It's open late June to early September, Monday through Friday from 8:30am to 8:30pm, and weekends from 10:30am to 6:30pm (closed weekends outside the peak summer season).

EXPLORING TWILLINGATE

As you reach Twillingate's harbor on Route 340, you'll arrive at a "T" intersection at Main Street. You can go right or left; both directions merit exploration.

Turning left leads to **Long Point** and the region's most prominent lighthouse. Along the way you'll pass the **Twillingate Museum & Craft Shop** (ℂ 709/884-2825; www. tmacs.ca) housed in a 1914 white clapboard building that was formerly the rectory for St. Peter's Anglican Church. Inside the handsome home you'll find displays of goods that might have been found in this outport community late in the 19th century, including hooked rugs, cranberry glass, dolls, and fashions. There's also a display of local artifacts from the Maritime Indian culture, and a display about Georgina Stirling, a soprano from town who was once the toast of European opera houses, performing as

Madame Toulinguet (she's buried at St. Peter's). The museum also houses an inviting gift shop with a selection of hand-knit sweaters, jams, and local history books. It's open daily from May through mid-October, 9am to 8pm. Admission is C$1 (US90¢/50p) adults, C50¢ (US45¢/25p) children.

Continuing on, the road to Long Point passes through a few small communities before entering undeveloped barrens riven with coves and cliffs. You'll soon pass **Seabreeze Municipal Park** ⋇ (small admission charge in summer), with picnic tables and dramatic hiking trails along the cliffs. The rusted equipment in the meadows is from a short-lived copper mine that operated here briefly between 1908 and 1917, and the ancient lava flows exposed in the cliff faces will be of interest to geologists.

A few minutes' drive beyond the park is the **Long Point Lighthouse** ⋇, Twillingate's must-see destination. The red-and-white, milk bottle–shaped lighthouse, built in 1876, isn't open to the public, but you can park along the cliffs and enjoy the sweeping views from these high headlands. (Unfortunately, antennae and microwave towers share the headland with the light, making it a poorer photo opportunity than you'd expect.) Whales and icebergs can often be spotted from here.

Turning right at Twillingate's main intersection takes you on a winding road through clustered homes along the harbor's edge. In 2km (1¼ miles) you'll come to the **Auk Island Winery** (© 877/639-4637; www.aukislandwinery.com), which has produced Notre Dame fruit wines since 1998. Among the varieties available here are dogberry, gooseberry, partridgeberry, blueberry, and strawberry-rhubarb wines. You're probably thinking they taste like Kool-Aid, but actually some of the wines are far drier than you might imagine. You can learn about the process and pick up bottles at the retail store; there's a small charge for a winery tour, but call ahead if you're thinking of taking it to see if that's possible, as there's no set schedule.

Continue along the road until you reach the CAUTION: ONE LANE traffic sign. Park here and continue on by foot to find some wonderful **hiking trails** ⋇⋇. The lane leads to a summer cottage and private property, but foot traffic is still permitted so far. To the left is a broad cobblestone beach; to the right are rocky, open hills and headlands laced by a network of informal hiking trails (look for cairns) that lead to oceanside cliffs and spectacular views. In mid- to late summer, bring containers and gather from the bountiful crop of raspberries and blueberries that grow in profusion here; they're among the plumpest and sweetest you'll find on the island. None of the trails here are very long or demanding; allow about 2 hours or so at most.

WHERE TO STAY

Camping is available in season at **Dildo Run Provincial Park** ⋇ (© 709/629-3350) on Route 340 in Virgin Arm, about 20 minutes south of Twillingate. The park has 55 sites, many along the water. A nicely maintained hiking trail winds along the remote coastline to Black Head, a hike of about an hour. Rates are C$13 (US$12/£6.50) per night.

One of Atlantic Canada's most dramatically sited campgrounds is at **Seabreeze Municipal Park** ⋇⋇ near the Long Point Lighthouse. It offers primitive camping (no showers or washrooms) from June through mid-October, with sites that are grassy and perched at the edge of soaring cliffs. The sunsets can't be beat.

Anchor Inn Motel The Anchor Inn is a well-maintained, relatively modern hotel just off the harbor. It was extensively updated in 1995, and has been kept up well enough since. Don't expect fancy, though: It's boxy and bland, with beige siding, and the rooms are standard motel units with durable chain-hotel furniture and decor. The

A 'Berg in the Hand: Spotting Icebergs

Twillingate is famous for the number of icebergs that float into the area and often run aground, providing a theatrical backdrop. That's not to say you'll be guaranteed icebergs if you arrive in midsummer: Some years are good for sighting icebergs; some aren't. Numerous factors conspire to determine when and if the 'bergs will show up, ranging from the thickness of sea ice in a given year to the prevailing direction of ocean currents to the summer temperature in the Arctic the previous year (which is when the glaciers in Greenland calved to produce the 'bergs that float past Newfoundland).

If icebergs *are* in the area, you should be able to spot them from the Long Point lighthouse or any of the other headlands or bays around Twillingate. (As anyone who's seen *Titanic* knows, icebergs tend to be neither subtle or elusive.) Your best bet is to arrive in June or July, although the occasional stray 'berg has been spotted in August as well.

Speaking of *Titanic,* you can get the best view of icebergs by taking a boat tour, two of which are offered right from Twillingate harbor. **Twillingate Island Boat Tours** (© 800/611-2374 or 709/884-2242; www.icebergtours.ca) has been operating since 1985 and offers iceberg and whale-watching tours. It's based out of the Iceberg Shop, painted with colorful murals of icebergs, at 50A Main St. (Turn right on Main St. when you enter Twillingate.) There are three cruises daily, May to September, taking 2 hours each. Also offering tours is Captain Perry Young's **Twillingate Adventure Tours** (© 888/447-8687 or 709/884-5999; www.daybreaktours.com), with a 40-passenger vessel. These 2-hour tours run from mid-May to Labor Day; also inquire about the outfit's sunset cruises.

Iceberg boat tours typically run about C$30 (US$27/£15) per adult, while children's fares might be discounted to half that.

best deals by far are the eight efficiency units in a separate building on a rise above the motel. They're larger and have small kitchens (you can buy fresh seafood in town and cook it yourself). Ask for a room with a harbor view. If you can't snag a room with a kitchen, there's also a restaurant on the premises.

Main St. (P.O. Box 550), Twillingate, NL A0G 4M0. © 800/450-3950 or 709/884-2777. Fax 709/884-2326. www. anchorinnmotel.ca. 22 units. C$84 (US$76/£42) double. AE, MC, V. **Amenities:** Restaurant. *In room:* TV.

Harbour Lights Inn B&B ⚜ *Value*   This attractive home on a hill across the road from the harbor was built in the 19th century for a British customs collector. It's been updated since, with vinyl siding and wood furniture that could have come from a '70s suburb. Guest rooms are located on the upper two floors and have an airy, whitewashed feel, a bit like Florida Keys bungalows—a neat trick in misty Newfoundland. The best units are higher-priced room nos. 4 and 5, which have burnished pine floors, in-room Jacuzzis, and wonderful views of the harbor. They're worth the extra few dollars.

189 Main St. (P.O. Box 729), Twillingate, NL A0G 4M0. © 877/884-2763 or 709/884-2763. Fax 709/884-2763. www. harbourlightsinn.com. 9 units. Mid June to late Aug C$109–C$139 (US$98–US$125/£55–£70) double; rest of the year C$79–C$125 (US$71–US$113/£39.50–£62.50) double. MC, V. *In room:* TV, hair dryer, Jacuzzi (2 rooms), no phone.

WHERE TO DINE

Options for dinner out are limited in Twillingate, despite the growing influx of travelers. The **Anchor Inn Motel** dining room (see above) and **R&J Restaurant,** on Main Street (© **709/884-2212**), remain the local favorites. Both serve family fare; you'll find an abundance of burgers, sandwiches, pizza, fried chicken, and the like.

GANDER

Gander (pop. 13,000) has historic resonance for aviation buffs. In the 1930s, when the island was still a British colony, the British Air Ministry developed a new airfield here. As the nearest fog-free spot to England, this was envisioned as a key link in transcontinental passenger air traffic. When World War II erupted less than a decade later, the air base suddenly took on an outsize importance of a different kind: as a staging area and refueling depot for troops and supplies heading overseas. After the war, the airstrip became a familiar sight to a generation of groggy tourists headed for Europe, as planes needed to stop here for refueling before or after making the leap across the Atlantic.

But aircraft technology was advancing fast, and the Boeing 707—which could cross the Atlantic from New York to Europe in a single bound—diminished Gander's importance in a single stroke; today the airfield is a shadow of its former self. The airport still exists and still gets a fair amount of commercial traffic (especially when St. John's is fogged in), but the city's Trans-Canada Highway gas stations are now usually the only thing travelers see of Gander—and only briefly at that—before resuming their journeys east or west across the island.

The **visitor information center** (© **709/256-7110**), open from 9am to 9pm in summer and 9am to 5pm the rest of the year, is well marked on the south side of the Trans-Canada Highway (next to the Aviation Museum and across from the Albatross Motel) as you drive through town.

EXPLORING GANDER

The Trans-Canada Highway skirts the southern edge of the downtown, which isn't really worth a detour; the commercial center was developed after the advent of the automobile, and as a result you'll find a handful of cheerless shopping plazas and fast-food joints. It's just a place to stock up on supplies on the way to Twillingate or Terra Nova National Park.

A handful of hotels, restaurants, and gas stations are situated on the Trans-Canada Highway. You'll also find the **North Atlantic Aviation Museum** (© **709/256-2923;** www.naam.ca) here. In fact, you can't miss it—it's the hangarlike building with the butt-end of a plane sticking out of the side. A couple of historic planes can be viewed on the grounds, including a Tiger Moth and a very handsome firefighting plane. With its emphasis on aviation arcana, the museum will be of interest chiefly to confirmed airplane addicts. It's open from 9am to 9pm daily in summer; fall through spring it's open Monday through Friday from 9am to 4pm. The cost is C$4 (US$3.60/£2) adults, C$3 (US$2.70/£1.50) seniors and children 6 to 16.

Just east of town, look for a sign directing you to the **Silent Witness Memorial.** This memorial marks the site where a plane carrying members of the U.S. 101st Airborne mysteriously went down shortly after takeoff in 1985. The plane was returning from a peacekeeping mission in the Middle East; all 259 on board were killed, marking it as the worst aviation disaster on Canadian soil. The breathtaking view of Gander Lake from the crash site makes visiting the memorial an especially bittersweet experience.

WHERE TO STAY & DINE

Two largish hotels right on the Trans-Canada Highway offer the best accommodations in town, although neither will win personality awards. The **Albatross Hotel** (© **800/ 563-4900** in Canada, or 709/256-3956) has 97 modern rooms and a ground-floor restaurant and cocktail lounge. Prices range from C$82 to C$165 (US$74–US$149/ £41–£83). Nearby is the **Hotel Gander** (© **800/563-2988** in Canada, or 709/256-3931), with 148 rooms, an aviation theme, a small indoor pool, modest fitness facil- ities, and a chain hotel-style restaurant that offers many traditional Newfoundland specialties. Room rates are C$89 to C$129 (US$80–US$116/£45–£65). Both are popu- lar with bus tours, conference planners, and wedding parties. Another option is **Sin- bad's Hotel,** Bennett Drive (© **800/563-8330** or 709/651-2678), a 111-room hotel/ motel with suites off the highway that has an above-average dining room. Rates are C$84 to C$162 (US$76–US$146/£42–£81).

7 Terra Nova National Park ★

You may have heard other travelers rave about Gros Morne National Park as you dis- cussed your impending trip to Newfoundland. At the same time, you might have received only deafening silence upon mention of the island's other national park, Terra Nova, on the island's eastern shore.

There's a reason for that. Words like *dramatic* and *grandeur* don't get tossed around here much. This is an exceedingly pleasant spot with lots of boreal forest and coastal landscape, along with a surplus of low, rolling hills. Within its boundaries, forest and shoreline are preserved for wildlife and recreation and make for excellent exploration. But the terra, however nova it is, isn't likely to take your breath away. (With one pos- sible exception: the cliffs and hills at the mouth of Newman Sound.) More than likely, a visit here will simply leave you soothed and relaxed.

Activities and facilities at Terra Nova have mostly been designed with families in mind. There's always something going on, from games with starfish at the interpreta- tion center to movies at the park's main campground. Terra Nova also has a fine jun- ior naturalist program, and many of the hikes are just the right duration for younger kids; there's also a fine (and relatively warm) swimming area at Sandy Pond.

If your goal is to put some distance between yourself and the noisy masses, head for the backcountry section of the park. A number of campsites are accessible by foot, canoe, or ferry only; once there, you'll be able to scout for bald eagles and shooting stars in complete silence.

ESSENTIALS

GETTING THERE   Terra Nova is located on the Trans-Canada Highway. It's about 232km (144 miles) from St. John's, and 609km (378 miles) from Port aux Basques.

VISITOR INFORMATION   The **Visitor Interpretation Centre** (© **709/533- 2801**) at the Saltons Day-Use Area, about 5km (3 miles) north of the Newman Sound Campground, is open daily June to mid-October from 9am to 7pm (limited hours after Labor Day; closed from Oct to early Jan). There's a kiosk at the campground as well, open 8am to 12 midnight in high season, shorter hours out of season.

FEES   A park entry fee is required of all visitors, even those just overnighting at a park campground. Fees are C$5.45 (US$4.90/£2.75) per day adults, C$4.70 (US$4.25/ £2.35) seniors, C$2.70 (US$2.45/£1.35) children 6 to 16, C$14 (US$13/£7) families.

Annual passes are available for about C$27 (US$24/£14) per adult or C$68 (US$61/£34) per family.

EXPLORING THE PARK

A trip to the park should begin with a visit to the spiffy, modern Visitor Information Centre (see above). It's located on a scenic part of the sound, encased in verdant hills, and from here the sound looks suspiciously like a lake. Oceangoing sailboats tied up at the wharf will suggest otherwise, however.

The center has a handful of exhibits focusing on local marine life, and many are geared toward kids. There's a touch tank where you can scoop up starfish and other aquatic denizens, and informative displays on life underwater. Especially nifty is an underwater video monitor that allows you to check out the action under the adjacent wharf with a joystick and zoom controls. There's also a **wet lab,** where you can conduct experiments under the guidance of a park naturalist. The center is free with your paid park admission. You'll also find a snack bar and gift shop here.

Check with a ranger on duty for your options in exploring the park. They're good at pointing you in the right direction, whether your interests are in soft adventure or in getting face to face with wild nature in the backcountry.

HIKING & BOATING

The park has 77km (48 miles) of maintained **hiking trails.** Many of these are fairly easy treks of an hour or so through undemanding woodlands. The booklet you'll receive when you pay your entrance fee offers descriptions of the various trails. Among the more popular is the 4.5km (2.8-mile) **Coastal Trail** ✦✦, which runs between Newman Sound Campground and the information center. You get great views of the sound, and en route you pass the wonderfully named **Pissing Mare Falls.**

The most demanding hike is probably the **Outport Trail,** a 46km (29-mile) round-trip that winds in and around the south shore of Newman Sound past abandoned settlements. It's possible to overnight at two backcountry sites along the way. Each direction can be completed in about 7½ hours, but with camping layovers the whole trip typically takes 2 to 3 days, with the going sometimes slowed by bogs and wet trail sections.

For **canoeing,** head to either Sandy Pond or Southwest Arm. Canoes are available for rent at Sandy Pond by the hour or day. You can cobble together a very attractive 10km (6-mile) one-way trip from Sandy Pond by paddling to Beachy Pond (this requires a 400m/1,312-ft. portage), then continuing onward to Dunphy's Pond.

The park also lends itself quite nicely to **sea kayaking.** If you've brought your own boat, ask for route suggestions at the information center. (Overnight trips to Minchin and South Broad coves are good options, as are day trips to Swale Island.)

For a more passive view from the water, consider a tour with **Ocean Watch Tours** (© **709/533-6024**), which sails in a converted fishing boat four times daily from the wharf at the visitor center. You're all but certain to spot bald eagles and, with some luck, whales and icebergs. The tours typically cost around C$35 (US$32/£18) for a 2-hour tour and around C$45 (US$41/£23) for a 3-hour tour, half-price for children. Reservations are recommended during peak season, when the tours take place three times daily.

CAMPING

Terra Nova's main campground is at **Newman Sound.** It has 355 campsites (mostly of the gravel-pad variety) set in and around spruce forest and sheep laurel clearings. Amenities include free showers, limited electrical hookups, a grocery store and snack bar, evening programs, a laundromat, and hiking trails. Be aware that the campground can be quite noisy and bustling in peak season. Fees are C$18 to C$28 (US$16–US$25/£9–£14), depending on level of services and time of year.

At the park's northern border is the somewhat more rustic **Malady Head** 🎔 camping area. This is the better destination for those looking for quiet. It has 99 campsites, along with showers and access to a popular hiking trail. If you want your own campfire, head here; at Newman Sound, fires are restricted to shared community fire pits. The fee is about C$16 to C$19 (US$14–US$17/£8–£9.50) per site.

The park also maintains a handful of backcountry campsites. Between four and eight parties can camp at each site, and all but Beachy Pond allow open fires. Dunphy's Island is accessible by canoe only and involves a 400m (1,312-ft.) portage; on the shore across from the island site is another site, which is also accessible via a 5km (3-mile) footpath. These cost about C$15 (US$14/£7.50) per site.

For a more coastal backcountry experience, head for either **Minchin Cove** or **South Broad Cove.** Both can be reached via demanding hikes (11km/6.8 miles and 16km/9.910 miles, respectively) on the **Outport Trail** 🎔, which departs from Newman Sound Campground (see above). You can also arrange to be dropped off by boat, then picked up later; ask at the visitor center for details. Backcountry campers need to register in advance and pay a small access fee for the privilege.

WHERE TO STAY & DINE

Campgrounds are the only option within the park itself. At the north end of the park, the town of Eastport (see "Nearby Excursions," below) is 16km (10 miles) from the Trans-Canada Highway on Route 310 and offers several places to stay overnight. From May through the end of October, try **The Doctor's Inn Bed & Breakfast,** 5 Burden's Rd., Eastport, NL A0G 1Z0 (© **877/677-3539** or 709/677-3539), with six rooms priced at C$70 to C$95 (US$63–US$86/£35–£48); there's a large patio here and breakfast is included. Right on a sandy beach are the **Seaview Cottages,** 325 Beach Rd., Eastport, NL A0G 1Z0 (© **709/677-2271**), open May through September, with 23 basic cottages, a small indoor heated pool, minigolf, a barbecue area, and other family-friendly amenities. Rates are C$60 to C$75 (US$54–US$68/£30–£38).

At the southern edge of the park you'll also find the larger-scale Terra Nova Golf Resort (see below).

Terra Nova Golf Resort 🎔 (Kids   This modern three-story resort on 88 hectares (217 acres) of oceanfront property is a short drive off Route 1, about 2km (1¼ miles) south of the park's southern entrance. Even better, it's adjacent to both the 6,546-yard, par-71 **Twin River Golf Course** 🎔🎔—one of Atlantic Canada's most scenic, best-regarded courses, even if it's sometimes overlooked in favor of Nova Scotian courses—and the 9-hole Eagle Creek Golf Course. This hotel isn't lavish at all—it features bland, cookie-cutter rooms, but it's clean, comfortable, and well-located for a golfing holiday or exploring the park. It's a popular spot with families, since kids can roam the grounds, splash around in the pool, and congregate around the downstairs video games. Note that about two-thirds of the rooms consist of two double beds; the rest are king-bedded or queen-bedded, have pullout sofas, or (in a few cases) are suites with full kitchens. The resort's Clode Sound Dining Room, offering standard resort fare with an emphasis on chicken and beef, is open daily for breakfast and dinner; there's also a pub downstairs, open from lunchtime.

Rte. 1, Port Blandford, NL A0C 2G0. © **709/543-2525.** Fax 709/543-2201. www.terranovagolf.com. 89 units. C$101–C$157 (US$91–US$141/£51–£79) double. AE, DC, DISC, MC, V. **Amenities:** 2 restaurants; bar; outdoor pool; 2 tennis courts; Jacuzzi; sauna; game room. *In room:* A/C, TV, kitchenette (some units).

NEARBY EXCURSIONS

Route 310 runs along the northern edge of Terra Nova National Park and winds along inlets and hillsides to the Eastport peninsula. In and around the town of Eastport are a number of fine **sandy beaches,** hidden in coves and laid out in long strands edging the road. Some of the best are located along Route 310 (between Eastport and Salvage; this route also passes through the wonderfully named village of Happy Adventure), as well as in the aptly named village of **Sandy Cove.** Follow signs to the right when you enter Eastport.

Across from the Sandy Cove beach is the start of **The Old Trails** ⚑. The main trail in this system winds along a wooded ridge and past remote ponds about 8km (5 miles) to the village of Salvage; bear in mind that the trail is still under development, so hiking may be a bit rugged. Bring lunch, sturdy boots, and a compass, and plan to make an adventure of it. Brochures with general descriptions of the trails are sometimes available in local visitor information centers.

From Eastport, continue on toward the fishing village of **Salvage** ⚑⚑, about 10km (6 miles) farther along. The road runs alongside the water, except for the periodic detour up into the hills. The village itself is tucked into and around several coves, and everywhere great slabs of rock protrude from the earth, lending a cinematic drama to the landscape. More about the region's history can be found at the **Salvage Fisherman's Museum** ⚑, set on a low hill overlooking the harbor (☎ 709/677-2414). It's housed in the oldest building in the area—an 1860 home that's now filled with displays on the whys and hows of fishing. It's open daily mid-June to early September from 10am to 6pm (sometimes shorter hours; check ahead), and there's a small admission charge.

A longer excursion is the ferry trip that winds through a beautiful archipelago to remote **St. Brendan's Island** ⚑. From **Burnside,** just north of Eastport, 1-hour-long ferries (☎ 709/466-4121 or 709/677-2204) run three to five times daily, with one-way fares of C$8.25 (US$7.45/£4.15) for a car and driver, C$2.75 (US$2.50/£1.40) for additional passengers, C$2 (US$1.80/£1) for seniors and students. Pay when leaving the island. The island is home to several small communities located along some 9km (5⅔ miles) of unpaved road, although St. Brendan's offers little in the way of services for travelers—just a few general stores, and no restaurants or overnight accommodations.

The island makes a good destination for adventurous mountain bikers. Otherwise, just take the ferry out and back as a low-budget, scenic boat tour. The islands between Burnside and St. Brendan's are uninhabited, wild, and beautiful: You might spot **bald eagles** perched along the shore during the 45-minute crossing.

Also in Burnside, if you've made it this far, be sure to check out the **Burnside Archaeology Centre museum** ⚑⚑ (☎ 709/677-2474) on Main Street, easily recognizable by the replica *mamateek* (aboriginal Canadian birch-bark house) standing outside. The museum displays artifacts from local archaeological digs that have been going on here for about 20 years; some are as many as 5,000 (yes, 5,000) years old. This is a fascinating record of the Beothuk people who inhabited Newfoundland at the time of the first Viking and European contact. You can also watch staff sifting, cleaning, and cataloguing some of the finds. The center sometimes runs a very scenic 4-hour **boat tour** of the area dig sites, including a stop for a hilltop walk along a hiking trail with expansive views at Bloody Bay Cove; inquire about times and prices.

The museum, which is open mid-June through October daily from 9am to 7pm (but check ahead before coming), is also a good place to park and stretch your legs for a scenic walk around the little village.

8 The Bonavista Peninsula ★

The Bonavista Peninsula juts northeast into the sea just south of Terra Nova National Park. It's a worthy side trip for travelers fascinated by the island's past. You'll find a historic village, a wonderfully curated historic site, and one of the province's most intriguing lighthouses. It's also a good spot to see whales, puffins, and icebergs.

Along the south shore of the peninsula is **Trinity,** an impeccably maintained old village. (It's the only village in Newfoundland where the historic society has say over what can and cannot be built.) Some longtime visitors grouse that it's becoming overly popular and a bit dandified with B&Bs and traffic restrictions. That may be, but there's still a palpable sense of tradition in this profoundly historic spot. Anyway, it's the place for miles to find good shelter and a decent meal.

From Trinity it's about 40km (25 miles) out to the tip of the peninsula. Somewhere along the route, which isn't particularly scenic, you'll wonder whether it's worth it. But keep going; it will be. Plan to spend at least a couple of hours exploring the dramatic, ocean-carved point and the fine fishing village of **Bonavista,** with its three excellent historic properties.

Note that there's little in the way of interesting accommodations or restaurants this far out, so it's better to plan this as a day trip (perhaps from Trinity) rather than an overnight. The one sight possibly worth seeing is the **Bonavista North Regional Museum** (© **709/536-2110**), open daily from 10am to 6pm July through September. It features displays on fishermen and the local fishing industry, as well as some items depicting community life here during the early 20th century.

ESSENTIALS

GETTING THERE   Depending on the direction you're coming from, the Bonavista Peninsula can be reached from the Trans-Canada Highway via Route 233, Route 230, or Route 230A. Route 230 runs all the way to the tip of the cape; Route 235 forms a partial loop back and offers some splendid water views along the way. The round-trip from Clarenville to the tip is approximately 232km (144 miles).

VISITOR INFORMATION   Consult the **Discovery Trail Tourism Association** (© **866-420-3255** or 709/466-3845; www.thediscoverytrail.org) at 54 Manitoba Dr. in Clarenville with your questions; they have the best information about this stunningly lovely and historically fascinating region. Get there by car by taking Route 230A off the Trans-Canada Highway; the association is located nearly at the junction of the two roads. This is about 40km (25 miles) south of Terra Nova National Park, and from here it's about another 75km (47 miles) down the side road to Trinity.

The tourism association also maintains a greatly helpful website, which can be found on the Web at **www.thediscoverytrail.org.**

TRINITY ★

The tiny coastal hamlet of Trinity, with a year-round population of just 200, once had more residents than St. John's. For more than 3 centuries, from its first visit by Portuguese fishermen in the 1500s until well into the 19th century, Trinity benefited from a long and steady tenure as a hub for traders, primarily from England, who supplied the booming fishing economy of Trinity Bay and eastern Newfoundland.

Technological advances (including the railroad) doomed Trinity's merchant class, and the town lapsed into an extended economic slumber. But even today, you can see lingering traces of the town's former affluence, from the attractive flourishes in much of the architecture to the rows of white picket fences all around the village.

In recent years, the provincial government and concerned individuals have taken a keen interest in preserving Trinity, and it's clearly benefiting from a revival in which many homes have been preserved and a good number made over as bed-and-breakfasts. Several buildings (see below) are open to the public as provincial historic sites, two others as local historical museums. Most are open mid-June to early October, then shuttered the remainder of the year. Allow about 3 hours to wander about and explore.

Days on which the popular historic pageant is held (see "Tours & Shows," below) bring a flood tide of visitors to Trinity, making parking and rooms scarce and meals sometimes difficult to obtain. The village is also well worth seeing on nonpageant days, when a great quiet settles in.

Start your voyage into the past at the **Trinity Interpretation Centre** (© 709/464-2042) at the Tibbs House, open 10am to 5:30pm daily from mid-May through late September. (It's a bit tricky to find, since signs don't seem to be a priority. Follow the one-way road around the village and continue straight past the parish hall. Look on the left for the pale green home with the prominent gable.) Here you can purchase tickets, pick up a walking-tour map, and get oriented with a handful of history exhibits. Entry costs C$3 (US$2.70/£1.50) per adult. This ticket also admits you to the Lester-Garland property and the Hiscock House (see below), which keep the same seasons and hours as the interpretation center.

A minute's walk away is the brick **Lester-Garland Premises** (© 709/464-2042), often the first stop on travelers' Trinity itineraries. Here you can learn about the traders and their times. This handsome Georgian-style building is a convincing replica (built in 1997) of one of the earlier structures, built in 1819. The original was occupied until 1847, when it was abandoned and began to deteriorate. It was torn down (much to the horror of local historians) in the 1960s, but parts of the building hardware, including some doors and windows, were salvaged and warehoused until the rebuilding.

Next door is the Ryan Building, where a succession of the town's most prominent merchants kept shop. The grassy lots between these buildings and the water were once filled with warehouses, none of which survived. The **Rising Tide Theatre** (© 888/464-3377 or 709/464-3232) was architecturally styled after one of the warehouses (a good imagination is helpful in envisioning the others). This 255-seat theater is a good stop if you enjoy the arts and offers a surprisingly full card of dramatic productions from mid-June through the fall. Performances here are top-rate, and well worth the admission cost; that's remarkable in such a remote outpost.

A short walk away, just past the parish house, is the **Hiscock House** (© 709/464-2042), a handsome home where Emma Hiscock raised her children and kept a shop after the untimely death of her husband in a boating accident at age 39. The home has been restored to appear as it might have in 1910, and helpful guides fill in the details. Again, the combination Trinity ticket gets you in here for C$3 (US$2.70/£1.50) per adult; children under 13 enter for free.

The **Trinity Historical Society Museum** on Church Road (© 709/464-3599), in a late-19th-century home, contains more than 2,000 everyday artifacts that one might have seen in Trinity a century or more ago; it's open mid-June through mid-October, 10am to 5:30pm daily. The adjacent fire pump dates from 1811 and is intriguing.

Also nearby, the **Green Family Forge Blacksmith Museum** ℛ (on Church Rd., just beyond St. Paul's Anglican Church)—operated by the museum folks—will teach you about what was one of the essential local industries in the early 18th century. This current smithy was built about a century later, and used until 1955; in 1999, it was restored and began operating once more. The smith and museum are open the same season and hours as the museum.

TOURS & SHOWS

An entertaining way to learn about the village's history is from the summertime **Trinity Pageant.** Local actors lead a peripatetic audience through the streets, acting out episodes from Trinity's past. For dates and tickets, contact the innovative **Rising Tide Theatre** (see above); also check with the theater about performances throughout the summer, most depicting island episodes or themes. In the past, the cast staged their shows at impromptu venues around town (upstairs at the parish hall, in a field at the water's edge, on the front porch of a B&B, and the like).

Also recommended is the 2-hour historical walking tour of Trinity led daily at 10am by **Kevin Toope** (© 709/464-3723). Toope's family has been in the area for generations, and Kevin (a schoolteacher in St. John's most of the year) has put together an informed and entertaining tour of the village he knows so well. After a tutored loop around the winding streets, you'll come away with lots of fascinating facts and bits of color that help bring the town to life. The tours cost C$8 (US$7.20/£4) per adult, free for kids. (One tidbit you'll learn: Whatever happened to the family of one of the town's merchant princes, who owned practically everything but treated his employees with contempt? Historians have traced a single descendent: a derelict in London.)

OUTDOOR PURSUITS

A trail system on the Bonavista Peninsula is being created through woodlands and over headlands. The **Discovery Trail Tourism Association** (© 709/466-3845; see above) has been working with other groups to develop and promote hiking trails on the peninsula, and a trail guide is now available.

There is a superb hike about a 15-minute drive south of Trinity, outside the fishing village of New Bonaventure: the **Kerley's Harbour Trail** ✴✴, which starts from the end of the parking area adjacent to St. John's Anglican Church; make the first right as you enter New Bonaventure, and then drive uphill to the end of the road. This 2km (1.2-mile) trail—a grassy lane that winds over rolling hills and past a pristine pond—requires about 35 minutes of walking, and ends at the abandoned outport of Kerley's Harbour, a well-protected cove flanked by rocky hills and open meadows dotted with fallen homes. Along the waters are remnants of fishing stages, and a new extension trail leads to a resettled community—in the early 1900s the government moved remote communities to a more central area in order to provide them with better services—which is no longer inhabited but can still be visited on foot.

WHERE TO STAY

All the properties mentioned below are in the heart of Trinity's historic area. Reservations are essential during the peak summer season, especially when the pageant is scheduled. Those who come unprepared risk a drive back to Clarenville (about 45 miles) to find a room.

Lockston Path Provincial Park (© 709/464-3553) is a 15-minute drive from Trinity in Port Rexton and one of the better-outfitted of the province's parks for camping. From mid-May to mid-September, there are 56 campsites available here (about one-third with water and electrical hookups), and the park now has a modern comfort station with free hot showers. You can swim at a big sandy beach, though there is no lifeguard. Campsites at Lockston Path cost C$20 (US$18/£10) each.

If you're still stuck for a room, the good **Eriksen Premises** restaurant on West Street (see "Where to Dine," below) is part of a smart bed-and-breakfast operation renting out seven well-appointed suites in an 18th-century home. Rooms run from C$90 to C$120 (US$81–US$108/£45–£60) per night; most are simple and sturdy, though one also has a Jacuzzi. Call ✆ **877/464-3698** or 709/464-3698 for details.

Bishop White Manor Bed & Breakfast   This historic house with early woodwork and tin ceilings was home to Newfoundland's first native-born bishop, and is convenient to just about everything in Trinity. It's more serviceable than elegant, and the small rooms are *very* small. The extra cost for a larger room is worth it, especially if it's a rainy day. There's limited common space on the first floor, although the rear deck is a nice spot to unwind if the weather's sunny.

Gallavan's Lane (P.O. Box 58), Trinity, NL A0C 2S0. ✆ 877/464-3698 or 709/464-3698. Fax 709/464-2104. www.trinity experience.com. 9 units. C$80–C$95 (US$72–US$86/£40–£48) double. Rates include full breakfast. AE, MC, V. Closed mid-Oct to mid-May. *In room:* No phone.

Campbell House Bed & Breakfast Inn ✿ (Finds)   This handsome 1840 home and two nearby cottages are set amid lovely gardens on a twisting lane overlooking Fisher Cove. Two rooms are on the second floor of the main house, and these have a nice historic flair, even to the point that they require some stooping under beams if you're over 5 feet, 10 inches tall. Two rooms are located in a lovely and simple pine-paneled house just beyond the gardens, and they feature an adjacent waterfront deck and a full kitchen on the first floor. The Twine Loft (home to a restaurant) also overlooks the water. An affiliated property, the **Artisan Inn,** offers three similar simple rooms at C$115 to C$135 (US$104–US$122/£58–£68) double occupancy. Innkeeper Tineke Gow and her family are great sources of information on local adventures and maintain a wine cellar on the premises. Reserve well in advance for July and August, when the inn rarely has a free room.

High St., Trinity, Trinity Bay, NL A0C 2S0. ✆ 877/464-7700 or 709/464-3377. www.trinityvacations.com. 3 units plus 3 units in Artisan Inn. C$109–C$230 (US$98–US$207/£55–£115). Rates include full breakfast. AE, DC, MC, V. Closed Nov–May. **Amenities:** Laundry. *In room:* TV, kitchenette, dataport, hair dryer, iron, no phone.

Village Inn   This handsome old inn, located on what passes for a busy street in Trinity (busy with pedestrians, that is), has a pleasantly lived-in feel with its eclectic-but-leaning-toward-Victorian furniture, front porch for relaxing, and small dining room that feels as if it hasn't changed a whit in 75 years. The folksy sitting room, with its fireplace, piano, and collections of books and board games, is a popular chill-out spot. Innkeepers Christine and Peter Beamish do a fine job of making guests feel at home here; they also run Ocean Contact, a whale-watch operation that uses an 8m (26-ft.) rigid-hull inflatable. Ask about tour availability when you book.

Taverner's Path (P.O. Box 10), Trinity, Trinity Bay, NL A0C 2S0. ✆ 709/464-3269. Fax 709/464-3700. www.oceancontact. com/inn/inn.html. 6 units. From C$100 (US$90/£50) double. Packages available. MC, V. Closed except by arrangement Nov–Apr. Small, well-behaved pets allowed. **Amenities:** 2 dining rooms; pub. *In room:* No phone.

WHERE TO DINE

Eriksen Premises ✿ TRADITIONAL   Despite some inelegant touches, this is Trinity's best restaurant, and it offers good value. The restaurant shares the first floor of a B&B with a gift shop, and has a homey feel with oak floors, beadboard ceiling, and

> ## *Tips* Bonavista: Taking the High Road
>
> If you're approaching Bonavista on Route 230, I'd suggest detouring down Route 238 through **Elliston** ✿ first. This is a pretty coastal village worth the few extra kilometers. More to the point, this route will take you into the town of Bonavista via a nicely scenic road that crosses through high upland barrens. You'll get great **views** ✿ of the whitewashed town with its expansive bay beyond as you crest the hill, and maybe an iceberg or two—this is a great vantage point from which to check for them before heading back down to sea level and the town.

Victorian accents. (There's also dining on an outside deck, which is especially inviting at lunchtime.) Meals are mostly traditional: cod tongue, broiled halibut, scallops, liver and onion, chicken, and the like. The service and food are a notch above the expected, though. Desserts, like the cheesecake with fresh berry toppings, are especially good.

West St. ✆ **877/464-3698** or 709/464-3698. Reservations recommended during peak season. Main courses C$5–C$7 (US$4.50–US$6.30/£2.50–£3.50) at lunch, C$10–C$19 (US$9–US$17/£4.50–£9.50) at dinner. MC, V. Daily 8am–9:30pm. Closed Nov–May.

Village Inn ✿ *(Finds* TRADITIONAL   The pleasantly old-fashioned dining room at the Village Inn (see "Where to Stay") has been known to serve good vegetarian meals, which is an extremely rare species in the Newfoundland kitchen. The options might include a lentil shepherd's pie or a rice-nut casserole. Of course, those looking for comfort food are also well served, with options like chowder, meatloaf, fried cod, liver and onions, a ham plate, or a seafood platter. This is country cooking at its best—everything made from scratch, soups to dessert.

Taverner's Path. ✆ **709/464-3269.** Main courses C$8–C$20 (US$7.20–US$18/£4–£10); lunch items less. MC, V. Daily 8am–9pm.

BONAVISTA ✿

Bonavista is a 45-minute drive from Trinity and is a strongly recommended day trip for those spending a night or two in the area. The bay here is noted for its icebergs, which can linger into middle or late summer, so watch for them closely if you're here at that time; scan the horizon with the kids for icebergs and "bergy bits."

EXPLORING THE TOWN

The **Ryan Premises National Historic Site** ✿ (✆ **709/468-1600**) opened in 1997, with Queen Elizabeth herself presiding over the ceremonies. Located in downtown Bonavista, the newish site is a very photogenic grouping of white clapboard buildings at the harbor's edge. For more than a century, this was the town's most prominent salt-fish complex, where fishermen sold their catch and bought all the sundry goods needed to keep an outport functioning. Michael Ryan opened for business here in 1857; his heirs kept the business going all the way up until 1978. (One elderly resident recalled that you could "get everything from a baby's fart to a clap of thunder" from the Ryans.) The spiffy complex today features an art gallery, a local museum, a gift shop, a handcrafted-furniture store, and an exhibit on the role of the codfish in

Newfoundland's history. An hour or two here will go a long way toward helping you make sense of the rest of your visit to this singular island.

The property is open daily mid-May through late October from 10am to 6pm. Admission is C$3.95 (US$3.55/£2) adults, C$3.45 (US$3.10/£1.75) seniors, C$1.95 (US$1.75/£1) youths, and C$9.90 (US$8.90/£4.95) families.

On the far side of the harbor, and across from a field of magnificent irises, is the beautiful **Mockbeggar Plantation** (© 709/468-7300). Named after an English seaport that shared characteristics with Bonavista, the home was occupied by prominent Newfoundland politician F. Gordon Bradley. It's been restored to how it appeared when Bradley moved here in 1940, and it features much of the original furniture. With a few telltale exceptions (note the wonderful 1940s-era carpet in the formal dining room), it shows a strong Victorian influence. The house is managed as a provincial historic site, and admission is C$3 (US$2.70/£1.50) adults, free for children 12 and under; this ticket also gets you admission to the Cape Bonavista Lighthouse (see below). The house is open to the public daily from mid-May to late September, 10am to 5:30pm.

A replica of the *Matthew* (© 877/468-1497 or 709/468-1493), the ship John Cabot sailed when he first landed in Newfoundland in 1497, floats in Bonavista's harbor. This compact ship is an exacting replica, based on plans of the original ship. (Don't confuse this ship with the other *Matthew* replica, which crossed the Atlantic and sailed around Newfoundland in 1997.) An interpretive center and occasional performances staged wharfside provide context for your tour aboard the ship, which is designed as a floating museum. Because it's an exact copy and looks roughly as it did 500 years ago, the ship doesn't have an engine or any modern safety devices, and thus isn't allowed to leave the dock for passenger cruises. It stays tied up along the dock in summer and is stored in an architecturally striking white clapboard boathouse in the off season.

The ship is open from June to mid-October, daily from 10am to 6pm (to 8pm in summer). Admission is C$6.50 (US$5.85/£3.25) adults, C$6 (US$5.40/£3) seniors, C$2.25 (US$2.05/£1.15) children ages 6 to 16, C$16 (US$14/£8) per family; plan to spend an hour touring the ship.

JUST NORTH OF TOWN

The extraordinary **Cape Bonavista Lighthouse Provincial Historic Site** ⊕ (© 709/ 468-7444) is located 6km (3¾ miles) north of town on a rugged point. Built in 1843, the lighthouse is essentially a stone tower around which a red-and-white wood-frame house has been constructed. The keepers' quarters (the lightkeeper and his assistant both lived here) have been restored to the year 1870; today, you can clamber up narrow stairs to the light and inspect the ingenious clockwork mechanism that kept six lanterns revolving all night, every night, between 1895 and 1962. (With some help— it took 15 min. to wind the counterweight by *hand,* a job that needed to be repeated every 2 hr . . . all night long.) This light served mariners until its role was usurped in very recent times by an inelegant modern steel tower and beacon.

The lighthouse is open daily from mid-May to late September from 10:30am to 5:30pm; admission is C$3 (US$2.70/£1.50) per adult, free for children 12 and under. (This ticket also includes admission to the Mockbeggar Plantation; see above.)

Below the lighthouse on a rocky promontory cleft from the mainland is a lively **puffin colony** ⊕⊕. Dozens of these stumpy, colorful (and endangered) birds hop around the grassy knob and take flight into the sea winds. They're easily seen from just below the lighthouse; bring binoculars for a clearer view, but don't disturb them. Red-footed common murres dive for fish below as well, and whales are often sighted just offshore. (You just might catch sight of whales and puffins through your binoculars at the same moment—with beautiful icebergs just out of frame.)

Also nearby is a **statue of John Cabot.** Although no one can prove it, long-standing tradition holds that Cape Bonavista was the first land spotted by the Italian explorer (who was working for the English) in 1497. The statue is located in the handsome **Landfall Municipal Park,** next to the lighthouse, where you'll find picnic tables and an exceptional example of a quiggly fence, a traditional Newfoundland windbreak made of vertically woven whips or saplings.

En route to the lighthouse you'll pass a turnoff to **Dungeons Provincial Park.** It's about 2km (1¼ miles) down a gravel road through cow, goat, and sheep pastures. Park and follow the short trail to a punchbowl-like cavity some 50 yards across. Relentless waves carved two tunnels beneath the pasture, and eventually the grassy roof collapsed, leaving this gaping hole to be flushed by the surf. Admission is free.

9 The Baccalieu Trail

The Baccalieu Trail forms a loop around the long, narrow, unnamed peninsula that separates Conception Bay from Trinity Bay. It doesn't have the distinguished 18th-century pedigree of neighboring Bonavista Peninsula, which was the region's mercantile center in the early days, but the history here is actually more intriguing, in a quirky kind of way—local episodes feature the mysterious Amelia Earhart, the cranky Rockwell Kent, and the pioneers of both Arctic exploration and transatlantic communication.

Be aware that the drive isn't uninterruptedly picturesque. It's notably unscenic for a long stretch south of Carbonear on the Conception Bay side. But elsewhere you will come upon vistas that will leave you absolutely speechless.

ESSENTIALS
GETTING THERE   The Baccalieu Trail is composed of routes 80, 70, and 60. The entire detour to Bay de Verde and back from the Trans-Canada Highway is about 250km (155 miles).

VISITOR INFORMATION   The **Provincial Interpretive and Information Center (© 709/759-2170)** is on the Trans-Canada Highway just west of Route 80 in Whitbourne. It's open daily in season from 8:30am to 8:30pm. The local tourism agency can be found on the Web at **www.baccalieutourism.com**.

DILDO
The pretty (if undeniably oddly named) fishing town of Dildo consists of homes clustered along a hilly harbor's edge and a forested prominence rising near the outer point. (It's located about 12km/7½ miles north of the Trans-Canada Hwy. on Rte. 80.) While fishing has ground to a near halt since cod-protection measures kicked in, cultural tourism has picked up some of the slack, with visitors now trekking here to view traces of a once-thriving Indian culture. One highlight is a visit to an island in the mouth of the harbor, which was occupied at various times by Beothuk, Dorset Eskimo, and modern Indians.

A good place to start a tour is the **Dildo Interpretation Centre** (© 709/582-3339), on the harbor as you come into town. (Look for the giant squid made of fiberglass in the parking lot, an actual-size model of one caught locally in 1933.) The center opened in 1997 and features displays of some of the nearly 6,000 Eskimo artifacts recovered by archaeologists on the island, including harpoon end blades, knives, soapstone bowls and lamps, and scrapers. The center also features a touch tank with crabs and starfish for kids and exhibits on the more recent lumber and fishing industries of the region. The center is open June through September daily from 10am to 6pm; admission costs C$2 (US$1.80/£1) for adults, C$1 (US90¢/50p) for children, and C$5 (US$4.50/£2.50) for families.

Oh, yes . . . the town's name. (I suspect you might have been wondering?) The generally accepted theory around here is that it was named by early Spanish sailors for some person or place in Spain, and the spelling was changed later. Other theories: It may be from a local Indian word meaning "still waters," or—and there's less historical provenance for this one—taken from the chorus of some old ballad or another. The truth is, nobody really knows. Just rest assured: It wasn't named for *that*. Let's move on.

HEART'S CONTENT

Now this is a town with a *much* better name. Heart's Content was named either after an early ship that docked here or because of its vaguely heart-shaped harbor. Either way, it's a pleasing coastal village that claims a prominent footnote in the annals of telecommunications history. In 1858, the **first trans-Atlantic telegraph cable** was brought ashore, connecting England with Newfoundland (and beyond, to the United States), and Queen Victoria and U.S. president James Buchanan exchanged messages. After 27 days and 732 messages, the cable mysteriously failed, however, and another cable—again to Heart's Content—was installed in 1866.

This cable was to blossom as a vital link between the New and Old Worlds for years. It also provided employment for about 300 people in the little village and brought a measure of culture and prosperity that the area was sorely needing. In the late 1800s, as many as 1,200 people lived here; since the 1950s, however, the population has hovered around 600 and the cable has obviously long since passed out of use. You can still see rusted and frayed cables jutting from an embankment near the center of town.

The brick cable station, with its distinctive gingerbread trim, still stands just across the road at the **Heart's Content Cable Station Historic Site** (© **709/583-2160**). Here you can see the impressively bulky antique equipment and learn more about how involved this historic enterprise really was. It's open daily from mid-May through late September from 10am to 5:30pm; admission is C$3 (US$2.70/£1.50) adults, free for children 12 and under.

Another worthy attraction lies at the rocky point at the mouth on the north side of the harbor. A relatively modern barber pole-striped **lighthouse** is set there amid impressive, rounded rocks that seem to heave up from the earth. Wonderful views of Trinity Bay can be had from here; it's a good spot for a picnic.

BACCALIEU ISLAND

Cliff-girded **Baccalieu Island,** about 3.5km (2¼ miles) off the peninsula's tip, is 5km (3 miles) long and has a rich history as a fishing center and location of an important lighthouse. Today, it's better known for its vast colonies of seabirds, 11 species of which breed here. They include puffins, northern fulmar, common murre, northern gannets, thick-billed murre, and razorbills, as well as a truly staggering three-million-plus colony of Leach's storm petrels. Alas, boat tours to the island haven't been offered on a regular basis in recent years. Committed birders might be able to drum up a local fisherman who'd be willing to make the trip; ask at the provincial information center in Whitbourne for suggestions, if you're keen on seeing them.

The village of **Bay de Verde** at the northern tip of the peninsula is worth an excursion even if you're going to visit the island. A road now reaches this remote fishing village, but it still has the feel of a place thoroughly untouched by modern times. The village is dominated by trim, old-fashioned homes on rocky terraces overlooking the scenic harbor.

HARBOUR GRACE ⊛

The historic town of Harbour Grace sprawls along a waterfront with views out to Conception Bay. It's not a picture-perfect town—there's plenty of charmless modern architecture mixed among the historic—but you'll get a good sense of the region's rich history after poking around for an hour.

The town's octagonal **visitor center** (𝄐 **709/596-3042**) at the south end of town is an attraction in and of itself; referred to here as a "tourist chalet" (whatever that is), it closely resembles a local lighthouse. It's open from June through September and contains a special "*Kyle* room" with information about the local steamer anchored just offshore (see below).

Near this visitor center are two modest memorials to the age of transportation before cars took over. The *Spirit of Harbour Grace,* a cargo transport that was later modified into a DC-3 commuter aircraft, is mounted in a graceful banked turn, like a trout rising to take a fly. Just offshore and slightly out of kilter is the **SS *Kyle*,** a handsome coastal steamer that lies aground and listing to port. The *Kyle* was one of the last of the wood-and-coal-burning coastal steamers. Launched in 1913, it plied Newfoundland's waters until 1967, when a nor'easter blew her from her moorings and she came to rest on a mussel bed. A paint job in 1997 made her somewhat more festive.

Harbour Grace also occupies a prominent niche in the history of early-20th-century aviation: A cluster of pioneer pilots used the town airfield as a jumping-off point for crossings of the Atlantic, during an era when Newfoundland was abuzz with daring aviators. (The first nonstop crossing of the Atlantic, by J. Alcock and A. W. Brown, was from Harbour Grace, Newfoundland, to Ireland in 1919; this was 8 full years before Charles Lindbergh crossed the Atlantic solo.) In 1928, Amelia Earhart flew to Wales from Newfoundland, and in 1932—when she became the **first woman to cross the Atlantic solo**—Earhart took off from Harbour Grace.

You can revisit this rich history at the **Harbour Grace Airfield** ⊛, which was the first aerodrome in Newfoundland. It's a stunningly beautiful and pristine spot on a hillside overlooking the harbor and the town, and it appears not to have changed much since Earhart took off for Europe more than a half-century ago, though the strip is growing over and planes very rarely land here anymore. You can scramble atop the monolith at the north end of the airfield to get a sweeping view out to Conception Bay, with the lush, grassy airstrip stretching out below.

Find the airfield by driving 1.5km (1 mile) north of the tourist information center on Route 70, then turning left. The paved road soon ends; keep at it along the dirt road, continuing 1.5km (1 mile) past Route 70, then turn right on yet another dirt road. Continue another 1.5km (1 mile), passing the end of the airstrip, and then turn right and drive to the top of the low hill. There's a small plaque here commemorating the early fliers.

More local history is on view at the very red **Conception Bay Museum** (𝄐 **709/596-5465**) at 1 Water St. Located on a low bluff overlooking the harbor and distant sea stacks, the museum occupies a three-story brick-and-granite building that was a customs station when it was built in 1870. Inside you'll find artifacts and costumed guides, who offer walking tours of the town's **Heritage District** ✿ by appointment. The museum is open daily from June through September, 10am to 5pm (though often closed at lunch), closed the rest of the year. Admission is about C$2 (US$1.80/£1) per adult, C$1 (US90¢/50p) for seniors and children ages 10 to 18.

WHERE TO STAY & DINE

There are a couple of motels along the Baccalieu Trail, especially on the southern stretches of Route 70. Carbonear has two basic, serviceable motels: **Fong's Motel** (✆ 709/596-5114) and the **Carbonear Motel** (✆ 877/596-5662 or 709/596-5662). Rooms at both run about C$60 to C$75 (US$54–US$68/£30–£38).

NaGeira House Bed & Breakfast Inn ✿✿ (Finds)   The NaGeira House is named after an Irish princess who was kidnapped in the 17th century and spirited away to Carbonear, where she lived out her life. The inn opened in 1999 in a wonderful old gabled home (registered as a historic property), and the innkeepers have a good eye for detail, from down duvets and quality linens to delicious breakfasts. The rooms vary widely as to size, from the very small (and least expensive) to a luxurious and spacious master suite with an in-room Jacuzzi and fireplace. Even if you opt for the smallest room, you'll still have access to a cozy library, living room, and bar—as well as a pub and gardens.

7 Musgrave St., Carbonear, NL A1Y 1A4. ✆ **800/600-7757** or 709/596-1888. Fax 709/596-4622. www.nageira house.com. 4 units. C$99–C$149 (US$89–US$134/£50–£75) double. Rates include full breakfast. Discounts available in off-season. AE, MC, V. **Amenities:** Bar. *In room:* TV (3 units), dataport.

Rothesay House Inn ✿ (Value)   The Queen Anne–style Rothesay House dates from 1910, and sits on a low-rise looking across the street to the harbor beyond. It's well situated for exploring Harbour Grace and the Baccalieu Trail, and has four comfortable guest rooms, each with a private bathroom. The inn's popular restaurant is open for three meals daily; make a reservation. The menu changes with the availability of goods, but tends to have a lot of selections for carnivores—a nice break from the usual emphasis on seafood islandwide. The day's or night's menu might include pork loin chops with an apple and cream sauce, chateaubriand, or an orange basil chicken. Of course, there are also dishes of salmon and cod, as you would expect.

34 Water St. (P.O. Box 577), Harbour Grace, NL A0A 2M0. ✆ **877/596-2268.** Fax 709/596-0317. www.rothesay.com. 4 units. C$95–C$125 (US$86–US$113/£48–£63). Rates include full breakfast. MC, V. **Amenities:** Dining room. *In room:* No phone.

BRIGUS

The trim and tidy harborfront village of Brigus is clustered with wood-frame homes and narrow lanes that extend out from the harbor. Brigus is remembered by some art historians as the town that gave the boot to iconoclastic American artist Rockwell Kent, who lived here (briefly) in 1914 and 1915. World War I was raging, and Kent was suspected of "pro-German activities." His crime? Singing songs in Pennsylvanian Dutch. Kent eventually returned to Newfoundland in 1968 as a guest of the premier and forgave the province and the people.

Near the harbor, look for the **"Brigus Tunnel,"** built in the summer of 1860 by Capt. Abraham Bartlett, whose deepwater dock was on one side of a low, rocky ridge but whose warehouses were on the other. He resolved the problem by hiring a Cornish miner to create a pathway. Although the dock and warehouses are gone and local teens have adorned the tunnel with graffiti, you can still stroll through and be rewarded with a fine view of the harbor.

If you're in town come evening, the **Baccalieu Players** (ⓒ 709/528-4044) stage various shows and dinner cabarets and host comedy nights at various venues in Brigus and beyond. For information, ask at any shop locally. Performance tickets generally cost C$6 to C$40 (US$5.40–US$36/£3–£20); the more expensive shows include three-course dinners.

Also in town, the whitewashed, Gothic Revival **St. George's Anglican Church** ⓡⓡ hosts local musicians year-round; tickets are generally C$10 to C$15 (US$9–US$14/£5–£7.50) per performance. There's also an art gallery at the church, and local writers sometimes read from their work (small donations requested).

Finally, inquire about the annual **Blueberry Festival** ⓡ (ⓒ 709/528-3201) if you happen to be visiting Brigus in August, which includes 3 days of concessions, crafts sales, a Missed Blueberry competition, fireworks—and, of course, blueberry-spiked foods.

Hawthorne Cottage National Historic Site   This elaborate gingerbread cottage on a lovely landscaped yard in the town center was the home of one Capt. Bob Bartlett, one of the tough support crew members who accompanied Admiral Robert E. Peary on his successful trip to the North Pole in 1909. (Bartlett has been lauded in some quarters as the "greatest ice navigator of the century.") This cottage was originally built in 1830, then moved here from about 10km (6¼ miles) away in 1833; today, it is furnished much as it might have been by the local gentry at the turn of the 20th century. Allow 2 to 3 hours if you're intrigued by Bartlett's story; otherwise, 45 minutes should be plenty of time.

Village Center (P.O. Box 5542), Brigus. ⓒ 709/528-4004. Admission C$4 (US$3.60/£2) adults, C$3.50 (US$3.15/£1.75) seniors, C$3.20 (US$2.90/£1.60) children 6–16, C$10 (US$9/£5) families. July–Aug daily 9am–7pm; mid-May to June and Sept Wed–Sun 9am–5pm.

Ye Olde Stone Barn Museum ⓡ   This might be one of the finest small museums in the province; it opened in 1991 and focuses on local history inside a reconstructed 1820 stone barn that had served as the local customs house and also an actual barn. Inside is a limited but well-chosen selection of artifacts. They include a beautiful plate hand-painted by Rockwell Kent during his short and controversial residency here and some steel spikes used during the construction of the Brigus tunnel. Plan to spend 30 minutes here.

4 Magistrate's Hill. ⓒ 709/528-4982. Admission C$1 (US90¢/50p) adults, C50¢ (US45¢/25p) children. Mid-June to Labor Day daily 11am–6pm; Sept–Oct weekends only 11am–6pm. Closed Nov to mid-June.

10 St. John's ⓡⓡ

St. John's (always abbreviated, never spelled out) is a world apart from the rest of Newfoundland. The island's small fishing villages and long empty roads through spruce and bog are imbued with loneliness, quietude, and wildness. St. John's, on the other hand, is surprisingly vibrant, cultured, and bustling. Coming into this port city of more than 100,000 after traveling the hinterlands is like stepping from Kansas into Oz—the picture suddenly seems to burst with color and life.

Like Halifax, Nova Scotia, and Saint John, New Brunswick, St. John's also serves as a magnet for youth culture throughout the entire province, and the clubs and restaurants tend to have a more cosmopolitan feel and sharper edge than you might expect from such a provincial, conservative island. The presence of Memorial University—the province's premier institution of higher learning, less than 2 miles west of the harbor—gives the city yet another shot in the cultural arm.

St. John's

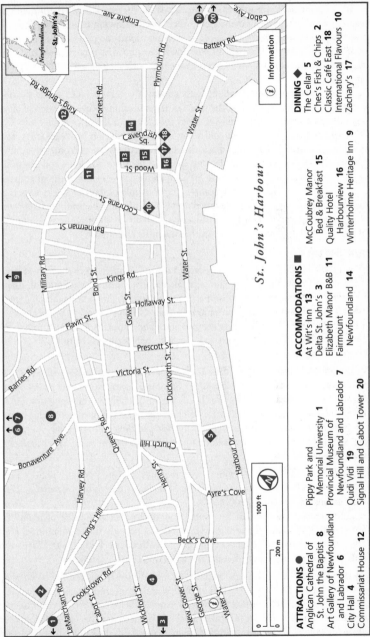

ATTRACTIONS ●

Anglican Cathedral of
St. John the Baptist **8**
Art Gallery of Newfoundland
and Labrador **6**
City Hall **4**
Commissariat House **12**

Pippy Park and
Memorial University **1**
Provincial Museum of
Newfoundland and Labrador **7**
Quidi Vidi **19**
Signal Hill and Cabot Tower **20**

ACCOMMODATIONS ■

At Wit's Inn **13**
Delta St. John's **3**
Elizabeth Manor B&B **11**
Fairmount
Newfoundland **14**

McCoubrey Manor
Bed & Breakfast **15**
Quality Hotel
Harbourview **16**
Winterholme Heritage Inn **9**

DINING ◆

The Cellar **5**
Ches's Fish & Chips **2**
Classic Café East **18**
International Flavours **10**
Zachary's **17**

St. John's Harbour

ⓘ **Information**

St. John's harbor is impressive, protected from the open seas by stony hills and accessible only through a pinched gap called The Narrows, a rocky defile of the sort you'd expect to see Atlas straddling. The Narrows sits at the north end of the harbor, hidden from view from much of the downtown, so first-time visitors may think they've stumbled upon a small lake—albeit one with tankers and other oceangoing ships in it.

This is still very much a working harbor today, the hub of much of the province's commerce; as such, don't expect the place to be very quaint. Across the way are charmless oil-tank farms and offloading facilities for tankers, a major container-ship wharf occupies the head of the harbor, and along the water's edge on Harbour Street downtown you'll often find hulking ships tied up. Pedestrians are welcome to stroll and gawk—but wholesale commerce remains the focus here, not boutiques and fine dining.

If you can arrange for it, come to St. John's after you've explored the more remote parts of Newfoundland. At that point—after a couple of days or weeks days eating endless seafood, staying in simple motel rooms, and camping beneath the stars—you'll truly appreciate the city's urban attitude, its diversity of culture, the wide choice of hotels and motels here, and the varied cuisine in its restaurants.

ESSENTIALS

GETTING THERE   St. John's is located 127km (79 miles) from the ferry at Argentia, 874km (543 miles) from Port aux Basques. **St. John's International Airport** (© 709/758-8500; www.stjohnsairport.com) receives flights from Halifax, Montréal, Ottawa, Toronto, and even internationally. See "Getting There" at the beginning of this chapter for ferry and airline information. The airport is 6.5km (4 miles) from downtown; taxis from the airport to downtown hotels cost C$15 to C$20 (US$14–US$18/£7.50–£10).

VISITOR INFORMATION   The city's main **tourist information office** (© 709/576-8106) is located at 348 New Water St., and is open year-round (9am–5pm in summer, weekdays 9am–4:30pm in the off season). St. John's produces a free, informative, and comprehensive pocket-size brochure detailing walking and driving tours of the metro area; it's an outstanding resource for planning and executing your visit to the city. Ask for it at the tourist information office (see above). The city's tourism web site is at **www.stjohns.ca**.

GETTING AROUND   Metrobus serves much of the city. Fares are C$2 (US$1.80/£1) for a single trip. Route information is available at the visitor information center or by calling © **709/722-9400.**

Taxis are plentiful around St. John's; they charge an initial fee of about C$3 (US$2.70/£1.50) plus about C$2 (US$1.80/£1) per additional mile. One of the larger and more dependable outfits in the city is **Bugden's Taxi** (© **709/726-4400**). You can tour the city by taxi for about C$30 (US$27/£15) per hour.

ORIENTATION   St. John's is built on the side of a steep hill, and the downtown is oriented along three streets—**Harbour, Water,** and **Duckworth**—that run parallel to the water's edge. (Duckworth and Water sts. contain the bulk of the downtown's shops and restaurants.) These are relatively level, each following the hill's contours, one above the other. Cross streets linking these main drags run the gamut from moderately challenging inclines to clutch-smoking vertical hills.

Outside of the central downtown, St. John's is an amalgam of confusing roads that run at peculiar angles to one another and suddenly change names on a whim. You can try to navigate with a map, but it's just as easy to orient yourself by some landmark—such as Signal Hill—and then point your car in the general direction you want to go. The city's small enough that you'll never get too lost, and you'll eventually end up on the main ring road (which of course goes by various names, including Columbus Dr., Confederation Pkwy., and Prince Philip Dr.).

SPECIAL EVENTS The great annual **Newfoundland and Labrador Folk Festival** ★★ began in 1976 and is well worth a visit. This 3-day shindig is usually held during the first weekend in August and includes performers from all over the province, who gather to play at Bannerman Park in downtown St. John's. (Bring a lawn chair.) Even after all these years, tickets are still very affordable: It costs just C$12 (US$11/£6) per adult (less for seniors and children) for an afternoon pass or evening pass allowing you access to the entire slate of performers, or C$50 (US$45/£25) for an all-weekend pass. That's a bargain.

Contact the festival specialists at the **Newfoundland and Labrador Folk Arts Council** (✆ **800/576-8508** or 709/576-8508; www.nlfolk.com) for schedules and information about how to purchase tickets.

EXPLORING ST. JOHN'S

Parking is rarely a problem in downtown St. John's, so long as you bring loonies and quarters to feed the meters. Once you park, you can continue easily by foot; the downtown area is compact. St. John's drivers seem to be uncommonly respectful of pedestrians as well—a nice bonus. If you so much as take a step off the curb (or even let a look cross your face suggesting you just might want to do so), drivers will come to a halt and wave you across. So bring a good pair of walking shoes and use them.

DOWNTOWN ATTRACTIONS

Anglican Cathedral of St. John the Baptist This impressive hillside cathedral was constructed in stages from 1843 to 1885, with additional rebuilding following the great fire of 1892. Designed in high Gothic Revival style by noted English architect Sir George Gilbert Scott, the cathedral has very fine stained glass, lavish oak carvings, and bluestone walls from nearby quarries. (The sandstone of the arches and bays was shipped from Scotland.) After you admire the historically significant architecture and the small one-room museum, stop by the crypt, where sweets and tea are served weekdays. It's an hour peacefully spent.

16 Church Hill. ✆ **709/726-5677.** Free admission; free tours June–Sept daily 10am–5pm.

Art Gallery of Newfoundland and Labrador ★★ This gallery has moved downtown into The Rooms, a multifunction cultural facility and very appropriate home for it. Permanent and rotating exhibits mostly showcase Newfoundland talent, but the occasional touring show highlights other Canadian artists as well. Consult the local newspaper to see what's on display. Plan to spend a couple of hours here, should the current exhibitions catch your fancy.

9 Bonaventure Ave. ✆ **709/757-8040.** www.therooms.ca/artgallery. C$5 (US$4.50/£2.50) adults, C$4 (US$3.60/£2) seniors, C$3 (US$2.70/£1.50) children 6–16, C$15 (US$14/£7.50) families. Additional charge for special exhibits; free Wed 6–9pm. June to mid-Oct Mon–Sat 10am–5pm (Wed–Thurs to 9pm), Sun noon–5pm; mid-Oct to May closed Mon.

Commissariat House This stellar Georgian house built in 1821 has served varied purposes over the years. Originally constructed as offices and living quarters to serve Fort William and other military installations, the home subsequently served as a rectory, nursing home, and children's hospital. Now a provincial historic site, the home has been restored to look as it might have in 1830, with the English china, fine paintings, and elaborate furnishings that would befit an assistant commissary general. Fans of historic architecture and 19th-century period furnishings could while away an enjoyable hour here.

King's Bridge Rd. ℂ 709/729-6730. C$3 (US$2.70/£1.50) adults, free for children age 12 and under. Mid-May to late Sept daily 10am–5:30pm.

Provincial Museum of Newfoundland and Labrador 𝒦𝒦 *Kids*   This downtown museum found a new home in 2005, moving to a complex known as The Rooms (the Provincial Art Gallery and Provincial Archives are also located here; see above). It offers a good introduction to the natural and cultural history of the island, through exhibits that both kids and adults can understand and enjoy. The second level features a lesson on canoe-building from an Innu native, while the third level focuses on the processes of change as glaciers retreated and native peoples settled the province. You'll also learn about flora and fauna here, finding out for example that the moose is in fact *not* native to Newfoundland. The fourth level suggests how 19th-century life was lived by the province's British settlers and features a re-created fort, stories about Newfoundland's fisheries, and a history of the constabulary (in other words, the fuzz). In addition, look for delicate carvings of bear heads and exhibits highlighting the awesome power of the polar bear; special exhibitions include a Canadian heritage quilt project. Allow about an hour for a leisurely tour.

9 Bonaventure Ave. ℂ 709/757-8020. www.therooms.ca/museum. C$5 (US$4.50/£2.50) adults, C$4 (US$3.60/£2) seniors, C$3 (US$2.70/£1.50) children 6–16, C$15 (US$14/£7.50) families. Additional charge for special exhibits; free Wed 6–9pm. June to mid-Oct Mon–Sat 10am–5pm (Wed–Thurs to 9pm), Sun noon–5pm; mid-Oct to May closed Mon.

Signal Hill 𝒦𝒦 *Value*   You'll come for the history, but stay for the views. Signal Hill is St. John's most visible and visit-worthy attraction. This rugged, barren hill is the city's preeminent landmark, rising up above the entrance to the harbor and topped with a craggy "castle" complete with flag fluttering overhead—the "signal" referred to in the name. The layers of history here are rich and complex: Flags have flown atop this hill since 1704, and over the centuries a succession of military fortifications have occupied these strategic slopes, as did three different hospitals. The castlelike structure (which is officially called Cabot Tower) dates from 1897, when it was built in honor of Queen Victoria's diamond jubilee and the 400th anniversary of John Cabot's arrival in the new world. The hill secured its spot in history in 1901, when Nobel laureate Guglielmo Marconi received the **first wireless transatlantic broadcast**—three short dots indicating the letter *S* in Morse code, sent from Cornwall, England—on an antenna raised 120m (394 ft.) on a kite in powerful winds.

A good place to start a tour is in the interpretive center, where you'll get a briefing about the hill's history. (Military drills and cannon firings still sometimes take place in the field next to the center; check here if you're interested.) From the center, you can follow serpentine trails up the hill to the tower, where you'll be rewarded with breathtaking **views** 𝒦 of the Narrows and the open ocean beyond—Cape Spear can even be seen in the distance to the south, and look for icebergs in the early summer and whales anytime. Interpretive placards, scattered about the summit, feature engaging photos from various epochs.

Atop Signal Hill at the entrance to St. John's harbor. ℂ 709/772-5367. Free admission to grounds; admission to interpretive center C$3.95 (US$3.55/£2) adults, C$3.45 (US$3.10/£1.75) seniors, C$1.95 (US$1.75/£1) children 6–16, C$9.90 (US$8.90/£4.95) families. Grounds open year-round; Interpretation Center mid-May to mid-Oct daily 10am–6pm, rest of the year Mon–Fri 8:30am–4:30pm; Cabot Tower Apr to mid-Jan daily 9am–5pm, closed mid-Jan to March.

EXPLORING FARTHER AFIELD

The Fluvarium *Finds Kids*   This low, octagonal structure at the edge of Long Pond (near Memorial University, a few miles west of downtown) actually descends three stories into the earth. The second level features exhibits on river ecology, including life in the riffles (that's where trout spawn) and in shallow pools, which are rich with nutrients. On the lowest level you'll find yourself looking up into a deep pool that's located alongside the building. Watch for brown trout swimming lazily by. Plan to spend about 45 minutes here.

Pippy Park, off Allandale Rd. © 709/754-3474. www.fluvarium.ca. Admission C$5.50 (US$4.95/£2.75) adults, C$4.50 (US$4.05/£2.25) seniors and students, C$3.50 (US$3.15/£1.75) children under 14. Hours variable but weekdays usually daily 9am–5pm in summer, closed or shorter hours weekends in off season. Guided tours on the half-hour in summer; feeding time 4pm.

Memorial University Botanical Garden   An abundant selection of northern plants makes this garden well worth seeking out (it's tucked over a wooded ridge on the city's western edge, behind Pippy Park). The main plots are arranged in gracious "theme gardens," including a cottage garden, a rock garden, and a peat garden. Among the most interesting is the Newfoundland Heritage Garden, with examples of 70 types of perennials traditionally found in island gardens. The floral displays aren't as ostentatious or exuberant as you'll find in other public gardens in Atlantic Canada (the gardens of Halifax and Annapolis Royal come to mind), but they will be of great interest to amateur horticulturists curious about boreal plants. Behind the gardens are winding hiking trails leading down to marshy Oxen Pond. Allow an hour for this visit.

306 Mt. Scio Rd. (take Thorburn Rd. past Avalon Mall; turn right on Mt. Scio Rd.). © 709/737-8590. www.mun.ca/botgarden. Summer admission C$5 (US$4.50/£2.50) adults, C$3 (US$2.70/£1.50) seniors, C$1.15 (US$1.05/£60) children 6–18, C$10 (US$9/£5) families; spring and fall rates discounted. May–Sept daily 10am–5pm; Oct 10am–4pm.

Quidi Vidi   Pronounced "kitty vitty," this tiny harbor village sets new standards for the term *quaint*. The village is tucked in a rocky defile behind Signal Hill, where a narrow ocean inlet provides access to the sea. It's photogenic in the extreme and a wonderful spot to investigate by foot or bike (it's rather more difficult by car). The village consists mostly of compact homes, including the oldest home in St. John's, with very few shops. Visit here while you can; in recent years, following rancorous local debate, development plans were approved for the addition of modern housing in the area. (There's a microbrewery already, if you're into that.)

To get to Quidi Vidi, follow Signal Hill Road to Quidi Vidi Road, then turn right onto Forest Road. From here you can easily connect to Quidi Vidi Lake, where St. John's Regatta is held the first Wednesday in August, as it has been since 1826. Look for the trail leading to the lake from near the entrance to Quidi Vidi, or ask locally.

OUTDOOR PURSUITS

Pippy Park (© 709/737-3655) is on the city's hilly western side adjacent to the university and contains 1,340 hectares (3,311 acres) of developed recreation land and quiet trails. You should definitely visit if you're coming with kids. This popular park is home to the city campground and The Fluvarium (see above), as well as miniature golf and regulation-size golf courses, picnic sites, playgrounds, hiking trails, and more.

For bike rentals, head downtown to **Canary Cycles** at 294 Water St. (© 877/4CANARY or 709/579-5972; www.canary-cycles.com). It offers several different types of bikes, with rates around C$30 (US$27/£15) per day (C$5/US$4.50/£2.50 extra for locks and helmets), as well as new and used bike sales and a repair service.

Charging Up to the Battery

When in St. John's, one highly recommendable hike (but only if you are *not* afraid of heights) is the **North Head Trail** 🐦🐦, which runs from **Signal Hill** to an improbable cluster of small buildings between the rock face and the water called **The Battery.** Don't tackle this unless you are reasonably fit; it's no easy stroll.

Here's how to get there: On foot, follow Duckworth Street between the Hotel Newfoundland and **Devon House,** then bear right onto Battery Road. Stay on the main branch (a few smaller branches may confuse you) as the pathway narrows, rises, and falls while skirting a rock face. First you reach the so-called **Outer Battery.** The former fishermen's homes here are literally inches from the road—and not much farther from the water—and most have drop-dead views of the Narrows and the city skyline. There's a whimsical, storybook character to this place, and this real estate is now much-sought-after by city residents.

At the end of the Battery, you'll cross someone's front porch (it's okay), and it's here that the North Head Trail begins in earnest. It runs along the **Narrows,** past old gun emplacements, up and down heroic sets of steps, and along some narrow ledges (chains are bolted to the rocks as handrails for a little extra security in one place). The trail ascends an open headland before looping back and starting a final climb up Signal Hill. After some time exploring and soaking up the view, you can save time on the return by walking a paved road back downhill to Duckworth Street where you began.

Allow about 2 hours total, assuming a departure and return from the vicinity of the Hotel Newfoundland.

The **Grand Concourse** (☎ 709/737-1077) is an ambitious project to link much of St. John's with pedestrian pathways. More than 120km (75 miles) have been completed to date, with more walkways being developed all the time; two of the most inviting segments are the **loop around Quidi Vidi Lake** and the **Rennie's River Trail** running between Pippy Park and Quidi Vidi Lake. Bikes are not permitted on the trails, however. Ask at the tourist information center for trail status and map availability.

SHOPPING

A number of downtown shops tout "traditional Newfoundland" crafts and souvenirs, though their offerings can range from high-quality finery to tourist schlock.

The Bird House and Binocular Shop   This is a great stop for both serious and aspiring birders. The shop stocks a selection of field guides, binoculars, and spotting scopes, along with backyard bird supplies. Binoculars are also available for rent, and the shop distributes a brochure with a checklist of local species and suggested birding areas around St. John's. 166 Duckworth St. ☎ **709/726-2473.**

Devon House Craft Centre 🐦   The nonprofit Devon House (operated by the Craft Council of Newfoundland & Labrador) displays the works of more than 150 of the province's artisans in an attractive old house across from the Hotel Newfoundland;

the shop specializes in works in clay. There's also a gallery of current crafts and design. 59 Duckworth St. ✆ **709/753-2749.**

Downhome Shoppe & Gallery   This might be the best destination in town for your basic Newfoundland souvenirs. It's located at the offices of a folk-life magazine publisher and is stocked with T-shirts, coffee mugs, postcards, dolls in tartans, and so on. 303 Water St. ✆ **709/722-2970.**

Fred's   There's a great selection of Newfoundland and other music here on record, tape, and CD, and a knowledgeable sales staff to boot. You can sample any of the CDs on headphones before you buy. 198 Duckworth St. ✆ **709/753-9191.**

Newfoundland Weavery   This shop started as a weaving supply store in 1972, and has since expanded to become a showcase for local arts and crafts, including pottery, oilskin coats, and pewter work. 177 Water St. ✆ **709/753-0496.**

O'Brien's Music Store   A popular hangout for local musicians looking for equipment (tin whistles? natch), O'Brien's also carries an excellent selection of local tapes and CDs, and the staff is wise about all things musical. Newfoundland music can also be ordered by mail or via the store's website (www.obriens.nf.ca). 278 Water St. ✆ **709/753-8135.**

Wordplay Bookstore   This is a great one-stop shop for books about Newfoundland and Labrador, books by Newfoundlanders, and even good books written by anyone else (including me, hopefully). 221 Duckworth St. ✆ **800/563-9100** or 709/726-9193.

EXCURSIONS FROM ST. JOHN'S

Some 11km (6¾ miles) southeast of downtown is North America's most easterly point, home to dramatic **Cape Spear National Historic Site** (✆ **709/772-5367**). Here you'll find a picture-perfect lighthouse dating from 1836 and underground passages from abandoned World War II gun batteries. A visitor center will orient you; leave plenty of time to walk the hiking trails and scout for whales surfacing at sea. Admission to **the lighthouse,** which has been restored to its 1839 appearance and opens from 10am to 6pm, is C$3.95 (US$3.55/£2) for adults, C$3.45 (US$3.10/£1.75) for seniors, C$1.95 (US$1.75/£1) for children ages 6 to 16, and C$9.90 (US$8.90/£4.95) for families. The lighthouse and interpretive center are closed mid-October to mid-May, but the grounds are open year-round.

Just 14km (8¾ miles) west of St. John's is Portugal Cove, from which frequent ferries depart for **Bell Island** 🐟 year-round, except in very stormy weather. This is a handsome and historic island, with abrupt cliffs edging its eastern shore. It was once a thriving community early in the 20th century; an iron mine employed hundreds of locals from 1895 to 1966, after which it no longer made economic sense to scratch ore out of the earth in these parts. Today the island is honeycombed with impressive mine shafts, many extending far out under the sea. You'll find simple accommodations, a few lowbrow seafood restaurants, and an art gallery; check the island's website (www.bellisland.net) to get its flavor before coming.

The **ferry** ride over and back costs C$6.25 (US$5.65/£3.15) for a car and driver and C$2.25 (US$2.05/£1.15) per extra adult passenger; less for students, children over age 6, and seniors. It runs every 40 minutes from about 6am until about 10:30pm most days. The crossing takes about 20 minutes. Contact the ferry office at ✆ **709/488-2842** or 709/895-3491 for more details about the journey.

The no. 2 mine on the island has been maintained as a museum of sorts, the **Bell Island Community Museum and Mine Tour** (✆ **709/488-2880**), where visitors can relive the life of a typical miner, who made his way through the perpetual underground night with a carbide lantern. During a 40-minute tour, you'll descend by foot 195m (640 ft.) underground to the point near where flooding makes the mineshaft impassable. (The mine actually descends another 510m/1,673 ft. into the earth, and is 3–5km/2–3 miles long in total.) Tours are offered frequently daily in summer; combo tickets incorporating the tour and museum admission cost C$7 (US$6.30/£3.50) adults, C$5 (US$4.50/£2.50) seniors, C$3 (US$2.70/£1.50) for children under 12. Tickets for the museum alone are just C$2 (US$1.80/£1), though frankly, that's less fun. The museum is open daily from 11am to 7pm, June through September.

While on Bell Island, ask locals about the **Grebe's Nest,** a rocky point marked by an offshore sea stack. Down on the shore, there's a man-made tunnel leading to a secluded beach surrounded by towering, crumbling cliffs.

WHERE TO STAY

Campers arriving in St. John's should head straight for the municipally owned **Pippy Park Campground** 🅰 (© 877/477-3669 or 709/737-3669), just a couple miles from downtown off Allandale Road. The campground has nearly 200 sites, most with full hookups, and a sociable tenting area. Rates in the past have ranged from about C$16 (US$14/£8) for an unserviced site to about C$24 (US$22/£12) for a fully serviced site. It often books up in summer, so it's wise to call ahead for reservations. It's open from May through September.

EXPENSIVE

Delta St. John's Hotel 🅰🅰 *(Kids)*   The sleek and modern Delta St. John's is located downtown near City Hall and caters largely to businesspeople. It must be doing something right: It has nearly doubled in room count in recent years. The Delta lacks the views and ineffable sense of class that you'll find at the Fairmont (see below), but has nice touches like ship models in the lobby and a handsome pool table as the centerpiece of the lounge. It's also well situated for prowling the city and features a number of amenities that choosy travelers will appreciate, such as hair dryers and coffeemakers in all of the rooms. Management runs a number of children's programs and offers babysitting services as well. The hotel's chummy Mickey Quinn's restaurant off the lobby offers breakfast, lunch, and dinner daily; the dinner menu, as expected, emphasizes both local provincial seafood and heavier fare such as steaks.

120 New Gower St., St. John's, NL A1C 6K4. © 888/890-3222 or 709/739-6404. Fax 709/570-1622. www.delta hotels.com. 403 units. C$99–C$650 (US$89–US$585/£50–£325) double. AE, DC, DISC, MC, V. Valet parking C$18 (US$16/£9), self-parking C$8 (US$7.20/£4) per day. Pets allowed with advance permission. **Amenities:** Restaurant; indoor pool; health club; Jacuzzi; sauna; children's program; concierge; limited room service; babysitting; laundry service; dry cleaning. *In room:* A/C, TV, minibar, fridge (some units), coffeemaker, hair dryer, iron.

The Fairmont Newfoundland 🅰🅰   The Newfoundland was built in 1982 in a starkly modern style, yet it boasts a refined sensibility and attention to detail that's vaguely reminiscent of a lost era. The designers and architects have been subtle about their best surprises; the lobby has one of the best views of the Narrows in town, but you have to hunt around to find it. It's a wonderful effect, and one that's used nicely throughout. (This helps compensate for the somewhat generic, conference-hotel feel of much of the decor.) The rooms themselves are standard size and unremarkable, though all have coffeemakers and bathrobes. About half have harbor views. The hotel's lobby is home to three dining establishments: The rather formal **Cabot Club** 🅰🅰 ranks among the best restaurants in the city, and is known for tableside Caesar salads, caribou soup, and entrees like pan-fried cod and halibut with saffron-truffle butter. The colorful Mediterranean-inspired Bonavista Cafe is lighter on the wallet, with lunches of burgers and sandwiches and dinners like Greek lamb chops, vegetable fettuccine, and poached salmon. The Narrows lounge is the spot for a nightcap.

115 Cavendish Sq. (P.O. Box 5637), St. John's, NL A1C 5W8. © **800/441-1414** or 709/726-4980. Fax 709/576-0554. www.fairmont.com. 301 units. C$219–C$349 (US$197–US$314/£110–£175) double. AE, DC, DISC, MC, V. Valet parking C$17 (US$15/£8.50) per day, self-parking free. Pets C$20 (US$18/£10) extra per night. **Amenities:** 3 restaurants; indoor pool; health club; Jacuzzi; sauna; concierge; business center; salon; 24-hr. room service; babysitting; laundry service; dry cleaning. *In room:* A/C, TV, minibar.

Winterholme Heritage Inn 🏆🏆 This stout, handsome Victorian mansion was built in 1905 and is as architecturally distinctive a place as you'll find in Newfoundland, with prominent turrets, bow-front windows, bold pediments, elaborate molded plaster ceilings, and woodwork extravagant enough to stop you in your tracks. (The oak woodwork was actually carved in England and shipped here for installation.) Room no. 1 is oval-shaped (the original master bedroom to the home) and occupies one of the turrets; it has a Jacuzzi, as well as a king bed. Room no. 7 is another of the most lavish; this former billiards room features a fireplace and a two-person Jacuzzi, along with a plasterwork ceiling and a supple leather wing chair. Attic-level rooms here are less extraordinary, but still appealing with their odd angles and nice touches. The mansion is located about a 10-minute walk from downtown. Limited spa services are available at the inn by appointment.

79 Rennies Mill Rd., St. John's, NL A1C 3R1. © **800/599-7829** or 709/739-7979. Fax 709/753-9411. www.winterholme. com. 11 units. C$129–C$249 (US$116–US$224/£65–£125) double. Rates include full breakfast. AE, DC, MC, V. Free parking. *In room:* TV/DVD, coffeemaker, hair dryer, iron.

MODERATE

At Wit's Inn 🏆🏆 *(Finds* Forgive the innkeepers their pun. This lovely century-old home was wonderfully restored and opened as an inn in 1999 by a former Toronto restaurateur. Decorated with a sure eye for bold color and simple style, this is a welcoming urban oasis just around the corner from the Fairmont. The four rooms are not terribly spacious, but neither are they uncomfortably small, and each is nicely furnished with down duvets and VCRs. (The largest room is on the top floor, requiring a bit of a hike.) The beautifully refinished floors and elaborately carved banister here are notable, as are many of the old fixtures (such as the servant's intercom) that have been left intact. A full breakfast is served in the first-floor dining room, wine and cheese are offered in the late afternoon, and there's a butler's pantry for snacking in between times. At Wit's Inn offers luxury touches at a relatively affordable price.

3 Gower St., St. John's, NL A1C 1M9. © **877/739-7420** or 709/739-7420. www.atwitsinn.ca. 4 units. C$109–C$139 (US$98–US$125/£55–£70) double. Rates include breakfast. Free parking. AE, MC, V. *In room:* TV/VCR.

Elizabeth Manor B&B 🏆 *(Value* Lodging history note: This is said to have been the first modern B&B proper in St. John's. The Elizabeth—long known as the Prescott, until a recent ownership change—is composed of an unusually attractive grouping of wood-frame town houses. They were substantially renovated and upgraded in 2004, adding more Jacuzzis, as well as sleigh and four-poster beds. Some rooms have carpeting; others have hardwood floors. All are furnished with antiques; the lower-priced rooms are among the city's better bargains. Guests are welcome to relax on the shared balcony that runs along the back of the building. The same owners also manage a group of suites known as the Randall-Shea suites; inquire about those if you've brought a family.

21 Military Rd. (P.O. Box 204), St. John's, NL A1C 2C3. © **888/263-3786** or 709/753-7733. Fax 709/738-7434. www. elizabethmanor.nl.ca. 6 units. Peak season C$80–C$199 (US$72–US$179/£40–£100) double; off season C$60–C$169 (US$54–US$152/£30–£85) double. Rates include full breakfast. AE, DC, MC, V. Free parking. Pets allowed. *In room:* TV, fridge, Jacuzzi (some).

McCoubrey Manor Bed & Breakfast 🏃🏃 *(Kids)*   McCoubrey Manor offers a convenient downtown location with Victorian charm, and yet also a nicely casual atmosphere. These adjoining 1904 town houses are decorated in what might be called a "contemporary Victorian" style, and its six rooms are quite inviting. Upstairs rooms have private double Jacuzzis; room no. 1 is brightest and faces the street, while room no. 2 has a sunken Jacuzzi, oak-mantled fireplace, and trim of British Columbian fir. Just around the corner, the property manages a few other spacious apartments with full kitchens—what they lack in elegance, they make up for in space—so families take note. Evening tea get-togethers and breakfasts in the main inn only add to its charm.

6–8 Ordnance St., St. John's, NL A1C 3K7. © **888/753-7577** or 709/722-7577. Fax 709/579-7577. www.mccoubrey. com. 6 units plus 4 off-site apartments. Peak season C$139–C$199 (US$125–US$179/£70–£100) double; off season C$89–C$179 (US$80–US$161/£4–£950) double. Rates include full breakfast. AE, DC, MC, V. Free parking. **Amenities:** Laundry. *In room:* A/C (some units), TV/VCR, kitchenette (some units), fridge (some units), no phone (most units).

Quality Hotel Harbourview   Courteous service and a great downtown location with free parking are among the merits of this modern chain hotel. The rooms are standard size but comfortable and clean; they're set apart mainly by their views—ask for one overlooking the Narrows. You can easily walk downtown to restaurants and attractions in a few minutes; the Battery and Signal Hill are a pleasant hike in the other direction. The better-than-average restaurant on-site serves three meals daily.

2 Hill O'Chips, St. John's, NL A1C 6B1. © **800/228-5151** or 709/754-7788. Fax 709/754-5209. 160 units. C$99–C$159 (US$89–US$143/£50–£80) double. Off-season discounts available. AE, DC, DISC, MC, V. Free parking. **Amenities:** Restaurant. *In room:* A/C, TV, coffeemaker, hair dryer, iron.

WHERE TO DINE

Budget travelers should wander up the city's hillside to the intersection of LaMarchant and Freshwater streets. Within a 2-block radius, you'll find numerous options for cheap eats at both eat-in and takeout establishments.

One local favorite is **Ches's Fish and Chips,** at 9 Freshwater Rd. (© **709/726-2373**), which has been serving up pleasingly unhealthy portions of fried fish, chicken wings, and burgers since 1958. Amazingly, it's open as late as 2am even on weekdays—and they deliver, too. For good coffee right in town, head for **HavaJava** at 216 Water St. (© **709/753-5282**).

EXPENSIVE

The Cellar 🏃🏃 ECLECTIC   The classy interior is a surprise here—the restaurant looks nondescript from the outside. Inside, however, it's as intimate and warm (though never as stuffy) as a fine gentleman's club. The kitchen has been turning out fine meals for a while now, developing a local following for its creativity and consistency. Look for standbys like gravlax, homemade bread, and pastas. Fish is prepared especially well; cuts are often paired with innovative flavors such as ginger or pear. Lunches are an even better bargain: Past menus have featured such tasty and offbeat offerings as baked brie in phyllo with a red-currant chutney, and scallop crepes.

189 Water St. © **709/579-8900.** Reservations recommended. Main courses C$9–C$21 (US$8.10–US$19/ £4.50–£11) at lunch, C$10–C$34 (US$9–US$31/£5–£17) at dinner. AE, DC, DISC, MC, V. Mon–Fri 11:30am–2:30pm and 5:30–9:30pm (Fri until 10:30pm); Sat 5:30–10:30pm; Sun 5:30–9:30pm.

MODERATE

Classic Café East CANADIAN   This come-as-you-are eatery is appropriately named: It's your classic St. John's spot, and everyone in town seems to drop by here at some point. Breakfast is served until 4pm daily, but don't expect toast and tea: The macho entrees (sirloin with eggs, toast, home fries, and baked beans is one) appeal to everyone from burly longshoremen to hungover musicians. Lunch and dinner portions, running to usual diner fare and seafood, are equally generous and surprisingly good.

73 Duckworth St. ☎ **709/726-4444.** Main courses C$6–C$8 (US$5.40–US$7.20/£3–£4) at breakfast and lunch, C$8–C$17 (US$7.20–US$15/£4–£8.50) at dinner. DC, MC, V. Daily 24 hr.

Zachary's TRADITIONAL   This informal spot with wood-slat booths offers a slew of Newfoundland favorites, such as fish cakes, fried bologna (really), and Acadian-style *toutons* (dough fried in pork fat)—and that's just for breakfast. Dinners emphasize seafood—entrees might include grilled salmon, seafood fettuccine, pan-fried cod, and lobster most of the year—but you'll also find plenty of steaks and chicken. Desserts here are homemade; especially tempting are the cheesecake, carrot cake, and date squares. You'll find more inventive spots for dinner, but you probably can't do better for reliable quality when on a budget. Breakfasts, served all day, are outstanding.

71 Duckworth St. ☎ **709/579-8050.** Reservations recommended. Main courses C$3.30–C$7.50 (US$3–US$6.75/£1.65–£3.75) at breakfast, C$6–C$9 (US$5.40–US$8.10/£3–£4.50) at lunch, C$11–C$20 (US$9.90–US$18/£5.50–£10) at dinner. AE, MC, V. Daily 7am–11pm.

INEXPENSIVE

International Flavours *(Value)* INDIAN   This is my favorite cheap meal in St. John's. This storefront restaurant has just five tables, and all the dinners are priced at less than C$8 (US$7.20/£4), which includes a decent mound of food. You'll usually have a choice of four or so dishes. Smart money gets the basic curry. Also recommended is the very satisfying mango milkshake.

124 Duckworth St. ☎ **709/738-4636.** Dinner plates C$6.95–C$7.95 (US$6.25–US$7.15/£3.50–£4). V. Mon–Tues and Thurs–Sat 11:30am–6:30pm; Wed 11:30am–7pm (often later).

ST. JOHN'S AFTER DARK

The nightlife in St. John's is extraordinarily vibrant, and you will be doing yourself an injustice if you don't spend at least one evening on a pub crawl.

Your first stop for local music and cordial imbibing should be **George Street** ⚓, which runs for several blocks near New Gower and Water streets, close to City Hall. Every St. John's resident confidently asserts that George Street is home to more bars per square foot than anywhere else on the planet; being unable to track down a global authority that tracks and verifies pubs per square foot, I cannot verify this mighty large boast. But a walk down George does nothing to refute this claim.

The street is packed with energetic pubs and lounges—some fueled by beer, others by testosterone, still others (these are my favorite) by lively Celtic fiddling. The best strategy for selecting a pub is to do a slow ramble down the strip around 10pm or a bit later, stopping to peek inside those with appealing music wafting from the door. If the feel's right, just go with it. At places with live music, cover charges are universally cheap, and rarely top C$5 (US$4.50/£2.50).

For blues and traditional music, there's the lively **Fat Cat Blues Bar,** 5 George St. (☎ **709/739-5554**), with acts scheduled almost every single night. (It's closed Mon, however.) For a more upscale spot with lower decibel levels, try **Christian's Bar,** 23 George St. (☎ **709/753-9100**), which also serves specialty coffees.

Trapper John's, 2 George St. (© **709/579-9630**), is known for its outstanding provincial folk music; in addition, it tries a bit harder (or too hard) to attain that Ye Olde Newfoundland character and atmosphere you will either be ardently seeking out, or ardently seeking to avoid. (This is also a traditional "screeching in" spot for visitors—a local ritual which involves cheap Newfoundland rum and some embarrassment; don't ask if you don't want to know.)

If George Street's beery atmosphere just reminds you a little *too* uncomfortably of certain nights in college that you'd just as soon forget, **The Ship Inn,** at 265 Duckworth St. (© **709/753-3870**), is tucked down an alley a few blocks away and is better known for its genial public-house atmosphere and local patronage. It's a St. John's mainstay featuring a variety of local musical acts that complement rather than overwhelm the place's cozy atmosphere.

11 The Southern Avalon Peninsula ★★

The Avalon Peninsula—or just "The Avalon," as it's commonly called—is home to some of Newfoundland's most memorable and dramatic scenery, including high coastal cliffs and endless bogs. More good news: It's also relatively compact and manageable, and is close enough to the big city that it can be viewed either on longish day trips from St. John's or in a couple of days of poking around. It's a good destination for anyone who's short on time yet wants to get a taste of the islander's particular brand of wildness. The area is especially notable for its bird colonies, as well as its herd of wild caribou. The bad news? It's physically thrust out into the North Atlantic, a place where cold and warm currents collide—resulting in legendary fogs and blustery, moist weather. Bring a rain suit and come prepared for bone-numbing dampness and occasionally sluggish driving through pea-soup conditions.

While snooping about, also listen for the distinctive Irish-influenced brogue of the residents. You'll find no more vivid testimony to the settlement of the region by Irish pioneers than this.

ESSENTIALS
GETTING THERE   Several well-marked and well-maintained highways follow the coast of the southern Avalon Peninsula, though few roads cross the damp and spongy interior. A map is essential.

VISITOR INFORMATION   Your best bet is to stop in the **St. John's tourist information office** (see earlier in this chapter) or at the well-marked tourist bureau just up the hill from the Argentia ferry before you begin your travels. Witless Bay has a **tourist information booth** (© **709/334-2609**) stocked with a handful of brochures. It's open irregularly.

WITLESS BAY ECOLOGICAL RESERVE
The Witless Bay area, about 34km (21 miles) south of St. John's, makes an easy day trip from the city, or can serve as a launching point for an exploration of the Avalon Peninsula. The main attraction here is the **Witless Bay Ecological Reserve** ★ (© **709/635-4520**), comprising four islands a short boat ride offshore. Literally millions of seabirds nest and fish here, and it's a spectacle even if you're not a bird watcher.

On the islands you'll find the largest puffin colony in the western Atlantic Ocean, with some 60,000 puffins burrowing into the grassy slopes above the cliffs, and awkwardly launching themselves from the high rocks. The tour boats are able to edge right along the shores, about 6 or 7.5m (20 or 25 ft.) away, allowing puffin watching on even foggy days. Also on the islands is North America's second-largest murre colony.

While the islands are publicly owned and managed, access is via privately operated tour boat, several of which you'll find headquartered along Route 10 in Bay Bulls and Bauline East. It's worth shopping around since prices can vary considerably.

Bay Bulls is the closest town to St. John's, and is home to three of the more popular tours: **Mullowney's** (© 877/783-3467 or 709/334-3666), operating late May to late September; **O'Brien's** (© 877/639-4253 or 709/753-4850), operating mid-April to mid-October; and **Gatherall's** (© 800/419-4253 or 709/334-2887). Two-and-a-half-hour tours from here range generally between C$32 and C$45 (US$29–US$41/£16–£23) per adult, though you'll want to check ahead for the latest rates.

LA MANCHE PROVINCIAL PARK 🐾

La Manche means "the sleeve" in French, and the area is so named because of the long, narrow cove found here. This well-protected site was settled in 1840. Around 50 people still occupied homes on the steep hillsides flanking the cove as late as 1966, when a powerful storm all but destroyed the village. The occupants resettled elsewhere, leaving the remote village to be reclaimed by the elements.

Hikers can today follow a 30-minute pathway to the village's cove-side site, which is beautiful and a bit melancholy. Stone and concrete foundations can be found amid the grass and weeds; meanwhile, towering gray-black cliffs rise above the cove, where a river gorge meets the sea. It's a perfect place to while away an afternoon.

La Manche Provincial Park (© 709/685-1823) is well marked on Route 10, about 52km (32 miles) south of St. John's. There's a C$5 (US$4.50/£2.50) per car admission charge. The hike to the cove departs from the park campground's fire-exit road, and camping for the night at La Manche costs C$13 (US$12/£6.50) per site.

FERRYLAND 🐾

Historic Ferryland is among the most picturesque of the Avalon villages, set at the foot of rocky hills on a harbor protected by a series of abrupt islands at its mouth.

Ferryland was among the first permanent settlements in Newfoundland. In 1621, the Colony of Avalon was established here by Sir George Calvert, First Baron of Baltimore (he was also behind the settlement of Baltimore, Maryland). Calvert sunk the equivalent of C$4 million into the colony, which featured luxe touches like cobblestone roads, slate roofs, and fine ceramics and glassware from Europe. So up-to-date was the colony that privies featured drains leading to the shore just below the high-tide mark, making these the first flush toilets in North America. (Or so the locals insist.) Later the Dutch, and then the French, sacked the colony during ongoing squabbles over territory, and eventually it was abandoned.

Recent excavations have revealed much about life here nearly 4 centuries ago. Visit the **Colony of Avalon Interpretation Centre** 🐾 (© 877/326-5669 or 709/432-3200) with its numerous glass-topped drawers filled with engrossing artifacts, and then ask for a tour of the six archaeological sites currently being excavated (the tour is included in the cost of admission). Other interpretive exhibits include a reproduction of a 17th-century kitchen and three gardens of the sort you might have seen had you lived 400 years ago. After your tour, take a walk to the lighthouse at the point (about 1-hr. round-trip), where you can scan for whales and icebergs. Ask for directions at the museum.

The site is open daily mid-May to early October, usually from 9am to 7pm (10am–5pm May–June); admission is C$6 (US$5.40/£3) adults, C$5 (US$4.50/£2.50) seniors,

C$4 (US$3.60/£2) students, C$3 (US$2.70/£1.50) children ages 5 to 14, and C$15 (US$14/£7.50) families.

WHERE TO STAY & DINE

The Downs Inn   Overlooking the harbor, this building served as a convent between 1914 and 1986, when it was converted to an inn. The rather simple furnishings might reflect its heritage as an institution, rather than a historic building. (Much of the religious statuary was left in place.) Ask for one of the two front rooms, where you can watch for whales from your windows. The front parlor has been converted to a tearoom, where you can order a pot of tea and a light snack such as carrot cake or a rhubarb tart.

Irish Loop Dr. (P.O. Box 69), Ferryland, NL A0A 2H0. © 877/432-2808 or 709/432-2808. Fax 709/432-2659. acostello@nf.sympatico.ca. 4 units. C$55–C$75 (US$50–US$68/£28–£38) double. Rates include full breakfast. MC, V. Closed mid-Nov to mid-May. Small pets allowed. **Amenities:** Laundry service. *In room:* No phone.

AVALON WILDERNESS RESERVE

Where there are bogs, there are **caribou** 🦌. Or at least that's true in the southern part of the Avalon, which is home to the island's largest caribou herd, numbering some 13,000 of these magnificent animals. You'll see signs warning you to watch for them along the roadway. The caribou roam freely throughout a 1,700-sq.-km (656-sq.-mile) reserve, so it's largely a matter of happenstance to find them. Your best bet is to scan the high upland barrens along Route 10 between Trepassey and Peter's River—an area that's actually just outside the reserve.

On Route 90 between St. Catherines and Hollyrood is the **Salmonier Nature Park** 🦌🦌 (© **709/229-7189**), where you're certain to see caribou—along with other wildlife—if you can't find the herd on the reserve described above. This intriguing and well-designed park is fundamentally a 2.5km (1.6-mile) nature trail, almost entirely on boardwalk, which tracks through boglands and forest and along streams and ponds. Along the route are more than a dozen unobtrusive pens, in which orphaned or injured wildlife can be observed. (It's the only such facility in the province.) Among the animals represented: arctic fox, snowy owl, moose, bald eagle, mink, otter, beaver, and lynx. It's located 11km (6¾ miles) south of the Trans-Canada Highway, and admission is free. The gates open in summer daily from 10am to 6pm, then to 4pm from Labor Day until (the Canadian) Thanksgiving Day, when the park closes for winter. It remains closed from early October through the end of May.

WHERE TO STAY & DINE

The Salmonier Nature Park website, **www.env.gov.nl.ca/snp**, also handily lists a number of local lodgings and eateries.

Trepassey Motel & Restaurant   Trepassey is an unvarnished fishing village of about 1,200 souls south of the wildlife reserve, near Newfoundland's southernmost tip. This is an area often visited by whales and unusual birds during migrations. The village motel's 10 rooms are clean and basic, arrayed along a single hallway that connects to the restaurant. The local specialty is cod tongues (yep, cods have tongues), but you can also find a variety of other basic dishes including pork chops, turkey, and roast beef. The view from the solarium here of the Atlantic is splendid. Almost everything on the menu is inexpensive; at breakfast, try a partridgeberry muffin if it's offered.

Rte. 10, Trepassey, NL A0A 4B0. © 888/438-2934 or 709/438-2934. Fax 709/438-2722. 10 units. C$79 (US$71/£40) double. AE, MC, V. **Amenities:** Restaurant. *In room:* TV/VCR.

CAPE ST. MARY'S ✸✸

Cape St. Mary's Ecological Reserve ranks high on my list of favorite places on Newfoundland. Granted, it's off the beaten track—some 97km (60 miles) from the Trans-Canada Highway—but it's worth every mile. The terrain in this southwest portion of the Avalon is rather unique, mostly consisting of open barrens covering low, rolling hills. At times along Route 92 between North Harbour and St. Bride's, you might be convinced that you were driving through, say, Oklahoma.

On your way here, the 46km (29-mile) **scenic drive along Route 100** ✸ between St. Bride's and Placentia is like a miniature Cape Breton Island: The road climbs to open headlands, then swoops down to river valleys and through small villages. At every turn another extraordinary view of Placentia Bay unfolds.

Cape St. Mary's Ecological Reserve ✸✸   This natural reserve is home to some 5,500 pairs of northern gannets: big, noisy, beautiful, graceful white birds with cappuccino-colored heads and black wingtips. While they can be seen wintering off the coast of Florida and elsewhere to the south, they're seldom seen in such cacophonous numbers as they are here. Most are nesting literally right on top of one another on a compact, 100m (328-ft.) sea stack. At any given moment, hundreds are flying above, around, and below you, too, which is all the more impressive given their huge, nearly 2m (6½-ft.) wingspan.

You needn't take a boat ride to see the colony. Start your visit at the visitor center, which offers a quick and intriguing introduction to the indigenous bird life. Then walk 15 minutes along a grassy cliff-top pathway—through harebell, iris, and dandelion—until you arrive at a dizzying cliff just a couple of dozen yards from the sea stack (it's close enough to be impressive even in a dense fog). You'll be looking straight down onto the birds. Also nesting on and around the island are some 10,000 pairs of murre, 10,000 kittiwakes, and 100 razorbills. Guided tours are offered for a fee and are worthwhile; so is the summer performance series of evening concerts, if it's on. This extensive and unique wildland is worth several hours to a half-day for die-hard shutterbugs or birders. Admission to the reserve was free in 2007, though this could change in the future.

14km/8¾ miles off Rte. 100 (5km/3 miles east of St. Bride's). ✆ **709/277-1666.** Free admission. 1½-hr. guided tours C$7 (US$6.30/£3.50). Daily 9am–7pm. Grounds open year-round; interpretive center closed Nov–Apr.

WHERE TO STAY & DINE

Atlantica Inn and Restaurant   The Atlantica won't win points for charm—it's a basic, aluminum-sided box among some of the newer houses in the village. But it offers great value at the price, and the three rooms are well enough maintained and comfortable, if a bit small. The attached restaurant is by and large the only game in town, offering inexpensive meals daily.

Rte. 100, St. Bride's, NL A0B 2Z0. ✆ **888/999-2860** or 709/337-2860. Fax 709/337-2860. 3 units. C$45–C$55 (US$41–US$50/£23–£28) double. MC, V. **Amenities:** Restaurant. *In room:* No phone.

Bird Island Resort ✸ *Value* *Kids*   This modern, unaffected motel (as a "resort," it is *really* unaffected) is located behind the town food market, where you'll stop in to ask for a room. It's the best choice in town, especially for families, and offers unexpected amenities, such as a laundry room open to guests, tiny fitness room, and minigolf course (rooms come with clubs and balls). Rooms themselves vary in size; three-quarters of them are cottages. The double-efficiency cottage units feature separate sitting rooms, and some have good newish kitchenettes, which come in handy given the

Ghost of a Temporary City

An instant city of 26,000 people sprung up and occupied Argentia for a time during World War II, and U.S. forces still used this military base as late as 1994. The area is recorded in wartime annals for a significant event that occurred just offshore: U.S. President Franklin D. Roosevelt and British Prime Minister Winston Churchill met on a ship moored nearby as part of the Atlantic Conference. During that meeting, they hammered out their goals for ending the war. A monument commemorating the meeting is located at **Ship Harbour,** about 24km (15 miles) north of Dunville, east of Argentia.

Today, however, the once-sprawling military base is now shuttered up and forlorn-looking, the buildings lonely against the scrappy hills; only the heartbreakingly beautiful views of Placentia Sound remain. The base lands and their views have not gone to waste, however. As part of its conversion back to civilian use, the base authority agreed to establish the **Backland Trail** ⚑, which travels wooded hills and passes bunkers, lookouts, and old radar sites. Ask for information about the trail at Argentia's information center (see above); the road to the trailhead departs from Route 100, just downhill from the center.

dearth of restaurants in town. Families with kids will especially appreciate those. Room nos. 1 through 5 all have these kitchenettes and all face the ocean—which means terrific views, assuming the fog hasn't moved in yet. The motel units here are basic, but as clean and updated as those at a Hampton This or a Comfort That.

Rte. 100, St. Bride's, NL A0B 2Z0. ⓒ 888/337-2450 or 709/337-2450. Fax 709/337-2903. www.birdislandresort.com. 20 units. C$69–C$99 (US$62–US$89/£35–£50) double. AE, MC, V. *In room:* TV, kitchenette (some units), coffeemaker.

PLACENTIA & ARGENTIA

Placentia was settled by the Spanish in 1662 along a cove that proved to be perfect for a summer fishing base. Although the town has since grown and modernized some, it remains smallish, and it doesn't take much effort to imagine what it looked like centuries ago when the Spanish and (better-equipped) Basques grappled for fish and drying space during the short season.

It's especially easy to let your imagination go when viewing Placentia from **Castle Hill National Historic Site** ⚑ (ⓒ **709/227-2401**), just outside of town. This prominent hill overlooking the harbor was fortified variously by the French and English in the 17th and 18th centuries. The **visitor center** is expertly done, with historic maps and dioramas showing how the hilltop fortress once looked. Afterward, stroll to the summit to explore the fort's ruins and take in the expansive views of town and sea. This is a great first stop if you're just arriving via ferry. You'll get significant background on European settlement here to prime your visit to the rest of the island, and you'll learn plenty about the long historical importance of the cod fisheries here.

The site's grounds are open year-round; in summer (mid-May to mid-Sept), the visitor center opens daily from 10am to 6pm. Viewing the exhibits in the visitor center costs C$3.95 (US$3.55/£2) adults, C$3.45 (US$3.10/£1.75) seniors, C$1.95 (US$1.75/£1) ages 6 to 16, C$9.90 (US$8.90/£4.95) families.

The town of Argentia, a former military base, is on the far side of Castle Hill from Placentia. The helpful **visitor information center** (© **709/227-5272**) on Route 100 has an informative exhibit explaining how a historic fishing village became displaced by the base during World War II (see box). The center is open quite variable hours, usually from 9am (but sometimes 6am) depending on the schedule of the incoming ferry. They can point you to good scenic hiking trails nearby.

12 Labrador

For an English-speaking place on a media-saturated continent, there's still quite a lot of mystery and confusion surrounding Labrador. Let's debunk these myths, one by one. First, Labrador is *not* an island (like its cousin Newfoundland); it is part of mainland Canada, joined to the wild eastern reaches of Québec province in the same way that eastern New Hampshire butts up against Maine. (It *is* part of a bigger peninsula that includes parts of Québec, which is confusingly also called the Labrador Peninsula.)

Second, you *cannot* drive directly from Newfoundland into Labrador; to get here from The Rock, you must take a car ferry across the Labrador Straits to Québec, then drive a short distance to the provincial border, making it a nifty three-province commute. You could also take a lonely train from the hinterlands of Québec.

Third, Labrador is *not* a separate province; the province is officially called "Newfoundland and Labrador," and the two sections are joined at the hip administratively even though they are separated physically. (All the provincial governance takes place in faraway St. John's.) Finally, Labrador is *not* a French or Inuit or Beothuk word meaning "lake of gold" or "lots of fish, not so many people" or something like that. In fact, it was simply named for the Portuguese sailor—a guy named Lavrador—who spied its crags from a ship one day late in the 15th century.

So, yes, Labrador may be highly remote and poorly understood. Despite that, however, it has long played an outsize role in the history of Atlantic Canada. For centuries, its many-toothed coastline was famed for robust fisheries, and itinerant fleets plied these waters for a bounty of Atlantic seafood. The empty landscape here has served much the same function that the American West frontier has played in the course of American history—it has become a land of opportunity, seemingly bottomless with natural resources (once fish and furs, but now primarily raw ore), as well as a place where tough outdoorsmen historically test their mettle against a harsh environment, stalking big game, big salmon, big views, and big quiet.

Although Labrador is sparsely settled, people have been part of its landscape for centuries. The Innu (American Indian) culture in Labrador goes back 8,000 years, and the Inuit (Eskimo) culture 4,000 years. Vikings first sighted Labrador in 986 (although they actually didn't step onto the shore and start building things until 1010). In fact, traces of the horn-helmeted ones still remain in the shape of "fairy holes"—deep, cylindrical holes bored into local rocks at angles away from the sea. The Vikings are thought to have used them to tie up their boats against the rough tides here.

The 16th century brought Basque whalers, as many as 2,000 of them, who returned to Europe with tens of thousands of barrels of whale oil in what must have been one of the planet's original oil booms. It has been said that the whale oil of Newfoundland and Labrador was as valuable to the Europeans as the gold of South America was; vestiges of a whaling station remain even today on Saddle Island, off the coast of Red Bay on the Labrador Straits.

Next came British and French fishermen, fur traders, and merchants, who first visited only in summer to fish, hunt, and trade here, finally establishing permanent settlements during the 18th century. Many of these Europeans married Innu and Inuit women, but tensions between the Inuit whalers and their European counterparts along the southern coast eventually prompted most of the Inuit communities to move farther north, where they remain today.

Only about 30,000 people live in all of Labrador: about 13,000 in western Labrador, about 8,000 in Happy Valley–Goose Bay, and the remainder spread thinly along and around the many-tongued coast. Approximately four-fifths of those born here remain here for life; strong ties bind family and neighbors, although these close-knit communities typically welcome visitors warmly.

Many visitors come here for the sportfishing of brook trout, Atlantic salmon, Arctic char, lake trout, white fish, and northern pike. Others come for wilderness adventure, hiking, and camping beneath the undulating northern lights. Still others are simply curious to see such a remote part of the world.

Labrador basically boils down to three destinations, assuming your definition of *destination* includes places to park your car, stay overnight, and eat. (If you've come with a tent and supplies, it's a totally different story—the entire howling landmass is your destination.) First there's Labrador West, including **Labrador City** and **Wabush;** this region is reached by train from Sept-Îles, Québec (pronounced "Set-*teel*") or via Route 389 from Québec.

The second area—let's call it Central Labrador, since that's what it is—includes the commercial and industrial hub centered around **Happy Valley–Goose Bay.** Finally, there are the **Labrador Straits,** easily accessible from the main island of Newfoundland via ferry, offering small fishing villages and glimpses of Labrador's rich history at several sites.

The most scenic route here—and the only way to visit some of Labrador's outports—is by coastal ferry, along the so-called **Iceberg Alley** ☆☆. The ferry that serves this remote coast offers cabin accommodations as well as facilities for day passengers—and it's the only means of transportation along much of the Atlantic coast of Labrador. See "Getting There," under "Exploring Newfoundland & Labrador," at the beginning of this chapter, for more information.

SPECIAL-INTEREST/ADVENTURE TOURS   Those considering a trip to Labrador would do well to consider a packaged adventure tour. The rough terrain, limited transportation, and paucity of visitor services add up to one inescapable conclusion: Let someone familiar with this place do the planning. If you enjoy fishing, know that Labrador is considered a world-class destination among anglers. Nearly 50 fishing camps are scattered throughout the region; many can arrange floatplane access. Whether you're seeking out fish, fowl, or fun on a bike or kayak, **Newfoundland and Labrador Tourism** (© **800/563-6353**) can provide you with a list of outfitters catering to your specific interests and abilities; get in touch with them first.

THE LABRADOR STRAITS ☆

The Labrador Straits are the easiest part of Labrador to explore from Newfoundland. The southeast corner of Labrador is served by ferries shuttling between St. Barbe, Newfoundland, and Blanc Sablon, Québec (which is almost right on the Québec–Labrador border). From Blanc Sablon, you then travel on the (only) road, which runs 77km (48 miles) northward, dead-ending at the hamlet of Red Bay; plans call for extending this road in the future, but that could take another decade.

Labrador

Ferries are timed such that you can cross over in the morning, drive to Red Bay, and still be back for the later ferry to Newfoundland. Such a hasty trip isn't recommended, however. It's better to spend a night, when you'll have a chance to meet the people, who offer the most compelling reason to visit.

The **MV** *Apollo* (© **866/535-2567**) ferry runs from mid-April until ice season, usually sometime in mid-January. The crossing takes about 1 hour and 30 minutes, and reservations are encouraged in summer because some seats are first-come, first-served. The one-way fares in 2007 were C$23 (US$21/£12) for a car and driver, C$7.50 (US$6.75/£3.75) per additional passenger; there are discounts for seniors and youths. Remember that you pay a nonrefundable C$10 (US$9/£5) deposit if you do reserve in advance; miss the boat and you don't get it back.

The terrain along the Labrador Straits is rugged, the colors muted except for a vibrant stretch of green along the Pinware River. The few small houses are clustered close together; during winter, it's nice to have neighbors so nearby. Homes here are often brightened up with "yard art"—replicas of windmills, wells, churches, and the like.

In summer, icebergs float by the coast while whales breach and spout offshore. The landscape is covered with cotton grass, clover, partridgeberries, bakeapples, fireweed, buttercups, and bog laurel. Fogs roll in frequently; they will either stay a while or roll right back out again. Capelin come and go as well—these tiny migrating fish crash-land onshore by the thousands during a week in late June or early July, and local residents rush to the beach, scoop up the fish, and carry them proudly home where they become the unfortunate stars of quick and easy suppers.

In past years, there has been a "Gateway to the Labrador Straits" visitor information center set up in the small, restored St. Andrews Church in **L'Anse-au-Clair,** the first town after the ferry landing; check to see if it's open as you're passing through. The local tourism association has also developed several footpaths and trails in the area.

If you come in mid-August, plan to attend the annual **Bakeapple Folk Festival,** celebrating the local berry that stars in desserts both here and in Newfoundland.

EXPLORING THE LABRADOR STRAITS

Drive the "slow road" that connects the villages of the Labrador Straits. Traveling southwest to northeast, here's some of what you'll find along the way.

In L'Anse-au-Clair, **Moores Handicrafts,** 8 Country Rd., just off Route 510 (© **709/931-2186**), sells handmade summer and winter coats, traditional cassocks, moccasins, knitted items, handmade jewelry, and other crafts, as well as homemade jams. They also embroider Labrador cassocks and coats, and if you stop on the way north and choose your design, they'll finish it by the time you return to the ferry—even the same day. Prices are quite reasonable. The shop, run by the Moores family, is open daily in season from 9am to as late as 10pm.

The **Labrador Straits Museum** (© **709/927-5234**) is just outside L'Anse-Amour (pop. 25), about 19km (12 miles) from L'Anse-au-Clair. Two exhibit rooms focus mainly on the role of women in the history of the Labrador coast. You can also see photographs of the pilots who flew the first nonstop east-to-west transatlantic flight; they flew off course in April 1928 and landed on Greely Island, off the Labrador–Québec coast. The museum is open daily mid-June to mid-September (call for hrs.); a small admission fee is charged. The attached **gift shop** ✿, Labrador Crafts, is also an excellent stop.

The **Point Amour Lighthouse** ✿✿ (© **709/927-5825**), at the western entrance to the Strait of Belle Isle, is the tallest lighthouse in the Atlantic Provinces and the second tallest in all of Canada. The walls of this slightly tapered, circular tower (built in 1858) are 2m (6 ½-ft.) thick at the base; the dioptric lens up top was imported from Europe for the princely sum of C$10,000—a mint at the time. This light kept watch for submarines during World War II and is still in use; in fact, it was maintained by a resident lightkeeper right up until 1995. Remember to climb the 122 steps to reach the views from the top. The lighthouse is open to the public daily from mid-May to September, 10am to 5:30pm, with an admission fee of C$3 (US$2.70/£1.50) adults, free for children 12 and under. This is about a 3km (2-mile) detour off the main road.

After you pass the fishing settlements of **L'Anse-au-Loup** ("Wolf's Cove") and **West St. Modeste,** the road follows the scenic Pinware River, where the trees start becoming noticeably taller. Along this stretch of road, you'll also see glacial erratics—big odd boulders deposited by the melting ice cap. **Pinware River Provincial Park** ⚓ (℗ **709/ 927-5516**), open June to mid-September, is about 42km (26 miles) from L'Anse-au-Clair and offers a picnic area, hiking trails, and 15 simple campsites with neither flush toilets nor showers for C$10 (US$9/£5) per night. There's a C$5 (US$4.50/£2.50) fee per car to enter the park. The 81km-long (50-mile) Pinware River, which passes through the park, is known for its trout and salmon fishing; ask the rangers about the provincial rules and license requirements if you're interested.

The highway ends in **Red Bay.** Here, the interesting **Red Bay National Historic Site** ⚓⚓ (℗ **709/920-2051** or 709/920-2142) showcases artifacts from the late 1500s, when Basque whalers came here in numbers to hunt right and bowhead whales. Beginning in 1977, excavations began turning up whaling implements, pottery, glassware, and even partially preserved seamen's clothing. If you're really gung-ho about this sort of thing, you can arrange a tour of sites on **Saddle Island** ⚓, the home of Basque whaling stations in the 16th century. Or you can simply scope out the island from afar: The observation deck on the third floor of the visitor center has a good view of it. Admission to the historic site complex is C$7.15 (US$6.45/£3.60) adults, C$5.90 (US$5.30/£2.95) seniors, C$3.45 (US$3.10/£1.75) ages 6 to 16, C$18 (US$16/£9) families. The site is open 9am to 6pm daily from early June to early October, closed the rest of the year.

WHERE TO STAY

Beachside Hospitality B&B ⚓   A stay here offers an excellent opportunity to meet a local family and learn firsthand about life in this region of Labrador. Three bedrooms each have separate entrances, though two must share use of a bathroom. There's a whirlpool bath in the house, and guests have access to a communal phone and television room. Home-style meals are available by arrangement, or you can cook your own in a kitchen or outdoors on the grill; the friendly owners also sell homemade breads, jams, and jellies, and sometimes arrange accordion-powered Newfoundland jigs or other events. Ask about the "iceberg" drink, too.

9 Lodge Rd., L'Anse-au-Clair, Labrador, NL A0K 3K0. ℗ 709/931-2338. Fax 709/931-2275. 3 units, 1 with private bathroom. C$45 (US$41/£23) double. Rates include continental breakfast. MC, V. **Amenities:** Jacuzzi. *In room:* Kitchenette, no phone.

Grenfell Louie A. Hall Bed & Breakfast (Value   History buffs love the Grenfell Hall—it was built in 1946 by the International Grenfell Association as a nursing station, and there's plenty of reading material about the coast's early days. The rooms here are furnished with basic, contemporary-country furniture, and all share bathrooms; there's also a common room with a TV, VCR, and fireplace. A sixth unit, a private cottage, sports four double beds. The innkeepers can arrange to transport you to and from the ferry, if needed. (If you're just curious about the place and want to visit it, museum-style, you're invited to stop in for a small donation.) Evening meals are available by advance arrangement, and usually feature seafood such as cod or salmon along with homemade bread, preserves, and dessert. A full breakfast costs extra.

3 Willow Ave. (P.O. Box 137), Forteau, Labrador, NL A0K 2P0. ℗ 877/931-2916 or 709/931-2916. Fax 709/931-2916. 6 units, 5 with shared bathroom. Inn rooms C$50–C$65 (US$45–US$59/£25–£32.50) double; cottage C$75–C$100 (US$68–US$90/£37.50–£50). Rates include continental breakfast. MC, V. Closed Nov–Apr. *In room:* Iron, no phone.

Lighthouse Cove B&B   Hosts Cecil and Rita Davis have lived in this simple home overlooking rocks, water, and beach for more than 4 decades, so they can tell you much about the region—and since they live here, it's one of the rare inns in the province that stays open year-round. A light breakfast is included in your room rate; a full breakfast and seafood supper can be requested, with a charge for the dinners. From the house you can walk a footpath right to the Point Amour Lighthouse, a great bonus.

3 Main St. (P.O. Box 225), L'Anse-Amour, Labrador, NL A0K 3J0. ℭ 709/927-5690. Fax 709/927-5690. 3 units share 2½ bathrooms. C$40 (US$36/£20) double. Rates include continental breakfast. MC, V. *In room:* No phone.

Northern Light Inn 🔒 *Kids*   The largest and most modern hotel in the region, and the one closest to the ferry, the Northern Light has long offered comfortable, well-maintained rooms, a good gift shop, friendly staff, and a big dining room. All the inn's rooms possess modern, business-hotel amenities such as air-conditioning, hair dryers, voicemail, and even (in some cases) Jacuzzis. In addition to the pasta and seafood doled out in the dining room, there are fried-chicken and pizza chain outlets on-site as well, making this perhaps a good choice for those with restless kids.

58 Main St. (P.O. Box 92), L'Anse au Clair, Labrador, NL A0K 3K0. ℭ 800/563-3188 from Atlantic Canada or 709/931-2332. Fax 709/931-2708. www.northernlightinn.com. 59 units. C$89–C$159 (US$80–US$143/£45–£80) double. AE, DC, MC, V. **Amenities:** Restaurant; business center; laundry service. *In room:* A/C, TV, hair dryer, Jacuzzi (some units).

WHERE TO DINE
SeaView Restaurant HOME COOKING   This family-style restaurant in Forteau, 13km (8 miles) northeast of L'Anse-au-Clair, offers eat-in or takeout meals. Seafood dishes are the specialty, and the seafood basket is especially popular. There's an adjacent grocery store and bakery where you can buy homemade bread, peanut-butter cookies, and more. The motel here has eight units for about C$90 (US$81/£45) per night.

35 Main St., Forteau. ℭ 866/931-2840 or 709/931-2840. Meal items C$3–C$20 (US$2.70–US$18/£1.50–£10). AE, MC, V. Daily 9am–11:30pm.

LABRADOR WEST
The most affluent and industrialized part of Labrador, Labrador West lies on the Québec border and is home to the twin towns of **Wabush** and **Labrador City,** 6.5km (4 miles) apart. The two towns share many attractions, activities, and services. This region offers top-notch **cross-country skiing** and has hosted two World Cup events. Labrador West is also home to the largest open-pit iron-ore mine in North America, which reportedly produces nearly half of Canada's ore. To begin getting a handle on information about activities in this region, first contact the **Labrador West Tourism Development Corporation** (ℭ 709/944-7631; www.labradorwest.com).

Either Labrador City or Wabush makes an equally decent good base for hiking, canoeing, and birding trips. Ask for directions to **Crystal Falls,** where a short hike takes you to the falls and a view over the city. You can also play 18 holes at the **Tamarack Golf Course** (ℭ 709/944-3007), open June through September, for greens fees of about C$33 (US$30/£17). Other outdoorsy choices include windsurfing, scuba diving, and sailing on one of the many surrounding lakes. If you come in the winter, go cross-country skiing at the **Menihek Nordic Ski Club** (ℭ 709/944-5842), a complete ski center with about 34km (21 miles) of groomed trails for all skill levels, a few kilometers of which are lighted. Short sled dog rides are also offered for a small charge. The facility opens from November through April, weather permitting.

Labrador City is a stop on the oft-overlooked **Tshiuetin Rail Line** 🔒 (ℭ 866/960-0988 or 418/962-5530), the only passenger train in all of Newfoundland and Labrador. Tshiuetin Rail Transportation is a native-Canadian company that took over the passenger services of the Québec North Shore and Labrador Railway (QNS&L) in 2005. Its trains depart from Sept-Îles, Québec, twice weekly for an 8- to 10-hour trip to Labrador City; some of the cars continue farther north to Schefferville, so check when you board. The trip covers 419km (260 miles), running across 19 bridges, through 11 tunnels, and along or through riverbanks, forests, rapids, mountains, waterfalls, and subarctic vegetation.

In previous summers, a highlight has been the vintage 1958 **dome car** with sofa seats that was once part of the Wabash Cannonball; call the rail line directly to confirm the dome car and current rates. A round-trip typically costs about C$150 (US$135/£75) for adults, C$75 (US$68/£38) for seniors and children 5 to 11. This train line has been getting big government infusions of cash to guarantee its continued existence as a sort of commuter service between strung-out communities, but you never know. Always check ahead.

If you're overnighting in Sept-Îles on this trip, by the way, the 70-room **Hôtel Sept-Îles** (© **800/463-1793** from Québec only or 418/962-2581) is a decent place to stay. It's located at 451 Ave. Arnaud, down on the waterfront.

CENTRAL LABRADOR

From the North West River and Mud Lake to the Mealy Mountains, a visit to the interior of Labrador will bring you deep into a land of lakes, rivers, and spruce forests, where the horizon looks the same in every direction. Some believe that the Lake Melville area is the "Markland, land of forests" from old Viking sagas.

Outdoor activities include berry picking from August to the first snowfall of November, excellent sportfishing, canoeing the famed **Churchill River,** kayaking the rapid-filled Kenamou River, and snowmobiling. Look for *Them Days* (© **709/896-8531**), a quarterly magazine that chronicles the stories and memories of Labrador's people. It's published in Happy Valley–Goose Bay and sold everywhere in the region.

Three displays of local history are exhibited at the local mall, the **Northern Lights Building** (© **709/896-5939**) at 170 Hamilton River Rd. You'll see examples of regional animals in the displays, including the black bear, wolf, fox, lynx, otter, beaver, bald eagle, loon, duck, and Canada goose. A simulated trapper's brook has actual running water and its associated soothing sounds. Also here is the **Northern Lights Military Museum** (© **709/896-5939**), with uniforms, weapons, and other items from the Royal Newfoundland Regiment. Then there's a **model railway display** ("one of the largest collections of O-gauge Lionel toy trains on the east coast of Canada"). Admission to all exhibits is free and the building is open year-round, Tuesday to Saturday.

In 1997, Labrador's first provincial museum was built near Happy Valley–Goose Bay; the opening was attended by none other than Queen Elizabeth II herself. The **Labrador Interpretation Centre** is located on Lake View Drive in North West River (© **709/497-8566**) and is home to displays of some of Labrador's finest art. It's also free of charge. It's usually open June through September, Tuesday and Wednesday from 1 to 4pm, Thursday and Friday from 10am to 4pm, and weekends from 1:30 to 4:30pm, but check ahead if you're coming.

To take a little bit of Labrador home with you, stop by **Labrador Crafts and Supplies,** 367 Hamilton River Rd. (© **709/896-8400**), in Happy Valley–Goose Bay, which sells Innu tea dolls, grass work, soapstone carvings, labradorite jewelry, hooked rugs, parkas, and the like.

WHERE TO STAY

Convenient to the airport, the Trans-Lab Highway, and the ferry dock, the full-service **Labrador Inn** (𝕽 (𝒞 **800/563-2763** in Atlantic Canada, or 709/896-3351; www. labradorinn.nf.ca) at 380 Hamilton River Rd. has 66 modern business-hotel rooms with air-conditioning and TVs; there's a guest laundry on the premises as well. Doubles at the inn cost from C$84 to C$120 (US$76–US$108/£42–£60), suites from C$105 to C$150 (US$95–US$135/£53–£75). The restaurant serves chicken and ribs, as well as Italian dishes and some local specialties. Yes, indeed, that means this is the place to get your fresh caribou burgers.

THE NORTH COAST

The Inuit live along Labrador's North Coast, largely in Makkovik, Rigolet, Hopedale, and Nain, where they continue to fish, hunt, and carry on many aspects of their traditional culture in splendid isolation. Though it's somewhat inaccessible, skilled outdoor enthusiasts find their ways here for good hiking, sea kayaking, camping, and climbing in the Torngat Mountains.

There's also history to be found. In 1771, a small group of Moravian missionaries began to arrive on the North Coast, bringing with them prefabricated buildings from Germany, some of which are still standing. The wood-frame structure they raised in 1782 is considered the oldest such building east of Québec City. It's located in the village of **Hopedale,** accessible via the local ferry which travels from Happy Valley–Goose Bay to Nain (see below). Tours are by advance appointment only.

Inquire about the museum and other local sights at the adjacent **Amaguk Inn** (𝒞 **709/933-3750;** www.labradoradventures.com), a suitable lodging offering the bonus of historical and fly-fishing tours of the area (ask at the desk). Double rooms at the inn cost about C$135 (US$122/£68), and all have televisions, phones, and access to wireless Internet service. If you're in town on Sunday morning, check out the religious services, which occur twice: first in Inuit (including choral music), and then in English.

Unless you've brought your own cruising boat or airplane (I'm taking a wild guess you haven't), about the only way to explore the remainder of the coast in detail is aboard the **MV *Northern Ranger,*** a working supply vessel operated by provincial ferry services. The full excursion from Goose Bay to Nain, Labrador—with numerous stops at tiny ports of call along the way—takes a week round-trip. The cabins are cozy but all have views; you'll eat your meals in the ship's cafeteria with the crew and local passengers. It's a unique way to experience what's arguably the last frontier left on the Atlantic seaboard.

Cruises generally start in mid-June and run through to late November, though this is all dependent on the ice conditions. The rides aren't cheap; one-way passage from Goose Bay all the way to Nain costs C$142 (US$128/£71) per adult, with an extra charge per night for sleeping bunks—this can get expensive if you need a private room. You choose from among a standard cabin, deluxe cabin, or shared bunks in an economy sleeping room; the best accommodation costs C$573 (US$516/£287) one-way for the entire cabin. The hefty tariff does includes your meals, at least—on-ship, of course. No autos are allowed on the boat.

For the latest information on schedules and fares, contact the ferry line at 𝒞 **866/ 535-2567** or check the website at **www.tw.gov.nl.ca/ferryservices**. (Click on "Schedules," then click on the "H" ferry line along the map's northern Labrador coast.)

Appendix:
A Nature Guide to
the Atlantic Provinces

The human history of eastern Canada is usually thought of as beginning in or around the 17th century with the arrival of European colonists—or, from what we can guess about Viking settlements in Newfoundland, maybe as far back as the 11th century. But the clock actually turns back much farther than that—beginning thousands of years ago, when Native American tribes fished Atlantic shores and hunted these hills. Even *they* were here for only a sliver of the long period of time required to create this place; situations like this call for the word *eons*. The rocks upon which you climb, sun yourself, and picnic are old—staggeringly old.

Before arriving, then, it's a good idea to acquaint yourself with the natural history of the place. Armed with a little respect and appreciation for the landscape before you, you just might treat it more reverently while you're here—and help ensure that it remains for future generations to behold for many years.

1 The Landscape

The beginnings of this region are perhaps a half billion years old. You read right: That's *billion,* with a *B*. At that time, deep wells of liquid rock known as magma were moving upward, exploding in underground volcanoes, then hardening—still underground, mind you—into granitelike rocks. Later, natural forces such as wind and water wore away and exposed the upper layers of these rocks. Their punishment was only beginning, however; soon enough (geologically speaking, that is), what is now eastern North America and most of Europe began to shove up against each other, slowly but inexorably.

This "collision" (which was more like an *extremely* slow-motion car wreck) heated, squeezed, transformed, and thrust up the rocks that now form the backbone of the coastline. Ice ages came and went, but the rocks remained; the successive waves of great glaciation and retreat scratched up the rocks like old vinyl records, and the thick tongues of pressing ice cut deep notches out of them. Huge boulders were swept up and deposited by the ice in odd places. When the glaciers finally retreated for the last time, tens of thousands of years ago, the water melting from the huge ice sheet covering North America swelled the level of the Atlantic high enough to submerge formerly free-flowing river valleys and give the coastline and places like Newfoundland their distinctively rocky, knuckled faces. (Inland, at Prince Edward Island, the boulders laid down tons of silt and sand in their wake; that's what the island is, basically: a big sandbox.)

Once the bones of this landscape were established, next came the flesh: plants and animals. After each ice age, conifers such as spruce and fir trees—alongside countless grasses and weeds—began to reform, then decompose and form soils. It was tough work: Most of eastern Canada is a rocky, acidic place. Yet they persevered (as plants tend to do), and soon spruces, firs, and hemlocks formed an impenetrable thicket covering much of the coastal bedrock. Again, PEI was the exception: Mostly grasses, weeds, flowers, and pine trees sprouted up in the red mud and sand dumped here by the glaciers—because such an environment is inhospitable to almost everything else.

As the trees and flowers and fruits became reestablished, animals wandered back here, too—some now extinct but some still thriving today in the fields, hills, and woods of the region.

Eastern Canada's unique position—it is near the warm Gulf Stream—also bequeathed it plenty of marine (and economic) life: The current passes over the high, shallow undersea plateau known as Georges Bank, bringing an astonishing variety of microorganisms, and the marine life that follows, right to these provinces' doorsteps. Migrating whales make for a wonderful spectacle twice each year; seabirds travel similar passages, lighting upon the rocks and lakes of the region. And the waters teem—though not as they once did: Two of the three species of striped bass in the Bay of Fundy have disappeared from overfishing—along with fish, lobsters, crabs, dolphins, and a great deal more.

Then there are the coast's tidal pools, that precarious zone where land and rock meet ocean; a closer look at these pools reveals an ever-changing world of seaweed, snails, barnacles, darting water bugs, clams, shellfish, mud-burrowing worms, and other creatures. Interestingly, the type of life you find changes in well-marked "bands" as you get closer to water; rocks that are always submerged contain one mixture of seaweed, shellfish, and marine organisms, while rocks that are exposed and then resubmerged each day by the tides have a different mix. It's fascinating to note how each particular organism has found its niche. Move it up or down a foot and it would perish.

What follows is only the barest sketch of some of the nature life you'll find in eastern Canada. For a real look at it, go see it yourself. Whether you explore the provinces on foot, by bicycle, by kayak, by charter boat, or some other way, you're almost certain to see something that you've never seen before. If you're attentive, you'll come away with a deeper respect for things natural—not only here, but everywhere.

2 The Flora

Balsam fir   The best-smelling tree in the provinces must be the mighty balsam fir, whose tips are sometimes harvested to fabricate aromatic Christmas-tree wreaths. They're most common in Newfoundland but are also found in pockets of New Brunswick and Nova Scotia. It's sometimes hard to tell a fir from a spruce or hemlock, though the balsam's flat paddlelike needles (white underneath) are unique—only a hemlock's are similar. Pull one off the twig to be sure; a fir's needle comes off clean, a hemlock's ragged. Still not sure you've got a fir tree on your hands? The long, glossy, almost purplish cones are absolutely distinctive. You can find tree farms around the Lunenburg, Nova Scotia, area.

Balsam Fir   *Red Pine*

Red and white pine These pines grow in sandy soils and like some (or a lot of) sunlight. The **eastern white pine** is the familiar "King's pine" once prevalent throughout the northeast portions of North America; you can recognize it by its very long, strong needles that are always arranged five to a clump, like a hand's fingers. Its trunk was prized for the masts of ships of war in the 16th to 19th centuries, and countless huge pines were floated down Canadian rivers by logger men. Sadly, old-growth white pines are virtually nonexistent today, but you can still find the tree throughout eastern Canada. The **red pine,** not so common, can be distinguished by its pairs of needles and pitchy trunk; it grows on PEI (where it loves the sandy soil), but also in parts of New Brunswick and Nova Scotia.

White Pine

Red and sugar maple These two maple trees look vaguely alike when turning color in fall, but they're actually quite different, from the shapes of their leaves to the habitats they prefer. **Red maples** have skinny, gray trunks and like a swampy or wet area; often, several of the slim trunks grow together into a clump, and in fall the red maples' pointy leaves turn a brilliant scarlet color almost at once. **Sugar maples,** on the other hand, are stout-trunked trees with lovely, substantial leaves (marked with distinctive *U*-shaped notches), which autumn slowly changes to red and flame-orange. Sugar maples grow in or at the edges of mixed forests, often in combination with birch trees, oak trees, beech trees, and hemlocks. Their sap, of course, is collected and boiled down to make delicious maple syrup—big business in eastern Canada.

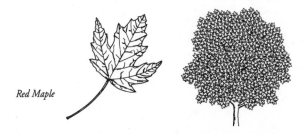

Red Maple

Lowbush blueberry Canada is the world's largest producer of wild blueberries, officially known as lowbush blueberries, cultivating nearly $70 million worth annually. With shrubby, tealike leaves and thick twigs, the plants lie low on exposed rocks on sunny hillsides, or sometimes crop up in shady woods; most of the year, the berries are inconspicuous and trail harmlessly underfoot. Come late summer, however, they're suddenly very popular—for bears as well as people. The wild berries ripen slowly in the sun (look behind and beneath leaves for the best bunches) and make for great eating off the bush, pancake baking, or jam making.

3 The Fauna

MAMMALS

LAND MAMMALS

Beaver   Often considered symbolic of Canada, beavers almost became extinct in the early 1900s due to a brisk world trade in beaver pelts and the rapid development of wetlands. But today the beaver's lodge-building, stick-chewing, and hibernating habits are well known once again; you'll find them in streams, lakes, and ponds.

Beaver

Black Bear

Black bear   Black bears still occur in eastern Canada, though in small numbers (still, you may want to keep a cover on that campfire food). The bears are mostly—emphasis on *mostly*—plant eaters and docile; they're the smallest of the North American bears and don't want trouble. Though they'll eat just about anything, these bears prefer easily reached foods on the woodland floor such as berries, mushrooms, nuts . . . and campers' leftovers. (Suspend leftovers in a "bear bag" away from your tent if you're camping in bear territory.) Black bears fatten up in fall for a long winter hibernation that averages 6 months.

Moose

Moose   Nothing says Canada like a moose, and the huge, skinny-legged, vegetarian moose is occasionally seen in the deep woods of eastern Canada; in Nova Scotia, they're listed as a provincially endangered species, but New Brunswick holds an annual lottery dispensing hunting permits resulting in about 2,000 moose kills a year. They're commonly seen by the road in Newfoundland. (But there are *no* moose—or even deer—on PEI.) The animal prefers deep woods, lakes, ponds, and uninhabited areas, and you can't miss it: The rack of antlers on the male, broad linemanlike shoulders, spindly but quick legs, and sheer bulk (it's as big as a truck) ensure you won't mistake it for anything else. Be careful driving on highways through remote wooded areas late at night: A collision with a moose is often fatal for the driver.

WHALES, DOLPHINS, PORPOISES & SEALS

Finback whale   A seasonal visitor to eastern Canada's waters twice a year when migrating between polar and equatorial waters, the finback is one of the biggest whales, and also one of the most collegial. It often travels in pairs or groups of a half-dozen or more (most whales are relatively solitary), though it does not travel close to shore or in shallow waters; you'll need a whale-watch boat to spot it. Find it by its rather triangular head and a fin that sweeps backward (like a dolphin's) rather than straight up like many other whales'. There are only 100 to 1,000 finbacks left in the waters off eastern Canada, according to the latest estimates.

Finback Whale

Humpback whale   Though this whale's Latin name roughly translates to "large-winged New England resident," the gentle, gigantic humpback isn't often seen from shore in eastern Canada, except in the Digby, Nova Scotia, area. (That's mostly because they were easy targets in the heyday of whaling.) Whale-watch tours often pass humpbacks, and if you see them, you'll never forget the sight: They are huge, jet-black, blow tremendous amounts of water when surfacing, and perform amazingly playful acrobatics above water. The males also sing haunting songs, sometimes for as long as 2 days at a time. The world population has shrunk to perhaps 20,000 whales.

Minke Whale

Minke whale   The smallest (and most human-friendly) of the whales, the minke swims off the coast of Canada, usually moving in groups of two or three whales—but much larger groups collect in feeding areas and during certain seasons. It has a unique habit of approaching and congregating around boats and ships, making this a whale you're quite likely to see while on a whale-watch tour. The minke is dark gray on top, the throat has grooves, and each black flipper fin is marked with a conspicuous white band.

Pilot Whale

Pilot whale   A smallish whale, the pilot is often seen in Atlantic Canadian waters by whale-watching boats, but it's still poorly understood: Its habits, true population, and diet are mostly unknown. It *is* known to congregate in large groups, sometimes numbering up to several hundred, and even to swim with other species of whale at sea. But pilot whales sometimes become stranded (as happened in 2006 on Big Tancook Island off Chester, Nova Scotia) by changing tides. Nearly unique among whales in this part of the world, the pilot has teeth; the roundish fin is swept back like a dolphin's.

Atlantic White-Sided Dolphin

Dolphins   Two very similar-looking species of dolphin—the **Atlantic white-sided dolphin** and the **white-beaked dolphin**—come to the Atlantic coast of the eastern provinces. Cute and athletic, these dolphins also occasionally turn up on beaches, for the same reason as pilot whales: Large groups are occasionally stranded by the tides, then perish when they cannot get back to sea in time.

White-Beaked Dolphin

Harbor porpoise   Quiet in behavior and habit, the porpoise is not the same thing as the dolphin; in fact, it's darker, much less athletic, and with a blunter, triangular fin. (The dolphin jumps out of the water and has a sharper fin that sweeps backward.)

Harbor Porpoise

Harbor seal   Related to sea lions, the whiskered harbor seal is common in all seasons in the Atlantic provinces. It's best seen by using a charter-boat service, as you'll often find it basking in the sun on rocks offshore. You'll easily recognize it: The seal's flippers have five claws, almost like a human hand; its neck is stocky and strong (as are its teeth); and then there is its fur, and those whiskers.

INVERTEBRATES
American lobster   Everyone knows the lobster by sight and taste; what few know is that it was once considered ugly, tasteless, and unfit to eat. There was a time not long ago when prisoners were served lobster and lobster stew three times a day. Today, the situation is quite different: This is one of eastern Canada's major exports. Lobsters are related to crabs, shrimp, and even spiders and insects (sorry to spoil your appetite); they feed by slowly scouring the ocean bottom in shallow, dark waters, locating food by smell (they see very poorly). The hard shell, which is periodically shed in order to grow larger, is the lobster's skeleton: A greenish-black or rarely blue color when alive, it turns bright red only after the lobster is cooked.

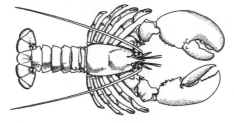

American Lobster

BIRDS
WATERFOWL
Ducks   Between one and two dozen species of ducks and ducklike geese, brant, and teal seasonally visit the lakes, ponds, and tidal coves of eastern Canada every year, including—though hardly limited to—the **red-breasted merganser** and the **common eider.** Mergansers, characterized by very white sides and very red bills (in males) or reddish crests (in females), occur year-round but are more common in winter months. So is the eider, which inhabits offshore islands and coastal waters rather than provincial freshwater lakes; in winter, these islands forms huge rafts of birds. Males are marked with a sharp black-and-white pattern.

Red-Breasted Merganser

Common Eider

Great blue heron   Everyone knows a great blue at once, by its prehistoric flapping wings, comb of feathers, and spindly legs. These magnificent hunters wade through tidal rivers, fishing with lightning strikes beneath the surface, from May through around October. The smaller, stealthier green heron and yellow-crowned night heron are rarely seen.

*Great Blue
Heron*

Loons   Two species of loon visit the region's lakes and tidal inlets, fishing for dinner. The **red-throated loon,** grayish with a red neck, is a spring passer-through and very rare in summer or winter. The **common loon** is, indeed, much more common—it can be distinguished by a black band around the neck, as well as black-and-white stripes and dots—and can be found in Canada year-round, though it's most easily spotted in late spring and late fall. It summers on lakes and winters on open patches of ocean inlets, giving a distinctively mournful, almost laughing call. Both loons have been decimated by environmental changes such as oil spills, acid rain, and airborne mercury.

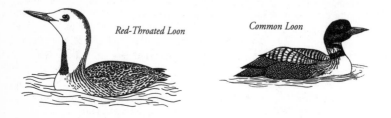

Red-Throated Loon   *Common Loon*

Plovers   Plovers inhabit and breed in certain muddy tidal flats, and their habitat is precarious; a single human step can crush an entire generation of eggs. Four species of plover visit eastern Canada in a few spots, and they're here only for a relatively short time. The **lesser golden-plover** flocks in considerable numbers in September while passing through, and the **greater golden-plover** occasionally lands in Newfoundland during migration. The **semipalmated plover,** with its quite different brownish body and white breast, has a similar life cycle and is also usually only seen in spring, passing through.

Semipalmated Plover

Seagulls   No bird is as closely associated with the sea as the seagull. But, in fact, there's more than one kind of gull in eastern Canada. A number of gulls are found here year-round, a few species visit seasonally, and a few more pop up only occasionally. Most common is the grayish **herring gull,** which is also the gull least afraid of humans. It's found in prevalence every month of the year. The **great black-backed gull** is similarly common, and is nearly all white (except for that black back and wings). This aggressive bird will even eat the eggs of another gull but in general avoids humans. There's a huge colony on Lake George outside Yarmouth, Nova Scotia. You might also see **glaucous, ring-billed,** and even **laughing** and **Bonaparte's gulls** (rarely, and usually only in summer), not to mention the related **black-legged kittiwake.**

Herring Gull

Great Black-Backed Gull

Bonaparte's Gull

Storm petrels   The tiny storm petrel is a fascinating creature. These plucky little birds fly astonishing distances in winter, eating insects on the wing, only to return to the coast each spring like clockwork, usually in May. They spend an amazing 4 months incubating, hatching, and tending to their single, white eggs in nests eked out of rocks. **Wilson's storm petrels** sometimes follow behind offshore boats; the much less common **Leach's storm petrel** restricts its visits and nests solely to far-offshore rocks and islands and is also mostly nocturnal, which reduces the chances of seeing it further. Both breed in summer, then head south for winter.

Wilson's Storm Petrel

LAND BIRDS

Bald eagle   Yes, they're here in Atlantic Canada—year-round—and even breed here, though they're difficult to find and hardly conspicuous, except on Cape Breton Island in Nova Scotia. (Their endangered status means you shouldn't really seek them out anyway.) The bald eagle's black body, white head, and yellow bill make it almost impossible to confuse with any other bird. It was nearly wiped out in the 1970s, mainly due to environmental poisons such as DDT-based pesticides, which caused female eagles to lay eggs that were too weak to sustain growing baby chicks. However, the bird is beginning to make a comeback.

Bald Eagle

Songbirds   There are literally dozens of species of songbirds that roost in Acadia's open fields, forests, and dead snags—even in the rafters and bird boxes of houses. They are not so common in remote rocky places like Newfoundland as in suburbia (greater Halifax, for instance) or in the farmlands of the provinces. One thing is for certain: Songbirds love human company, so look for them near the settled areas. The region hosts a dozen or so distinct types of chirpy little **warblers,** each with unique and often liquid songs; a half-dozen **thrushes** occurring in significant numbers; winter **wrens, swallows, sparrows, vireos, finches, creepers,** and **thrashers;** the whimsical **black-capped chickadee;** and occasionally lovely **bluebirds, cardinals,** and **tanagers,** among many other species.

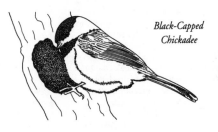

Black-Capped Chickadee

Index

See also Accommodations and Restaurant indexes, below.

ACCOMMODATIONS— NEW BRUNSWICK

ACCOMMODATIONS— PRINCE EDWARD ISLAND

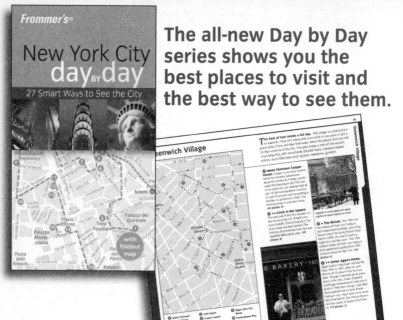

FROMMER'S® COMPLETE TRAVEL GUIDES

Alaska
Amalfi Coast
American Southwest
Amsterdam
Argentina
Arizona
Atlanta
Australia
Austria
Bahamas
Barcelona
Beijing
Belgium, Holland & Luxembourg
Belize
Bermuda
Boston
Brazil
British Columbia & the Canadian
  Rockies
Brussels & Bruges
Budapest & the Best of Hungary
Buenos Aires
Calgary
California
Canada
Cancún, Cozumel & the Yucatán
Cape Cod, Nantucket & Martha's
  Vineyard
Caribbean
Caribbean Ports of Call
Carolinas & Georgia
Chicago
Chile & Easter Island
China
Colorado
Costa Rica
Croatia
Cuba
Denmark
Denver, Boulder & Colorado Springs
Eastern Europe
Ecuador & the Galapagos Islands
Edinburgh & Glasgow
England
Europe
Europe by Rail

Florence, Tuscany & Umbria
Florida
France
Germany
Greece
Greek Islands
Guatemala
Hawaii
Hong Kong
Honolulu, Waikiki & Oahu
India
Ireland
Israel
Italy
Jamaica
Japan
Kauai
Las Vegas
London
Los Angeles
Los Cabos & Baja
Madrid
Maine Coast
Maryland & Delaware
Maui
Mexico
Montana & Wyoming
Montréal & Québec City
Morocco
Moscow & St. Petersburg
Munich & the Bavarian Alps
Nashville & Memphis
New England
Newfoundland & Labrador
New Mexico
New Orleans
New York City
New York State
New Zealand
Northern Italy
Norway
Nova Scotia, New Brunswick &
  Prince Edward Island
Oregon
Paris
Peru

Philadelphia & the Amish Country
Portugal
Prague & the Best of the Czech
  Republic
Provence & the Riviera
Puerto Rico
Rome
San Antonio & Austin
San Diego
San Francisco
Santa Fe, Taos & Albuquerque
Scandinavia
Scotland
Seattle
Seville, Granada & the Best of
  Andalusia
Shanghai
Sicily
Singapore & Malaysia
South Africa
South America
South Florida
South Korea
South Pacific
Southeast Asia
Spain
Sweden
Switzerland
Tahiti & French Polynesia
Texas
Thailand
Tokyo
Toronto
Turkey
USA
Utah
Vancouver & Victoria
Vermont, New Hampshire & Maine
Vienna & the Danube Valley
Vietnam
Virgin Islands
Virginia
Walt Disney World® & Orlando
Washington, D.C.
Washington State

FROMMER'S® DAY BY DAY GUIDES

Amsterdam
Barcelona
Beijing
Boston
Cancun & the Yucatan
Chicago
Florence & Tuscany

Hong Kong
Honolulu & Oahu
London
Maui
Montréal
Napa & Sonoma
New York City

Paris
Provence & the Riviera
Rome
San Francisco
Venice
Washington D.C.

PAULINE FROMMER'S GUIDES: SEE MORE. SPEND LESS.

Alaska
Hawaii
Italy

Las Vegas
London
New York City

Paris
Walt Disney World®
Washington D.C.

FROMMER'S® PORTABLE GUIDES

Acapulco, Ixtapa & Zihuatanejo
Amsterdam
Aruba, Bonaire & Curacao
Australia's Great Barrier Reef
Bahamas
Big Island of Hawaii
Boston
California Wine Country
Cancún
Cayman Islands
Charleston
Chicago
Dominican Republic

Florence
Las Vegas
Las Vegas for Non-Gamblers
London
Maui
Nantucket & Martha's Vineyard
New Orleans
New York City
Paris
Portland
Puerto Rico
Puerto Vallarta, Manzanillo & Guadalajara

Rio de Janeiro
San Diego
San Francisco
Savannah
St. Martin, Sint Maarten, Anguila & St. Bart's
Turks & Caicos
Vancouver
Venice
Virgin Islands
Washington, D.C.
Whistler

FROMMER'S® CRUISE GUIDES

Alaska Cruises & Ports of Call

Cruises & Ports of Call

European Cruises & Ports of Call

FROMMER'S® NATIONAL PARK GUIDES

Algonquin Provincial Park
Banff & Jasper
Grand Canyon

National Parks of the American West
Rocky Mountain
Yellowstone & Grand Teton

Yosemite and Sequoia & Kings Canyon
Zion & Bryce Canyon

FROMMER'S® WITH KIDS GUIDES

Chicago
Hawaii
Las Vegas
London

National Parks
New York City
San Francisco

Toronto
Walt Disney World® & Orlando
Washington, D.C.

FROMMER'S® PHRASEFINDER DICTIONARY GUIDES

Chinese
French

German
Italian

Japanese
Spanish

SUZY GERSHMAN'S BORN TO SHOP GUIDES

France
Hong Kong, Shanghai & Beijing
Italy

London
New York
Paris

San Francisco
Where to Buy the Best of Everything.

FROMMER'S® BEST-LOVED DRIVING TOURS

Britain
California
France
Germany

Ireland
Italy
New England
Northern Italy

Scotland
Spain
Tuscany & Umbria

THE UNOFFICIAL GUIDES®

Adventure Travel in Alaska
Beyond Disney
California with Kids
Central Italy
Chicago
Cruises
Disneyland®
England
Hawaii

Ireland
Las Vegas
London
Maui
Mexico's Best Beach Resorts
Mini Mickey
New Orleans
New York City
Paris

San Francisco
South Florida including Miami & the Keys
Walt Disney World®
Walt Disney World® for Grown-ups
Walt Disney World® with Kids
Washington, D.C.

SPECIAL-INTEREST TITLES

Athens Past & Present
Best Places to Raise Your Family
Cities Ranked & Rated
500 Places to Take Your Kids Before They Grow Up
Frommer's Best Day Trips from London
Frommer's Best RV & Tent Campgrounds in the U.S.A.

Frommer's Exploring America by RV
Frommer's NYC Free & Dirt Cheap
Frommer's Road Atlas Europe
Frommer's Road Atlas Ireland
Retirement Places Rated

CLOSED
due to
accidental demolition

WEGEN BISSIGEN
EICHHÖRNCHEN GESCHLOSSEN

CERRADO
CABRAS

Κλειστό
Μετεωρίτες

POOL CLOSED
ELECTRIC EELS
プールも
閉鎖中

Hotel
closed for
facelifting

FERMÉ POUR
RAISON
DE GRÈVE
DES BONNES

FECHADO!
POR CAUSA DE
ATAQUES DOS CROCODILOS

— I don't speak
sign language.

©2007 Travelocity.com LP. CST# 2056372-50

A hotel can close for all kinds of reasons.
Our Guarantee ensures that if your hotel's undergoing construction, we'll
let you know in advance. In fact, we cover your entire travel experience.
See www.travelocity.com/guarantee for details.

*** travelocity*
You'll never roam alone.